Conversational
Spanish for
Medical Personnel

SECOND EDITION

Conversational Spanish for Medical Personnel

Essential Expressions, Questions, and Directions for Medical Personnel to Facilitate Conversation with Spanish-Speaking Patients and Coworkers

ROCHELLE K. KELZ, Ph.D.

Adjunct Associate Professor of Spanish
North Park College
Visiting Assistant Professor of Medical Spanish
University of Illinois at Chicago
Chicago, Illinois

DELMAR PUBLISHERS INC.®

NOTICE TO THE READER

Publisher and author do not warrant or guarantee any of the products described herein or perform any independent analysis in connection with any of the product information contained herein. Publisher and author do not assume, and expressly disclaim, any obligation to obtain and include information other than that provided to them by the manufacturer.

The reader is expressly warned to consider and adopt all safety precautions that might be indicated by the activities described herein and to avoid all potential hazards. By following the instructions contained herein, the reader willingly assumes all risks in connection with such instructions.

The publisher and author make no representations or warranties of any kind, including but not limited to, the warranties of fitness for particular purpose or merchantability, nor are any such representations implied with respect to the material set forth herein, and the publisher and author take no responsibility with respect to such material. The publisher and author shall not be liable for any special, consequential or exemplary damages resulting, in whole or in part, from the readers' use of, or reliance upon, this material.

For information, address Delmar Publishers Inc.
2 Computer Drive West, Box 15-015
Albany, New York 12212

Printed in the United States of America
Published simultaneously in Canada
By Nelson Canada
A Division of The Thomson Corporation

10 9 8 7 6 5 4 3 2 1

ISBN 0-8273-42659

A Max y Melissa
que aún no comprenden por qué no puedo jugar
con ellos a cada rato y
A mis padres que sí comprenden

Preface to the Second Edition

There is no longer room in our society for the "culturally encapsulated" health care practitioner. Effective communication with minorities is becoming increasingly necessary. The primary purpose of this book is to show how basic language skills can be applied to medicine and health care for the Hispanic patient and to provide information about the impact of Hispanic culture on health care.

The term *Hispanic*, as I use it here, is a generic label for a diverse group of Spanish-speaking people in the United States who reflect varied histories and who have a wide range of cultural values. There are over 14.6 million Hispanos in the United States, over 6 percent of the total U.S. population, ranking them this country's second largest minority group. Estimates for 1980 for those residing in the United States illegally range from 6 to 12 million. The Hispanic people are a highly mobile population, but they are concentrated in certain major urban areas such as New York City, Los Angeles, Chicago, San Antonio, Houston, El Paso, Miami, San Jose, San Diego, and Phoenix.

Among the Hispanic population, beliefs and attitudes about health care differ widely. Many cultural attitudes shared in common, however, account for the way they view illness, the way they use medical services, and the way they follow the advice and prescriptions of their physicians. The problems of providing adequate health care to this population have long been recognized by hospital staff members. Those administering to the Hispanic patient, even ancillary personnel, should be given appropriate information about this cultural background and basic language instruction to enable them to understand and be understood by the Hispanic patient. This book is intended for the diverse group of people who work with those Hispanic patients. Specifically, it is written for professionals and students in the health care services—physicians, dentists, nurses, therapists, technicians, dieticians, and paramedics—and I believe that it will also be useful to educators and people in the human services fields—social workers, psychologists, counselors —as well as to Spanish-speaking people who wish to learn English.

Health programs for the Hispanic population must include bilingual personnel and staff. The most common barrier is that of communication. Personalizing health services to the Hispanic population includes a basic speaking knowledge of their language and, more important, an understanding of the cultural attitudes governing patients' behaviors.

vii

This text emphasizes the differences among written, formal, and academic Spanish (*el español oficial*) and casual, everyday, and, at times, regional Spanish (*el español popular o corriente*). Difficulty occurs when dealing with Spanish-speaking people who have limited medical knowledge. Many medical terms may be expressed in different ways in Spanish. There are technical expressions, many of which mean little to people who are not familiar with medicine; slang or street Spanish; and ordinary Spanish. An example of these differences in vocabulary occurs in the ways of denoting German measles: **rubéola** (technical), **sarampión alemán** (popular), and **fiebre de tres días** or **alfombría** (colloquial).

This text is adaptable to varying needs and methods of presentation. It is for students whose primary objective is the development of conversational skills using terminology and concepts related to health care. Since the composition of classes varies, instructors will probably choose material pertinent to their students' job requirements and previous skills.

Chapter 1 is a discussion of linguistics. The second chapter is now an introductory grammar. Although the grammar section has been expanded greatly, it is still streamlined. Unlike traditional texts, the basic points of grammar, which are simply stated, are organized on the basis of parts of speech. For example, all information pertaining to nouns is discussed in the section on nouns, rather than being interspersed throughout the grammar. Both in the grammar chapter and in the text itself the second-person plural forms have been entirely eliminated, and the second-person singular forms are found only in the grammar section; it is easier for health care professionals to learn and use only the formal, polite forms, which are more appropriate in interactions between health care professionals and patients. Chapter 3 contains pertinent cultural information, as well as phrases needed for rudimentary, polite conversation and morning rounds. Chapter 4 adds readings and problem-solving exercises on the metric system. Chapter 5 contains additional regional vocabulary and new physiological drawings. Chapters 6 and 7, containing conversations for medical, paramedical, and administrative personnel, have been expanded to include additional vital materials on oral surgery, family planning, birthing, proctoscopic examinations, drug abuse, poisonings, breast self-examination, and the insertion of NG tubes. Cultural notes have been added primarily in these chapters. Illness is not merely the loss of health; it involves the attitudes of patients and their families. The person who is providing health care must have an understanding of the various attitudes that different cultures have about illness and those who are sick. Some new forms have been added to Chapter 8. Specialized vocabulary dealing with drug abuse terminology, blood component and excretion terminology, places in the hospital, and principal medical abbreviations have been added to Chapter 9, providing the tools for interviewing patients. The text concludes with a bilingual dictionary of the medical terminology used in the book.

My contacts with the medical schools and hospitals in the Chicago area have made possible the personal testing and gradual refinement of the text and have provided the direct experience upon which many of the dialogues are based.

I thank the many unnamed students to whom I have taught this course, who have offered insightful suggestions and advice about what they most need to know.

As is true with any project of this nature, this book could not have been written without the encouragement and moral support of many people. I wish to express my heartfelt thanks and gratitude to my parents, Dr. and Mrs. Samuel Kanter, for their assistance, which freed me from many of my household tasks and enabled me to devote many long hours researching and writing the revised, expanded manuscript. I am grateful to Andrea Stingelin, my editor, for her comments, criticisms, and suggestions, and to the many typists and other assistants who brought their efforts to this project. To all, my sincerest appreciation is clearly forthcoming.

Rochelle K. Kelz

Preface to the First Edition

More than a dozen good Samaritans swarmed to the scene of an automobile wreck in Texas where a woman was quietly sitting behind the steering wheel. Most of the would-be helpers ignored her "No puedo mover las piernas." One woman, however, knew that this meant she couldn't move her legs, and stopped the good-willed but amateurish rescue effort so that the injured woman could be removed from the car by the ambulance assistants who soon arrived. Permanent spinal damage and perhaps even death were thus avoided because a passerby knew the correct Spanish words.

A San Diego physician took his month's vacation in central Peru, donating his medical skills to an impoverished area that could not possibly afford his talent if he charged his usual fee. Spanish did not come easily to him. He could have gotten by without any knowledge of Spanish because his Peruvian assistants spoke English quite well. But he learned how to greet his patients, thank them, bid them good-by, and added some Spanish medical terms to his vocabulary. A few words spoken in Spanish to a poor Peruvian makes his eyes "light up like a full moon," he explained. He could tell that patients had more confidence in him after he spoke just a few words in their own language.

A nurse who works the night shift in one of Chicago's North Side hospitals empathizes with men whose wives are in the delivery room. For most of them it is a difficult experience; for those who speak only Spanish, it is pure agony. She speaks just a few phrases, like "Todo va bien" (All is going well) or "¿Le gustará café?" (Would you like coffee?), which bring smiles of relief from the fathers-to-be that she will remember forever.

These situations illustrate how a rudimentary understanding of medical Spanish has helped non-native Spanish-speaking citizens and medical personnel make life easier for themselves or others. Not many of us have the opportunity to save a life because we understand another language, but there are many times when we can make certain experiences more tolerable for ourselves and others. This book, as part of the trend in career education, is designed to eliminate any artificial separation between the academic and vocational worlds. As such, the goal of this work is to aid communication between medical personnel and Spanish-speaking people. Millions of Spanish-speaking persons who know little or no English live in the United States. Their inability to communicate poses a serious problem when these people seek medical attention.

Conversational Spanish for Medical Personnel: Essential Expressions, Questions, and Directions for Medical Personnel to Facilitate Conversation with Spanish-Speaking Patients and Coworkers is a teaching manual that assists non-Spanish-speaking personnel in health-related fields in effective communication with Spanish-speaking patients and coworkers. While the book is not (nor is it meant to be) a grammar text, essential grammar, both in English and Spanish, is thoroughly explained to facilitate comprehension of the basic structures of speech in both languages. Often, medical personnel, though highly motivated, have minimal exposure to language study. But effective health care depends on efficient communication, and communication implies comprehension of certain grammar points not necessarily considered essential in traditional study of the Spanish language. Thus, the concise explanations of grammar points given in this book, illustrated by examples using medical vocabulary, reinforce active communication and aid in the ability to deal with occupational roles in the second language. The book also provides variations of Spanish words and phrases, listing many regionalisms, slang, and basic alternatives to the traditional expressions in an effort to avoid misunderstandings by medical practitioners or patients. At all times, the emphasis is on speaking to the sick patient—never on doing exercises in grammar.

The expressions appearing in this book are primarily those used in the Latin American countries located closest to the United States. Frequently these words or expressions are unknown or little used in Spain because many local Indian words enrich American Spanish. In addition, words and meanings often vary from one Spanish-speaking country to another. I have chosen the word or words most widely understood throughout the entire Spanish-speaking world. Most frequently these words or expressions derive from Spain. Words that are unique to one or two Latin American countries are noted as such so that people who deal with patients from that particular locality may acquire the necessary word or colloquialism, as well as the general term used elsewhere. The designation *Sp. Am.* is used with any variant current in a number of Spanish-American countries.

The English translations opposite the Spanish expressions are given principally for the benefit of English-speaking students but may also be used by Spanish-speaking medical personnel who wish to acquaint themselves with conversational usage in American English.

ROCHELLE K. KELZ

Contents

1

1

PRONUNCIATION
PRONUNCIACION

2

27

ESSENTIAL GRAMMAR
GRAMATICA BASICA

3

183

COMMON EXPRESSIONS
EXPRESIONES CORRIENTES

4

197

NUMERICAL EXPRESSIONS
EXPRESIONES NUMERICAS

5

221

ANATOMIC AND PHYSIOLOGIC VOCABULARY
VOCABULARIO ANATOMICO Y FISIOLOGICO

6

241

CONVERSATIONS FOR MEDICAL AND PARAMEDICAL PERSONNEL
CONVERSACIONES PARA PERSONAL MEDICO Y PARAMEDICO

7

397

CONVERSATIONS FOR ADMINISTRATIVE PERSONNEL
CONVERSACIONES PARA PERSONAL ADMINISTRATIVO

8   413

AUTHORIZATIONS AND SIGNATURES
AUTORIZACIONES Y FIRMAS

9   425

CRUCIAL VOCABULARY FOR MEDICAL PERSONNEL
VOCABULARIO CRUCIAL PARA PERSONAL MEDICO

APPENDIX **A**   467

ENGLISH–SPANISH VOCABULARY
VOCABULARIO INGLES–ESPAÑOL

APPENDIX **B**   491

SPANISH–ENGLISH VOCABULARY
VOCABULARIO ESPAÑOL–INGLES

                                                           517

SELECTED BIBLIOGRAPHY
BIBLIOGRAFIA SELECTA

                                                            525

ESSENTIAL GRAMMAR INDEX
INDICE DE GRAMATICA BASICA

                                                            531

INDEX
INDICE

Conversational Spanish for Medical Personnel

CHAPTER 1

Pronunciation

Pronunciación

THE ALPHABET

EL ALFABETO

The Spanish alphabet has thirty letters. They are:

Letter	Name	Transliteration	Letter	Name	Transliteration
A	a	ah	Ñ	eñe	eh-nyay
B	be	bay	O	o	oh
C	ce	say	P	pe	pay
CH	che	chay	Q	cu	coo
D	de	day	R	ere	eh-ray
E	e	ay	RR	erre	er-rray
F	efe	eh-fay	S	ese	eh-say
G	ge	hay	T	te	tay
H	hache	ah-chay	U	u	oo
I	i	ee (ē)	V	ve/uve	bay or oo-bay
J	jota	hoe-tah	W	doble ve;	do-blay bay;
K	ka	kah		doble u;	do-blay oo;
L	ele	eh-lay		ve doble	bay do-blay
LL	elle	l-yay	X	equis	eh-keys
M	eme	h-may	Y	i griega	ē grē-ay-gah
N	ene	eh-nay	Z	zeta	zeh-tah

GENERAL REMARKS

OBSERVACIONES GENERALES

Spanish is pronounced the way it is written. Spanish letters are treated as feminine nouns, and each has one sound except for *C, D, E, G, N, O, S, X,* and *Y,* which have at least two sounds. The letters *K* and *W* appear only in foreign words. The letter combinations *CH, LL, Ñ,* and *RR* each have one sound, are each considered to be one consonant, and are alphabetized as such. Excluding prefixes and suffixes, *C, R,* and *L* are the only three consonants that may be doubled in Spanish.

The Spanish alphabet is divided into vowels (**vocales**) and consonants (**consonantes**). The vowels *A, E, I, O,* and *U* are the same as in English. *Y* is a vowel when it is the last letter in a word and a consonant when it begins a word or a syllable. Thus, *Y* serves two functions. An example of *Y*'s use as a vowel is **hoy** (today); as a consonant, **inyección** (injection).

All vowels in Spanish are short, pure sounds. *A, I,* and *U* each have one sound, although there will be slight variations according to placement within the phrase or word.

Spanish Phonetics *Fonética española*

Spanish consists of specific speech-sounds classified as *phonemes* (**fonemas**). The Spanish of Spain (except the southwest) has 24 different phonemes, and 22 exist in the Spanish of most of Spanish America and southwestern Spain. Thirty arbitrary graphic symbols, called the letters of the alphabet, represent these phonemes. (Phonemes always refer to sounds, never to spelling.) Phonemes are conventionally placed between slant lines—/a/, /s/.

Some Spanish phonemes are represented by different "sounds" in different contexts. These phonemic variants are called *allophones* (**alofonas**). Allophones are conventionally enclosed in square brackets—[o], [ə].

The pronunciation sections in this book compare the sound systems of English and Spanish. They do not offer a complete description of either sound system, but they present many pointers so that the student, using his native language as a point of reference, can better understand these elements of the foreign language.

Certain standardized terminology, based on the positions and movements of the various speech organs (Chart 1), is used to accurately describe the sounds of speech. The description includes four minimum features: (1) the distinction between *voiced* and *voiceless*; (2) the name of the articulator; (3) the name of the point of articulation; (4) the sound type. The following nomenclature is used:

PHONATION: the production of voice.

VOCAL BANDS: a pair of bundles of cartilage and muscle, about $\frac{3}{5}$ of an inch in length, attached to the walls of the larynx, and adjustable in many ways.

VOICELESS: refers to the completely open position of the vocal bands. The glottis, or opening between the vocal bands, allows air to pass unobstructed. The vocal bands do not vibrate.

VOICED: refers to the vibration of the vocal bands as air passes through the glottis.

ARTICULATION: refers to the changes in the shape and size of the air passages and resonating cavities resulting in the production of different sounds.

RESONATING CAVITIES: pharynx (or pharyngeal cavity), nasal cavity, oral cavity (or mouth).

ARTICULATORS: various moveable organs that affect tone or noise. The main *articulators* are the tongue, the lower lip, the velum (or "soft" palate) and the uvula. The main points of *articulation* are the upper lip, the upper teeth, the alveolar ridge, the palate, and the velum again (see Chart I). The following terms are used when certain combinations of articulator and point of articulation occur:

	Articulator	*Point of Articulation*
Bilabial	lower lip	upper lip
Labiodental	lower lip	upper teeth
Dental	tip of tongue	upper teeth
Interdental	tip of tongue	upper and lower teeth
Alveolar	tip of tongue	upper gums
Velar	back of tongue	velum (soft palate)
Alveopalatal	front of tongue	far front of palate
Palatal	front of tongue	hard palate

STOP: occurs when the speech organs used to produce sounds press together to stop the outgoing air stream and then abruptly open to release it (also called a *plosive* or an *occlusive*)

AFFRICATE: a special type of stop in which a slight friction noise is heard upon the gradual release of the air stream.

FRICATIVE: occurs when the speech organs touch lightly or not quite at all to allow the air stream to continue flowing through (also called *spirant*).

SONORANT: a third type of general sound. It results from movement of the articulator so as to produce noise, but not stop or constrict the air stream. Nasals, laterals, vowels and semivowels are sonorants.

Nasal: consonantal phoneme, which is produced by the passage of air through the nose instead of the mouth.

Lateral: characteristic continuant sound produced by placing part of the tongue against the roof of the mouth, thus closing off most of the air passage of the mouth except for openings on the sides of the tongue.

Vowel: found in the center of a syllable and the most prominent sound in syllable; it is formed without any stoppage or constriction of the oral cavity. Vowels are *a, e, i, o, u*.

Semivowel: very brief and always in the same syllable with a true vowel. *U, i,* and final *y* are semivowels.

FLAP: the sound of the tongue briefly touching some point of articulation (i.e., alveolar ridge) and withdrawing sharply before either a stop or an affricate can be produced.

TRILL: the momentary, but rapid, vibration of an articulator (i.e., tip of the tongue) against some point of articulation (i.e., alveolar ridge).

CHART I

Organos principales del habla   Principal Speech Organs

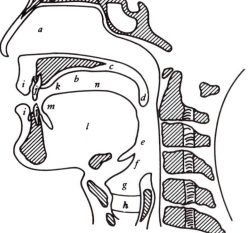

(*a*) **cavidad nasal**   nasal cavity; (*b*) **paladar**   palate; (*c*) **velo del paladar** velum; (*d*) **úvula**   uvula; (*e*) **faringe**   pharyngeal cavity; (*f*) **epiglotis**   epiglottis; (*g*) **laringe**   larynx; (*h*) **cuerdas vocales**   vocal bands; (*i*) **labios**   lips; (*j*) **dientes**   teeth; (*k*) **alvéolos**   alveolar ridge; (*l*) **lengua**   tongue; (*m*) **ápice** apex; (*n*) **cavidad bucal**   oral cavity.

SYLLABLE: the smallest sound group in a language.

> *Open Syllable:*   one which ends in a vowel, including final *y*.
>
> *Closed Syllable:*   one which ends in one or two consonants, excluding final *y*.
>
> *Tonic Syllable:*   the stressed syllable.
>
> *Atonic Syllable:*   an unaccented syllable.

RULES OF PRONUNCIATION
REGLAS DE LA PRONUNCIACION

A*   sounds like *A* in father and is pronounced as a clipped *ah.*   /a/

adrenal adrənál *adrenal*	**aparato** aparáto *apparatus*
abdomen abdómĕn *abdomen*	**amígdala** amígdəlɐ *tonsil*

* Here, and throughout the chapter, the asterisk instructs the reader to see **Dialectal Variations** on page 12–15.

B is pronounced exactly like *V*. Thus the sounds of **a ver** and **haber** and **las aves** and **la sabes** are the same. Pronunciation of these two letters depends on their position in the word, phrase, or sentence. When *B* appears at the beginning of a sentence, a breath group, or follows *M* or *N*, *B* has the *B* sound of *boy*.   /b/

hombro	ọmbrɔ	*shoulder*	**brazo**	brásɔ/bráθɔ	*arm*
miembro	mjémbrɔ	*limb*	**bazo**	básɔ/báθɔ	*spleen*

Note that in all other positions, especially when the *B* or *V* occurs between two vowels (intervocalic), the sound softens. They should then be pronounced with less lip pressure. Do not quite close the lips, but allow air to escape through the slight opening between them.   [b]

cabeza	kabésɐ/kabéθɐ	*head*	**aborto**	abọrtɔ	*abortion*

C has two sounds.

1. Before *A*, *O*, *U*, or a consonant, *C* generally has a hard sound, as in *cap*.*   /k/

carne	kárnɔ	*flesh*	**córnea**	kọrnɐ	*cornea*
cadáver	kaɖábɘɹ	*corpse*	**clavículas**	klabíkulas	*clavicles*
cuerpo	kwẹrpɔ	*body*	**cúbito**	kúbị̣to	*ulna*

2. *C* before *E* or *I* is pronounced like the *C* in *city* throughout most of Latin America and in the southern part of Spain. In Spain, except Andalusia, *C* followed by *E* or *I* is pronounced approximately like *TH* in the English word *thin*.   /s/ or /θ/ Castilian

cintura	sịṇtúrɐ/θịṇtúrɐ *waist*
cerebro	serébrɔ/θerébrɔ *cerebrum*
cirujano	sirụxánɔ/θirụxánɔ *surgeon*
contracepción	kọṇtrasẹbsjọ́n/kọṇtraθẹpθjọ́n *contraception*

*CH** is pronounced as the *CH* of *child*.   /ĉ/

chinelas	ĉinélɐs	*slippers*	**mucho**	múĉɔ	*much, a lot*
chaleco	ĉalékɔ	*vest*	**gancho**	gáṇĉɔ	*clasp (for a dental bridge)*
chicle	ĉíklɔ	*chewing gum*	**noche**	nóĉɔ	*night, evening*

D has two sounds.

1. At the beginning of a sentence, after a pause, an *N* or an *L* it is a hard, strongly dentalized sound. The tip of the tongue presses against the back of the upper front teeth.   /d/

domingo	domĩ́ŋgɔ *Sunday*
dolor	dolọ́ɹ *pain*
dos veces al día	dọz bésɐs ạl díɐ/dọz béθes ạl díɐ *twice a day*

NOTE: Care must be taken to articulate this Spanish *D* as a dental sound, and not as an alveolar as it is in English. Intervocalic *D* in English, as in mu*dd*y, la*dd*er, is the equivalent of Spanish *R*.

2. In other positions, *D* approaches the *TH* of *the*.*   [d̪]

médicos	méd̪ɪkǫs	*physicians*	**mojado**	moxá^dɔ	*wet*
codo	kód̪ɔ	*elbow*	**radio**	r̄ád̪jɔ	*radius*

E   has two sounds.

1. When no other letter follows it in the syllable, it is like the long *A* sound in m*a*te.   /e/

higiene	ɪxjénǝ	*hygiene*	**pelo**	pélɔ	*hair*
teléfono	teléfɔno	*telephone*	**vena**	bénɐ	*vein*

2. When followed by a consonant in the same syllable, or in contact with /r̄/ or before /x/, even though final in the syllable, *E* is like the *E* in m*e*t.*   [ę]

abertura	abęrtúrɐ	*opening*	**regla**	r̄églɐ	*menstrual period*
técnica	tęgnɪka/tęknɪka	*technician*	**oreja**	oręxɐ	*ear*

*F**   is pronounced essentially the same as in English.   /f/

afeitar	afęɪtáɹ	*to shave*	**fumar**	fumáɹ	*to smoke*
familia	famílɐ	*family*	**fémur**	fému̜ɹ	*femur*

G   before *A*, *O*, *U*, or a consonant has two sounds.

1. When initial after a pause or after *N*, the *G* is hard, like the *G* in g*i*rls.   /g/

lengua	léŋgwɐ	*tongue*	**gotero**	gotérɔ	*dropper*
garganta	gargáņtɐ	*throat*	**glándulas**	gláņdu̜las	*gland*

2. In all other positions the *G* before *A*, *O*, *U*, or a consonant has the weaker *G* of English su*g*ar. The back of the tongue is raised toward the soft palate but does not touch it.*   [g̱]

su gotero	su gotérɔ	*your dropper*	**hago**	ágɔ	*I am doing. I am making.*
las gafas	laz gáfɐs	*the glasses*		

G before *E* or *I* is a soft guttural sound that does not exist in English. Formed in the back of the throat, it is like the *CH* in German A*ch* or in the Scottish Lo*ch*.   /x/

virgen	bɪ́rxǝn	*virgin*	**ginecólogo**	xinǝkólɔgo	*gynecologist*
ingerir	ɪŋxerɪ́ɹ	*to ingest*	**gemelos**	xemélɔs	*twins*

Occasionally a silent *U* will precede the *E* or *I* to indicate that the *G* is hard as in English g*u*est.

pagué	pagé	*paid*	**guijón**	gɪxǫ́n	*tooth decay*

To keep the *U* sound in the *gue* or *gui* combination, a diaeresis (¨) is inserted over the *U*.

vergüenza bɛrgwénsɐ/bɛrgwéṇθɐ   *shame*
ungüento uŋgwéṇtↄ   *ointment*
bilingüe bilíŋgwə   *bilingual*

H   is the only silent consonant.

hormonas ↄrmõnɐs   *hormones*
hematólogo emɐtólↄgo   *hematologist*
heroína eroínɐ   *heroin*
hígado ígaᵈↄ   *liver*

I   is like the *I* in machine. /i/

infarto iɱfártↄ   *infarct*
interno iṇtérnↄ   *intern*
irritación iɾ̣itasʝↄ́n/iɾ̣itaθʝↄ́n   *irritation*

J   is pronounced just like the soft Spanish *G*. /x/

aguja agúxɐ   *needle*   **joven** xóbən   *young person*
juanete xwanétə   *bunion*   **jeringa** xeríŋgɐ   *syringe*

K   is pronounced as in English. /k/

kilo kílↄ   *kilo*   **kilogramo** kilográmↄ   *kilogram*
kilómetro kilómətro   *kilometer*

L*   is pronounced almost the same as in English, but with the tip of the tongue against the upper front teeth. /l/

líquido líkɪɖo   *liquid*
lágrimas lágrɪmas   *tears*
laceración laserasʝↄ́n/laθerɐθʝↄ́n   *laceration*

LL*   is considered to be one consonant in Spanish. In Mexico, many parts of South America, and in some parts of Spain it usually sounds like the *Y* of *yes*. In most parts of Spain, Paraguay, most of Peru, and in Bogota, Colombia *LL* approximates the *LLI* in the English word Wi*lli*am. /y/ or /ḽ/ Castilian

costilla kↄstíyɐ/kↄstíḽɐ   *rib*
espaldilla espaḽdíyɐ/espaḽdíḽɐ   *shoulder blade*
cuchillada kuĉɪyáᵈɐ/kuĉiḽáᵈɐ   *gash*
mellizos meyísↄs/meḽíθↄs   *twins*

M   is pronounced essentially the same as in English. /m/

miope mɪópə   *myopia*
metabolismo metabolízmↄ   *metabolism*
médula méɖula   *marrow*
mejilla məxíyɐ/məxíḽɐ   *cheek*

N has three pronunciations.

1. It is pronounced generally as in English. It is short and clipped. /n/

noche nóĉə *night*   **novacaína** nobakaínɐ *novocaine*
nalgas nálgɐs *buttocks*   **negro** négrɔ *black*

2. *N* is pronounced like *M* before *B, F, P, M,* and *V.* [m]

enfermo ẽm̩fẹ́rmɔ *ill*   **un viejo** ųm bɹéxɔ *an old man*
enfermera ẽm̩fɔ̃rmérɐ *nurse*   **un brazo** ųm brásɔ/ųm bráθɔ *an arm*
un pulmón ųm pųlm̩ǫ́n *a lung*
un metatarso ų̃ₙᵐ metatársɔ *a metatarsus*

3. *N* assumes a nasal quality similar to English *N* in ri*n*g before *CA, CU, CO, K, G, J, QU,* or *HUE.* [ŋ]

un hueso ųŋ wésɔ *a bone*   **un cúbito** ųŋ kúbɪtɔ *an ulna*
un kilo ųŋ kílɔ *one kilo*   **estancado** eʂtɐŋkáᵈɔ *stagnant*
sangre sáŋgrə *blood*   **estangurria** eʂtɐŋgúɹ̃jɐ *catheter*
un jarro ųŋ xáᵬɔ *a pitcher*   **estanquidad** eʂtɐŋkɪdáᵈ *watertightness*

Ñ sounds like the *NI* in o*ni*on or the *NY* in ca*ny*on. It always begins a syllable. /ɲ/

riñón r̃ɪ̃ɲǫ́n *kidney*   **señor** seɲǫ́ɹ *sir, Mr.*
niño nípɔ *child*

O has two pronunciations.

1. When it ends a syllable it is comparable to the English *O* in *o*ak.* /o/

agotamiento agotamɹ̃ẹ́ntɔ *exhaustion*
muslo múzlɔ *thigh*
enérgico enérgɪko *energetic*
oreja orẹ́xɐ *ear*
emocional emosjonál̩/emoθjonál̩ *emotional*
no nó *no*

2. When followed by a consonant in the same syllable it sounds like *O* in *o*r. [ɔ]

ombligo ǫmblígɔ *navel*   **hormona** ɔrmónɐ *hormone*
órgano ǫ́rgɐno *organ*   **cónyuge** kǫ́nŷųxə *spouse*

P is pronounced as in English. /p/

pañal paɲál *diaper*   **pecho** péĉɔ *chest, breast*
pijama pɪxámɐ *pajamas*   **pestaña** peʂtáɲɐ *eyelash*

In a few words the *P* before *S* is retained in print, but is silent. Some authorities now omit this initial *P*.

psicología sikɔlɔ́xíɐ *psychology*
psicoterapia sikɔterápjɐ *psychotherapy*
psiquíatra sikíɐtra *psychiatrist*

Q appears only before *UE* or *UI*. The *U* is always silent and the *Q* has a *K* sound. /k/

quejar kɐxáɹ *to complain*   **bronquios** brɔ́ŋkjɔs *bronchia*
quijada kɪxáᵈɐ *jaw*   **química** kímɪka *chemistry*

R* has two pronunciations.

1. It is slightly trilled when not in an initial position. /r/

primo hermano prímɔ ɐrmǎnɔ *first cousin*
sufrir sufríɹ *to suffer*

2. It is strongly trilled when initial or after *S*. /r̄/

roséola r̄osécla *roseola*
roncha r̄ɔ́ŋ̃ĉɐ *rash*; *welt*
los ricos lɔɹ r̄íkɔs *the wealthy*
reumatismo r̄eumɐtízmɔ *rheumatism*

RR* is very strongly trilled. *RR* often affects the sound of the vowel preceding it. /r̄/

sarro sár̄ɔ̌ *tartar of the teeth*   **gonorrea** gonɔr̄éɐ *gonorrhea*
diarrea djar̄éɐ *diarrhea*

S has two pronunciations.

1. *S* is usually pronounced as *ESS* in the English dr*ess*. /s/

saliva sɐlíbɐ *saliva*   **toser** toséɹ *to cough*
sudor suđóɹ *sweat*

2. *S* before *B, D, G, L, M, N,* and *V* has the *Z* sound in to*y*s. [z]

asma ázmɐ *asthma*   **los dientes** lɔz đjéŋtəs *the teeth*
desgana dezgánɐ *loss of appetite*

T is similar to English, but the tip of the tongue must go directly behind the upper front teeth. *T* is dental in Spanish, but alveolar in English; i.e., the tongue touches slightly above the gums. /t/

tijeras tɪxérɐs *scissors*
teléfono teléfcno *telephone*
asistente de hospital asɪṣtéŋtə đe ɔspɪtál *orderly*

NOTE: The sound the English *T* sometimes has when it occurs between vowels (wa*t*er, clu*tt*er) is the equivalent of Spanish *R*.

U sounds like the *U* in r*u*le. /u/

mujer	muxéɹ *woman*	**empujar**	empu̥xáɹ *to push*
pulso	pu̥lsɔ *pulse*	**agudo**	agúdɔ *acute*

V* has the same sound as Spanish *B*. /b/ or [b̆]

vaginal	baxɪnạl *vaginal*	**vena**	bénɐ *vein*
vacunar	baku̥náɹ *to vaccinate*	**la vena**	la bénɐ *the vein*
verruga	bɛɾúgɐ *wart*	**la vida**	la bídɐ *the life*

W occurs only in foreign words and keeps the pronunciation of the original language. /w/

X has two pronunciations.

1. Before a consonant, it is usually a hissing *S* as in *s*it.* /s/

excelente essǝléṇtǝ/eşθǝléṇtǝ *excellent*
ambidextro ambɪdéştrɔ *ambidextrous*

2. Between vowels *X* is like the *X* in e*x*amine. [gs]

sexual sɛgswạl *sexual*   **tóxico** tógsɪko *toxic*

In Mexico the words *México*, *mexicano*, and *Texas* are written with an *X*, but pronounced with Spanish *J*. In Spain these words are spelled with a *J*.

Y* has three pronunciations.

1. As a consonant it is generally pronounced like the *Y* in *y*es. /y/

yo	yó I	**yeso**	yésɔ *plaster*
yodo	yódɔ *iodine*	**yerno**	yɛ́rnɔ *son-in-law*
yeyuno	yeyúnɔ *jejunum*		

2. Consonantal *Y* is usually pronounced like the *J* in *j*udge when it follows an *N*. [ŷ]

cónyuge kǫ́ṇŷu̥xǝ *spouse*   **inyectar** ịṇŷɛktáɹ *to inject*
inyección ịṇŷɛksɹǫ́n/ịṇŷ̧ɛgθɹǫ́n *injection*

3. When it stands alone or at the end of a word, *Y* is considered a vowel and is pronounced as the Spanish *I*. /i/

y i *and*   **estoy** eştǫ́i̧ *I am*

Z is pronounced the same way as *C* before *E* or *I*. Thus, in Spanish America and in southern Spain it has the *S* sound of *sit*. In central and northern Spain *Z* has the *TH* sound of *th*ink. /s/ or /θ/ Castilian

embarazada embaɾɐsáᵈɐ/embaɾɐθáᵈɐ *pregnant*
izquierdo, -a ɪskjéɾdɔ, -ɐ/ɪθkjéɾdɔ, -ɐ *left*
zurdo sṵ́ɾdɔ/θṵ́ɾdɔ *left-handed*

DIALECTAL VARIATIONS OF SPANISH

VARIANTES DIALECTALES DE ESPAÑOL

In Spain any educated speaker can easily be understood by any other educated Spanish-speaker. This is due both to unanimity of linguistic standards and to uniformity of education. Dialectal differences are great, however, among the uneducated masses.

In Spanish America the Spanish differs from that of Spain principally in vocabulary and pronunciation. The most acceptable dialect of Spanish throughout Spanish America is apparently that spoken in southern Mexico, the Yucatan peninsula, Guatemala, Honduras, El Salvador, Nicaragua, Costa Rica, the interior of Venezuela, Ecuador, most of Colombia, Peru, and Chile.[1]

The following discussion briefly describes dialectal variations that exist both in Spain and in Spanish America, Remember, any educated Spanish-speaker can easily understand and be understood by any other educated Spanish-speaker regardless of country of origin.

Vowels *Vocales*

A In central Mexico and parts of Ecuador, words with an unstressed *A* at the end are occasionally quite relaxed, almost to the *UH* sound, in rapid conversation.

E In the Caribbean region Spanish-speakers frequently use the pronunciation of the English *E* as in b*e*t, even when no other letter follows it in the syllable.

I Has no important dialectal variations.

O In parts of Cuba, Mexico, and Colombia a final unstressed *O* is pronounced as the *U* in English r*u*le. This usually does not cause confusion.

U Has no important dialectal variations.

Consonants *Consonantes*

C In all dialects of Spanish the hard *C* sound at the end of a syllable or at the end of a foreign word is often eliminated when it occurs in rapid speech.

doctor > **dotor** dǫktǫ́ɹ > dǫtǫ́ɹ *doctor*
Nueva York > **Nueva Yor** nwébɐ yǫ́rk > nwébɐ yǫ́r *New York*

The syllable final hard *C* generally tends to voice to /g/:

doctor > **dogtor** dǫktǫ́ɹ > dǫgtǫ́ɹ *doctor*
técnico > **tégnico** tékn̩ko > tégn̩ko > tégn̩ko *technician*

CH In Panama, Cuba, and the Dominican Republic a variation of this sound (similar to English *sh*ell) is freely used in which the tongue assumes almost the same position as for the *CH*, except that the front of the tongue never touches the front palate.

D Sometimes the intervocalic *D* completely disappears in all dialects of Spanish. Even educated Spanish-speakers will frequently drop it in words ending in *-ado*:

operado > **operao** opəráᵈɔ > opəráɔ > opəráɔ > opəráṳ *operated*

It is usually eliminated when occurring at the end of a word:

Madrid > **Madri** mađríd > mađríᵈ > mađrí *Madrid*
usted > **uste** ṳstęđ > ṳstęᵈ > ṳsté *you (formal, sg)*

The omission of this *D* in any other combination is considered substandard:

nada > **naa** or **na** náđɐ > náɐ > ną *nothing*

F In many parts of Spanish America a rural variant of the *F* sound exists, particularly after the *M* sound and before the diphthong *UE*. This free variation is a softened *P*:

enfermo > **epermo** em̩fę́rmɔ > epę́rmɔ *ill*
fuerte > **puerte** fwę́rtə > pwę́rtə *strong*

G This sometimes disappears at the end of a syllable:

indigno > **indino** ın̩dígnɔ > ın̩dínɔ *unworthy*

Many uneducated or rural Spanish-speakers will use dialectal variations of *GU* for *BU*. This is considered substandard Spanish and is indicated orthographically by the use of *GÜ*:

abuela > **agüela** aþwélɐ > agwélɐ *grandmother*
buenos días > **güenos días** bwénǫẕ díɐs > gwénǫẕ díɐs *good morning,*
good day, hello

Many educated speakers, however, will pronounce words with *HU* as though they were spelled *GU* or *GÜ* or even *BU*:

hueso > **güeso** or **bueso**   wésɔ > gwésɔ or bwésɔ   *bone*

The uneducated speakers make these same sounds stops, instead of fricatives, especially before nasals:

un hueso   ų̊ŋ gwésɔ/ų̊m bwésɔ   *a bone*

/X/   In southern Spain, the Caribbean, and Central America, *J*, *GE*, and *GI* are pronounced [h].

L   When *L* occurs at the end of a syllable, it is often replaced by *R* by uneducated Spanish-speakers in the Caribbean, along the coast of Colombia, and parts of Chile.

bolsillo > **borsillo**   bɔlsíyɔ > bɔ ɹsíyɔ   *pocket*

LL   In Uruguay, Argentina, and neighboring countries, *LL* sometimes sounds like *S* in plea*s*ure [ž] and sometimes like *J* in *j*udge [ŷ]. In these countries the consonant *Y* has the *LL* pronunciation.

calle   kážə   *street*   **hallo**   ážɔ/áŷɔ   *I find*

NS   In the syllables *INS*, *CONS*, and *TRANS*, the *N* is often nasalized or lost in semieducated and uneducated speech.

constipado   kɔnʂtipáɖɔ > kɔⁿʂtıpáᵈɔ > kõʂtıpáᵈɔ > kɔʂtıpą̊ɔ   *head cold*

PC   The *P* in the *PC* group of certain learned words is often lost; in ordinary conversation the *P* is often modified to *B*.

suscripción   sų̊skrıpsjɔ́n/sų̊skrıpθjɔ́n > sų̊skrısjɔ́n/sų̊skrıθjɔ́n   *subscription*
concepción   kɔnsępsjɔ́n/kɔn̦θępθjɔ́n > kɔnsębsjɔ́n/kɔn̦θębθjɔ́n   *conception*

PS   In uneducated speech the *P* is suppressed when the *PS* occurs within a word.

cápsula   kápsula > ką̊ų̊sula   *capsule*
autopsia   ą̊ų̊tópsja > ą̊ų̊tósja   *autopsy*

In Cuba, Central America, Colombia, and Venezuela *PS* is pronounced *KS*:

pepsi cola   péksi kóle   *Pepsi Cola*

PT   is pronounced *KT* and vice versa:

apto   áptɔ > áktɔ   *apt*

R Many Spanish-speaking people, even educated speakers, in the Caribbean, the coastal region of Colombia, and parts of Chile, will replace syllables ending with *R* with an *L*:

enfermo > **enfelmo** eɱfélmɔ *ill*   **carne** > **calne** kȧlnə *meat*

The sounds of Spanish *R* is similar to the English *D* or *T* sounds of mu*dd*y, bu*dd*y, bu*tt*er, or wa*t*er. This frequently causes confusion in hearing and speaking for English-speakers of Spanish:

cata   **cada**   **cara**
moto   **modo**   **moro**

The syllable final *R* and the *RR* are strongly assibilated in Guatemala, Costa Rica, Bolivia, Chile, Paraguay and parts of Colombia, Ecuador, and Argentina: [ř][řř]

mujer mṵxéř *woman*

RR Spanish-speakers in Cuba, Puerto Rico, the Dominican Republic, Panama, and coastal Colombia pronounce the *RR* so that the tongue strikes either the uvula or the velum. This type of sound exists in French (*rouge*) and German (*rot*).

S The Spanish spoken in Cuba, Puerto Rico, the Dominican Republic, and the coastal regions of Chile, Argentina, and Uruguay substitutes an aspirated *H* sound for both voiced and unvoiced *S*. This pronunciation is common among educated speakers, especially in rapid conversation:

espero ęʰpérɔ *I am waiting*   **los codos** loʰ kódɔs *the elbows*
los chicos loʰ ĉikɔs *the children*

S is pronounced *R* among the uneducated:

exceso essésɔ/eʂθésɔ > ęɹsésɔ/ęɹθésɔ *excess*
los dientes loẓ djéntəs > loɹ djéntəs *the teeth*

In southern Spain *S* before a voiced consonant drops out, and the voiced consonant becomes unvoiced.

V The occasional use of the *V* sound is not a matter of dialect. Rather, it is a hypercorrection. The *V* sound has never been used consistently in modern Spanish and is best avoided.

X In Cuba, Puerto Rico, the Dominican Republic, Venezuela, and parts of Argentina and Uruguay, *X* before a consonant has an aspirated *H* sound:

extraño ęʰtráṇɔ *strange*

Y In eastern Argentina, Uruguay, and central Colombia, *Y* is pronounced like the *S* in plea*s*ure. [ž]

ayer ažḛɹ *yesterday*

DIPHTHONGS

DIPTONGOS

The vowels are divided into two groups: strong vowels—*A, E, O*; weak vowels—*U, I (Y)*.

Spanish vowels retain their basic sound when they form part of a diphthong, but they are pronounced more rapidly in succession and form one syllable. A diphthong consists of a strong and weak vowel, a weak and strong vowel, or two weak vowels in one syllable.

AU   about like "ow" in "cow."   [aṷ]

    causa káu̯sɐ *cause*   **primeros auxilios** primércs au̯gsíljcs *first aid*

UA   about like "wa" in "waffle."   [wa]

    juanete xwanétɐ *bunion*   **sublingual** sublíŋgwál *sublingual*

AI or *AY*   about like "ai" in "aisle," or "y" in "rye."   [ai̯]

    hay ái̯ *there is, there are*   **suprainguinal** supraiŋgɪnál *suprainguinal*

IA   about like "ya" in "yard."   [ja]

    arteria artérjɐ *artery*   **tenia** ténjɐ *tapeworm*

EU   an "e" plus "u" *sound.*   [eṷ]

    terapéutico terɐpéṷtɪko *therapeutic*   **leucorrea** leṷkọřéɐ *leukorrhea*

UE   about like "we" in "wet."   [we]

    hueso wésc *bone*   **cuerpo** kwẹrpc *body*

EI or *EY*   about like "ei" in "eight" or "ey" in "they."   [ei̯]

    aceite asẹi̯tɐ/aθẹi̯tɐ *oil*   **ley** lẹi̯ *law*

IE   about like "ye" in "yes."   [je]

    diente djéntɐ *tooth*   **tienta** tjéntɐ *surgical probe*

OI or *OY*   about like the "oy" in "toy."   [ọi̯]

    hoy ọi̯ *today*   **sigmoidoscopio** sigmọi̯dɔskópjc *sigmoidoscope*

IO   about like "yo" in "yoke."   [jo]

    ovario obárjc *ovary*   **labio** lábjc *lip*

UO   about like "wo" in "woke."   [wo]

    duodeno dwodénc *duodenum*   **sinuoso** sinwósc *sinuous*

IU   about like "ew" in "chew."   [ju]

di*u*rético djurétɪko *diuretic*   **di*u*rno** djúrnɔ *diurnal*

UI or *UY*   like "we."   [wi]

m*uy* mwí *very*   **c*ui*dado** kwiđáᵈɔ *care*

The stress in a diphthong is always on the strong vowel, or on the second of two weak ones.

The combinations *QUE, QUI, GUE,* or *GUI* are *not* diphthongs: the *U* is silent.

sang*ui*neo saŋgínǝo *blood* (adj)   **in*qui*rir** iŋkɪríɹ *to inquire into*

Two strong vowels never form a diphthong:

íleon í-lǝ-ǫn *ileum*   **coágulo** kɔ-á-gʉ-lo *clot*
cráneo krá-nǝ-o *skull*

When the weak vowel in a strong and weak vowel combination is stressed, a written accent on the weak vowel breaks up the diphthong:

frío fríɔ *cold*   **cocaína** ko-ka-í-nɐ *cocaine*

REMARKS CONCERNING THE FORMATION OF SOME SPANISH WORDS AND THEIR CORRESPONDING ENGLISH EQUIVALENTS

CORRESPONDENCIA DE PALABRAS

The Spanish ending *ción* corresponds to the English *tion.*

esterilización sterilization   **obfuscación** obfuscation
recuperación recuperation

The Spanish endings *dad* and *tad* correspond to the English *ty.*

dificultad difficulty   **sexualidad** sexuality
mortalidad mortality

The Spanish endings *dad* and *tad* may also correspond to the English *ness.*

enfermedad illness

The Spanish endings *cia* and *cio* correspond to the English *ce.*

servicio service   **edificio** edifice
impotencia impotence

The Spanish ending *cia* may also correspond to the English *tia.*

exodoncia exodontia   **demencia** dementia
ortodoncia orthodontia

The Spanish endings *ia* and *io* correspond to the English *y.*

directorio directory   **laboratorio** laboratory
familia family

The Spanish ending *ia* also corresponds to the English *y.*

disentería dysentery   **histerectomía** hysterectomy
vasectomía vasectomy

The Spanish ending *oso* (*osa* in the feminine) corresponds to the English *ous.*

cauteloso (cautelosa) cautious   **nervioso (nerviosa)** nervous
generoso (generosa) generous

The Spanish ending *ico* (*ica* in the feminine) corresponds to the English *ical.*

biológico (biológica) biological   **físico (física)** physical

The Spanish ending *itis* corresponds to the English *itis.*

mastitis mastitis   **laringitis** laryngitis

The Spanish ending *scopio* corresponds to the English *scope.*

microscopio microscope   **estetoscopio** stethoscope

The Spanish ending *ólogo* corresponds to the English *gist.*

patólogo pathologist   **oftalmólogo** ophthalmologist
neurólogo neurologist

The Spanish ending *'tico* (*'tica* in the feminine) corresponds to the English *otic.*

narcótico narcotic   **neurótico (neurótica)** neurotic

The Spanish ending *logía* corresponds to the English *logy.*

serología serology   **biología** biology

The Spanish ending *ómetro* corresponds to the English *ometer.*

termómetro thermometer   **esfigmomanómetro** sphygmomanometer

Many English words that begin with *s* and a consonant, insert *e* before the *s* for the corresponding Spanish word.

esfigmomanómetro sphygmomanometer   **escroto** scrotum
esquizofrénico schizophrenic

English words that have the *ph* sound are spelled in Spanish with an *f*.

físico physical   **fósforo** phosphorus
flebitis phlebitis

The English vowel *y* is replaced in Spanish by the *i*.

esfigmomanómetro sphygmomanometer   **hímen** hymen

Many English words ending in silent *e*, drop the *e* and add *o* or *a* in Spanish.

medicina medicine   **caso** case
intenso (intensa) intense   **dentífrico** dentifrice

Many English words that end in a consonant add *o*, *a*, or *e* in Spanish.

accidente accident   **mucho** much
víctima victim

The endings *ar*, *er*, and *ir* are added to some English infinitives that end in a consonant to form the corresponding verbs in Spanish.

permitir permit   **comprender** comprehend
inyectar inject

Many English infinitives ending in silent *e*, drop the *e* and add *ar* or *ir* to form the Spanish equivalent.

terminar terminate   **revivir** revive
cauterizar cauterize

ACCENTUATION
ACENTUACION

Stress is the prominence given to certain syllables: *HOS-pi-tal*. Spanish has only two degrees of stress—strong and weak:

docTOR weak + strong   **enFERmo** weak + strong + weak

In English, stress is occasionally used to differentiate between words:

wind (n)   wind (v)
live (adj)   live (v)

In Spanish the same use of stress occurs:

praTIco (I practice)
practiCÓ (he practiced)
PRÁtico (practical, medical practitioner)

Spanish words do not usually bear a written accent (´). Rules for determining the stressed syllable are clear:

1. Words ending in a vowel, an -*N*, or -*S*, stress the next to the last syllable:

a-ci-DO-sis acidosis　　　**BUS-can** they are looking for
me-di-CI-na medicine

2. Words ending in a consonant other than -*N* or -*S*, are stressed on the last syllable:

pe-OR worst　　　**es-pa-ÑOL** Spanish

NOTE: Final *Y*, although pronounced as a vowel, is considered a consonant for the purpose of written accentuation.

3. Words that do not follow rules 1 and 2 must have a written accent mark (´) on the syllable stressed.

Á-ci-do acid　　　**ac-NÉ** acne
tam-PóN tampon　　　**MÉ-di-co** physician

NOTE: Spanish has only one written accent, which always indicates that the syllable bearing it is *stressed*.

1. Interrogative words are always accented:

¿qué? what?　　　**¿cuánto?** how much?
¿cuándo? when?

2. A written accent differentiates similarly spelled words, usually monosyllabic, with different meanings:

él	he	**el**	the
dé	give (command)	**de**	of, from
sí	yes	**si**	if
sé	I know	**se**	himself, etc.
sólo	only (adv)	**solo**	alone (adj)

The accent mark may be omitted over capital letters: **PRONUNCIACION DE CONVERSACION MEDICA.**

DIVISION OF WORDS INTO SYLLABLES

SEPARACION DE LAS SILABAS

Spanish words are syllabified according to simple but rigid rules:

1. A word has as many syllables as it has vowels, diphthongs, and triphthongs.

2. A single consonant, including *CH*, *LL*, *RR*, goes with the following vowel:

   sa-rro   tartar   **ni-ño**   little boy
   mu-cha-cha   girl

3. Two consonants are usually separated:

   som-no-len-cia   sleepiness   **a-del-ga-zar**   to lose weight
   bar-bi-lla   chin

   (*a*) A combination of a consonant and an *L* or an *R* (which can begin a word in English) goes with the following vowel in Spanish:

   re-tra-í-do   withdrawn   **pla-no**   plain
   sa-cro   sacrum

   (*c*) There is one exception: *-S* plus a consonant. Since this combination cannot begin a syllable, the *-S* goes with the preceding syllable:

   as-cen-sor   elevator   **es-to-ca-da**   stab

4. Three consonants are usually divided after the first one, unless the second is an *S*:

   in-gle   groin   **abs-ten-ción**   withdrawal
   tem-blar   to tremble

5. Four consonants between vowels are a very rare Spanish combination. They are always divided after the second:

   obs-truc-ción   blockage   **trans-plan-te**   transplant
   re-cons-truc-ti-vo   reconstructive

PRACTICE *PRACTICA*

Rewrite the following words. Divide them into syllables and indicate the stressed syllable.

therapist   **terapeuta**   _____
to rinse   **enjuagar**   _____
vulva   **vulva**   _____
umbilicus   **ombligo**   _____

red-haired **pelirrojo**	_____
X-ray therapy **radioterapia**	_____
ammonia **amoníaco**	_____
vaccination **inoculación**	_____
diaphragm **diafragma**	_____
enema **lavativa**	_____
dressing **parche**	_____
drainage **drenaje**	_____
crutch **muleta**	_____
infarct **infarto**	_____
hoarseness **carraspera**	_____
lump **borujo**	_____
measles **sarampión**	_____
nit **liendra**	_____
malarial fever **chucho**	_____
German measles **rubéola**	_____

PRONUNCIATION PRACTICE _PRACTICA DE LA PRONUNCIACION_

Contrast the two sounds.

Practice the contrasting _b_ sounds.

		/b/	/ƀ/
vagina	the vagina	**vagina**	**la vagina**
beard	the beard	**barba**	**la barba**
mouth	the mouth	**boca**	**la boca**
I drink	I drink	**bebo**	**yo bebo**
he came	he came	**vino**	**él vino**
bladder	the bladder	**vejiga**	**la vejiga**

Practice the contrasting _d_ sounds.

		|d|	|đ|
finger	my finger	**dedo**	**mi dedo**
weakness	the weakness	**debilidad**	**la debilidad**
pain	a little pain	**dolor**	**poco dolor**
doubt	the doubt	**duda**	**la duda**
slender		**delgado**	

Practice the contrasting _g_ sounds.

		(g)	/ɡ/
it pleases	I like	**gusta**	**me gusta**
drop	a drop	**gota**	**una gota**
expenses	your expenses	**gastos**	**sus gastos**

Practice the contrasting *r* sounds.

		/r̄/	/r/
knee	the knee	**r**odilla	la **r**odilla
cold		**r**esfriado	
diarrhea		dia**rr**ea	
	uterus		**ú**tero
rabies		**r**abia	
	urethra		u**r**etra
rectum		**r**ecto	
	relative		pa**r**iente
kidney		**r**iñón	
	ear		o**r**eja
gonorrhea		gono**rr**ea	
	nose		na**r**iz

READING EXERCISE   *EJERCICIO DE LECTURA*

Read the following aloud for pronunciation practice.

Un doctor me dijo que no podía quedarme en este lugar y que tendría que dormir más, hacer más ejercicios y comer menos.

—Pero, doctor, ¿adónde iré para vivir de este modo? No puedo dormir tanto si me despiertan temprano todos los días. Y no me gusta divertirme con deportes.

El perro de San Roque no tiene rabo porque Ramón Ramírez se lo ha cortado.

PUNCTUATION

PUNCTUACION

Spanish punctuation is the same as English punctuation with the following exceptions:

1. A question has an inverted question mark (¿) at the beginning of the question as well as the regular question mark (?) at the end.

   ¿Dónde está el médico?   Where is the physician?

2. An inverted exclamation point (¡) precedes exclamations and a regular exclamation mark (!) concludes them.

   ¡Qué magnífica enfermera es!   What a magnificent nurse she is!

3. In quotations a dash (—) is generally used to indicate a change of speaker instead of quotation marks.

El doctor dijo:—¿Qué es lo que Vd. padece?—Siento mucha opresión en el pecho.—respondió Pablo.

The doctor said: "What is the matter with you?" "I feel a lot of congestion in my chest," responded Paul.

Common Punctuation Symbols

Frecuentes símbolos de punctuación

apostrophe	'	**apóstrofo**
asterisk	*	**asterisco**
braces	{ }	**corchetes**
brackets	[ ]	**paréntesis cuadrados**
colon	:	**dos puntos**
comma	,	**coma**
dash	—	**raya**
diaeresis	ä	**crema / diéresis**
exclamation point	¡ !	**principio de exclamación (¡); fin de exclamación (!)**
hyphen	-	**guión**
parentheses	( )	**paréntesis**
period	.	**punto**
question mark	¿ ?	**principio de interrogación (¿); fin de interrogación (?)**
quotation marks	" "	**comillas**
semicolon	;	**punto y coma**
suspension points	. . .	**puntos suspensivos**

The conjunction *o* is accented between numbers to avoid confusion with zero.

Tengo 7 ó 8.   I have 7 or 8.

CAPITALIZATION

USO DE MAYUSCULAS

Capital letters are not used as frequently in Spanish as in English. Only proper nouns and topographic nouns are capitalized.

The pronoun **yo** (I) is not capitalized, except at the beginning of a sentence.

The days of the week and the months of the year are not capitalized except at the beginning of a sentence. Names of political parties, languages, and titles are not capitalized.

Hoy es miércoles   Today is Wednesday.

Es el veinte de agosto.   It is the twentieth of August.

El es republicano, no demócrato.   He is a Republican, not a Democrat.

An adjective of nationality is not capitalized. Some authors capitalize adjectives of nationality used as nouns while others do not.

Dígalo Vd. en inglés.   Say it in English.

Hablo con un español. ⎫
                           ⎬   I am speaking to a Spaniard.
Le hablo a un Español. ⎭

The followed words are capitalized when they are abbreviated:

usted-Vd. (Ud.)   ustedes-Vds. (Uds.)   you

señor-Sr.   señora-Sra.   señorita-Srta.   Mr.   Mrs.   Miss

The following nouns are also capitalized:

1. Divine attributes

    Creador   Creator   **Redentor**   Redeemer

2. Titles and nicknames which designate specific people

    el Duque de Windsor   the Duke of Windsor

3. Names of important positions and public powers when they are equivalent to proper names

    el Rey   the King   **el Presidente**   the President

4. Certain collective nouns

    la Nación   the Nation   **el Reino**   the Kingdom

EXERCISES   *EJERCICIOS*

A. Rewrite the following passages, inserting proper punctuation and capitals.

1. qué causa la alta presión arterial   el 90–95% de todos los casos de alta presión arterial es debido a una causa desconocida

2. el tiempo en la sala de recuperación varía de una hora a 3 o 4 horas o más

3. la siguiente información es exigida por la administración de alimentos y drogas de los estados unidos   la píldora es el más eficaz de todos los anticonceptivos si sigue completamente las instrucciones sobre su uso.

4. por favor vaya a llamar al dr. garcía del departamento de psiquiatría a ver si puede continuar con el examen

5. inglaterra tiene un sistema de la medicina socializada en que el gobierno paga los gastos médicos

B. Examine the following sentences. Note the differences between the Spanish writing system and the English writing system. Draw circles around examples of such differences.

1. —¡Hola, Carlos! ¿Qué tal? ¿Cómo estás?

2. —Muy bien, gracias, ¿y tú?

3. —¿Cómo está usted, doctor Ortega?[2]
4. —Estoy bien, gracias. ¿Y Vd., señor Burgos?[2]

Notes *Notas*

1. Pedro Henríquez Ureña, "Observaciones sobre el español de América," *Revista de filología española* VIII (1921): 357–390.

2. Note that the titles **doctor** (Dr.) and **señor** (Mr.) are not capitalized as they would be in English. Spanish uses a capital with these titles only when they are abbreviated. See page 25.

CHAPTER

Essential Grammar

Gramática básica

PARTS OF SPEECH

LAS PARTES DE LA ORACION

In Spanish as well as in English, there are eight parts of speech: nouns, pronouns, verbs, adjectives, adverbs, prepositions, conjunctions, and interjections.

NOUNS *LOS SUSTANTIVOS*

A *noun* is the name of a person, place, or thing.

physician **médico**   clinic **clínica**
speculum **espéculo; espejo vaginal**

PRONOUNS *LOS PRONOMBRES*

A *pronoun* is a word that takes the place of, or is used instead of, a noun.

he (3rd person, sg, subject pronoun) **él**
us (1st person, pl, object pronoun) **nos**

VERBS *LOS VERBOS*

A *verb* is a word that shows action, being, or state of being.

Nurse Gómez takes the ECG. **La enfermera Gómez le hace un electro-cardiograma.** (action)

Robert is an anesthesiologist. **Roberto es anestesiólogo.** (being)

The child is constipated. **El niño está estreñido.** (state of being)

ADJECTIVES *LOS ADJETIVOS*

An *adjective* is a word that modifies (limits or describes) a noun or pronoun.

dehydrated **deshidratado** (m, sg), **deshidratados** (m, pl)
            deshidratada (f, sg), **deshidratadas** (f, pl)

Delimiting adjectives precede the noun that they modify; *descriptive adjectives* usually follow the noun that they modify.

my son **mi hijo**

my constipated son **mi hijo estreñido**

3 syringes **tres jeringas**

3 hypodermic syringes **tres jeringas hipodérmicas**

ARTICLES *LOS ARTICULOS*

Articles are the most frequent of Spanish adjectives. Unlike English, the Spanish article agrees in number and gender with the noun that it modifies. Both the definite and indefinite articles precede the noun. The definite article modifies a definite person, place, or thing.

the attending physician   **el médico de cabecera**

the bones   **los huesos**

the operating room   **la sala de operaciones**

the arteries   **las arterias**

The indefinite article denotes an indefinite person, place, or thing.

a surgeon   **un cirujano**

an emergency room   **una sala de urgencia**

a thermometer   **un termómetro**

ADVERBS *LOS ADVERBIOS*

An *adverb* is a word, phrase, or clause that modifies a verb, an adjective, or another adverb. Unlike an adjective, an adverb shows no agreement with the word that it modifies. It is helpful to group adverbs into categories. Adverbs answer the questions *where?* (place), *how?* (manner), *when?* (time). They are also grouped according to *quantity, negation, affirmation, order, doubt,* and *concession.*

He doesn't operate *blindly.*   **El no opera *a ciegas.*** (adverbial phrase modifying a verb)

Jane is *very* constipated.   **Juana está *muy* estreñida.** (simple adverb modifying an adjective)

The clinic is *quite* near.   **La clínica está *bastante* cerca.** (simple adverb modifying an adverb)

The patient waited in the recovery room *until the surgeon released him.* **El paciente esperó en la sala de recuperación *hasta que el cirujano le dio de alta.*** (adverbial clause)

PREPOSITIONS *LAS PREPOSICIONES*

A *preposition* is a word that shows the relation of a noun, pronoun, infinitive, or adverb following it to some other word in a sentence or expression.

toward the doctor   **hacia el médico** (preposition + noun)

around her   **alrededor de ella** (preposition + pronoun)

after operating   **después de operar** (preposition + infinitive)

for tomorrow   **para mañana** (preposition + adverb)

Prepositional phrases function either as adjectives or as adverbs.

the wheelchair **la silla *de ruedas*** (adj)
Take the pills after eating. **Tome Vd. las píldoras *después de comer*.** (adv)

CONJUNCTIONS *LAS CONJUNCIONES*

A *conjunction* is a word (or a combination of words) that joins words or groups of words to other words or groups of words.

> The stethoscope *and* the speculum are here, *but* the sphygmomanometer isn't. **El estetoscopio *y* el espejo vaginal están aquí, *pero* el baumanómetro no está.**

INTERJECTIONS *LAS INTERJECCIONES*

An *interjection* is a word or combination of words that expresses strong or sudden feeling without any grammatical connection to what precedes or follows.

> What a pity! **¡Qué lástima!**

DECLARATIVE WORD ORDER

ORDEN DE LAS PALABRAS EN LA ORACION ENUNCIATIVA

A sentence is a group of words that expresses a complete thought. There are two parts to the sentence: the subject (noun or pronoun) and its modifiers, and the predicate (verb) and its modifiers.

Spanish word order is much more flexible than English word order. The meaning is not usually affected by a change in the order of the words.

El médico encuentra a las enfermeras en el hospital en la sala de emergencia.

En el hospital en la sala de emergencia el médico encuentra a las enfermeras.

En el hospital el médico encuentra a las enfermeras en la sala de emergencia.

El médico encuentra en el hospital a las enfermeras en la sala de emergencia.

Encuentra el médico a las enfermeras en el hospital en la sala de emergencía.

The physician meets the nurses in the hospital in the emergency room.

It may be helpful to remember that the subject of the Spanish sentence, though it frequently precedes the verb, may follow it, especially when the subject is longer than the predicate.

Aquí se ven muchas operaciones.   Many operations are seen here.

The two parts of a compound verb are *never* separated.

Le haría daño a los ojos.   It would harm your eyes.

INTERROGATIVE WORD ORDER
INTERROGACION

A question is ordinarily formed in Spanish by placing the verb before the subject, which is done in English in the case of the verbs *be* and *have*, and the other auxiliary verbs.

> **Usted es enfermera.**   (statement)
> **¿Es usted enfermera?**   (question)

A declarative sentence may be turned into a question by using the expression **¿verdad?** or **¿no es verdad?** or simply **¿no?** at the end of a statement.

Usted habla español, ¿verdad?   You speak Spanish, don't you?

In questions the Spanish word order may be:

$$\text{Verb} + \begin{cases} \text{Adverb} \\ \text{Noun Object} \\ \text{Predicate Adjective} \end{cases} + \text{Subject}$$

If an interrogative word is used in the question, normally this word is placed in the same position as in the English sentence.

¿Por qué necesita primeros auxilios?   Why do you need first aid?

EXERCISES *EJERCICIOS*

A.   Change the following sentences to interrogatives, according to the model.

> **La enfermera trabaja en el hospital.**
> **¿Trabaja la enfermera en el hospital?**
> **¿Trabaja en el hospital la enfermera?**

1. **Tú practicas en la clínica.**
2. **El médico está en el hospital.**

3. El doctor López practica aquí.
4. Ella consulta ahora.
5. El doctor y las enfermeras operan en el quirófano.
6. Nosotros examinamos a los pacientes.
7. El doctor Valdés necesita ayuda.
8. Usted trabaja en el hospital.
9. Tú operas en la sala de operaciones.
10. Yo opero en el hospital.

B. Say the following in Spanish.

1. Does Dr. Rivera practice in the hospital?
2. Are they consulting?
3. Do you (familiar) work in the hospital?
4. Does the doctor operate in the clinic?
5. Are they examining the patients?

NEGATION

NEGACION

The most frequently used negative word in Spanish is **no.** To form a negative statement or question, place the word **no** immediately before the verb.

¿Sufre Vd.?   Do you suffer?

Vd. no sufre.   You do not suffer. You are not suffering.

¿No sufre Vd.?   Don't you suffer?

El médico examina al paciente.   The physician examines the patient.

El médico no examina al paciente.   The doctor doesn't examine the patient.

Only the reflexive, indirect, and direct object pronouns (the R.I.D. pronouns) may come between **no** and the verb it negates.

La enfermera le pone una inyección al enfermo.   The nurse gives the sick man an injection.

La enfermera no le pone una inyección al enfermo.   The nurse doesn't give the sick man an injection.

La enfermera se la pone a él.   The nurse gives it to him.

La enfermera no se la pone a él.   The nurse doesn't give it to him.

In order to answer a yes or no question negatively, two **no**'s are used, the first responds to the question, and the second negates the verb.

¿Opera él? No, él no opera.   Does he operate? No, he doesn't operate.

EXERCISES *EJERCICIOS*

Make the following sentences negative.

1. **Ella menstrua ya.**
2. **El médico está en el hospital.**
3. **Yo consulto en la clínica.**
4. **Las enfermeras operan.**
5. **Usted examina al paciente.**
6. **Nosotros necesitamos primeros auxilios.**
7. **El doctor opera en la sala de emergencia.**
8. **Nosotros ayudamos a los pacientes.**
9. **Roberto necesita a un médico.**
10. **La enferma está en el hospital.**

Spanish uses other negative words. The most common negative expressions and their affirmative counterparts are the following.

Negative	*Affirmative*
no no, not	**sí** yes
nadie no one, nobody, not anyone	**alguien** someone, somebody
nada nothing, not anything	**algo** something
ninguno, -a, -os, -as no, none, not any	**alguno, -a, -os, -as** some, any
ni . . . ni neither . . . nor, not . . . nor	**o . . . o** either . . . or
nunca/jamás never, not ever	**siempre** always
	algunas veces/a veces sometimes
	muchas veces often
	alguna vez ever, at sometime
tampoco neither, not either	**también** too, also
sin without	**con** with
todavía not yet	**ya** already

Double negation is correct and common in Spanish, although not in English. Double negation means that the negative word **no** precedes the verb, and that the other negative word follows it.

> *No* **he tenido** *nunca* **(***jamás***) sarampión.**   I have *never* had measles.

To be more emphatic, however, Spanish places the negative word before the verb, omitting the **no**.

> *Nunca* **(***Jamás***) he tenido sarampión.**   I have *NEVER* had measles.

Compare the following uses of Spanish negatives and their indefinite affirmative counterparts.

NADIE: refers only to people and may be used as the subject or object of a sentence. In the latter case, the personal **a** is retained when the emphatic form is used.[1] This rule also applies to **alguien**.

No **opera** *nadie* **hoy.** ⎫
Nadie **opera hoy.** ⎭   *No one* is operating today.

Alguien **opera hoy.**   *Someone* is operating today.

La partera no examina *a nadie.* ⎫   The midwife does *not* examine *any one.*
A nadie **examina la partera.** ⎭   The midwife examines *no one.*

La partera examina *a alguien.*   The midwife is examining *someone.*

NADA, ALGO: refer only to things.

La embarazada *no* **aprieta** *nada.* ⎫   The pregnant woman does *not* squeeze
                                   ⎬   *anything.*
La embarazada *nada* **aprieta.** ⎭   The pregnant woman squeezes *nothing.*

No **está** *nada* **en el ojo.** ⎰ Nothing is in the eye.
                              ⎱ Not anything is in the eye.

Nada **está en el ojo.** ⎰ *Nothing* is in the eye.
                         ⎱ Not *anything* is in the eye.

Algo **está en el ojo.**   Something is in the eye.

NOTE: **Nada** and **algo** have an additional use as adverbs.

Esa operación es *algo* **difícil.**   That operation is *somewhat* (*rather*) difficult.

La recuperación *no* **es** *nada* **complicada.**   The recuperation is *not at all* (*not a bit*) complicated.

NINGUNO: A form of **ninguno** is used to make a noun negative. **Ningún** is used with masculine nouns, and **ninguna** with feminine ones. The two plurals are used only with nouns that appear in the plural. Both **ninguno** and **alguno** may refer to people or things.

Ningún **paciente sabe la resucitación cardiopulmonar.**   *No* patient knows CPR. (*No* patients know CPR.)

Ninguna **paciente amamanta ahora.**   *No* patient is nursing now. (*No* patients are nursing now.)

No **voy a firmar de** *ningún* **modo.** ⎫
                                ⎬   In *no* way am I going to sign.
No **voy a firmar de** *ninguna* **manera.** ⎭

Voy a firmar de *algún* **modo.** ⎫
                                ⎬   *Somehow* I am going to sign.
Voy a firmar de *alguna* **manera.** ⎭

Ninguno, used as an adjective, may be replaced by **alguno**. If so, **alguno** follows the noun and is not as emphatic as **ninguno**.

No examino *a ninguna* **paciente.**   I do *not* examine *any* patients.

No **examino a paciente** *alguna.*   I examine *no* patient.

When used as pronouns, **ninguno (-a)** and **alguno (-a)** are used. **Ninguno (-a)** is usually used in the singular.

> *Ninguno* **de los pacientes tiene una tos crónica.**   *None* of the patients has a chronic cough.
>
> *Algunos* **de los pacientes tienen una tos crónica.**   *Some* of the patients have a chronic cough.

TAMBIEN: shows agreement with an affirmative statement, **tampoco**, with a negative one.

> **El doctor Gómez va al quirófano ahora.**   Dr. Gómez is going to the OR now.
>
> **Yo** *también.*   Me, *too.* (I am *also.*)
>
> **Tú** *también.*   You, *too.* (You are *also.*)
>
> **El doctor no opera.**   The doctor doesn't operate.
>
> **Yo** *tampoco.*   Me *neither.* (Neither do I.)
>
> **Nosotros** *tampoco.*   We *neither.* (*Neither* do we.)

With the expression **ni . . . ni,** the verb is used in the plural if the **ni . . . ni** introduces the subject.

> *Ni* **el médico** *ni* **la enfermera están aquí.**   *Neither* the doctor *nor* the
> *No* **están aquí** *ni* **el médico** *ní* **la enfermera.**   nurse are here.

But a singular verb may be used if the expression introduces the direct object.

> *No* **encuentro** *ni* **el pulso de la carótida** *ni* **la respiración normal.**   I find *neither* the carotid pulse *nor* normal breathing.
>
> *O* **Juana** *o* **María va a dar luz mañana.**   *Either* Jane *or* Mary is going to deliver tomorrow.

NUNCA, JAMAS: are interchangeable in a negative sentence. They have several affirmative counterparts:

> *Nunca (Jamás)* **tengo catarro.**   I *never* have a cold.
>
> *No* **tengo** *nunca (jamás)* **catarro.**   I do *not ever* have a cold.
>
> *Algunas veces (A veces)* **tengo catarro.**   *Sometimes* I have a cold.
>
> *Muchas veces* **tengo catarro.**   I *often* have a cold.
>
> *Siempre* **tengo catarro.**   I *always* have a cold.
>
> *Alguna vez* **he tenido catarro.**   *At some time* I have had a cold.

The expression **jamás** may be used additionally in affirmative questions as **ever.**

> ¿**Ha tenido** *jamás* **catarro?**   Have you *ever* had a cold?

TODAVIA: is used mostly in negative sentences.

YA: is used in affirmative or interrogative-affirmative sentences.

> *No* **ha recuperado** *todavía.*   He has *not* recuperated *yet.*
>
> **Ha recuperado** *ya.*   He has *already* recuperated.
>
> *¿No* **ha recuperado** *todavía?*   Has he *not* recuperated *yet?*

In Spanish many negative words can be used in the same sentence.

> *Nadie* **deja** *nunca ninguna* **esponja dentro de un paciente.**   *No one ever* leaves *any* sponge in a patient.

In Spanish a negative is used after a comparative.

> **El doctor Ruiz opera más que** *nadie.*   Dr. Ruiz operates more than *anyone.*

EXERCISES *EJERCICIOS*

A.   Rewrite the following sentences in the negative.

1.   **El anestesiólogo tiene algo en la mano.**
2.   **Alguien está sobre la mesa de partos.**
3.   **Siempre tiene catarro durante los inviernos.**
4.   **La chica nació en la clínica también.**
5.   **Veo a alguien en la sala de recuperación.**
6.   **Oigo algo.**
7.   **A veces opera por la tarde.**
8.   **¿Tienes algún problema?**
9.   **¿Ha tenido viruelas jamás?**
10.   **¿Tiene alguna cicatriz?**

B.   Answer negatively in Spanish.

1.   **¿Es Vd. partera?**[2]
2.   **Yo no veo bien. ¿Y Vd.?**
3.   **¿No tienes reconocimiento físico mañana?**
4.   **¿No opera ella?**
5.   **¿Tiene Vd. dolores agudos con frecuencia?**

C.   Rewrite the following using the less emphatic form.

1.   **Nunca sufre.**
2.   **El pobre ni dinero ni seguro de hospital tiene.**
3.   **Ningunas drogas están al alcance de niños.**
4.   **Nada sabe de la hipertensión.**
5.   **Ningunos dientes le quedan en la boca.**

D. Change the following to affirmative statements.

1. **Vd. no compra nada en la farmacia.**
2. **Vd. no conoce a ninguno de los pacientes.**
3. **Jamás tomo la medicina tres veces al día.**
4. **Nunca quiere quedarse en la cama.**
5. **No come ni pan ni toronjas.**

NOUNS

LOS SUSTANTIVOS

A noun is the name of a person, place, or thing. A noun may be modified by an adjective but never by an adverb. A proper noun is the name of a specific person, place, or thing.

Juan John
San Francisco San Francisco
el doctor Gómez Dr. Gómez

A common noun is a name for persons, places, or things that are of the same type or class.

médico doctor   **hospital** hospital

Other categories of nouns also exist: *collective*, *count* (or *concrete*), and *mass* (or *abstract*) nouns. A *collective noun* names a collection or aggregate of individuals by a singular form (**la gente** people; **la familia** family; **el personal** staff). Usually collective nouns are followed by singular verbs because the group is thought of as a whole. At times when the component individuals are of primary importance, the noun may take a plural verb.

The staff decides it. **El personal lo decide.**
The majority *are* physicians. **La mayoría son médicos.**

Count nouns are objects that can be counted as well as perceived by the senses. Count nouns may be singular or plural. In Spanish, count nouns are often introduced by the indefinite article or by a number.

two physicians **dos médicos**   a stretcher **una camilla**

Mass nouns are usually singular. They express things that you cannot count but of which you can take a certain quantity, or else they express a complete abstract concept. In English, mass nouns cannot be introduced by *a* or *an*. They are frequently without a determiner but may be introduced by *some* or *any*. When used as subjects, Spanish mass nouns occur with the definite article.

Penicillin is the cure. **La penicilina es la cura.**

Spanish count nouns occur in the plural after a quantitative expression, mass nouns follow the quantitative expression in the singular.

a box of band aids   **una caja de** *curitas* (count noun)

a cup of pills   **una taza de** *píldoras* (count noun)

a wad of cotton   **una mota de** *algodón* (mass noun)

two pieces of gauze   **dos pedazos de** *gasa* (mass noun)

Gender of Nouns   *Género de los sustantivos*

In English nouns are classified as masculine, feminine, or neuter. In Spanish nouns are either masculine or feminine. There is no neuter gender. The Spanish gender distinction is purely arbitrary.

The gender of a noun is almost as important as its meaning. All words that modify nouns, such as articles and adjectives, agree with the noun in gender. The following guidelines exist to help determine a noun's gender.

GENDER BY MEANING   *GENERO SEGUN LA SIGNIFICACION*

The following are usually masculine:

1. Nouns referring to male beings:

   un padre   a father   **el hijo**   the son

2. Nouns referring to "masculine" occupations:

   el doctor   the physician   **el químico**   the chemist

   There is a tendency in modern spoken Spanish to differentiate the gender of nouns of occupation and profession due to the changing role of the woman in society. When a woman holds a "male" occupation, either a new noun is created (**la doctora**; **la arquitecta**   architect; **la jefa**   "boss," chief), or the definite article indicates the gender (*la químico*).

3. The days of the week, months of the year, cardinal numbers, cardinal points, musical notes, and names of languages:

   el miércoles   Wednesday   **el abril**   April   **el norte**   north

   el dos   the second   **el español**   Spanish   **el do, el re**   do, re

4. The proper names of rivers, seas, lakes, volcanoes, and mountains:

   el Atlántico   the Atlantic   **los Pirineos**   the Pyrenees

5. The names of most fruit trees:

   el naranjo   the orange tree   **el cerezo**   the cherry tree

The following are usually feminine:

1. Nouns referring to female beings:

la madre   the mother   **una hija**   a daughter

2. Nouns referring to "feminine" occupations:

la nodriza   the wet nurse   **la enfermera**   the nurse
la modelo   the model

When a man occupies the same profession, either a new noun is created (**el enfermero**   the male nurse) or the definite article indicates the gender (**el modelo**   the model).

3. The names of the letters of the alphabet:

la jota   J   **la ese**   S

4. The names of some cities, towns, and countries ending in **-a.**

GENDER BY ENDING   *GENERO SEGUN LA TERMINACION*

The following are usually masculine:

1. Nouns ending in **-o**:

el quirófano   the operating room   **el laboratorio**   the laboratory

NOTE: Some exceptions which are feminine exist:

la mano   the hand   **la soprano**   the soprano

2. Nouns ending in **-ón, -el, -al, -ente, -ador,** and **-or**:

el corazón   the heart   **el papel**   the paper
el cabezal   the compress   **el astringente**   the astringent
el esterilizador   the sterilizer

The following are usually feminine:

1. Nouns ending in **-a**:

la clínica   the clinic   **la píldora**   the pill

NOTE: Nouns of Greek origin, ending in **-a, -ma, -ta, -pa,** are an exception; they are masculine.

el día   the day   **el síntoma**   the symptom
el astronauta   the astronaut

2. Nouns ending in **-tad, -dad, -ción, -sión, -tión, -ez, -ie, -xión, -sis, -ud**, and **-umbre**:

la dosis the dose **la reflexión** the reflexion
la oclusión the occlusion

Exceptions:

el análisis the analysis **el énfasis** the emphasis

NOTE: A small number of nouns ending in **-ie** and **-ión** are masculine:

el pie the foot **el sarampión** the measles

Nouns not ending in **-o** or **-a** should be memorized with the definite article.

1. Certain masculine nouns which refer to people occasionally use a different form for the feminine:

el hombre the man **la mujer** the woman

2. A few nouns which are assigned gender and are modified accordingly, may refer to subjects of either sex:

María es *la víctima*. Mary is the victim.
Pablo es *la víctima*. Paul is the victim.
Ella es *una buena persona*. She is a good person.
El es *una buena persona*. He is a good person.

3. Some nouns, especially those ending in **-ista**, have the same form for both masculine and feminine gender. The article indicates the sex of the person.

el(la) cónyuge the spouse **el(la) dentista** the dentist
el(la) estudiante the student **el(la) joven** the youth, young person

4. Some nouns change their meaning but not their form, according to differences in gender:

el frente the (battle) front **la frente** the forehead
el calavera the reckless fellow **la calavera** the skull
el radio the radius **la radio** the network
el cura the priest **la cura** the cure
el coma the coma **la coma** the comma

5. Nouns referring to certain animals and birds *often* have different words for the sexes:

el gallo the rooster **la gallina** the hen
el caballo the horse **la yegua** the mare

6. For animals whose sex is not indicated by the ı. un itself, the words **macho** (male) or **hembra** (female) are added :

el ratón hembra   the female mouse

EXERCISES *EJERCICIOS*

Read the following and indicate whether the nouns are masculine or feminine.

proteína	ovulación	esfigmomanómetro
pólipo	certidumbre	enfermería
legumbre	juventud	virgen
sarampión	factor	cuerpo
corazón	hospital	tirantez
cansancio	punto	vial
algodón	dolor	frigidez
pulmón	pentatol	estudiante
problema	astringente	miércoles
gasa	especialista	reflexión

Formation of the Plural of Nouns
El plural de sustantivos

Nouns in Spanish, as in English, are either singular or plural. Unlike English, the articles that accompany Spanish nouns also show gender and number. A noun is made plural by adding either **-s** or **-es** to the singular form according to the following rules.

1. A noun ending in an unaccented vowel, accented **-é**, or a diphthong, forms the plural by adding **-s**.

   el pie   the foot   > **los pies**   the feet

   el café   the cafe   > **los cafés**   the cafes

   la ambulancia   the ambulance > **las ambulancias**   the ambulances

2. A noun ending in a consonant, a triphthong, or accented **-á**, **-í**, **-ú**, or **-ó**, geлı-erally adds **-es**.

   el tisú   the tissue   > **los tisúes**   the tissues

   el doctor   the physician > **los doctores**   the physicians

   Exceptions :   **el papá**   the daddy   > **los papás**   the daddies

               la mamá   the mommy > **las mamás**   the mommies

NOTE: A noun ending in **-z** changes the **-z** to **-c**, and then adds **-es**. A noun ending in **-c** changes the **-c** to **-qu**, and then adds **-es**.

la cicatriz   the scar > **las cicatrices**   the scars
el tic   the tic   > **los tiques**   the tics

3. Nouns whose final syllable is unstressed and ends in the /s/ phoneme use the same form for both singular and plural. The article shows the number.

el tórax   the thorax > **los tórax**   the thoraxes
la dosis   the dose   > **las dosis**   the doses
el análisis   the test   > **los análisis**   the tests

4. Most surnames are invariable in number.

los Gómez   the Gómez' > **los García**   the Garcías

5. The plural of loan words is usually arbitrary since native speakers frequently use irregular plurals.

el club   the club   > **los clubs**   the clubs
el suéter   the sweater > **los suéters/los suéteres**   sweaters
el cóctel   the cocktail > **los cóctels/los cócteles**   cocktails

6. Compound nouns are nouns that consist of two elements, usually two words fused into one, or two words in apposition functioning as one unit. Many compound nouns form their plural regularly. However, some show a plural change in both elements, and others show no change at all.

Regular: **el anteojo**   telescope   > **los anteojos**   eyeglasses
            el sobretodo   overcoat > **los sobretodos**   overcoats
Both elements: **el gentilhombre**   gentleman
            los gentileshombres   gentleman
First element: **cualquiera**   anyone
            cualesquiera   anyone
            la casa cuna   daycare center
            las casas cuna   daycare centers
Invariable: **el cuentagotas**   dropper   > **los cuentagotas**   droppers
            el sacabalas   ball forceps > **los sacabalas**   ball forceps
            el lavamanos   washstand > **los lavamanos**   washstands

7. The masculine plural of nouns expressing relationship or rank may be used to refer to members of both sexes.

los esposos   the husband and wife/the husbands
tus hijos   your children (sons and daughters)/your sons

Accents *Los acentos*

The spoken stressed or accented syllable remains the same for both singular and plural nouns, pronouns, adjectives, and participles.

el cálculo renal the kidney stone	**los cálculos renales** kidney stones	
la úlcera the ulcer	**las úlceras** ulcers	

Three noun exceptions exist in which the stress changes in the plural:

el carácter the character	**los caracteres** the characters
el espécimen the specimen	**los especímenes** the specimens
el régimen the government	**los regímenes** the governments

When a word ends in **-n**, **-s**, or a stressed vowel, however, the addition of **-es** does affect the orthography. Singular nouns whose last syllable bears a written accent and whose plural is formed by adding **-es** drop the accent mark in the plural:

la hinchazón   swelling   **las hinchazones**   swellings

For multisyllabic singular nouns ending in **-n**, add an accent mark in the plural to show that the stress remains the same despite the addition of **-es**.

el himen hymen	**los hímenes** hymens	
la virgen virgen	**las vírgenes** virgens	

EXERCISES *EJERCICIOS*

A.   Make the following words plural.

doctora	**enfermera**	**médico**
hospital	**clínica**	**terapia**
asistente	**dolor**	**calmante**
himen	**inmunización**	**aspirina**
placenta	**aborto**	**colesterol**
clítoris	**circuncisión**	**abrasión**
nariz	**acidez**	**factor**

B.   Change the following phrases to the singular form.

1.   **los médicos** (the physicians)   el médico _____
2.   **las hojas clínicas** (the clinical charts) _____
3.   **las jeringuillas** (the syringes) _____
4.   **las infecciones** (the infections) _____
5.   **los accidentes** (the accidents) _____
6.   **los pacientes felices** (the happy patients) _____
7.   **las noticias buenas** (the good news) _____
8.   **las narices largas** (the long noses) _____

9. **los huesos frágiles** (the brittle bones) _____

10. **las clavículas rotas** (the broken clavicles) _____

C. Change the following phrases to the plural form.

1. **la almohada** (the pillow) las almohadas _____

2. **el cuñado enfermo** (the sick brother-in-law) _____

3. **la enfermera del turno de noche** (the night-shift nurse) _____

4. **el especialista** (the specialist) _____

5. **la quijada fracturada** (the fractured jawbone) _____

6. **el riñón** (the kidney) _____

7. **la crisis** (the crisis) _____

8. **la voz** (the voice) _____

9. **el domingo** (on Sunday) _____

10. **el tisú** (the tissue) _____

Diminutives and Augmentatives
Diminutivos y aumentativos

Diminutive and augmentative suffixes are commonly used in Spanish with nouns, adjectives, and pronouns, especially in colloquial speech. They not only make the language more colorful, but they add additional connotations to the basic meanings of the words from which they are derived. Non-native speakers of Spanish have to be careful when using these forms because of the multiple meanings of these diminutive and augmentative endings, meanings other than those given in the following discussion.

Diminutives generally end in **-ito** or **-ita**. These endings express smallness and are sometimes used to express endearment. Diminutive endings that convey the idea of contempt and adversity are **-uelo** and **-uela**. Diminutives follow the number and gender of the nouns from which they are formed.

For words ending in **-co**, **-go** (**-ca**, **-ga**), the suffixes **-quito** (**-a**) and **-guito** (**-a**) are substituted:

chico > **chiquito**   **amiga** > **amiguita**

Diminutives of monosyllabic words ending in a consonant are formed by adding **-ecito** (**-a**):

pan > **panecito**   **flor** > **florecita**

Words of more than one syllable that end in a consonant other than **-n** or **-r**, add **-ito** (**-a**):

lápiz > **lapicito**

When the word ends in **-e, -n,** or **-r,** add **-cito (-a)**:

mujer > mujercita

Other diminutive endings that imply beauty, grace, and endearment are **-illo** **(-a)** and **-ico (-a).** Common endings for proper names are **-ito (-a)**:

Juan > Juanito.

Augmentatives are formed by adding **-ón, -ote, -azo** (m), **-ona, -ota, -aza** (f), and imply contempt, aversion, or unnatural size.

hombre > hombrón, hombrote, hombrazo a big, strong man
mujer > mujerona a big, strong woman

The suffix **-azo** when applied to English nouns of neuter gender, such as stick or sword, means "a blow struck"

bastón cane > **bastonazo** a blow struck with a cane

The suffix **-ada** is similarly applied

puñal > puñalada a stab with a dagger (or knife)

The ending **-azo** applies to blunt instruments, **-ada** applies to sharp ones. The simple idea of large or small size is expressed, as in English, by the adjectives **grande** and **pequeña.**

EXERCISES *EJERCICIOS*

A. Give diminutives for each of the following words.

1. **la jeringa** (syringe)
2. **el vaso** (glass)
3. **la botella** (bottle)
4. **un momento** (a moment)
5. **la chica** (girl)
6. **la cuchara** (spoon)
7. **la cucharada** (spoonful)
8. **el cigarro** (cigar)

B. Give the augmentatives that indicate "a blow struck" or "stabbed with."

1. **látigo** (whip) _____ (whiplash)
2. **bala** (bullet) _____ (bullet wound)
3. **codo** (elbow) _____ (a jab with the elbow)
4. **escopeta** (gun) _____ (gunshot)
5. **cuchilla** (razorblade) _____ (gash with a blade)

PRONOUNS

LOS PRONOMBRES

A pronoun is a word that takes the place of, or is used instead of, a noun. A pronoun has an antecedent, which is the word, idea, person, or thing, whether word, phrase, or clause, to which the pronoun refers. Interrogative pronouns (*who* **quién, quiénes**; *which* **cuál, cuáles**; *what* **qué**) request the identity of the antecedent. Negative pronouns (*nobody* **nadie**; *nothing* **nada**; etc.) imply that the antecedent is nonexistent.

Personal Subject Pronouns
Los pronombres personales nominativos

The subject pronouns are:

yo	I	**nosotros (nosotras)**	we
tú	you (fam.)	**vosotros (vosotras)**	you (fam. pl.)
él	he	**ellos**	they
ella	she	**ellas**	they (feminine)
usted	you (form.)	**ustedes**	you (form., pl.)

The word *it* as the subject of a verb need not be translated:

Soy yo. It is I.   **Está por aquí.** It is through here.

Subject pronouns are usually omitted in Spanish since their meaning is included in the meaning of the verb.[3] They are used only for clarification or emphasis. Subject pronouns are also used in combination with a noun or another pronoun to form a compound subject.

él tiene laringitis   he has lariginitis

ella tiene sarampión   she has the measles

opero   I operate.

yo **opero**   *I* operate.

Ana y tú son enfermeras.   Ana and you are nurses.

Vd. y yo operamos.   You and I are operating.

Subject pronouns for inanimate nouns or for nonhuman animate nouns are rarely used. There is really no Spanish subject pronoun for *it* or its plural *they* and, consequently, subject pronouns of this nature are either repeated or the stated subject is omitted.

Las radiografías mostraron que es una fractura seria de la tibia.   The x-rays showed that it is a serious fracture of the tibia.

(Las radiografías nos dieron una visión gráfica de la fractura.) (The x-rays gave us a graphic vision of the break.)

(Nos dieron una visión gráfica de la fractura.) (They gave us a graphic vision of the break.)

Often the word *you* is expressed in Spanish by **usted** when speaking to one person, by **ustedes** when addressing more than one person. Both pronouns use the same verb endings as any other third person pronoun. The familiar form of address in Spanish, **tú**, derives from Latin. This form has a special conjugation, and the pronoun is usually omitted since the verb ending alone indicates the subject of the sentence. This form is generally reserved for close friends, relatives, children, and pets and, sometimes, for social inferiors. A shift from **tú** to **usted** with close friends may show respect. However, it could also indicate displeasure or anger. Likewise, the reverse shift from **usted** to **tú** when addressing an older person or a social superior would indicate contempt. The plural of **tú** is **vosotros**. This used to be used when speaking to a group of people who would be addressed individually with **tú**. However, all of Latin America and many parts of Spain use **ustedes** for the familiar plural as well as the polite plural. It should be noted that in Guatemala, El Salvador, Honduras, Nicaragua, Costa Rica, and parts of Colombia, Argentina, and Uruguay, **vos** is used as a singular familiar second person pronoun.

You may be translated into Spanish as follows:

	Familiar	*Formal (Polite)*
Singular	**tú** **(vos)**	**usted (Vd.** or **Ud.)**
Plural	**vosotros** **ustedes (Vds.** or **Uds.)**	**ustedes (Vds.** or **Uds.)**

Examples: You are competent. **Tú eres competente.**
Vos eres competente.
Usted (Vd., Ud.) es competente.
Vosotros sois competentes.
Ustedes (Vds., Uds.) son competentes.

A. Fill in the blanks with the corresponding subject pronouns.

1. _____ **voy a la clínica ahora.** <u>I</u> am going to the clinic now.
2. **¿Prefiere** _____ **el pentotal de sodio?** Do <u>you</u> prefer sodium pentothal?
3. **¿Ponen** _____ **a María en la camilla?** Are <u>you</u> putting Mary on the stretcher?
4. _____ **esperamos la ambulancia.** <u>We</u> are waiting for the ambulance.
5. _____ **traen las píldoras.** <u>They</u> (f.) are bringing the pills.

6. _____ **están en la cafetería.** They (f.) are in the cafeteria.

7. _____ **abre la boca.** She is opening her mouth.

8. _____ **examina la pierna del joven.** He examines the youth's leg.

9. _____ **necesitan tratamiento médico.** They (mixed group) need medical treatment.

10. _____ **irás al cuarto de fisioterapia.** You will go to physical therapy.

B. In the blanks at the left, insert the necessary subject pronouns. In those sentences where a choice is possible, include all possibilities to the right.

1. _____ **eres anestesiólogo.**   _____

2. _____ **es médico consultor.**   _____

3. _____ **somos dentistas.**   _____

4. _____ **es la madre del enfermo**   _____

5. _____ **soy terapeuta.**   _____

6. _____ **es española.**   _____

7. _____ **es una enfermera graduada.**   _____

8. _____ **son los médicos del hospital.**   _____

9. _____ **eres camillero.**   _____

10. _____ **un médico famoso.**   _____

Direct Object Pronouns
Los pronombres objetivos directos

The direct object (noun or pronoun) of a sentence is acted upon by the subject; it directly receives the action of the verb. It answers "what" when it is referring to things.

> The nurse prepares the booster shot.

> What does the nurse prepare?   Answer: the *booster shot*; therefore, *booster shot* is the direct object noun.

> My brother has bursitis.

> What does my brother have?   Answer: *bursitis*; therefore, *bursitis* is the direct object noun.

The direct objects shown above are nouns. When a pronoun replaces each noun, the sentences read:

> The nurse prepares *it*.   My brother has *it*.

In conversation, direct object nouns are not usually repeated after they have already been established; they are replaced with direct object pronouns. Since all nouns are either masculine or feminine in Spanish, object pronouns that agree both in number and gender must replace the direct object nouns. Spanish direct object pronouns for things are:

lo it (m)   **los** them (m)
la it (f)   **las** them (f)

The direct object can also refer to a person or persons. In this case it answers the question "whom?".

Jane sees the nurse.

Whom does Jane see?   Answer: the *nurse*; therefore, *nurse* is the direct object noun.

Paul visits the patients.

Whom does Paul visit?   Answer: the *patients*; therefore, *patients* is the direct object.

In Spanish, whenever the direct object is a definite person noun, it is preceded by the personal **a** (see pages 164–165).

Juana ve a la enfermera.   Jane sees the nurse.

Pablo visita a los pacientes.   Paul visits the patients.

If the direct object nouns are replaced with pronouns, the sentences read:

Jane sees *her*.   Paul visits *them*.

The following are the direct object pronouns for persons:

	Singular			*Plural*	
me	me		**nos**	us	
te	you (familiar)		**os**	you (familiar)	
le	(preferred in Spain)	} him	**les**[4]	(preferred in Spain)	} them (m)
lo	(commoner in Sp. Am.)		**los**	(commoner in Sp. Am.)	
la	her		**las**	them (f)	
le, lo (m); **la** (f) you			**los** (m), **las** (f) you		

Position of Object Pronouns
El orden de los pronombres objetivos

In English the noun's change to the pronoun does not affect the position of tne direct object. It is in final position.

The doctor prescribes the medicine. (subject/verb/direct object noun)

The doctor prescribes it. (subject/verb/direct object pronoun)

In Spanish the direct object noun occurs at the end of the sentence as in English.

El médico receta la medicina. (subject/verb/direct object noun)

The direct object pronoun does not follow the verb, except in three cases: the infinitive, the gerund, and the direct affirmative command. Notice the use of the accent mark over the syllable that normally takes the stress.[5]

¡Lláme*me* a las dos!   Call me at two!

Quiero ver*los*.   I want to see them.

Estamos estudiándo*las*.   We are studying them.

Object pronouns immediately precede a conjugated verb.

Juan *la* toma.   John takes it.

Object pronouns immediately precede the conjugated form of the verb **haber** when dealing with the compound tenses.

Juan *la* ha recetado.   John has prescribed it.

Object pronouns may immediately precede the conjugated form of the verb **estar** or may be attached to the present participle when dealing with the progressive tenses.

Juan *la* está recetando.
Juan está recetándo*la*. $\Big\}$ John is prescribing it.

If ambiguity exists when third person direct object pronouns are used, they may be clarified by the use of prepositional pronouns (see page 61).

Le examina (a él).   He is examining him.

EXERCISES *EJERCICIOS*

A.   Complete the following with the appropriate direct object pronoun.

1.   **Yo examino a la muchacha. Yo _____ examino.**
2.   **La enfermera trae las pastillas. La enfermera _____ trae.**
3.   **El paciente lee la receta. El paciente _____ lee.**
4.   **Tenemos sólo un cuarto individual. ¿_____ quiere Vd.?**
5.   **La paciente ha tomado el formulario de entrada y _____ ha llenado.**
6.   **¿Dónde está el enfermero de noche? No _____ he visto todavía.**
7.   **¿Conocen Vds. al especialista? No, no _____ conocemos.**
8.   **¿Compras el jarabe? Sí, _____ compro en seguida.**

B.   Repeat the following statements, changing the direct object nouns to pronouns.

1.   **Quiero ver a aquellas enfermeras.**
2.   **Tengo que llenar esta receta.**
3.   **¿Puedo devolver los uniformes si no me van bien?**
4.   **Tengo que acompañar al médico.**
5.   **¿Piensa Vd. ver a la trabajadora social?**

C. Rewrite Exercise B, changing the verbs to formal, singular commands. Use direct object pronouns.

D. Translate the following sentences into Spanish.

1. The night nurse has to change it (the bandage).
2. Where is the Admission's Office? I don't see it.
3. I have to fill out the admission form, but I don't have it.
4. The nurse has the pills. You must take them.
5. Where are my children? I want to see them.

E. Answer the following with complete Spanish sentences. Change the direct object nouns to pronouns in your response.

1. **¿Conoce Vd. el problema?**
2. **¿Le aviso cuando siento dolor?**
3. **¿Tiene Vd. seguro de salud?**
4. **¿Ha tenido Vd. paperas?**
5. **¿Qué buscan Vds.? ¿Los rayos equis?**

Indirect Object Pronouns
Los pronombres objetivos indirectos

Indirect object nouns or pronouns name the person or persons to whom or for whom the subject gives or does something. The indirect object pronoun may suggest that the person stands to lose or gain by the action of the sentence; that he is emotionally involved in an event or that he is the possessor.

The indirect object pronoun shows the person *for whom* a (dis)service is performed if the direct object is his possession: for example, parts of the body, articles of clothing, personal belongings. English uses the possessive. Although in English the indirect object may be considered a prepositional phrase, in Spanish the indirect object is never considered as such. The indirect object answers the questions "to whom" or "for whom".

Dr. Gómez writes John a prescription. (Dr. Gómez writes a prescription for John.)

For whom does Dr. Gómez write a prescription?   Answer: for *John*; therefore, *John* is the indirect object.

She gives Paul a bedpan (She gives a bedpan to Paul.)

To whom does she give a bedpan?   Answer: to *Paul*; therefore, *Paul* is the indirect object.

Upon substituting pronouns for nouns, the sentences will read:

> Dr. Gómez writes *him* a prescription. (Dr. Gómez writes a prescription for *him*.)
>
> She gives *him* a bedpan (She gives a bedpan to *him*.)

Indirect object pronouns are expressed in English and Spanish as follows:

Singular		*Plural*	
me	me	**nos**	us
te	you (familiar)	**os**	you (familiar)
le	him, her, you	**les**	them, you

Since **le** has three meanings, the speaker may clarify further by adding a prepositional phrase **a Vd.**, **a él**, or **a ella**. **Les** may also be clarified by adding **a Vds.**, **a ellos.**, or **a ellas**.

The position of indirect object pronouns in Spanish is the same as the position of direct object pronouns.

Many medically oriented verbs require indirect objects. The verb *to give* is an example. It is expressed in Spanish in two ways. **Dar** is used with something for the person to take.

> **Le doy a Vd. un baño.**   I am giving you a bath.

Poner is used to express the idea of putting something into a person, on a specific part of him, or under him.

> **Le pongo a Vd. una transfusión.**   I am giving you a transfusion.

Both forms require the indirect object in Spanish. Other verbs that require indirect objects include:

cambiarle la venda, las sábanas   to change (someone's) bandage, sheets

darle un calmante, drogas, una enema, un purgante, oxígeno   to give (someone) a sedative, drugs, an enema, a laxative, oxygen

hacerle una biopsia, un tacto rectal   to do a biopsy on (someone), a rectal examination on (someone)

ligarle los tubos uterinos   to tie (someone's) tubes

ponerle un catéter/una sonda   to catheterize (someone)

ponerle el bacín, una enema, una inyección, suero intravenoso, un torniquete, una transfusión   to give (someone) a bedpan, an enema, an injection, an IV, to apply a tourniquet (to someone), to give (someone) a transfusion

quitarle los puntos   to remove (someone's) stitches

rasurarle la barba, el pelo púbico, el vello   to shave (someone's) beard, pubic hair, hair

repararle la mandíbula, la nariz   to set (someone's) jaw, nose

sacarle + organ of body   to remove/take out + organ of body

tomarle la presión, el pulso, los signos vitales, la temperatura   to take (someone's) blood pressure, pulse, vital signs, temperature

The indirect object pronoun indicates the person *to whom* something is given or done.

El médico me escribió la receta.   The doctor wrote me the prescription.

Le hablaré después de la operación.   I will speak to her after the operation.

Nos explicó la situación.   He explained the situation to us.

The indirect object pronoun indicates the person *for whose* advantage something is done.

Le traje las flores a ella.   I brought the flowers for her.

Se lo hice a él.   I did it for him.

The indirect object pronoun indicates the person *from whom* something is bought, taken away, or removed.

La enfermera le quitó las píldoras a él.   The nurse took the pills away from him.

Le suspendieron el permiso para operar.   They took his privilege to operate away from him.

Me compró la silla de ruedas.   She bought the wheelchair from me.

Yo le compro la medicina al farmacéutico.   I buy the medicine from the pharmacist.

El le pide prestada la almohadilla eléctrica a la enfermera de guardia.   He borrows the electric heating pad from the nurse on duty.

Indirect objects are used with the following verbs in Spanish, even though there is frequently no English correspondence.

ayudar   to help

comprar   to buy

dar   to give

deber   to owe

doler (ue)   to ache, hurt

escribir   to write

molestar   to annoy

pagar   to pay (for)

pedir (i)   to ask (for); to request, petition, beg; to order (in a restaurant); to claim

pedir prestado[6]   to borrow

sangrar   to bleed

The Spanish indirect object pronoun may express the subject of certain English sentences. This unusual construction involves **gustar** (to please), **faltar** (to be lacking, wanting), **hacer falta** (to need, be lacking), **quedar** (to stay, remain, be left over), **parecer** (to seem, appear), and a few others. Whereas most Spanish verbs use the same subjects and objects as their English counterparts, these reword the English sentence. That is, the subject of the English sentence becomes the indirect object of the Spanish one. The English direct object is expressed as the subject of the Spanish sentence. When the Spanish subject is plural, the verb is also plural. The Spanish pattern is: negative word (if any) + indirect object pronoun + verb + subject.

Gustar is the most important verb in this category. To express the English sentence *He likes the clinic*, the English object, which is *clinic*, becomes the Spanish subject. The subject of the English sentence, *he*, becomes the indirect object of the Spanish construction. Rewording this, the sentence becomes *The clinic is pleasing to him*. This is then translated directly into Spanish. To clarify or emphasize the indirect object pronoun, the preposition **a** and the appropriate object of the preposition are used, usually at the beginning of the sentence. Although the English object may lack an article, the Spanish subject generally requires its use.[7]

> Mary likes hospitals > To Mary hospitals are pleasing.   **A María le gustan los hospitales.**
>
> I like hospitals > To me hospitals are pleasing.   **Me gustan los hospitales.**

When English expresses a fondness for a certain action, Spanish always uses the third person singular of **gustar** followed by the infinitive as the subject of the sentence.

> We like to intubate > To intubate is pleasing to us.   **Nos gusta entubar.**

To express liking with regard to people, Spanish uses the expression **caer bien**. Dislike of people is expressed with the idiom **caer mal**. The English subject rewords itself with these idioms to become the indirect object in Spanish.

> I like the young doctor > The young doctor "falls" well to me.   **Me cae bien el joven médico.**
>
> We don't like the nurse on duty.   {**Nos cae mal la enfermera de guardia.**
> **No nos cae bien la enfermera de guardia.**}

Both **faltar** and **hacer falta** are like **gustar** in all respects. Although the verb **necesitar** can and does replace these verbs, some familiarity with them is helpful in recognizing and understanding them when they are used by others.

> I need a syringe. > { To me is lacking (missing) a syringe.   **Me falta una jeringa.**
> To me a syringe makes a lack.   **Me hace falta una jeringa.**
> **Necesito una jeringa.** }

The other verbs that follow the pattern of **gustar** are **parecer** and **quedar**. **Parecer** is usually followed by an adjective. The subject may either precede the indirect object or follow the adjective:

El hospital nos parece muy moderno. } The hospital seems very
    Nos parece muy moderno el hospital. }   modern to us.

The question **¿Qué le parece a Vd. el hospital?** literally means *How does the hospital seem (appear) to you?* It is equal to saying *How do you like the hospital?* or *What do you think of the hospital?*

We have one pill left > One pill is left (remaining) to us. **Nos queda una píldora.**

Selected verbs of emotion—worry, interest, delight, surprise, amazement—are used in the passive voice in English but in the active voice in Spanish, following the **gustar** word order.[8] In Spanish what causes the emotion is the subject, and the person is the indirect object.

I am interested in antihistamines > To me antihistamines are interesting. **Me interesan los antihistamínicos.**

He is worried about this operation > This operation worries him. **A él le preocupa esta operación.**

They were delighted with the results > The results delighted them. **Les encantaron los resultados.**

EXERCISES *EJERCICIOS*

A. Answer negatively, following the model.

       ¿Quieres píldoras para dormir?
       No, gracias, no me gustan píldoras para dormir.

1. **¿Quieres usar el método del ritmo?**
2. **¿Quieres novocaína?**
3. **¿Quieres un termómetro rectal?**
4. **¿Quieres hormonas?**
5. **¿Quieres pastillas para la tos?**

B. Answer following the model.

       No quiero un cuarto semiprivado.
       ¿Por qué? ¿No te gusta un cuarto semiprivado?

1. **No quiero un examen físico.**
2. **No quiero paragórico.**
3. **No quiero amamantar.**
4. **No quiero alimentación intravenosa.**
5. **No quiero anteojos.**

C. Answer according to the model.

¿Por qué no operó Paco?
Porque no le gusta operar.

1. **¿Por qué no estuvo a dieta la paciente?**
2. **¿Por qué no usó un hule?**
3. **¿Por qué no inyectó en la nalga?**
4. **¿Por qué no le dio de alta al paciente?**
5. **¿Por qué no tuvo una máscara de oxígeno?**

D. Answer according to the model.

¿Prefieren Vds. comadrona u obstetra?
Nos gusta más el obstetra.

1. **¿Qué anestesia prefieren Vds. para el parto, anestesia paracérvica o caudal?**
2. **¿Prefieren Vds. enfermero o ayudante de enfermera?**
3. **¿Prefieren Vds. inyección intramuscular o subcutánea?**
4. **¿Prefieren Vds. la picazón o la pomada?**
5. **¿Prefieren Vds. la penicilina u otro antibiótico?**

E. Answer according to the model.

¿Quieren medicinas ellos?
Sí, les gustan mucho las medicinas.

1. **¿Quieren las pastillas ellos?**
2. **¿Quieren recetas ellas?**
3. **¿Quieren sedativos ellos?**
4. **¿Quieren la leche de magnesia ellos?**
5. **¿Quieren los urinálisis ellos?**

F. Answer in Spanish.

1. **¿Te gusta anestesia regional?**
2. **¿Les gusta respirar hacia adentro profundamente?**
3. **¿Le gusta a Vd. fumar?**
4. **¿Le preocupa a Vd. su cirujía?**
5. **¿Cuántas píldoras nos quedan?**

G. Say in Spanish.

1. They like the medicine.
2. I don't like hospitals.
3. Do you like fruits?
4. I like to eat vegetables.
5. Does she like the IUD?
6. We like the wheelchair.

7. José has six pills left.
8. She doesn't like to be in the hospital.
9. You need another shot.
10. We are delighted with your progress.

Double Object Pronouns
Dos pronombres objetivos

When there are two object pronouns the indirect always precedes the direct, and they both precede or follow the verb according to the rules.

Me las van a sacar. ⎫
Van a sacármelas. ⎭ They are going to take them out (of me).

If both object pronouns are in the third person (i.e., begin with **l-**), the indirect (**le, les**) changes to **se.**

Se la receto. I prescribe it for you (for him, for them, for her, etc.).

It is also possible to have double object pronouns using a reflexive and a direct object pronoun. In this case, the reflexive precedes the direct object pronoun, and they both precede or follow the verb according to the rules.

Póngasela Vd. Put it on.
No se la ponga Vd. ahora. Don't put it on now.

EXERCISES *EJERCICIOS*

A. Rewrite the following, changing the object nouns to pronouns. Watch the order.

1. **La enfermera le da las drogas a la mujer.**
2. **El cirujano le hizo una biopsia a la paciente.**
3. **Mi ginecólogo acaba de hacerme un tacto rectal.**
4. **Le ligaron los tubos uterinos a María.**
5. **¿Puedo cambiarle las sábanas ahora?**

B. Rewrite the following in the affirmative.

1. **No se lo vende Vd.**
2. **No nos la sirva Vd.**
3. **No me la explique Vd.**
4. **No se la ofrezca Vd. a ella.**
5. **No me la prepare Vd.**
6. **No me los saque Vd.**

C. Rewrite the following according to the model.

> **El auxiliar va a llevar la bandeja al paciente.**
> **El auxiliar va a llevársela a él.**
> **El auxiliar se la va a llevar a él.**

1. **Tengo que devolver los resultados al doctor Sánchez.**
2. **La enfermera prefiere darle un calmante a ese tipo.**
3. **Ellos piensan quitarle los puntos al paciente mañana.**
4. **El médico quiere explicarme las complicaciones.**
5. **¿Puedo mostrarles la radiografía?**

D. Rewrite the following according to the model.

> **Ella está tomándole la temperatura a él.**
> **Ella se la está tomando a él.**
> **Ella está tomándosela a él.**

1. **Su recepcionista sigue mandándome los resultados.**
2. **El está devolviéndonos las radiografías.**
3. **El dietista está preparándome una dieta especial.**
4. **Estamos sirviendo la cena a los pacientes.**
5. **Ese hombre sigue trayendo las flores a la enferma.**

E. Say in Spanish.

1. The doctor wrote it for me. (the prescription)
2. The pharmacist sells it to him. (the cough syrup)
3. My mother has to buy it for me. (the medicine)
4. The nurse takes it to her. (the medicine)
5. The technician does them for him. (the tests)

F. *General Review.* Say in Spanish.

1. Can I help you?
2. Can you help me?
3. I want to examine her.
4. Take it.
5. He tells me it.
6. He wants to tell me it.
7. I see John. Do you see him?
8. They see us.
9. He explains it to them.
10. I can't feel it.
11. The doctor gives him a prescription.

12. Here are the pills. You must take them.
13. The patient doesn't want to tell it to her.
14. She is teaching me to walk.
15. Do you want to see them?
16. The nurse wants to help you.
17. Do you live in a house? I want to see it.
18. The aide has to bring it to me.
19. The technician sends (**mandar**) them to him.
20. We have to do some tests. The nurse is going to explain them to you.

Reflexive Pronouns *Los pronombres reflexivos*

Reflexive pronouns are used with certain verbs when the subject and the object pronoun are the same person or thing; that is, when the subject acts upon itself. A verb is made reflexive by the use of the following reflexive pronouns[9]:

me myself
te yourself
se himself, herself, yourself, itself, oneself
nos ourselves
—   —
se themselves, yourselves

The reflexive pronouns follow the same rule for their position as do the direct and indirect object pronouns.[10] When multiple object pronouns are used the order is reflexive + indirect + direct (R.I.D.). Reflexive verbs are written with the third person reflexive pronoun attached in the infinitive form for vocabulary and dictionary purpose.

SE ME CONSTRUCTIONS   EL USO DE SE ME

The reflexive pronoun **se** is used together with an indirect object pronoun in ways that have no English parallel. The verb is conjugated in the third person. This construction expresses either unplanned or involuntary actions.

The **se me** construction is used for physiologic states that arise within a person. The indirect object pronoun is the person affected by the process that occurs within him, as well as the source of the process.

Se me subió la presión arterial. My blood pressure rose.
Se le bajó la fiebre a ella. Her fever dropped.
Se les llenaron los ojos de lágrimas. Their eyes filled with tears.

To express accidental or unexpected actions, Spanish uses the reflexive pronoun **se** and the appropriate indirect object pronoun together with the third person verb. The verbal agreement is with the English direct object.

Se	**me**	**olvidó el termómetro.**	I forgot the thermometer.
↑	↑	↑	(The thermometer forgot it-
(reflexive +	indirect +	verb)	self to me.)

Se te olvidó el termómetro. You forgot the thermometer.

Se le olvidó el termómetro. He (she, you) forgot the thermometer.

Se nos olvidó el termómetro. We forgot the thermometer.

NOTE: The Spanish verb always agrees with the English direct object in number.

Se me olvidaron la jeringa y el alcohol. I forgot the syringe and the alcohol.

Se le rompió el termómetro. She (he, you) broke the thermometer.

Se me cayó el microscopio. I dropped the microscope.

Se les perdió la carta. They lost the chart.

RECIPROCAL USE *USO RECIPROCO*

Reflexive pronouns may be used in the plural form (**nos, se**) to express a mutual or reciprocal relationship. The translation of the reflexive pronoun is "(to) each other" or "(to) one another."

Los pacientes *se* **ayudan.** The patients help each other.

Nos **visitamos con frecuencia.** We visit one another frequently.

For clarification or emphasis, an additional phrase, **uno(s) a otro(s)**, may be added.

El médico y Juan se miran uno a otro. The doctor and John look at one another.

Only when both persons are female is the feminine **una(s) a otra(s)** used.

Las especialistas *se* **hablan** *una a otra*. The specialists talk to each other.

El médico y la enfermera *se* **hablan** *uno a otro* **a menudo.** The doctor and the nurse frequently talk to one another.

EXERCISES *EJERCICIOS*

Say in Spanish.

1. They help each other always.
2. They like to visit each other.
3. Do you (pl) write one another?

4. We look at each other.

5. We need one another.

6. You (pl) visit one another often.

Prepositional Pronouns
Los pronombres preposicionales

When the object of a preposition is a pronoun, prepositional pronouns must be used. These are the same as the subject pronouns with two exceptions—the first and second persons singular.

Singular		*Plural*	
mí	me	**nosotros (-as)**	us
ti	you (fam.)	— —	
él	him	**ellos**	them
ella	her	**ellas**	them
Vd.	you (formal)	**Vds.**	you (formal)

Prepositional pronouns can never be substituted for the indirect object pronouns. The indirect object pronouns can stand alone; the prepositional pronouns cannot.

With the preposition **con** (with), the first and second person singular pronouns combine to form **conmigo** (with me) and **contigo** (with you).

Prepositional Forms of the Reflexive Pronouns
Las formas preposicionales de los pronombres reflexivos

When a reflexive pronoun is used as the object of a preposition other than *con* and *entre*, the special prepositional reflexive pronoun must be used. These forms are the same as the other prepositional pronouns, except for the third person **sí**. See above.

Singular		*Plural*	
mí	myself	**nosotros (-as)**	ourselves
ti	yourself	— —	
sí	himself, herself, yourself, itself	**sí**	themselves, yourselves

After **con** the special forms **conmigo**, **contigo**, and **consigo** must be used. The preposition **entre** (among, between) requires the subject forms: **entre tú y yo**,

entre nosotros. The adjective **mismo** is added to these prepositional reflexives for emphasis or clarity.

> **Ella habla para sí misma.** She was talking to herself.
> **El paciente no podía vestirse a sí mismo.** The patient couldn't dress himself.

USE *USO*

The prepositional reflexive pronouns are used to distinguish between reflexive sentences and reciprocal sentences when they are in the plural.

> **Ellos se bañan a sí mismos.** They bathe themselves.
> **Ellos se bañan entre sí.** They bathe each other.

EXERCISES *EJERCICIOS*

Translate into English.

1. La enfermera se compró un uniforme a sí misma.
2. Me llevaron consigo.
3. El se lo llevó consigo.

Recap of Personal Pronouns
Repaso de los pronombres personales

See chart on page 63.

Interrogative Pronouns
Los pronombres interrogativos

«**Cuál(es)**?» meaning "which?" refers to persons or things and is used to choose one or more from a larger group. In questions asking "which" + noun, either **cuál** or **qué** may be used.

> **¿Cuál enfermera es suya? (¿Qué enfermera es suya?)** Which nurse is yours?
> **¿Cuál es su enfermera?** Which (one) is your nurse?

«**¿Cuál?**» meaning "what?" precedes **ser**, except when definition is asked for, in which case «**¿qué?**» is used.

> **¿Cuál es su nacionalidad?** What is your nationality?
> **¿Qué es esto?** What is this?

PERSONAL PRONOUN CHART *GRAFICA DE LOS PRONOMBRES PERSONALES*

Singular

Subject Pronouns	Object of Preposition Pronouns		Reflexive Object Pronouns	Indirect Object Pronouns	Direct Object Pronouns
	Regular	Reflexive			
yo I	**mí** me	**mí** me, myself	**me** (to) myself	**me** (to/for) me	**me** me
tú you	**ti** you	**ti** you, yourself	**te** (to) yourself	**te** (to/for) you	**te** you
él he	**él** him, it (m)	**sí** himself, itself (m),	**se** (to) himself, itself,	**le (se)** (to/for) him, it	**le** him (Spain)
					lo him, it (m)
ella her	**ella** her, it (f)	herself, itself (f),	(to) herself, itself,	(to) her, it (f)	**la** her, it (f)
usted you	**usted** you	yourself	(to) yourself	(to) you	**le** you (m, Spain)
					lo you (m)
					la you (f)

Plural

Subject Pronouns	Object of Preposition Pronouns		Reflexive Object Pronouns	Indirect Object Pronouns	Direct Object Pronouns
	Regular	Reflexive			
nosotros, -as we	**nosotros, -as** us	**nosotros, -as** us, ourselves	**nos** (to) ourselves	**nos** (to) us	**nos** us
ellos they	**ellos** them	**sí** themselves	**se** (to) themselves	**les (se)** (to) them	**les** them (m, Spain)
					los them (m)
ellas they (f)	**ellas** them (f)				**las** them (f)
ustedes you	**ustedes** you	yourselves	(to) yourselves	(to) you	**les** you (m, Spain)
					los you (m)
					las you (f)

«¿Qué?» translates the English interrogative "what?" in all other cases, except in idioms.

¿Qué estudia Vd.? What are you studying?

«¿Quién» or «quiénes?» meaning "who?" or "whom?" refer to persons only.

¿Quién tiene mi medicina? Who has my medicine?

¿Con quiénes vive Vd.? With whom do you live?

«¿De quién?» or «¿de quiénes?» meaning "whose?" is always followed immediately by the verb.

¿De quién es esta tarjeta verde? Whose green card is this?

«¿Cuánto (cuánta)?» meaning "how much?" and «¿cuántos (cuántas)?» meaning "how many?" are used both as pronouns and as adjectives.

¿Cuántos van al hospital? How many are going to the hospital?

¿Cuánto cuesta mi cuenta? How much is my bill?

EXERCISES *EJERCICIOS*

A. Complete the following using **qué, cuál,** or **cuáles** as required.

1. ¿———— **médico vive en Houston?**
2. ¿———— **de los termómetros prefiere Vd. más? ¿El rectal o el oral?**
3. ¿———— **es un electrocardiograma?**
4. ¿———— **es la especialidad del doctor Gómez?**
5. ¿———— **periódico tiene Vd. en la mano?**

B. Say in Spanish.

1. How many people are suffering from that illness?
2. Whose medicine is this?
3. What is your occupation?
4. Who has a cold?
5. What did the doctor say?

Demonstrative Pronouns
Los pronombres demonstrativos

	Singular		Plural	
Near the speaker:	**éste** (m)	this one	**éstos** (m)	these
	ésta (f)	this one	**éstas** (f)	these
Near the listener:	**ése** (m)	that one	**ésos** (m)	those
	ésa (f)	that one	**ésas** (f)	those
Away from both speaker and listener:	**aquél** (m)	that one	**aquéllos** (m)	those
	aquélla (f)	that one	**aquéllas** (f)	those

Three neuter forms also exist: **esto** (this), **eso** (that), **aquello** (that).

As can be seen, the Spanish demonstrative pronouns differ from the demonstrative adjectives only on paper.[11] Each demonstrative pronoun bears a written accent over the stressed **e**. These pronouns agree in number and gender with the nouns whose place they take.

Doctor, éste es mi estetoscopio. Doctor, this is my stethoscope.

¿Qué máquina debo usar? ¿Ésta de aquí o ésa de ahí. Which machine should I use? This one here or that one there?

As is the case for the demonstrative adjectives, the forms of **ése** (that) refer to objects near the person being addressed, and the forms of **aquél** (that) refer to objects which are distant from both speaker and listener.

Éste es mi termómetro. This is my thermometer.

Ése es el de Vd. That one is yours.

Aquél que está allí es del otro doctor. That one over there is the other doctor's.

Forms of **éste** are frequently used in the sense of *the latter* and forms of **aquél**, in the sense of *the former*. Unlike English usage, in Spanish, when both pronouns are used in the same sentence, *the latter* always precedes:

El señor Franco y su esposa cancelaron su turno porque ésta no se siente bien. Mr. Franco and his wife cancelled their appointment because the latter doesn't feel well.

Pablo y Juan estudian para médicos. Éste quiere especializarse en la pediatría; aquél no tiene ninguna preferencia todavía. Paul and John are studying to be doctors. The latter (i.e., John) wants to specialize in pediatrics; the former (i.e., Paul) still has no preference.

An alternative exists, which has the force of demonstrative pronouns. The forms of the definite article (**el, la, los, las**) combine with either **de** or **que**. They may refer to persons or things and translate into English as "the one(s) with / of," "that / those of / with / in," "the . . . one."

Tengo dos pacientes gravemente enfermos. Uno está para morir, pero el de la nariz inflamada va a mejorarse. I have two seriously ill patients. One is about to die, but the one with the inflamed nose is going to get better.

Las que salen ahora son mis pacientes. The ones (Those) who are leaving now are my patients.

El que no puede ver es ciego. He who (The one who) cannot see is blind.

The neuter demonstrative pronouns, none of which has gender nor written accent, are used when the gender of an object has not yet been established, or when the object itself has not been identified. They are also used to refer to general ideas and situations, or to previous statements.

¿Qué es esto? What is this?   **¿Quién dijo eso?** Who said that?

EXERCISES *EJERCICIOS*

A. Answer affirmatively using the appropriate demonstrative pronoun.

   1. ¿Le gusta a Vd. este uniforme?
   2. ¿Está inflamado este ojo?
   3. ¿Es necesaria esta operación?
   4. ¿Cuándo ve Vd. a ese médico?
   5. ¿Vienen a la clínica aquellas pacientes?

B. Answer according to the model.

   —¿Cuántas píldoras le quedan a Vd.?
   —No tengo más que ésta.
   —¿Y ésta a mi lado?
   —Esa no es mía. No sé de quién es.

   1. ¿Cuántas cápsulas le quedan a Vd.? ¿Y éstas a mi lado?
   2. ¿Cuántos sedantes le quedan a Vd.? ¿Y éstos a mi lado?
   3. ¿Cuántas tabletas le quedan a Vd.? ¿Y ésta a mi lado?
   4. ¿Cuántos frascos de insulina le quedan a Vd.? ¿Y éste a mi lado?
   5. ¿Cuántas jeringuillas le quedan a Vd.? ¿Y ésta a mi lado?

C. Supply the correct Spanish demonstrative pronoun.

   1. **Este especialista y** *that one* (near you).
   2. **Ese auxiliar y** *that one* (yonder).
   3. **Aquel formulario y** *this one.*
   4. **Esas puertas y** *those* (yonder).
   5. **Aquel hospital y** *this one.*
   6. **Estos médicos y** *those.*
   7. **Aquellos pasillos y** *these.*
   8. **Esto y** *that* (which he said).

D. Replace each of the italicized expressions with a neuter demonstrative pronoun.

   1. *Lo que Vd. ve* **es agradable.**
   2. **Creo en** *lo que dices.*
   3. *Lo que observo* **me gusta.**
   4. **Piense Vd. en** *lo que digo.*
   5. **No es posible repetir** *lo que él me dijo.*

Relative Pronouns   *Los pronombres relativos*

A relative pronoun is a word that introduces a dependent clause. The clause may be essential to the meaning of the sentence, or it may be parenthetical (i.e., separated by commas from the main clause). In English the relative pronoun is often omitted; this is never the case in Spanish.

> You know the pain (that) I have. **Vd. bien sabe el dolor que tengo.** (The clause is essential to the meaning of the sentence.)
>
> Dr. Smith, who just arrived, is talking to the nurse. **El doctor Smith, quien acaba de llegar, habla a la enfermera.** (The clause is parenthetical to the meaning of the sentence.)

USES OF RELATIVE PRONOUNS *USOS DE LOS PRONOMBRES RELATIVOS*

The pronoun **que** means "who," "whom," "which," or "that." It refers to persons or things, masculine or feminine, singular or plural.

Que is used as the subject or direct object of the dependent clause.

> The test that you did is negative. **La prueba *que* hizo es negativa.**
>
> The doctor who is examining him is Dr. García. **El doctor *que* le examina es el doctor García.**

Que is used after monosyllabic prepositions when referring to things. It then means "which."

> The bed in which I am does not have side rails. **La cama en *que* me quedo no tiene barandillas laderas.**
>
> The case to which I refer was ended yesterday. **El caso a *que* me refiero se terminó ayer.**

Que is invariable in form.

The pronouns **quien** and **quienes** refer to persons only. They are both masculine and feminine, but must agree with the antecedent in number. **Quien** or **quienes** are used to indicate "who" or "whom" when the dependent clause is parenthetical. **Que,** which is more widely used in conversation, may also be used in this type of construction.

> That technician, who is very handsome, is going to do my chest x-ray. **Ese técnico, *quien (que)* es muy guapo, va a hacerme una radiografía del pecho.**

Quien or **quienes** are used as the object of prepositions when the antecedent is a person. When **quien(es)** is the direct object of a verb, the personal **a** is required.

> The doctors for whom the receptionist works are nice. **Los médicos para *quienes* la recepcionista trabaja son simpáticos.**
>
> The nurse with whom I must speak is here now. **La enfermera con *quien* debo hablar está aquí ahora.**
>
> The specialist (whom) we saw yesterday . . . **La especialista a *quien* vimos ayer . . .**

The longer forms of relative pronouns, **el cual, la cual, los cuales, las cuales** or **el que, la que, los que, las que** (who, whom, that which) are used with both persons and things to avoid ambiguity when there are two possible antecedents. They are also used after the prepositions **tras, por,** and **sin,** and after multisyllabic prepositions.

> Here is the door I had to go through to get to the OR.   **Aquí tiene Vd. la puerta por** *la que* **(***la cual***) tuve que entrar para llegar al quirófano.**
> I visited Mary's father, who had a heart attack.   **Visité al padre de María,** *el cual* **(***el que***) sufrió un ataque al corazón.**

EXERCISES *EJERCICIOS*

A.   Join the two sentences together by making the second a relative clause of the first. Use the relative pronoun **que.**

  1.   **Aquella señora es Marta. Marta trabaja en la clínica.**
  2.   **El hombre es el doctor. El hombre está allí.**
  3.   **La madre de Felipe no saldrá hoy. Felipe está enfermo.**
  4.   **El doctor operará más tarde. Habló con la doctora.**
  5.   **La carne tiene mal sabor. Compramos la carne.**

B.   Continue as above. This time use either **que** or **quien** as a relative pronoun.

  1.   **Aquella señora es la doctora Navas. Quiero hablar con ella.**
  2.   **La familia consulta con ese doctor. El doctor nunca llega a tiempo.**
  3.   **Conocimos al hombre ayer. Es técnico.**
  4.   **Anita compró un uniforme. Es lindo.**
  5.   **Uso termómetro oral. Es plástico.**

C.   Follow the model.

> **Me despido del paciente. Es puertorriqueño.**
> **Me despido del paciente, quien es puertorriqueño.**
> **El paciente de quien me despido es puertorriqueño.**

  1.   **Ayer conocí a ese doctor. Es especialista.**
  2.   **Llamé a aquella enfermera. Trabaja cerca de aquí.**
  3.   **Vi al auxiliar. Es mexicano.**
  4.   **Ellos hablan de una farmacia. Es farmacia de guardia** (all night).

D.   Combine the two sentences that follow. Use an appropriate form of **el cual.**

  1.   **La madre de Carlos no saldrá hoy. La madre de Carlos está enferma.**
  2.   **La hermana de Juan está en el hospital. Ella se ha torcido la pierna.**
  3.   **Los padres de Berta viven en Cuba. Ellos son médicos.**
  4.   **Visité a la madre del doctor. Me saludó con cortesía.**

Cuyo (cuya, cuyos, cuyas) is a relative possessive adjective meaning "whose," "of whom," or "of which." It agrees in number and gender with the noun it modifies.

I know the young specialist whose mother is a nurse. **Conozco al joven especialista cuya madre es enfermera.**

He is a scientist whose discoveries are famous throughout the world. **El es cientista cuyos descubrimientos son famosos por el mundo entero.**

| Concepts | Classes of Pronouns | | |
	Interrogatives	Demonstratives	Relatives
Persons	¿quién? ¿quiénes?	éste, ése, aquél	que, quien
Things	¿qué?	esto, eso, aquello	que
Possession	¿de quién?	mío, tuyo, suyo, etc.	cuyo
Quantity	¿cuánto?		

The interrogative, demonstrative, and relative pronouns present the correlation as shown in the table regarding the concepts they express.

Possessive Pronouns *Los pronombres posesivos*

Possessive pronouns are used to replace a noun modified by a possessive adjective. A possessive pronoun agrees with the noun for which it stands in number and gender, not the possessor. The following are the forms used:

Singular	Plural	Singular	Plural	
el mío	los míos	la mía	las mías	mine
el tuyo	los tuyos	la tuya	las tuyas	yours (fam)
el suyo	los suyos	la suya	las suyas	his
el suyo	los suyos	la suya	las suyas	hers
el suyo	los suyos	la suya	las suyas	yours
el nuestro	los nuestros	la nuestra	las nuestras	ours
el suyo	los suyos	la suya	las suyas	theirs (m)
el suyo	los suyos	la suya	las suyas	theirs (f)
el suyo	los suyos	la suya	las suyas	yours

To avoid confusion, instead of **el suyo** use **el de él, el de ella, el de Vd.**, etc. Instead of **la suya** use **la de él, la de ella, la de Vd.**, etc. Instead of **los suyos** use

los de él, los de ella, los de Vd., etc. Instead of **las suyas** use **las de él, las de ella, las de Vd.**, etc.

> **Tengo bastante con esta insulina y la mía.** I have enough with this insulin and mine.
>
> **sus instrumentos y los de ella** his instruments and hers
>
> **la medicina de Vds. y la nuestra** your medicine and ours

After the verb **ser,** the definite article preceding the possessive pronoun is generally omitted when it answers the question *whose.*

> **Estos instrumentos son míos.** These instruments are mine.
>
> **Este no es mi libro. ¿Es tuyo?** This is not my book. Is it yours?
>
> **No, tengo el mío.** No, I have mine.

The definite article is used, however, after **ser** and before the possessive pronoun when it answers the question *which.*

> **¿Cuál de esos uniformes es el suyo?** Which of those uniforms is yours?
>
> **Ese a la izquierda es el mío.** The one on the left is mine.

EXERCISES *EJERCICIOS*

A. Replace the possessive adjective and noun with the proper possessive pronoun.

1. **mis pacientes y los pacientes de Vd.**
2. **nuestros formularios y el formulario de él**
3. **mi maletín y el maletín del doctor Ruiz**
4. **nuestro consultorio y el consultorio tuyo**
5. **la solicitud de ella y la solicitud de él**

B. Answer according to the model.

> **¿De quién es este termómetro? ¿Es del pediatra?**
> **Sí, es suyo.**
> **Sí, es de él.**

1. **¿De quién es este espejo vaginal? ¿Es de la ginecóloga?**
2. **¿De quién es esta crema? ¿Es del dermatólogo?**
3. **¿De quién son estas radiografías? ¿Son del radiólogo?**
4. **¿De quién son estas píldoras? ¿Son de la enfermera?**
5. **¿De quién es este maletín? ¿Es del internista?**
6. **¿De quiénes son estos pañuelos? ¿Son de los bebés?**

C. Answer the questions affirmatively.

1. **Hay dos pastillas. ¿Es ésta la mía?**

2. **¿De quién son estas pastillas? ¿De Vds.?**

3. **¿Es éste el abrigo de Vd.?**

4. **¿Son de Vd. estos documentos?**

5. **Esta es mi radiografía. ¿Es ésa la tuya?**

ADJECTIVES
LOS ADJETIVOS

An adjective is a word that modifies (limits or describes) a noun or a pronoun.

enfermo sick   **dolorido** painful
alta high   **amargo** sour

Agreement *Concordancia*

Adjectives agree in number and gender with the nouns or pronouns that they modify.

el brazo roto the broken arm   **la tobilla rota** the broken ankle

GENDER OF ADJECTIVES *GENERO DE ADJETIVOS*

Adjectives ending in **-o** form the feminine by changing the **-o** to **-a**.

roto > **rota** broken

Adjectives ending in **-e** or a consonant have the same form for both genders.

el hueso grande the large bone   **la glándula grande** the large gland

Adjectives (and nouns) of nationality ending in a consonant add **-a** for the feminine.

el médico español the Spanish physician
la enfermera española the Spanish nurse

An adjective modifying two nouns of different genders is generally masculine.

las manos y los pies limpios the clean hands and feet

Adjectives ending in **-án**, **-ón**, **-or** add **-a** to form the feminine. (This does not apply to comparative forms ending in **-or**.)

holgazán, holgazana   idle, lazy

el paciente llorón }
la paciente llorona }   the weeping patient

el mejor paciente }
la mejor paciente }   the best patient

When more than one adjective modifies plural nouns denoting units, the adjectives agree in gender but are singular.

las enfermeras francesa y americana   the French and American nurses (singled out from a group)

las enfermeras francesas y americanas   the French and American nurses (two large groups)

FORMATION OF PLURAL OF ADJECTIVES
FORMACIÓN DE LOS PLURALES DE LOS ADJETIVOS

Adjectives form their plurals in the same way as nouns. If they end in a vowel, they form plurals by adding **-s**; if they end in a consonant, they form plurals by adding **-es**; if they end in **-z**, add **-es** after changing the **-z** to **-c**.

Singular	*Plural*	
español (m)	**españoles** (m) }	Spanish
española (f)	**españolas** (f) }	
robusto (m)	**robustos** (m) }	healthy
robusta (f)	**robustas** (f) }	

Position of Adjectives   *El orden de los adjetivos*

Limiting adjectives are numbers and other expressions of quantity, possessives, demonstratives, and so on. They generally precede the noun that they modify.

muchos técnicos   many technicians   **ese hospital**   that hospital

nuestro médico   our physician

Descriptive adjectives are those that indicate such things as color, shape, size, or nationality. They usually follow the noun that they modify.

muchas enfermeras buenas   many good nurses

el dolor torácico   the thoracic pain

Descriptive adjectives that normally follow the noun precede it when they indicate an expected or inseparable characteristic of the word described.

la roja sangre   the red blood

Certain adjectives vary in meaning when they precede or follow the noun modified.

	Before	*After*
algún/alguno	some	any at all
antiguo	old, former	old, ancient
bajo	low, vile	short, low
caro	dear	expensive
cierto	a certain	sure, definite
dichoso	annoying	lucky, fortunate
gran/grande	great	large (size)
medio	half	average
mismo	same, very	himself, herself, etc.
nuevo	another, new	new, brand new
pobre	poor (unfortunate)	poor (indigent)
propio	own	proper, suitable
raro	rare	strange, odd
único	only	unique
viejo	old (long-time)	old (elderly)

La operación tendrá un éxito cierto.   The operation will have a sure success.

Idiomatic Use of Adjectives
Uso idiomático de adjetivos

An adjective may be used as a noun.

El ciego lo necesita.   The blind man needs it.
La enferma acaba de morir.   The sick lady has just died.

Interrogative Adjectives
Los adjetivos interrogativos

In colloquial speech **¿cuál . . .?** is frequently used in place of **¿qué . . .?**. Technically **cuál** is a pronoun and should not be used as an adjective.

Which hospital do you prefer?
- **¿Cuál hospital prefiere Vd.?** (colloquial)
- **¿Qué hospital prefiere Vd.?**
- **¿Cuál de los hospitales prefiere Vd.?**

Possessive Adjectives *Los adjetivos posesivos*

SHORT FORMS *ANTES DEL SUSTANTIVO*

	Singular				*Plural*		
mi	my	**nuestro**⎫	our	**mis**	my	**nuestros**⎫	our
tu	your	**nuestra**⎭		**tus**	your	**nuestras**⎭	
su	his, its (m)	**su**	their (m)	**sus**	his, its (m)	**sus**	their (m)
su	her, its (f)	**su**	their (f)	**sus**	her, its (f)	**sus**	their (f)
su	your	**su**	your	**sus**	your	**sus**	your

In Spanish the possessive adjectives agree in number and gender with the thing possessed rather than with the possessor.

mi seguro my insurance	**mis seguros** my insurances
mi enfermera my nurse	**mis enfermeras** my nurses
nuestra clínica our clinic	**nuestras clínicas** our clinics
nuestro hospital our hospital	**nuestros hospitales** our hospitals

Possessive adjectives in the short form precede the nouns they modify and are repeated before each noun.

nuestra enfermera y su ayudante our nurse and their orderly

Su and **sus** have so many different meanings that they are often replaced by expressions that clarify the meaning. When a prepositional phrase is used for clearness, the definite article replaces the possessive adjective.

Tengo sus gotas. I have his (her, your, their, etc.) drops.

but

Tengo las gotas de él. I have his drops.

Tengo las gotas de ellos. I have their drops.

Tengos las gotas de ella. I have her drops.

Tengo las gotas de ellas. I have their drops.

Tengo las gotas de Vd. I have your drops.

Tengo las gotas de Vds. I have your drops.

LONG FORMS *DESPUÉS DEL SUSTANTIVO*

These forms are the same as the possessive pronouns:

mío, mía, míos, mías my

tuyo, tuya, tuyos, tuyas your

suyo, suya, suyos, suyas his, her, its, your, their

nuestro, nuestra, nuestros, nuestras our

These stressed adjectives follow their nouns and are used to translate "of mine," "of his," etc., or "my" as used in an exclamation.

> **¡Dios mío!** My goodness!
>
> **El doctor González es un amigo mío.** Dr. Gonzalez is a friend of mine.
>
> **Un primo nuestro es dentista.** A cousin of ours is a dentist.

NOTE: With parts of the body and articles of clothing being worn, the definite article replaces the possessive adjective.

> **Me pongo *la* chaqueta pero él no se pone *la* chaqueta.** I put on *my* jacket but he doesn't put on *his* jacket.
>
> **Me duele *la* cabeza.** *My* head hurts.

EXERCISES *EJERCICIOS*

A.   Rewrite the following placing the adjective given in parentheses in the proper position.

1.   **Hay enfermeras. (veinte)**
2.   **Recuerdo sus ojos. (hundidos)**
3.   **La sala de operaciones está en el piso. (tercer)**
4.   **Es una especialista. (suiza)**
5.   **Brota de granos. (muchos, rojos)**

B.   Say in Spanish.

1.   The poor (unfortunate) child has the mumps.
2.   They have a new laboratory.
3.   She is wearing a new (different) uniform.
4.   He is an only child.
5.   Dr. Ruiz is my old anatomy professor.

C.   Give the short form of the possessive adjective.

1.   (my) _____ **doctor**
2.   (my) _____ **doctora**
3.   (your) (fam.) _____ **estetoscopio**
4.   (their) _____ **paciente**
5.   (our) _____ **clínica**
6.   (his) _____ **herida**
7.   (their) _____ **muestra**
8.   (her) _____ **cita**
9.   (our) _____ **hijos**
10.   (her) _____ **pacientes**

D. Clarify the phrases below according to the model.

$$(her) \; \textbf{paciente} > \begin{cases} \textbf{la paciente de ella} \\ \textbf{el paciente de ella} \end{cases}$$

1. (your) **termómetro**
2. (his) **problemas**
3. (his) **medicina**
4. (their) **respuestas**
5. (her) **píldoras**
6. (their) **pacientes**

E. Repeat Exercise C, this time using the long forms of the possessive adjective.

(my) **doctor** > **un doctor mío**

F. Answer affirmatively, using possessive adjectives.

¿Es suyo el termómetro? Sí, es mío.

1. **¿Es tuyo este libro?**
2. **¿Son suyas estas píldoras?**
3. **¿Es nuestra esta enfermera?**
4. **¿Son suyas estas recetas?**
5. **¿Es suya esta radiografía?**

G. Say in Spanish.

1. We see with our eyes.
2. We have a tongue and thirty-two teeth in our mouths.
3. The doctors have to wash their hands first.
4. My feet hurt.
5. The patient puts on his gloves and hat before leaving.

Demonstrative Adjectives
Los adjetivos demonstrativos

Demonstrative adjectives are the same as demonstrative pronouns but lack a written accent mark.

Singular	*Plural*	
este hospital (m)	**estos hospitales** (m)	this (these) hospital(s)
ese hospital (m)	**esos hospitales** (m)	that (those) hospital(s)
aquel hospital (m)	**aquellos hospitales** (m)	that (those) hospital(s) (yonder)
esta clínica (f)	**estas clínicas** (f)	this (these) clinic(s)
esa clínica (f)	**esas clínicas** (f)	that (those) clinic(s)
aquella clínica (f)	**aquellas clínicas** (f)	that (those) clinic(s) (yonder)

Apocopation of Adjectives
Apócope de adjetivos

Before a masculine singular noun the following adjectives drop the final vowel.

primero first		**tercero** third	
bueno good		**cualquiera** any	
malo bad		**alguno** some	
ninguno some		**uno** a, an	

Eres un buen técnico.   You are a good technician.

Grande becomes **gran**.

el gran médico   the great physician

el médico grande   the big physician (physically)

Ciento becomes **cien** before any noun.

Necesito cien dólares.   I need a hundred dollars.

EXERCISES *EJERCICIOS*

A.   Rewrite the following in the plural.

1. **Este caso es interesante.**
2. **Ese niño está enfermo.**
3. **Aquella señora es cirujana.**
4. **Ese estetoscopio que tiene es mío.**
5. **Esta prueba requiere mucho tiempo.**

B.   Rewrite the following in the singular.

1. **Aquellas mujeres no vienen a la clínica.**
2. **Estos oídos están enrojecidos.**
3. **Estos sonidos son difíciles de oír.**
4. **Aquellos pacientes son mis hermanos.**
5. **Esos tónicos son caros.**

C.   Supply the correct form in Spanish.

1. **Este es su** (first) _____ **aborto.**
2. **Compré** (100) _____ **píldoras.**
3. **Busco** (some) _____ **remedio.**
4. **La técnica necesita** (any) _____ **individuo.**
5. **Hay** (100) _____ **pacientes enfermizos.**
6. **Examinó al** (third) _____ **paciente.**
7. **Ayer sufrí del** (first) _____ **ataque.**
8. **Jonas Salk es un** (great) _____ **doctor.**

D. Say in Spanish.

1. I don't like this syrup.
2. That hospital is in Texas.
3. Those pains come and go.
4. These patients do not know English.
5. This girl has (is suffering from) measles.

Comparison of Adjectives
El comparativo de adjetivos

In English two ways exist to compare adjectives (and adverbs):

Positive	*Comparative*	*Superlative*
dark	darker	darkest
beautiful	more beautiful	most beautiful

In Spanish the comparison of adjectives is formed like the second example above. Regular adjectives add **más** (or **menos**) to the positive form for the comparative degree; **el más (la más)** or **el menos (la menos)** are added to form the superlative.

Positive	*Comparative*	*Superlative*
obscuro dark	**más obscuro** darker	**el más obscuro** darkest
rojo red	**menos rojo** less red	**el menos rojo** the least red

Some adjectives are irregular in their comparison:

Positive	*Comparative*	*Superlative*
bueno good	**mejor** better	**el mejor** best
malo bad	**peor** worse	**el peor** worst
grande large	**mayor** older	**el mayor** oldest[12]
pequeño small	**menor** younger	**el menor** youngest[12]

Este paciente es mayor que el otro, pero es más pequeño. This patient is older than the other, but he is smaller.

In a comparative sentence the English word "than" is usually expressed in Spanish by **que**. However, before numbers, **de** is used.

Su presión arterial está más alta que la última vez. Your blood pressure is higher than last time.

Un análisis de la orina necesita menos tiempo que un análisis de sangre. A urinalysis takes less time than a blood chemistry.

Un cuarto doble debe costar más de cien dólares. A semi-private room must cost more than $100.

The superlative form of the adjective generally follows the noun that it modifies.

El cirujano más importante acaba de llegar. } The most important surgeon
El más importante cirujano acaba de llegar. }   has just arrived.

In English the superlative is usually followed by *in*. This is translated by **de** in Spanish.

María es la mejor enfermera del hospital. Mary is the best nurse in the hospital.

Absolute Superlative *El superlativo absoluto*

This superlative is expressed in English when the adverbs *very*, *extremely*, or *highly* modify the adjective. The Spanish counterpart is formed by adding the suffix **-ísimo** to the adjective (or adverb).

hospitales modernísimos extremely modern hospitals

Comparison of Equality
El comparativo de igualdad

In English the constructions "as . . . as" "as many . . . as," and "as much . . . as" are called the comparative of equality. In Spanish these forms are translated by:

tan . . . como as . . . as
tanto (tanta) . . . como as much . . . as
tantos (tantas) . . . como as many . . . as

In the first case the comparison is of an adjective, and the word **tan** is an adverb and is invariable. In the other two, comparisons are of number and amount of nouns, and the words expressing the amount or number are adjectives and, therefore, agree in number and gender with the word modified.

La dentistería es *tan* importante *como* la medicina. Dentistry is *as* important *as* medicine.

Tengo *tantas* píldoras *como* Eduardo. I have *as many* pills *as* Edward.

Hay *tanto* suero en este jarro *como* en aquél. There is *as much* IV in this bottle *as* in that one.

EXERCISES *EJERCICIOS*

A. Complete the following with the appropriate words for the comparative.

1. **La niña tiene fiebre _____ alta _____ su hermana.**
2. **El doctor examina a _____ pacientes _____ yo.**

   3. **Hay pacientes _____ enfermos _____ nosotros.**

   4. **Su cicatriz es _____ grande _____ la mía.**

   5. **El asistente es _____ gordo _____ la enfermera.**

B. Answer the following using complete Spanish sentences.

   1. **¿Opera Vd. menos que el otro doctor?**

   2. **¿Es Vd. más alto (-a) o más bajo (-a) que el camillero?**

   3. **¿Es la salud más importante que el dinero?**

   4. **¿Son Vds. más o menos inteligentes que Lola?**

   5. **¿Es Vd. mejor que el otro cirujano?**

C. Complete the following with the appropriate words.

   1. **El doctor Sánchez es viejo. Es _____ el doctor Ruiz pero no es _____ del hospital.**

   2. **Esta sala de espera es mala. Es aún _____ la otra pero no es _____ todas.**

   3. **Paquito es joven. Es _____ su hermana pero no es _____ la familia.**

   4. **Este hospital es bueno. Es _____ el otro pero no es _____ todos.**

D. Complete the following with the correct form of **tanto ... como.**

   1. **Vd. tiene _____ pacientes _____ el doctor Martín.**

   2. **La enfermera tiene _____ paciencia _____ él.**

   3. **La farmacia tiene _____ píldoras _____ la droguería.**

   4. **Hacemos _____ análisis _____ los otros técnicos.**

   5. **Leo _____ planillas de admisión _____ Vd.**

E. Complete with the appropriate words to express the comparative of equality.

   1. **La doctora es _____ conocida _____ su esposo.**

   2. **Aquella enfermera es _____ aplicada _____ las otras.**

   3. **Esta clínica es _____ famosa _____ la Clínica de los Mayos.**

   4. **Esta parte del hospital no es _____ vieja _____ la otra parte.**

ARTICLES

LOS ARTICULOS

In Spanish definite and indefinite articles are adjectives and, thus, precede the noun they modify and agree with it in number and gender.

Definite Article *El artículo definido*

The definite article (*the*) is translated in four different ways: **el** before a masculine singular noun; **la** before a feminine singular noun; **los** before a masculine plural noun; **las** before a feminine plural noun.

el hospital the hospital   **los hospitales** the hospitals
la clínica the clinic   **las clínicas** the clinics

NOTE: **El** is used in the singular instead of **la**, when the feminine noun begins with stressed **a** or **ha** and the definite article immediately precedes. Only proper names are excluded. This does not imply a change in the gender of the noun.

el hambre the hunger

mucha hambre very hungry (much hunger)

el acta de nacimiento the birth certificate

las actas de nacimiento the birth certificates

There are *only* two contractions in Spanish:

a + el = al to/at the

de + el = del of/from the

Voy al hospital, no a la clínica. I am going to the hospital, not the clinic.

El viene del hospital, no de la clínica. He is coming from the hospital, not from the clinic.

USES OF THE DEFINITE ARTICLE
USOS DEL ARTICULO DEFINIDO

In addressing someone by his or her full name, John García, we say: **Sr. Juan García, Juan García,** or **Sr. García.** When speaking of a person, the titles **señor** and **señora** require the definite article before them.

El Sr. García está aquí. Mr. García is here.

The definite article replaces possessive adjectives when alluding to parts of the body and personal possessions that are being worn. Often the possessor is indicated by an indirect object pronoun or by a reflexive pronoun:

El se quita la ropa. He removes his clothes.

Te ha bajado la fiebre. Your fever has gone down.

The definite article is used with the names of languages in Spanish unless immediately following the verb **hablar** or the prepositions **de** and **en**. However, colloquial Spanish also omits the definite article after the verbs **aprender, comprender, estudiar,** and **saber.**

El paciente comprende (el) inglés, pero no sabe hablar inglés. The patient understands English, but does not know how to speak English.

El descargo está escrito en español. The release is written in Spanish.

When used with the days of the week, the definite article has the meaning of *on* (see page 216). The definite article is used with the seasons only in a general sense, or after the preposition **en.**

El médico no trabaja *los* **miércoles.**   The doctor doesn't work on Wednesdays.

El **invierno es la estación más fría del año.**   Winter is the coldest season of the year.

Ella no tiene que quedarse en case en *el verano.*   She doesn't have to stay home in the summer.

Spanish uses the definite article before nouns that are abstract or that refer to all members of the whole in general. (The definite article is omitted to show the idea of "some," "a few," or "any.")

Me gusta *la* **leche.**   I like milk.

Tomo leche en el desayuno.   I drink milk for breakfast.

La **salud es una cosa magnífica.**   Health is a wonderful thing.

EXERCISES *EJERCICIOS*

A.   Rewrite the following in the singular.

1.   **Las aguas son muy buenas.**   The waters are very good.
2.   **Las hachas son peligrosas.**   Axes are dangerous.
3.   **Las áreas son enormes.**   The areas are enormous.
4.   **Las águilas atacan al niño.**   The eagles are attacking the child.
5.   **Las ayas hablan al médico.**   The governesses speak to the physician.

B.   Supply the appropriate definite article.

＿＿＿ **intestinos**	＿＿＿ **enfermero**	＿＿＿ **enfermera**	＿＿＿ **mano**
＿＿＿ **cirujano**	＿＿＿ **infección**	＿＿＿ **trabajo**	＿＿＿ **huesos**
＿＿＿ **hospital**	＿＿＿ **anestesia**	＿＿＿ **terapeuta**	＿＿＿ **síntoma**
＿＿＿ **especialización**	＿＿＿ **bronquios**	＿＿＿ **diafragma**	＿＿＿ **día**

C.   Complete the following with the appropriate definite article when necessary.

1.   ＿＿＿ **doctor Ortega está en la clínica.**
2.   **¿Cómo se siente hoy, ＿＿＿ señora Torres?**
3.   **El médico escribe la receta en ＿＿＿ inglés.**
4.   **La enfermera aprende ＿＿＿ español.**
5.   **La paciente piensa mucho en ＿＿＿ muerte.**
6.   **No nos gustan ＿＿＿ inyecciones.**
7.   ＿＿＿ **enfermedades son terribles.**
8.   **Soy alérgica a ＿＿＿ aspirina.**
9.   ＿＿＿ **señora Torres está mala.**
10.   ＿＿＿ **ciencia es importante.**

11. A ella le duele _____ pecho.
12. Te quitas _____ ropa.
13. Ella se puso _____ bata.
14. Nos duele _____ cabeza.

Indefinite Article *El artículo indefinido*

The indefinite article is translated as "a" or "an" in the singular, and "some" or "a few" in the plural: **un** before a masculine singular noun; **una** before a feminine singular noun; **unos** before a masculine plural noun; **unas** before a feminine plural noun.

Normally an article is used before each noun and agrees in number and gender with the noun.

un ayudante   an orderly   **unas enfermeras**   some nurses

OMISSION OF INDEFINITE ARTICLE
FALTA DEL ARTICULO INDEFINIDO

The indefinite article (**un, una, unos, unas**) is omitted in the following instances:

1. before unmodified predicate nouns indicating profession, occupation, religion, political affiliation or nationality.

   Es ayudante.   He is an orderly.

   Mi amiga es enfermera.   My friend is a nurse.

   Raúl es español.   Raul is Spanish.

   but: **Mi padre es un buen médico.**   My father is a good physician.

2. before **ciento, cierto, mil, otro**.

   cien (mil) camas   a hundred (a thousand) beds

   otro hospital   another hospital

3. after the exclamatory **¡qué!** (what a).

   ¡Qué error!   What a mistake!

EXERCISES *EJERCICIOS*

A. Give the correct indefinite article.

_____ esfigmomanómetro   _____ solicitud (application)

_____ termómetro   _____ descargo

_____ sala de reconocimiento   _____ flujo vaginal (vaginal discharge)

_____ píldoras   _____ consultorio

_____ camilla   _____ radiografía

B. Supply the correct indefinite article when needed.

1. **Necesito _____ otra píldora más fuerte.**
2. **El doctor García es _____ anestesiólogo.**
3. **¿Busca Vd. _____ receta?**
4. **¡Qué _____ médica!**
5. **Tú eres _____ buen demócrato.**
6. **La paciente es _____ católica fiel.**
7. **Ese hombre es _____ médico distinguido.**
8. **Necesita _____ operación pronto.**
9. **La mujer es _____ puertorriqueña.**
10. **¿Qué es? Es _____ estudiante de medicina.**

VERBS
LOS VERBOS

A verb is a word that shows action, being, or state of being.

Dr. Jones *takes* my temperature. (action)
Mary *is* a nurse. (being)
Paul *is* sick. (state of being)

Spanish verbs are divided into three conjugations, according to the endings of their infinitives: **-ar**, **-er**, and **-ir**. Some Spanish verbs are conjugated by removing the final **-ar**, **-er**, or **-ir**, leaving a base or stem and then adding a series of endings, which express distinctions of person, number, tense, and mood. The base, or stem, of the verb embodies the meaning of the verb. To conjugate in the present and past tenses, endings are added to the unchanged stem of the regular verb. To conjugate in the future and conditional tenses, endings are added to the entire infinitives.

In Spanish, verbs are conjugated to show mood, tense, person, and number. Most verbs are conjugated after a regular pattern. Those verbs that do not follow the pattern are considered to be irregular and must be memorized.

Present Indicative Tense
El tiempo presente de indicativo

The present tense has three English meanings.

Estudio medicina.
{
I study medicine.
I do study medicine.
I am studying medicine.
}

Regular Spanish verbs are conjugated in the present indicative tense by dropping the infinite ending (**ar**, **er**, or **ir**) and, to what is left, which is the stem, attaching the following endings:

Subject pronoun	-ar	-er	-ir
yo	-o	-o	-o
tú	-as	-es	-es
él, ella, usted	-a	-e	-e
nosotros (-as)	-amos	-emos	-imos
	— 13	— 13	— 13
ellos, ellas, ustedes	-an	-en	-en

The present indicative tense in Spanish signifies that the time under consideration is present, and points out a thing as existing. It may be used to make a statement or a question, either affirmatively or negatively.

-AR VERBS (FIRST-CONJUGATION VERBS)

The majority of Spanish verbs end in **-ar**. To conjugate in the present tense drop **-ar** and attach **-o**, **-as**, **-a**, **-amos**, **(-áis)**, or **-an**. The following list includes many common medically oriented **-ar** verbs.

aliviar   to alleviate
agravar   to aggravate
amputar   to amputate
aspirar   to aspirate
ayudar   to alleviate, to help
consultar   to consult
doblar   to bend, to flex
esperar   to hope (for), to wait (for)
examinar   to examine
hallar   to find
hinchar   to swell
llamar   to call
llegar   to arrive
llorar   to cry
mejorar   to improve, to get better
menstruar   to menstruate
molestar   to annoy
operar   to operate
orinar   to urinate

pasar   to pass, to spend time
quejar   to complain
quitar   to remove, to take off
radiografiar   to take x-rays
recetar   to prescribe
recuperar   to recuperate
respirar   to breathe
resucitar   to resuscitate
sacar   to take out
sangrar   to bleed
tomar   to take, to drink
trabajar   to work
vendar   to bandage
vomitar   to vomit

EXERCISES *EJERCICIOS*

A.   Give the corresponding forms of the following regular verbs.

	operar	trabajar	examinar	consultar
yo				
tú				
el médico				
la enfermera				
usted				
nosotros				
los médicos				
las enfermeras				
ustedes				

B.   Item Substitution. Repeat the following sentences, substituting the new subjects. Make sure that the verbs agree.

1.   **Yo opero en el quirófano. (tú / tú y yo / ella / ellos)**
2.   **Nosotros trabajamos con los pacientes. (La terapeuta / yo / él / ustedes)**
3.   **Ella consulta en la clínica. (Vds. / María / Juan y ella / él / yo)**
4.   **Vd. examina en el hospital. (yo / ellos / Pablo / Pablo y yo)**

C.   Say in Spanish.

1.   He examines in the clinic.
2.   We consult with the patients.
3.   She works in Chicago.
4.   They work in the hospital.
5.   I operate in the clinic.

-ER VERBS (SECOND-CONJUGATION VERBS)

To conjugate **-er** verbs in the present tense drop **-er** and add **-o**, **-es**, **-e**, **-emos**, (**éis**), or **-en**. Some health-oriented **-er** verbs are:

comer   to eat
comprender   to understand
meter   to insert, to put
responder   to respond
romper   to break
suceder   to happen
temer   to fear
toser   to cough

-IR VERBS (THIRD-CONJUGATION VERBS)

From the infinitive of all regular **-ir** verbs, drop the **-ir** ending and to the stem, attach the following endings: **-o**, **-es**, **-e**, **-imos**, (**ís**), or **-en**. Some health-oriented **-ir** verbs are:

abrir   to open
escupir   to spit
permitir   to permit, to allow
prescribir   to prescribe
revivir   to revive
sufrir   to suffer
vivir   to live

EXERCISES *EJERCICIOS*

A.   Give the corresponding forms of the following regular verbs.

1.   **yo: comer, toser, responder, temer**
2.   **tú: comprender, aprender, toser, romper**
3.   **la enfermera: suceder, responder, meter, comer**
4.   **el doctor y yo: temer, meter, comprender, toser**
5.   **Luis y usted: toser, responder, comer, aprender**

B.   Item Substitution. (Change the verbs according to the new subjects.)

1.   **Yo revivo a la paciente. (él / los médicos / Vd. / tú)**
2.   **Ella sufre mucho. (el viejo / tú / yo / Juan y ella / Vd. / tú y yo)**
3.   **El médico prescribe muchas drogas. (yo / Juan y María / Vd. / tú)**
4.   **Ella abre la boca. (tú / yo / Vd. / ellos)**
5.   **Recibo la medicina de la enfermera. (nosotros / Juan / Juan y él / tú)**

C. Review of Regular Verbs. Change these sentences from **yo** to **tú** and to **Vd**.

1. **Yo *leo* la carta del paciente todos los días. Tú *lees* . . . ; Vd. *lee* . . . .**
    I read the patient's chart daily.

2. **Yo *necesito* la máquina ultrasónica.** _____
    I need the ultrasound machine.

3. **Yo *camino* por el cuarto de estar.** _____
    I walk through the waiting room.

4. **Yo *vivo* cerca de la clínica.** _____
    I live near the clinic.

5. **Yo *desinfecto* la lesión.** _____
    I disinfect the wound.

6. **Yo le *debo* mucho al hospital.** _____
    I owe the hospital a lot.

7. **Yo *bebo* demasiado café.** _____
    I drink too much coffee.

8. **Yo *recibo* la cama de ruedas del asistente.** _____
    I receive the gurney from the orderly.

NOTE: For further practice with these verbs, repeat the above exercises orally, this time changing **yo** to **él**. (**El lee** la carta del paciente todos los días, etc.) Repeat again, this time changing **yo** to **nosotros**. (**Nosotros leemos** la carta del paciente todos los días, etc.)

IRREGULAR VERBS *VERBOS IRREGULARES*

The following irregular verbs are necessary for mastery of the Spanish language. They must be memorized since they do not follow the regular verb pattern. The English auxiliary verbs *do*, *does*, *am*, *are*, and *is* also apply to these verbs.

	Dar to give
yo *doy*	I give, I am giving, I do give
tú *das*	you give, you are giving, you do give
él, ella, Vd. *da*	he, she, it gives; you give; he, she, it is giving; you are giving; he, she, it does give; you do give
nosotros (-as) *damos*	we give, we are giving, we do give
—	—
ellos, ellas, Vds. *dan*	they, you give, are giving, do give

	Decir to say, to tell
yo *digo*	I say, tell
tú *dices*	you say, tell

él, ella, Vd. *dice*	he, she, it says, tells; you say, tell
nosotros (-as) *decimos*	we say, tell
—	—
ellos, ellas, Vds. *dicen*	they, you say, tell

Haber   to have (auxiliary verb)

yo *he*	I have
tú *has*	you have
él, ella, Vd. *ha*	he, she, it has; you have
nosotros (-as) *hemos*	we have
—	—
ellos, ellas, Vds. *han*	they, you have

Haber is always followed by the past participle and never stands alone.

Yo he vomitado mucho.	I have vomited a lot.
Ella ha comido uvas.	She has eaten grapes.
Nosotros hemos sufrido demasiado.	We have suffered too much.

Hacer   to do, to make

yo *hago*	I do, make
tú *haces*	you do, make
él, ella, Vd. *hace*	he, she, it does, makes; you do, make
nosotros (-as) *hacemos*	we do, make
—	—
ellos, ellas, Vds. *hacen*	they, you do, make

Ir   to go

yo *voy*	I go
tú *vas*	you go
él, ella, Vd. *va*	he, she, it goes, you go
nosotros (-as) *vamos*	we go
—	—
ellos, ellas, Vds. *van*	they, you go

Ir may be followed by **a** plus an infinitive. In this case it has the future meaning "to be going to do something."

Voy a examinarle.	I am going to examine you.

Oír   to hear

yo *oigo*	I hear
tú *oyes*	you hear
él, ella, Vd. *oye*	he, she, it hears; you hear
nosotros (-as) *oímos*	we hear
—	—
ellos, ellas, Vds. *oyen*	they, you hear

Poder   to be able

yo *puedo*	I can, am able
tú *puedes*	you can, are able
él, ella, Vd. *puede*	he, she, it can, is able; you can, are able
nosotros (-as) *podemos*	we can, are able
—	—
ellos, ellas, Vds. *pueden*	they, you can, are able

Poder is followed directly by an infinitive.

Yo puedo comer ahora.	I am able to eat now.
Podemos estudiar más.	We can study more

Poner   to put, to place

yo *pongo*	I put, place
tú *pones*	you put, place
él, ella, Vd. *pone*	he, she, it puts, places; you put, place
nosotros (-as) *ponemos*	we put, place
—	—
ellos, ellas, Vds. *ponen*	they, you put, place

Querer   to want, wish

yo *quiero*	I want, wish
tú *quieres*	you want, wish
él, ella, Vd. *quiere*	he, she, it wants, wishes; you want, wish
nosotros (-as) *queremos*	we want, wish
—	—
ellos, ellas, Vds. *quieren*	they, you want, wish

Querer is followed by an infinitive.

El médico quiere salir del hospital.	The physician wants to leave the hospital.

Saber   to know

yo *sé*	I know
tú *sabes*	you know
él, ella, Vd. *sabe*	he, she, it knows, you know
nosotros (-as) *sabemos*	we know
—	—
ellos, ellas, Vds. *saben*	they, you know

Saber may be followed directly by an infinitive, in which case it has the meaning of "to know how to."

Sé leer un libro español.   I know how to read a Spanish book.

Salir   to leave

yo *salgo*	I leave
tú *sales*	you leave
él, ella, Vd. *sale*	he, she, it leaves, you leave
nosotros (-as) *salimos*	we leave
—	—
ellos, ellas, Vds. *salen*	they, you leave

Tener   to have

yo *tengo*	I have
tú *tienes*	you have
él, ella, Vd. *tiene*	he, she, it has, you have
nosotros (-as) *tenemos*	we have
—	—
ellos, ellas, Vds. *tienen*	they, you have

Traer   to bring

yo *traigo*	I bring
tú *traes*	you bring
él, ella, Vd. *trae*	he, she, it brings, you bring
nosotros (-as) *traemos*	we bring
—	—
ellos, ellas, Vds. *traen*	they, you bring

Venir   to come

yo *vengo*	I come
tú *vienes*	you come
él, ella, Vd. *viene*	he, she, it comes, you come
nosotros (-as) *venimos*	we come
—	—
ellos, ellas, Vds. *vienen*	they, you come

Ver   to see

yo *veo*	I see
tú *ves*	you see
él, ella, Vd. *ve*	he, she, it sees, you see
nosotros (-as) *vemos*	we see
—	—
ellos, ellas, Vds. *ven*	they, you see

Ser, Estar   to be

ser	estar	
yo *soy*	yo *estoy*	I am
tú *eres*	tú *estás*	you are
él, ella, Vd. *es*	él, ella, Vd. *está*	he, she, it is, you are
nosotros (-as) *somos*	nosotros (-as) *estamos*	we are
—	—	—
ellos, ellas, Vds. *son*	ellos, ellas, Vds. *están*	they, you are

Both verbs translate in English as *to be*, but they are NOT interchangeable!
Both are irregular in the present indicative tense.

USES OF SER   *USOS DE SER*

1. **Ser** expresses an inherent or relatively permanent quality.

   Vd. es joven.   You are young. (age)
   La mujer es pobre.   The woman is poor. (wealth)
   Mi hermano es alto.   My brother is tall. (size)
   La mesa es redonda.   The table is round. (shape)
   El traje es azul.   The suit is blue. (color)
   El libro es mío.   The book is mine. (possession)
   La nieve es fría.   Snow is cold. (characteristic)

2. **Ser** is used with predicate nouns, pronouns, or adjectives.

   El es dentista.   He is a dentist.
   ¿Quién soy yo?   Who am I?
   Somos católicos.   We are catholic.

3. **Ser** indicates origin, source, material, or ownership.

   El ayudante es de Nueva York.   The orderly is from New York.
   La bata es de algodón.   The bathrobe is cotton.
   Las flores son de Vd.   The flowers are yours.

4. **Ser** tells time.

   Es la una. It is one o'clock.   **Son las seis.** It is six o'clock.

5. **Ser** is used with adverbs of location. In this case, **ser** is synonymous with **tener lugar** or **ocurrir** (to occur, to take place).

   La operación es la semana que viene. The operation is next week.

   ¿Cuándo fue la conferencia? When was the lecture?

6. **Ser** is used with **para** to indicate either the recipient of an action or for what an item is intended.

   El urinálisis es para aquella paciente. The urinalysis is for that patient.

   ¿Para quién son las píldoras? For whom are the pills?

   Es una dieta para adelgazar. It is a weight-reducing diet.

7. **Ser** is used in impersonal expressions.

   Es posible. . . It is possible. . .   **Es que. . .** The fact is that. . .

8. **Ser** is used with the past participle to form the true passive voice (see page 128).

RECAP: **Ser** is used when the attribute is inherent or essential to the subject and implies a permanent quality of things, or persons, rank, condition, position, profession, and possession. It answers the questions: "what?" "of what?" "for what?" "for whom?" and "whose?"

EXERCISES *EJERCICIOS*

A. Answer the following using the directed responses.

   1. **¿Cómo es la enfermera?** (paciente)
   2. **¿Qué es Vd.?** (terapeuta)
   3. **¿De dónde son los pacientes?** (Puerto Rico)
   4. **¿Cómo es el especialista?** (competente)
   5. **¿Cómo eres tú?** (joven, guapo, simpático)

B. Complete the following with the appropriate form of the verb **ser**.

   1. **Carlos _____ ginecólogo.**
   2. **Nosotros _____ enfermeros.**
   3. **Ellos _____ dentistas.**
   4. **La clínica _____ moderna.**
   5. **¿Qué hora _____?**
   6. **Aquella doctora _____ de Puerto Rico.**
   7. **La máquina no _____ de madera, sino metal.**
   8. **Esos pacientes _____ borrachos.**
   9. **¿De quién _____ el reloj de pulsera?**
   10. **¿_____ tú la nueva auxiliar de enfermeras?**

USES OF ESTAR *USOS DE ESTAR*

1. **Estar** expresses location (both temporary and permanent).

   Chicago está en Illinois. Chicago is in Illinois.
   Yo estoy en la clase. I am in class.

2. **Estar** expresses conditions of health.

   ¿Cómo está Vd.? How are you?
   Estoy muy bien. I am fine.
   Estamos enfermos. We are ill.

3. **Estar** expresses a temporary quality or characteristic.

   Ella está nerviosa. She is nervous.
   Estoy atenta. I am attentive.
   Vd. está ausente. You are absent.

NOTE: When **tiempo** (weather) is used in connection with adverbs or adjectives, the verb **estar** is used instead of **hacer**.

   ¿Cómo está el tiempo hoy? How is the weather today?
   El tiempo está hermosísimo. The weather is very beautiful.
   El día está frío. The day is cold.
   La tarde está calurosa. The afternoon is warm.

4. **Estar** is used with the gerund to form the progressive tenses (see pages 118–120).

RECAP: **Estar** is used when the state or condition, quality or position of the subject is accidental, temporary, or transitory. It answers "where?" "how?" and "who?"

EXERCISES *EJERCICIOS*

A. Complete the following with the appropriate form of the verb **estar**.

1. **La clínica _____ en la Avenida Primera.**
2. **Evanston _____ en Illinois.**
3. **Los visitantes _____ en la sala de espera.**
4. **El quirófano _____ en el quinto piso.**
5. **Los instrumentos quirúrgicos _____ en la mesa.**

B. Answer the following using the directed responses.

1. **¿Dónde están las almohadas** (pillows)**?** (on the bed)
2. **¿Dónde estás?** (the doctor's office)
3. **¿Está la mujer estreñida** (constipated)**?** (yes)
4. **¿Cómo están Vds.?** (better than yesterday)
5. **¿Cómo estamos?** (still ill)

C. Complete the following sentences using the appropriate forms of **ser** and **estar**. Make all necessary changes.

   1. **Tú eres rico pero no estás contento.**

   2. **Ella _____ pero no _____.**

   3. **Nosotros _____ pero no _____.**

   4. **Vd. _____ pero no _____.**

   5. **La bata es nueva pero está sucia.**

   6. **La sábana _____ pero _____.**

   7. **Los uniformes _____ pero _____.**

   8. **El uniforme _____ pero _____.**

D. Complete the following with the correct form of **ser** or **estar**.

   1. **Mañana _____ lunes.**

   2. **¿_____ Vd. satisfecha?**

   3. **Vds. _____ médicos.**

   4. **¿Qué _____ su tío?**

   5. **Juan _____ de Puerto Rico; _____ puertorriqueño.**

   6. **Mi enfermera no _____ en la oficina porque _____ enferma.**

   7. **Nuestros pacientes _____ jóvenes.**

   8. **Esta oficina _____ del doctor Ruiz.**

Some adjectives may be used with either **ser** or **estar**. The meaning of the adjective varies, however.

   El paciente es aburrido.   The patient is boring.

   El paciente está aburrido.   The patient is bored.

Additional examples include:

	with **ser**	with **estar**
alegre	gay, light-hearted (by nature)	gay (at the moment)
bueno	good	well, in good health
callado	silent (by nature)	not talking
cansado	tiresome	tired
divertido	amusing, funny	amused
embarazada	embarrassed	pregnant
enfermo	sickly	sick
listo	clever, intelligent	ready
malo	bad (in behavior)	ill, not well
pálido	pale-complexioned	pale (condition)
seguro	safe (reliable)	sure (state of mind)
tonto	dull-witted, not bright	silly

triste	dull	sad
verde	green (in color)	green (not ripe)
vivo	lively, bright (color)	alive, living

EXERCISES *EJERCICIOS*

Complete the following using the correct forms of **ser** or **estar** according to the meaning conveyed in the sentence.

1. **Pepe** _____ **muy malo; tiene catarro.**
2. **Yo** _____ **seguro de que Pedro lo hará.**
3. **Se acuesta temprano porque** _____ **muy cansado.**
4. **El** _____ **listo para operar.**
5. **Los médicos** _____ **listos.**
6. **Los colores** _____ **muy vivos.**

Tener   to have (verb of possession)

yo *tengo*	I have
tú *tienes*	you have
él, ella, Vd. *tiene*	he, she, it has, you have
nosotros (-as) *tenemos*	we have
—	—
ellos, ellas, Vds. *tienen*	they, you have

IDIOMS USING **TENER**   *MODISMOS CON TENER*

tener _____ **años**   to be _____ years old
tener calor (m)   to be warm
tener cuidado   to be careful
tener la culpa   to be guilty
tener deseos (de)   to desire (to)
tener éxito   to be successful
tener frío   to be cold
tener ganas (de)   to feel like
tener hambre (f)   to be hungry
tener lugar   to take place
tener miedo   to be afraid
tener murria   to be blue
tener prisa   to be in a hurry
tener que + infinitive   to have to (must) (shows strong obligation)

tener razón   to be right
no tener razón   to be wrong
tener retraso   to be late
tener sed (f)   to be thirsty
tener sueño   to be sleepy
tener vergüenza   to be ashamed

EXERCISES   *EJERCICIOS*

A. Substitution.

1. **Tengo un termómetro. (tú / él / Vds. / tú y yo / ella)**
2. **Ella no tiene dolor ahora. (María / Vd. / yo / nosotros / tú)**
3. **La paciente tiene una fiebre alta. (Vd. / tú / ellos / yo / María y yo)**

B. Complete the following sentences, using the first one as a model and making all the necessary changes suggested by the cues.

1. **Yo tengo hambre.**
2. **_____ prisa.**
3. **Tú _____ .**
4. **_____ calor.**
5. **Nosotros _____ .**
6. **_____ frío.**
7. **_____ miedo.**
8. **Ella _____ .**
9. **_____ sed.**
10. **_____ sueño.**
11. **Vds. _____ .**
12. **_____ razón.**

C. Answer the following questions with complete sentences.

1. **¿Tiene sueño la enfermera de guardia?**
2. **¿Cuántos años tiene el paciente?**
3. **¿Tienen prisa los médicos?**
4. **¿Tienes miedo?**
5. **¿Tiene ella mucha hambre?**

SELECTED HEALTH EXPRESSIONS USING **TENER**
TENER ENFERMEDADES

tener artritis   arthritis
tener asma   asthma
tener bronquitis   bronchitis

    tener cáncer cancer
    tener catarro a cold
    tener cirrosis hepática cirrhosis of the liver
    tener conjuntivitis conjunctivitis
    tener dermatitis dermatitis
    tener diabetes diabetes
    tener encefalitis encephalitis
    tener escarlatina scarlet fever
    tener faringitis pharyngitis
    tener fiebre a fever
    tener gangrena gangrene
    tener hepatitis hepatitis
    tener laringitis laryngitis
    tener leucemia leukemia
    tener náuseas be nauseous
    tener neuralgia neuralgia
    tener otitis otitis
    tener paludismo malaria
    tener paperas mumps
    tener la presión alta high blood pressure
    tener la presión baja low blood pressure
    tener pulmonía pneumonia
    tener rubéola german measles
    tener sarampión measles
    tener sífilis syphilis
    tener tifus typhus
    tener viruelas smallpox

RADICAL OR STEM-CHANGING VERBS
VERBOS QUE CAMBIAN DE RADICAL

Certain **-ar**, **-er**, and **-ir** verbs show a change in the radical or stem vowel when the stress falls on it. When the last stem vowel is a stressed **e** or **o**, it changes to **ie** or **ue**. These changes occur in all persons except the first and second persons plural of the present indicative (and present subjunctive).

    All **-ar** and **-er** verbs that show this stem-changing trait are classified as Class I verbs. The stem-changing **-ir** verbs are divided into Class II and Class III verbs. Class II verbs are those **-ir** verbs whose stem vowel is either an **e**, which changes to **ie**, or an **o**, which changes to **ue**, when stressed in the present tenses.

Class III verbs undergo a special change in the stem. Their last stem vowel is an **e** which, when stressed, changes to **i** in the present indicative. Class II and Class III verbs make a vowel change in the entire singular and third person plural of the present indicative tense, and in the third person of the preterite tense.

The radical changes of Classes I, II, and III are often indicated in verb lists with parentheses following the infinitives—**(ie)**, **(ue)**. Verbs that make changes in both tenses show two items within parentheses—**(ie, i)**, **(ue, u)**, **(i, i)**. The first item shows the present tense change; the second, the preterite.

The following represent common radical-changing verbs.

CLASS I (IE), (UE)

acordarse   to remember

acostar(se)   to go to bed, to lie down

almorzar   to have lunch

cerrar   to close

colgar   to hang

comenzar   to begin

confesar   to confess

contar   to count

costar   to cost

demostrar   to demonstrate, to show

despertar(se)   to wake up

devolver   to return, to give back

doler   to hurt, to ache

empezar   to begin

encender   to light, to turn on

encontrar   to find

entender   to understand

mostrar   to show

mover   to move

negar   to deny

pensar   to think

perder   to lose

probar   to prove, to test, to try out

querer   to want, to love

recordar   to remember

rogar   to beg

sentar(se)   to sit down
soler   to be in the habit of
soñar (con)   to dream (of)
tender   to stretch, to unfold
torcer   to twist, to turn
volver   to return, to come back

CLASS II (IE, I), (UE, U)

advertir   to warn
arrepentir(se)   to repent
consentir   to consent
convertir(se)   to turn into
discernir   to discern
divertirse   to amuse oneself
dormir   to sleep
dormirse   to fall asleep, to doze off
herir   to wound, to hurt
mentir   to lie
morir   to die
preferir   to prefer
referir   to refer
sentir   to feel, to regret
sentirse   to feel
sugerir   to suggest
transferir   to transfer

CLASS III (I, I)

competir   to compete
concebir   to conceive
conseguir   to obtain, to get
despedirse (de)   to say goodbye (to)
elegir   to choose
impedir   to prevent
pedir   to ask (for), to request
perseguir   to pursue
reír   to laugh
repetir   to repeat

reñir   to quarrel

seguir   to follow

servir   to serve

sonreír   to smile

vestir(se)   to dress (oneself)

NOTE: The verb **decir** (to tell, to say) undergoes the same change. It also has an irregular first person singular: **yo digo**.

EXERCISES *EJERCICIOS*

A.   Item Substitution.

    1.   **Yo empiezo la operación. (tú / nosotros / ellos / el médico)**

    2.   **La enfermera no entiende el español. (yo / ellos / Vd. / Vds.)**

    3.   **Tú quieres consultar. (el médico y yo / él / ellos / yo)**

B.   Complete the following sentences.

    1.   **La paciente _____ (morir).**

    2.   **Yo _____ (pedir) ayuda.**

    3.   **¿Cómo _____ (dormir) Vd.?**

    4.   **Yo _____ (poder) volver mañana.**

    5.   **El _____ (repetir) las instrucciones.**

    6.   **El _____ (pensar) ordenar el análisis.**

    7.   **El doctor _____ (probar) la jeringa.**

    8.   **¿Qué _____ (sugerir) Vd.?**

    9.   **¿Cuándo _____ (poder) él volver?**

    10.   **Nosotros _____ (servir) a la una.**

C.   Conjugate in the first person singular and plural of the present indicative.

cerrar	_____	_____
acostar	_____	_____
encontrar	_____	_____
perder	_____	_____
encender	_____	_____
negar	_____	_____
herir	_____	_____
referir	_____	_____
concebir	_____	_____
mostrar	_____	_____

D.   Say in Spanish.

    1.   You can use a diaphragm (**un diafragma**).

    2.   It is used (serves) in order to cover part of the vagina.

    3.   Do I ask for an appointment for (**para**) next week?

4. The patient is sleeping now.
5. We count calories.
6. I am following a strict diet.
7. Are you following your doctor's orders?
8. I feel some pain when I sit down.
9. The nurse tries the syringe.
10. She shows me where it hurts her.

Preterite Indicative Tense
El tiempo pretérito

The preterite indicative tense expresses a definitely completed past action. Grammarians have called this tense the historical past, the past definite, or the absolute past. The preterite is translated as *did* plus the meaning of the verb, or as the simple past tense: "I operated," "I did operate." In negative or interrogative verbs, however, "I did not" or "did I" may indicate either preterite or imperfect. The preterite tense is formed as follows for regular verbs:

For **-ar** verbs, remove the infinite ending (**-ar**) and add:

-é, -aste, -ó, -amos, —, -aron

For **-er** and **-ir** verbs, remove the infinite endings (**-er** and **-ir**) and add:

-í, -iste, -ió, -imos, —, -ieron

Subject Pronouns	*examinar*	*comer*	*sufrir*
yo	examin*é*	com*í*	sufr*í*
tú	examin*aste*	com*iste*	sufr*iste*
él, ella, Vd.	examin*ó*	com*ió*	sufr*ió*
nosotros(-as)	examin*amos*	com*imos*	sufr*imos*
—	**—**	**—**	**—**
ellos, ellas, Vds.	examin*aron*	com*ieron*	sufr*ieron*

Thus, **examiné** means I examined, or I did examine.

All regular preterite verbs have a written accent over the final vowel in the first and third person singular. Any time a definite past action is expressed, the preterite is used. A specific time need not be mentioned.

Seventeen verbs are irregular in the preterite. Fourteen of these verbs, although possessing irregular stems, use the same irregular preterite endings: **-e, -iste, -o, -imos, —, ieron**.

NOTE: (1) No written accent appears on any of these endings.
(2) Those verbs whose stem ends in **j** use **-eron** for the third person plural.
(3) The third person singular of **hacer** is spelled **hizo**, the **c** changes to **z** in order to retain the original soft "**c**" sound.

Irregularities   Irregularidades

Infinitive	*Irregular Stem*	*Conjugation*
andar	anduv-	anduve, anduviste, anduvo, anduvimos, —, anduvieron
caber	cup-	cupe, cupiste, cupo, cupimos, —, cupieron
conducir	conduj-	conduje, condujiste, condujo, condujimos, —, condujeron
decir	dij-	dije, dijiste, dijo, dijimos, —, dijeron
estar	estuv-	estuve, estuviste, estuvo, estuvimos, —, estuvieron
haber	hub-	hube, hubiste, hubo, hubimos, —, hubieron
hacer	hic-	hice, hiciste, hizo, hicimos, —, hicieron
poder	pud-	pude, pudiste, pudo, pudimos, —, pudieron
poner	pus-	puse, pusiste, puso, pusimos, —, pusieron
querer	quis-	quise, quisiste, quiso, quisimos, —, quisieron
saber	sup-	supe, supiste, supo, supimos, —, supieron
tener	tuv-	tuve, tuviste, tuvo, tuvimos, —, tuvieron
traer	traj-	traje, trajiste, trajo, trajimos, —, trajeron
venir	vin-	vine, viniste, vino, vinimos, —, vinieron

ser and **ir** have the same forms in the preterite:

fui, fuiste, fue, fuimos, —, fueron

Dar is conjugated like a regular **-er** or **-ir** verb in the preterite tense, but without the written accent marks:

di, diste, dio, dimos, —, dieron

ORTHOGRAPHIC CHANGES IN THE PRETERITE
CAMBIOS DE ORTOGRAFIA EN EL PRETERITO

When the stem of **-er** or **-ir** verbs ends in a vowel, change the third person singular and plural from **-ió** to **-yó**, and from **-ieron** to **-yeron**. In all the other forms the **i** has a written accent.

EXCEPTIONS: **traer** (to bring), **atraer** (to attract), and all verbs ending in **-guir** (the **u** is silent.)

caer	to fall,	**creer**	to believe,
leer	to read,	**oír**	to hear

Verbs whose infinitive ends in **-car**, **-gar** and **-zar** show an orthographic change only in the first person singular. In order to preserve the original sound, **c** changes to **qu**, **g** changes to **gu**, and **z** changes to **c**.

sacar	sa*qué*	I removed
pagar	pa*gué*	I paid
comenzar	comen*cé*	I began

Class II and Class III radical changing verbs undergo a stem change in the third singular and plural. The **o** of the stem changes to **u**, and the **e** changes to **i**.

El murió. He died.   **Ellos lo sintieron.** They regretted it.

USES OF THE PRETERITE TENSE   *USOS DEL PRETERITO*

1. The preterite is used to indicate the beginning or the end of an action or event that happened in the past. Additionally, it may also narrate a complete event—beginning and end.

   La operación comenzó a las nueve.   The operation began at 9:00. (beginning)
   Cesó de operar a las cinco.   He stopped operating at 5:00. (end)
   El médico me examinó ayer.   The doctor examined me yesterday. (complete)

2. Because of the use of the preterite to express instantaneous, completed acts, special meanings are ascribed to the verbs **conocer** (to know), **poder** (to be able), **querer** (to want), **saber** (to know), and **tener** (to have).

   La *conocimos* en el hospital.   We *met* her in the hospital. (began to know)
   El *pudo* convencer a su paciente.   He *managed* to convince his patient. (finally was able)
   ***No pude* concentrar.**   I *could not* concentrate. (tried to but couldn't)
   El equipo médico *quiso* ayudarme.   The medical team *tried to* help me. (final decision)
   Ellos *no quisieron* sacármela.   They *refused to* remove it from me. (final decision)
   ***Supo* que no tiene cáncer.**   He *found out* (that) he doesn't have cancer. (began to know)
   ***Tuve* los resultados de las radiografías anoche.**   I *received* the results of the X-rays last night. (came into my possession)

EXERCISES   *EJERCICIOS*

A. Item Substitution.

1. **El técnico limpió la herida. (tú / Vds. / yo / nosotros / las enfermeras)**
2. **Tú abriste la incisión. (él / el doctor / yo / la enfermera y yo / Vds.)**
3. **El paciente no comió nada después de medianoche. (yo / tú / los pacientes / Vd.)**
4. **Perdí la planilla de admisión. (la enfermera / tú / Vds. / el terapéutico / nosotros)**
5. **El médico ordenó un análisis de sangre. (yo / los especialistas / tú / Ana)**
6. **El anestesiólogo escribió las instrucciones. (yo / la enfermera y Juan / tú / nosotros / ella)**
7. **Fui a llamar a la ambulancia. (ellas / Vd. / Vds. / tú / la enfermera)**

    8.   **Yo le di las pinzas. (tú / las enfermeras / Vd. / nosotros)**

    9.   **Ella fue enfermera. (tú / yo / María y yo / Vds. / Vd.)**

B. Answer according to the model.

> **¿Van Vds. a llenar la planilla de admisión?**
> **Ya la llenamos.**

    1.   **¿Van Vds. a tomar una cucharada de jarabe?**

    2.   **¿Van Vds. a ordenar un análisis de orina?**

    3.   **¿Van Vds. a examinar las radiografías?**

    4.   **¿Van Vds. a recibir la planilla de admisión?**

    5.   **¿Van Vds. a terminar el aparato ortopédico?**

    6.   **¿Van Vds. a masticar bien los alimentos?**

C. Answer according to the model.

> **¿No vas a tragar las cápsulas ahora?**
> **Ya las tragué.**

    1.   **¿No vas a regañar (scold) al paciente?**

    2.   **¿No vas a llenar un formulario en la sala de admisión?**

    3.   **¿No vas a beber mucho jugo de naranja?**

    4.   **¿No vas a levantar la cabecera de la cama?**

    5.   **¿No vas a enyesar la pierna?**

D. Change to the preterite.

    1.   **¿Quién manda la operación?**

    2.   **¿Limpias el cuarto?**

    3.   **¿Comprendes?**

    4.   **¿Abren su estómago?**

    5.   **¿Cuándo regresa el doctor?**

    6.   **El padre llega tarde a la sala de esperar.**

    7.   **Los asistentes salen para el quirófano.**

    8.   **¿A qué hora llegan Vds. al hospital?**

    9.   **Ya aprendo la técnica del cirujano.**

   10.   **El doctor Peña opera por la mañana.**

E. Answer according to the model.

> **Hoy voy a la clínica. > Ayer fui a la clínica.**

    1.   **Hoy tú vas para el emético.**

    2.   **Hoy vamos al quirófano.**

    3.   **Hoy el doctor va a la conferencia.**

    4.   **Hoy las enfermeras van a la sala de recuperación.**

    5.   **Hoy voy a la sala de radioterapia.**

F.   Answer according to the model.

> **Ahora no soy drogadicto** > **Ayer no fui drogadicto.**

1.   **Ahora los niños no son drogadictos.**
2.   **Ahora tú no eres drogadicta.**
3.   **Ahora no somos drogadictas.**
4.   **Ahora no es drogadicto.**
5.   **Ahora no son drogadictas.**

G.   Answer in Spanish with complete sentences.

1.   **¿Cuándo fue la última vez que tuvo Vd. un reconocimiento físico?**
2.   **¿Le recetó el médico algo para reducir la presión arterial?**
3.   **¿Cuándo empezaron a ocurrir las contracciones a intervalos de tres minutos?**
4.   **¿Quiere indicarme cómo comenzó el dolor?**
5.   **¿Cómo encontró la médica al paciente?**

H.   Say in Spanish.

1.   When did your pains begin?
2.   Did you smoke?
3.   He felt nothing.
4.   What did the nurse give you?
5.   When was your last period?
6.   Did you sleep well last night?
7.   When was your child born?
8.   How much did she weigh at birth?
9.   Did you see the doctor yesterday?
10.   He had (suffered) a heart attack.

Imperfect Tense   *El tiempo imperfecto*

The imperfect tense indicates the continuance of a past event or action, or it describes a situation in past time. No mention of start or finish of the event is made. It is expressed in English by *was* or *were* plus the present participle, or by *used to* plus the infinitive. Occasionally, this construction is translated by *would* plus the infinitive.

The imperfect tense is formed as follows for regular verbs:

For **-ar** verbs drop the **-ar** and add:

> **-aba, -abas, -aba, -ábamos, —, -aban**

For **-er** or **-ir** verbs, drop **-er** and **-ir** and add:

> **-ía, -ías, -ía, -íamos, —, -ían**

Subject Pronouns	*examinar*	*comer*	*sufrir*
yo	examin*aba*	com*ía*	sufr*ía*
tú	examin*abas*	com*ías*	sufr*ías*
él, ella, Vd.	examin*aba*	com*ía*	sufr*ía*
nosotros (-as)	examin*ábamos*	com*íamos*	sufr*íamos*
—	—	—	—
ellos, ellas, Vds.	examin*aban*	com*ían*	sufr*ían*

Thus, **yo examinaba** means I was examining, I used to examine, or I would examine.

IRREGULARITIES *IRREGULARIDADES*

Only three verbs are irregular in the imperfect tense. They are **ser**, **ir**, and **ver**.

> **ser** to be: **era, eras, era, éramos, —, eran**
>
> **ir** to go: **iba, ibas, iba, íbamos, —, iban**
>
> **ver** to see: **veía, veías, veía, veíamos, —, veían**

USES OF THE IMPERFECT *USOS DEL IMPERFECTO*

1. It describes people or things in the past.

   La paciente era joven. The patient *was* young.
   El quirófano estaba lleno de enfermeras. The OR *was* full of nurses.

2. It expresses what was occurring, used to occur, or occurred repeatedly in the past.

   Operábamos todos los días por la mañana. We *used to operate* everyday in the morning.
   Cuando era niña, sufría de asma. When she *was* a child, she would suffer from asthma.

3. It describes a mental state in the past with such verbs as **creer** (to believe), **pensar** (to think), **querer** (to want), and **saber** (to know).

   Querían ir de vacaciones. They *wanted* to go on vacation.
   Creía (Pensaba, Sabía) que Juan estaba muriendo. He *believed* (*thought, knew*) that John was dying.

4. It tells time in the past.

   Eran las dos. It *was* two o'clock.

5. Combined with the preterite, it describes a situation that was going on (*imperfect*) when an event or action occurred (*preterite*).

   Operaban cuando sufrió un ataque cardíaco. They *were operating* when he *had* a heart attack.

NOTE: *Was* or *were* with the present participle usually indicate the imperfect tense in Spanish, but *was* or *were* alone do not always imply the imperfect.

Ella era pálida.   She was pale complexioned. (description)

Ella estuvo pálida.   She was pale. (condition)

Vd. estaba contento.   You were happy. (situation)

Vd. estuvo contento.   You were glad. (became glad)

RECAP: Use the imperfect indicative tense to state whatever the person or persons: (1) was or were; (2) had [possession]; (3) wanted; (4) knew; (5) needed; (6) intended; or (7) owed.

EXERCISES *EJERCICIOS*

A.   Item Substitution.

1.   **Todos los días yo visitaba a los pacientes. (tú, el cirujano, Vds., Juan y yo)**
2.   **La enfermera traía el estetoscopio en el bolsillo. (él, Vd., Vds., yo, nosotros)**
3.   **Muy a menudo Vd. escribía recetas para penicilina. (el médico, tú, Vds., yo)**
4.   **Nunca iba en ambulancia. (tú, él, Vds., nosotros, ellas, yo)**
5.   **Eras médico. (Vd., yo, ellos, nosotros, él, Vds.)**
6.   **Veía a los pacientes cada día. (tú, Vd., él, Vds., yo, nosotros, ellas)**

B.   Answer according to the model.

> **El doctor Ruiz salió del hospital ayer.**
> **Yo no sabía que salía.**

1.   **El doctor Ruiz llegó al hosital ayer.**
2.   **El doctor Ruiz volvió al hospital ayer.**
3.   **El doctor Ruiz regresó al hospital ayer.**
4.   **El doctor Ruiz vino al hospital ayer.**
5.   **El doctor Ruiz caminó al hospital ayer.**

C.   Answer according to the model.

> **Acabo de operar.**
> **¿Eh? Recuerdo que cuando era médico residente operaba.**

1.   **Acabo de examinar a los pacientes.**
2.   **Acabo de ponerles una inyección.**
3.   **Acabo de tomarle la temperatura.**
4.   **Acabo de estudiar las radiografías.**
5.   **Acabo de hacerles una radiografía del pecho.**

D.   Change the verb from the present to the imperfect.

1.   **Todos los días se baña.**
2.   **La ves cada día.**

3. Conoce aquella clínica.
4. Nunca examinamos al paciente.
5. Somos trabajadores sociales.
6. Siempre busco la planilla de admisión.
7. Muchas veces le tomas la temperatura.
8. Cada mes me trae una muestra de orina.
9. Vamos al hospital todos los días.
10. Muchas veces le traigo las pastillas.

E. Rewrite the following in the past tense, putting the first verb in the imperfect and the second in the preterite.

1. Mientras preparamos, él se lava las manos.
2. Mientras estudio las radiografías, el paciente llega.
3. Mientras duerme la paciente, le sacan la vejiga biliar.
4. Mientras espero, ella se viste.

F. Rewrite the following using the imperfect to describe both simultaneously occurring actions.

1. Mientras estudio la radiografía, la enfermera trabaja.
2. Yo me visto mientras (que) él se afeita.
3. Nosotros estudiamos mientras (que) ellos descansan.
4. La nene llora mientras (que) la pediatra la examina.

G. Rewrite the following changing the first verb to the preterite and the second verb to the imperfect.

1. Llama a su siquíatra porque tiene murria y está deprimida.
2. Cuando la ambulancia llega, llueve.
3. El médico dice que quiere operar.
4. Veo que hay muchos pacientes en la sala de espera.
5. Buscan un médico porque él se siente enfermo.

H. Fill in the correct form of the verb. Use either the preterite or imperfect.

1. Mientras yo _____ (leer), la enfermera _____ (llamar).
2. Al poco rato ella _____ (mirar) el reloj; _____ (ser) las doce y _____ (tener) que salir en seguida.
3. El paciente _____ (querer) saber si el doctor _____ (poder) hacer visita facultativa.
4. Generalmente la pediatra _____ (llegar) al consultorio a las nueve.
5. Esta mañana ella _____ (llegar) a las diez porque _____ (hacer) una visita facultativa.
6. Los pacientes la _____ (esperar) cuando _____ (entrar).
7. Yo _____ (tener) sueño.
8. Cuando la bebé _____ (despertarse), nosotros _____ (comer).

I. Answer the following questions in Spanish with complete sentences.

1. ¿A qué facultad de medicina asistía Vd. cuando era estudiante?
2. ¿Se lastimaba cuando era joven?
3. Cuando era niño (-a), ¿llevaba anteojos o veía bien?
4. Cuando era joven, ¿qué carrera quería estudiar?
5. ¿Cuánto tiempo hacía que trabajaban en la clínica?

J. Say in Spanish.

1. We were talking when the phone rang.
2. We were talking while the phone was ringing.
3. The child always cried when(ever) she saw him.
4. The child cried when she saw him.
5. The child was crying when she saw him.
6. Didn't you see that the patient left?
7. Didn't you see that the patient was leaving?
8. Didn't you (ever) see that the patient was leaving?
9. He wrote (from time to time) that he was getting shots.
10. He wrote (once) that he was getting shots.
11. He wrote that he got shots (for a period of time).
12. The old man was living in Florida when he died.

Reflexive Verbs *Los verbos reflexivos*

In Spanish some verbs are called reflexive. These verbs can be recognized by their ending (-se attached to the infinitive). When conjugated in any tense they must be preceded by the appropriate reflexive pronouns.[14] Reflexive pronouns are:

me	myself	**nos**	ourselves
te	yourself	—	—
se	himself, herself, yourself	**se**	themselves, yourselves

Remember that a verb is reflexive when the subject acts upon itself, or does something to itself. Many Spanish reflexive verbs are not reflexive in English, and therefore cannot be literally translated into English:

yo *me* llamo   my name is (I call myself)

tú *te* llamas   your name is (you call yourself)

él, ella Vd., *se* llama   his, her, your name is (he, she, you call yourself)

nosotros (-as) *nos* llamamos   our name is (we call ourselves)

— —

ellos, ellas, Vds. *se* llaman   their, your name is (They call themselves)

Reflexive verbs fall into three categories:

1. Those that are reflexive logically, according to whether the subject acts upon itself (reflexive), or upon someone or something else (nonreflexive). The personal hygiene verbs fall into this category. Any transitive verb may be made reflexive if its meaning permits.

2. Those that when reflexive assume a new meaning. Many of these verbs are not used reflexively in English, and so must be memorized.

3. Those verbs that are always reflexive in Spanish, but not in English. These must be memorized.

Selected reflexive verbs include:

abstenerse (de) to abstain (from)
acercarse to get close
acordarse (de) (ue) to remember
acostarse (ue) to go to bed, to lie down
acostumbrarse (a) to get used to
afeitar(se)/rasurar(se) to shave
asustarse to get frightened
atragantarse to choke
bajarse to get down (off)
bañar(se) to bathe, to take a bath
caerse to fall down
calmar(se) to calm down
callarse to be quiet
cambiar(se) to change (oneself)
cansarse to get tired
casarse (con) to marry, to get married (to)
cepillarse los dientes to brush one's teeth
cortarse to cut (oneself)
curarse to recover, to recuperate, to get well
desayunarse to eat breakfast
desmayarse to faint
desnudarse/desvestirse (i) to undress, to get undressed
despedirse (de) (i) to say goodbye (to), to take leave (of)
despertarse (ie) to awaken, to get up
divertirse (ie) to have a good time, to amuse oneself
dormirse (ue) to fall asleep, to doze

ducharse   to shower, to take a shower
echarse gases   to expel gas
enfadarse/enojarse   to get angry
enjuagar(se)   to rinse (out)
enjugarse/secarse   to dry off
envenenar(se)   to poison (oneself)
equivocarse   to be mistaken
esconderse   to hide
especializarse (en)   to specialize (in)
familiarizarse (con)   to familiarize oneself (with)
golpearse   to hit oneself
hacerse + noun of profession—to become (that profession)
inyectar(se)   to inject (oneself)
irse   to go away
lastimarse/hacerse daño   to hurt onself
lavar(se)   to wash (oneself)
levantarse/pararse   to stand up, to get up
limpiar(se)   to clean (oneself)
llamarse   to be called, to be named
marcharse   to go away
mejorarse   to improve, to get better
moverse (ue)   to move (to change positions)
pararse   to stop; to stand up
peinarse   to comb one's hair
ponerse + noun   to put on (clothing)
           + adj. of emotion/mental state   to become, to turn + adj.
  ponerse azul   to turn blue
  ponerse tenso (-a)   to tense up
preocuparse   to worry
quedarse   to remain, to stay
quejarse (de)   to complain (about)
quemarse   to burn oneself
quitarse la ropa   to take off one's clothing
rascarse   to scratch (oneself)
relajarse   to relax
romperse/fracturarse   to break
sentarse (ie)   to sit down
sentirse (ie)   to feel

subirse to climb up

  subirse la manga to roll up one's sleeve

suicidarse to commit suicide

torcerse (ue) to twist

vestirse (i) to get dressed

volverse (ue)/darse vuelta to turn (over)

USES OF REFLEXIVES *USOS DE LOS REFLEXIVOS*

1. Transitive verbs may be used with direct reflexive objects.

  a. As in English:

    El se miró. He looked at himself.

    Nos miramos. We looked at each other.

  b. The action of the verb affects the subject. This form frequently translates into English as "get" or "become."

    Me canso. I get tired.

    Se me olvidó hacerlo. I forgot to do it.

2. Transitive verbs may be used with indirect reflexive objects.

  a. True indirect object:

    Se permite hacerlo. He permits himself to do it.

  b. Interest or intensification:

    Me rompí la pierna. I broke my leg.

    Me sacó (ese diente). He extracted it (that tooth).

  c. Possession:

    Enjugándose los ojos, . . . Drying his eyes, . . .

  d. Separation or the opposite:

    Ella se quita la ropa. She takes off her clothing.

    Ella se pone la bata. She puts on the gown.

3. Transitive verbs may be used with reflexive objects to show interest, intensification of action, and so forth.

  Me río. I laugh.

  Me duermo. I fall asleep. (I doze off.)

  Me muero. I am dying.

  Me caigo de espaldas. I fall down backwards.

4. Normally reflexive verbs.

Me lastimé. I hurt myself. (I got hurt. I was hurt.)

Me quejo de jaquecas. I complain about headaches.

5. Reflexives may be used as the subject or as a substitute for the passive voice (see pages 130–131).

No se ve nada. One sees nothing. (Nothing is seen.)

Se le invita. He is invited. (They invite him.)

Se habla español. Spanish is spoken. (They speak Spanish.)

EXERCISES *EJERCICIOS*

A. Supply the reflexive pronoun required in each sentence.

  1. **El paciente _____ acuesta sobre la mesa de reconocimientos.**

  2. **¿A qué hora _____ levantas, Juanito, generalmente?**

  3. **Yo también _____ despierto temprano todos los días.**

  4. **¿Cómo _____ llama la pediatra?**

  5. **Yo _____ canso si tengo que caminar mucho o subir escaleras.**

  6. **Nosotros _____ quedamos en casa cuando estamos enfermos.**

  7. **La enfermera _____ peina cuidadosamente.**

  8. **A veces ella _____ mira el espejo (mirror).**

  9. **La dietista _____ enoja mucho si como demasiado azúcar.**

  10. **Vd. _____ enferma si toma una dosis excesiva.**

B. Item Substitution.

  1. **La paciente se queja de dolores. (tú, Vds., nosotros, la recepcionista, yo)**

  2. **Juan se cepilla los dientes ahora. (el médico, tú, el técnico y yo, las pacientes)**

  3. **El técnico se pone el escudo (shield). (la paciente, las enfermeras, yo, tú)**

  4. **Vd. se sube la manga. (el paciente, los pacientes, yo, nosotros, tú)**

C. In the blanks supply the correct form, present tense, of the verbs given.

  1. **¿Cómo (llamarse) _____ la enfermera del pelo rubio?**

  2. **Si yo no (equivocarse) _____, Vd. está embarazada.**

  3. **Los pacientes siempre (desayunarse) _____ antes de que llegue el médico.**

  4. **Tú (ponerse) _____ nervioso antes del electrocardiograma.**

  5. **El señor García (quedarse) _____ en el hospital tres semanas.**

  6. **Yo (enfermarse) _____ raras veces.**

  7. **El paciente (afeitarse) _____ con una máquina eléctrica de afeitar.**

  8. **Ella no está en su cama. (Ducharse) _____.**

  9. **El médico (enojarse) _____ con los pacientes de vez en cuando.**

  10. **El niño (echarse) _____ gases.**

D. Change to the plural.

1. **Tú te preocupas mucho por la operación.**
2. **Me baño con un jabón** (soap) **especial.**
3. **¿A qué hora se despierta la paciente?** 〻
4. **Ese paciente se queja mucho.**
5. **El paciente se olvida de todo.**

E. Supply the infinitive form, together with the correct reflexive pronoun.

1. **La paciente no puede** (take a bath) _____ **ya.**
2. **Tú debes** (comb your hair) _____ **con más cuidado.**
3. **Ella tiene que** (take off) _____ **la blusa y el sostén.**
4. **A nadie le gusta** (get sick) _____ .
5. **Vamos a** (stay) _____ **en el hospital mañana.**

F. Answer in Spanish using complete sentences.

1. **¿A qué hora se acuesta Vd. por la noche?**
2. **¿Siente Vd. dolor cuando se mueve?**
3. **¿Cómo se siente Vd. hoy?**
4. **¿De qué se queja la enferma?**
5. **¿Por qué se siente la paciente tan nerviosa?**

G. Say in Spanish.

1. What is the new patient's name?
2. The patient is getting dressed now.
3. The nurse wakes the patient (up) at 7 A.M.
4. The old man is complaining a lot.
5. You have to wake up now because you have to take a bath.

Future Tense   *El tiempo futuro*

The future tense generally expresses a future action and parallels English. In Spanish the future tense is formed by adding to the infinitive the following endings:

-é, -ás, -á, -emos, —, -án[15]

In English the future tense is rendered by *shall* in the first person, and by *will* in the second and third persons.

Subject Pronouns	*examinar*	*comer*	*sufrir*
yo	examinar**é**	comer**é**	sufrir**é**
tú	examinar**ás**	comer**ás**	sufrir**ás**
él, ella, Vd.	examinar**á**	comer**á**	sufrir**á**
nosotros (-as)	examinar**emos**	comer**emos**	sufrir**emos**
—	—	—	—
ellos, ellas, Vds.	examinar**án**	comer**án**	sufrir**án**

Thus, **yo examinaré** means I shall examine or I will examine.

IRREGULAR FORMS *IRREGULARIDADES*

Although all verbs in Spanish use the same endings, which are added to the infinitive, not all verbs use the entire infinitive. The following use a modified form of the infinitive but are regular in the use of the future endings.

decir	**decir**	**dir-**	**diré,** etc.	I shall say
hacer	**hacer**	**har-**	**haré,** etc.	I shall do, make
querer	**querer**	**querr-**	**querré,** etc.	I shall want
saber	**saber**	**sabr-**	**sabré,** etc.	I shall know
poder	**poder**	**podr-**	**podré,** etc.	I shall be able
haber	**haber**	**habr-**	**habré,** etc.	I shall have (auxiliary verb)
tener	**tener**	**tendr-**	**tendré,** etc.	I shall have (possession)
poner	**poner**	**pondr-**	**pondré,** etc.	I shall put
venir	**venir**	**vendr-**	**vendré,** etc.	I shall come
salir	**salir**	**saldr-**	**saldré,** etc.	I shall leave
valer	**valer**	**valdr-**	**valdré,** etc.	I shall be worth

SPECIAL USE OF THE FUTURE *USO ESPECIAL DEL FUTURO*

The future tense is used in Spanish to express conjecture or probability in the present tense. This is often rendered in English by "I wonder," "do you suppose. . .," "probably," "must," and "can." None of these English words is translated into Spanish, however.

¿Dónde estará el médico? I wonder where the doctor is. (Where do you suppose the doctor is? Where can the doctor be?)

¿Qué hora será? I wonder what time it is. (What time can it be? What time must it be?)

Serán las ocho y media. It is probably 8:30. (It must be 8:30. I bet it is 8:30.)

EXERCISES *EJERCICIOS*

A. Change to the future tense.

1. **El paciente sale del hospital hoy.**
2. **Tengo que ir a la clínica hoy.**
3. **La paciente puede caminar hoy.**
4. **Las doctoras hacen los exámenes.**
5. **Los médicos tienen los resultados.**
6. **El técnico hace el análisis pronto.**
7. **La paciente quiere salir del hospital.**
8. **Hacemos los análisis de orina.**

9. **El enfermero me pone la inyección.**

10. **Los técnicos hacen las radiografías.**

B. Say in Spanish.

1. The patient must be in her room.

2. Do you suppose there is an accident?

3. He must have fallen.

4. He is probably examining her leg.

The Infinitive *El infinitivo*

In Spanish the infinitive is often used as a nominal. It may also be followed by either a subject or object pronoun:

operar   operate, operating

¿Operar él?   He (Him) operate?

Examinarlo.   To examine it.

The infinitive is the form of the verb that is used after a preposition and is commonly translated as an English gerund.

Al *entrar* en el quirófano. . .   Upon entering the operating room. . . (When I [he, you, etc.] entered the OR. . .)

Tómelas antes de *comer*.   Take them before eating (before you eat).

With the verbs **dejar, hacer, mandar, ordenar, permitir,** and **prohibir,** the infinitive may be used instead of the subjunctive—even with a change of subject (see pages 151–152).

El médico me deja *tomar*las 2 veces al día.   }   The doctor lets me take
El médico me deja que las tome 2 veces al día. }   them twice a day.

When followed by a verb other than **ser,** the infinitive is usually preceded by the definite article **el.**

***El operar* se aprende difícilmente.**   Operating is learned with difficulty.

On signs and with instructions the infinitive is often used as a command.

No *fumar* aquí.   No smoking here. (Do not smoke here.)

After verbs of perception like **ver** (to see) or **oír** (to hear), the infinitive is used. The infinitive precedes the noun, unlike English.

El médico vio *morir* a muchos heridos.   The doctor saw many wounded die.

Oí *llorar* al nene.   I heard the baby cry.

EXERCISES *EJERCICIOS*

A. Say in Spanish.

1. I saw the boy fall.
2. I heard the boys shout.
3. I saw the doctor enter.
4. I heard the ambulance arrive.
5. I listened to the woman scream.
6. I watched the doctors operate.

B. Answer according to the model.

> **¿Quién mandó traer los resultados?**
> **Yo los mandé traer.**

1. **¿Quién oyó discutir los resultados?**
2. **¿Quién dejó abrir el maletín?**
3. **¿Quién hizo escribir las recetas?**
4. **¿Quién mandó preparar la dieta?**

C. Change the dependent clause to **al** + infinitive.

1. **Cuando llegaron al hospital, se sentían malos.**
2. **Cuando me despierto, me visto inmediatamente.**
3. **Cuando te despides de ellos, tienes que besarlos.**
4. **Cuando entran Vds. en el hospital, hay que pedir el número de su cuarto.**
5. **Cuando nos sentamos a la mesa, tenemos mucha hambre.**

The Present Participle *El gerundio*

The Spanish present participle is formed by adding **-ando** to the stem of **-ar** verbs and **-iendo** to the stem of **-er** and **-ir** verbs. Classes II and III radical changing verbs (i.e., those **-ir** verbs whose stem vowel changes from **e** to **ie**, **o** to **ue**, or **e** to **i** in the present indicative tense) change from **e** to **i** and **o** to **u** in the present participle.

> **morir (ue) mu*r*iendo** dying
> **sentir (ie) s*i*ntiendo** regretting
> **pedir (i) p*i*diendo** asking

The present participle is invariable in form. Pronouns used as objects follow a present participle and are attached to it, forming a single word. Thus, the participle requires an accent mark (**recetándolas** prescribing them). In the progressive tenses, the object pronoun may either precede the verb or be attached to the present participle.

> **El médico estaba recetándolas.** }
> **El médico las estaba recetando.** } The doctor was prescribing them.

USES OF THE PRESENT PARTICIPLE
USOS DEL GERUNDIO

1. The leading use is as a verbal adjective in explanatory or parenthetical clauses. The present participle modifies a noun or a pronoun but functions largely as a verb.

    Cerrando **los ojos, el paciente perdió su conocimiento.**   *Closing* his eyes, the patient lost consciousness.

    La enfermera encontró a la familia *esperando* **al médico en la sala de espera.**   The nurse found the family *waiting* for the doctor in the waiting room.

2. The present participle states the condition under which an act takes place. It often refers to the subject of the sentence, but may equally apply to the object.

    Pasamos muchas horas en el hospital *visitando* **a Alvarez.**   We spent many hours in the hospital *visiting* Alvarez. (referring to the subject)

    Veo a los infantes *llorando* **constantemente.**   I see the newborns *crying* constantly. (referring to the object)

3. Although the Spanish present participle is called **el gerundio**, it does not serve the same function as the English gerund. The Spanish **gerundio** never is used as a noun or as a pure adjective.

    a. The noun function of the English gerund is normally translated into Spanish by an infinitive. This Spanish verbal noun often takes the definite article, but not after a preposition.

    El operar **no es fácil.**   *Operating* is not easy.

    Está adicto a *beber*.   He is addicted to *drinking*.

    b. Since the Spanish present participle cannot be used as an adjective, its meaning is expressed with special participial adjectives that derive from Latin. These forms end in **-ante**, **-iente**, or **-ente**, or are expressed with a **que** clause in Spanish.

    arder   to burn > **ardiente**   burning

    calentar   to heat > **caliente**   heating (hot)

    causar   to cause > **causante**   causative

    crecer   to grow > **creciente**   growing

    interesar   to interest > **interesante**   interesting

    perseverar   to persevere > **perseverante**   persevering

    seguir   to follow > **siguiente**   following

    Fue una operación *emocionante*.   It was an *exciting* operation.

    Ese hombre *que se acerca* **es su especialista.**   That man *approaching* is your specialist.

4. The most common use of the present participle is to combine with the verb **estar** (*never* **ser**) to form the *progressive tenses*. The progressive is a word-for-word translation of the English verb. It stresses the fact that an event is (was or will be) in progress, or is continuing at a given moment in time.

NOTE: The present participle remains the same for *all* persons in *all* tenses. Only the conjugation of **estar** changes to agree with the subject.

The progressive tenses are very emphatic and graphic. They are not used with great regularity. The simple tenses are preferred since they contain the idea of some form of the verb *be* and the present participle. Unlike in English, the progressive tense is *not* used:

1. to refer to situations in the future time.

Me harán unos análisis la semana que viene. ⎱ I am taking some tests
Van a hacerme unos análisis la semana que viene. ⎰ next week.

2. with verbs that do not describe true actions (i.e., **estar, tener, sentirse, querer,** etc.).

¿Cómo te sientes?   How are you feeling?

The verbs **ir**[16], **andar, seguir, continuar,** and **venir** are also used with the present participle for an even stronger continued action. Each of these imparts a different meaning:

1. **ir** implies that the progression is gradual or stresses the fact that the action is beginning.

El enfermo va empeorando.   The sick man is gradually growing worse.
Va perdiendo sangre a pesar de todo.   She keeps on losing blood in spite of everything.

2. **andar** suggests perfunctory action, or implies that something is carried out in a busy way.

El ayudante anda buscando muestras de orina.   The orderly goes around (about) looking for urine specimens.

3. **Seguir** and **continuar** mean to keep on or to continue.

Siga tomando su medicina.   Keep on taking your medicine.

4. **Venir** indicates that an action begun in the past continues in the present.

Hace mucho tiempo que su situación viene siendo muy crítica.   His situation has been very critical for a long time.

EXERCISES *EJERCICIOS*

A. Rewrite these phrases changing the infinitive to the present participle.

1. **sufrir mucho**
2. **sentirse mal**
3. **masticar bien**
4. **vomitar un poco**
5. **hacer un análisis**
6. **repetir las instrucciones**
7. **levantarse a las seis**
8. **decir la verdad**
9. **dormir tarde**
10. **esperar al ayudante**

B. Rewrite these sentences, changing the infinitive to the present participle.

1. **Pablo, (abrir) los ojos, se puso muy nervioso.**
2. **El viejo hablaba despacio, (pronunciar) las palabras claramente.**
3. **Pasamos el tiempo (estudiar).**
4. **(Ver) a mis parientes en la distancia, empecé a andar hacia ellos.**
5. **Carmen, (pensar) en el enfermo, compró unas flores.**

C. Express in Spanish using **que** clauses.

1. That woman talking is my nurse.
2. The child running is called José.
3. I found the patient sleeping.
4. We helped those people feeling sick.
5. That nurse walking by (**pasar**) is going to physical therapy.

D. Change the verbs below to the present progressive.

1. **La enferma no come.**
2. **Lo dice el cirujano.**
3. **Tú lo decides.**
4. **¿Vas a subir o bajar?**
5. **El trae los resultados.**
6. **Yo consulto con muchos médicos.**
7. **Ellos leen el nuevo libro de histología.**
8. **Nosotros tomamos su temperatura constantemente.**
9. **Vds. empiezan a comprender la situación.**
10. **El señor García trata de levantarse de la cama.**

E. Complete these sentences using a form of **seguir**, **ir**, **venir**, or **andar**.

1. **Los técnicos** (continued working).
2. (I was beginning to accustom myself) a **la cirugía**.

3. **Ese pobre enfermo** (goes around asking for) **trabajo**.
4. (We gradually arrived) **a una decisión**.
5. **La vieja** (keeps on complaining).

F. Say in Spanish, using the simple tense, the progressive tense, or both, if it seems appropriate.

1. She is coming to the hospital.
2. They will continue working.
3. She continues suffering.
4. What medicine are you taking?
5. Keep on taking the same medicine.
6. We are going to the clinic today.

The Past Participle *El participio pasivo*

The past participle of regular verbs is formed by adding **-ado** to the stems of **-ar** verbs, and **-ido** to the stems of **-er** and **-ir** verbs.

examinar > **examin***ado*   examined
toser > **tos***ido*   coughed
revivir > **reviv***ido*   revived

A group of common Spanish verbs (and their compounds) have irregular past participles.

abrir > **abierto**   open(ed)
cubrir > **cubierto**   covered
decir > **dicho**   said, told
escribir > **escrito**   written
hacer > **hecho**   done, made
morir > **muerto**   dead
poner > **puesto**   put
romper > **roto**   broken
ver > **visto**   seen
volver > **vuelto**   returned

The following past participles require a written accent over the **í**.

caer > **caído**   fallen
creer > **creído**   believed
leer > **leído**   read
oír > **oído**   written
traer > **traído**   brought

EXERCISE *EJERCICIO*

Give the past participle of the following.

ver	**consultar**	**morir**	**ser**
operar	**tener**	**cortar**	**quebrar**
hacer	**romper**	**vendar**	**limpiar**
sentir	**decir**	**poner**	**salir**
abrir	**terminar**	**entrar**	**aprender**

USES OF THE PAST PARTICIPLE *USOS DEL PARTICIPIO PASIVO*

First Use: The basic function of the past participle is in the formation of the perfect tenses with the auxiliary verb **haber**. No word can come between the auxiliary verb and the past participle. When the past participle is part of a perfect tense, it is invariable.

The present perfect indicative tense (also called the "perfect" or **el perfecto**) is formed by the present of **haber** plus the past participle. The English equivalent is *have (has)* plus the past participle of the main verb.

Other Spanish perfect tenses and their formation are as follows:

pluperfect	**pluscuamperfecto**	imperfect of **haber**	+past
preterite perfect[17]	**pretérito perfecto**	preterite of **haber**	participle
future perfect	**futuro perfecto**	future of **haber**	of the
conditional perfect	**potencial perfecto**	conditional of **haber**	main verb

FORMATION OF THE PRESENT PERFECT TENSE
FORMACION DEL TIEMPO PERFECTO

examinar	**toser**	**revivir**
he examin*ado*	*he* tos*ido*	*he* reviv*ido*
has examin*ado*	*has* tos*ido*	*has* reviv*ido*
ha examin*ado*	*ha* tos*ido*	*ha* reviv*ido*
hemos examin*ado*	*hemos* tos*ido*	*hemos* reviv*ido*
—	—	—
han examin*ado*	*han* tos*ido*	*han* reviv*ido*

USES OF THE PRESENT PERFECT *USOS DEL PERFECTO*

The Spanish present perfect tense is basically the same as in English.

El cirujano ha operado ya.   The surgeon has already operated.

The present perfect and the preterite are both used to express certain past actions. The present perfect translates recent past actions connected to the present by a given unit of time, such as **esta mañana** (this morning), **esta semana** (this week), **este mes** (this month). The preterite is used when past action occurs before that given unit of time—**ayer** (yesterday), **la semana pasada** (last week), **el mes pasado** (last month).

> **Esta mañana he puesto dos inyecciones.** This morning I gave two shots.
>
> **Ayer puse dos inyecciones.** Yesterday I gave two shots.

EXERCISES *EJERCICIOS*

A. Item substitution.

1. **El médico ha escrito la receta. (yo, nosotros, Vds., él, tú)**
2. **El cirujano ha operado esta mañana. (tú, los médicos, yo, ellos, ellos y yo)**
3. **Ella se ha sentido mal este mes. (los niños, yo, tú, nosotros, Vds.)**
4. **Yo he visto al doctor. (tú, la enfermera, él, nosotros, ellos)**
5. **Tú has tenido todas las enfermedades. (nosotros, él, Vd., Vds., yo)**

B. Change the following to the present perfect tense.

1. **El estudia para médico.**
2. **Siempre me siento bien.**
3. **El paciente murió.**
4. **Van a la sala de primeros auxilios.**
5. **La nene tiene roséola.**

C. Answer in Spanish, using complete sentences.

1. **¿Te han puesto una inyección?**
2. **¿Ha tenido Vd. sarampión?**
3. **¿Ha sido operado (-a) alguna vez?**
4. **¿Ha ido la paciente al hospital?**
5. **¿Por qué le han vendado el brazo?**
6. **¿Se ha roto Vd. la pierna alguna vez?**
7. **¿Ha habido algún caso de diabetes aquí?**
8. **¿Le han hecho radiografías del pecho?**
9. **¿Han tenido Vds. un accidente esta mañana?**
10. **¿Hemos tenido problemas médicos últimamente?**

FORMATION OF THE PLUPERFECT
FORMACION DEL PLUSCUAMPERFECTO

examinar	toser	revivir
había examin*ado*	*había* tos*ido*	*había* reviv*ido*
habías examin*ado*	*habías* tos*ido*	*habías* reviv*ido*
había examin*ado*	*había* tos*ido*	*había* reviv*ido*
habíamos examin*ado*	*habíamos* tos*ido*	*habíamos* reviv*ido*
—	—	—
habían examin*ado*	*habían* tos*ido*	*habían* reviv*ido*

USE OF THE PLUPERFECT *USO DEL PLUSCUAMPERFECTO*

The Spanish pluperfect corresponds to the English pluperfect tense.

Ya yo había estudiado las radiografías. I had already studied the x-rays.

EXERCISES *EJERCICIOS*

A. Change the following to the pluperfect.

1. **he llamado**
2. **ha muerto**
3. **han hecho**
4. **he visto**
5. **han puesto**
6. **hemos comido**
7. **te has despertado**
8. **te has acostado**
9. **ha entubado**
10. **hemos abierto su estómago.**

B. Rewrite the following, changing the italicized verb to the pluperfect tense.

1. **Tú *ves* la radiografía.**
2. **El *dice* que es alérgico.**
3. **Me *operaron* de amigdalitis.**
4. **Nosotros no *hacemos* nada.**
5. **Siempre ella *se sentía* bien.**
6. **La enfermera me *pone* una inyección.**

C. Say in Spanish.

1. The orderly had cleaned my wound.
2. The nurse had not disinfected it.
3. The ambulance had not yet arrived.
4. They had taken the R$_x$ to the pharmacy.
5. You had not had the chickenpox when you were young.

Second Use of Past Participle: In Spanish, as in English, the past participle (**examinado, tosido, sufrido**) may be used as an adjective. As such it agrees in number and gender with the noun it modifies.

El paciente es un hombre de *avanzada* edad. The patient is a man of *advanced* age.

Empezó la carta: "*Distinguidos* cirujanos." He began the letter: "*Distinguished* Surgeons."

Occasionally the Spanish past participle is translated with an English present participle. The most common examples are:

aburrido   boring

acostado   lying (down)

atrevido   daring

bien parecido   good looking

descreído   unbelieving

divertido   amusing

dormido   sleeping

sentado   sitting

Está *acostada* **en la cama.**   She is *lying down* on the bed.

Hace 5 horas que la señora *sentada* **en el banco está en la clínica.**   The lady *sitting* (*seated*) on the bench has been in the clinic for 5 hours.

EXERCISES *EJERCICIOS*

A.   Give the past participle of the verbs in parentheses.

1.   **La cadera está (romper).**
2.   **El brazo está (romper).**
3.   **Las piernas están (romper).**
4.   **Los huesos están (romper).**
5.   **La herida está (vendar).**
6.   **La etiqueta indica "(hacer) en Puerto Rico."**
7.   **Perdió mucha sangre por la herida (abrir).**
8.   **Nosotros estamos muy (ocupar) hoy.**
9.   **Las enfermeras están muy (cansar).**
10.   **El médico está muy (preocupar) por ella.**

B.   Say in Spanish.

1.   The x-ray lab is closed.
2.   The infected wound began to suppurate.
3.   Do you have swollen ankles in the morning?
4.   Is any part of your body swollen?
5.   Are you frequently tired?

Third Use of Past Participle: Some Spanish past participles may be used as nouns. Some have been made nouns so often that they are permanently considered nouns. Most of these past participles correspond to parts of speech other than English past participles.

el acabado   the finish
los casados   the married couple
el desconocido   the stranger
el dicho   the saying
el empleado   the employee
la entrada   the entrance
el graduado   the graduate
el hecho   the deed/fact
el herido   the wounded person
la herida   the wound
los invitados   the guests
el muerto/la muerta   the dead person
la parada   the stop
el pedido   the order/request
el puesto   the job, stand, position
la respuesta   the answer
el resultado   the result
la salida   the exit
el significado   the meaning
el vestido   the dress
Los _heridos_ están en la enfermería.   The _wounded_ (men) are in the infirmary.

Other past participles may be nominalized by omitting the noun.[18]

Miremos al nene recién nacido.   Let us look at the newborn baby.
Miremos al recién nacido.   Let us look at the newborn.

EXERCISE   _EJERCICIO_

Say in Spanish.

1. How many employees work here?
2. The wound was infected.
3. The entrance to the OR is on the left.
4. Give me the results of the EEG.
5. Here is the order for a CBC.

Fourth Use of Past Participle: The past participle is used with the verb **ser** to form the true passive voice. See the explanation of the passive voice.

Passive Voice   *La voz pasiva*

Two voices, active and passive, exist in both Spanish and English. While active and passive sentences contain the same information, they maintain a different focus of emphasis. In the active voice the subject does the action of the verb:

El cirujano le saca las amígdalas del chico.   The surgeon removes the boy's tonsils.

The subject of a passive verb receives the action. It remains passive, being acted upon by a specific or implied agent.

Las amígdalas del chico son sacadas por el cirujano.   The boy's tonsils are removed by the surgeon. (specified agent)

Las amígdalas del chico son sacadas.   The boy's tonsils are removed. (implied agent)

THE TRUE PASSIVE   *LA VERDADERA VOZ PASIVA*

The true passive voice in Spanish corresponds to English usage. In English the passive voice is formed with the verb "to be" and the past participle of a transitive verb. Some form of the verb **ser** plus the past participle of the main verb make up the Spanish true passive. The Spanish past participle agrees in number and gender with the subject. The agent (by whom the action is done) is introduced by the preposition **por**. The true passive, unlike most Spanish sentences, translates word for word into English in a direct declarative sentence.

subject	+ **ser**	+ past participle	+ **por**	+ agent
La enfermedad	**fue**	**causada**	**por**	**una reacción alérgica.**
(The illness	was	caused	by	an allergic reaction.)
Juan	**fue**	**atropellado**	**por**	**un auto.**
(John	was	run over	by	a car.)

Occasionally the preposition **de** replaces **por** to indicate the agent, especially when the action is mental or emotional, and with certain verbs such as **acompañar** (to accompany), **preceder** (to precede), **seguir** (to follow), **rodear** (to surround).

Ella es amada *de* todos.   She is loved *by* everyone.

La cirugía es seguida *de* mucho dolor.   The surgery is followed *by* much pain.

The tenses of the passive correspond to the tenses of the verb **ser** being used.

INDICATIVE   *EL INDICATIVO*

Son examinados.   They are examined. (present)

Eran examinados.   They were examined. (imperfect)

Fueron examinados. They were examined. (preterite)
Serán examinados. They will be examined. (future)
Han sido examinados. They have been examined. (present perfect)
Habían sido examinados. They had been examined. (pluperfect)
Hubieron sido examinados. They had been examined. (preterite perfect)
Habrán sido examinados. They will have been examined. (future perfect)

SUBJUNCTIVE *EL SUBJUNTIVO*

(que) sean examinados   (that) they be examined (present)
(que) fueran/fuesen examinados   (that) they were examined (imperfect)
(que) hayan sido examinados   (that) they have been examined (present perfect)
(que) hubieran/hubiesen sido examinados   (that) they had been examined
  (pluperfect)

EXERCISES *EJERCICIOS*

A. Item substitution.

1. **Los enfermos fueron traídos al hospital por la noche. (yo, él, las mujeres, tú)**
2. **El había sido operado. (Vds., tú, la enferma, nosotros, Vd.)**
3. **La paciente ha sido anestesiada por él. (yo, ellas, él, Vd., nosotros)**
4. **Yo seré llevada al quirófano por el asistente. (la paciente, él, nosotros, Vds.)**

B. Pattern drill. Answer according to the model.

   ¿Es verdad que la enfermera puso la inyección?
   Sí, la inyección fue puesta por la enfermera.

1. **¿Es verdad que el interno admitió al paciente?**
2. **¿Es verdad que el técnico tomó la radiografía?**
3. **¿Es verdad que ella tomó veinte pastillas?**
4. **¿Es verdad que nosotros tragamos dos cucharas de jarabe?**
5. **¿Es verdad que el paciente da su autorización?**

¿Ya han llamado al cirujano?
No, el cirujano será llamado mañana.

1. **¿Ya han confirmado la cirujía?**
2. **¿Ya han notificado a la familia?**
3. **¿Ya han traído a los niños?**
4. **¿Ya han firmado las autorizaciones?**
5. **¿Ya han enviado los resultados de la radiografía?**

C. Change from the active to the passive voice.

1. **El doctor Gómez empleó a esa enfermera.**
2. **La técnica no toma los signos vitales.**

    3. **El anestesiólogo escribirá un artículo para JAMA.**

    4. **El dentista prepara el diente para un empaste.**

    5. **El director del hospital entrevista a los internos.**

D. Say in Spanish.

    1. The hospital was built in 1981.

    2. The ECG was done by the technician.

    3. Aspirins are sold in this pharmacy.

    4. The orders are written by the attending.

    5. The patient will be discharged from the hospital soon.

ALTERNATES FOR THE TRUE PASSIVE
ALTERNATIVOS PARA LA VOZ PASIVA

Spanish uses the passive voice rather sparingly and most often in the preterite. The true passive is used (1) when the "agent" is mentioned, or (2) when the subject is a person; otherwise a pseudo- or impersonal passive is used which, in reality, is an active sentence.

1. Use of the **se** construction   **Uso de** *se*

    a. Whenever the English passive states a general condition without mentioning the person who does the action, Spanish tends to use the pronoun **se** with a transitive verb. The subject of the sentence is a thing, and the verb agrees in number with the subject. (A specific act done by a specified agent is expressed with the true passive.)

        Se venden aspirinas en la farmacia.   Aspirins are sold in the pharmacy.

        Las aspirinas son vendidas en la farmacia por un dependiente.   Aspirins are sold in the pharmacy by a clerk.

        NOTE: The reflexive verb will normally precede the subject when it is used passively.

    b. When the subject of the English passive construction is a person (or the equivalent), Spanish uses an impersonal **se**, which functions as the subject of the Spanish sentence. Thus, it replaces the impersonal English pronouns *one* and *people*, and the impersonally used pronouns *you*, *we*, and *they*. The verb is always in the third person singular. The English subject becomes the object of the Spanish sentence and is preceded by the personal **a** if it is a noun.[19]

        Se me enseñó el quirófano.   I was shown the OR.

        No se le llamó al médico a tiempo.   The doctor was not called on time.

        Se nos explicó lo que es la esterilización.   Sterilization has been explained to me.

NOTE: The impersonal reflexive construction can take either a direct or an indirect object, but only **le** and **les** may be used for the third person masculine.

¿A qué hora se le dio de alta al paciente?   When was the patient discharged?

¿Se le admitió a la paciente a causa de un accidente?   Was the patient admitted because of an accident?

Se ve a la enfermera con frecuencia.   The nurse is seen often.

Se llamó al médico.   The doctor was called.

Se le llamó.   He was called. (direct)

Se llamó a los médicos.   The doctors were called.

Se los llamó.   They were called.

Se le escribió una receta a él.   An R$_x$ was written for him. (indirect)

Se le escribió una receta a ella.   An R$_x$ was written for her.

2. If the subject of the sentence is a *person*, the tendency is to avoid both the passive voice and the impersonal construction, and to change the whole sentence back to the active voice, using the third person plural as a substitute for the passive. This assumes that the agent is not expressed. (This construction is somewhat more common in oral Spanish.)

No llamaron al médico a tiempo.   The doctor was not called on time. (Literally: They didn't call the doctor on time.)

¿Le vacunaron contra la viruela?   Were you vaccinated against smallpox? (Literally: Did they vaccinate you against smallpox?)

The third person plural substitutes for both the reflexive and the true passive constructions when double object pronouns are present. To use the reflexive in such a case would mean using three consecutive object pronouns (reflexive, indirect, and direct). To use the true passive would be awkward since the indirect object refers to a human.

Me los enseñaron a las seis.   I was shown them at 6 o'clock.

Se lo pusieron.   He was given it.

EXERCISES *EJERCICIOS*

A.   Express the following using an alternate form for the passive voice.

El hospital fue construido. > Se construyó el hospital.

1.   **Los resultados serán analizados.**
2.   **La oficina fue abierta a las 7.**
3.   **Las medicinas han sido compradas.**
4.   **Sus consejos habían sido aceptados.**
5.   **Las radiografías son estudiadas cuidadosamente.**

B. Substitute appropriate forms for the true passive.

Los hombres fueron heridos > $\left\{\begin{array}{l}\textbf{Hirieron a los hombres.}\\ \textbf{Se hirió a los hombres.}\\ \textbf{Se les hirió.}\end{array}\right.$

1. **Los médicos fueron llamados.**
2. **La paciente fue llevada al quirófano.**
3. **María será traída al hospital mañana.**
4. **El paciente fue admitido a la clínica.**
5. **Los heridos son llevados al hospital en una ambulancia.**

C. Complete the following, using the true passive voice or the alternate construction of the verbs in parentheses.

1. **La clínica (fundar) _____ por ese médico.**
2. **En el quirófano (operar) _____ a las siete.**
3. **¿Cómo (decir) _____ "tisis" en inglés?**
4. **Eso no (hacer) _____.**
5. **(Comer) _____ mucho maíz en Méjico.**

Orthographic Irregularities
Irregularidades ortográficas

1. Verbs ending in **-cer** or **-cir**, preceded by a vowel, change **c** to **zc** in the first person singular only of the present indicative and in all persons of the present subjunctive. Some health-oriented **-cer** verbs are:

agradecer   to thank for, to be grateful for

conocer   to know, to be acquainted with

convalecer   to convalesce

crecer   to grow

enronquecerse   to become hoarse

estremecerse   to shiver

fortalecer   to strengthen

nacer   to be born

padecer   to suffer

parecer   to seem

reconocer   to recognize

2. Verbs ending in **-cer** or **-cir**, preceded by a consonant, change **c** to **z** before **a** and **o**. This affects the first person singular only of the present indicative and all persons of the present subjunctive. Some health-oriented verbs are:

convencer   to convince

ejercer   to practice (a profession); to exert (one's rights)

torcer (ue)   to twist

3. Verbs ending in **-ger** or **-gir** change **g** to **j** before **a** and **o**. This affects the first person singular only of the present indicative and all persons of the present subjunctive. Some health-oriented verbs are:

coger   to pick (up)
dirigir   to direct
encoger   to bend (elbow, legs), to pull in/up (legs, knees)
escoger   to choose, to select
exigir   to demand
proteger   to protect
recoger   to pick up

4. Verbs ending in **-ducir** have the same changes as verbs in the first paragraph above. However, they make additional changes in the preterite and the imperfect subjunctive:

Preterite: **traduje, tradujiste, tradujo, tradujimos, —, tradujeron**
Imperfect Subjunctive: **tradujera,** etc.   **tradujese,** etc.

Some examples are:

conducir   to drive
introducir   to introduce
producir   to produce
reducir   to reduce, diminish
seducir   to seduce, charm
traducir   to translate

5. Verbs ending in **-uir** (except **-guir** and **-quir**), insert **y** between the stem **u** and the vowels **a**, **e**, and **o** of the conjugated endings. This affects the present participle, the entire singular of the present indicative as well as the third person plural, all of the present subjunctive, the third person singular and plural of the preterite, and all forms of the imperfect subjunctive. Some health-oriented verbs are:

concluir   to conclude, to end
constituir   to form, to constitute
construir   to construct
contribuir   to contribute
destruir   to destroy
disminuir   to diminish
distribuir   to distribute
huir   to flee
incluir   to include

instruir   to instruct

obstruir   to block, to obstruct

substituir   to substitute

6. Verbs ending in **-guir** change **gu** to **g** before **a** and **o**. This affects only the first person singular of the present indicative and the entire present subjunctive. Some health-oriented examples include:

conseguir (i)   to obtain

distinguir   to distinguish

seguir (i)   to follow, continue

7. Verbs whose stems end in **ll** or **ñ** drop the i of the diphthongs **ié** and **ió**. This occurs in the present participle, the third person singular and plural of the preterite, and all forms of the imperfect subjunctive. Examples include:

bullir   to boil

ceñir (i)   to tighten

desteñir (i)   to discolor, fade, bleach

gruñir   to grunt, growl, grumble

reñir (i)   to scold, quarrel

teñir (i)   to dye, tinge

8. Stem-changing verbs whose infinitive ends in **-eír** require a written accent mark over the stressed **i**. When there are supposed to be two **i**'s together, they reduce to one. This occurs in the present participle, the entire singular and third person plural of the present indicative, all of the present subjunctive, the third person both singular and plural of the preterite, and all forms of the imperfect subjunctive. Some health-oriented verbs include:

freír   to fry

reír   to laugh

reírse (de)   to laugh at

sonreír   to smile

Special Uses of Selected Verbs
Usos especiales de verbos escogidos

TO BECOME   *EQUIVALENTES DE*

The idea of "becoming" expressed in English by such verbs as to go, to get, to become, to turn, is also expressed in Spanish in a variety of ways. Frequently there is only one way to use *become* in Spanish, but other times two or more ways are possible. While the idea of "becoming" is implicit in certain verbs when they are used reflexively,[20] the four common Spanish equivalents are **hacerse, llegar a ser, ponerse,** and **volverse.**

Hacerse and **llegar a ser** are used with predicate nouns or adjectives.[21] **Hacerse +** noun/adjective implies achieving the status suggested by the noun or adjective as a result of one's conscious efforts. It is usually applied to professions. **Llegar a ser** + noun/adjective stresses achieving the status suggested as the end result in a process.

> **Pablo se hizo médico.** ⎫
> **Pablo llegó a ser médico.** ⎬ Paul became a doctor.

> **Por fin Carlos llegó a ser director del hospital.** Charles finally became director of the hospital.

> **Llegó a ser riquísimo.** He became extremely wealthy.

Ponerse and **volverse** are used only with predicate adjectives. **Ponerse +** adjective means to become whenever there is a physical, mental, or emotional change, usually temporary. **Volverse** + adjectives implies a basic or violent change.

> **María se ponía nerviosa en el ascensor.** Mary would become nervous in the elevator.

> **Me pongo muy deprimida cuando los veo.** I become very depressed when I see them.

> **El paciente se puso muy delgado.** The patient became very thin.

> **Juan se volvió loco.** John became mad/crazy.

Among the other translations that exist are **meterse a, ser de, hacerse de,** and **convertirse en. Meterse a** is used specifically for religious orders.

> **El joven se metió a cura.** The young man became a priest.

Ser de and **hacerse de** are synonyms. They imply the idea of "what has become of" someone or something.

> **¿Qué es del ayudante?** ⎫
> **¿Qué se hizo del ayudante?** ⎬ What has become of the orderly?

Convertirse en + noun implies a physical or chemical change.

> **Con el frío el agua se convierte en hielo.** With the cold the water becomes ice.

EXERCISES *EJERCICIOS*

A. Complete these sentences with the correct translation of "to become."

    1. ¿Qué _____ las pinzas?

    2. **La pobre** _____ **enferma.**

    3. **Ella** _____ **monja** (nun).

4. **El** _____ **presidente.**

5. **Después del accidente** _____ **ciego.**

6. **Mi tía** _____ **gorda en las vacaciones.**

7. **Ultimamente Juan** _____ **muy triste.**

8. **Nunca** _____ **un buen médico si no estudias.**

9. **Al morir Paco, Pepe** _____ **dueño del café.**

10. **Los enfermos** _____ **tan nerviosos.**

B. Say in Spanish.

1. He became very indifferent.

2. They became insane.

3. The situation became dangerous.

4. The woman went crazy after her son died.

5. Pablo worked a lot and became very rich.

TO HURT *EQUIVALENTES DE*

To hurt can be expressed in Spanish in a variety of ways. **Dolerle (algo a alguien)** means "to feel pain in" (see page 53).

> **Me duele la cabeza.**   I have a headache. (I feel pain in my head.)

Lastimar and **hacerle daño** are synonyms. Both mean "to hurt" (in a physical sense). Both verbs can be used reflexively as well.

> **No quiero lastimarla.**
> **No quiero hacerle daño a ella.**   } I don't want to hurt her.
>
> **Me lastimé.**
> **Me hice daño.**   } I hurt myself.

Herir (ie) means "to wound," or "to hurt (feelings)."

> **Su sarcasmo me hiere.**   His sarcasm hurts me.
> **Se hirió con un cuchillo.**   She hurt (wounded) herself with a knife.

EXERCISE *EJERCICIO*

Fill in the correct verb.

1. **Me** _____ **los ojos.**

2. **La carta que Berta recibió la** _____ **.**

3. **Hubo un accidente y Pablo** _____ **.** (2 ways)

4. **No quiero demostrar mis habilidades en karate porque puedo** _____ **a Vd.** (2 ways)

SOME IDIOMATIC USES OF **HACER**
*ALGUNOS USOS IDIOMATICOS DE **HACER***

Hace + expressions of time = For (+ certain time)

An action that began in the past and is still going on now is expressed in English with the present perfect tense followed by the length of time: I have been sick for two days.

This concept is expressed in Spanish with **hace** + expression of time + **que** + the simple present tense of a verb. An alternative exists in which the verb precedes the time expression:

Present perfect English + for + time.
$\begin{cases} \textbf{Hace} + \text{time expression} + \textbf{que} + \\ \quad \text{present tense verb.} \\ \text{Present tense verb} + \textbf{desde hace} + \\ \quad \text{time expression.} \end{cases}$

I have been sick for two days.
$\begin{cases} \textit{Hace} \textbf{ dos días } \textit{que} \textbf{ estoy enfermo.} \\ \textbf{Estoy enfermo } \textit{desde hace} \textbf{ dos días.} \end{cases}$

The same pattern can be expressed in English in the pluperfect tense and in Spanish in the imperfect tense:

Pluperfect English + for + time.
$\begin{cases} \textbf{Hacía} + \text{time expression} + \textbf{que} + \\ \quad \text{imperfect verb.} \\ \text{Imperfect verb} + \textbf{desde hacía} + \\ \quad \text{time expression.} \end{cases}$

I had been sick for two days.
$\begin{cases} \textit{Hacía} \textbf{ dos días } \textit{que} \textbf{ estaba enfermo.} \\ \textbf{Estaba enfermo } \textit{desde hacía} \textbf{ dos días.} \end{cases}$

The preceding English sentences may be expressed in Spanish by a word-for-word translation, but the **hace** construction is preferable.

I have been sick for two days.   **He estado enfermo por dos días.**

I had been sick for two days.   **Había estado enfermo por dos días.**

A similar construction exists using **desde** alone and gives the idea of *since*. **Desde** is used to indicate a general point of time in the past, as opposed to specific units of time (like days, years, or minutes). In a complex sentence, when an occurrence began in the past, it is introduced with **desde que**.

How long have you been ill?   **¿Desde cuándo está Vd. enfermo?**

I have been ill since yesterday.   **Estoy enfermo desde ayer.**

Since your illness I have been working.   **Desde su enfermedad, trabajo.**

She has been calling me daily since I got sick.   **Ella me llama todos los días desde que enfermé.**

He has been suffering from heart trouble since he was a young man.   **Sufre del corazón desde que era joven.**

Hace + expression of time = Ago

The only possible translation for the word *ago* is the idiomatic use of **hace**. In English the construction is the length of time + ago, whereas the Spanish construction is **hace** + time.

English past tense verb + length of time + ago.	Preterite main verb + **hace** + time. **Hace** + time + **que** + preterite verb.

She died five days ago.	**Ella murió *hace* cinco días.** ***Hace* cinco días que ella murió.**

EXERCISES *EJERCICIOS*

A. Answer the following questions, using complete Spanish sentences.

1. **¿Cuánto tiempo hace que le duele la cabeza? (dos días)**
2. **¿Cuánto tiempo hace que tiene problemas del estómago? (un mes)**
3. **¿Cuánto tiempo hace que le hacen una radiografía del pecho? (un año)**
4. **¿Cuánto tiempo hace que tiene el paciente dolores muy fuertes (dos horas)**
5. **¿Cuánto tiempo hace que no viene a la clínica. (tres años)**

B. Change to the past.

1. **Hace un mes que tomo las píldoras.**
2. **Hace dos horas que espero aquí.**
3. **Hace tres días que el niño no obra.**
4. **Hace una semana que tengo el salpullido.**

C. Rewrite Exercise B, putting the time clause at the end of the sentence. Then, do the same for the modified version of Exercise B—the imperfect tense version.

THE SUBJUNCTIVE MOOD

EL MODO SUBJUNTIVO

Three moods exist in both Spanish and English—the indicative, the imperative, and the subjunctive.

The indicative mood is based upon facts or certainties; it indicates that something either does or does not exist. (**Juan es médico.** John is a doctor.)

The imperative mood commands; it is used when the person to whom the command is directed is addressed as **tú**. (**Tómalas, Juan.** Take them, John.)

The subjunctive mood is probably the most difficult for the English-speaking person studying Spanish because few Americans are aware of using the subjunctive on a daily basis. In both languages the subjunctive mood expresses an attitude, tinged with subjectivity and unreality. It is dependent upon the main idea expressed in an independent clause of desire, emotion, doubt, uncertainty, or causation. Subjunctive occurs whenever there is an implication of a command, of something contrary to fact, of something indefinite or unreal, of an emotionally charged statement. These concepts produce the subjunctive mood in Spanish; in English many substitute forms replace the subjunctive.

The subjunctive is found in dependent clauses; it never asks a direct question nor makes a direct statement. It is only in the third person singular of the present (English) subjunctive that the verb form is different, and in the past and present subjunctive forms of the verb "to be." The auxiliaries "may" and "might" express the subjunctive ideas in English. English examples of the subjunctive include: "Come what may." "If I were a doctor..." "I want you to study medicine." Modern Spanish uses four subjunctive tenses. For more advanced study of the subjunctive, the student is advised to consult Ramsey-Spaulding's *A Textbook of of Modern Spanish* (New York, Holt, Rinehart & Winston, 1963).

Formation of the Present Subjunctive
Formación del presente de subjuntivo

The present subjunctive is formed like the formal commands: if the first person singular of the present indicative ends in **-o**, the **-o** is dropped. New present subjunctive endings are added to what is left. This applies to regular, stem-changing, and irregular verbs alike. Below are the subjunctive endings for the present tense[22]:

For **-ar** verbs add: **-e, -es, -e, -emos, —, -en**

For **-er** and **-ir** verbs add: **-a, -as, -a, -amos, —, -an**

Subject Pronouns	examinar	comer	sufrir
yo	examine	coma	sufra
tú	examines	comas	sufras
él, ella, Vd.	examine	coma	sufra
nosotros (-as)	examinemos	comamos	suframos
—	—	—	—
ellos, ellas, Vds.	examinen	coman	sufran

Thus, **que yo examine** means (that) I may examine, (that) I examine, "for me to examine."

NOTE: Even if a verb is considered to be "irregular" in the first person, if this form ends in an **-o**, the subjunctive formation is regular based on the above endings. The "irregularity" of the first person singular of the present indicative will be kept in all persons of the present subjunctive.

Verb	First Person Singular Present Indicative	Stem Used	First Person Singular Present Subjunctive
caber (to fit)	**quepo**	**quep-**	**quepa**
caer (to fall)	**caigo**	**caig-**	**caiga**
conocer (to know)	**conozco**	**conozc-**	**conozca**

EXERCISE *EJERCICIO*

Give the appropriate form of the verb listed in infinitive form, first in the present indicative and then in the present subjunctive.

Infinitive	Person	Present Indicative	Present Subjunctive
	yo		
operar		_____	_____
hallar		_____	_____
ayudar		_____	_____
revivir		_____	_____
	tú		
prescribir		_____	_____
comprender		_____	_____
hacer		_____	_____
	él, ella, Vd.		
tener		_____	_____
auscultar		_____	
venir		_____	_____
toser		_____	_____
	nosotros (-as)		
aspirar		_____	_____
ver		_____	_____
decir		_____	_____
escupir		_____	_____
	ellos, ellas, Vds.		
consultar		_____	_____
aliviar		_____	_____
permitir		_____	_____
oír		_____	_____
traer		_____	_____

NOTE: Class I radical changing verbs show the same stem changes in the present subjunctive as in the present indicative. Classes II and III make the same type of stem change in the present subjunctive as in the present indicative; however, they make an additional stem change in the first (and second) person plural: **e** > **i** and **o** > **u**.

Class I

despertar	mostrar	querer	mover
despierte	muestre	quiera	mueva
despiertes	muestres	quieras	muevas
despierte	muestre	quiera	mueva
despertemos	mostremos	queramos	movamos
—	—	—	—
despierten	muestren	quieran	muevan

Class II

sentirse	dormir
me sienta	duerma
te sientas	duermas
se sienta	duerma
nos sintamos	durmamos
—	—
se sientan	duerman

Class III

seguir
siga
sigas
siga
sigamos
—
sigan

EXERCISE   *EJERCICIO*

Give the appropriate form of the verb listed in infinitive form, first in the present indicative and then in the present subjunctive.

Infinitive	Person	Present Indicative	Present Subjunctive
	yo		
acostarse		_____	_____
reñir		_____	_____
herir		_____	_____
	tú		
cerrar		_____	_____
soñar		_____	_____
querer		_____	_____

Infinitive	Person	Present Indicative	Present Subjunctive
	él, ella, Vd.		
doler		_____	_____
pedir		_____	_____
probar		_____	_____
	nosotros (-as)		
referir		_____	_____
perseguir		_____	_____
acostarse		_____	_____
	ellos, ellas, Vds.		
negar		_____	_____
concebir		_____	_____
perder		_____	_____

Orthographic Changes *Cambios ortográficos*

The present subjunctive shows several spelling changes due to pronunciation requirements. (Remember, in Spanish it is important to maintain the same basic sound, even though the spelling must be modified.) Orthographic changes, which occur in all conjugated forms of the present subjunctive, are found in verbs that end in **-car**, **-gar**, **-guar**, and **-zar**. (NOTE: These verbs are not considered to be "irregular" in the present subjunctive even with this spelling change.)

c > qu *masticar*	*g > gu* *tragar*	*g > gü* *averiguar*	*z > c* *comenzar*
mastique	trague	averigüe	comience
mastiques	tragues	averigües	comiences
mastique	trague	averigüe	comience
mastiquemos	traguemos	averigüemos	comencemos
—	—	—	—
mastiquen	traguen	averigüen	comiencen

Additional spelling changes occur throughout the present subjunctive for verbs ending in:

    -ger or **-gir**: elegir (i) (g > j) elijo > elija

    -guir: seguir (i) (gu > g) sigo > siga

    -(vowel) + **cer** or **cir**: conocer (c > zc) conozco > conozca

    -ducir: traducir (c > zc) traduzco > traduzca

    -(consonant) + **cer**: torcer(ue) (c > z) tuerzo > tuerza

Irregular Verbs   *Verbos irregulares*

There are six verbs that are completely irregular in the present subjunctive. They must be memorized.

dar	estar	haber	ir	saber	ser
dé	esté	haya	vaya	sepa	sea
des	estés	hayas	vayas	sepas	seas
dé	esté	haya	vaya	sepa	sea
demos	estemos	hayamos	vayamos	sepamos	seamos
—	—	—	—	—	—
den	estén	hayan	vayan	sepan	sean

EXERCISE   *EJERCICIO*

Fill in the correct form of the verb, first in the present indicative and then in the present subjunctive.

Infinitive	*Person*	*Present Indicative*	*Present Subjunctive*
	yo		
explicar		_____	_____
ir		_____	_____
llegar		_____	_____
lanzar (to hurl)		_____	_____
	tú		
escoger (to choose)		_____	_____
saber		_____	_____
colgar (ue)		_____	_____
	él, ella, Vd.		
dirigir (to direct)		_____	_____
convencer (to convince)		_____	_____
estar		_____	_____
sacar		_____	_____
	nosotros (-as)		
gozar (to enjoy)		_____	_____
ser		_____	_____
obligar (to oblige)		_____	_____
	ellos, ellas, Vds.		
equivocarse (to be mistaken)		_____	_____
encoger las rodillas (to pull up one's knees)		_____	_____
dar		_____	_____

Formation of the Past Subjunctive
Formación del imperfecto de subjuntivo

There are two forms used for the past subjunctive, both of which, without any exception, are based on the third person plural of the preterite. (Any irregularity found in the third person plural of the preterite is also found throughout the past (or imperfect) subjunctive. Both the **-ra** and **-se** forms drop the **-ron** and add the following endings (which are the same for all verbs):

-ra, -ras, -ra, -'ramos, —, -ran

-se, -ses, -se, -'semos, —, -sen

There are no irregularities, and both forms may be used interchangeably.

examinaron (examinar)		*comieron (comer)*	
examin*ara*	examina*se*	comi*era*	comie*se*
examin*aras*	examina*ses*	comi*eras*	comie*ses*
examin*ara*	examina*se*	comi*era*	comie*se*
examin*áramos*	examin*ásemos*	comi*éramos*	comi*ésemos*
—	—	—	—
examin*aran*	examina*sen*	comi*eran*	comie*sen*

sufrieron (sufrir)	
sufri*era*	sufrie*se*
sufri*eras*	sufrie*ses*
sufri*era*	sufrie*se*
sufri*éramos*	sufri*ésemos*
—	—
sufri*eran*	sufrie*sen*

Thus, **que yo examinara (examinase)** means (that) I examined, (that) I might examine, "me to examine."

EXERCISE *EJERCICIO*

Supply the third person plural, preterite of the verbs given in infinitive form. Then, give the appropriate form of the past subjunctive, using the **-ra** forms first, and the **-se** next.

Infinitive	*Preterite*	**-ra**	**-se**
ayudar	_____	que yo _____	_____
venir	_____	que yo _____	_____
sentir	_____	que tú _____	_____
querer	_____	que tú _____	_____
estar	_____	que él _____	_____

saber	_____	que él _____	_____
explicar	_____	que ella _____	_____
obligar	_____	que ella _____	_____
sacar	_____	que Vd. _____	_____
leer	_____	que Vd. _____	_____
oír	_____	que nosotros _____	_____
ser	_____	que nosotros _____	_____
poner	_____	que ellos _____	_____
poder	_____	que ellos _____	_____
afeitarse	_____	que Vds. _____	_____
acostarse	_____	que Vds. _____	_____
ir	_____	que ellas _____	_____

Formation of the Present Perfect Subjunctive
Formación del perfecto de subjuntivo

The present perfect subjunctive is composed of the present subjunctive of **haber** (**haya, hayas, haya, hayamos, —, hayan**) plus the past participle of the verb (**haya examinado, haya comido, haya sufrido**, etc.).

Formation of the Pluperfect Subjunctive
Formación del pluscuamperfecto de subjuntivo

The pluperfect subjunctive is composed of either the **-ra** or **-se** form of the imperfect subjunctive of **haber** (**hubiera, hubieras, hubiera, hubiéramos, —, hubieran** or **hubiese, hubieses, hubiésemos, —, hubiesen**) plus the past participle of the verb (**hubiera examinado, hubiera comido, hubiera sufrido**, etc. or **hubiese examinado, hubiese comido, hubiese sufrido**, etc.).

SEQUENCE OF TENSES *SECUENCIA DE TIEMPOS*

Main Clause	*Dependent Clause*
Present Future Imperative (command) Present Perfect	Same tense as in English
Imperfect Preterite Pluperfect	Imperfect subjunctive or pluperfect subjunctive

Me alegro de que ella se mejore. I am glad that she is improving.

Será imposible que yo venga mañana. It will be impossible for me to come tomorrow.

Dígale a ella que se mejore. Tell her to get better.

El médico ha tenido miedo de que su paciente muera. The doctor has been afraid that his patient is dying.

El paciente se alegra de que su familia haya llegado antes de la operación. The patient is glad that his family has arrived before the operation.

Me alegro de que la familia le viera/viese antes de su muerte. I am glad that the family saw him before his death.

La familia me pidió que operara/operase. The family asked me to operate.

Me alegraba de que no fuera/fuese cáncer. I was glad that it was not cancer.

Me alegraba de que no hubiera/hubiese sido cáncer. I was glad that it had not been cancer.

La enfermera nos había pedido que saliéramos/saliésemos. The nurse had asked us to leave.

Uses of the Subjunctive
Usos del subjuntivo

The subjunctive is always introduced in a dependent or subordinate clause by the relative **que**, which is frequently not translated into English. The subjunctive is used to reflect the speaker's attitude about a specific state or action. Usually it is possible to classify this attitude as either reflecting some type of desire or some type of uncertainty. Expressions of will, need, approval, permission, purpose, fear, joy, command, and so on, fall into the first category. Notions of doubt, possibility, probability, permissibility, and hypotheticals fall into the second category. Subjunctive is found in both the main and subordinate clauses.

Subjunctive in the Main Clause
Subjuntivo en la oración principal

COMMANDS *LOS MANDATOS*

1. Direct Command *El mandato directo*

   a. *Polite, Formal Command El mandato formal.* Polite, formal commands of most verbs are formed from the first person singular of the present indicative tense, provided that it ends in **-o**. The **-o** is dropped and the following endings are added:

For **-ar** verbs, **-e**; for **-er** or **-ir** verbs, **-a**.

In *all* cases the plural of these commands will be formed by adding **-n** to the singular. Use **no** before the affirmative command to state the polite negative command.

> **Tome Vd. la medicina.**   Take the medicine.
>
> **No tome Vd. la medicina.**   Don't take the medicine.

b. *Irregularities   Irregularidades.* Certain orthographic changes are made for verbs ending in **-car** or **-gar** when forming polite commands. In order to retain the *k* sound in any verb ending in **car**, change the **c** to **qu** before adding **e** or **en**.

> **Búsquelo Vd.   Búsquenlo Vds. (buscar)**   Look for it.

In order to retain the hard *g* sound in any verb ending in **-gar**, change the **g** to **gu** before adding **e** or **en**.

> **Pague Vd. ahora.   Paguen Vds. ahora. (pagar)**   Pay now.

The following verbs are totally irregular in their polite commands and must be memorized:

	Singular	*Plural*
estar to be	**esté Vd.**	**estén Vds.**
ser to be	**sea Vd.**	**sean Vds.**
dar to give	**dé Vd.**	**den Vds.**
ir to go	**vaya Vd.**	**vayan Vds.**
saber to know	**sepa Vd.**	**sepan Vds.**

Object pronouns—indirect and direct—and reflexive pronouns are attached to the affirmative commands. Written accent marks are necessary in order to retain the original stress.[23]

> **Hábleme Vd.**   Speak to me.
>
> **Dígamelo.**   Tell it to me.

In the negative commands object pronouns precede the verb.

> **No me hable Vd.**   Don't speak to me.

c. *Hortatory Command   El Mandato con "nosotros"*[24]. This is formed by using the first person plural of the present subjunctive. Object pronouns—direct and indirect—as well as reflexive pronouns are attached to the affirmative command, but precede the negative command. With a reflexive verb the final **-s** of the first person plural is omitted in the affirmative.

> **Operemos.**   Let us operate.
>
> **Escribámoslas.**   Let's write them.
>
> **Divirtámonos.**   Let's have a good time.
>
> **No nos durmamos ahora.**   Let's not doze now.

d. *The Imperative   El imperativo.* The imperative is used to issue an affirmative command when the person to whom the command is given is addressed in the familiar voice. In the hospital context, it is best to avoid the familiar form of address because of the very real difference between the intimacy conveyed by **tú** and the formality conveyed by **usted**. However, the imperative may be used comfortably with children who are hospitalized.

The familiar command of regular verbs is formed by using the third person singular of the present indicative tense as it is. The subject **tú** may be used *following* the verb. Object pronouns are attached to the end of the command, as is the reflexive pronoun **te**, if needed. An accent mark is then used over the syllable that was stressed originally.

> **Encoge tú el codo, Juanito.**   Bend your elbow, Johnny.
>
> **Despiértate.**   Wake up.

The negative familiar command is obtained by adding an **-s** to the polite, formal singular command (see page 146).

> **No encojas tú el codo, Juanito.**   Don't bend your elbow, Johnny.
>
> **No te despiertes, María.**   Don't wake up, Mary.

The following irregular verbs do not follow this rule for the formation of the familiar affirmative command. They must be memorized. Note that the negative command is regular, however.

> **decir > di   no digas**
> **hacer > haz   no hagas**
> **ir > ve   no vayas**
> **poner > pon   no pongas**
> **salir > sal   no salgas**
> **ser > sé   no seas**
> **tener > ten   no tengas**
> **venir > ven   no vengas**

2. Indirect Command   *El mandato indirecto*

The indirect command has the same form as the third person of the present subjunctive. It is a command issued indirectly to a third party. Object pronouns and reflexive pronouns precede the indirect command. The main verb is generally omitted; the clause is introduced by **que**.

> **Que escriba la receta el médico.**   Let the doctor write the prescription.
>
> **Que los examine en seguida.**   Have her examine them at once.

3. Impersonal Command   El mandato impersonal

These are used to give instructions or directions. The third person singular or plural of the present subjunctive is used together with the pronoun **se**.

Manténgase en el refrigerador.   Keep in the refrigerator.

Guárdese afuera del alcance de niños.   Keep out of the reach of children.

Tómense las píldoras con agua.   Take the pills with water.

WISHES *LOS DESEOS*

These are used as exclamations. They may begin with **ojalá**, which loosely translates as *I* (*we, etc.*) *hope that...*, or *would that....* (**Ojalá** is of Arabic derivation and is an imprecation to Allah.) Wishes usually begin with **que**.

Que se mejore pronto su madre.   May your mother get well soon. (I hope) (that) your mother gets well soon.

¡Que Dios te bendiga!   (May) God bless you!

Ojalá que se cure pronto.   I (We) hope that you recuperate soon.

¡Bien venido sea, doctor!   Welcome, doctor! (May you be welcome.)

HYPOTHETICAL EVENTS *LOS ACONTECIMIENTOS HIPOTETICOS*

The subjunctive is used after certain adverbs of probability, **acaso**, **quizá(s)**, **tal vez**, which all mean *perhaps*, when the speaker has strong doubt in mind. (If there is no doubt, the indicative is used.)

Quizá no tenga fiebre.   Perhaps she doesn't have a fever.

Acaso se haya dormido.   Perhaps she might have fallen asleep.

But: **Se ha dormido tal vez.**   Perhaps she has fallen asleep.

POLITE STATEMENTS *LOS RUEGOS CORTESES*

The imperfect subjunctive forms **debiera**, **quisiera**, and **pudiera** are used as the main verb instead of the present indicative. These forms convey the idea of respect or courtesy and are more polite than **debo**, **quiero**, and **puedo** when making a request.

Vds. debieran consultar con la especialista.   You ought to (should) consult with the specialist.

¿Pudiera Vd. llenar esta receta?   Could you fill this prescription?

Quisiera consultar con mi familia.   I'd like to consult my family.

Subjunctive in the Dependent Clause
El subjuntivo en la cláusula subordinada

NOUN CLAUSES *LA CLAUSULA SUBSTANTIVA*

A noun clause is a group of words having a subject and a predicate, which act as a noun. This type of clause is always introduced in Spanish by **que**. For the verb in the noun clause to be in the subjunctive, two requirements have to be fulfilled: (1) the main verb must require subjunctive in the dependent clause; (2) the subject of the dependent clause must be different from that of the main verb (in most cases). The following categories of main verbs require this type of subjunctive.

1. Verbs of wishing or desiring   Verbos que expresan deseo

> **Quiero que Vd. flexione los pies.**   I want you to flex your feet.
> **Deseo que tú describas tu hemorragia menstrual.**   I want you to describe your menstrual flow.
> *but:* **Deseo describir mi hemorragia menstrual.**   I want to describe my menstrual flow.

2. Verbs of emotion   Verbos que expresan emociones
The subjunctive is used in Spanish after all verbs of emotion provided that there is a change of subject in the subordinate clause. If there is only one subject, the infinitive is used. Verbs of emotion include:

> **alegrarse (de)**   to be glad, to be happy
> **avergonzarse (de) (ue)**   to be ashamed, to be embarrassed
> **encantarle (a uno)**   to be delighted
> **enojarle (a uno)**   to be angry, to be mad
> **esperar**   to hope (for)
> **extrañarle (a uno)**   to be surprised
> **gustarle (a uno)**   to like (to be pleasing to)
> **lamentar**   to regret
> **molestarle (a uno)**   to be annoyed, to be bothered
> **preocuparse**   to worry
> **quejarse de**   to complain
> **sentir (ie)**   to regret, to be sorry
> **sorprenderle (a uno)**   to be surprised
> **temer**   to be afraid, to fear
> **tener miedo de**   to be afraid, to fear
> **Temo que el paciente muera.**   I am afraid (that) the patient is dying.
> **Me alegro de que Vd. se sienta mejor que ayer.**   I am glad (that) you feel better than yesterday.
> *but:* **Me alegro de sentirme mejor que ayer.**   I am glad that I feel better than yesterday.

3. Verbs of commanding or requesting   Verbos que expresan mandatos o ruegos
Spanish uses the subjunctive in subordinate clauses when the speaker tells, requests, forbids, prevents, advises, persuades, suggests, insists, compels, or

demands that someone else do something. Within this category there are two types of verbs—those that communicate information and those that influence.

If the verbs only communicate information, the indicative is used, even if there is a change in subject. Verbs of communication include:

decir   to tell

escribir   to write

indicar   to indicate

Dígale que ha llegado el paciente.   Tell him that the patient has arrived.

Unlike the verbs of wanting and wishing, or those of emotion, many verbs of influence are used with an indirect object. These include:

aconsejar   to advise

advertir (ie)   to warn

avisar   to advise

convencer   to convince

exigir   to demand

impedir (i)   to prevent

mandar   to order

pedir (i)   to ask, to request

permitir   to allow, to permit

persuadir a   to persuade

preferir (ie)   to prefer (no object pronoun used)

prohibir   to forbid

proponer   to propose, to suggest

recomendar (ie)   to recommend

rogar (ue)   to beg

sugerir (ie)   to suggest

Ella me dice que deje de fumar.   She tells me to stop smoking.

Le ruego que tome precauciones.   I beg you to take precautions.

There are some verbs of influence that are used with a direct object:

dejar   to allow, to let

hacer   to make

invitar   to invite

obligar a   to force

Doctora García, la invitamos a que tome algo con nosotros.   Dr. García, we invite you to have something with us.

A few verbs of influence may be followed by an infinitive instead of the subjunctive, even when the subject of the subordinate clause is different from that of the main clause. The use of the infinitive is more common with **dejar, hacer, impedir, mandar,** and **permitir.**

Le hice venir al médico.   I had the doctor come.

[*rather than*: **(Le) hice que viniese/viniera el médico.**]

Nos mandará ir por la médica.   She'll have us (order us to) go for the doctor.

[*rather than*: **Nos mandará que vayamos por la médica.**]

4. Verbs of doubt, denial, uncertainty   Verbos que expresan duda, o negación, o incertidumbre.

Verbs of doubt, denial, and uncertainty require the subjunctive in a subordinate clause when there is a change of subject. Also included in this group are verbs of *belief used negatively.* The following verbs fall into this category:

dudar   to doubt

negar (ie)   to deny

no considerar   not to think

no creer   not to think, not to believe

no decir   not to say

no pensar (ie)   not to think

no querer decir (ie)   not to mean

no significar   not to mean

no sospechar   not to suspect

Dudo que alguien pueda ayudarme.   I doubt that anyone can help me.

Vd. niega que ella haya ingresado al hospital.   You deny that she has been admitted to the hospital.

No creo que sea posible.   I don't believe that it is possible.

When the main verb implies certainty, the subordinate clause is in the indicative. **No creer** can be followed by the indicative if there is certainty on the part of the speaker.

Creo que alguien puede ayudarme.   I believe (that) someone can help me.

No dudo que ella ha ingresado al hospital.   I don't doubt that she has been admitted to the hospital.

Creo que es posible.   I believe that it is possible.

When used in questions **creer, no creer, pensar,** and **no pensar** can be followed by either the indicative or the subjunctive, depending on the speaker's belief. The beliefs of the person being addressed have nothing to do with the subordinate verb choice.

¿Cree Vd. que ese paciente muere?   Do you think that that patient is dying? (I do; I want to see if you agree.)

¿Cree Vd. que ese paciente muera?   Do you think that that patient is dying? (I don't know; what do you think?)

5. After impersonal expressions   Después de expresiones impersonales

The subjunctive is used after many impersonal expressions that do not stress a fact. If the impersonal expression indicates a fact or certainty, it is followed by the indicative. If these expressions are used without specific subjects in the dependent clause, an infinitive is used. Some are

es aconsejable   it is advisable

es bueno   it is good

es deseable   it is desireable

es difícil   it is unlikely, it is difficult

es extraño   it is strange

es fácil   it is likely, it is easy

es fantástico   it is fantastic

es importante   it is importante

es (im)posible   it is (im)possible

es lamentable   it is regrettable

es lástima   it is a pity/shame

es malo   it is bad

es maravilla   it is a wonder

es mejor   it is better

es menester/necesario/preciso   it is necessary

es natural   it is natural

es probable   it is probable

es raro   it is odd, it is rare

es triste   it is sad

es una pena   it is a pain, it is (really) inconvenient

basta (con) que   it is enough

conviene   it is suitable, it is right

importa   it is important

más vale/vale más   it is better

parece mentira   it seems incredible

puede ser   it may be

The following impersonal expressions are followed by the indicative:

es cierto   it is certain

es evidente   it is evident

es obvio   it is obvious

está seguro   it is sure

es verdad   it is true

no hay duda   there is no doubt

Es necesario que Vd. vaya al hospital.   It is necessary for you to go to the hospital.

but: **Es necesario ir al hospital.**   It is necessary to go to the hospital.

ADJECTIVE CLAUSES   *SUBJUNTIVO EN LA CLAUSULA ADJETIVA*

Subjunctive is used in adjective clauses when the antecedent is hypothetical, indefinite, nonexistent, or negative. If the antecedent is definite, the indicative is used. When the object is indefinite, omit the personal **a**.

¿**Conoce Vd. alguien que sepa colocarme un marcapasos?**   Do you know anyone who knows how to implant a pacemaker (in me)?

No hay nadie que le haga un lavado de estómago a él.   There is no one who will pump his stomach.

but: **Conozco a alguien que sabe colocarme un marcapasos.**   I know someone who knows how to implant a pacemaker (in me).

Hay alguien que le hace un lavado de estómago a él.   There is someone who is pumping his stomach.

ADVERBIAL CLAUSES   *SUBJUNTIVO EN LA CLAUSULA ADVERBIAL*

1. Adverbs of time   Adverbios de tiempo

When the verb in the main clause is in the future tense, the verb in the adverbial dependent clause is in the present subjunctive, since one cannot be certain that the action in the adverbial clause will occur in the future. However, if the main verb is in the past, the subordinate verb in the adverbial clause of time is in the indicative, since the action has already happened and, hence, is a fact.

Le daré la inyección a Vd. cuando venga.   I will give you the shot when you come.

but: **Le dí la inyección a Vd. cuando vino.**   I gave you the shot when you came.

Some adverbial conjunctions of time which are followed by the subjunctive are:

cuando   when

en cuanto, luego que, tan pronto como   as soon as

después de que   after

hasta que   until

NOTE: The conjunction **antes de que** (before) is an exception to the above requirement. It is *always* followed by the subjunctive. The imperfect subjunctive is used after it if the main verb is in the past.

Saldrá antes de que empiece la operación. He will leave before the operation begins.

Salió antes de que empezara/empezase la operación. He left before the operation began.

2. Adverbs of purpose and provision   Adverbios de propósito y condición
The subjunctive is used after the following conjunctive expressions:

a fin de que, para que   in order that

a menos que   unless

a pesar de que   in spite of

con tal que   provided that

de manera que, de modo que[25]   so that, so

en caso de que   in case

Iremos para que Vd. reciba una transfusión de sangre. We will go so that you will receive a blood transfusion.

La enfermera vendrá con tal que Vd. guarde cama. The nurse will come provided you stay in bed.

3. Without   **Sin que**
Because of the negative results, clauses beginning with **sin que** are always in the subjunctive.

Salimos sin que nadie nos dé los resultados del urinálisis. We are leaving before anyone gives us the results of the urinalysis.

4. Even if/even though   **Aunque**
The subjunctive is used with **aunque** if the clause expresses concession. In this case it has the meaning of *even if*. The indicative is used if the subordinate verb states a fact. In this case it has the meaning of *even though*.

Aunque no le guste, tendrá que tragarlo. Although you may not like it, you have to swallow it.

Aunque no le gusta, tendrá que tragarlo. Although you do not like it, you have to swallow it.

EXERCISES *EJERCICIOS*

A. Complete the following with the correct subjunctive form of the indicated verb.

1. **Yo quiero que Vds. _____.** (mejorarse, guardar cama, tomarme el pulso)

2. **¿Por qué espera el médico que yo _____?** (curarse, no sentir dolor, comprarlos)

3. **Insisten en que el técnico lo _____.** (hacer, terminar, aprender, leer)

4. **Creo que el cirujano _____.** (estar aquí, llegar tarde, lavarse las manos)

5. **La familia esperará hasta que el médico _____.** (terminar, explicarlo, examinarle)

B. Complete the following with the appropriate form of the indicated verb.

1. **El doctor me dice que** _____ . **(guardar cama)**
2. **El doctor me dice que él** _____ . **(guardar cama)**
3. **¿Te extraña mucho que Alberto todavía** _____ **enfermo? (estar)**
4. **Ellos nos aconsejan que lo** _____ **poco a poco. (tragar)**
5. **No dudo que el paciente** _____ **fiebre. (tener)**

C. Rewrite the following sentences in the negative.

1. **Hay algún doctor que lo tiene.**
2. **Hay algo que me ayuda.**
3. **Tiene algo que sirve.**
4. **Hay un enfermero que es competente.**
5. **Hay un diccionario médico que contiene todas las palabras en español.**

D. Rewrite the following sentences, introducing each by the indicated expression.

1. **El paciente está enfermo. Es lamentable**
2. **El cirujano hace todo lo posible. Importa**
3. **Volvemos pronto. No hay duda**
4. **Le dan de alta mañana. Es difícil**
5. **Mañana es día de trabajo. Es verdad**

E. Change the following sentences to the future. Make all necessary changes.

1. **Esperé hasta que vino.**
2. **Se la di cuando me pagó.**
3. **El paciente vivió allí hasta que murió.**
4. **La voluntaria me dio las cartas tan pronto como me vio.**

F. Say in Spanish.

1. I hope to be able to finish the tests today.
2. I had the midwife come.
3. The doctor ordered me to leave immediately.
4. It is best for them to wait outside.
5. I want you to follow a low-carbohydrate diet.

ADVERBS

LOS ADVERBIOS

El adverbio explains certain conceptual qualities and circumstances. Adverbs may modify verbs, adjectives, other adverbs, and whole sentences. Basically they are correlated with the four interrogative adverbs: time **¿cuándo?**; manner **¿cómo?**; place **¿dónde?**; extent or intensity **¿cuánto?**

Adverbs of time *Adverbios que concretan tiempo*

already **ya**[26]
always **siempre**
at once **en seguida**
before, earlier **antes**
early **temprano**
last night **anoche**
late **tarde**
later **después, luego**
never **nunca**
still **todavía**
still, yet **aún**[27]
then **entonces**
today **hoy**
tomorrow **mañana**
yesterday **ayer**

Unlike English, adverbs do not occur between the auxiliary and the main verb:

Todavía **está operando.**   He is *still* operating.

¿Está operando *todavía***?**   Is he *still* operating?

Adverbs of manner *Adverbios que expresan modo*

badly, poorly **mal**
better **mejor**
low **bajo**
slowly **despacio**
thus **así**
well **bien**
worse **peor**

Additional adverbs of manner are formed by adding **-mente** (which corresponds to *ly* in English) to the feminine singular form of the adjective:

lenta slow   **lentamente** slowly
rápida rapid   **rápidamente** rapidly

NOTE: The written accent mark of the adjective is kept in the new adverbial form (**rápidamente**).

Frequently an adverbial phrase is used instead of the adverb.

Adverb	*Adverbial Phrase*	
cuidadosamente	**con cuidado**	carefully
finalmente	**por fin, al fin**	finally

In a series of two or more adverbs, both of which normally end in **-mente**, the suffix is used only with the last:

> **El opera lenta y cuidadosamente.**   He operates slowly and carefully.

> **La paciente ya respira *profunda*, *rápida* y *fácilmente*.**   The patient now is breathing *deeply*, *rapidly*, and *easily*.

In Spanish, adverbs of manner usually follow the verb immediately.

> **El Sr. Gómez sigue *mucho mejor* gracias a la operación.**   Mr. Gómez is *much better* thanks to the operation.

Adverbs of manner never occur between an auxiliary and a main verb as in English:

> **El ha tomado baños calientes *repetidas veces*.**   He has *repeatedly* taken hot baths.

Adverbs of place   *Adverbios que determinan lugar*

> back, in the back   **atrás**
> down, downstairs   **abajo**
> far, far away   **lejos**
> here   **acá**
> in, inside   **adentro**
> inside, within   **dentro**
> near by, close by   **cerca**
> opposite, across from   **enfrente**
> outside, out   **afuera**
> over there   **allá**
> (right) here   **aquí**
> (right) over there, there   **allí**
> there   **ahí**
> up, upstairs   **arriba**

With the exception of **atrás**, **cerca**, and **lejos**, the other adverbs of place may be used with verbs of motion to indicate direction, or with verbs of location to indicate position or location.

> **Vaya *arriba* a la sala de espera.**   Go *upstairs* to the waiting room.
> **Está *abajo*.**   She is *downstairs*.

Adverbs of Intensity
Adverbios que expresan cantidad

almost   **casi**

enough, considerably, sufficiently   **bastante**

enough, sufficiently   **suficiente**

less   **menos**

little, not much   **poco**

more   **más**

much, a lot, very much   **mucho (muy)**

scarcely   **apenas**

so   **tan**

too much   **demasiado**

very much   **tanto**

Adverbs of intensity take the same position in Spanish as in English.

Es *tan* tarde.   It is *so* late.

Sentence Modifiers
Modificativos de oraciones

Additional adverbs exist that do not answer the four traditional interrogatives. These adverbs modify sentences.

AFFIRMATIVE ADVERBS   *ADVERBIOS QUE SIRVEN PARA AFIRMAR*

also, too   **también**

certainly   **ciertamente**

of course   **por supuesto**

surely   **seguramente**

truly   **verdaderamente**

undoubtedly   **sin duda**

yes   **sí**[28]

NEGATIVE ADVERBS[29]   *ADVERBIOS QUE SIRVEN PARA NEGAR*

neither/not either   **ni**

neither/not either   **tampoco**

never/not ever   **nunca / jamás**

no   **no**

Spanish often uses a double negative. In this case the adverb **no** precedes the verb and the second negative adverb either follows the verb or appears at the end of the sentence. The alternative is to omit the **no** and have the negative adverb precede the verb.

No tomo *nunca/jamás* **barbitúricos.**⎫
Nunca/jamás **tomos barbitúricos.**⎬ I *never* take barbiturates.
                                     ⎭
Ni yo *tampoco.* *Neither* do I.

ADVERBS OF DOUBT *ADVERBIOS QUE SIRVEN PARA DUDAR*

perhaps **acaso, quizá, quizás, tal vez**

EXERCISE *EJERCICIO*

Answer in Spanish with complete sentences.

1. **¿Desde cuándo tiene esa condición?**
2. **¿Cuántas calorías tiene eso?**
3. **¿Dónde le duele?**
4. **¿Cuándo tomo la medicina?**
5. **¿Cómo la tomo?**

Comparison of Adverbs
El comparativo de los adverbios

This is the same as for adjectives (see above, pages 78–79) except that in the superlative case the definite article is omitted.

Positive	Comparative	Superlative
rápido fast	**más rápido** faster	**más rápido** fastest
despacio slow	**más despacio** slower	**más despacio** slowest

The comparison may be of a lesser degree rather than a greater degree. If this is so, the word **menos** replaces **más**. In the above examples the word **menos**, meaning *less*, could replace **más** giving the opposite idea.

There are four adverbs that are compared irregularly:

Positive	Comparative	Superlative
bien well	**mejor** better	**mejor** best
mal badly	**peor** worse	**peor** worst
mucho much	**más** more	**más** most
poco little	**menos** less	**menos** least

Absolute Superlative of Adverbs
El superlativo absoluto de los adverbios

The absolute superlative of adverbs is formed by adding the ending **-mente** to
the feminine form of the absolute superlative of the adjective.

> **Trabaja diligentísimamente.** He works most diligently.

The same idea can be expressed by using the adverb **muy** before the adjective;
however, the absolute form is more emphatic. **Muy** cannot be correctly used before
mucho or any of its variants. Therefore, to translate the expression *very much*,
muchísimo must be used.

EXERCISES *EJERCICIOS*

A. Complete the following using the appropriate forms of the adverb.

1. **¿Quién hace** _____ (less)? **¿El asistente o el camillero?**
2. **El auxiliar de enfermera trabaja** _____ (as much as) **los otros pero gana** _____ (less).
3. **Este cirujano opera** _____ (more carefully than) **aquél.**
4. **La paciente se vistió de nuevo** _____ (as fast as) **pudo.**
5. **La médica residente explicó procedimiento** _____ (less clearly) **de lo que esperábamos.**

B. Change the following sentences according to the model.

> **El examina tan cuidadosamente como yo.** (equality)
> **El examina más cuidadosamente que yo.**
> **El examina menos cuidadosamente que yo.**

1. **Vd. sufre tanto como los demás.**
2. **No diagnostico tan bien como tú.**
3. **No hay nadie que coma tan poco como ella.**
4. **No hay nadie que escriba tan mal como ese médico.**
5. **El paciente sube la escalera tan rápidamente como los demás.**

PREPOSITIONS
LAS PREPOSICIONES

A preposition is a word that shows the relation of the noun or pronoun following
it to some other word. Prepositions are invariable; very few Spanish prepositions
correspond exactly with English prepositions. Their use is one of the most difficult
things to master because prepositional usage is largely idiomatic. Observe and

learn, through repetition and practice, the prepositional usages that differ from English. The simple prepositions are:

a   at, by, for, in, to, upon
ante   before
bajo   under
con   with
contra   against
de   about, from, of, to
desde   from, since
durante   during
en   at, in, into, on
entre   among, between
excepto   except
hacia   toward
hasta   as far as, until, up to
mediante   by means of
menos   but, except
no obstante   notwithstanding
para   around, for, on, to
por   because of, by, for, in, through
salvo   except, save
según   according to
sin   without
sobre   about, on, over
tras   after, behind

There are many compound prepositions and prepositional phrases used in Spanish. Prepositions that require **a** include:

con respecto a   with respect to
conforme a   according to, in accordance with
contrario a   contrary to
en cuanto a   as for, in regard to
frente a   in front of
igual a   the same as
junto a   next to
respecto a   with respect to
tocante a   concerning, with reference to

Prepositions which require **de** include:

a causa de   because of, on account of
a excepción de   with exception of
a fuerza de   because of, by means of
a pesar de   in spite of
a través de   through
acerca de   about, concerning
además de   beside(s)
alrededor de   about, around
antes de   before
arriba de   above
cerca de   close to, near
debajo de   below, under, underneath
delante de   before, in front of
dentro de   inside of, within
después de   after
detrás de   behind
en contra de   against
en frente de   in front of
en lugar de   instead of
en vez de   in place of
encima de   above, on, on top of, over, upon
fuera de   outside of
lejos de   far from
más allá de   beyond

In Spanish the object of a preposition may be a noun (*al* **médico**   to the physician), a pronoun[30] (*de* **usted**   from you), a pronomial adverb (*para* **acá**   over here), an infinitive (*antes de* **inyectarse**   before injecting), an adjective (*en* **serio**   in earnest), or a clause that functions as a noun (**No comprendo** *de que* **me hablas.** I don't understand what you are talking about.).

The Preposition A   *La preposición A*

USES   *USOS*

1. **A** is used to introduce all indirect object nouns. (See page 51.)

   *A*l **doctor Peña le falta un termómetro.**   Dr. Peña needs a thermometer.

2. **A** is used to indicate a spacial relationship.

El laboratorio está *a* mano izquierda. The laboratory is on the left-hand side.

3. **A** is used in the phrase **al** + an infinitive. It translates as *on, upon,* or *when.*

***A*l sufrir un ataque cardíaco. . .** Upon having a heart attack. . .

4. **A** expresses the way or means of doing something.

***a* pie** on (by) foot
***a* máquina** machine-made
escrito *a* mano handwritten

5. **A** is used in expressions of time.

***A*l principio** At (ln) the beginning
***A* las 8** At 8:00

6. **A** is used before measurements of speed, percent, price, and so forth.

Las curitas se venden *a* 25¢ la docena. The bandages sell for 25¢ a dozen.
La fiebre del niño está *a* ciento dos grados. The child's fever is 102°.

7. **A** is used after verbs of motion (beginning, learning, teaching, etc.) when these verbs are followed by an infinitive.

El cirujano ya empieza *a* operar. The surgeon is beginning to operate now.

EXERCISE *EJERCICIO*

Say in Spanish.

1. Come at two o'clock.
2. Stop eating at midnight.
3. Turn (**torcer**) to the right.
4. He is teaching me to diagnose better.
5. The uniform is machine-made.
6. Come on the following day.

THE PERSONAL **A** *A PERSONAL*

The preposition **a**, untranslated, is always used:

1. When the direct object noun refers to a specific, particular person.

Vio *al* médico. She saw the doctor.

2. When the indefinite pronouns **alguien, alguno, nadie, ninguno, cualquiera,** or the demonstratives, interrogatives, possessives, or relative pronouns refer to people.

Llámeme *a* alguno de los internos.   Call me one of the interns.

Recuerdos *a* los tuyos.   Regards to your relatives.

3. When both the subject and direct object are things or animals to avoid ambiguity.

La recuperación sigue a la operación.
A la operación sigue la recuperación. } Recuperation follows the operation.

4. When an abstract noun or animal is personified.

Temo *a* la muerte.   I fear death.

5. With geographical nouns unless they are preceded by the definite article.

Desean visitar *a* Nueva York; no quieren ver el Canadá.   They want to visit New York; they do not want to see Canada.

6. The personal **a** may be omitted with **tener** when it means to have (possess).

Tiene una hija.   She has a daughter.

7. The personal **a** may be omitted if the direct object noun does not refer to a specified individual.

Vamos a buscar un médico con mucha experiencia.   We are going to look for a very experienced doctor. (unknown)

Vamos a buscar *a* un médico con mucha experiencia.   We are going to look for a very experienced doctor. (known)

EXERCISE   *EJERCICIO*

Use the personal **a** if necessary.

1. **Veo** _____ **mis hermanas.**   I see my sisters.
2. **Buscan** _____ **sus libros.**   They are looking for their books.
3. **Busco** _____ **mi médico.**   I am looking for my doctor.
4. **Tengo** _____ **varios amigos en México.**   I have several friends in Mexico.
5. **Enseña** _____ **muchos internos.**   He teaches many interns.
6. **Pregunto** _____ **enfermera de guardia.**   I question the nurse on duty.
7. **El contesta** _____ **médico de cargo.**   He answers the attending physician.
8. **Examina** _____ **los tubos de Falopio.**   He examines the fallopian tubes.
9. **Adoro** _____ **Chicago.**   I adore Chicago.
10. **Esto precede** _____ **pentotal de sodio.**   This precedes sodium pentothal.

The Preposition Con *La preposición CON*

USES *USOS*

1. **Con** is used with a noun to form an adverbial phrase.

   La paciente anda *con cuidado*. The patient walks carefully.

2. **Con** shows accompaniment.

   Tragó la píldora *con* agua. She swallowed the pill with water.

3. **Con** indicates the instrument or means.

   El cirujano congeló la córnea *con* aguja especial. The surgeon froze the cornea with a special needle.

4. **Con** is used with select verbs when an infinitive follows (see page 173).

   El médico cuenta *con* hacer el análisis. The doctor is counting on doing the test.

EXERCISE *EJERCICIO*

Say in Spanish.

1. The nurse arrives with the doctor.
2. You have the flu. (You are with flu.)
3. I am worried about the operation.
4. The orderly moved rapidly.
5. Her allergy comes with spring.

The Preposition DE *La preposición DE*

1. *The Possessive Case El caso posesivo.* The possessive case of nouns corresponding to the English 's or s', is expressed in Spanish by means of the preposition **de** placed before the possessor.

   la muestra del paciente the patient's specimen/the specimen of the patient
   el padre de las chicas the girls' father/the father of the girls

2. *Use of preposition **de** to replace adjectival nouns Uso especial de **de**.* In Spanish a noun cannot be used as an adjective to show the material of which an item is made, as in English. In Spanish it is necessary to construct a prepositional phrase joining the material to the object by means of the preposition **de**.

   la silla de ruedas the wheelchair (the chair of wheels)

3. In Spanish, **de** + an infinitive are used as an adjectival phrase. In English this concept is expressed by an infinitive directly following the noun or adjective it precedes. In Spanish **de** + the infinitive describe the function of a machine or other equipment. Only if the infinitive answers the unstated question "for what purpose?" does Spanish replace **de** with **para**.

Es difícil *de* **examinarla.**   It is difficult to examine her.

la hora *de* **acostar**   bedtime (time to go to bed)

una máquina de calcular   a calculator

but: **un bacín para vomitar**   an emesis basin

4. **De** is used to introduce a phrase that gives a specific, often inseparable, characteristic of an individual. In this instance it often is translated by *with* or *in*. (If the phrase is not considered inseparable, **con** is used.)

el paciente de los ojos hundidos   the patient with the sunken eyes

but: **el auxiliar con el periódico**   the aide with the newspaper

5. **De** is used to express content and origin.

un termómetro *de* **vidrio**   a glass thermometer

6. **De** is used to indicate the way something happens.

Mañana Vd. tiene que ponerse *de* **pie.**   Tomorrow you have to stand up.

7. **De** indicates cause.

Murió *de* **cáncer.**   He died of cancer.

8. **De** is used with specific time to indicate A.M. or P.M.

a las seis *de* **la mañana.**   at 6 A.M.

9. **De** is used in a superlative sentence to translate "in."

Es el mejor anestesiólogo del hospital.   He is the best anesthesiologist *in* the hospital.

10. **De** is used to express a partial amount (as a partitive).

un poco *de* **agua**   a little water

una docena *de* **curitas**   a dozen bandages

EXERCISE   *EJERCICIO*

Say in Spanish.

1. a glass of water
2. deaf in the left ear
3. The white gown is the doctor's.
4. nearsighted (**miope**) in both eyes.

5. It is very hard (**duro**) to suffer.
6. This test is the least difficult of all.

The Prepositions POR and PARA
Las preposiciones POR y PARA

These two prepositions have more than one meaning. Each has definite uses and cannot be interchanged with the other without changing the meaning of the sentence.

USES OF **POR**

1. To introduce the agent in the true passive voice.[31]

   Yo seré llevada allí *por* **el ayudante.**   I will be taken there *by* the orderly.

2. To express *for* meaning *in exchange for*.

   Me dio su espéculo *por* **mi fetoscopio.**   He gave me his speculum *for* my fetoscope.

3. To express approximate location or vague position.

   La terapia ocupacional está *por* **aquí.**   Occupational therapy is some place around here.

4. To express *per* in expressions of measure or rate.

   por **docenas**   *by* the dozen   *por* **hora**   *per* hour

5. To indicate *by* what means.

   Se me sacó la muela *por* **fuerza.**   My tooth was removed *by* force.

6. To express motion with the English prepositions *through, around, along, by*.

   Paseo *por* **el hospital.**   I walk *through* (*around*) the hospital.
   Pasé *por* **el consultorio.**   I went *by* the office.

7. To express the *reason for*.

   Jonas Salk es célebre *por* **su vacuna.**   Jonas Salk is famous *for* his vaccine.

8. To introduce certain periods of time.
   a. To express a period of time during which an action occurs.[32] It is often translated by *in*.

   Padecía de la fatiga *por* **muchos años.**   She suffered from asthma *for* many years.

   Estuvo en la unidad de cuidado intensivo *por* **una semana.**   He was in the ICU *for* a week.

b. To express approximate time.

Vuelva *por* junio.   Return *around* June.

9. To express *for* meaning *in favor of, on account of, for the sake of,* or *(on) in behalf of.*

Todo lo hace *por* sus hijos.   He does everything *for* his children.
Hay que observar *por* sí mismo.   It is necessary to watch *for* yourself.

10. To express *out of, because of, through.*

Se quejaron *por* miedo.   They complained *out of* fear.
No puedo hacerlo *por* la enfermedad.   I can't do it *because of* illness.

11. To express *for* meaning *in search of.* It is used in this way after the verbs **ir** (to go), **mandar, enviar** (to send), **llamar** (to call), **preguntar** (to ask), **venir** (to come), and **volver** (to return).

Fue *por* el médico.   He went *for* the doctor.
Envía por la medicina.   She sends for the medicine.

12. To express *to* meaning *with the desire to,* and after expressions of strong feeling.

Estudio medicina *por* complacer a Juan.   I'm studying medicine to please John.

13. To express what remains to be done when introducing an infinitive.

Operaciones *por* empezar. . .   Operations *yet* to begin. . .

14. In oaths, assertions and other expressions.

por Dios for heaven's sake	**por lo menos** at least	
por ejemplo for example	**por lo pronto** for the time being	
por favor please	**por supuesto** of course	

15. To indicate the opinion or estimation that is held. It is the equivalent of **como** (as).

Se le tenía *por* un gran médico.   He was considered a great physician.

16. Idiomatically with **estar** (to be in favor of), **quedar** (to remain to), **terminar** (to eventually. . .), **acabar** (to end up as/by), **pasar** (to be considered), and **interesarse** (to take an interest in).

Estoy *por* operar.   I *am in favor of* operating.
Quedaba poco *por* hacer.   There *was* little left to do.
Terminará *por* acostumbrarse.   You will *eventually* get used to it.
Ese viejo pasa *por* autoridad.   That old man *is considered* an authority.

USES OF **PARA**

1. To indicate purpose.[33]

   Este hospital es *para* ancianos.   This hospital is *for* old people.
   Estudia *para* aprender.   He studies (*in order*) *to* learn.

2. To express certain English compound nouns where the secondary noun expresses the purpose or use for which the first is intended.

   un remedio *para* fiebres   a fever remedy
   una escuela *para* médicos   a medical school

3. To express destination with place names.

   Salimos *para* Mayo Clinic.   We left *for* Mayo Clinic.

4. To indicate a definite point in the future. It specifies occasions and due dates.

   Fijaron la operación *para* el 3 de enero.   They set the operation *for* January 3.
   Tengo otro turno *para* el viernes por la mañana.   I have another appointment *for* Friday morning.
   Llegarán *para* la una.   They will be here *around* (*by*) one.

5. To indicate the recipient of an action or object.

   Tengo dos aspirinas *para* Vd.   I have two aspirins *for* you.

6. To express *for* meaning *considering* (*that*), *compared with, with respect to.*

   ***Para* un viejo, puede hacer todo.**   *For* an old man, he can do everything.

7. To express an objective or goal. **Para** also means **para ser.**

   No tiene las aptitudes necesarias *para* enfermera.   She does not have the aptitude required *to be* a nurse.
   Tome Vd. dos aspirinas *para* la fiebre.   Take two aspirins *for* the fever.

8. To express *in order to.*

   Le dio una inyección *para* calmarla.   He gave her a shot *to* calm her down.

9. Idiomatically with *estar* meaning *to be about to, to be on the verge of.*

   Estaban *para* operar cuando el paciente sufrió un ataque cardíaco.   They *were about to* operate when the patient suffered a heart attack.

EXERCISES *EJERCICIOS*

A. Complete the following sentences using either **por** or **para.**

   1. **Pagué diez dólares _____ el análisis de esputo.**
   2. **El delantal de plomo** (lead) **es _____ la paciente.**

3. Pase Vd. _____ la clínica _____ verme.
4. Necesito el análisis _____ pasado mañana.
5. Todo estará listo _____ el miércoles.
6. Voy _____ el médico.
7. Entran en el quirófano _____ la puerta principal.
8. Hay que tomar la medicina _____ aliviar el dolor.
9. _____ un cirujano nuevo, opera bien.
10. ¿Dónde está el bacín _____ vómitos?
11. El especialista pasará _____ el piso quirúrgico a eso de las nueve.
12. Me han dado cinco dólares _____ la medicina.
13. Vamos a terminarlo _____ diciembre.
14. Tome Vd. dos aspirinas _____ fiebre.
15. _____ estar enferma no puedo asistir.

B. Answer the following questions with complete Spanish sentences.

1. ¿Va a quedarse en el hospital por una semana o por dos?
2. ¿Está el cirujano por operar o por esperar?
3. ¿Prefiere Vd. trabajar por la noche, por la mañana, o por la tarde?
4. ¿Por qué pasillo está la sala de espera?
5. ¿Para qué hora va a terminar?

Prepositions Before Infinitives
Las preposiciones antes de infinitivos

In Spanish the only verb form that may follow a preposition is the infinitive, regardless of what is used in English.

> *Después de ponerle* **una inyección, voy a tomarle la temperatura.** *After giving* you a shot, I am going to take your temperature.

The subject of both the main verb and the infinitive will be the same whenever prepositions are used. If the subjects are different, a clause must be used, involving **que** and a "conjugated" verb in either the indicative or subjunctive.

> *Después de tomarle* **la temperatura, le puse una inyección.** *After taking* his temperature, I gave him a shot.

> *Después de que* **la enfermera le** *tomó* **la temperatura, le tomé el pulso.** *After* the nurse *took* his temperature, I took his pulse.

> **Me alegro** *de mejorarme.* I am glad to be better.

> **Me alegro** *de que Vd. se mejore.* I am glad that you are getting better.

Verbs Requiring Prepositions
Los verbos que requieren preposiciones

In Spanish many verbs require the use of a preposition when an infinitive or other dependent element follows, although no preposition may be needed in English.

VERBS REQUIRING a BEFORE AN INFINITIVE OR AN OBJECT

acercarse a   to approach

acertar a   to happen to (by chance)

acostumbrarse a   to become accustomed to

aficionarse a   to become fond of

ajustarse a   to adjust to

alcanzar a   to succeed in

aprender a   to learn (how to)

apresurarse a   to hasten/hurry to

asistir a   to attend (lecture, etc.)

asomarse a   to look out of (window, etc.)

aspirar a   to aspire to

atreverse a   to dare to

ayudar a   to help/aid to

bajar a   to come/go down to

comenzar a (ie)   to begin to

condenar a   to condemn to

convidar a   to invite to

dar a   to overlook

decidirse a   to decide to

dedicarse a   to devote oneself to

detenerse a   to pause to

dirigirse a   to address, go toward, speak to

disponerse a   to get ready to

echarse a   to begin to, to start

empezar a (ie)   to begin to

enseñar a   to teach to

invitar a   to invite to

ir a   to go to

jugar a (ue)   to play (sports, cards, etc.)

llegar a   to become, to come to, to arrive at, to reach

negarse a   to refuse to

obligar a   to compel to, to obligate, to oblige to
oler a (ue)   to smell like
parecerse a   to look like
ponerse a   to begin to
prepararse a   to prepare to
principiar a   to begin to
referirse a (ie)   to refer to
regresar a   to return to, to . . . again
resignarse a   to resign oneself to
resolverse a (ue)   to make up one's mind to
saber a   to taste of
salir a   to go out to
sonar a (ue)   to sound like
subir a   to go up to, to get into
venir a   to attain, to end up by
volver a (ue)   to return to, to . . . again

El fisioterapeuta le *enseñó a* **caminar.**   The physiotherapist taught her to walk.
Comenzó a **operar.**   He began to operate.

VERBS REQUIRING con BEFORE AN INFINITIVE OR AN OBJECT

acabar con   to finish off, to put an end to
amenazar con   to threaten to
casarse con   to marry
conformarse con   to put up with, to resign oneself to
contar con (ue)   to count on, to rely on
contentarse con   to be satisfied with
cumplir con   to fulfill
dar con   to meet
encontrarse con (ue)   to meet (by chance), to run into
entenderse con (ie)   to come to an understanding with
meterse con   to pick a quarrel with
preocuparse con   to be concerned with/about, to be preoccupied with
relacionarse con   to be related to
soñar con (ue)   to dream of/about
tropezar con (ie)   to collide, to come upon, to meet, to run into, to strike
  against

Pablo *sueña con* **hacerse médico.**   Pablo dreams of becoming a doctor.
Me contento con **los resultados de la prueba.**   I'm satisfied with the test results.

VERBS REQUIRING **de** BEFORE AN INFINITIVE OR AN OBJECT

abstenerse de   to refrain from

abusar de   to abuse, to overindulge in

acabar de + inf.   to have just + past participle

acordarse de (ue)   to remember to

alegrarse de   to be glad to, to be happy about

apartarse de   to move away from

apoderarse de   to take possession of

aprovecharse de   to take advantage of

burlarse de   to make fun of

cambiar de (ropa)   to change (clothing)

cansarse de   to become tired of

carecer de   to lack

cesar de   to stop

compadecerse de   to feel sorry for, to pity

constar de   to consist of

cuidar de   to care for, to take care of

deber de   must, ought to (indicates probability)

dejar de   to fail, to leave off, to stop

depender de   to depend on

deshacerse de   to get rid of

despedirse de (i)   to say goodbye to, to take leave of

disfrutar de   to enjoy

enamorarse de   to fall in love with

encargarse de   to take charge of

enterarse de   to find out about

fiarse de   to trust

gozar de   to enjoy

haber de   to be supposed to, to be to

ocuparse de   to attend to (a job, etc.)

olvidarse de   to forget (to)

partir de   to leave

pensar de (ie)   to think of, have an opinion of

preocuparse de   to worry about

quejarse de   to complain about

reírse de (i)   to laugh at

salir de   to leave

servir de (i)   to serve as, to be used as

tratar de   to try to, to deal with, to treat of

tratarse de   to be a question of

La mujer *se queja de* **un dolor constante.**   The woman complains of a constant pain.

Por fin la herida *cesó de* **sangrar.**   Finally the wound stopped bleeding.

VERBS REQUIRING en BEFORE AN INFINITIVE OR AN OBJECT

complacerse en   to be pleased to, to delight in

confiar en   to be confident about, to rely on, to trust in

consentir en (ie)   to agree to, to consent to

consistir en   to consist of

convenir en (ie)   to agree to

empeñarse en   to insist on

entrar en   to enter

esforzarse en (ue)   to strive, to try hard to (verb may also use **por**)

fijarse en   to notice

insistir en   to insist on

meterse en   to get into, to plunge into

pensar en (ie)   to think about, consider

quedar en   to agree on

reparar en   to pay attention to

tardar en   to be late in, to delay in, to take long to

Vd. tiene que *confiar en* **el cirujano.**   You have to trust in the surgeon.

No tarde en visitarme.   Don't delay in visiting me.

VERBS FOLLOWED DIRECTLY BY AN INFINITIVE OR AN OBJECT

agradecer   to thank for

aprovechar   to take advantage of

bastar   to be enough, to be sufficient

buscar   to look for

conseguir (i)   to succeed in

convenir (ie)   to be advisable, to be fitting

deber   must, ought to

decidir   to decide

dejar   to allow, to let, to permit

desear   to desire, to want, to wish

escuchar   to listen to

esperar   to expect, to hope for, to wait (for)

faltar   to be lacking

gustar   to be pleasing to, to "like"

hacer   to make, to do, to have (something done)

impedir (i)   to prevent

importar   to be important, to matter

interesar   to interest

lograr   to succeed in

mandar   to command, to have, to order

merecer   to deserve, to merit

mirar   to look at, to watch

necesitar   to need

oír   to hear

olvidar   to forget

parecer   to appear, to seem

pensar (ie)   to intend to, to plan

permitir   to allow, to let, to permit

poder (ue)   to be able (to), can

preferir (ie)   to prefer

pretender   to attempt

prometer   to promise

querer (ie)   to want, to wish

resolver (ue)   to resolve

saber   to know how (to), can

sentir (ie)   to be sorry, to regret

soler (ue)   to be accustomed to

temer   to fear

ver   to see

¿*Suele* estar estreñido?   Are you usually constipated?

No me *dejan* salir de la cama.   They don't let me out of bed.

EXERCISE   *EJERCICIO*

Fill in the correct preposition, if necessary. Indicate if not needed.

1. **Asisto _____ una conferencia que trata _____ la medicina legal.**
    (I am attending a lecture that deals with forensic medicine.)

2. **La enfermera siempre sueña** _____ **casarse** _____ **un médico joven.**
   (The nurse always dreams of marrying a young physician.)

3. **¿Necesita Vd. una píldora para hacerle** _____ **dormir?**
   (Do you need a pill to make you sleep?)

4. **No me encargaré** _____ **firmar el descargo.**
   (I will not take charge of signing the release.)

5. **El doctor no tardará** _____ **venir.**
   (The doctor will not be long in coming.)

CONJUNCTIONS
LAS CONJUNCIONES

A conjunction is a word that links a word or group of words to another word or group of words. There are three classes: coordinate, subordinate, and correlative.

Coordinate Conjunctions
Las conjunciones coordinantes

A coordinate conjunction is one that joins two or more words, phrases, or classes of equal grammatical rank. Coordinate conjunctions include:

and	**y**	but	**pero, mas,**[34] **sino**
nor	**ni**[35]	or	**o**[35]

NOTE: Before words beginning with **i** or **hi**, the conjunction **y** changes to **e** in order to prevent synalepha (the blending into one syllable of the vowels of two adjacent syllables). No change occurs before **hie** or **y**.

labia and hymen **labios *e* himen** *but* bandages and ice **curitas *y* hielo**
cardiologist and internist **cardiólogo *e* internista**
but mercurochrome and iodine **mercurocromo *y* yodo**

NOTE: Before words beginning with **o** or **ho**, the conjunction **o** becomes **u** in order to prevent synalepha.

clinic or hospital **clínica *u* hospital** *but* hospital or clinic **hospital *o* clínica**
pounds or ounces **libras *u* onzas** *but* ounces or pounds **onzas *o* libras**

The conjunctions **pero** and **sino** are synonyms. Their use, however, is not interchangeable. **Sino** introduces an affirmative contradictory phrase when the first part of the sentence is negative. **Sino que** introduces a contradictory affirmative clause that follows a negative beginning. In all other cases **pero** is used. An example of two complete and noncontradictory ideas follows:

It is a dull pain *but* it is very strong at night. **Es un dolor sordo *pero* aumenta durante la noche.**

The following is an example in which the second part contradicts or corrects the first part of the sentence:

My head doesn't hurt me, *but* (*rather*) my stomach does. **No me duele la cabeza, *sino* el estómago.**

Pero is used in the following example because the first part of the sentence is not negative:

It hurts me where you are pressing, *but* not anywhere else. **Me duele donde Vd. aprieta, *pero* no me duele en otros lugares.**

Sino que is required below because a clause follows:

It doesn't hurt me elsewhere, *but* it does hurt me where you are pressing. **No me duele en otros lugares, *sino que* me duele donde Vd. aprieta.**

EXERCISES *EJERCICIOS*

A. Supply the correct form of *or*.

1. **bebiendo** _____ **orinando**
2. **ocho** _____ **nueve**
3. **centro médico** _____ **hospital**
4. **hombres** _____ **mujeres**

B. Supply the correct form of *and*.

1. **dieta** _____ **ejercicios**
2. **curitas** _____ **yodo**
3. **píldoras rojas** _____ **azules**
4. **grave** _____ **incurable**
5. **medicinas útiles** _____ **importantes**

C. Supply the correct form of *but*.

1. **Tiene fiebre,** _____ **estará bien mañana.**
2. **Juanito no quiere hacerse abogado** _____ **médico.**
3. **Fuimos a la clínica** _____ **nadie estuvo allí.**
4. **La enfermera habla español** _____ **sabe hablar portugués.**
5. **El quirófano no es grande** _____ **es limpio.**

Subordinate Conjunctions
Las conjunciones subordinantes

A subordinate conjunction subordinates a clause to a sentence. The subordinate clause, introduced by the conjunction, contains a subject and verb, but is dependent on the main clause. Common Spanish subordinate conjunctions include:

after   **después de que**

although   **aunque**

as, since   **como**

as if   **como si**

as soon as   **así que, en cuanto, luego que, tan pronto como**

because   **porque, que**

before   **antes de que**

if, whether   **si**

in case   **en caso de que**

in order that   **a fin de que, para que**

now that   **ahora que, ya que**

provided that   **con tal que**

since   **como, desde que, puesto que, ya que**

so that   **así que, de modo que**

that   **que**

until   **hasta que**

when   **cuando**

where   **donde**

whether   **si**

while   **mientras que**

without   **sin que**

Many Spanish prepositions are formed from the adverb by adding **de**. Adding **que** and retaining (or omitting) the **de** turns the prepositional form into a conjunction. Frequently English uses the same word in three different capacities—adverb, preposition, and conjunction. Spanish requires distinct forms.

We left *afterward*. (adverb)   **Salimos** *después*.

The specialist left after the nurse. (preposition)   **El especialista salió** *después de* **la enfermera.**

The specialist left after the physiotherapist took him to the parallel bars.   **El especialista salió** *después de que* **el fisioterapista le llevó a las barras paralelas.**

The specialist left *after* examining him.   **El especialista salió** *después de* **examinarle.**

The subjunctive mood is used after many of these subordinate conjunctions, especially those expressions of supposition, purpose, result, provision, or concession. The subjunctive is also used after conjunctive expressions when the future is either expressed or implied. (See pages 154–155.)

Correlative Conjunctions
Las conjunciones correlativas

Correlative conjunctions are pairs of conjunctions used in a sentence with words intervening. Examples include:

as well as **así como**

both **tanto** (invariable) . . . **como**

either . . . or **o . . . o**

neither . . . nor **ni . . . ni**

now . . . now **ya . . . ya**

scarcely . . . when **apenas . . . cuando**

whether . . . or not **sea . . . o sea**

The verb will be plural when singular nouns (or pronouns), linked by **ni** or **o**, precede the verb. It may be singular when the subject follows the verb.

Neither the doctor nor the nurse knows him.

Ni el médico ni la enfermera le conocen.
No le conoce ni el médico ni la enfermera.

EXERCISE *EJERCICIO*

Say in Spanish.

1. Either we operate or you die.
2. Both the nurse and the intern fainted.
3. He scarcely got better (**mejorarse**) when she broke her arm.
4. The pills as well as the syrup were in the kitchen.
5. Neither the anesthesiologist nor the cardiologist arrived on time.

Notes *Notas*

1. This is also true for **ninguno** and **alguno** when referring to direct objects that are persons. For use of the **personal a**, see pages 164–165.
2. In this book **usted** is abbreviated as **Vd**.
3. See **Verbs**, page 84. Many beginning students of Spanish, however, find it easier at first to include all subject pronouns. Naturally there is no prohibition against such usage.
4. This book uses only **los** for the masculine plural direct object pronoun, but uses both **le** and **lo** as direct object pronouns referring to a man.
5. See page 20.

6. **Prestado** agrees with the item borrowed in number and gender.

7. A common noun that is the subject of a sentence is usually preceded by its corresponding article.

8. See **Passive Voice Construction**, pages 128–132.

9. See **Reflexive Verbs**, pages 110–115.

10. See **Position of Object Pronouns**, page 49.

11. See **Demonstrative Adjectives**, page 76.

12. **Grande** and **pequeño** also compare regularly, in which case they retain the meanings of *larger* and *smaller*. Old (**viejo**) and young (**joven**) can also be compared regularly, but these are generally for animals and things.

13. As previously noted (see above p. 47), in all of Latin America and many parts of Spain the second person plural is replaced by the third person plural. Hence, this book does not show those verb forms.

14. See **Reflexive Pronouns**, page 59. When a reflexive verb is used in the infinitive form, the reflexive pronoun must agree with the subject of the sentence:.

> **Quiero bañarme.** *I want to take a bath.*

15. Note the similarity between these endings and the conjugated present tense forms of **haber**: **he, has, ha, hemos, —, han.**

16. The present participle of the verb **ir** is **yendo.**

17. The preterite perfect is not used in conversation and is infrequently used in contemporary literature.

18. See **Nominalization of Descriptive Adjectives**, page 73.

19. See **Personal A**, pages 164–165.

20. To become angry   **enfadarse/enojarse**
    To become embittered   **amargarse**
    To become glad   **alegrarse**
    To become impatient   **impacientarse**
    To become insane, to go mad   **enloquecerse**
    To become sad   **entristecerse**
    To become sick   **enfermarse**
    To become surprised   **asombrarse**
    To become tired   **cansarse**
    To become worried   **afligirse**

21. A predicate noun is one used in the predicate of the sentence as the complement of a linking verb: *Mary became a nurse.* A predicate adjective is an adjective used in the same way: *Mary became ill.*

22. It is common to teach that the "opposite" vowels are added. Note that the first and third person singular use the same endings; hence, it is advisable to use subject pronouns in the dependent clause to avoid confusion.

23. See page 20.

24. An alternative to this consists of **vamos a** + infinitive: **Vamos a operar.** Let's operate.

25. When **de modo que** and **de manera que** introduce clauses in which the desired result occurred, these dependent clauses are always in the indicative.

> **Se sentía mejor de manera que no tomó las aspirinas.**   She felt better so she didn't take the aspirins.

26. **Ya** translates as *already* or *now* in an affirmative sentence; in negative ones, as *no longer*:

> **¿Ya toma Vd. la medicina?**   Are you taking the medicine *now*?
> **Ya no la tomo.**   I am *no longer* taking it.

27. **Aún** in an affirmative sentence is equivalent to *still*; it translates as *yet* in negative ones:

> **Aún está en el quirófano.**   She is *still* in the OR.
> **Aún no ha llegado el terapeuta.**   The therapist hasn't arrived *yet*.

28. In Spanish **sí** may be used as the equivalent of an emphatic *do, by all means*, or any lexical word:

> **Eso sí que es.**   *By all means.*
> **Sí que es demasiado gordo.**   He is *indeed* too fat.
> **El no tuvo fiebre, pero yo sí.**   He didn't have a fever, but I *did*.

29. See **Negation**, pages 32–37.
30. See **Prepositional Pronouns**, pages 61–62.
31. See **Passive Voice**, page 128.
32. *For* in time expressions is more commonly expressed by **hace**, etc. (see page 137).
33. With verbs of motion **a** often replaces **para**.
34. **Mas** is a literary form that sometimes replaces **pero**. It bears no accent.
35. For a full discussion on the use of **ni** and **o**, see **Negation**, page 35.

CHAPTER

Common Expressions

Expresiones corrientes

Hispanos trace their origins to Mexico, Puerto Rico, Cuba, the Caribbean, Central and South America, and other Spanish cultures. Hispanos are Latinos, but Latinos need not be Hispanos. (Latinos have their origin in countries where the languages derive from Latin.[1]) Hispanos were the second largest ethnic minority in the United States in 1980 accounting for over 6% of the total United States population (14.6 million). An additional estimated 7 million **indocumentados** (aliens without proper documents) are said to reside in the United States illegally.

Most ethnomedical research on the Hispanic population in the United States has focused on Mexican-Americans (Chicanos), with more limited attention directed toward Puerto Ricans and Cubans. In part this may be because Chicanos comprise the largest group of Hispanos in this country. This focus may also be attributed to the great numbers of post–1965 immigrants from Mexico, Puerto Rico, and Cuba, who dwell in major urban areas where medical anthropologists and others have easy access to them. Those Hispanos who trace their origin to Central and South America, and who now constitute about 20% of the persons of Hispanic heritage in the United States, have been studied to a lesser extent.

Most researchers note that there is no single theory of disease common to all Hispanos, yet certain cultural attitudes about health and illness are peculiar to many of them. Education and acculturation have produced some change in the medical beliefs held by many Spanish-speaking and Hispanic-American individuals. However, modern ideas taught in school rarely are enough to dispel contrary parental teachings. For the health-care professional, therefore, knowledge of existing beliefs and practices in medicine is of utmost importance; nonetheless, "an unsystematic collection of scraps of information may lead to an exaggerated respect for taboos and an underestimation of the importance of features of the society which may throw a medical program out of gear."[2]

Researchers who have studied the principal features of folk medicine in Latin American countries and among Hispanos in the United States point to the eclectic nature of Latin American folk medicine. Hispanos are influenced by a combination of Spanish medicine based on ancient and medieval concepts, spiritualism, indigenous beliefs, patent remedies, homeopathic therapy, and the professional biomedical traditions. Even the most sophisticated Hispano sometimes relies on **curanderismo**, or folk medicine, although he may be unwilling to admit it to others. While not all Spanish-speakers and Hispanic-Americans subscribe to these beliefs at all times, faith in folk medicine seems to be strongest among members of the lower class. The middle classes generally accept Anglo medical ways. For many, folk beliefs and practices provide a culturally acceptable explanation for the unusual happenings within and around the patient.[3]

Research has been conducted on the Hispanic concept of mental health, which embodies the balance of body, mind, and spirit. This research centers on the Chicano and his use of psychiatric treatment agencies in Texas and California.[4] Originally studies in those states showed that Chicanos *appeared* to have a lower prevalence of major mental disorders.[5] Among the possible interpretations for this was Madsen's suggestion that the Mexican-American family provided a mechanism for anxiety-sharing and anxiety-reduction. He also noted that the family often turned to **curanderos**[6] to reduce stress. Finally, he concluded that Chicanos do not worry about the possibility of mental illness to the extent that Anglos do.[7] Karno, Edgerton, and their colleagues studied Chicanos in East Los Angeles and found that they did not perceive nor define mental illness in markedly different ways than Anglos did.[8] There was little to suggest that the underrepresentation of Chicanos in psychiatric treatment facilities was due to the practice of folk psychiatry, because their data showed a decreased reliance on folk curers.[9] Edgerton and Karno found that respondents born in Mexico who used Spanish as their primary language believed that the recovery of mentally ill people *within* the family was desirable, while respondents born in the United States who were interviewed in English agreed with the Anglos that a mentally ill person would *not* best recover from his illness by staying with his family.[10] This knowledge is important for health-care professionals who should be concerned with both the traditional qualities of Hispanic culture as well as its changing aspects.

It is important for the Anglo health-care practitioner to be able to make small talk before proceeding with the physical examination. The typical health worker fails to establish the close affective relationship with Hispanic-American patients, which is so characteristic of the **curandero**-client relationships. The most obvious explanation is the language barrier. A second reason has to do with the "clinical attitude" of most American physicians. Hispanos expect medicine to be practiced within the familiar context of their beliefs. They are more likely than Anglos to need and prefer a personal element at hospitals and clinics. To the Hispano, the openness, frankness, directness, and simplicity so highly valued by Anglos may seem blunt, rude, and disrespectful. Hispanos value politeness and courtesy, and observe many social amenities. Coffee and conversation come first. The illness is mentioned only after a suitable interval of time has passed. Hispanos want and expect the medical practitioner to be sympathetic toward them, caring about what happens to the sick individual. They feel that illness is always a matter of family concern. The **curandero** is never too busy to sit down and discuss the problem with the patient and his family, and listen to their concepts of illness. Those professionals who visit the home, such as visiting nurses and case workers, must make a concerted effort to remember this.

Hispanic-Americans are highly sensitive to the authoritarian attitude that health-care personnel often assume. They do not accept the superiority of the physician over other people. In their culture it is the father and the family group who have the authority, not the doctor. Hispanos generally regard such "non-medical" aspects of life as jobs, use of leisure time, and child rearing, to be beyond the scope of the doctor.

Hispanos generally value tact and diplomacy. When misunderstanding occurs between the health-care worker and the patient, many Spanish-speaking people will not voluntarily call attention to the misunderstanding. They are likely to answer leading questions in a way they think the health-care worker would like them answered. They are also likely to appear to agree to what is being asked of them even when they disagree, and to state that they fully understand even when they do not.[11] Health-care workers must communicate with these patients slowly and in simple terms, avoiding vague concepts and technical words that are meaningless to lay people in either English or Spanish.

Health-care practitioners must not ridicule the Spanish-speaking patients' self-diagnosis.[12] It is common for Hispanos to define disease by symptoms. Anglo practitioners should attempt to treat symptoms, as well as investigate causes of diseases, if possible. Nothing is gained by ridiculing these beliefs, and conflicts between traditional folk practices and scientific modern medical practices can lead to the rejection of American health care. In fact, harmless folk remedies should be allowed or overlooked. For example, the patient who eats a daily garlic clove to reduce hypertension is in no danger, provided that he follows the measures prescribed by his treating physician. This may even increase his trust in Anglo medicine. Or, for another example, the physician treating an Hispano for a fever should not neglect the patient's concern about inadequate defecation. Knowing that fever often dehydrates feces, making stool hard and perhaps difficult to expel, the health practitioner should attempt to "treat" this problem as well. If the latter notes only the fever and concentrates on finding its cause, the patient might seek treatment of **empacho** (an indigestion problem).[13] Studies have shown that Hispanos living in the United States consult **curanderos** more commonly if their experience with Anglo medicine is unsatisfactory.[14] Many illnesses are treated with herbal remedies. An example of useful knowledge of both cultures is shown by George M. Foster[15]: A doctor who was treating a baby for diarrhea and dehydration prescribed a weak tea made with an herb with which the mother was familiar. Had he merely prescribed boiled water, the mother might not have cooperated. However, the treatment seemed sensible to the woman. In prescribing a remedy that the mother knew was "good," the doctor strengthened the relationship between himself and the family.

The Spanish-speaking do not recognize illness in the absence of symptoms. There is thus some problem accepting the Anglo germ theory of disease. If these germs or **animalitos** cannot be seen, they cannot exist.[16] Hispanos will not return for further medical care if the doctor does "nothing" for them at the visit. They feel deceived when they are told that "everything is fine, come back in two weeks."

One difficult problem is any discussion of body functions. The early teachings that "genitals are dirty" and the "hands off" attitude possibly account for the general lack of interest in pelvic anatomy and physiology. Hispanic women prefer a woman physician to do a genital exam. Many of these problems can be minimized if materials are disseminated in conversations involving only the patient and a single medical practitioner, preferably of the same sex.

To the Anglo, illness is an impersonal event caused by nonemotional, natural agents, such as germs. To the Hispano, however, illness is very personal and emotional. Illness relates to an individual's life, his community, his interpersonal relationships, and above all, to his God. Under these conditions illness is both a social and a biological fact.

Finally, there are cultural differences toward time.[17] In English the *clock runs* while in Spanish **el reloj anda** (the clock walks). Routine medical appointments do not have the same importance for the Spanish-speaking patient. Distant appointments should not be scheduled if possible. Also, when prescribing medication for the Spanish-speaking, it is better to associate the medicine with specific times such as at mealtime or before going to bed, rather than at arbitrary intervals of every four hours. The clock is not as important in Hispanic homes.

GREETINGS
SALUDOS

1. Good morning (good day).
   Buenos días.

2. And to you.
   Muy buenos.

3. Good afternoon (used from noon until evening).
   Buenas tardes.

4. Good afternoon (response).
   Muy buenas.

5. Good evening.
   Buenas noches.

6. Good evening (response).
   Muy buenas.

INTRODUCTION
PRESENTACION

1. Hello (hi).
   Hola.

2. Let me introduce myself.
   Déjeme presentarme.
   Permita usted que me presente.

3. Let me introduce you to _____.
   Déjeme presentarle a _____.

4. My name is _____.
   Me llamo _____, para servirle (-la).

5. I am _____.
   Soy _____, para servirle (-la).

6. What is your name?
   ¿Cómo se llama usted?

7. I am glad to meet you.
   Me alegro de conocerle (-la).

8. I am glad to see you.
   Me alegro de verle (-la).

9. It's been a real pleasure.
   Tanto gusto.
   He tenido un verdadero gusto.

10. I am pleased to meet you.
    Estoy encantado (-a) de conocerle (-la).

11. The pleasure is mine.
    El gusto es mío.

COMMUNICATION
COMMUNICACION

1. Do you speak English?·
   ¿Habla usted inglés?

2. Do you speak Spanish?
   ¿Habla usted español?

3. Do you understand English?
   ¿Comprende usted (el) inglés?

4. Do you understand Spanish?
   ¿Comprende usted (el) español?

5. Repeat, please.
   Repita, por favor.

6. Please speak more slowly.
   Hable usted más despacio, por favor.
   Favor de hablar más despacio.

7. I do not understand Spanish very well.
   No comprendo el español muy bien.

8. Please answer my questions slowly, showing me, nodding your head for "yes," or shaking it for "no."

Por favor, conteste Vd. a mis preguntas despacio, señalándome, moviendo la cabeza para arriba y para abajo cuando quiere decir "sí," o moviéndola de un lado a otro cuando quiere decir "no."

9. Am I speaking clearly?
   ¿Hablo claramente?

10. Answer as briefly as possible, please.
    Conteste Vd. lo más breve posible, por favor.

11. Answer in a different way, please.
    Conteste de otra manera, por favor.

12. Be calm, please.
    Cálmese Vd., por favor.

13. Don't be frightened.
    No se asuste Vd.
    No tenga Vd. miedo.

14. Don't talk so fast.
    No hable Vd. tan de prisa.

15. Tell me, please.
    Dígame, por favor.
    Favor de decirme.

16. What's the matter?
    ¿Qué pasa?

17. Do you need something?
    ¿Necesita usted algo?

18. Do you want something?
    ¿Desea usted algo?

19. How can I help you?
    ¿En qué puedo servirle (-la)?

20. How do you say _____?
    ¿Cómo se dice _____?

21. You say _____.
    Se dice _____.

22. What does _____ mean?
    ¿Qué quiere decir _____?
    ¿Qué significa _____?

23. It means _____.
    Quiere decir _____.
    Significa _____.

24. How do you spell it?
    ¿Cómo se deletrea?
    ¿Cómo se escribe?

25. Write it here, please.
    Escríbalo aquí, por favor.

26. Please speak louder.
    Hable usted en voz más alta, por favor.
    Favor de hablar en voz más alta.

CONVERSATION FOR MORNING ROUNDS

CONVERSACION PARA VISITAS DE RUTINA

1. How are you?
   ¿Cómo está usted?

2. How do you feel today?
   ¿Cómo se siente hoy?

3. How are things?
   ¿Cómo le va?

4. How goes it?
   ¿Qué tal?

5. Fine, thank you.
   Bien, gracias.

6. Very well, thanks.
   Muy bien, gracias.

7. Marvelous, thanks.
   Maravilloso (-a), gracias.

8. So, so. (Fair.)
   Así, así.
   Regular.
   Pasándolo.
   Pasándola. (Mex.)
   Así no más. (Sp. Am.)

9. Better than yesterday.
   Mejor que ayer.

10. And (how are) you?
    ¿Y usted?

11. I am slightly ill.
    Estoy un poco enfermo (-a).
    Estoy un poco malo (-a).

12. I feel blue.
    Tengo murria.

13. I feel okay.
    Me siento bien.

14. I feel bad.
    Me siento mal.

15. I feel better.
    Me siento mejor.

16. I feel worse.
    Me siento peor.

17. Please sit up.
    Haga Vd. el favor de sentarse recto.

18. Breathe slowly.
    Respire Vd. despacio.

19. Cough please.
    Tosa Vd., por favor.

20. Please be quiet for a moment.
    Haga Vd. el favor de callarse un momento.

21. Please lie down.
    Haga Vd. el favor de acostarse.

22. You cannot eat yet.
    Vd. no puede comer todavía.

23. You have to eat.
    Vd. tiene que comer.

24. You cannot drink yet.
    Vd. no puede beber todavía.

25. You have to drink.
    Vd. tiene que beber.

26. You have to stay in bed.
    Vd. tiene que quedarse en la cama.

27. You may walk around today.
    Vd. puede caminar hoy.

28. You are doing very well.
    Vd. va muy bien.

COURTESY

CORTESIA

1. Please.
   Por favor.

2. Excuse me. (I must leave. I'd like to pass, etc.)
   Con permiso.

3. Pardon (me). (for interrupting, but . . .)
   Perdón.
   Perdóneme usted.
   Dispense usted.

4. You are welcome.
   De nada.

5. Don't mention it.
   No hay de que.

6. Gladly. (I'd be glad to.)
   Con mucho gusto.

7. My deepest sympathy.
   Mi sentido pésame.

8. I am sorry.
   Lo siento.

FAREWELLS

DESPEDIDAS

1. I will talk with you later.
   Le hablaré más tarde.

2. I will explain it to your family when they come.
   Se lo explicaré a su familia cuando venga.

3. Good-bye.
   Adiós.
   ¡Que le vaya bien!

4. Well, good-bye.
   Pues, adiós.

5. So long. (See you later.)
   Hasta luego.
   Hasta lueguito. (Chile, Arg.)

6. Till we meet again.
   Hasta la vista.

7. Until tomorrow.
   Hasta mañana.

8. I'll see you.
   Nos veremos.
   Nos vemos. (Mex.)

9. Until next time.
   Hasta la próxima vez.

10. Come again.
    Vuelva otra vez.

11. Regards to the family.
    Recuerdos a la familia.

EXERCISES *EJERCICIOS*

A. Practice the above greetings and farewells with others in your class, making up your own variations.

B. The following is a conversation between a nurse and a patient in the hospital. Take the part of the nurse, filling in her comments and reactions. Use the new vocabulary that you have just learned.

NURSE: Good morning, I am Mary, your nurse.

ENFERMERA : _____ _____

PATIENT: Good morning. I am Mrs. García.

PACIENTE : **Muy buenos. Me llamo señora García.**

NURSE: I am glad to meet you.

ENFERMERA : _____ _____

PATIENT: The pleasure is mine.

PACIENTE : **El gusto es mío.**

NURSE: How do you feel today?

ENFERMERA : _____ _____

PATIENT: Better than yesterday, but I still am slightly ill.

PACIENTE : **Mejor que ayer, pero todavía un poco enferma.**

NURSE: What is the matter?

ENFERMERA : _____ _____

PATIENT: I have the chills.

PACIENTE : **Tengo escalofríos.**

NURSE: Do you need something?

ENFERMERA : _____ _____

PATIENT: I would like another blanket.

NURSE: Gladly.

PACIENTE: **Me gustaría otra manta.**

ENFERMERA: _____

PATIENT: Pardon me.

NURSE: Yes?

PACIENTE: **Perdóneme Vd.**

ENFERMERA: _____

PATIENT: Do you understand Spanish?

NURSE: A little.

PACIENTE: **¿Comprende Vd. el español?**

ENFERMERA: _____

PATIENT: My family is coming this afternoon and they do not understand English.

NURSE: I will be pleased to meet them. So long.

PATIENT: Well, good bye.

PACIENTE: **Mi familia vendrá esta tarde y ellos no comprenden el inglés.**

ENFERMERA: _____

PACIENTE: **Pues, adiós.**

Notes *Notas*

1. *Diccionario de la Lengua Española*, Real Academia Española, XIX ed., Madrid: Espasa-Calpe, S. A., 1970, p. 713.

2. Raymond Firth, "Acculturation in Relation to Concepts of Health and Disease," in *Medicine and Anthropology*, XXI, New York: Books of Libraries Press, 1971, pp. 153–154.

3. William Holland, "Mexican-American Medical Beliefs: Science or Magic?" in *Hispanic Culture and Health Care: Fact, Fiction, Folklore*, St. Louis: C. V. Mosby, 1978, pp. 99–119; C. Martínez and H. Martín, "Folk Diseases Among Urban Mexican-Americans," *JAMA*, Vol. 196, No. 2 (April 11, 1966), pp. 161–164.

4. E. G. Jaco, "Mental Health of the Spanish-American in Texas," in *Culture and Mental Health*, New York: Macmillan, 1959, pp. 467–485; W. Madsen, "Mexican-Americans and Anglo-Americans: A Comparative Study of Mental Health in Texas," in *Changing Perspectives in Mental Illness*, New York: Holt, Rinehart, 1969, pp. 217–240; M. Karno and R. Edgerton, "Perception of Mental Illness in a Mexican-American Community," *Archives of General Psychiatry*, Vol. 20 (1969), pp. 233–238.

5. Karno and Edgerton, "Perception of Mental Illness."

6. The **curandero(-a)** is a person who has a more extensive knowledge of herbs and household remedies than other individuals in the community, and to whom people turn for problems concerning "internal medicine." These individuals are lay practitioners who have no formal training in medicine or allied health fields. See O. I. Romano V., "Charismatic Medicine, Folk-Healing, and Folk-Sainthood," *American Anthropologist*, Vol. 67 (1965), pp. 1151–1173.

7. Madsen, "Mexican-Americans and Anglo-Americans," pp. 238–240.

8. Karno and Edgerton, "Perception of Mental Illness," pp. 236–237.

9. R. Edgerton, M. Karno, and I. Fernández, "Curanderismo in the Metropolis," *Archives of General Psychiatry*, Vol. 24 (1970), pp. 124–134.

10. R. Edgerton and M. Karno, "Mexican-American Bilingualism and the Perception of Mental Illness," *Archives of General Psychiatry*, Vol. 24 (1971), pp. 286–290.

11. See Margaret Clark, *Health in the Mexican-American Culture*, 2nd ed., Berkeley: University of California Press, 1970, pp. 162–217; and Pedro Poma, "Hispanos: Impact of Culture on Health Care," *Illinois Medical Journal*, Vol. 156, No. 6 (Dec. 1979), pp. 451–458.

12. See note 3, page 386 and note 7, pages 387–390.

13. See page 387.

14. See P. Poma, "Hispanos," p. 455; J. Kreisman, "The Curandero's Apprentice: A Therapeutic Integration of Folk and Medical Healing," *American Journal of Psychiatry*, Vol. 132, No. 1 (Jan. 1975), pp. 81–83.

15. George M. Foster, "Relationships Between Theoretical and Applied Anthropology: A Public Health Program Analysis," *Human Organization*, Vol. II (Fall 1952), 5–16.

16. See William Madsen, "Health and Illness," in J. Burma, ed., *Mexican-Americans in the United States: A Reader*, Cambridge: Schenkman Publishing Co., 1970, pp. 333f.

17. See Margaret Mead, ed., *Cultural Patterns and Technical Change*, Paris: United Nations Educational, Scientific, and Cultural Organization, 1953, pp. 179–180.

CHAPTER **4**

Numerical Expressions

Expresiones numéricas

NUMBERS

NUMEROS

Cardinals *Cardinales*

1	uno, un, una
2	dos
3	tres
4	cuatro
5	cinco
6	seis
7	siete
8	ocho
9	nueve
10	diez
11	once
12	doce
13	trece
14	catorce
15	quince
16	dieciséis, diez y seis
17	diecisiete, diez y siete
18	dieciocho, diez y ocho
19	diecinueve, diez y nueve
20	veinte
21	veintiuno, veintiún, veintiuna, veinte y uno, veinte y un, veinte y una
22	veintidós, veinte y dos
23	veintitrés, veinte y tres
24	veinticuatro, veinte y cuatro
25	veinticinco, etc.
26	veintiséis
27	veintisiete
28	veintiocho
29	veintinueve
30	treinta
31	treinta y uno (un, una)
32	treinta y dos, etc.
40	cuarenta
50	cincuenta
60	sesenta
70	setenta
80	ochenta
90	noventa

100	**ciento, cien**
105	**ciento cinco**
200	**doscientos, -as**
300	**trescientos, -as**
400	**cuatrocientos, -as**
500	**quinientos, -as**
600	**seiscientos, -as**
700	**setecientos, -as**
800	**ochocientos, -as**
900	**novecientos, -as**
999	**novecientos noventa y nueve**
1.000[1]	**mil**
1.009	**mil nueve**
2.000	**dos mil**
7.555	**siete mil quinientos cincuenta y cinco**
27.777	**veintisiete mil setecientos setenta y siete**
100.000	**cien mil**
1.000.000	**un millón**
2.000.000	**dos millones**
4.196.234	**cuatro millones ciento noventa y seis mil doscientos treinta y cuatro**

Ordinals *Ordinales*[2]

1st	**primer(o), -a (1er, 1°, 1^a)**
2nd	**segundo, -a (2°, 2^a)**
3rd	**tercer(o), -a (3er, 3°, 3^a)**
4th	**cuarto, -a (4°, 4^a)**
5th	**quinto, -a (5°, 5^a)**
6th	**sexto, -a (6°, 6^a)**
7th	**séptimo, -a (7°, 7^a)**
8th	**octavo, -a (8°, 8^a)**
9th	**noveno, -a (9°, 9^a)**
10th	**décimo, -a (10°, 10^a)**

Ordinals above ten are rarely used; they are replaced by cardinals. When a cardinal is used for an ordinal, it is placed after the noun it modifies.

segunda lección   second lesson

lección doce   twelfth lesson

In Spanish ordinal numbers do not occur with the same frequency as in English. Ordinal numbers when used as adjectives agree with the nouns they modify in gender. The formation of the feminine and the plural of ordinals is regular in Spanish.

el segundo quirófano   the second operating room

la segunda cirugía plástica   the second plastic surgery

las segundas copias   the second copies

Primero and **tercero** drop the **o** when they precede a masculine singular noun.

el primer paciente ⎫
la primera paciente ⎭   the first patient

los primeros pacientes ⎫
las primeras pacientes ⎭   the first patients

With the exception of *primero* (first), cardinal numbers and not ordinals are used in Spanish to express the days of the month.

el primero de diciembre   December 1st

but: **el dos de octubre**   October 2nd

el diez de mayo   May 10th

Spanish does not use ordinal numbers to designate centuries, unlike English.

el siglo veinte   the twentieth century

Ordinal numbers are used to designate monarchs up to only ten.

Alfonso sexto   Alfonso VI

Isabel segunda   Isabel II

but: **Alfonso trece**   Alfonso XII

Aniversario is one noun, however, that always calls for an ordinal number.

en el primer aniversario   on the first anniversary

el octogésimo segundo aniversario   the 82nd anniversary

Position of numbers   *Posición de los números*

Cardinal numbers usually precede the noun. If they are used to substitute for ordinals, they follow.

Operó quince horas.   He operated for 15 hours.

Estuvo en la Unidad de cuidado intensivo tres días.   She was in ICU for three days.

El quirófano está en el piso veintiuno del hospital.   The OR is on the twenty-first floor of the hospital.

Ordinal numbers may precede or follow the noun that they modify. Generally they follow when they indicate a member of a recognized series. Cardinal numbers may precede or follow ordinal numbers.

Las tres primeras suturas ⎫
las primeras tres suturas ⎬ the first three sutures
⎭

EXERCISES *EJERCICIOS*

A. Write the cardinal numbers in Spanish.

1. 14 _____ **espéculos**
2. 3 _____ **baños de asiento**
3. 50 _____ **píldoras**
4. 21 _____ **cápsulas**
5. 36 _____ **aspirinas para niños**
6. 1 _____ **tobillera**
7. 31 _____ **transfusiones de sangre**
8. 16 _____ **radiografías**
9. 64 _____ **onzas**
10. 77 _____ **curitas**

B. Say the following in Spanish.

1. 2,000,000
2. 17,592
3. 8,653
4. 706
5. 911
6. 1492
7. 875
8. 1,812
9. $25
10. 2598
11. 1124
12. 100,400
13. 3,247
14. 449

Fractions *Fracciones*

$\frac{1}{2}$ **un medio (la mitad)**
$\frac{1}{3}$ **un tercio (la tercera parte)**
$\frac{1}{4}$ **un cuarto (la cuarta parte)**

$\frac{2}{3}$ **dos tercios**

$\frac{3}{4}$ **tres cuartos**

$\frac{4}{5}$ **cuatro quintos**

$\frac{9}{16}$ **nueve dieciseisavos**

$\frac{7}{20}$ **siete veintavos**

$\frac{1}{50}$ **un cincuentavo**

$\frac{28}{75}$ **veintiocho setentaicincoavos**

NOTE: The numerator of a fraction is a cardinal number. The denominators from $\frac{1}{4}$ to $\frac{1}{10}$ are the corresponding ordinals. From $\frac{1}{11}$ to $\frac{1}{99}$, the denominators end in the suffix **-avo**, which is added to the cardinal after the final **e** or **a** has been dropped. There are two exceptions to the apocopation of the final **e**—**siete** and **nueve**.

$\frac{2}{7}$ **dos siet*e*avos** $\frac{1}{19}$ **un diecinuev*e*avo**

The word **parte(s)** may be used to express all fractions higher than, and including, one-third.

$\frac{4}{7}$ **las cuatro séptimas partes**

Symbols   *Símbolos*

The equal symbol (=) is pronounced **es igual a**. The plus symbol (+) is pronounced **más**.

1/4 pastilla = un cuarto o la cuarta parte
de una pastilla

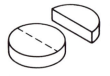

1/2 pastilla = media pastilla

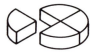

1 1/2 pastilla = una pastilla y media

1/8 pastilla = un octavo de una pastilla

Decimals *Números decimales*

Fractions in the form of so many tenths (**décimas**) or hundredths (**centésimas**) or thousandths (**milésimas**) are called decimal fractions (**quebrados decimales**), from the Latin word for *ten*. The decimal point (**punto decimal**) marks off integers (units [**unidades**], tens [**decenas**], hundreds [**centenas**], etc.) from fractions (**fracciones decimales**).

Additional decimal equivalents are:

ten thousandths **diezmilésimas**

hundred thousandths **cienmilésimas**

millionths **millonésimas**

ten millionths **diezmillonésimas**

hundred millionths **cienmillonésimas**

Spanish decimals are read in several ways. The number 12.435,678 can be expressed

12 unidades, 4 décimas, 3 centésimas, 5 milésimas, etc. or

12 unidades, 435,678 millonésimas or

12 unidades, 435 milésimas, 678 millonésimas

Social security numbers *Números del seguro social*

The nine digits in the social security numbers are expressed in Spanish according to the following breakdown:

123-45-6789 **123-45-67-89** or

ciento veintitrés, cuarenta y cinco, sesenta y siete, ochenta y nueve

Some Spanish-speakers will express their social security number as: **1-2-3-45-6-7-8-9** or **uno, dos, tres, cuarenta y cinco, seis, siete, ocho, nueve**.

Street addresses *Señas del domicilio*

Addresses in Spanish are given with the street number following the name of tne street. Street direction is the last item mentioned:

651 West Main Avenue **Avenida Main, número seiscientos cincuenta y uno, oeste**

street **calle** (f)   boulevard **paseo** (m)   lane **callejuela** (f)

Dimensions *Las dimensiones*

Dimension is expressed with **ser**[3] or with **tener**.[3] The nouns and adjectives needed to express dimension are:

Nouns	*Adjectives*
la altura height	**alto** tall, high
la anchura width	**ancho** wide
la longitud length	**largo** long
la profundidad depth	**profundo** deep
el espesor thickness	**grueso** thick

The interrogative pronoun **¿cuánto?** followed by **de** + an adjective of dimension ask for the dimension of a person or thing.

How deep is the wound? **¿Cuánto de profundo es la llaga?**

How wide is the cyst? **¿Cuánto de ancho es el lobanillo?**

De plus the adjective form express the dimension when the number precedes the dimension.

How long is the baby? **¿Cuánto de largo es el nene?**

The baby is 50 centimeters long. $\left\{\begin{array}{l}\text{\bf El nene tiene (es) una longitud de cincuenta}\\ \text{\bf centímetros. El nene es (tiene) cincuenta}\\ \text{\bf centímetros de largo.}\end{array}\right.$

CONVERSION

CONVERSION

Fahrenheit/Centigrade *Fahrenheit/Centígrado*

32 degrees (**grados**) Fahrenheit (**Fahrenheit**) (F) = 0° centigrade (**centígrado**)
Each centigrade degree is equal to 1.8 Fahrenheit degrees.

To change degrees F to degrees C, subtract 32 and multiply by $\frac{5}{9}$.

$(F - 32) \times \frac{5}{9} = C$

To change degrees C to degrees F, multiply by $\frac{9}{5}$ and add 32.

$(C \times \frac{9}{5}) + 32 = F$

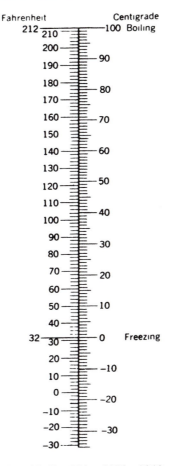

Fahrenheit	96°	97°	98°	98.6°	99°	100°	101°	102°	103°	104°	105°
Centigrade	35.6°	36.1°	36.7°	37°	37.2°	37.8°	38.3°	38.9°	39.4°	40°	40.6°

Decimal/Metric *Decimal/Métrico*

1 centimeter (**centímetro**) = .393 inches (**pulgadas**)
1 inch = 2.54 centimeters
1 meter (**metro**) = $\begin{cases} 39.37 \text{ inches} \\ 3.28 \text{ feet (\textbf{pies})} \\ 1.903 \text{ yards (\textbf{yardas})} \end{cases}$
1 foot = .304 meters
1 yard = .914 meters
1 kilometer (**kilómetro**) = .621 miles
1 mile (**milla**) = 1.609 kilometers
1 gram (**gramo**) = .035 ounces (**onzas**)

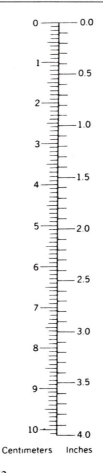

Centimeters   Inches

1 hectogram (**hectogramo**) = 3.53 ounces
1 ounce = 28.35 grams
1 kilogram (**kilo**) = $\begin{cases} 2.204 \text{ pounds (\textbf{libras})} \\ 35.273 \text{ ounces} \end{cases}$
1 pound = .453 kilograms (**kilogramos**)
1 liter (**litro**) = $\begin{cases} 2.113 \text{ pints (\textbf{pintas})} \\ 1.056 \text{ quarts (\textbf{cuartos})} \\ .264 \text{ gallons (\textbf{galones})} \end{cases}$
1 pint = .473 liters
1 quart = .946 liters
1 gallon = 3.785 liters

EXERCISES *EJERCICIOS*

In the United States we are used to using a measuring system that is not used in other parts of the world. The metric system is the universally accepted system of measurement.

Length is perhaps the most familiar measure. The ruler is used to measure something. For Americans the yard is the most commonly used measure. The yard does not exist in the metric system, nor do the foot or inch. The basic unit of measure in the metric system is the meter. It is called the basic unit because the metric systems of weight and volume are derived from the meter.

The meter can easily be divided into 100 or 1,000 equal parts: centimeters or millimeters. Since one part of 1,000 is called a millimeter (mm), then a metric ruler consists of 1,000 mm. Ten millimeters make up a centimeter. There are 100 centimeters (cm) in a meter (m).

$$1 \text{ m} = 1,000 \text{ mm} = 100 \text{ cm} \qquad 10 \text{ mm} = 1 \text{ cm}$$

In the metric system volume is measured in liters. There is a similarity between the liter and the meter. The liter can also be divided into 1,000 equal parts (milliliter). Therefore, 1 liter = 1,000 ml.

Volume means the quantity of material that a cube can hold. The volume of a cube is measured by dividing the length, width, and height. If a 10 cm cube holds one liter in quantity (10 cm × 10 cm × 10 cm = 1,000 cc [cc = cubic centimeter]), 1 liter = 1,000 cc.

Just as a metric system of length and volume exists, so too there is one for weights. The kilo is the measure used to weigh materials in this system. It also can be divided into 1,000 equal parts, which are called grams (g).

The metric system is easier than the English system. It can easily be divided into hundreds or thousands, which can be reduced to decimals. Moreover, length, volume, and weight are related.

En los Estados Unidos nos hemos acostumbrado a usar un sistema de medidas que no se usa en otras partes del mundo. El sistema métrico es el sistema de medidas aceptado universalmente.

El largo es tal vez la medida más familiar. La regla se usa para medir algo. La medida más comúnmente usada es la yarda para los estadounidenses. La yarda no existe en el sistema métrico, tampoco el pie ni la pulgada. La unidad fundamental de medida en el sistema métrico es el metro. Se llama la unidad fundamental porque es del metro que se derivan los sistemas métricos de peso y volumen.

El metro se puede dividir fácilmente en 100 o 1000 partes iguales: centímetros o milímetros. Puesto que una parte de 1000 se denomina milímetro (mm), entonces una regla métrica consta de 1000 mm. Diez milímetros se agrupan en un centímetro. Hay 100 centímetros (cm) en un metro (m).

$$1 \text{ m} = 1000 \text{ mm} = 100 \text{ cm} \qquad 10 \text{ mm} = 1 \text{ cm}$$

En el sistema métrico, el volumen se mide en litros. Existe una afinidad entre el litro y el metro. El litro también puede dividirse en 1000 partes iguales (mililitro). Por lo tanto, 1 litro = 1000 ml.

Volumen quiere decir la cantidad de material que un cubo puede contener. El volumen de un cubo se mide multiplicando la longitud y el ancho y el alto. Si un cubo de 10 cm contiene un litro en cantidad (10 cm × 10 cm × 10 cm = 1000 cc [cc = centímetro cúbico]), 1 litro = 1000 cc.

Así como existe un sistema métrico de longitud y volumen, de la misma manera existe uno para los pesos. El kilo es la medida que se usa para pesar materiales en este sistema. También se puede dividir en 1000 partes iguales llamadas gramos (g).

El sistema métrico es más fácil que el sistema inglés. Se puede dividir con facilidad en cientos o miles, los cuales se pueden reducir a décimos. Además, longitud, volumen y peso están relacionados en sí.

A. Convert the following.

1. 50 mm = _____ cm
2. 50 cm = _____ m
3. 75 mm = _____ cm
4. 500 mm = _____ m

B. Answer the following in Spanish.

1. ¿Cuántos cm hay en un pie?
2. ¿Cuántos mm hay en un pie?
3. ¿Cuál es su altura en pies, metros, centímetros?
4. ¿Cuál es la unidad básica de medida en la yarda?
5. ¿Cuál es la unidad básica de medida en el metro?
6. ¿Cuántas pulgadas hay en una yarda? ¿en un metro?

C. Solve the following problems.

1. A man tells you that he is 185 centimeters tall (**ciento ochenta y cinco centímetros**). How tall is he in feet and inches? (conversion: 1 cm = .4 [.393] in.)

2. A woman says that her baby weighs 5 kilos (**cinco kilos**) now. How much does the baby weigh in pounds? (conversion: 1 k = 2 lb [2.204])

3. A man arrives at the hospital with a gash made by a knife that was about 8 centimeters long by 2 centimeters wide. How long and how wide was the knife? (conversion: 1 cm = .4 in.)

4. A woman says that she cannot walk more than 30 meters before she begins to have trouble breathing. How many feet can she walk? (conversion: 1 m = 3 ft [3.28])

Medicines are packaged by weight—in grams (**gramos[g]**) and milligrams (**miligramos[mg]**). 1,000 mg = 1 g (**mil miligramos es igual a un gramo**). 1 mg = .001 g = 1/1,000 g (**un miligramo es una milésima de un gramo**). In some countries medicines are still weighed in grains (**grano[gn]**). 1 gn = 65 mg.

EXERCISES *EJERCICIOS*

1. Convert the following according to the model.
   How many mg does a 5 gn aspirin contain? (conversion: 1 gn = 65 mg)
   How many mg = 0.5 g? (conversion: 1 g = 1,000 mg)

2. Terramycin comes in capsules (**cápsulas**) of 50 mg, 100 mg, and 250 mg doses. Convert to 50 mg and 100 mg doses an R$_x$ that reads: **Tome Terramicina, 4 cápsulas de 250 mg diarias.**

TELLING TIME

LA HORA

1. What time is it?
   ¿Qué hora es?
   ¿Qué horas son? (Sp. Am.)

2. Do you know what time it is?
   ¿Sabe usted la hora?

3. I cannot say because I haven't any watch.
   No puedo decir porque no tengo reloj.

4. It is one o'clock.
   Es la una.

5. It is two o'clock.
   Son las dos.

6. It is three o'clock.
   Son las tres.

7. **Son las cuatro.**

8. It is five o'clock.
   Son las cinco.

9. It is six o'clock.
   Son las seis.

10. **Son las siete.**

11. It is eight o'clock.
    Son las ocho.

12. It is nine o'clock.
    Son las nueve.

13. It is ten o'clock.
    Son las diez.

14. It is eleven o'clock.
Son las once.

15. **Son las doce.**

16. It is one thirty.
Es la una y media.

17. It is 4:30.
Son las cuatro y media.

18. It is 11:30.
Son las once y media.

19. It is 1:15.
Es la una y cuarto.

20. It is 2:15.
Son las dos y cuarto.

21. It is 2:10.
Son las dos y diez.

22. It is 11:10.
Son las once y diez.

23. It is 10:10 P.M.
Son las veintidós y diez.[4]

24. **Son las diez y veinte.**

25. It is 12:05.
Son las doce y cinco.

26. It is 2:45.
Son las tres menos cuarto.

27. **Son las ocho menos cuarto.**

28. **Son las diez menos cuarto.**

29. It is 6:55. (It is five to seven.)
    Son las siete menos cinco.

30. **Es la una menos veinte.**

31. It is 6 A.M.
    Son las seis de la mañana.

32. It is 5 P.M. (in the afternoon).
    Son las cinco de la tarde.

33. It is 8 P.M. (in the evening).
    Son las ocho de la noche.

34. It is exactly three o'clock.
    Son las tres en punto.

35. It is approximately nine.
    Son las nueve, más o menos.

36. It is noon.
    Es mediodía.

37. It is midnight.
    Es medianoche.

38. At 3:00.
    A las tres.

39. At 5:05.
    A las cinco y cinco.

40. At 12:50 (at ten to one).
    A la una menos diez.

41. My watch is slow.
    Mi reloj se atrasa.

42. My watch is fast.
    Mi reloj se adelanta.

43. My watch has stopped.
    Mi reloj ha parado.

PRACTICE *PRACTICA*

¿Qué hora es?

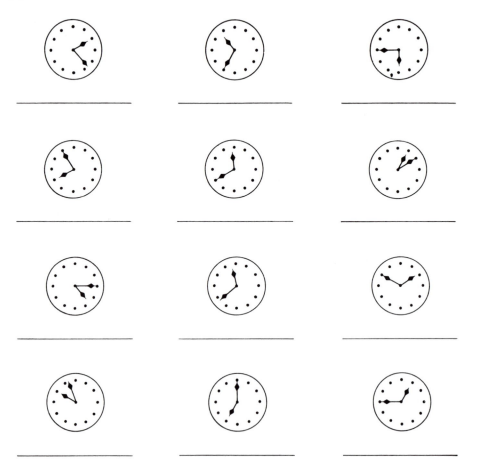

Notes on Telling Time   *Observaciones acerca de la hora*

The verb **ser** is always used in telling time. The singular verb **es** is used to express one o'clock; from two o'clock on, the plural verb **son** is used. Note that the definite article **la** stands for **la hora**, and **las** stands for **las horas**. These definite articles are loosely translated as *o'clock*. **Media** ($\frac{1}{2}$) is a feminine adjective that agrees with the understood **hora**; **cuarto** ($\frac{1}{4}$) is a masculine noun and therefore does not have to agree in gender with **hora**. To express time from the hour to the half hour, minutes are added to the hour by **y**. When the number of minutes past the hour is greater than thirty, minutes are subtracted from the next hour, using the word **menos**. Thus, "six thirty-eight" becomes "seven minus twenty-two." Remember that from 12:31 to 1:30 singular verb **es** and the article **la** are used.

Colloquially it is acceptable to say **"Faltan diez para las diez"** instead of **"Son las diez menos diez."**

The Spanish "day" is divided into **mañana** (from sunrise to noon), **tarde** (from noon to sunset), **noche** (from sunset to midnight), **madrugada** (from midnight to sunrise). When the hour is specified, **de** must be used to translate *in* and *at* in the expressions **de la mañana**, and so on. When there is no definite hour specified, **por** is used for *in* or *at*: **por la mañana** (in the morning), **por la tarde** (in the afternoon, evening), and **por la noche** (in the evening, at night).

Additional Expressions of Time
Más expresiones horarias

a short while ago   **hace poco**
a week from today   **de hoy en ocho**
after meals   **después de comer**
as of now   **por ahora**
at bedtime   **al acostarse**
at the same time   **a la vez**
before meals   **antes de comer**
by that date   **para esa fecha**
by then   **para entonces**
constantly   **constantemente**
daily   **diario**
during the day   **durante el día**
early   **temprano**
every hour   **(a) cada hora**
every other day   **cada tercer día**

every hour **(a) cada hora**
first time **primera vez**
for how long? **¿por cuánto tiempo?**
for many years **por muchos años**
for the time being **por ahora**
four a day **cuatro veces al día**
from time to time **de vez en cuando**
how many times? **¿cuántas veces?**
how often? **¿cada cuánto tiempo?, ¿con qué frecuencia? ¿cada qué tiempo?**
immediately, at once **en seguida**
in a few minutes, shortly **dentro de poco**
last time **última vez**
late **tarde**
lately **últimamente**
minute **minuto**
moment **momento**
month **mes**
monthly **mensual, mensualmente**
next month **el mes que viene**
next week **la semana que viene**
next year **el año que viene**
now **ahora**
occasionally **a veces**
often **a menudo, seguido** (Mex.)
on time **a tiempo**
once **una vez**
once a day **una vez al día**
per day **al (por) día**
per month **al (por) mes**
per week **a (por) la semana**
second **segundo**
since when? **¿desde cuándo?**
the day after tomorrow **pasado mañana**
the day before yesterday **anteayer, antier** (Mex.)
three a day **tres veces al día**
today **hoy**
tomorrow **mañana**
tonight **esta noche**

twice a day   **dos veces al día**
two weeks from today   **de hoy en quince**
upon getting up   **al levantarse**
upon waking up   **al despertarse**
week   **semana**
weekly   **semanal**
year   **año**
year round   **todo el año**
yearly   **anual, anualmente**
yesterday   **ayer**

THE CALENDAR

EL CALENDARIO

Days of the Week   *Los días de la semana*

Sunday   **el domingo**
Monday   **el lunes**
Tuesday   **el martes**
Wednesday   **el miércoles**
Thursday   **el jueves**
Friday   **el viernes**
Saturday   **el sábado**

Seasons   *Las estaciones*[5]

spring   **la primavera**
summer   **el verano**
autumn   **el otoño**
winter   **el invierno**

Months of the Year   *Los meses del año*

January   **enero**
February   **febrero**
March   **marzo**
April   **abril**
May   **mayo**

June **junio**
July **julio**
August **agosto**
September **septiembre**
October **octubre**
November **noviembre**
December **diciembre**

Observe that in Spanish the months, seasons, and days of the week are not capitalized. The masculine definite article is used with the days of the week except when the days of the week are preceded by the adjectives **cada**, **muchos**, **pocos**, by any number, or by the verb **ser**. When the English *on* is expressed or implied before a day of the week or month, the definite article **el** (or **los**) is used.

on Saturday **el sábado**   on April 23 **el veintitrés de abril**
on Wednesdays **los miércoles**

In expressing dates, **primero** is used for the first day of the month. All other days of the month are counted in Spanish by the cardinal numbers, preceded by the definite article. The month and year, when expressed, are connected with the date by the preposition **de**:

on April 1 **el primero de abril**
January 7, 1970 **el siete de enero de mil novecientos setenta**

When the month is omitted, it is common to place the word **día**, day, before the number.

Today is the 23rd. **Hoy es el día veintitrés.**

There are several ways to ask the day of the month. All are acceptable. When answering, the response should use the same terms as the question.

What day of the month is it?
 ⎧ **¿A cuántos estamos?**
 ⎪ **¿A cómo estamos?**
 ⎪ **¿Cuál es la fecha?**
 ⎪ **¿Qué fecha tenemos?**
 ⎨ **¿Qué día del mes tenemos?**
 ⎪ **¿Qué día del mes es hoy?**
 ⎪ **¿A qué fecha estamos?**
 ⎩ **¿A qué día del mes estamos?**

(Today) It is the 23rd of April.
 ⎧ **Hoy es el veintitrés de abril.**
 ⎨ **Tenemos el veintitrés de abril.**
 ⎩ **Estamos a veintitrés de abril.**

More Calendar Vocabulary *Más vocabulario del calendario*

birthday **cumpleaños** (m, sg)

calendar **calendario** (m)

century **siglo** (m)

date **fecha** (f)

day **día** (m)

daylight **luz de día** (f)

eve **víspera** (f)

fortnight **quincena** (f)

holiday **fiesta** (f); **día de fiesta** (m); **día festivo** (m)

   Christmas **Navidad** (f)

   Christmas Eve **Nochebuena** (f)

   Easter **pascua de resurrección** (f), **pascua florida** (f), **pascua de flores** (f); **día de la coneja** (m, Chicano)

   Independence Day (USA) **día de la independencia** (m)

   Labor Day (USA) **día del trabajo** (m)

   Memorial Day (USA) **día (de recordación) de los caídos** (m)

   New Year's Eve **víspera de año nuevo** (f)

   Pentecost **pascua del espíritu santo** (f), **pascua de Pentecostés** (f)

hour, time **hora** (f)

   daylight saving time **hora de verano** (f)

   standard time **hora legal** (f), **hora normal** (f)

minute **minuto** (m)

midnight **medianoche** (f)

month **mes** (m)

noon **mediodía** (m)

week **semana** (f)

weekend **fin de semana** (m)

workday **día de trabajo** (m), **día laborable** (m)

saint's day **(día del) santo** (m)

year **año** (m)

   fiscal year **año económico** (m)

   leap year **año bisiesto** (m)

   school year **año escolar** (m), **año lectivo** (m)

Spanish Adage   *Un refrán español*

Treinta dias tiene noviembre,
con abril, junio y septiembre;
veintiocho tiene uno,
y los demás treinta y uno.

EXERCISES *EJERCICIOS*

A.   Translate the following into Spanish.

    1.   Conchita was born February 17, 1973.

    2.   The operation is going to cost $985.

    3.   At what time does the technician arrive here?

    4.   It is 3:45 P.M., November 29, 1982.

    5.   Two hundred children are sick today.

    6.   They operate at 6:30 A.M.

    7.   We do not work on Wednesdays.

    8.   She goes to the laboratory every Saturday.

    9.   The baby always has a cold in the winter.

    10.   I have an appointment with my doctor every Tuesday morning at the clinic during the summer.

B.   Answer in Spanish.

    1.   ¿Qué dia es hoy? (Hoy es lunes, etc. . . .)

    2.   ¿Qué dia es mañana?

    3.   ¿Qué dia fue (was) ayer?

    4.   Si hoy es lunes, ¿qué dia es mañana? (Si hoy es lunes, mañana es ...)

    5.   Si hoy es lunes, ¿qué día fue ayer?

    6.   Si hoy es jueves, ¿qué día es mañana?

    7.   Si hoy es miércoles, ¿qué dia fue ayer?

    8.   Si hoy es martes, ¿qué dia es pasado mañana?

    9.   Si hoy es martes, ¿qué dia fue anteayer?

    10.   Si hoy es domingo, ¿qué dia es pasado mañana?

    11.   ¿Cuáles son (Which are) los meses de la primavera? ¿ del verano? ¿del otoño? ¿del invierno?

    12.   ¿En qué mes estamos ahora?

    13.   ¿Cuál es la fecha de hoy?

    14.   ¿En qué mes celebramos (do we celebrate) la Navidad? ¿La independencia de los Estados Unidos (United States)?

    15.   ¿En qué mes tiene Vd. su cumpleaños (do you have your birthday)? (Tengo mi cumpleaños en . . .)

Notes *Notas*

1. Note that in Spanish a period is used to punctuate thousands; a comma is used as a decimal point.

2. Ordinal numbers do exist for *11th* to *100th*. These are for reference use only. (11th **undécimo, -a**; 12th **duodécimo, -a**; 13th **décimo tercero, -a**; 14th **décimo cuarto, -a**; 15th **décimo quinto, -a**; 20th **vigésimo, -a**; 30th **trigésimo, -a**; 40th **cuadragésimo, -a**; 50th **quincuagésimo, -a**; 60th **sexagésimo, -a**; 70th **septuagésimo, -a**; 80th **octogésimo, -a**; 90th **nonagésimo, -a**; 100th **centésimo, -a**).

3. See pages 92 and 96.

4. Official time in Spain and other Spanish-speaking countries is expressed on a 24-hour basis. This applies to radio, television, train, and airline schedules among other things. To figure out the equivalent time after 12 noon and before midnight (P.M.) you would need to subtract 12 hours. Thus, **las diecinueve** is 7:00 P.M., **las veintitrés** is 11:00 P.M.

5. In much of Hispanic America, from Guatemala through Peru, there are no seasons of hot and cold, since summer and winter depend on altitude. Therefore, in these countries (Guatemala, El Salvador, Honduras, Nicaragua, Costa Rica, Panama, Colombia, Venezuela, Ecuador and Peru) the term **invierno** refers to the wet periods, and **verano,** to the dry.

Anatomic and Physiological Vocabulary

Vocabulario anatómico y fisiológico

PARTS OF THE BODY

LAS PARTES DEL CUERPO

Miscellany   *Miscelánea*

albumin   **albúmina** (f)
aorta   **aorta** (f)
artery   **arteria** (f)
   brachial artery   **arteria humeral**
   carotid artery   **arteria carótida**
   coronary artery   **arteria coronaria**
   facial artery   **arteria facial**
   pulmonary artery   **arteria pulmonar**
   subclavian artery   **arteria subclavia**
   temporal artery   **arteria temporal**
articulation   **articulación** (f); **coyuntura** (f)
blood   **sangre** (f)
body   **cuerpo** (m)
   ciliary body   **cuerpo ciliar**
bone   **hueso** (m)
breath   **aliento** (m)
capillary   **capilar** (m)
cardiovascular system   **aparato cardiovascular** (m); **sistema cardiovascular** (m)
cartilage   **cartílago** (m)
cholesterol   **colesterol** (m); **grasa en las venas** (f)
circulation   **circulación** (f)
circulatory (hematologic) system   **aparato circulatorio (o hematológico)** (m); **sistema circulatorio (o hematológico)** (m)
crow's feet   **patas de gallo** (f)
diastole   **diástole** (f)
digestive system   **aparato digestivo** (m); **sistema digestivo** (m)
endocrine system   **aparato endócrino** (m); **sistema endócrino** (m)
enzyme   **enzima** (f); **jugo digestivo** (m)
epidermis   **epidermis** (f)
excretion   **excreción** (f); **excremento** (m)
extrasystole   **extrasístole** (f)

fibroid   **fibroideo** (adj)
flesh   **carne** (f)
follicle   **folículo** (m)
freckles   **pecas** (f)
gastrointestinal system   **aparato gastrointestinal** (m); **sistema gastrointestinal** (m)
genitourinary system   **aparato genitourinario** (m); **sistema genitourinario** (m)
hairy   **peludo** (adj); **tarántula** (adj, Chicano)
hormone   **hormona** (f); **hormón** (m)
joint   **articulación** (f); **coyuntura** (f)
ligament   **ligamento** (m)
limb   **miembro** (m); **extremidad** (f)
lingual   **lingual** (adj)
lymph node   **nódulo linfático** (m); **nudo linfático** (m, colloq)
marrow   **médula** (f)
membrane   **membrana** (f)
mole, birthmark   **lunar** (m)
muscle   **músculo** (m)
   involuntary muscle   **músculo involuntario**
   smooth muscle   **músculo liso**
   striated muscle   **músculo estriado**
   voluntary muscle   **músculo voluntario**
nerve   **nervio** (m)
   cranial nerve   **nervio craneal**
   motor nerve   **nervio motor**
   parasympathetic nerve   **nervio parasimpático**
   sensory nerve   **nervio sensorial**
   sympathetic nerve   **nervio simpático**
nervous system, autonomic   **aparato nervioso autónomo** (m); **sistema nervioso autónomo** (m)
nervous system, central   **aparato nervioso central** (m); **sistema nervioso central** (m)
olfactory   **olfatorio** (adj)
organ   **órgano** (m)

periosteum   **periostio** (m)
perspiration   **sudor** (m)
pore   **poro** (m)
pulse   **pulso** (m)
reflex   **reflejo** (m)
reproductive system   **aparato reproductivo** (m); **sistema reproductivo** (m)
respiratory system   **aparato respiratorio** (m); **sistema respiratorio** (m)
sense   **sentido** (m)
   sense of feel (tactile)   **sentido del tacto**
   sense of hearing (auditory)   **sentido del oído**
   sense of sight (visual)   **sentido de la vista**
   sense of taste (gustatory)   **sentido del olfato**
sensorial   **sensorial** (adj)
skeleton   **esqueleto** (m); **armazón** (f)
skin   **piel** (f); **cuero** (m)
   flap of skin   **pellejo** (m)
sphincter   **esfínter** (f)
systole   **sístole** (f)
tactile   **tácil** (adj)
tendon   **tendón** (m)
tissue   **tejido** (m)
urine   **orina** (f); **orín** (m); **orines** (m)
valve   **válvula** (f)
vein   **vena** (f)
   brachial vein   **vena humeral**
   deep vein   **vena profunda**
   facial vein   **vena facial**
   great cardiac vein   **vena coronaria mayor**
   inferior vena cava vein   **vena cava inferior**
   jugular vein   **vena yugular**
   pulmonary vein   **vena pulmonar**
   small cardiac vein   **vena coronaria menor**

The Head   *La cabeza*

Adam's apple   **nuez de Adán** (f); **bocado de Adán** (m); **manzana** (f, Mex.)
adenoids   **adenoides** (m, pl)
beard   **barba** (f)
blood vessel   **vaso sanguíneo** (m)

brains   **sesos** (m)
cell   **célula** (f)
   ciliated cell   **célula ciliada** (f)
cerebral cortex   **corteza cerebral** (f); **materia gris** (f, colloq)
cerebral hemisphere   **hemisferio cerebral** (m)
cerebrum   **cerebro** (m)
   anterior chamber of cerebrum   **cámara anterior del cerebro** (f)
   posterior chamber of cerebrum   **cámara posterior del cerebro** (f)

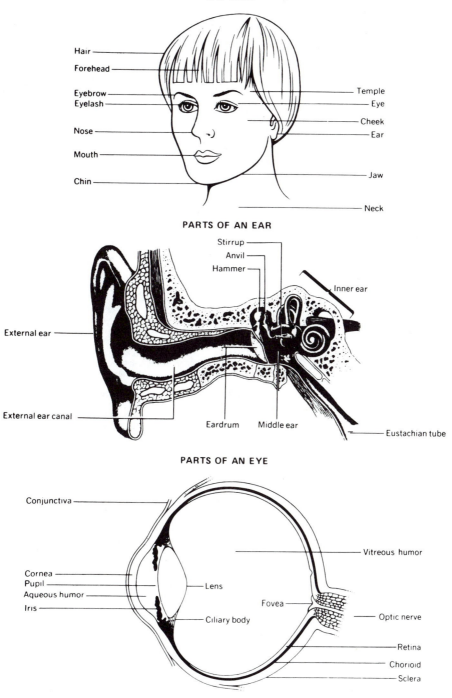

THE HEAD

Hair
Forehead
Eyebrow
Eyelash
Nose
Mouth
Chin

Temple
Eye
Cheek
Ear
Jaw
Neck

PARTS OF AN EAR

Stirrup
Anvil
Hammer
Inner ear
External ear
External ear canal
Eardrum
Middle ear
Eustachian tube

PARTS OF AN EYE

Conjunctiva
Cornea
Pupil
Aqueous humor
Iris
Lens
Ciliary body
Fovea
Vitreous humor
Optic nerve
Retina
Choroid
Sclera

223

cheek **mejilla** (f); **carrillos** (m);
  cachete (m); **cacha** (f)
cheekbone **pómulo** (m)
chin **barbilla** (f); **mentón** (m);
  barba (f); **piocha** (f); **talache** (m)
cranium **cráneo** (m)
  base of the cranium **base
  del cráneo** (f)
crown of the head **mollera** (f)
ear **oreja** (f)
  auditory **auditivo** (adj)
  ear (organ of hearing) **oído** (m)
  earwax **cerumen** (m); **cera de
  los oídos** (f); **cerilla** (f)
  Eustachian tube **trompa de
  Eustaquio** (f)
  external ear **oído externo** (m);
  **pabellón externo de la
  oreja** (m); **aurícola** (f)
    external ear canal **conducto**[1]
    auditivo externo (m)
  lobe of the ear **pulpejo** (m);
  lóbulo (m)
  eardrum (tympanic membrane)
  tímpano (m)
  inner ear **oído interno** (m)
    cochlea **cóclea** (f); **caracol**
    (m)
    semicircular canal **conducto
    semicircular** (m)
  middle ear **oído medio** (m)
    anvil (incus) **yunque** (m)
    hammer (malleus)
    martillo (m)
    stirrup (stapes) **estribo** (m)
  saccule **sáculo** (m)
eye **ojo** (m)
  aqueous humor **humor
  acuoso** (m)
  chorioid **corioides** (f, sg)
  cone **cono** (m)
  conjunctiva **conjuntiva** (f)
  cornea **córnea** (f)
  eyeball **globo del ojo** (m); **globo
  ocular** (m); **tomate** (m, slang,
  Chicano)
  eyebrow **ceja** (f)
  eyelash **pestaña** (f)
  eyelid **párpado** (m)
  eye socket **cuenca de los ojos** (f)
  fovea centralis **fóvea central** (f)
  iris **iris** (m)

lachrymal **lacrimal** (adj);
  lagrimal (adj)
lens (of eye), crystalline
  cristalino (m)
optic nerve **nervio óptico** (m)
pupil **pupila** (f); **niña del ojo** (f)
retina **retina** (f)
rod **bastoncillo** (m)
sclera **esclerótica** (f)
tear duct **conducto lagrimal**
  (m)
tear sac **bolsa de lágrimas** (f)
vitreous humor **humor
  vítreo** (m)
face **cara** (f); **rostro** (m);
  carátula (f, slang, Chicano)
features **facciones** (f)
fontanelle **fontanela** (f);
  mollera (f)
forehead **frente** (f)
fossa **fosa** (f)
frontal **frontal** (adj)
ganglion **ganglio** (m)
hair **cabello** (m); **pelo** (m);
  chimpa (f, Chicano)
  curl of hair **rizo** (m);
  tirabuzón (m); **chino** (m,
  Chicano)
  curly hair **pelo crespo; pelo
  rizado**
  kinky hair **pelo grifo** (Chicano);
  pelo pasudo
  (premature) gray hair **canas
  (verdes)** (f, pl)
  straight hair **pelo liso**
  wavy hair **pelo quebrado**
jaw **mandíbula** (f); **quijada** (f)
jawbone **mandíbula** (f)
larynx **laringe** (f)
lip **labio** (m)
lymph glands **glándulas
  linfáticas** (f)
maxillar **maxilar** (adj)
moustache **bigote** (m);
  mostacho (m)
mouth **boca** (f)
mucus **moco** (m)
nape (of neck) **nuca** (f)
nose **nariz** (f); **nayotas** (f, pl,
  slang, Chicano)
  bridge of the nose **caballete de
  la nariz** (m)

nostril **fosa nasal** (f); **ventana de la
  nariz** (f); **ventanilla de la nariz** (f)
occipital **occipital** (adj)
palate **paladar** (m)
  hard palate **paladar duro** (m);
  bóveda ósea del paladar (f)
  soft palate **paladar blando** (m);
  velo del paladar (m)
parotid gland **glándula parótida** (f)
pharynx **faringe** (f)
pituitary gland **glándula
  pituitaria** (f)
saliva **saliva** (f)
salivary gland **glándula salival** (f)
scalp **piel de la cabeza** (f); **cuero
  cabelludo** (m)
septum **tabique** (m)
sinus **seno** (m)
skin (of the face) **cutis** (m)
  light skinned/complexioned
  despercudido (adj)
  olive skinned/complexioned
  trigueño (adj)
  very dark skinned, but lacking
  Negroid features **pinto** (adj);
  retinto (adj)
skull **cráneo** (m); **calavera** (f,
  Chicano)
  top of the skull **tapa de los
  sesos** (f, colloq)
sputum **esputo** (m); **saliva** (f);
  desgarro (m, Sp. Am.); **pollo** (m,
  Chicano)
sublingual gland **glándula
  sublingual** (f)
submaxillary gland **glándula
  submaxilar** (f)
suture **sutura** (f); **comisura** (f)
tear **lágrima** (f)
tear gland **glándula lagrimal** (f)
temple **sien** (f)
throat **garganta** (f)
tongue **lengua** (f)
tonsils **amígdalas** (f); **anginas** (f,
  Mex., Ven.); **tonsils** (m,
  Chicano)
tooth **diente** (m)
trachea **tráquea** (f); **gaznate** (m)
uvula **úvula** (f); **campanilla** (f,
  colloq); **galillo** (m, colloq)
vocal cord **cuerda vocal** (f)
wrinkle **arruga** (f)

The trunk   *El tronco*

abdomen **abdomen** (m); **vientre**
  (m); **panza** (f, colloq)
alveolus **alvéolo** (m)
anus **ano** (m); **agujero** (m,
  vulgar, Chicano); **chicloso** (m,
  vulgar, Chicano); **chiquito** (m,
  vulgar, Chicano); **fundillo** (m,
  Mex.); **istantino** (m, colloq)

appendix **apéndice** (m); **apendix**
  (f); **tripita** (f, colloq)
back **espalda** (f); **dorso** (m)
backbone **columna vertebral** (f)
belly **barriga** (f); **panza** (f, colloq)
bile **bilis** (f); **hiel** (f)
bladder **vejiga** (f); **vesícula**
bosom **senos** (m, pl)

bowel **intestino inferior** (m)
bowels **entrañas** (f); **tripa** (f,
  colloq)
breast **pecho** (m); **busto** (m);
  agarraderas (f, Chicano);
  chichas (f, pl, C.R.); **chichi** (f,
  Mex.); **teta** (f, slang); **tele** (f)
breastbone **esternón** (m)

bronchia **bronquios** (m)
buttock **nalga**[2] (f); **sentadera** (f);
  anca (f); **aparato** (m, Chicano);
  pellín (m, Chicano); **común** (m,
  Mex.); **fondillo** (m, Cuba);
  fundillo (m, Mex.); **olla** (f, slang,
  Chicano); **fondongo** (m, slang);
  buche (m, vulgar, Chicano)
cervix **cervix** (f); **cerviz** (f);
  cuello de la matriz (m)
chest **pecho** (m); **tórax** (m)
clitoris **clítoris** (m); **bolita** (f,
  slang); **pelotita** (f, slang); **pepa**
  (f. slang)
coccyx **cóccix** (m); **cócciz** (m,
  Chicano); **colita** (f);
  coxis (m)
collar bone/clavicle **clavícula** (f);
  cuena (f, Chicano)

colon **colon** (m)
coronary **coronario** (adj)
crotch **entrepiernas** (f, pl)
diaphragm **diafragma** (m)
disc **disco** (m)
duodenum **duodeno** (m)
epididymis **epidídimo** (m)
esophagus **esófago** (m);
  tragante (m, Chicano)
Fallopian tubes **trompas de
  Falopio** (f); **tubos** (m)
flank **costado** (m)
foreskin **prepucio** (m)
gallbladder **vesícula biliar** (f);
  vejiga de la bilis (f)
gastric juice **jugo gástrico** (m)
genitals **órganos genitales** (m);
  partes (f, slang); **partes ocultas** (f,
  slang)

gland **glándula** (f)
adrenal gland **glándula
  suprarrenal** (f)
carotid gland **glándula
  carótidea** (f)
endocrine gland **glándula
  endocrina** (f)
lymph gland **glándula
  linfática** (f)
mammary gland **glándula
  mamaria** (f)
parathyroid gland **glándula
  paratiroides** (f)
prostrate gland **próstata** (f);
  glándula de la próstata (f);
  glándula prostática (f)
sebaceous gland **glándula
  sebácea** (f)

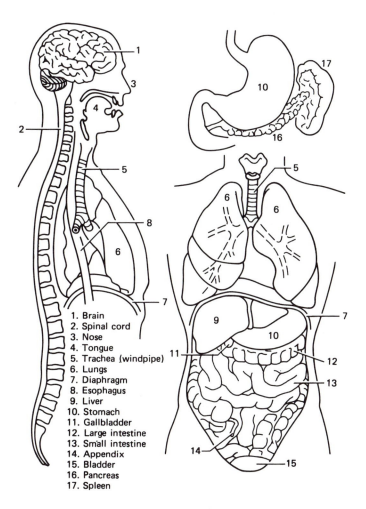

1. Brain
2. Spinal cord
3. Nose
4. Tongue
5. Trachea (windpipe)
6. Lungs
7. Diaphragm
8. Esophagus
9. Liver
10. Stomach
11. Gallbladder
12. Large intestine
13. Small intestine
14. Appendix
15. Bladder
16. Pancreas
17. Spleen

MALE GENITOURINARY SYSTEM
FRONT VIEW

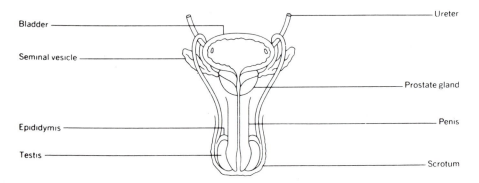

Bladder

Seminal vesicle

Epididymis

Testis

Ureter

Prostate gland

Penis

Scrotum

MALE GENITOURINARY SYSTEM
SIDE VIEW

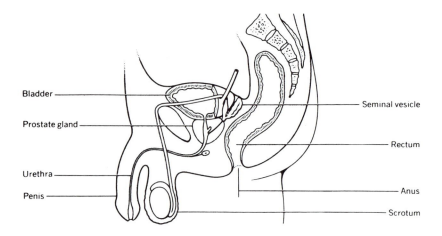

Bladder

Prostate gland

Urethra

Penis

Seminal vesicle

Rectum

Anus

Scrotum

FEMALE GENITOURINARY SYSTEM
FRONT VIEW

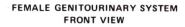

Fallopian tube

Ovary

Vagina

Uterus

Cervix

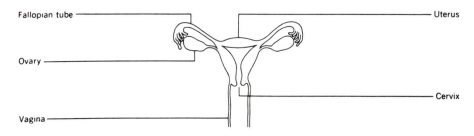

226

sweat gland **glándula sudorípara** (f)
thyroid gland **glándula tiroides** (f)
glans (penis) **glande** (m); **bálano** (m); **cabeza** (f, slang)
gluteal region **región glutea** (f); **gluteo** (m)
heart **corazón** (m)
  apex of the heart **punta del corazón** (f)
  auricle **aurícula** (f)
  heart valve **válvula del corazón** (f)
  ventricle **ventrículo** (m)
hip **cadera** (f); **cuadril** (m, Mex., Chicano)
ileum **íleon** (m)
intestines **intestinos** (m); **tripas** (f)
  large intestine **intestino grueso** (m)
  small intestine **intestino delgado** (m)
jejunum **yeyuno** (m)
kidney **riñón** (m)
lap **regazo** (m)
liver **hígado** (m)
loin **lomo** (m)
lung **pulmón** (m); **bofe** (m, Chicano, Sp. Am.)
marrow **médula** (f)
myocardium **miocardio** (adj)
navel **ombligo** (m)
neck **cuello** (m)
  back of neck **nuca** (f); **cerviz** (f)
nipple (female) **pezón** (m); **chichi** (f, slang)
nipple (male) **tetilla** (f)
ovary **ovario** (m)

pancreas **páncreas** (m)
pelvis **pelvis** (f)
penis **pene** (m); **miembro** (m); **pito** (m, slang); **verga** (f, slang); **pija** (f, slang, Arg.); **balone** (m, Chicano); **chale** (m, vulgar, Chicano); **chalito** (m, vulgar, Chicano); **chicote** (m, slang); **chile** (m, slang); **chorizo** (m, vulgar); **güine** (m, vulgar); **palo** (m, slang); **picha** (f, vulgar); **pichón** (m, vulgar); **pilinga** (f, vulgar); **pilonga** (f, slang, vulgar); **pinga** (f, vulgar); **reata/riata** (f, vulgar)
pubic hair **pelitos** (m, pl, Chicano)
pubis **pubis** (m)
rectum **recto** (m)
rib **costilla** (f)
  false/floating rib **costilla falsa o flotante** (f)
  true rib **costilla verdadera** (f)
sacroiliac **sacroilíaco** (adj)
sacrum **sacro** (m)
sciatic **ciático** (adj)
scrotum **escroto** (m); **bolsa de los testículos** (f)
semen **semen** (m); **esperma** (f)
seminal vesicle **vesículo seminal** (m)
shoulder blade (scapula) **espaldilla** (f); **omóplato** (m); **escápula** (f); **paletilla** (f)
side **costado** (m); **lado** (m)
skin **piel** (f)
spinal column **columna vertebral** (f); **espina dorsal** (f)
spinal cord **médula espinal** (f)
spleen **bazo** (m); **esplín** (m)

stomach **estómago** (m); **vientre** (m)
stomach (pit of) **boca del estómago** (f)
testicle **testículo** (m); **huevos** (m, pl, slang); **compañones** (m, pl, slang); **cuates** (m, pl, slang, Chicano); **blanquillo** (m, slang, Chicano); **bola** (f, pl, slang)
thoracic cavity **caja torácica** (f)
thorax **tórax** (m)
thymus **timo** (m)
thyroid **tiroides** (m)
umbilical cord **cordón umbilical** (m)
umbilicus **ombligo** (m)
ureter **uréter** (m)
urethra **uretra** (f), **canal urinario** (m); **caño urinario** (m)
urinary bladder **vejiga de la orina** (f)
urinary tract **vías urinarias** (f)
uterus **útero** (m); **matriz** (f)
vagina **vagina** (f); **panocho** (m, slang); **pan** (m, slang, vulgar); **cueva** (f, slang, vulgar, Chicano); **linda** (f, slang); **partida** (f, vulgar); **agujero** (m, vulgar, Chicano); **concha** (f, vulgar, Arg., Chile, Ur.)
vas deferens **conducto deferente** (m)
vertebra **vértebra** (f)
vulva **vulva** (f); **panocha** (f, slang); **rajada** (f, vulgar)
waist **cintura** (f)
womb **matriz** (f); **útero** (m)

FEMALE GENITOURINARY SYSTEM
SIDE VIEW

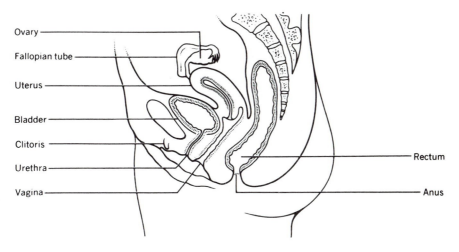

Ovary
Fallopian tube
Uterus
Bladder
Clitoris
Urethra
Vagina
Rectum
Anus

Upper extremities *Las extremidades superiores*

arm **brazo** (m)
  bend of the arm **flexura del brazó** (f)
armpit **sobaco** (m); **axila** (f); **arca** (f, Mex.)
biceps **biceps** (m); **conejo** (m, sg. Chicano); **mollero** (m, Cuba, Sp., colloq)
cuticle **cutícula** (f)
elbow **codo** (m)
finger **dedo** (m)
  ball of thumb **pulpejo** (m)

fleshy tip of the finger **yema** (f)
index **índice** (m)
knuckle **nudillo** (m)
little finger **meñique** (m)
middle finger **dedo del medio** (m); **dedo del corazón** (m)
ring finger **dedo anular** (m)
thumb **pulgar** (m); **dedo gordo** (m)
fist **puño** (m)
forearm **antebrazo** (m)

hand **mano** (f)
  back of the hand **dorso de la mano** (f)
  palm of the hand **palma de la mano** (f)
humerus **húmero** (m)
nail **uña** (f)
phalanx **falange** (f)
radius **radio** (m)
ulna **cúbito** (m)
wrist **muñeca** (f)

Lower extremities *Las extremidades inferiores*

ankle **tobillo** (m)
big toe **dedo grueso o gordo** (m)
bunion **juanete** (m)
callus **callo** (m)
femur **fémur** (m)
fibula **peroné** (m)
foot **pie** (m)
groin **ingle** (f); **empeine**[3] (m)
heel **talón** (m); **calcañar** (m)

hip **cadera** (f)
instep **empeine**[3] (m)
knee **rodilla** (f)
  knee (back of the) **corva** (f); **flexura de la pierna** (f)
  kneecap **rótula** (f); **choquezuela** (f)
leg **pierna** (f)
  calf of the leg **pantorrilla** (f);

canilla (f); **chamorro** (m, Chicano)
shin **espinilla** (f); **canilla** (f)
shinbone **tibia** (f)
sole of the foot **planta del pie** (f)
tendon **tendón** (m)
thigh **muslo** (m); **changa** (f)
toe **dedo (del pie)** (m)

DENTAL VOCABULARY

VOCABULARIO DENTAL

abscess **absceso** (m)
acrylic **acrílico** (adj)
amalgam **amalgama** (f)
artificial, false teeth **dientes postizos** (m)
block the nerve, to **obstruir el nervio**
bite, to **morder (ue)**
braces **aparato ortodóntico** (m); **frenos** (m, Mex.)
bridge (dental) **puente** (m)
  fixed dental bridge **puente fijo** (m)
  removable bridge **puente movible** (m)
brush one's teeth, to **cepillarse los dientes**
burr **fresa** (f)
canker sore **ulceración** (f); **postemilla** (f)
capillaries **capilares** (m); **vaso capilar** (m)
caries **caries** (f)
cavity **carie** (f); **diente picado** (m); **diente cariado** (m); **cavidad** (f) **picadura** (f); **guijón** (m)
cementum **cemento** (m)
chew, to **mascar**

clasp **gancho** (m)
cleaning **limpieza** (f)
crown **corona** (f)
  acrylic jacket crown **corona acrílica** (f)
  porcelain jacket crown **corona de porcelana** (f)
cut teeth, to **dentar (ie)**; **endentecer**
deaden the nerve, to **adormecer el nervio**
dental **dental** (adj)
dental drill **taladro** (m)
dental floss **hilo dental** (m); **seda encerada** (f)
dental forceps **pinzas** (f, pl); **tenazas de extracción** (f, pl); **gatillo** (m)
dental hygienist **higienista dental** (m or f)
dental office **clínica dental** (f)
dentine **dentina** (f)
denture **dentadura (postiza)** (f)
  full denture **dentadura completa** (f)
  partial denture **dentadura parcial** (f)
diet, liquid **dieta de líquidos** (f)

drill **taladro** (m); **torno** (m); **trépano** (m)
drill, to **perforar; taladrar**
emesis basin **riñonera** (f)
enamel **esmalte** (m)
extraction **extracción** (f)
fauces **fauces** (f, pl)
feel nothing, to **no sentir nada (ie)**
file down, to **limar**
fill, to **empastar; tapar; calzar; emplomar** (Arg.)
  fill with gold, to **orificar**
filling **empaste** (m); **empastadura** (f); **relleno** (m); **tapadura** (f); **emplomadura** (f, Arg.)
frenum of the tongue **frenillo** (m)
gargle (liquid) **gargarismo** (m)
gargle, to **hacer gárgaras; hacer buches (de sal)**
gold **oro** (m)
gums **encías** (f)
headrest **apoyo para la cabeza** (m)
impression **impresión** (f)
immobilization **inmovilización** (f)
impaction **impacción** (f)
inlay **incrustación** (f); **orificación** (f)

THE HUMAN BODY
FRONT VIEW

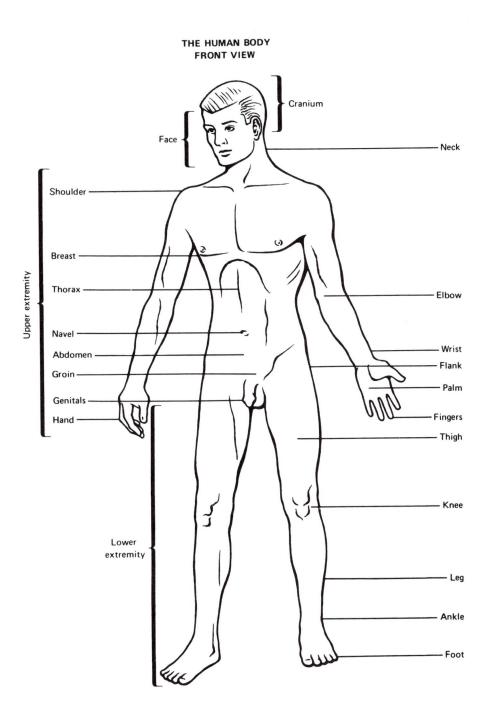

Cranium

Face

Neck

Shoulder

Breast

Thorax

Navel

Abdomen

Groin

Genitals

Hand

Upper extremity

Lower extremity

Elbow

Wrist

Flank

Palm

Fingers

Thigh

Knee

Leg

Ankle

Foot

229

**THE HUMAN BODY
REAR VIEW**

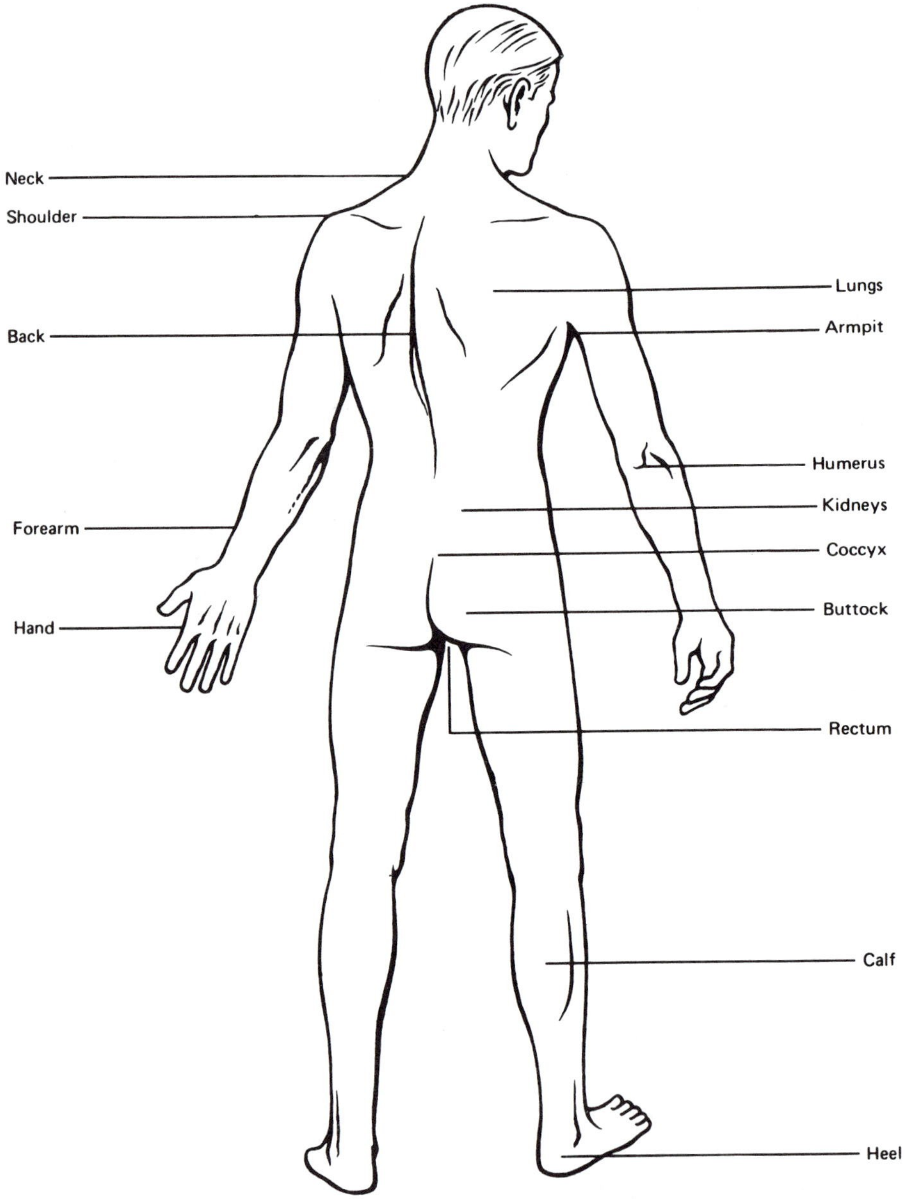

Neck

Shoulder

Lungs

Armpit

Back

Humerus

Kidneys

Forearm

Coccyx

Buttock

Hand

Rectum

Calf

Heel

230

jaw **quijada** (f); **mandíbula** (f)
  broken jaw **quijada rota** (f);
  mandíbula rota (f)
nerve **nervio** (m)
novocaine **novocaína** (f)
numb **entumecido** (adj);
  adormecido (adj); **entumido** (adj)
occlusion **oclusión** (f)
palate **paladar** (m)
plaque **placa** (f)
plate **placa** (f)
polish, to **limar**
porcelain **procelana** (f)
pressure **presión** (f)
  exert pressure on, to **ejercer**
  presión sobre
  sensations, pressure
  sensaciones de ser apretado
pull out, to **extraer**
pulp **pulpa** (f)
pulpotomy **pulpotomía** (f)
put to sleep, to **adormecer por**
  anestesia
pyorrhea **piorrea** (f)
reimplantation **reimplantacíon** (f);
  reinjertación (f)
remove the nerve, to **sacarle el**
  nervio a alguien; matarle el
  nervio a alguien
ridge **elevación** (f); **reborde** (m)
rinse, to **enjuagarse**
roof of the mouth **cielo de la**
  boca (m); **paladar** (m)
root **raíz** (f)
root canal **canal radicular** (m)
root canal work **extracción del**
  nervio (f); **curación del nervio**
  (f)
saliva **esputo** (m); **saliva** (f);
  expectoración (f)

set a fracture, to **reducir una**
  fractura; componer una fractura
show one's teeth, to **enseñar los**
  dientes (coll.); **mostrar los dientes**
side **lado** (m)
  upper right side **lado derecho**
  superior (m)
  lower right side **lado derecho**
  inferior (m)
  upper left side **lado izquierdo**
  superior (m)
  lower left side **lado izquierdo**
  inferior (m)
smooth, to **limar**
sodium pentothal **pentotal de**
  sodio (m)
spit in the bowl, to **escupir en la**
  taza
straighten the teeth, to **enderezar**
  los dientes
surface **superficie** (f)
  buccal surface **superficie bucal**
  distal surface **superficie distal**
  lingual surface **superficie lingual**
  mesial surface **superficie mesial**
  occlusal surface **superficie**
  oclusal
suture (dental) **sutura** (f)
tartar **sarro** (m)
teeth **dientes** (m); **mazorca** (f, sg,
  slang)
  bicuspids **bicúspides** (m);
  premolares (m)
  canine, eyeteeth **canino** (m);
  colmillo (m)
  deciduous teeth **dientes de**
  leche (m, pl)
  even teeth **dientes parejos** (m)
  incisors, front teeth **incisivos**
  (m)

lacking teeth **chimuelo** (adj,
  Chicano)
molars **molares** (m)
  third molar **tercer molar** (m)
  stained teeth **dientes**
  manchados (m)
  white teeth **dientes blancos** (m)
  wisdom teeth **muelas del juicio**
  (f); **muelas cordales** (f)
teething **dentición** (f); **salida de**
  los dientes (f)
temporary filling **empaste**
  provisional (m); **empaque** (m,
  Chicano)
tingling **hormigueo** (m)
tooth **diente** (m)
  baby tooth **diente mamón** (m);
  diente de leche (m)
  back tooth **muela** (f)
  impacted tooth **diente**
  impactado (m)
  large, misshapen tooth **diente**
  de ajo (m, colloq)
  lower tooth **diente inferior** (m)
  toothache **dolor de muelas** (m);
  dolor de dientes (m);
  odontalgia (f)
  toothbrush **cepillo de dientes**
  (m)
  toothpaste **pasta de dientes** (f);
  pasta dentífrica (f)
  toothpick **palillo de dientes** (m);
  mondadientes (m)
  tooth socket **alvéolo** (m)
  upper tooth **diente superior** (m)
  wall **pared** (f)
  waterpick **limpiador de agua a**
  presión (m)
  wire, to **atar con alambre**

EXERCISES   *EJERCICIOS*

The diagrams below correspond to those appearing on the previous pages. Fill in the Spanish names for each body part indicated.

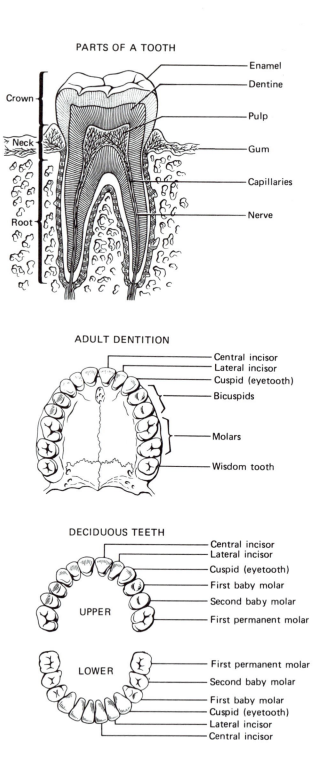

PARTS OF A TOOTH

Crown

Neck

Root

Enamel
Dentine
Pulp
Gum
Capillaries
Nerve

ADULT DENTITION

Central incisor
Lateral incisor
Cuspid (eyetooth)
Bicuspids

Molars

Wisdom tooth

DECIDUOUS TEETH

Central incisor
Lateral incisor
Cuspid (eyetooth)
First baby molar
Second baby molar
First permanent molar

UPPER

LOWER

First permanent molar
Second baby molar
First baby molar
Cuspid (eyetooth)
Lateral incisor
Central incisor

232

LA CABEZA

PARTES DE UN OIDO

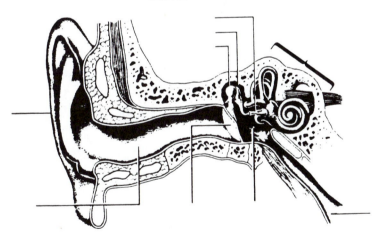

233

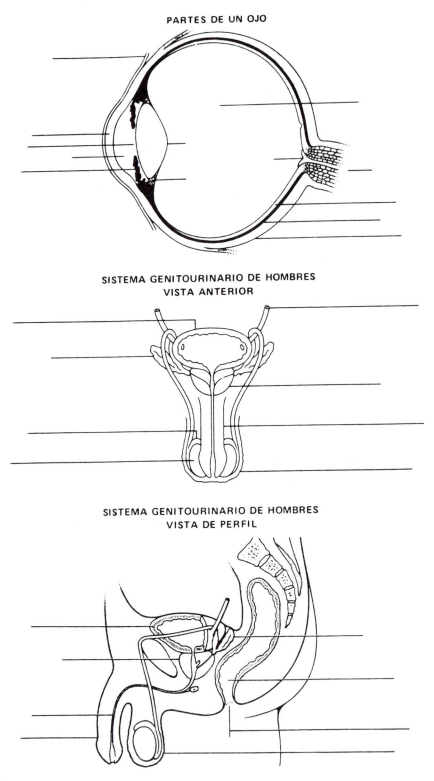

PARTES DE UN OJO

SISTEMA GENITOURINARIO DE HOMBRES
VISTA ANTERIOR

SISTEMA GENITOURINARIO DE HOMBRES
VISTA DE PERFIL

PARTES DE UN DIENTE

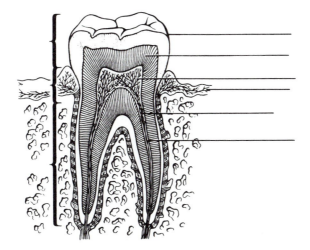

SISTEMA GENITOURINARIO DE MUJERES
VISTA ANTERIOR

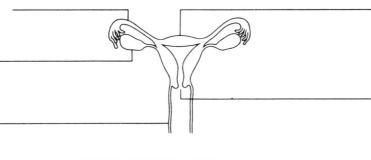

SISTEMA GENITOURINARIO DE·MUJERES
VISTA DE PERFIL

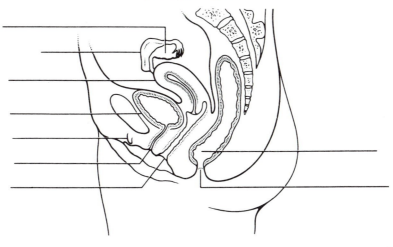

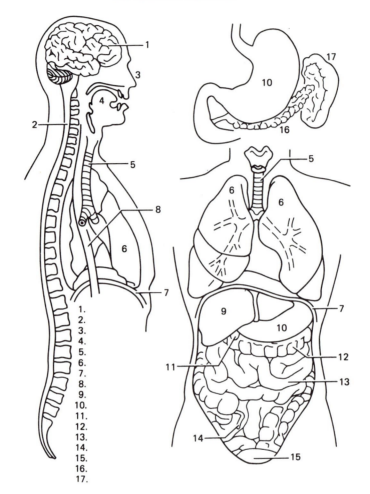

1.
2.
3.
4.
5.
6.
7.
8.
9.
10.
11.
12.
13.
14.
15.
16.
17.

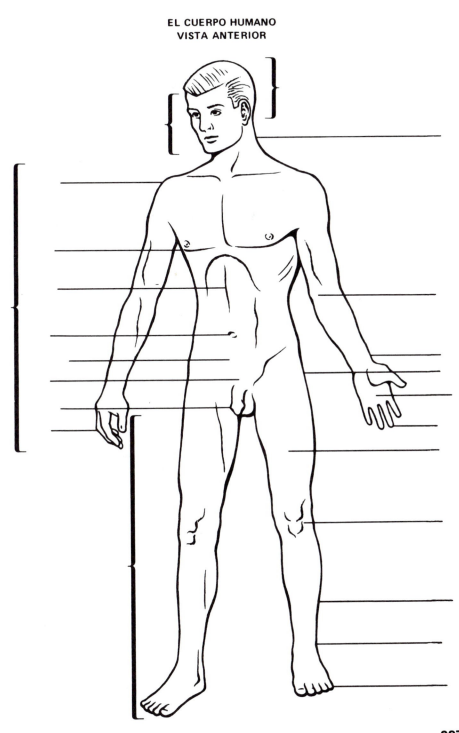

EL CUERPO HUMANO
VISTA ANTERIOR

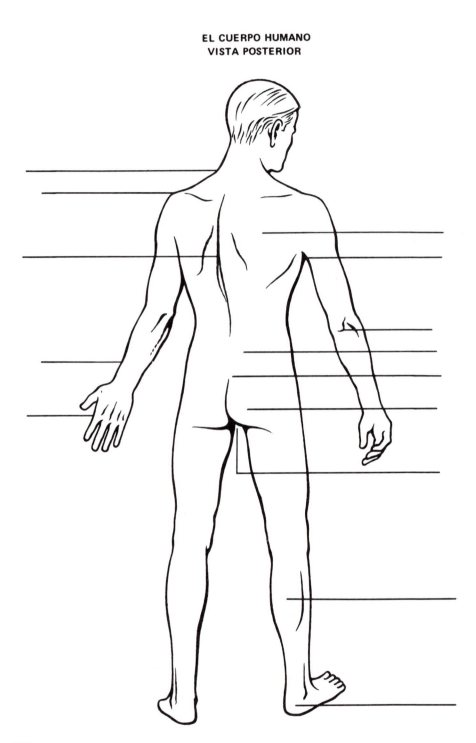

LA DENTADURA DEL ADULTO

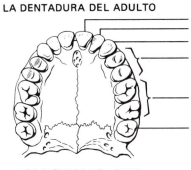

LOS DIENTES DE LECHE

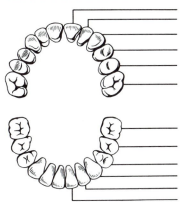

Note *Notas*

1. In Spanish **canal** is an open duct, **conducto** is closed.
2. The plural of **nalga** is less polite.
3. Multiple meanings of **empeine** (m) include these and ringworm.

CHAPTER 6

Conversations for Medical and Paramedical Personnel

Conversaciones para personal médico y paramédico

AMBULANCE[1]

AMBULANCIA

1. I cannot help the patient here.
   No puedo ayudar al (a la) paciente aquí.

2. We must take the patient to the hospital (to the clinic).[2]
   Tenemos que llevar al (a la) paciente al hospital (a la clínica).

3. We are going to move the patient to a stretcher.
   Vamos a pasar al (a la) paciente a una camilla.

4. Don't be afraid.
   No tenga Vd. miedo.

5. Someone ought to accompany the patient in the ambulance.
   Alguien debe acompañar al (a la) paciente en la ambulancia.

6. Is the patient comfortable?
   ¿Se siente el (la) paciente cómodo (-a)?

7. We will be at the hospital (clinic) soon.
   Estaremos al hospital (a la clínica) dentro de poco.

ADMISSION OF THE PATIENT TO THE ROOM[3]

ADMISION DEL PACIENTE AL CUARTO

1. I am _____.
   Soy _____.

2. I am the day nurse, night nurse, nurse on duty, nurse's aide, head nurse.
   Soy la enfermera de día, la enfermera de noche, la enfermera de guardia, la ayudante de enfermera, la jefa de enfermeras.

3. I am the public health nurse, visiting nurse.
   Soy la enfermera de salud pública, la enfermera ambulante.

4. Do you need a wheelchair?
   ¿Necesita Vd. una silla de ruedas?

5. Your family may accompany you to the room.
   Su familia puede acompañarle al cuarto.

6. You can accompany your wife (husband) to her (his) room.
   Vd. puede acompañar a su esposa (esposo) hasta el cuarto.

7. When is your family coming? I want to talk to them.
   ¿Cuándo viene su familia? Quiero hablarles.

8. I want to introduce you to _____ (other patient in the room).
   Quiero presentarle a _____.

9. Here is a hospital gown, please put it on. Do you need help?
   Aquí está una bata del hospital. Favor de ponérsela. ¿Necesita ayuda?

10. Instruct your family (or a friend) to take your suitcase home.
    Pida Vd. que su familia (amigo) devuelva su maleta a casa.

11. I need a urine specimen.
    Necesito una muestra de orina de Vd.

12. When you urinate, fill up this bottle and give it to the nurse on duty.
    Cuando Vd. orine, llene este frasco y déselo a la enfermera de guardia.

13. Here is a booklet that deals with the rules of the hospital.
    Aquí está un librito que trata de las reglas del hospital.

14. This is the buzzer (bell).
    Este es el timbre.

15. This is the call light.
    Esta es la luz para llamar a la enfermera.

16. If you need anything, press the button.
    Si Vd. necesita algo, oprima el botón.

17. The light over your door will stay on until a member of the nursing staff answers your call.
    La luz que está sobre la puerta se mantendrá prendida hasta que un miembro del personal de enfermeras conteste a su llamada.

18. This button raises the headboard.
    Este botón levanta la cabecera de la cama.

19. This button lowers the headboard.
    Este botón baja la cabecera de la cama.

20. This button raises (lowers) the bed.
    Este botón levanta (baja) la cama.

21. This button raises the foot of the bed.
    Este botón levanta el pie de la cama.

22. This button lowers the foot of the bed.
    Este botón baja el pie de la cama.

23. Call someone to help you.
    Llame a alguien para que le (la) ayude.

24. Do not turn without calling the nurse.
    No se voltee sin llamar a la enfermera.

25. Do you want me to raise your headboard?
   ¿Quisiera la cabecera de la cama más alta?
   ¿Quiere Vd. que le levante un poco la cabecera de la cama?

26. Do you want me to lower your headboard?
   ¿Quiere Vd. que le baje un poco la cabecera de la cama?

27. Do you want me to raise the knee rest (your knees)?
   ¿Quiere Vd. que le levante (suba) un poco las rodillas?

28. Do you want me to lower your knees?
   ¿Quiere Vd. que le baje un poco las rodillas?

29. The side rails on your bed are for your protection.
   Los rieles del costado están para su protección.
   Las barandas protectoras de la cama están para su protección.

30. Please do not try to lower or climb over the side rail.
   No pretenda bajarlos (bajarlas) o treparse sobre ellos.

31. Please wear slippers or shoes and a robe at all times when you are out of bed.
   Por favor, use Vd. pantuflas o zapatos y una bata en todo momento cuando no esté en la cama.

32. The bathroom is behind this door.
   El inodoro está detrás de esta puerta.

33. The bathtub is along the hall to the right (to the left).
   La bañera (la bañadera [Amer.]) está por el pasillo (corredor) a la derecha (a la izquierda).

34. This is a special denture cup to store your dentures in when you are not wearing them.
   Este es un recipiente especial para guardar su dentadura postiza cuando no la esté usando.

35. You must remove your dentures or any partial dentures before surgery or any procedure involving a general anesthetic.
   Vd. debe quitarse su dentadura postiza o cualquier diente postizo antes de la cirugía, o si Vd. está en la lista para algún tratamiento que envuelva anestesia general.

36. To place a local telephone call, dial 9, wait for the dial tone, then dial the number you wish.
   Para hacer una llamada local, marque 9 [nueve] y espere el tono, luego marque el número que Vd. desee.

37. For long distance or suburban calls, dial 0 and the operator will help you.
   Para llamadas de larga distancia o a los suburbios, marque 0 [cero] y la operadora lo (la) asistirá.

38. Telephone calls can (not) be added to your hospital bill.
   Las llamadas telefónicas (no) pueden ser agregadas en su cuenta de hospital.

39. Newspapers are sold each morning and evening throughout the hospital and are also available in the lobby.
   Se venden los periódicos todas las mañanas y todas las noches por todo el hospital y también están a disposición en el salón de entrada.

40. Television sets can be rented here in the hospital at a nominal cost.
    Se puede alquilar televisores (aparatos de televisión) aquí en el hospital por un pago nominal.

41. I will call the dietician to discuss your menu.
    Llamaré al dietista para que discutan su menú.

42. You will be given a choice of foods for your meals according to the diet prescribed by your doctor.
    Se le dará a elegir los alimientos para sus comidas según la dieta que su médico le prescribe.

43. Breakfast is served at 8 A.M.
    Se sirve el desayuno a las ocho de la mañana.

44. Lunch is served at 11:30.
    Se sirve el almuerzo a las once y media.

45. Dinner is at 5 P.M.
    Se sirve la cena a las cinco de la tarde.

46. A snack is served at 8:45 P.M.
    Se sirve una merienda (una colación) a las nueve menos cuarto de la noche.

47. The patients' chapel is located on the main floor and is open to members of all faiths.
    La capilla de los pacientes se halla en el piso principal y está a disposición de los miembros de todos los credos.

48. There are brief services there every Sunday at 10:30 A.M.
    Hay breves servicios allí todos los domingos a las diez y media de la mañana.

49. If you wish, your own priest, minister, or rabbi can come to visit you.
    Si Vd. desea, su propio sacerdote, ministro, o rabí puede venir a visitarle.

50. The head nurse is _____.
    La jefa de enfermeras es _____ .

51. Your doctor usually visits at _____.
    Su médico suele visitar a las _____ .

52. Do you need more blankets or another pillow?
    ¿Necesita Vd. más frazadas (cobijas) u otra almohada?

53. You may not smoke in the room.
    No se puede fumar en el cuarto.

54. Is the room too hot?
    ¿Hace demasiado calor en el cuarto?

55. Do you want me to open (close) the window?
    ¿Quiere que yo abra (cierre) la ventana?

56. Do you want me to turn on (turn off) the lights?
    ¿Quiere Vd. que encienda (apague) la luz?

57. Are you hungry?
    ¿Tiene Vd. hambre?

58. Are you thirsty?
    ¿Tiene Vd. sed?

59. Are you allergic to any medication?
    ¿Padece Vd. de alguna alergia?
    ¿Es Vd. alérgico (alérgica) a alguna medicina?

60. Are you on a restricted diet?
    ¿Sigue Vd. dieta rigurosa?

61. I am the orderly.
    Soy el ayudante.

62. I have come to take you for your tests.
    He venido para llevarle a que le hagan sus análisis.

63. Please move over to the stretcher.
    Acuéstese en la camilla, por favor.
    Por favor, pásese a la camilla.

64. Please sit down on the wheelchair.
    Siéntese Vd. en la silla de ruedas, por favor.

65. Wait here until you hear your name.
    Espere aquí hasta oír su nombre.
    que oiga su nombre.
    que escuche su nombre.

EXERCISES *EJERCICIOS*

A. Answer the questions using the cue given in parenthesis.

1. **¿Quién es Vd.? (la enfermera)**

    _____

2. **¿Quién es Vd.? (la enfermera de noche)**

    _____

3. **¿Quién es Vd.? (la jefa de enfermeras)**

    _____

4. **¿Quién es Vd.? (la ayudante de enfermera)**

    _____

5. **¿Quién es Vd.? (la enfermera de guardia)**

    _____

6. **¿Quién es Vd.? (la enfermera de salud pública)**

    _____

7. **¿Quién es Vd.? (la enfermera ambulante)**

    _____

8. **¿Quién es Vd.? (el enfermero)**

    _____

9. ¿Quién es Vd.? (el enfermero de salud pública)

_____

10. ¿Quién es Vd.? (el enfermero ambulante)

_____

11. ¿Quién es Vd.? (el ayudante de hospital)

_____

B. Make the appropriate substitutions.

1. **Este botón levanta la cabecera de la cama.
   (baja)** _____

2. **Este botón baja la cabecera de la cama.
   (la cama)** _____

3. **Este botón baja la cama.
   (levanta)** _____

4. **Este botón levanta la cama.
   (el pie de la cama)** _____

5. **Este botón levanta el pie de la cama.
   (baja)** _____

6. **Este botón baja el pie de la cama.**

VISITING HOURS

LAS HORAS DE VISITAS

1. Visitors are allowed unless you or your physician request "no visitors."
   Se permiten visitas a no ser que Vd. o su médico dispongan lo contrario.

2. Visitors are only allowed during visiting hours.
   Se admiten visitantes solamente durante las horas de visita.

3. The visiting hours are from _____ to _____.
   Las horas de visita son desde las _____ hasta las _____ de la tarde.

4. Visitors must obtain a pass from the information desk in the lobby.
   Los visitantes deben obtener un pase en la mesa de información del salón de entrada.

5. No more than two visitors at a time.
   No más de dos visitas (visitantes) al mismo tiempo.

6. Only two visitors per patient are allowed.
   Solamente se permiten dos visitantes por paciente.

7. Please return the passes when you leave.
   Por favor, no se olviden de devolver los pases cuando Vds. salgan.

8. There are too many visitors in the room.
   Hay demasiado visitantes en el cuarto.

9. Please do not smoke in the patient's room.
   Le(s) pedimos que siga(n) las reglas de no fumar en los cuartos de los pacientes.

10. Smoking is allowed in the wating room of each floor.
    Se permite fumar solamente en la sala de espera que está en cada piso.

11. Children under 14 are not able to visit patients.
    Los niños que no tienen catorce años no pueden visitar a los pacientes.

12. Children under 12 are not allowed to visit the patients.
    A los niños de menores de doce años, no se les permite visitar a los pacientes.

13. Children from 12 to 16 must be accompanied by an adult.
    Los visitantes entre la edad de doce a dieciséis años tienen que ser acompañados por un adulto.

14. Children accompanying visitors should not be left unattended in the lobby.
    No se debe dejar solos en el salón de entrada a los niños que acompañan a los visitantes.

15. Visiting hours for the Intensive Care Unit are:
    Las horas de visita para la Unidad de Cuidados Intensivos son:

16. Visiting hours for the Cardiac Care Unit are:
    Las horas de visita para la Unidad de Cuidados Coronarios son:

17. One (two) visitors for 5 minutes every hour on the hour beginning at _____ and ending with _____.[4]
    Un (dos) visitante(s) por cinco minutos cada hora en la hora comenzando a la _____ y terminando con _____.

18. One visitor for 5 minutes every hour on the half hour beginning at _____ and ending with _____.
    Un visitante por cinco minutos cada hora en la media hora comenzando a la _____ y terminando con _____.

CONVERSATION WITH THE PATIENT

CONVERSACION CON EL PACIENTE

Nursing Care   *Cuidados auxiliares*

1. May I help you?
   ¿En qué puedo servirle(-la)?

2. Did you call?
   ¿Me llamó Vd.?
   ¿Me ha llamado Vd.?

3. Did you sleep well?
   ¿Durmió Vd. bien?

4. Do you feel better today?
   ¿Se siente mejor hoy?

5. Do you still feel (very) weak?
   ¿Todavía se siente (muy) débil?

6. Are you sleepy?
   ¿Tiene Vd. sueño?

7. It is necessary to rest more.
   Es necesario descansar más.

8. Try to sleep.
   Trate de dormir.

9. Do you want to sit up?
   ¿Quiere Vd. sentarse?

10. Do you want to lie down?
    ¿Quiere Vd. acostarse?

11. Do you want the nurse?
    ¿Quiere Vd. a la enfermera?

12. Can I help you?
    ¿Puedo ayudarle (-la) en algo?

13. Can you help me?
    ¿Puede ayudarme?

Ambulation   *Tratamiento ambulatorio*

14. You are not well enough yet to get out of bed.
    Vd. no está bastante fuerte todavía para levantarse.

15. You are to remain in bed today.
    Vd. debe guardar cama hoy.
    Vd. debe permanecer en cama hoy.

16. You may get out of bed, but not by yourself.
    Vd. puede salir de la cama, pero no sin ayuda.

17. You may be able to get (up) out of bed tomorrow.
    Vd. podrá levantarse de la cama mañana.

18. You may get up for about 15 minutes this afternoon.
    Vd. puede levantarse por unos quince minutos esta tarde.

19. You will not be able to walk for ten days.
    No podrá caminar por diez días.

20. You must lie flat in bed until tomorrow.
    Vd. debe permanecer acostado (-a) hasta mañana.

21. You have to get out of bed.
    Vd. tiene que salirse de la cama.
    Vd. tiene que levantarse.

22. You may walk around today.
    Vd. puede caminar hoy.

Hygiene *Higiene*

23. You may take a bath.
    Vd. puede bañarse.

24. You may take a shower.
    Vd. puede darse una ducha.
    Vd. puede darse un regaderazo. (Mex.)
    Vd. puede ducharse.

25. You may take a sitz bath.
    Vd. puede darse un baño de asiento (un semicupio).

26. Take a hot sitz bath every four hours.
    Tome Vd. un baño de asiento (un semicupio) caliente cada cuatro horas.

27. Do not lock the door, please.
    No cierre Vd. la puerta con llave, por favor.

28. Call if you feel faint or in need of help.
    Llame si Vd. se siente débil, o si necesita ayuda.

29. Can you wash yourself or do you need help?
    ¿Puede Vd. lavarse, o necesita ayuda?

30. Do you want me to wash you?
    ¿Quiere Vd. que yo le (la) bañe?
    ¿Quiere Vd. que yo le (la) lave?

31. We are going to give you a (sponge) bath.
    Nosotros vamos a darle un baño (de esponja).

32. You may use the wash basin.
    Vd. puede usar la basija.
            jofaina.
            ponchera. (C. A.)
            palanga. (Mex.)

33. Wash your genitals.
    Lávese los privados (los [órganos] genitales).

34. Can you comb your hair without help?
    ¿Puede peinarse sin ayuda?

35. Can you shave yourself or do you want me to shave you?
    ¿Puede afeitarse a sí mismo, o quiere que yo le afeite?

36. Try to do it yourself.
    Trate de hacerlo por sí mismo (misma).

37. Call when you have to go to the toilet.
    Llame cuando tenga que ir al inodoro.
    a los servicios.
    al [cuarto de] baño.

38. Do you need the bed pan, or do you want to go to the bathroom?
    ¿Necesita Vd. la cuña o quiere ir al inodoro?
    la silleta o quiere ir al inodoro?
    el cómodo (Mex.) **o quiere ir al inodoro?**

39. I am going to put the bed pan on the table.
    Voy a dejar la cuña (el cómodo [Mex.]**) sobre la mesa.**

40. Flex your knees and raise your buttocks off the bed.
    Flexione Vd. las rodillas y levante las nalgas de la cama.

41. Use the signal cord to call as soon as you have urinated.
    Use Vd. el botón para llamar tan pronto como Vd. haya orinado.

42. Do you need tissues, toilet paper?
    ¿Necesita Vd. kleenex, papel de baño (pañuelo de papel)?

43. Are you constipated?
    ¿Está Vd. estreñido (estreñida)?

44. I will give you an enema.
    Le pondré una enema.

45. Turn on your left (right) side.
    Acuéstese Vd. sobre el lado izquierdo (derecho).

46. Turn over.
    Volteese del otro lado, por favor.
    Vírese Vd. del otro lado.
    Vuélvase del otro lado, por favor.

Diagnosis *Diagnosis*

47. I still don't know exactly what is wrong with you.
    Todavía no sé exactamente lo que Vd. tiene.

48. I think that we have found the cause of your illness.
    Pienso que hemos descubierto la causa de su enfermedad.

49. We are still trying to find the cause of your illness.
    Todavía estamos tratando de saber la causa de su enfermedad.

50. I (do not) know why you are sick.
    (No) sé por que está enfermo (-a).

51. It seems that you have heart disease.[5]
    Parece que Vd. tiene enfermedad cardíaca.

Prohibitions *Prohibiciones*

52. It is very harmful for you to smoke so much.
A Vd. le es muy dañino fumar tanto.

53. You have to stop smoking.
Vd. tiene que dejar de fumar.

54. Don't drink any alcohol.
No tome Vd. ninguna bebída alcohólica.

55. Don't have any sexual relations until are are treated.
No tenga relaciones sexuales hasta que se cure.

56. Avoid physical exercise.
Evite Vd. los ejercicios físicos.

57. Don't do any heavy work.
No haga Vd. ningún trabajo pesado.

58. Don't drive a car.
No conduzca Vd. el coche.

59. Don't lose weight.
No pierda Vd. peso.

60. Don't gain weight.
No aumente Vd. peso.

61. Avoid salt.
Evite Vd. sal.

62. Avoid tobacco.
Evite Vd. el tobaco.

63. Don't swim for the next few weeks.
No debe nadar durante las semanas que vienen.

64. Don't use this hand for the next few days.
No debe usar esta mano durante los días siguientes.

Appointments *Citas*

65. The doctor wants to see that prescription.
El médico quiere ver esa receta.

66. The doctor will examine you now.
El doctor le (la) examinará ahora.

67. The doctor wants to see how you are getting along.
El doctor (La doctora) quiere ver cómo (le) va.

68. Make an appointment to come back to the clinic to see me in two weeks.[6]
Haga Vd. una cita en la clínica para verme de hoy en quince días.

69. I will make an appointment for you to see Dr. Ortiz on Tuesday, February 17, at 11:30 A.M.
Le haré una cita a Vd. para ver a la doctora Ortiz el martes, el diecisiete de febrero, a las once y media de la mañana.

70. Here is an appointment card.
Aquí tiene Vd. una tarjeta con la información escrita.

71. Don't fail to return on the 17th (of February).[6]
No deje de volver el diecisiete (de febrero).

72. Don't forget.
No se olvide.

73. The appointment is important.
La cita es importante.

Discharge *El alta*

74. I think that you should not return home just yet.
Creo que Vd. no debe volver a su casa por mucho tiempo.

75. I think that you will be much better soon.
Creo que Vd. se sentirá mucho mejor dentro de poco.

76. I think that it may take you quite a while to recuperate.
Creo que no recobrará Vd. la salud por mucho tiempo.

77. You are going to be discharged (released) today.
A Vd. le van a dar de alta hoy.
A Vd. van a darle de alta hoy.

78. The patient was discharged this morning.
A la (Al) paciente le dieron de alta esta mañana.

79. If you have any questions, ask your doctor (ask for me).
Si Vd. quiere saber algo, pregunte por su doctor(a) (por mí).

Supplies *Materiales*

80. Do you need supplies?
¿Le faltan artículos (materiales)?

81. Do you need a sleeping pill?
¿Necesita Vd. una pastilla para dormir?
            una píldora somnífera?
            un somnífero?
            una soporífera?
            algo para ayudarle a dormir?

82. Do you need a stool softener?
¿Necesita Vd. una cápsula para ablandar sus evacuaciones?

PRESENT ILLNESS[7]

ENFERMEDAD ACTUAL

1. What is wrong with you?
   ¿De qué se queja Vd.?
   ¿Qué le pasa a Vd.?
   ¿Qué le sucede a Vd.?

2. Did you have an accident?
   ¿Tuvo Vd. un accidente?
   ¿Sufrió Vd. un accidente?

3. When did it occur?
   ¿Cuándo ocurrió?

4. Where did it happen?
   ¿Dónde ocurrió?

5. Were you hurt at work?
   ¿Fue lastimado en el trabajo?
   ¿Se lastimó en el trabajo?
   ¿Fue herido en el trabajo?

6. What is the name of your employer?
   ¿Para qué compañía trabaja Vd.?
   ¿Dónde trabaja Vd.?
   ¿Quién le emplea?

7. What is the address of your employer?
   ¿Cuál es la dirección de su trabajo?
   ¿Dónde está Vd. empleado (empleada)?

8. Did you faint before the accident?
   ¿Se desmayó Vd. antes del accidente?

9. Did you faint after the accident?
   ¿Se desmayó Vd. después del accidente?

10. Did you have a dizzy spell before the accident?
    ¿Tuvo Vd. mareos antes del acccidente?
    ¿Se sintió Vd. mareado (mareada) antes del accidente?

11. Did you lose consciousness after the accident?
    ¿Perdió Vd. el conocimiento después del accidente?

12. How long?
    ¿Por cuánto tiempo?

13. How did this illness begin?[8]
    ¿Cómo empezó esta enfermedad?
    ¿Cómo ha empezado esta enfermedad?

14. When were you first taken sick?
¿Cuándo ha empezado esta enfermedad?

15. Please try to remember dates and times accurately.
Por favor, trate de recordarse de las fechas y la hora exactas.

16. Have you taken any medicine for this?
¿Ha tomado Vd. alguna medicina para esto?

17. What have you taken?
¿Qué ha tomado Vd.?

18. Is the pain better after the medicine?
¿Siente Vd. alivio después de tomar la medicina?

19. Does it make it worse?
¿Lo aumenta?

20. Are you in pain?
¿Siente Vd. dolor?

21. When did your pains begin?
¿Cuándo empezaron sus dolores?

22. Where is the pain?
¿Qué le duele?
¿Dónde le duele?
¿Dónde siente Vd. el dolor?

23. In the head?
¿En la cabeza?

24. In the abdomen?
¿En el abdomen?

25. In the chest?
¿En el pecho?

26. In the side?
¿En el lado?
¿En su costado?

27. Which one?
¿En qué lado?

28. In the shoulder blades?
¿En los hombros?

29. In the back?
¿En la espalda?

30. In the legs?
¿En las piernas?

31. In the bones?
¿En los huesos?

32. Here?
    ¿Aquí?

33. Are you in pain now?
    ¿Tiene Vd. dolores ahora?
    ¿Siente Vd. dolores ahora?
    ¿Sufre Vd. de dolor ahora?

34. Does the pain radiate?
    ¿Se corre el dolor?

35. From where to where?
    ¿Hacia dónde?

36. Is it a constant pain or does it come and go?
    ¿Es un dolor constante, o va y vuelve (o le va y se le quita)?

37. Is it dull, sharp, steady pain, or a feeling of pressure?
    ¿Es un dolor sordo, agudo, continuo, o una sensación de presión?

38. Do you have pain here?
    ¿Siente Vd. dolor aquí?
    ¿Le duele aquí?

39. Has the pain eased a great deal?
    ¿Ha disminuido mucho el dolor?

40. How long have you had the pain?
    ¿Desde cuándo tiene Vd. el dolor?

41. Is there anything that makes the pain better?
    ¿Hay algo que lo alivie?

42. Is there anything that makes the pain worse?
    ¿Hay algo que lo aumente?

43. What is it?
    ¿Qué es?

44. Is there anything else that accompanies the pain?
    ¿Hay otras molestias que acompañen el dolor?

45. Does the pain go away when you rest?
    Al descansar, ¿se alivia el dolor?

46. Does the pain awaken you at night?
    ¿Le (La) despierta el dolor durante la noche?

47. Is the pain very strong at night?
    ¿Es mayor el dolor durante la noche?
    ¿Aumenta el dolor en la noche?

48. More during the daytime?
    ¿Mayor durante el día?

All the time?
¿Todo el tiempo?
Before eating?
¿Antes de comer?
After eating?
¿Después de comer?
While eating?
¿Al comer?
When it is (was) cold?
¿Cuando hace (hacía) frío?
When it is (was) hot?
¿Cuando hace (hacía) calor?
When it is (was) humid?
¿Cuando está (estaba) húmedo?
When you are (were) upset?
¿Cuando está (estaba) molesto (-a)?
When you are worried?
¿Cuando está (estaba) preocupado (-a)?
When you exercise(d)?
¿Cuando hace (hacía) ejercicios?
When you urinate(d)?
¿Cuando orina (orinaba)?
When you defecate(d)?
¿Cuando defeca (defecaba)?
When you have (had) sexual relations?
¿Cuando tiene (tenía) relaciones sexuales?
When you swallow(ed) liquids, solids, both?
¿Cuando traga (tragaba) líquidos, sólidos, ambos?
When you stand (stood)?
¿Cuando está (estaba) de pie?
When you sit (sat) down?
¿Cuando está (estaba) sentado (-a)?
When you lie (lay) down?
¿Cuando está (estaba) acostado (-a)?
When you walk (walked)?
¿Cuando camina (caminaba)?
When you climb(ed) stairs?
¿Cuando sube (subía) escaleras?
When you bend (bent) over?
¿Cuando se agacha (agachaba)?

49. Do you have a lot of pain in your left (right) leg?
    ¿Le duele mucho la pierna izquierda (derecha)?

50. Does it hurt more when I press, or when I stop pressing suddenly?
    ¿Le duele más cuando le comprimo o cuando dejo de comprimir rápidamente?

51. Does it hurt only where I am pressing, or somewhere else?
    Le duele solamente donde aprieto, o en otros lugares más?

52. Can you sleep with the pain?
    ¿Puede Vd. dormir con el dolor?

53. I will not hurt you.
    No voy a hacerle daño.

54. It is not painful.
    No le va a doler.

55. Tell me when you feel pain.
    Avíseme cuando sienta dolor.

56. Have you had a heart attack?
    ¿Sufrió Vd. un ataque cardíaco?

57. When did you have your first attack?
    ¿Cuándo sufrió Vd. su primer ataque?

58. Have you or another person in your family or neighborhood suffered from this same illness previously?
    ¿Ha padecido Vd. u otra persona de la familia o vecindad antes de esta misma dolencia?

59. What is bothering you most right now?
    ¿Qué es lo que más le molesta ahorita?

60. Do you know where you are?
    ¿Sabe Vd. dónde está?

61. You are in the hospital.
    Vd. está en el hospital.

62. What day is today?
    ¿Qué día es hoy?

63. What month is it?
    ¿Cuál es el mes?

64. You will be OK.
    Vd. va a estar bien.

65. You will need an operation.
    Vd. va a necesitar una operación.

66. I am calling a specialist to see you.
    Voy a llamar a un(a) especialista que le (la) vea.

REVIEW *REPASO*

Learn the following dialogue.

DOCTOR: Good afternoon. What is wrong with you?

DOCTOR: **Buenas tardes. ¿De qué se queja Vd.?**

PATIENT: I don't feel well.

PACIENTE: **No me siento muy bien.**

DOCTOR: Did you have an accident?

DOCTOR: ¿**Tuvo Vd. un accidente?**

PATIENT: Yes, a large box fell on my head.

PACIENTE: **Sí, una caja grande se me cayó en la cabeza.**

DOCTOR: When did it occur?

DOCTOR: ¿**Cuándo ocurrió?**

PATIENT: It happened at my factory during lunch.

PACIENTE: **Tuvo lugar en la fábrica donde trabajo, a mediodía.**

DOCTOR: What is the name of your employer?

DOCTOR: ¿**Quién le emplea?**

PATIENT: D & D Fabrics.

PACIENTE: **D & D Fabrics.**

DOCTOR: What is the address of your employer?

DOCTOR: ¿**Cuál es la dirección de su trabajo?**

PATIENT: 2312 East Noyes, Evanston.

PACIENTE: **Calle Noyes veintitrés doce Este, Evanston.**

DOCTOR: Did you faint after the accident?

DOCTOR: ¿**Se desmayó Vd. después del accidente?**

PATIENT: I suddenly lost consciousness.

PACIENTE: **De repente perdí el conocimiento.**

DOCTOR: How long?

DOCTOR: ¿**Por cuánto tiempo?**

PATIENT: A minute.

PACIENTE: **Un minuto.**

DOCTOR: Are you in pain now?

DOCTOR: ¿**Siente Vd. dolor ahora?**

PATIENT: Yes, and I feel dizzy.

PACIENTE: **Sí, y me siento mareado.**

DOCTOR: Where is the pain? Show me.

DOCTOR: ¿**Dónde le duele? Enséñeme.**

PATIENT: My head and neck hurt me.

PACIENTE: **Me duelen la cabeza y el cuello.**

DOCTOR: Is it a constant pain or does it come and go?

DOCTOR: ¿**Es un dolor constante, o va y vuelve?**

PATIENT: It is a constant pain.

PACIENTE: **Es un dolor constante.**

DOCTOR: Is it dull, sharp, steady, or a feeling of pressure?

DOCTOR: ¿**Es un dolor sordo, agudo, continuo, o una sensación de presión?**

PATIENT: It is a sharp pain in my head and a feeling of pressure on my neck.

PACIENTE: **En la cabeza es un dolor agudo, y en el cuello, una sensación de presión.**

DOCTOR: Has the pain eased a great deal?

DOCTOR: ¿**Ha disminuido mucho el dolor?**

PATIENT: It is better.

PACIENTE: **Es mucho mejor.**

DOCTOR: We must have more information. Please give the nurse the information she requests. You will also need some tests before we can make a diagnosis.

DOCTOR: **Debemos tener más informaciones. Tenga la bondad de contestar a las preguntas de la enfermera. Además, Vd. necesitará algunos análisis antes de que podamos hacer un diagnóstico.**

PAST MEDICAL HISTORY[9]

PREVIA HISTORIA MEDICA

1. Have you ever had...?
   ¿Ha sufrido Vd. alguna vez de...?
   ¿Ha padecido Vd. alguna vez de...?
   rheumatic fever
   fiebre reumática
   measles
   sarampión
   German measles
   rubéola; sarampión alemán; alfombría (Chicano); **fiebre de tres días**
   scarlet fever
   fiebre escarlatina
   mumps
   paperas; farfoyota (P.R.); **bolas** (slang)
   typhoid fever
   fiebre tifoidea
   polio
   polio
   chicken pox
   varicela; viruelas locas (slang)
   cholera
   cólera
   diphtheria
   difteria
   small pox
   viruela
   whooping cough
   tos ferina; tos convulsiva; coqueluche
   chronic tonsilitis
   amigdalitis crónica
   chronic laryngitis
   laringitis crónica
   tuberculosis
   tuberculosis
   amebic dysentery
   disenteria amebiana
   high blood pressure
   hipertensión arterial; presión arterial alta
   low blood pressure
   hipotensión arterial; presión arterial baja
   diabetes
   diabetes
   goiter
   bocio; buche (slang)

anemia
anemia (un número bajo de los glóbulos rojos)
venereal disease
enfermedades venéreas; la secreta (slang)
gonorrhea
gonorrea; purgación (slang)
syphilis
sífilis; sangre mala (slang)
heart disease
enfermedades cardíacas; enfermedad del corazón; cardiopatías
any kidney ailment
cualquier enfermedad del riñón
kidney stones
cálculos en el riñón
allergies
alergias
hay fever
fiebre del heno
sinusitis
sinusitis
arthritis
artritis
cystitis
cistitis (infección de la vejiga)
spastic colon
colon espástico; colitis mucosa
pneumonia
neumonia
emphysema
enfisema
varicose veins
venas varicosas; venas inflamadas
brain stroke
derrame cerebral; embolia cerebral; parálisis; hemorragia vascular; vascular hemorrage
blurred vision
vista borrosa
Parkinson's disease
la parálisis agitante; la enfermedad de Parkinson
chorea (any spastic paralysis)
corea; el mal o la danza o el baile de San Vito o de San Guido
tetanus
tétanos; el mal de arco (slang)
pancreatitis
pancreatitis
cirrhosis
cirrosis del hígado
epileptic attacks
ataques epilépticos; convulsiones

ulcers (stomach or duodenal)
úlceras de estómago o duodeno
mononucleosis
mononucleosis infecciosa
gall bladder attack
ataque de la vesícula; derrame de bilis; ataque vesicular
gall stones
cálculos en la vejiga
appendicitis
apendicitis
jaundice
derrame biliar; ictericia; piel amarilla (colloq)
hepatitis
hepatitis
pleurisy
pleuresía
large boils
furúnculos grandes
cancer
cáncer[10]
tropical diseases
enfermedades tropicales
diverticulitis
diverticulitis; colitis ulcerosa
any previous surgery
cualquier cirugía anterior; cirugía previa

2. Do you have problems with your thyroid gland?
   ¿Tiene Vd. problemas con la glándula tiroides?
   ¿Tiene Vd. problema de tiroides?

3. What immunizations have you had?
   ¿Qué clase de inmunizaciones ha tenido Vd.?
   cholera
   cólera
   yellow fever
   fiebre amarilla
   tetanus
   tétanos
   polio
   polio(melitis)—(la vacuna oral)
   measles
   sarampión
   BCG
   BCG para tuberculosis

4. Were you vaccinated against smallpox?
   ¿Le vacunaron contra la viruela?

5. Did you get an inoculation for typhoid?
   ¿Le pusieron una inoculación contra el tifus?

6. Were there many people in your town with that disease?
   ¿Había mucha gente en su pueblo con esa enfermedad?

7. Do you have asthma?
   ¿Sufre Vd. de asma?
   ¿Ha padecido Vd. de asma?
   ¿Sufre Vd. de fatiga? (colloq)

8. Are you allergic to
   ¿Tiene Vd. alergias a . . . ?
   ¿Es Vd. alérgico (alérgica) a . . . ?
   ¿Padece Vd. de alergias a . . . ?
   any food
   alguna comida
   penicillin
   penicilina
   aspirin
   aspirina
   sulfa
   sulfas
   sleeping pills
   píldoras para dormir
   dust or pollen or mold
   polvo o polen o moho
   animals
   animales
   insect bites
   mordeduras de insectos; picaduras de insectos

9. Have you ever had welts/rashes, itching, swelling or asthma after getting penicillin?
   ¿Ha tenido Vd. alguna vez ronchas, comezón, hinchazones o asma después de recibir penicilina?

10. Do you have any drug reactions?
    ¿Tiene Vd. alguna sensibilidad a productos químicos?

11. Have you been hospitalized within the last five years?
    ¿Ha estado Vd. hospitalizado (-a) por cualquier razón durante los últimos cinco años?

12. Why?
    ¿Por qué?

13. When did you come here (to the hospital) for the first time?
    ¿Cuándo vino Vd. aquí (al hospital) por primera vez?

14. How long had you been in the hospital?
    ¿Cuánto tiempo hacía que Vd. estaba[11] en el hospital?

15. Which hospital was it?
   ¿En qué hospital?

16. What is the address?
   ¿Cuál es la dirección?

17. How long have you been in the hospital?
   ¿Cuánto tiempo lleva Vd. internado (-a)?

18. Do you have your own doctor?
   ¿Tiene Vd. su propio médico (propia médica)?

19. What is his (her) name?
   ¿Cómo se llama?

20. Where is his (her) office?
   ¿Dónde está su consultorio?

21. What is the telephone?
   ¿Cuál es su número de teléfono?

22. When was the last time you saw a doctor?
   ¿Cuándo fue la última vez que visitó Vd. a un médico?
   ¿Cuándo fue la última vez que ha visitado a un médico?
   ¿Cuándo fue la última vez que ha visto a un médico?

23. What was the visit for?
   ¿Para qué consultó Vd. a su médico (-a)?

24. Have you seen another doctor or native healer for this problem?
   ¿Ha visto Vd. a otro médico o curandero tocante a este problema (por este problema)?

25. Why did you go to the doctor at that time?
   ¿Por qué fue Vd. a ver al médico entonces?

26. How long had you been sick?
   ¿Cuánto tiempo hacía que estaba enfermo (enferma)?
   ¿Cuánto tiempo lleva Vd. de estar enfermo (enferma)?

27. What was the name of the medicine that the doctor gave you?
   ¿Cómo se llama la medicina que el médico le recetó?
   ¿Cuál era el nombre de la medicina que le recetó el médico?

28. Are you taking any medicine, or are you undergoing any medical treatment at present?
   ¿Toma Vd. alguna medicina o está siguiendo algún tratamiento médico actualmente?

29. How many pills do you have at home?
   ¿Cuántas píldoras tiene Vd. en casa?

30. Have you ever had surgery?
   ¿Ha sido operado (-a) jamás?

31. How many times?
   ¿Cuántas veces?

32. Where were you operated on?
    ¿En qué parte fue operado (-a)?

33. Please show me.
    Muéstremela, por favor.

34. When was your last operation?
    ¿Cuándo fue la última operación?

35. Did you have much bleeding during or after the operation?
    ¿Sangró Vd. mucho durante la operación o después?

36. Did you receive blood transfusions?
    ¿Tuvieron que darle sangre?

37. Do you travel much abroad?
    ¿Viaja Vd. mucho al extranjero?

38. Were you sick?
    ¿Se puso enfermo (-a)?

39. Did you see a physician?
    ¿Vio Vd. a un(a) médico (-a)?

40. What did he (she) diagnose?
    ¿Qué diagnosticó?

41. What was the treatment?
    ¿Cuál fue el tratamiento?

42. How do you travel? By plane, train, boat, or car?
    ¿Por qué medio viaja Vd.?
    ¿Por avión, por tren, por barco, en auto?

43. How long do you spend away from the USA?
    ¿Cuánto tiempo pasa Vd. fuera de los Estados Unidos?

44. Where do you stay?
    ¿Dónde se queda Vd.?

45. Were you wounded while in the military service?
    ¿Fue Vd. herido o inhabilitado mientras que estuvo en el servicio militar?

46. Have you ever been wounded by a gun?
    ¿Jamás le dieron un balazo?
    ¿Ha tenido jamás escopetazo?

47. Were you ever cut with a knife?
    ¿Le cortaron jamás con un cuchillo (una daga, un puñal, una navaja)?

48. Were you hit with a stick, stone, fist?
    ¿Le pegaron con un palo, una piedra, el puño (la mano)?

49. Please show me where you were wounded.
    Muéstreme, por favor, donde fue herido (-a).

50. Have you ever been badly hurt in an automobile accident?
   ¿Ha sido gravemente herido (-a) en un accidente de automóvil?

51. In any other kind of accident?
   ¿En otra clase de accidente?

Although the drills that follow are designed to be done actively in class by the instructor and the students, they are arranged so that the student may do them individually outside the class. The student must cover the drill with a card, move the card down the page until the first question or response is visible, make the appropriate answer aloud, and then move the card down until the correct answer appears. This procedure is followed until the end of the drill, when the student may repeat the drill (for additional practice) or go on to the next one.

EXERCISES *EJERCICIOS*

A. Ask the following questions using the cues in parenthesis.

1. **¿Ha sufrido Vd. alguna vez de tuberculosis?**
    (reumatismo)

2. **¿Ha sufrido Vd. alguna vez de reumatismo?**
    (fiebre tifoidea)

3. **¿Ha sufrido Vd. alguna vez de fiebre tifoidea?**
    (tos ferina)

4. **¿Ha sufrido Vd. alguna vez de tos ferina?**
    (derrame biliar)

5. **¿Ha sufrido Vd. alguna vez de derrame biliar?**
    (enfisema)

6. **¿Ha sufrido Vd. alguna vez de enfisema?**
    (alergias)

7. **¿Ha sufrido Vd. alguna vez de alergias?**
    (enfermedades venéreas)

8. **¿Ha sufrido Vd. alguna vez de enfermedades venéreas?**
    (vista borrosa)

9. **¿Ha sufrido Vd. alguna vez de vista borrosa?**
    (rubéola)

10. **¿Ha sufrido Vd. alguna vez de rubéola?**
    (varicela)

11. **¿Ha sufrido Vd. alguna vez de varicela?**

B. Ask the hypothetical patients about immunizations, using the cues in parenthesis.

1. **¿Fue inmunizado Roberto contra la difteria?**
    (la viruela)

2. **¿Fue inmunizado Roberto contra la viruela?**
    (Roberto y Pablo)

3. **¿Fueron inmunizados Roberto y Pablo contra la viruela?**
    (la varicela)

4. ¿Fueron inmunizados Roberto y Pablo contra la varicela?
   (María)

5. ¿Fue inmunizada María contra la varicela?
   (la fiebre escarlatina)

6. ¿Fue inmunizada María contra la fiebre escarlatina?
   (la difteria)

7. ¿Fue inmunizada María contra la difteria?
   (el nene)

8. ¿Fue inmunizado el nene contra la difteria?
   (la cólera)

9. ¿Fue inmunizado el nene contra la cólera?
   (las chicas)

10. ¿Fueron inmunizadas las chicas contra la cólera?
    (el tifus)

11. ¿Fueron inmunizadas las chicas contra el tifus?

REVIEW OF SYSTEMS

REPASO DE SISTEMAS

General *General*

1. How much do you normally weigh?
   ¿Cuánto pesa Vd. por lo regular?

2. Do you have chills?
   ¿Tiene Vd. escalofríos?

3. Do the chills come every day?
   ¿Siente Vd. los escalofríos todos los días?
   every other day?
   cada dos días?
   every three days?
   cada tres días?

4. Are you hot or cold frequently?
   ¿Tiene Vd. calor o frío con frecuencia?[12]

5. Are you nervous?
   ¿Está Vd. nervioso (nerviosa)?

6. Are you depressed?
   ¿Está Vd. deprimido (deprimida)?
   ¿Sufre Vd. de depresiones severas?

PRACTICE *PRACTICA*

With a friend practice the following dialogue until you have mastered it.

DOCTOR: Good Afternoon, Mr. González. I would like you to answer my questions to the best of your ability.

DOCTOR: **Buenas tardes, señor González. Quiero que Vd. conteste a mis preguntas lo mejor posible.**

MR. GONZALEZ: Okay, Doctor.

SR. GONZALEZ: **Muy bien, doctor.**

DOCTOR: How much do you normally weigh?

DOCTOR: **Por lo regular, ¿cuánto pesa Vd.?**

MR. GONZALEZ: 140 pounds.

SR. GONZALEZ: **Ciento cuarenta libras.**

DOCTOR: What was you maximum body weight, and when was that?

DOCTOR: **¿Cuál fue su peso máximo, y cuándo pesaba eso?**

MR. GONZALEZ: A year ago I weighed 175 pounds.

SR. GONZALEZ: **Hace un año que pesé ciento setenta y cinco libras.**

DOCTOR: Then you have lost a lot of weight?

DOCTOR: **Entonces, ¿ha perdido mucho peso últimamente?**

MR. GONZALEZ: Yes, I have lost thirty-five pounds.

SR. GONZALEZ: **Sí, he perdido treinta y cinco libras.**

DOCTOR: What was your minimum body weight, and when?

DOCTOR: **¿Cuál fue su peso mínimo, y cuándo?**

MR. GONZALEZ: When I was in the army I weighed only 130 pounds.

SR. GONZALEZ: **Cuando estaba en el ejército pesaba solamente ciento treinta libras.**

DOCTOR: When were you in the army?

DOCTOR: **¿Cuándo estaba en el ejército?**

MR. GONZALEZ: I was in the army from 1972–1974. I was in the DMZ for a year.

SR. GONZALEZ: **Estuve en el ejército desde mil novecientos setenta y dos hasta setenta y cuatro. Estuve en la zona desmilitarizada en Vietnam por un año.**

DOCTOR: Were you ever ill while in the army?

DOCTOR: **¿Sufrió Vd. enfermedades mientras estaba en el ejército?**

MR. GONZALEZ: Never.

SR. GONZALEZ: **Nunca.**

DOCTOR: Do you sweat much?

DOCTOR: **¿Suda Vd. mucho?**

MR. GONZALEZ: No, I sweat very little.

SR. GONZALEZ: **No, sudo muy poco.**

DOCTOR: Do you have chills?

DOCTOR: **¿Tiene Vd. escalofríos?**

MR. GONZALEZ: Yes, I often have the chills.

SR. GONZALEZ: **Sí, a menudo tengo escalofríos.**

DOCTOR: Do the chills come every day?

DOCTOR: **¿Siente Vd. los escalofríos todos los días?**

MR. GONZALEZ: I have the chills every other day, usually in the evening.

SR. GONZALEZ: **Siento los escalofríos cada dos días, generalmente por la noche.**

DOCTOR: Are you nervous?

MR. GONZALEZ: Yes, I am very nervous, and I eat little.

DOCTOR: Very well, let's find out more about the problem.

DOCTOR: ¿Está Vd. nervioso?

SR. GONZALEZ: Sí, estoy muy nervioso, y como poco.

DOCTOR: Muy bien. Vamos a averiguar cuál es el verdadero carácter de su problema.

Skin, Hair *La piel, el pelo*

1. Do you have any bleeding problems if you cut yourself?
   ¿Tiene Vd. problemas de echar sangre (sangrar) si se corta?

2. How long does it last?
   ¿Cuánto tiempo le dura?

3. Does this happen frequently?
   ¿Ocurre con frecuencia?

4. Do you have any rash on your *face*?
   ¿Tiene Vd. alguna erupción en *la cara*?

5. Where else do you have the rash?
   ¿En qué otra parte tiene Vd. la erupción (el salpullido)?

6. How long have you had this rash?
   ¿Desde cuándo tiene Vd. esta erupción?

7. Have you had this before?
   ¿Ha tenido Vd. esto antes?

8. Has an insect bitten you?
   ¿Le (La) ha picado un insecto?

9. Have you eaten anything different lately?
   ¿Ha comido Vd. algo diferente últimamente (recientemente)?

10. Have you used a new soap lately, either for yourself or in the wash?
    ¿Ha usado Vd. un jabón nuevo últimamente o para usted mismo (misma) o cuando lava su ropa?

11. Does it irritate much?
    ¿Le (La) irrita mucho?

12. Is it itchy?
    ¿Le da comezón?

13. Does it hurt?
    ¿A Vd. le duele?

14. Did you take anything for it?
    ¿Ha tomado Vd. algo para curarlo?

15. Do you have chronic skin diseases, like psoriasis or seborhea?
¿Sufre Vd. de enfermedades crónicas de la piel, como psoriasis (la sarna [slang]) o seborrea?

16. Do you have any black or dark red moles that have changed in size?
¿Tiene Vd. lunares negros o marrones que hayan sufrido cambios?

17. Do you have any moles that bleed?
¿Tiene Vd. lunares que sangren?

18. Do you break out in hives?
¿Brota Vd. de urticarias severas en la piel?

19. Are you losing your hair?
¿Está Vd. perdiendo el pelo?

20. Does your scalp itch?
¿Le pica la cabeza?

Head   *La cabeza*

1. Do you get headaches?
¿Tiene Vd. dolores de cabeza?
¿Tiene Vd. jaquecas?
¿Le duele la cabeza?
¿Le dan dolores de cabeza?

2. Do you get migraines?
¿Tiene Vd. migrañas?

3. Do you ever feel dizzy?
¿Tiene Vd. vértigo alguna vez?
¿Suele Vd. tener mareos? (colloq)

4. How long do you feel dizzy?
¿Cuánto tiempo le duran los mareos?

5. How long have you had the headache?
¿Cuánto tiempo hace que Vd. tiene el dolor de cabeza?

6. Show me where it hurts you.
Enséñeme Vd. donde le duele.

7. Is it throbbing or is it a constant pain?
¿Le palpita o es un dolor constante?

8. Does your neck hurt?
¿Le duele el cuello?

9. Have you vomited?
¿Ha vomitado Vd.?

10. Is something else hurting you?
¿Le duele algo más?

11. Where?
    ¿Dónde?

12. Have you been feeling depressed?
    ¿Ha estado Vd. deprimido (-a)?

13. Have you ever been hit in the head? face? neck? eyes? nose?
    ¿Se ha golpeado jamás la cabeza? la cara? el cuello? los ojos? la nariz?

14. Have you ever lost consciousness?
    ¿Ha perdido jamás el conocimiento?

15. For how long?
    ¿Por cuánto tiempo?

16. When?
    ¿Cuándo?

17. What happened?
    ¿Qué le pasó?

18. Do you have or have you had frequent headaches?
    ¿Tiene Vd. o ha tenido dolor de cabeza frecuentemente?
                       colds?
                       catarros frecuentemente?
                       stuffed-up nose?
                       la nariz tapada frecuentemente?
                       pain in your forehead?
                       dolor en la frente?
                       pain under your eyes?
                       dolor debajo de los ojos?
                       trouble breathing through your nose?
                       dificultad al respirar por la nariz?

REVIEW *REPASO*

Practice the following dialogue.

DOCTOR: Do you have any bleeding problems, Mr. Gómez?

DOCTOR: ¿Tiene Vd. problemas de sangrar, señor Gómez?

MR. GOMEZ: No, Doctor, I don't have any bleeding problems if I cut myself.

SR. GOMEZ: No, doctor, no tengo problemas de sangrar si me corto.

DOCTOR: How long have you had this rash on your face?

DOCTOR: ¿Desde cuándo tiene Vd. esta erupción en la cara?

MR. GOMEZ: I have had it for a month.

SR. GOMEZ: La tengo desde hace un mes.

DOCTOR: Does it irritate much?

DOCTOR: ¿Le irrita mucho?

MR. GOMEZ: Yes, it itches me, but I don't scratch.

SR. GOMEZ: Sí, me irrita, pero no me rasco.

DOCTOR: Did you take anything for it?

MR. GOMEZ: Yes, I have been using a gray ointment.

DOCTOR: Discontinue using the ointment for now.

MR. GOMEZ: What should I use?

DOCTOR: After I do some more tests, I will give you a prescription. Do you get headaches?

MR. GOMEZ: I do; I have an awfully bad headache now.

DOCTOR: How long do the headaches generally last?

MR. GOMEZ: All day. The pain is especially bad over my left eye.

DOCTOR: Do you ever feel nauseated while you have a headache?

MR. GOMEZ: Yes, Doctor, and sometimes I vomit.

DOCTOR: What do you do for the headache?

MR. GOMEZ: I usually take two aspirins every three hours and stay in bed until I feel better.

DOCTOR: Very well, Mr. Gómez.

DOCTOR: ¿Ha tomado Vd. algo para curarla?

SR. GOMEZ: Sí, he usado una pomada gris.

DOCTOR: Deje Vd. de usar la pomada para ahora.

SR. GOMEZ: ¿Qué debo usar?

DOCTOR: Después de hacerle algunas pruebas más, le daré una receta. ¿Tiene Vd. dolores de cabeza?

SR. GOMEZ: Los tengo; me duele muchísimo la cabeza ahora.

DOCTOR: Generalmente, ¿cuánto tiempo le duran los dolores de cabeza?

SR. GOMEZ: Por lo común, todo el día. El dolor es aún más fuerte encima del ojo izquierdo.

DOCTOR: Mientras que tiene dolor de cabeza, ¿tiene náusea alguna vez?

SR. GOMEZ: Sí, doctor, y a veces vomito.

DOCTOR: ¿Qué hace para su jaqueca?

SR. GOMEZ: Por lo regular tomo dos aspirinas cada tres horas y guardo cama hasta que me sienta mejor.

DOCTOR: Muy bien, señor Gómez.

Eyes *Los ojos*

1. Do you wear glasses?
   ¿Usa Vd. anteojos? (general term)
   ¿Usa Vd. lentes? (Mex.)
   ¿Usa Vd. espejuelos? (Cuba)

2. for close-up?
   ¿para ver de cerca?
   for distance?
   ¿para ver de lejos?
   for reading?
   ¿para leer?
   all the time?
   ¿todo el tiempo?

3. Do you wear contact lenses?
 ¿Usa Vd. lentes de contacto?

4. Do you sometimes see things double?
 ¿Ve Vd. las cosas doble algunas veces?

5. Do you have blurred vision?
 ¿Ve Vd. borroso?

6. Do you see things through a mist?
 ¿Ve Vd. nubladas las cosas como a través de una neblina?

7. Do your eyes burn?
 ¿Le arden los ojos?

8. Do your eyes water much?
 ¿Le lagrimean mucho los ojos?

9. Your eyes seem inflamed (red).
 Sus ojos parecen inflamados (rojos).

10. Do you have eyestrain?
 ¿Sufre Vd. de cansancio de ojos?

11. Do you have eyeaches?
 ¿Sufre Vd. de dolores de ojos?

12. Does your (left) (right) eye hurt?
 ¿Le duele a Vd. el ojo (izquierdo) (derecho)?

13. Do both your eyes hurt?
 ¿A Vd. le duelen los dos ojos?

14. Do your eyes itch?
 ¿Tiene Vd. una picazón de los ojos?

15. Do you have a discharge from your eyes?
 ¿Le supuran los ojos?

16. Were your eyes stuck together when you awoke this morning?
 ¿Tenía los ojos pegados cuando se despertó Vd. esta mañana?

17. Does your eyeball feel as if it were swollen?
 ¿Le siente el ojo hinchado?

18. How long have your eyelids been swollen?
 ¿Desde cuándo tiene Vd. los párpados hinchados?

19. When did your eyes begin to look yellow?
 ¿Cuándo empezaban sus ojos a tener este color amarillo?

20. Did you ever have trouble with your vision?
 ¿Ha tenido alguna vez dificultades con su visión (vista)?

21. Did anything get in your eyes?
 ¿Le entró algo en los ojos?

22. A splinter of metal, wood, liquid?
¿Una esquirla de metal? de madera? un líquido?

23. Did it affect your vision?
¿Le afectó la vista?

24. When was the last time that you had a vision test?
¿Cuándo fue el último examen de la vista?

REVIEW *REPASO*

Practice the following dialogue.

DR. JONES: Hello, Mr. García. Please be seated.

DR. JONES: **Buenas tardes, señor García. Siéntese Vd. por favor.**

MR. GARCIA: Thank you, Doctor.

SR. GARCIA: **Gracias, doctor.**

DR. JONES: What seems to be your trouble?

DR. JONES: **Vamos a ver, ¿cuál parece ser la molestia?**

MR. GARCIA: My eyes hurt me.

SR. GARCIA: **Me duelen los ojos.**

DR. JONES: When were your eyes examined last?

DR. JONES: **¿Cuánto tiempo hace que se examinó la vista?**

MR. GARCIA: About three years ago.

SR. GARCIA: **Hace tres años, más o menos.**

DR. JONES: Did you ever have trouble with your vision?

DR. JONES: **¿Ha tenido alguna vez dificultades con su vista?**

MR. GARCIA: Yes, I had astigmatism in the left eye and they gave me a prescription for glasses.

SR. GARCIA: **Sí, tenía astigmatismo en el ojo izquierdo y me dieron una prescripción para anteojos.**

DR. JONES: Do you still wear glasses now?

DR. JONES: **¿Todavía lleva los anteojos?**

MR. GARCIA: No, I don't wear them because I lost my glasses last year and I didn't have enough money to buy new ones.

SR. GARCIA: **No, no los llevo porque se me perdieron los anteojos el año pasado y no tuve bastante dinero para comprar otros nuevos.**

DR. JONES: Do you feel pain in your right eye?

DR. JONES: **¿Siente dolor en el ojo derecho?**

MR. GARCIA: No, but my left eye hurts me, and I often have bad headaches.

SR. GARCIA: **No, pero me duele el izquierdo, y muchas veces tengo horribles dolores de cabeza.**

DR. JONES: Oh, really? Do you ever have eyeaches too?

DR. JONES: **¿De veras? ¿Sufre de dolores de ojos también?**

MR. GARCIA: My left eye aches me only when I read for a long time, and only at night.

SR. GARCIA: **Me duele el ojo izquierdo solamente cuando leo por mucho tiempo y entonces solamente por la noche.**

DR. JONES: Do you sometimes see things double?

DR. JONES: **¿Ve Vd. las cosas doble algunas veces?**

MR. GARCIA: No. When I have eyeaches I see things as though through a mist.

SR. GARCIA: **No. Cuando sufro de dolores de ojos veo nubladas las cosas como a través de una neblina.**

DR. JONES: Do your eyes burn?

DR. JONES: **¿Le arden los ojos?**

MR. GARCIA: No.

SR. GARCIA: **No.**

DR. JONES: Do your eyes water much?

DR. JONES: **¿Le lagrimean mucho los ojos?**

MR. GARCIA: Yes, very often my eyes water a lot.

SR. GARCIA: **Sí, muy a menudo me lagrimean mucho los ojos.**

DR. JONES: Your left eye seems inflamed now. Did anything get into your eye?

DR. JONES: **El ojo izquierdo parece inflamado ahora. ¿Le entró algo en el ojo?**

MR. GARCIA: I don't think so.

SR. GARCIA: **Creo que no.**

DR. JONES: Does your eyeball feel as if it were swollen?

DR. JONES: **¿Siente el ojo hinchado?**

MR. GARCIA: I don't understand. My left eye hurts me.

SR. GARCIA: **No comprendo. El ojo izquierdo me duele.**

DR. JONES: Very well. Let me see your eyes, and I will examine them.

DR. JONES: **Muy bien. Déjeme ver sus ojos, y los examinaré.**

Ears *Los oídos*

1. Do you ever have middle or inner ear infections?
   ¿Tiene Vd. alguna vez infecciones del oído medio o interno?

2. Are you (tone-deaf)hard of hearing, or deaf?
   ¿Es Vd. duro de oído, o sordo (sorda)?

3. Do you wear a hearing aid?
   ¿Lleva Vd. un aparato auditivo?

4. Do you have any hearing problems?
   ¿Tiene Vd. problemas de oído?
   ¿Padece Vd. de defectos de la audición?

5. Have you put anything in your ear?
   ¿Se ha puesto Vd. algo en el oído?

6. Do your ears run?
   ¿Le supuran los oídos?
   ¿Le sale material de los oídos?

7. Do you have a discharge from your left (right) ear?
   ¿Le supura el oído izquierdo (derecho)?

8. Do you usually get earaches?
   ¿Le duelen con frecuencia los oídos?

9. Are your ears clogged?
   ¿Siente Vd. los oídos taponados? (tapados [Mex.])?

10. Do your ears ring?
    ¿Siente Vd. un tintineo en los oídos?
    ¿Le rumban a Vd. los oídos?
    ¿Tiene Vd. como campanillas en los oídos?

11. Do you have ringing in your right (left) ear?
    ¿Le rumba el oído derecho (izquierdo)?

12. Do you ever have dizzy spells?
    ¿Tiene Vd. vértigo alguna vez?
    ¿Suele Vd. tener mareos? (colloq)
    ¿Tiene Vd. episodios de mareos?

13. Do you ever feel dizzy on getting up quickly from bed?
    ¿Tiene Vd. mareos al levantarse de la cama rápido?

Nose and Sinuses   *La nariz y los senos*

1. Do you have a stuffed nose?
   ¿Tiene Vd. la nariz obstruida?

2. Does your nose feel clogged?
   ¿Tiene Vd. la nariz tapada (Mex.)? tupida? taponada?

3. Do you have a cold?
   ¿Tiene Vd. un resfriado?
   ¿Tiene Vd. un catarro? (head cold)
   ¿Está Vd. resfriado (-a)?[13]
   ¿Está Vd. acatarrado (-a)?[13]

4. Did you catch cold?[14]
   ¿Se ha resfriado Vd.?
   ¿Se acatarró Vd.?

5. How many colds did you have last year?
   ¿Cuántos resfríos (resfriados; catarros) ha tenido Vd. el año pasado?

6. Do you have nose bleeds?
   ¿Le sangra la nariz a veces?
   ¿Presenta Vd. sangrado nasal?

7. Do you have a running nose?
   ¿La fluye a Vd. la nariz?
   ¿Moquea Vd.? (slang)

8. Do you have problems smelling?
   ¿Tiene Vd. problemas olfatorios?

Mouth and Throat *La boca y la garganta*

1. Are you frequently hoarse?
   ¿Tiene Vd. ronquera a menudo?
   ¿Está Vd. ronco (ronca) con frecuencia?

2. Does your tongue feel swollen, thick, or rough?
   ¿Le siente la lengua hinchada, gruesa, or dura?

3. Does your tongue feel furry?
   ¿Está su lengua con costra?
   ¿Se forman incrustaciones en su lengua?

4. How long has your tongue been that color?
   ¿Desde cuándo tiene la lengua de ese color?

5. Does your tongue burn?
   ¿Le arde la lengua?

6. Can you taste anything?
   ¿Puede Vd. saborear algo?

7. Do you have a sour taste in your mouth?
   ¿Siente Vd. un sabor agrio de boca?
   ¿Tiene Vd. una acidez en la boca?

8. Do you have sore throats?
   ¿Suele Vd. tener la garganta dolorida?
   ¿Le duele la garganta con frecuencia?

9. Does your throat hurt when you swallow?
   ¿Le duele la garganta cuando Vd. traga?
   ¿Tiene Vd. dolores o dificultades al tragar?

10. Is it just scratchy?
    ¿Está rascosa (raposa)?

11. Do you also have a cold?
    ¿Tiene catarro también?

12. Does your tongue feel sore?
    ¿Tiene Vd. la lengua dolorida?

13. Do your gums bleed frequently?
    ¿Le sangran las encías frecuentemente?

14. Do you have infections of the gum?
    ¿Tiene Vd. infecciones de las encías?

15. Do you have a toothache?
    ¿Tiene Vd. dolor de muelas?

16. Which tooth hurts?
    ¿Cuál de los dientes le duele?

17. Please point.
    Apunte Vd., por favor.

Neck   *El cuello*

1. Can you swallow?
   ¿Puede Vd. tragar?

Breasts   *Los pechos*

1. When was your last breast examination?
   ¿Cuándo fue su último examen de las mamas? / de los senos?

2. Do you know how to do breast self-examination?
   ¿Sabe Vd. autoexaminarse los senos?

3. Do you examine your breasts every month?
   ¿Hace Vd. un autoexamen mensual de los senos?

4. Have you noticed any lumps in your breasts?
   ¿Se ha fijado Vd. en algún tumor   de los pechos?
   alguna protuberancia
   algún abultamiento
   ¿Ha notado alguna bolita (algún tumorcito) en la mama? (colloq)

5. Have you notice a change
   ¿Se ha fijado Vd. algún cambio

   in the size of your breasts?
   en el tamaño de los senos?
   in the shape of your breasts?
   en la forma de los senos?

6. Do you have any pain or swelling of your breasts?
   ¿Tiene Vd. algún dolor o hinchazón de los senos?

   under your arms?
   debajo de los brazos?

7. Have you notice a change
   ¿Se ha fijado Vd. en algún cambio

   in the size of your nipples?
   en el tamaño de los pezones?
   in the shape of your nipples?
   en la forma de los pezones?

8. Do your nipples hurt you?
   ¿Le duelen los pezones?

9. Do you have a discharge from your nipples?
   ¿Le supuran los pezones?

10. What color is the discharge from your nipples?
    ¿De qué color es la material que sale de los pezones?

11. Your breasts are swollen. Do they hurt when you have your period?
    Vd. tiene los pechos hinchados. ¿Le duelen durante la regla?

12. Do your breasts begin to swell before your periods?
¿Empiezan a hincharse los pechos antes de la regla?

13. Have you nursed your child?
¿Ha dado de mamar a su criatura?

14. Did you nurse your child?
¿Amamantó a su criatura?

15. How long have you been nursing?
¿Desde cuánto tiempo da Vd. el pecho?

16. How long did you nurse?
¿Desde cuánto tiempo dió Vd. el pecho?

Respiratory *Respiratorio*

1. Can you breathe well?
¿Puede Vd. respirar bien?

2. Do you have any difficulty in breathing?
¿Tiene Vd. alguna dificultad para respirar?

3. How long can you hold your breath?
¿Durante cuánto tiempo puede Vd. retener la respiración?

4. Try it.
Pruébalo.

5. Are you short of breath?
¿Le falta la respiración?

> while exercising?
> **al hacer ejercicios?**
> when you are resting?
> **al descansar?**
> when you are upset?
> **cuando está trastornado (-a)?**

6. Do you have any difficulty in breathing
> **¿Respira Vd. con dificultad**
> at night?
> **por la noche?**
> sitting down?
> **sentado (-a)?**
> lying down?
> **acostado (-a)?**
> standing up?
> **de pie?**
> exercising?
> **al hacer ejercicios?**
> at rest?
> **al descansar?**

7. Do you perspire a lot, especially at night?
¿Suda Vd. mucho, sobre todo por la noche?

8. Do you cough a lot?
¿Tiene Vd. mucha tos?
¿Tose Vd. mucho?

9. How long have you been coughing?
¿Desde cuándo tiene Vd. tos?
¿Desde cuándo tose Vd.?

10. Does it hurt when you cough?
¿Le duele cuando tose (al toser)?

11. Are you coughing from an allergy?
¿Tose Vd. por alguna alergia?

12. Do you cough up phlegm?
Al toser, ¿arroja Vd. flemas?
¿Esgarra Vd.?

13. What color is the phlegm?
¿De qué color es la flema?
clear
incolora
gray or white
gris o blanca
yellow or green
amarilla o verde
red
roja
maroon or black
marrón o negra

14. Is it a dry cough?
¿Es una tos seca?

15. Is it a productive cough?
¿Es una tos con flema (esputo)?

16. Is the phlegm foul-smelling?
¿Es la flema apestosa?

17. Is it abundant?
¿Es abundante?

18. Is it thick or foamy?
¿Es espesa o espumosa?

19. Do you cough up blood?
Al toser, ¿arroja Vd. sangre?

20. Do you spit blood?
    ¿Escupe Vd. sangre?

21. Streaks of blood or clots?
    ¿Tose Vd. rayas de sangre o cuajarones?
    ¿Tose Vd. manchas de sangre o coágulos?

22. Do you spit a lot?
    ¿Escupe mucho?

23. Do you have pain when you cough?
    ¿Le duele al toser?

24. Do you breathe easier after you cough?
    ¿Respira Vd. mejor después de toser?

25. Is there any position
    ¿Hay alguna posición que lo

    that makes it better?
    alivie?
    that makes it worse?
    aumente?

26. Do you wheeze?
    ¿Le silba a Vd. el pecho?
    ¿Le sale un silbido al respirar?

27. Do you smoke?
    ¿Fuma Vd.?

28. How many per day?
    ¿Cuántos al día?

29. For how many years?
    ¿Por cuántos años?

30. Have you had asthma, emphysema, T.B.?
    ¿Ha padecido Vd. de asma, enfisema, tuberculosis (tisis)?

31. Do you get chills?
    ¿Le dan escalofríos?

32. Do you always feel cold?
    ¿Siente Vd. frío siempre?

33. Do you feel warm and feverish at night?
    ¿Se siente Vd. caliente y febril por la noche?

34. When was your last chest x-ray?
    ¿Cuándo fue su última radiografía del pecho (de los pulmones)?

35. What were the results?
    ¿Cuáles fueron los resultados?

REVIEW *REPASO*

Practice the following dialogue.

DR. SMITH: When did your illness begin, Mrs. Navas?

DR. SMITH: ¿Cuándo empezó su enfermedad, señora Navas?

MRS. NAVAS: It began Wednesday evening.

SRA. NAVAS: Empezó el miércoles por la noche.

DR. SMITH: Did you have any fever?

DR. SMITH: ¿Tuvo Vd. fiebre?

MRS. NAVAS: Yes, I had 102.

SRA. NAVAS: Sí, ciento dos grados Fahrenheit.

DR. SMITH: How long did the fever last?

DR. SMITH: ¿Por cuánto tiempo tuvo fiebre?

MRS. NAVAS: For almost two days.

SRA. NAVAS: Por casi dos días.

DR. SMITH: Did you vomit?

DR. SMITH: ¿Vomitó Vd.?

MRS. NAVAS: Yes, I vomited a lot, and I also coughed quite a bit.

SRA. NAVAS: Sí, vomité mucho y también tosía bastante.

DR. SMITH: How long have you been coughing?

DR. SMITH: ¿Desde cuándo tose Vd.?

MRS. NAVAS: For about a day.

SRA. NAVAS: Hace como un día.

DR. SMITH: Does it hurt when you cough?

DR. SMITH: ¿Le duele al toser?

MRS. NAVAS: Yes, my chest hurts, and so does my throat.

SRA. NAVAS: Sí, me duele el pecho, y la garganta también.

DR. SMITH: Do you cough up phlegm?

DR. SMITH: Al toser, ¿arroja Vd. flemas?

MRS. NAVAS: Sometimes.

SRA. NAVAS: A veces.

DR. SMITH: What color is the phlegm?

DR. SMITH: ¿De qué color son las flemas?

MRS. NAVAS: I am not sure. I think the phlegm is yellow.

SRA. NAVAS: No estoy segura. Creo que las flemas son amarillas.

DR. SMITH: Does anything else hurt you?

DR. SMITH: ¿Le duele algo más?

MRS. NAVAS: Right now my throat is sore.

SRA. NAVAS: Ahorita tengo la garganta dolorida.

DR. SMITH: Are you hoarse frequently?

DR. SMITH: ¿Está Vd. ronca con frecuencia?

MRS. NAVAS: Usually not.

SRA. NAVAS: Generalmente no.

DR. SMITH: Does your throat hurt when you swallow?

DR. SMITH: ¿Le duele la garganta al tragar?

MRS. NAVAS: Yes, and it is difficult for me to swallow.

SRA. NAVAS: Sí, y no puedo tragar muy bien.

DR. SMITH: I am going to give you a prescription for two medicines. One is for lozenges. Take one every four hours. The other is for a cough medicine. Take two teaspoonsful after every meal and at bedtime. Call me tomorrow.

DR. SMITH: **Voy a darle unas recetas para dos medicinas. Una es para pastillas. Tome una cada cuatro horas. La otra es para un jarabe para la tos. Tome dos cucharaditas después de cada comida y al acostarse. Llámeme mañana.**

Cardiovascular *Cardiovascular*

1. Do you feel (very) weak?
   ¿Se siente (muy) débil?

2. Do you have pains in your chest?
   ¿Tiene Vd. dolores en el pecho?
   ¿Ha estado teniendo dolores en el pecho?

3. In what part of the chest?
   ¿En qué parte del pecho?

4. In the middle, more towards the left side, more towards the right side?
   ¿En el medio, más hacia el lado izquierdo, más hacia el lado derecho?

5. Under the breastbone?
   ¿Debajo del esternón?

6. Does the pain extend to the arms, to the shoulders, to the neck?
   ¿Se extiende el dolor algunas veces hacia los brazos, hacia los hombros, o hacia el cuello?

7. Does the pain extend to the back or neck or jaw?
   ¿Se extiende el dolor hacia la espalda o el cuello o la quijada?

8. Where do you feel the pain?
   ¿Dónde siente Vd. el dolor?

9. Point to where it hurts.
   Apunte Vd. por favor, adonde le duele.

10. Does the pain stay in one place?
    ¿Se queda el dolor en un sólo lugar?

11. Does the pain radiate?
    ¿Se corre el dolor?

12. From where to where?
    ¿Hacia dónde?

13. How long have you had it?
    ¿Cuánto tiempo hace que lo tiene?

14. How long does (did) it last each time?
    ¿Cuánto le dura (duró) cuando le viene (vino)?

15. More than half an hour?
    ¿Más de media hora?

16. How often do you have the pain?
   ¿Con qué frecuencia tiene Vd. el dolor?

17. What is (was) the pain like?
   ¿Cómo es (era) el dolor?

18. Was it sharp?
   ¿Fue agudo?

19. Was it dull and crushing like a person standing on your chest?
   ¿Fue sordo y oprimido como si alguien estuviese colocado sobre su pecho?

20. Did you perspire when the pain came?
   ¿Sudó Vd. cuando le vino el dolor?

21. Did you black out?
   ¿Se desmayó Vd.?

22. Have you had it before?
   ¿Lo ha tenido antes?

23. Have you ever been told that you had heart trouble?
   ¿Sabe Vd. si ha tenido jamás enfermedad del corazón?

24. Have you ever had a heart attack?
   ¿Ha tenido alguna vez un ataque cardíaco?

25. How many?
   ¿Cuántas veces?

26. Do you have a heart condition?
   ¿Tiene Vd. problemas del corazón?

27. Do you take medicine for this pain?
   ¿Toma Vd. medicina para el dolor?
   nitroglycerin?
   ¿nitroglicerina?
   pills that you put under your tongue?
   ¿píldoras que se ponen debajo de la lengua?
   digitalis?
   ¿digital?
   water pills/diuretics?
   ¿píldoras para sacar el agua?

28. What is the name of the medicine?
   ¿Sabe Vd. el nombre de esta medicina?

29. Does your heart beat rapidly or irregularly?
   ¿Le late el corazón rápidamente o con irregularidad?

30. Can you remember ever having had irregular heart beats, or very rapid heart beats?
   ¿Puede Vd. recordar haber tenido alguna vez latidos irregulares o palpitaciones muy rápidas del corazón?

31. When?
    ¿Cuándo?

32. Do you have difficulty breathing through your nose when you walk?
    ¿Tiene Vd. dificultad en respirar por la nariz al caminar?

33. Have you noticed any shortness of breath lately?
    ¿Ha notado si ha tenido falta de aliento últimamente?

34. Do you get short of breath when you climb stairs? When you walk?
    ¿Le falta el aliento cuando sube Vd. por las escaleras? ¿Cuando camina?

35. How many flights of stairs can you climb without being short of breath?
    ¿Cuántos pisos puede Vd. subir sin que le falte el aliento?
    ¿Cuántas escaleras puede Vd. subir sin tener falta de aliento?

36. Did you ever have shortness of breath at night?
    ¿Ha tenido falta de aliento por la noche?

37. Do you awaken in the night because of shortness of breath?
    ¿Se despierta Vd. por la noche por falta de respiración?

38. How many pillows do you use to sleep on?
    ¿Cuántas almohadas usa Vd. para dormir?

39. Can you lay flat on the bed without pillows and not be short of breath?
    ¿Puede Vd. acostarse sobre la cama sin almohadas, y no tener falta de aliento?

40. Is any part of your body swollen?
    ¿Tiene Vd. alguna parte del cuerpo hinchada?

41. How long has it been swollen like this?
    ¿Desde cuándo está hinchado así?
    ¿Cuánto tiempo está hinchado así?

42. How many days?
    ¿Cuántos días?

43. How many weeks?
    ¿Cuántas semanas?

44. Are your ankles swollen in the morning when you awaken?
    ¿Tiene Vd. los tobillos hinchados por la mañana al despertarse?

45. Have you ever seen a bluish color in your lips?
    ¿Jamás ha visto Vd. que los labios se ponen morados?
    in your feet and hands?
    los pies y las manos se ponen morados?

46. Is there a coldness in your hands?
    ¿Se mantienen frías las manos?
    your feet?
    ¿Se mantienen fríos los pies?

47. Do you have a heart murmur or hypertension?
   ¿Tiene Vd. un murmullo de corazón o padece Vd. de la hipertensión?

48. When did you last have an electrocardiogram?
   ¿Cuándo fue la última vez que le hicieron un electrocardiograma?

49. What were the results?
   ¿Cuáles fueron los resultados?

Gastrointestinal *Gastrointestinal*

1. Do you eat between meals?
   ¿Come Vd. algo entre comidas?

2. Do you drink a lot of liquids?
   ¿Toma Vd. muchos líquidos?

3. Do you drink milk?
   ¿Bebe Vd. leche?

4. How much?
   ¿Cuánta?

5. Do you drink alcoholic beverages?
   ¿Toma Vd. algunas bebidas alcohólicas?

6. How many do you drink?
   ¿Cuánto bebe Vd.?

7. What type of alcoholic beverage do you drink?
   ¿Qué tipo (clase) de bebida alcohólica toma Vd.?

8. How much coffee or tea do you drink?
   ¿Cuántas tazas de café o de té bebe Vd.?

9. What type of coffee do you drink, regular or decaffeinated?
   ¿Qué clase de café toma Vd., regular o descafeinado?

10. How much water do you drink daily?
   ¿Cuántos vasos de agua bebe Vd. diariamente?

11. How much pop do you drink?
   ¿Cuántas bebidas gaseosas toma Vd. diariamente, como una Coca-Cola?

12. What food disagree with you?
   ¿Qué alimentos le caen mal?

13. Do you get gas pains?
   ¿Suele Vd. tener aire (flato)?

14. Do you belch (burp) a lot?
   ¿Eructa Vd. mucho?
   ¿Repite Vd. mucho? (Chicano)

15. Do you suffer from indigestion?
    ¿Padece Vd. de indigestión?

16. Do you get heartburn?
    ¿Suele tener ardor de estómago?
    ¿Tiene Vd. molestias en la parte superior del abdomen?

17. Do you have an upset stomach after eating fried or fatty foods?
    ¿Se siente descompuesto (descompuesta) del estómago después de comidas fritas o con grasa?

18. What exactly happens?
    ¿Qué le pasa exactamente?

REVIEW *REPASO*

Practice the following dialogue.

DR. BURNS: What is your problem, Miss Mendoza?

DR. BURNS: **¿Qué le sucede a Vd., señorita Mendoza?**

MISS MENDOZA: My stomach bothers me frequently.

SRTA. MENDOZA: **Me molesta mucho el estómago con frecuencia.**

DR. BURNS: How much do you weigh?

DR. BURNS: **¿Cuánto pesa Vd.?**

MISS MENDOZA: 125 pounds.

SRTA. MENDOZA: **Ciento veinticinco libras.**

DR. BURNS: What is your occupation?

DR. BURNS: **¿Cuál es su ocupación?**

MISS MENDOZA: I am a beautician.

SRTA. MENDOZA: **Soy peluquera.**

DR. BURNS: Do you like working in a beauty shop?

DR. BURNS: **¿Le gusta trabajar en un salón de belleza?**

MISS MENDOZA: Yes, but the hours are very long.

SRTA. MENDOZA: **Sí, pero las horas son larguísimas.**

DR. BURNS: Generally what hours do you work?

DR. BURNS: **Por lo común, ¿cuáles son las horas que trabaja?**

MISS MENDOZA: I work on Sundays from 10 until 3 in the afternoon, and on Tuesdays, Wednesdays and Thursdays I work from 9 until 6. On Fridays and Saturdays I work from 9 until 10 in the evenings.

SRTA. MENDOZA: **Los domingos trabajo desde las diez hasta las tres de la tarde, y los martes, miércoles y jueves, trabajo desde las nueve hasta las seis. Los viernes y los sábados trabajo desde las nueve de la mañana hasta las diez de la noche.**

DR. BURNS: How many meals do you normally eat?

DR. BURNS: **¿Cuántas comidas toma Vd. al día?**

MISS MENDOZA: Well, I always eat a good breakfast. Orange juice, two eggs, ham, some toast and coffee.

SRTA. MENDOZA: **Pues, siempre me desayuno bien. Jugo de naranja, dos huevos, jamón, unas tostadas y café.**

DR. BURNS: Do you eat lunch?

MISS MENDOZA: Usually I just drink black coffee all day long.

DR. BURNS: What about supper?

MISS MENDOZA: I am generally too tired to cook, so I have a hamburger and french fries, and a coke, or else fried chicken and french fries.

DR. BURNS: Do you have an upset stomach after eating such a supper?

MISS MENDOZA: Frequently my stomach hurts me after the chicken.

DR. BURNS: What exactly happens.

MISS MENDOZA: I have sharp pains here.

DR. BURNS: Do you drink milk?

MISS MENDOZA: I drink coffee because I don't like milk.

DR. BURNS: What type of coffee do you drink, regular or decaffeinated?

MISS MENDOZA: I drink regular.

DR. BURNS: How many cups do you drink daily?

MISS MENDOZA: I drink between fifteen and twenty.

DR. BURNS: How much water do you drink daily?

MISS MENDOZA: I almost never drink water.

DR. BURNS: Do you drink much pop?

MISS MENDOZA: Sometimes while I am working I drink two or three cans of pop.

DR. BURNS: Do you burp a lot?

MISS MENDOZA: Only after drinking the pop.

DR. BURNS: Do you get heartburn often?

DR. BURNS: ¿Almuerza Vd.?

SRTA. MENDOZA: **Generalmente solamente bebo café puro todo el día.**

DR. BURNS: **¿Y para la cena?**

SRTA. MENDOZA: **Con frecuencia estoy tan cansada que no tengo ganas de cocinar. Así compro una hamburguesa y papas fritas y una Coca, o pollo frito con papas fritas.**

DR. BURNS: **¿Se siente descompuesta del estómago después de comer tal cena?**

SRTA. MENDOZA: **Después del pollo muchas veces me duele el estómago.**

DR. BURNS: **¿Qué le pasa exactamente?**

SRTA. MENDOZA: **Sufro de dolores agudos aquí.**

DR. BURNS: **¿Bebe Vd. leche?**

SRTA. MENDOZA: **Tomo café porque no me gusta leche.**

DR. BURNS: **¿Qué clase de café toma Vd., regular o descafeinado?**

SRTA. MENDOZA: **Tomo regular.**

DR. BURNS: **¿Cuántas tazas de café bebe Vd. al día?**

SRTA. MENDOZA: **Tomo entre quince y veinte.**

DR. BURNS: **¿Cuántos vasos de agua bebe Vd. diariamente?**

SRTA. MENDOZA: **Casi nunca bebo agua.**

DR. BURNS: **¿Toma Vd. muchas bebidas gaseosas?**

SRTA. MENDOZA: **A veces mientras trabajo bebo dos o tres botes de soda.**

DR. BURNS: **¿Eructa Vd. mucho?**

SRTA. MENDOZA: **Solamente después de beber soda.**

DR. BURNS: **¿Suele tener ardor de estómago a menudo?**

MISS MENDOZA: Yes, I usually have heartburn after drinking too much coffee, or late in the evening after supper.

SRTA. MENDOZA: **Sí, por lo regular suelo tener ardor de estómago después de beber demasiado café o muy tarde por la noche después de la cena.**

DR. BURNS: You must eat more regularly— three meals a day, and you must drink more water and less coffee. Here is a list of foods which you should eat daily.

DR. BURNS: **Vd. debe comer con más regularidad—tres comidas al día y debe beber más agua y menos café. Aquí tiene una lista de las comidas que debe tomar diariamente.**

19. Do you feel bloated?
    ¿Se siente aventado (-a) (¿Siente ventosidad)?

20. Do you get sour regurgitation?
    ¿Le suben ácidos a la boca?

21. Do you have frequent stomach aches (bellyaches)?
    ¿Suele tener dolor de estómago (de vientre) a menudo?
    ¿Tiene Vd. dolor de estómago (de vientre) con frecuencia?

22. Do you feel nauseated?
    ¿Tiene Vd. ganas de vomitar?

23. Are you nauseated?
    ¿Tiene náusea(s)?

24. Are you going to vomit?
    ¿Va a vomitar?

25. Did you vomit?
    ¿Vomitó?

26. Did vomiting relieve your pains?
    ¿Le aliviaron los vómitos los dolores?

27. Can you hold down water without vomiting?
    ¿Puede detener agua sin vomitarla?

28. Do you have abdominal (stomach) pain?
    ¿Tiene Vd. dolor de estómago?

29. Where is the pain?
    ¿Dónde le duele?

30. Point to where it hurts.
    Apunte Vd. adonde le duele.
    with one finger.
    con un dedo.

31. Where was the pain when it started?
    ¿Dónde estaba el dolor cuando empezó?

32. What is the pain like?
    ¿Cómo es el dolor?

33. How long does the pain last?
    ¿Cuánto tiempo hace que tiene el dolor?

34. How often do you have it?
    ¿Con qué frecuencia lo tiene?

35. Do you have problems swallowing or chewing?
    ¿Tiene Vd. problemas al tragar o masticar?

36. Does eating (drinking milk) make the pain better?
    ¿Alivia el dolor al comer (tomar leche)?

37. Does eating make the pain worse?
    ¿Empeora el dolor al comer?

38. When you vomit, is it
    ¿Cuando Vd. vomita, es

    before eating?
    antes de comer?
    after eating?
    después de comer?
    while eating?
    mientras come?
    not related to when you eat?
    sin relación a cuando come?

39. Are you vomiting blood?
    ¿Vomita Vd. sangre?
    ¿Está vomitando sangre?

40. Are you vomiting something similar to what you have just eaten?
    ¿Vomita Vd. algo parecido a lo que acaba de comer?

41. Is it acidic in taste?
    ¿Es de sabor ácido?

42. Is it bitter?
    ¿Es de sabor amargo?

43. Do you keep vomiting?
    ¿Sigue Vd. vomitando?

44. Do you need a pan?
    ¿Necesita el bacín?

45. How are your stools?
    ¿Cómo son sus evacuaciones?

46. Do you move your bowels regularly?
    ¿Evacúa Vd. con regularidad?
    ¿Va Vd. al inodoro con regularidad?
    ¿Obra Vd. con regularidad? (Mex.)

47. Did you move your bowels yet?
    ¿Ya evacuó Vd.?
    ¿Obró ya? (Mex.)
    ¿Hizo caca ya? (slang)

48. When was your last bowel movement?
    ¿Cuánto tiempo hace que evacúa Vd.?

49. Is there anything unusual about your bowel movements?
    ¿Hay algo raro en su excremento?

50. Are you moving your bowels normally?
    ¿Evacúa Vd. normalmente?

51. How often do you have a bowel movement?
    ¿Cada cuánto evacúa el vientre?

52. Did you ever have any kind of rectal or intestinal problem before?
    ¿Tuvo Vd. jamás alguna enfermedad del ano o del intestino antes?

53. Have you had inguinal swollen glands?
    ¿Ha tenido Vd. las glándulas hinchadas el las ingles?

54. Do you have pain when you move your bowels?
    ¿Le duele evacuar el vientre?

55. Is the pain continuous or intermittent?
    ¿Es continuo o va y viene el dolor? (continuo o intermitente)

56. Do you have pain after you defecate? How long does it last?
    ¿Tiene Vd. dolor después de evacuar? ¿Cuánto tiempo le dura?

57. Does the anus swell? Is there a lump at the anus?
    ¿Se le hincha el ano? ¿Hay un bulto al ano?

58. Is it painful?
    ¿Le duele mucho?

59. Does the swelling have a discharge?
    ¿Tiene la hinchazón un desecho?

60. Does the rectum come out when you move your bowels?
    ¿Se le sale el recto al obrar?

61. Do you have to replace it manually or does it return by itself (spontaneously)?
    ¿Tiene Vd. que ponerlo en su sitio manualmente o se vuelve a su lugar por sí mismo (espontáneamente)?

62. Have you noticed any anal itching?
    ¿Se ha fijado en alguna picazón del ano?

63. Is this worse before or after a bowel movement?
    ¿Es peor antes o después de obrar?

64. Is the itching worse when you go to bed?
    ¿Se empeora la picazón al acostarse?

65. Does it awaken you?
    ¿Se le despierta?

66. Is there a history of rectal tumors or hemorrhages in your family?
    ¿Ha habido casos de tumores del recto o almorranas en su familia?

67. Have you ever seen worms in your bowel movements?
    ¿Ha visto jamás gusanos en el excremento?

68. Have you ever had hemorrhages?
    ¿Ha tenido Vd. hemorragias?

69. Do you have hemorrhoids?
    ¿Padece Vd. de hemorroides?
    ¿Sufre Vd. de almorranas?

70. Do you have bleeding hemorrhoids?
    ¿Tiene Vd. hemorroides sangrantes?

71. Do you have rectal bleeding?
    ¿Le sale sangre por el ano?
    ¿Echa sangre del recto?

72. Do you have blood in your stools?
    ¿Tiene sangre en las deposiciones intestinales?

73. Have you noticed the color of your stools?
    ¿Se ha fijado Vd. en el color de sus evacuaciones?

74. Is your stool dark black or light gray?
    ¿Son sus evacuaciones negras o grises claras?

75. Are you constipated?
    ¿Está Vd. estreñido (estreñida)?

76. Do you take enemas?
    ¿Usa Vd. enemas (lavativas)?

77. Do you often take laxatives?
    ¿Suele Vd. tomar laxantes?
    ¿Suele Vd. tomar medicina para evacuar el vientre?

78. How often?
    ¿Con qué frecuencia?
    Every day?
    ¿Cada día?
    About once a week?
    ¿Más o menos una vez por semana?
    Periodically?
    ¿De vez en cuando?

79. What laxatives do you take?
    ¿Qué purgantes toma Vd.?
    Mineral oil?
    ¿Aceite mineral?

Ex-Lax?
¿Ex-Lax?
Milk of magnesia?
¿Leche de magnesia?

80. Do you use suppositories?
¿Usa Vd. supositorios?

81. Do you use medicated suppositories for your hemorrhoids?
¿Usa Vd. supositorios medicados para sus almorranas?

82. Do you have diarrhea?
¿Tiene Vd. diarrea?
¿Tiene el chorrillo? (slang)
¿Tiene la cursera? (slang)
¿Están sus intestinos corrientes? (Mex.)

83. Is it diarrhea with mucus?
¿Es diarrea con moco?

84. Have you had diarrhea recently?
¿Ha tenido diarrea hace poco?

85. Since when have you had it?
¿Desde cuándo la ha tenido?

86. How often do (did) you have diarrhea?
¿Con qué frecuencia tiene (tenía) diarrea?

87. Do you have intestinal cramps with it?
¿Se acompaña de retortijones?

88. Do you have straining with it?
¿Se acompaña de pujo?

89. Is the diarrhea very foul-smelling?
¿Es la diarrea muy apestosa?

90. Is there mucus with it?
¿Hay moco con la diarrea?

91. When you finish, do you still feel as if you have to go?
Al terminar, ¿se queda Vd. con ganas de defecar?

92. Have you ever had typhoid fever?
¿Ha tenido alguna vez la fiebre tifoidea?

93. Have you ever had a (an inguinal) hernia?
¿Ha tenido alguna vez una hernia (una quebradura) inguinal (en la ingle)?

94. Have you ever had a barium x-ray where you swallowed barium or where you had a barium enema?
¿Le han hecho alguna vez una prueba de bario donde Vd. tragó el bario o donde le hicieron una lavativa de bario?

95. Have you ever had a gastrointestinal x-ray?
    ¿Le han hecho alguna vez una radiografía gastrointestinal?

96. Have you ever had a gallbladder x-ray?
    ¿Le han hecho alguna vez radiografía de la vesícula biliar?

97. What were the results?
    ¿Cuáles fueron los resultados?

98. Have you ever been told you have gallstones?
    ¿Le han dicho a Vd. alguna vez que tiene cálculos en la vesícula biliar?

Genitourinary *Génitourinario*

1. Can you urinate?
   ¿Puede Vd. orinar?

2. When you urinate do you notice a delay in beginning?
   Al orinar, ¿ha notado Vd. una demora en comenzar a orinar?

3. Are you unable to control your urine?
   ¿Tiene Vd. pérdidas involuntarias de orina?

4. How long has it been since you have urinated?
   ¿Desde cuándo no orina Vd.?

5. Do you feel like urinating constantly?
   ¿Tiene Vd. ganas de orinar seguido?

6. Have you ever passed urine involuntarily when you laugh?
   ¿Se le sale la orina involuntariamente cuando se ríe?
                              sneeze?
                              estornuda?
                              cough?
                              tose?

7. How frequently do you urinate?
   ¿Con qué frecuencia orina Vd.?

8. How much do you urinate?
   ¿Cuánto orina Vd.?

9. When you urinate do you pass a lot or a little urine?
   Al orinar, ¿pasa mucha o poca orina?

10. Do you awaken in the night to urinate?
    ¿Se despierta Vd. por la noche para orinar?
    ¿Se levanta Vd. de la cama para orinar por la noche?

11. How often?
    ¿Cuántas veces?

12. Did you urinate?
    ¿Orinó Vd.?
    ¿Hizo pipí? (slang)

13. Do you have or have you ever had pain from your kidneys or bladder?
    ¿Tiene Vd. o ha tenido jamás dolor de los riñones o de la vejiga?

14. Where is (was) the pain?
    ¿Dónde le duele (dolía)?

15. How long have (did) you had (have) the pain?
    ¿Cuánto tiempo hace (hacía) que Vd. tiene (tenía) el dolor?

16. How long does (did) it last?
    ¿Cuánto tiempo le dura (duraba)?

17. How often do (did) you have it?
    ¿Con qué frecuencia lo tiene (tenía)?

18. What is the pain like?
    ¿Cómo es el dolor?

19. Is it pain when you begin to urinate?
    ¿Es dolor al empezar a orinar?

20. Is it pain the entire time you urinate?
    ¿Es dolor por todo el tiempo que orina?

21. Is it pain at the end of urination?
    ¿Es dolor al terminar de orinar?

22. Does it hurt when you urinate?
    ¿Le duele cuando orina Vd.?

23. Is there a burning sensation when you urinate?
    ¿Hay un ardor (quemazón) al orinar?

24. Do you have a feeling of urgency to urinate?
    ¿Siente Vd. una urgencia para orinar?

25. Is there any difficulty starting to urinate?
    ¿Hay cualquier dificultad para empezar a orinar?

26. Is there an interrupted flow of urine?
    ¿Hay un chorro interrumpido de orina?

27. Do you notice dribbling after urination?
    ¿Se ha fijado en goteo al terminar de orinar?

28. Is there a decrease in the force of the flow of urine?
    ¿Hay una disminución de la fuerza del chorro de orina?

29. Are there small stones in your urine?
    ¿Orina Vd. con arenilla?

30. Have you ever had kidney stones?
    ¿Ha tenido alguna vez cálculos en los riñones?

31. Do you usually get backaches?
    ¿Suele Vd. tener dolores de espalda?

32. Do you ever have low back pain?
    ¿Suele Vd. tener dolores de la cintura?

33. Have you ever had a kidney (urinary) infection?
    ¿Ha tenido Vd. una infección en los riñones (una infección urinaria) alguna vez?

34. Was it treated?
    ¿Fue tratada?

35. What color is your urine?
    ¿De qué color es la orina?

36. Do you have blood in your urine?
    ¿Tiene Vd. sangre en la orina?

37. Is your urine cloudy?
    ¿Es nublosa la orina?

38. Does your urine look bloody?
    ¿Le parece que tiene sangre en la orina?

39. Do you have pus in your urine?
    ¿Orina Vd. con pus?
    ¿Tiene Vd. pus en la orina?

40. Do your ankles swell when you don't urinate?
    ¿Se le hinchan los tobillos cuando no orina Vd.?

41. Your kidneys aren't functioning.
    Sus riñones no funcionan.

REVIEW *REPASO*

Practice the following dialogue.

DR. GREEN: What is your problem, Miss Ruiz?

DR. GREEN: **¿Cuál es su problema, señorita Ruiz?**

MISS RUIZ: I am having problems with my urine.

SRTA. RUIZ: **Tengo problemas al orinar.**

DR. GREEN: Can you urinate?

DR. GREEN: **¿Puede Vd. orinar?**

MISS RUIZ: Oh, yes, Doctor, but I am unable to control my urine.

SRTA. RUIZ: **Ah, sí, doctor, pero tengo pérdidas involuntarias de orina.**

DR. GREEN: How long has it been since you have urinated?

DR. GREEN: **¿Desde cuándo no orina Vd.?**

MISS RUIZ: About five minutes.

SRTA. RUIZ: **Casi cinco minutos.**

DR. GREEN: How frequently do you urinate?

DR. GREEN: **¿Con qué frecuencia orina Vd.?**

MISS RUIZ: I feel like I have to urinate every few minutes.

SRTA. RUIZ: **Me parece que tengo que orinar cada cuantos minutos.**

DR. GREEN: When you urinate, do you pass a lot or a little urine?

DR. GREEN: **Al orinar, ¿pasa mucha o poca orina?**

MISS RUIZ: I only pass a few drops, but I feel like I have to go.

SRTA. RUIZ: **No paso más que unas gotas, pero me parece que tengo que orinar.**

DR. GREEN: Does it hurt when you urinate?

DR. GREEN: **¿Le duele cuando orina Vd.?**

MISS RUIZ: I don't think so.

SRTA. RUIZ: **Creo que no.**

DR. GREEN: Is there a burning sensation when you urinate?

DR. GREEN: **¿Hay un ardor al orinar?**

MISS RUIZ: No.

SRTA. RUIZ: **No.**

DR. GREEN: I am going to give you a prescription for some pills. Take one pill after each meal and at bedtime. Drink two glasses of water with each pill.

DR. GREEN: **Le daré una prescripción para unas píldoras. Tome una después de cada comida y antes de acostarse. Trague esta medicina con dos vasos de agua cada vez.**

MISS RUIZ: Yes, Doctor.

SRTA. RUIZ: **Sí, doctor.**

DR. GREEN: These pills may turn your urine different colors. Do not be afraid.

DR. GREEN: **Estas píldoras puedan cambiar su orina a varios colores. No se preocupe Vd.**

GENITOURINARY (MEN) *GENITOURINARIO (PARA HOMBRES)*

1. Do you get pains in the testicles?
   ¿Suede Vd. tener dolores de los testículos?
   de los huevos? (slang)
   de los compañones? (slang)

2. Do you pull back the foreskin on your penis when you wash in the genital region?
   ¿Se le pela Vd. al lavarse las partes?

3. Have you ever been impotent or sterile?
   ¿Ha padecido alguna vez de la impotencia o de la esterilidad?

4. Do you have a discharge from your penis?
   ¿Le supura el pene?

5. Have you ever had prostatitis (inflamed prostate)?
   ¿Ha padecido alguna vez de prostatitis (la prostata agrandada)?

6. Have you had any sores on your penis?
   ¿Ha tenido Vd. llagas (úlceras) en su pene?

GENITOURINARY (WOMEN): MENSTRUATION
GENITOURINARIO (PARA MUJERES): MENSTRUACION

1. When was your last menstrual period?
   ¿Cuándo fue su última menstruación? (general)
   ¿Cuándo fue su último período? (colloq)
   ¿Cuándo fue su última administración? (Mex.)
   ¿Cuándo fue su última regla? (Mex., P.R.)

2. How long did it last?
   ¿Cuánto tiempo le duró?

3. How often do you get your periods?
   ¿Cada cuánto le baja a Vd. la menstruación?
   ¿Cada cuánto menstrúa Vd.?

4. How many days does it last?
   ¿Por cuántos días pierde Vd. sangre?
   ¿Por cuántos días le dura?

5. Do you have it now?
   ¿La tiene ahora?

6. Do you have a light (heavy) flow?
   ¿Sale poca (mucha) sangre?

7. How old were you when you first began to menstruate?
   ¿A qué edad tuvo su primera menstruación (regla)?

8. Have your periods always been regular up to now?
   ¿Han sido regulares sus reglas hasta ahora?

9. Have you ever had menstrual problems?
   ¿Ha tenido alguna vez desórdenes menstruales?

10. Do you have pain with it?
    ¿Ha tenido dolor con ella?

11. Do you usually have pain with your periods?
    ¿Suele Vd. tener dolor con su regla?

12. Was it worse this time?
    ¿Fue más fuerte esta vez?

13. Was there more bleeding than usual?
    ¿Sangró Vd. más de lo ordinario?

14. How is your mood during your menstrual flow?
    ¿Cuál es su tipo de humor durante la menstruación?

15. Describe your menstrual flow.
    Describa Vd. su hemorragia menstrual.

16. Do you spot between periods (or after menopause)?
    ¿Tiene Vd. manchas de sangre entre períodos menstruales? (después de menopausia?)

17. Do you ever hemorrhage then?
    ¿Tiene Vd. hemorragia con sangre obscura o sangre roja entonces?

18. Are you bleeding heavily?
    ¿Está sangrando mucho?

19. How many sanitary pads or tampons did you use during your last menstrual cycle?
    ¿Cuántas toallas higiénicas ha usado Vd. en su última menstruación?

20. Do you gain weight during your period?
    ¿Tiene Vd. aumento de peso durante su período?

21. Do you have severe menstrual cramps?
    ¿Sufre Vd. de dolores fuertes del período?
    ¿Sufre Vd. de cólicos fuertes?

22. Are your breasts tender during your period?
    Con su período, ¿le duelen los senos?

PRACTICE *PRACTICA*

Read the following aloud both for fluency and comprehension. Then answer the questions based on the passage.

From the age of puberty until a woman enters menopause, she menstruates monthly. Once a month an egg is formed by the woman's ovaries and if the woman does not become pregnant, the lining of the uterus is cast off and replaced each month. This reproductive process, because it is repeated regularly every month, is called a menstrual cycle. The menstrual cycle is measured from the first day of menstruation to the first day of the next menstruation. Usually these cycles are 28 days long. Some women have longer menstrual cycles, others shorter ones. The menstrual cycle is controlled by hormones.

These hormones cause one of the ovaries to produce an egg each month. The hormones also cause changes in the lining of the uterus. If an egg is fertilized by sperm from a man, the egg attaches itself to the lining of the uterus.

If the egg is not fertilized the lining of the uterus is shed, accompanied by a flow of blood. The flow of blood passes from the uterus out through the vagina. This flow lasts from three to five days. Hormone secretions begin with the next menstrual cycle.

1. How long are menstrual cycles on the average?
2. What does the ovary produce?
3. How long does the flow of blood last?

Lea lo que sigue en voz alta para fluidez y comprehensión. Entonces conteste Vd. a las preguntas que siguen.

Desde la edad de pubertad hasta el cambio de vida, una mujer menstrúa una vez al mes. Una vez cada mes un óvulo se forma y a menos que la mujer esté embarazada, el forro o recubrimiento interior del útero es expulsado y reemplazado cada mes. Este proceso reproductivo, a causa de la repetición regular cada mes, se llama un ciclo menstrual. El ciclo menstrual empieza el primer día de la menstruación y dura hasta el primer día de la próxima menstruación. Generalmente estos ciclos duran veintiocho días. Para algunas mujeres estos ciclos duran más, para otras duran menos tiempo. El ciclo menstrual es controlado por unas hormonas.

Estas hormonas hacen que uno de los ovarios produzca un óvulo cada mes. Estas hormonas también producen cambios en el forro del útero. Si un óvulo es fertilizado por los espermatozoides de un hombre, el óvulo fertilizado se adhiere al forro del útero.

Si el óvulo no es fertilizado, el recubrimiento interior del útero es expulsado, acompañado de un flujo de sangre. El flujo sangrado pasa desde el útero hasta la vagina. El sangrado menstrual dura de tres a cinco días. La secreción de hormonas comienza de nuevo al empezar la menstruación.

1. ¿Por cuántos días duran los ciclos menstruales por lo regular?
2. ¿Qué produce un ovario?
3. ¿Por cuántos días duran el flujo sanguíneo?

VAGINAL DISCHARGE *SECRECION VAGINAL*

23. Do you have vaginal secretions?
    ¿Tiene Vd. secreciones vaginales?

24. Are they watery?
    ¿Son aguachentas?

25. Are they thick and yellow?
    ¿Son espesas y amarillas?

26. Are they thick and white?
    ¿Son espesas y blancas?

27. Are they frothy and greenish?
    ¿Son espumosas y verdosas?

28. Is your vagina itchy?
    ¿Tiene Vd. comezón en la vagina?

29. Have you had it before?
    ¿La ha tenido antes?

30. How long has the discharge been there?
    ¿Cuánto tiempo hace que le desecha?
    ¿Cuánto tiempo hace que le sale esta descarga?

31. Do you have a yellow-greenish or a whitish frothy, foul-smelling discharge that itches?
    ¿Tiene Vd. un desecho verde-amarillo o blancuzco, espumoso, apestoso con comezón?

32. Do you have a white discharge similar to "curds" that smells like mold or bread in the oven?
    ¿Tiene Vd. un desecho blanco, parecido a un cuajo con olor a moho o pan en el horno?

33. Do you have a milky, thick discharge, with a rancid odor?
    ¿Tiene Vd. un desecho color de leche, espeso, con olor rancio?

34. Do you have a coffee-colored discharge that is watery?
    ¿Tiene Vd. un desecho color café, como agua?

35. Do you have a lead-colored discharge, streaked with blood?
    ¿Tiene Vd. un desecho color plomo, rayado con sangre?

36. Have you ever had venereal disease (VD)?
   ¿Ha tenido jamás una enfermedad venérea (VD/EV)?

37. Is your husband circumcised?
   ¿Está circuncidado su esposo?
   Is your sexual partner circumcised?
   ¿Está circuncidada la persona con quien Vd. tiene relaciones sexuales?

38. Do you suffer from prolapse of the uterus?
   ¿Padece Vd. de la matriz caída?

39. When was your last pap smear?
   ¿Cuándo le han tomado un extendido vaginal para el test de Papanicolau?

40. Were the results normal (abnormal)?
   ¿Fueron normales (anormales) los resultados?

PREGNANCY *EMBARAZO*[15]

41. Have you ever been pregnant?
   ¿Ha estado embarazada alguna vez?
   ¿Ha estado encinta alguna vez?

42. How many times have you been pregnant?
   ¿Cuántos embarazos ha tenido Vd.?

43. Were all your pregnancies normal?
   ¿Fueron todos sus embarazos normales?

44. Was the birth natural or induced?
   ¿Fue el parto natural o provocado?

45. Was the delivery normal or did they use instruments?
   ¿Fue un parto normal o usaron fórceps (tenazas)?

46. Was the delivery by caesarean section?
   ¿Fue el parto por operación cesárea?

47. How many children do you have?
   ¿Cuántos hijos tiene Vd.?

48. How old is your oldest child? Your youngest?
   ¿Cuántos años tiene el (la) mayor? El (La) más joven (menor)?

49. Have you ever had an abortion or miscarriage?
   ¿Ha tenido alguna vez un aborto inducido o espontáneo, o un mal parto?

50. How many?
   ¿Cuántos?

51. How many weeks pregnant were you?
   ¿Cuántas semanas de embarazo tenía Vd. cuando tuvo el aborto (inducido/espontáneo)?

52. Have you ever had a baby who died at birth? How many?
   ¿Ha tenido jamás algún niño que haya muerto poco después de nacer? ¿Cuántos?

53. Have you ever had a stillborn child?
 ¿Jamás ha tenido Vd. un niño que haya nacido muerto?

54. Have you ever had a child who was born with the cord wrapped around the neck?
 ¿Jamás ha tenido un niño que haya nacido con el cordón umbilical alrededor del cuello?

55. Have you ever had a placenta previa?
 ¿Jamás ha tenido Vd. problema con la placenta previa?

56. Have you ever had postpartum hemorrhage?
 ¿Ha tenido Vd. alguna vez desangramiento después del parto?

57. How long was your labor with your first child?
 ¿Cuánto tiempo duró su labor con su primer hijo?
                      with other children?
                      con sus otros hijos?

58. What is the date of your last period?
 ¿Cuál fue la fecha de su última regla?

59. Are you pregnant now?
 ¿Está Vd. embarazada en este momento?

60. How many months?
 ¿Cuántos meses?

61. Was this a planned pregnancy?
 ¿Se planeó este embarazo?

62. When is your baby due?
 ¿Cuándo va a nacer el niño?

63. Have you had German measles during this pregnancy?
 ¿Ha tenido Vd. el sarampión de tres días durante este embarazo?

64. Do you have any hereditary diseases?
 ¿Sufre Vd. de alguna enfermedad hereditaria?

65. Do you have diabetes?
 ¿Sufre Vd. de diabetes?

66. Do you have high blood pressure?
 ¿Sufre Vd. de alta presión arterial?

67. Have you been using any medications?
 ¿Ha tomado algunas medicinas?

68. What type?
 ¿Qué clase?

69. What is the name?
 ¿Cómo se llaman?

70. Have you been taking drugs (narcotics) during this pregnancy?
 ¿Ha estado tomando drogas durante este embarazo?

71. Have you been drinking during this pregnancy daily?
    ¿Ha tomado alcohol durante este embarazo todos los días?

72. Have you had varicose veins or hemorrhoids during the pregnancy?
    ¿Ha tenido Vd. várices o hemorroides durante este embarazo?

73. Do you have nausea or vomiting?
    ¿Tiene Vd. náusea o vómitos?

74. Tiredness or low back pain?
    ¿Cansancio o dolor de la cintura?

75. Do you want to breastfeed this child?
    ¿Quiere Vd. criar a este niño?

76. Do you have any new aversion to certain foods?
    ¿Siente Vd. repugnancia para alguna comida?
    Cravings?
    ¿Antojos?

77. Do your breasts feel heavy and tight?
    ¿Siente los senos pesados y apretados?

78. If you see any bleeding, call me at once.
    Si Vd. echa sangre, o tiene un derrame o flujo sangriento, llámeme en seguida.

79. Call me immediately if you have any severe pain.
    Llámeme en seguida, si Vd. siente algunos dolores fuertes.
    severe and persistent headaches.
    dolores de cabeza severos y persistentes.
    stomachaches that do not go away when you move
    your bowels.
    **dolores abdominales continuos que no se alivien al
    evacuar el vientre.**

MENOPAUSE *LA MENOPAUSIA*

80. Have you noticed any change in your periods?
    ¿Se ha fijado en algún cambio en su período?

81. Do you have hot flashes?
    ¿Siente Vd. sensaciones de calor en la cara?
    ¿Le dan sofocones?

82. Do you have a decrease in your vaginal secretions?
    ¿Tiene Vd. una disminución de las secreciones vaginales?

83. Is there a dryness of your skin?
    ¿Hay una sequedad de su piel?

84. Are you feeling "sick" with grief, depression, nervousness?
    ¿Siente Vd. males como angustias, tristeza, nerviosidad?

85. You are going through menopause/change of life.
    Vd. pasa por la menopausia/el cambio de vida.

86. These symptoms are nomal for a woman between 40 and 50.
   Estos síntomas son normales para una mujer entre los 40 y 50 años de edad.

87. The symptoms will pass.
   Los síntomas pasarán.

88. After menopause, the majority of women again feel well.
   Después de la menopausia, la mayoría de la mujeres vuelven a sentirse bien.

GENITOURINARY (VENEREAL)   *GENITOURINARIO (VENEREA)*

89. Have you ever had any venereal disease (syphilis[16], gonorrhea)?
   ¿Ha padecido Vd. alguna vez de cualquier enfermedad venérea (sífilis, gonorrea)?

90. Did you receive treatment?
   ¿Recibió Vd. tratamiento?

91. When? Where?
   ¿Cuándo? ¿Dónde?

92. Do you have a discharge from your penis (vagina)?
   ¿Tiene Vd. un desecho de su pene (vagina)?

93. Do you have any sores on your penis (in or around your vagina)?
   ¿Tiene Vd. llagas (úlceras) en su pene (en o alrededor de su vagina)?

94. Is there itching?
   ¿Hay picazón de los genitales?

95. Do you have a burning sensation of your genitals?
   ¿Tiene Vd. un ardor de los genitales?

96. Is there swelling or tenderness of the inguinal area?
   ¿Hay hinchazón o dolor de la ingle?

97. Does it hurt to urinate?
   ¿Le duele al orinar?

98. Do any joints hurt you—wrist, ankle, knee?
   ¿Le duelen las coyunturas—las de la muñeca, del tobillo, de la rodilla?

99. Is your genital area red?
   ¿Tiene Vd. enrojecimiento de los genitales?

100. Do you have any rash on your body?
   ¿Tiene Vd. salpullido en el cuerpo?

101. How long has this been going on?
   ¿Cuánto tiempo hace que esto pasa?

102. Have you slept with a man (woman) recently?
   ¿Ha tenido relaciones sexuales con un hombre (una mujer) recientemente?

103. Do you know if that person with whom you have had sexual relations also has these symptoms?
¿Sabe Vd. si esa persona con quien Vd. ha tenido relaciones sexuales también tiene estos síntomas?

104. When was the last time that you had sexual relations?
¿Cuándo fue la última vez que tuvo relaciones sexuales?

105. Don't have sexual relations until you are completely cured.
No tenga relaciones sexuales hasta que esté completamente curado (-a).

106. Don't drink any alcoholic beverages until you are completely cured.
No tome ninguna bebida alcohólica hasta que esté completamente curado (-a).

107. Avoid physical exercise.
Evite Vd. ejercicios físicos.

108. You must go to the VD clinic.
Vd. tiene que ir a la clínica de enfermedades venéreas.

Extremities *Las extremidades*

1. Are your joints stiff in the morning?
¿Siente Vd. rígidas sus articulaciones por la mañana?
¿Están rígidas las coyunturas por la mañana? (colloq)

2. Have you had aches in your joints during the last year?
¿Ha tenido Vd. dolores en las articulaciones durante el último año?

3. Which joints are painful?
¿Cuáles son las articulaciones que le duelen?

4. Are your knees and wrists swollen or only your ankles and knees?
¿Tiene Vd. las rodillas y las muñecas hinchadas o solamente los tobillos y las rodillas hinchados?

5. Do you feel pain when you stand?
¿Siente Vd. dolor cuando se pone de pie?

6. Do you feel pain when you bend?
¿Siente Vd. dolor cuando se dobla?

7. Do the pains shoot down toward the legs?
¿Le bajan los dolores a las piernas?

8. Is the pain sharp or dull?
¿Es agudo o sordo el dolor?

9. Is your arm (leg) weak?
¿Está débil el brazo (la pierna)?

Neurological *Neurológico*

1. Do you feel (very) weak?
   ¿Se siente (muy) débil?

2. Do you ever feel dizzy (giddy)?
   ¿Suele Vd. tener mareos? (colloq.)
   ¿Tiene Vd. vértigo alguna vez?

3. Do you spin around?
   ¿Da Vd. vueltas?

4. Do objects spin around you?
   ¿A Vd. le dan vueltas los objetos?

5. Do you ever lose your coordination?
   ¿Pierde Vd. jamás su coordinación?

6. Do you ever lose your balance?
   ¿Pierde Vd. jamás su equilibrio?

7. Do you feel like falling?
   ¿Se siente Vd. como si se cayese/cayera?

8. Do you ever have trouble feeling heat on your skin?
   ¿Tiene Vd. algunas veces dificultad en distinguir el calor en la piel?
           feeling cold on your skin?
           en distinguir el frío en la piel?

9. Do you ever lose your sense of touch?
   ¿Le falta jamás la sensibilidad táctil?

10. Do you have tingling sensations?
    ¿Tiene Vd. hormigueos?

11. Do you have numbness in your hands or feet?
    ¿Tiene Vd. entumecimiento (calambres) en las manos o los pies?

12. Have you been sleeping on your arm?
    ¿Ha dormido Vd. encima del brazo?

13. Are some of the fingers numb?
    ¿Tiene Vd. algunos de los dedos adormecidos?

14. Come see me if your fingers become numb.
    Venga a verme si se le adormecen los dedos.

15. Do you have fainting spells?
    ¿Ha tenido Vd. desmayos?
    ¿Suele Vd. tener desvanecimientos?

16. Are you subject to them?
    ¿Se desmaya Vd. con frecuencia?

17. Do you have convulsions?
    ¿Le ha ocurrido a Vd. tener convulsiones o haber estado inconsciente?
    ¿Suele Vd. tener convulsiones?

18. When was your most recent one?
    ¿Cuándo fue la última?

19. When was your first one?
    ¿Cuándo fue la primera?

20. How often do you have them?
    ¿Con qué frecuencia las tiene Vd.?

21. Have you ever lost consciousness?
    ¿Perdió Vd. el sentido alguna vez?

22. For how long?
    ¿Por cuánto tíempo?

23. How frequently does this happen?
    ¿Con qué frecuencia ocurre?

24. When you have convulsions, do you ever bite your tongue?
    Cuando tiene Vd. convulsiones, ¿se muerde la lengua?

25. Are the convulsions preceded by any warning, like an odor, a strange feeling, pain, etc.?
    ¿Precede las convulsiones algún aviso, como un olor, una sensación rara, un dolor, etc.?

26. Are you disoriented afterwards?
    ¿Está Vd. desorientado (-a) después?

27. Do you take medicine for the convulsions?
    ¿Toma Vd. medicina para las convulsiones?

28. What kind?
    ¿Qué tipo?

29. Do you have headaches?
    ¿Sufre Vd. de jaquecas?

30. What type—mild, moderate, migraines?
    ¿Qué tipo—leves, moderadas, migrañas?

31. Describe the pain.
    Describa Vd. el dolor de la jaqueca.

32. Are the headaches preceded by any warning, like a strange feeling, an odor, nausea, etc.?
    ¿Precede las jaquecas algún aviso, como una sensación rara, un olor, náuseas, etc.?

33. Do you ever have trouble speaking clearly?
    ¿Tiene Vd. algunas veces dificultad cuando habla?

34. Do you ever have trouble when you read or write?
    ¿Tiene Vd. algunas veces problemas al leer o al escribir?

35. Do you ever have trouble understanding what someone asks?
    ¿Tiene Vd. algunas veces dificultad en entender cuando alguien le pregunta algo?

36. Have you ever had memory defects?
    ¿Ha tenido Vd. defectos de memoria?

37. Do you see double?
    ¿Ve Vd. doble?
    ¿Ve Vd. bizco? (C. A.)
    ¿Ve Vd. las cosas doble?

38. Do you have blurred vision?
    ¿Ve Vd. borrosamente?
    ¿Ve Vd. borroso?

39. Do you ever have spots before your eyes?
    ¿Tiene Vd. jamás manchas (moscos) volantes delante de los ojos?

40. Do you ever have pain behind your eyes?
    ¿Tiene Vd. jamás dolor que parece estar debajo de los ojos?

41. Have you ever had a problem distinguishing colors?
    ¿Ha tenido algunas veces problemas al distinguir los colores?

42. Have you ever had trouble smelling?
    ¿Ha tenido jamás problemas con el sentido olfatorio?

43. Have you ever had a change in taste sensations?
    ¿Ha tenido jamás un cambio del sentido del gusto?

44. Have you ever had difficulty in hearing?
    ¿Ha tenido jamás dificultad en oír?

45. Since when?
    ¿Desde cuándo?

46. How did it being—slowly or suddenly?
    ¿Cómo empezó—lentamente o de repente?

Musculoskeletal
Muscular-esquelético

1. Do you have any swelling?
    ¿Se le hincha a Vd. alguna parte del cuerpo?

2. Do you have a herniated disc?
    ¿Tiene Vd. una hernia del disco intervertebral?

3. Do you have varicose veins?
    ¿Tiene Vd. las venas inflamadas o venas varicosas?

4. Have you had any pain in your back?
    ¿Ha tenido Vd. algún dolor de espalda?

5. Where?
   ¿Dónde?

6. Have you been bothered recently by muscle spasms?
   ¿Ha tenido Vd. recientemente molestias o dolores en los músculos?

7. Have you had muscle weakness?
   ¿Ha tenido Vd. debilidad muscular?

Endocrine   *Endocrino*

1. Has there been a significant change in your weight recently? Gain? Loss?
   ¿Ha habido un gran cambio en su peso recientemente? ¿Aumento? ¿Pérdida?

2. Has there been any change in your facial features?
   ¿Ha habido algún cambio en la cara?

3. Has there been any change in your hair—either in texture, color, or quantity?
   ¿Ha habido algún cambio en el pelo de la cabeza—o en cuanto a la textura, el color o la cantidad?

4. Has there been any change in your skin?
   ¿Ha habido algún cambio en la piel?

5. Have you noticed any change in your desire to have sexual relations?
   ¿Se ha fijado en algún cambio en sus deseos de tener relaciones sexuales?

6. Are you more nervous than before?
   ¿Se pone Vd. más nervioso(-a) que antes?

7. Are you thirstier than usual?
   ¿Tiene Vd. más sed que lo normal?

8. Do you eat more than usual and not gain weight?
   ¿Come Vd. más que lo común y no se pone gordo (-a)?

9. Do you urinate more than usual?
   ¿Orina Vd. más que lo normal?

PERSONAL HISTORY

HISTORIA PERSONAL

Identification   *Identificación*

1. What is your name?[17]
   ¿Cómo se llama Vd.?

2. Where do you live?[18]
   ¿Dónde vive Vd.?

3. What is your telephone number?[19]
   ¿Cuál es el número de teléfono de su casa, por favor?

4. How old are you?
   ¿Cuántos años tiene Vd.?
   ¿Qué edad tiene Vd.? (colloq)

5. What is your birthdate?[20]
   ¿Cuál es la fecha de su nacimiento?

6. Where were you born?
   ¿Dónde nació Vd.?

7. Are you single or married?
   ¿Es Vd. soltero (soltera) o casado (casada)?

8. Are you single but living with your girlfriend (boyfriend)?
   ¿Es Vd. soltero (soltera) pero vive con su novia (novio)?
   ¿Está Vd. amancebado(-a)? (P.R.)

9. Are you divorced?
   ¿Es Vd. divorciado (divorciada)?

10. Are you a widow?
    ¿Es Vd. viuda?

11. Are you a widower?
    ¿Es Vd. viudo?

12. Have you been married before?
    ¿Ha estado casado(-a) alguna vez?

13. How long have you been married to your spouse?
    ¿Desde cuándo es Vd. casado(-a) con su esposa(-o)?

14. Are you happy with your spouse?
    ¿Está Vd. contento(-a) con su esposa(-o)?

15. Is your spouse in good health?
    ¿Goza su esposo(-a) de buena salud?

16. Do you have any children?
    ¿Tiene Vd. algunos hijos?

17. How many?
    ¿Cuántos?

18. How old is she/he (are they)?
    ¿Cuántos años tiene(n)?
    ¿Qué edad tiene(n)? (colloq)

19. Are your children in good health?
    ¿Gozan sus hijos de buena salud?

Job Data *Información del empleo*

20. What do you do? (How do you earn a living?)
    ¿Cómo gana Vd. la vida?
    ¿Qué clase de trabajo tiene Vd.?

21. What is your occupation?[21]
    ¿Cuál es su ocupación?

22. Where do you work?
    ¿Dónde trabaja Vd.?

23. How long have you worked there?
    ¿Desde cuándo trabaja Vd. allí?

24. What was your first job?
    ¿Cuál fue su primer empleo?

25. What other jobs have you had?
    ¿Qué otros empleos ha tenido Vd.?

26. How long did you work at each?
    ¿Cuánto tiempo trabajó Vd. en cada uno de estos empleos?

27. Why did you change jobs?
    ¿Por qué cambió Vd. de empleo?

28. Are you happy in your work?
    ¿Tiene Vd. satisfacción en el trabajo?

29. Do you work with
    En su empleo, ¿usa Vd. (¿está Vd. en contacto con . . .)
    paints?
    pinturas?
    insecticides?
    insecticidas?
    lead?
    plomo?
    plastics?
    plásticos?
    other synthetic materials?
    otras cosas sintéticas?
    drugs?
    drogas?
    dusts?
    polvos?
    chemicals?
    productos químicos?

30. How long are you in contact with them?
    ¿Por cuánto tiempo tiene Vd. tal contacto?

31. Do you take any precautionary measures?
    ¿Toma Vd. precauciones algunas?

32. What?
    ¿Cuáles son?

33. What is your religion?[22]
    ¿Cuál es su religión?

34. What is your nationality?[23]
    ¿Cuál es su nacionalidad?

35. How much education do you have?
    ¿Cuántos años de la escuela cumplió Vd.?
    grade school?
    ¿educación primaria?
    high school?
    ¿educación secundaria?
    college?
    ¿educación universitaria?
    graduate school?
    ¿educación graduada?
    professional school?
    ¿especializada profesional?

Allergy *Alergia*

36. Are you allergic to any medication? To any food? To dust or pollen?
    ¿Es Vd. alérgico (alérgica) a alguna medicina? ¿a alguna comida? ¿a polvo o a polen?

37. Do you have hay fever?
    ¿Tiene Vd. la fiebre del heno?

Weight Change *Cambio de peso*

38. How much do you normally weigh?
    Por lo regular, ¿cuánto pesa Vd.?

39. Have you gained or lost much weight recently, suddenly?
    ¿Ha ganado o perdido peso últimamente, de repente?

Diet *Dieta*

40. Do you have a good appetite?
    ¿Tiene Vd. buen apetito?

41. During the last year have you noticed an increase in your desire for sweets?
    ¿Ha observado Vd. durante el último año un aumento de apetito por dulces?

42. How many meals do you eat daily?
    ¿Cuántas comidas toma Vd. al día?

43. What do you eat for breakfast? lunch? dinner?
    ¿Qué toma Vd. para el desayuno? ¿para el almuerzo? ¿para la cena?

44. Do you eat between meals?
    ¿Toma Vd. algo entre comidas?

45. How much butter do you eat daily?
    ¿Cuánta mantequilla come Vd. al día?

46. How many eggs?
    ¿Cuántos huevos come Vd. por semana?

47. Do you drink coffee or tea?
    ¿Toma Vd. café o té?

48. How much coffee and tea do you drink a day?
    ¿Cuántas tazas de café o de té bebe Vd. al día?

49. Do you drink regular or decaffeinated coffee?
    ¿Toma Vd. café regular o descafeinado?

50. How much water do you drink daily?
    ¿Cuántos vasos de agua bebe Vd. al día?

Smoking, Drinking   *El fumar, el beber*

51. Do you drink alcoholic beverages?
    ¿Toma Vd. algunas bebidas alcohólicas?

52. Have you been drinking a lot?[24]
    ¿Ha estado tomando mucho alcohol (alcol)?

53. What type of alcoholic beverage do you generally buy?
    ¿Qué tipo de bebida alcohólica compra Vd. por lo regular?

54. How long does a bottle of alcohol last you?
    ¿Cuánto tiempo le queda una botella de alcohol?

55. How often during the week do you drink alcoholic beverages?
    ¿Cuántos días de la semana toma Vd. bebidas alcohólicas?

56. Do you sleep well?
    ¿Duerme Vd. bien?

57. What time do you go to bed?
    ¿A qué hora se acuesta por la noche, por lo regular?

58. What time do you get up in the morning?
    ¿A qué hora se despierta por la mañana, por lo regular?

59. It is important to rest more.
    Es importante descansar más.

60. Do you walk a lot at home?
    ¿Camina Vd. mucho en casa?

61. Do you walk a lot outside of the house?
    ¿Camina Vd. mucho afuera de la casa?

62. How many blocks do you walk on the average during the day?
    ¿Cuántas manzanas camina Vd. promedio durante el día?

63. Do you do your own shopping?
    ¿Va Vd. de compras sí mismo (misma)?

64. Do you smoke?
    ¿Fuma Vd.?

65. How much?
    ¿Cuántos cigarrillos al día?

66. If you smoke (or have smoked) how many years have you been smoking?
    Si Vd. fuma (o ha fumado antes) ¿por cuántos años ha venido haciéndolo?

67. I advise you to stop smoking or at least to reduce it to a minimum.
    Le aconsejo que deje de fumar o que lo reduzca a un mínimo.

Drugs[25] *Uso de drogas*

68. Do you use drugs regularly? Are you a drug addict?
    ¿Es Vd. adicto (-a) al uso de drogas?
    ¿Es Vd. drogadicto (-a)?
    ¿Acostumbra Vd. a tomar alguna droga?
    ¿Es Vd. un adicto (una adicta)?
    ¿Toma Vd. alguna droga?

69. How much money do you spend daily on your drug habit?
    ¿Cuánto dinero gasta Vd. por día para sus drogas?

70. Do you smoke marijuana?
    ¿Fuma Vd. la mariguana?

71. Do you take morphine?
    ¿Ingiere Vd. morfina?
    ¿Se administra Vd. morfina?
    ¿Es Vd. adicto (-a) a morfina?

72. Do you use heroin, cocaine, LSD?
    ¿Toma Vd. heroína, cocaína, drogas alucinantes (LSD)?

73. Do you use amphetamines?
    ¿Usa Vd. las anfetaminas?

74. Are you using barbiturates without medical supervision?
    ¿Toma Vd. los barbitúricos sin supervisión médica?

Medication *Medicación*

75. Do you use ...?
    ¿Ha tomado Vd. . . .?

    antihistamines?
    antihistamínicos?
    aspirin
    aspirinas
    sleeping pills
    píldoras para dormir (sedativos)
    birth control pills
    píldoras para control de embarazo
    diet pills
    píldoras para dieta
    laxatives
    laxantes
    diuretics
    píldoras diuréticas
    medication for diabetes
    medicación para diabetes
    digitalin or nitroglycerin
    digitalina o nitroglicerina
    antacids
    antiácidos
    antibiotics
    antibióticos
    tranquilizers
    tranquilizantes
    vitamins
    vitaminas
    thyroid pills
    medicación tiroides
    cortisone
    cortisona

76. How would you describe the feelings that you experience during coitus?
    ¿Cómo describiría Vd. las sensaciones que tiene durante el coito (relación sexual)?

EXERCISE *EJERCICIO*

¿Cómo se dice en español?

1. I normally weigh 125 pounds.
2. John eats three meals daily.
3. We never drink water.
4. The girl drinks coffee but I drink milk.
5. I have been smoking for five years.
6. I get up at 8 in the morning.

7. Paul goes to sleep at midnight.

8. You do not smoke now.

9. Why do you use barbiturates?

10. The widow has seven children.

SOCIAL HISTORY

HISTORIA SOCIAL

Economic and Insurance Data
Información financiera y de seguros

1. Who lives at home with you?
   ¿Quién vive en casa con Vd.?

2. Are you on relief?
   ¿Está Vd. en relief? (colloq)

3. Do you receive workmen's compensation?
   ¿Recibe Vd. compensación de obreros?

4. Do you support yourself?
   ¿Se mantiene Vd. mismo(-a)?

5. What do you earn per week, approximately?
   ¿Cuánto gana Vd. por semana, más o menos?

6. Are you the sole financial support of your family?
   ¿Es Vd. el único (la única) que sostiene a su familia?

7. What is the name of the person who supports you?
   ¿Cómo se llama la persona que le (la) mantiene?

8. Is this person a relative? a friend?
   ¿Es esta persona un pariente? ¿un amigo?

9. How many people in the family work for money?
   ¿Cuántas personas en la familia trabajan por dinero?

10. Do the people in the family who work contribute financially to the household?
    ¿Contribuyen las personas de la familia que trabajan a los gastos?

11. How many children attend school?
    ¿Cuántos niños asisten a la escuela?

12. Do you have money from other sources?
    ¿Recibe Vd. ayuda financiera de otras entradas?

13. Are there any city or religious agencies helping you or your family?
    ¿Hay algunas agencias de la ciudad o religiosas que le ayudan a Vd. o a su familia?

14. Do you have any savings? bonds? bank accounts?
    ¿Tiene Vd. ahorros? ¿bonos? ¿cuentos de banco?

15. Do you rent or own your own house?
    ¿Alquila Vd. o tiene casa propia?

16. How much rent do you pay?
    ¿Cuánto paga Vd. de renta?

17. How much is the mortgage?
    ¿Cuánto es la hipoteca?

18. Does anyone in your family own property?
    ¿Tiene propiedad alguno de su familia?

19. Do you have any unusual expenses?
    ¿Tiene Vd. gastos extraordinarios?

General Background *Fondo general*

1. Where do you live?
   ¿Dónde vive Vd.?

2. Is this an apartment or a house?
   ¿Es una casa de departamentos (de apartamentos) o una casa particular?

3. On what floor do you live?
   ¿En qué piso vive Vd.?[26]

4. How many rooms do you have?
   ¿Cuántos cuartos tiene Vd.?

5. How many people live in your apartment?
   ¿Cuántas personas viven en su apartamento?

6. How many are adults? Children?
   ¿Cuántos son adultos? ¿Niños?

7. How many people sleep in one room?
   ¿Cuántas personas duermen en un cuarto?

8. How many beds are there in one room?
   ¿Cuántas camas hay en un cuarto?

9. Is there a bathroom in your apartment?
   ¿Hay un cuarto de baño en su apartamento?

10. Do you share the bathroom?
    ¿Comparte Vd. el baño con otros?

11. Is there hot and cold water inside your house?
    ¿Hay agua caliente y fría dentro de su casa?

12. Are there any insects or rodents in your apartment?
    ¿Hay insectos o ratas en su apartamento?

Extracurricular   *Extracurricular*

1. Do you have many friends?
   ¿Tiene Vd. muchos amigos?

2. Do you have a large extended family?
   ¿Tiene Vd. una familia grande?

3. Do you enjoy the company of your friends/family?
   ¿Le gusta a Vd. la compañía de sus amigos/su familia?

4. Are you a member of a parish?
   ¿Pertenece a una parroquia?

5. Are you a member of any community club?
   ¿Pertenece Vd. a algún club o sociedad en la comunidad?

6. Do you belong to any sports organization?
   ¿Pertenece Vd. a algún grupo de deportes?

7. Who will take care of you when you leave the hospital?
   ¿Quién va a cuidarle(-la) cuando salga del hospital?

FAMILY HISTORY

HISTORIA FAMILIAR

1. Are your parents alive?
   ¿Todavía están vivos sus padres?
   ¿Todavía viven sus padres?

2. What did your mother die from?
   ¿De qué murió su madre?

3. What did your father die from?
   ¿De qué murió su padre?

4. How old were your grandparents when they died, or are they still alive?
   ¿Cuántos años tenían sus abuelos cuando murieron, o viven todavía?
   ¿A qué edad murieron sus abuelos, o están vivos todavía?

5. What did your grandmother die from?
   ¿De qué murió su abuela?

6. What did your grandfather die from?
   ¿De qué murió su abuelo?

7. What was your mother's maiden name?
   ¿Cuál era el nombre de soltera de su madre?

8. Where were you born?
   ¿Dónde nació Vd.?

9. Where were your parents born?
   ¿Dónde nacieron sus padres?

10. Do you have any brothers/sisters?
    ¿Tiene Vd. algunos hermanos? ¿hermanas?

11. How many?
    ¿Cuántos? ¿Cuántas?

12. Have any of your siblings died?
    ¿Han muerto algunos de sus hermanos (hermanas)?

13. How old was he (she)?
    ¿Cuántos años tenía?

14. Of what did he (she) die?
    ¿De qué murió?

15. Is there any family history of blood disease?
    ¿Hay alguna historia en su familia de enfermedades de la sangre?

16. Is there a history of lung trouble or diabetes?
    ¿Hay alguna historia de problemas pulmonares o de diabetes?

17. Does anyone in your family suffer from asthma or hay fever?
    ¿Padece alguien de su familia de asma o de fiebre del heno?

    extreme obesity
    obesidad extremada
    cancer or leukemia
    cáncer o leucemia
    heart attack
    ataque al corazón
    angina (pectoris)
    angina del pecho
    chronic anemia
    anemia crónica (sangre pobre [slang])
    stroke
    parálisis
    thyroid problems
    enfermedad de la tiroides
    stomach or duodenal ulcers
    úlceras de estómago o duodenales
    peptic ulcer
    úlcera péptica
    gall stones
    cálculos en la vesícula
    kidney stones
    cálculos en los riñones (cálculos renales)

18. Whom can we call in case of emergency?
    ¿A quién podemos llamar en caso de emergencia?

PREPARATION FOR PHYSICAL EXAMINATION

PREPARACION PARA EL RECONOCIMIENTO FISICO

1. Take off your clothes, please.
   Desvístase Vd., por favor.
   Favor de desvestirse.
   Take off your clothes except for your underwear, please.
   Desvístase Vd. por favor, menos la ropa interior.

2. Please take off your clothes down to your waist.
   Desvístase Vd. hasta la cintura, por favor.
   Quítese Vd. la ropa hasta la cintura, por favor.

3. Please take off your clothes from the waist down.
   Desvístase Vd. de la cintura para abajo, por favor.

4. Please take off your girdle and bra.
   Quítese Vd. la faja y el sostén (ajustador, portabustos [slang]), por favor.

5. Lower your trousers, please.
   Bájese Vd. los pantalones, por favor.

6. Please hang your clothes over there.
   Cuelgue Vd. la ropa ahí, por favor.

7. Put on the gown, please.
   Póngase Vd. la bata, por favor.

8. Sit on the table, please.
   Siéntese Vd. sobre la mesa, por favor.

9. Please lie down on the examining table.
   Acuéstese Vd. sobre la mesa de reconocimiento, por favor.

10. The doctor will examine you now.
    El doctor le (la) examinará ahora.

11. The doctor wants to examine your arm.
    El doctor quiere examinarle el brazo.

12. Are you comfortable?
    ¿Está cómodo(-a)?

13. I am sorry if this makes you uncomfortable.
    Lo siento si esto le molesta.

14. This won't hurt.
    Esto no le dolerá.

15. Does this hurt?
    ¿Le duele esto?

16. Can you feel this?
    ¿Puede sentir esto?

17. Hold still, please.
    No se mueva, por favor.

18. It will only take a minute more.
    No durará más de un minuto.

19. That's enough.
    Basta.

20. Just relax.
    Relaje Vd. el cuerpo.
    Relájese Vd.[27]

21. Please turn face up.
    Póngase Vd. boca arriba, por favor.

22. Please turn face down.
    Póngase Vd. boca abajo, por favor.

23. I am going to touch your knee with an instrument.
    Voy a tocar su rodilla con un instrumento.

24. You may get dressed now.
    Vd. puede vestirse ahora.

25. I want to talk with you when you are dressed.
    Quiero hablar con Vd. cuando se vista.

PHYSICAL EXAMINATION

RECONOCIMIENTO FISICO

Head *La cabeza*

1. I am going to examine your head.
   Voy a examinarle la cabeza.

2. Bend your head to the right, please.
   Doble Vd. la cabeza a la derecha, por favor.

3. Bend your head to the left, please
   Doble Vd. la cabeza a la izquierda, por favor.

4. Bend your head forward.
   Doble Vd. la cabeza hacia adelante.

5. Bend your head backwards.
   Doble Vd. la cabeza hacia atrás.

6. Turn your head to the right; to the left.
   Vuelva Vd. la cabeza hacia la derecha; hacia la izquierda.

7. Turn your head.
   Gire Vd. la cabeza.

Eyes   *Los ojos*

1. Let me see your eyes, please.
   Déjeme ver sus ojos, por favor.
   Déjeme mirar sus ojos.

2. I am going to examine your eyes (them).
   Voy a examinarle los ojos.
   Voy a examinárselos.

3. Look up.
   Mire Vd. hacia arriba.
   Mire Vd. para arriba.

4. Look down.
   Mire Vd. hacia abajo.
   Mire Vd. para abajo.

5. Look to the right.
   Mire Vd. para la derecha.

6. Look to the left.
   Mire Vd. para la izquierda.

7. Look at my finger.
   Mire Vd. mi dedo.

8. Look at this.
   Mire Vd. esto.

9. Look at the (red) light.
   Mire Vd. la luz (roja).

10. Keep looking at my nose.
    Siga mirándome en la nariz.

11. Keep looking here (there).
    Siga mirando aquí (allí).

12. Follow my finger with your eyes without moving your head.
    Siga Vd. mi dedo con los ojos sin mover la cabeza.

13. Open your eyes more (wider).
    Abra Vd. los ojos más.

14. Can you see this?
 ¿Puede Vd. ver esto?

15. Do you see this?
 ¿Ve Vd. esto?

16. How many fingers do you see?
 ¿Cuántos dedos ve Vd.?

17. Squeeze my fingers.
 Apriéteme los dedos.

18. Cover your eye like this.
 Tape Vd. el ojo así.

19. Don't blink.
 No parpadee Vd., por favor.

20. There is something in your eye.
 Hay algo en su ojo.

21. I am going to try to get it out.
 Voy a tratar de quitárselo.

22. I am going to put some drops (medicine) in your eye.
 Voy a ponerle gotas (medicina) en el ojo.

23. It will burn for a moment.
 Va a quemarle por un momento.

24. I am going to patch your eye.
 Voy a ponerle un parche sobre el ojo.

25. Leave it on for 24 hours.
 Déjeselo Vd. por veinticuatro horas.

26. I want to see your eye again tomorrow.
 Quiero examinarle el ojo de nuevo mañana.

Ears *Los oídos*

1. I am going to examine your ears.
 Voy a examinarle los oídos.

2. I am going to touch you with an instrument.
 Voy a tocarle con un instrumento.

3. Do you hear this tuning fork vibrating?
 ¿Oye Vd. vibrar este diapasón?

4. Tell me if it seems sharper to you on the left side than on the right.
 Dígame Vd. si le parece más agudo en el lado izquierdo que en el derecho.

5. Tell me when you can(not) hear this.
 Dígame Vd. por favor, cuando (no) pueda oír esto.

6. Is this the same in both ears?
   ¿Es esto igual en ambos oídos?

7. Is this louder in the right ear than in the left?
   ¿Oye Vd. mejor en el oído derecho que en el izquierdo?

8. Is there any difference?
   ¿Hay alguna diferencia?

9. Call me if there is any change.
   Avíseme Vd. si hay algún cambio.

10. You have an ear infection.
    Vd. tiene una infección del oído.

11. I am going to give you eardrops.
    Voy a darle gotas para el oído.

Mouth and Throat *La boca y la garganta*

1. I am going to examine your mouth (throat).
   Voy a examinarle la boca (garganta).

2. Can you open your mouth?
   ¿Puede Vd. abrir la boca?

3. Open your mouth, please.
   Abra Vd. la boca, por favor.

4. Say "ah."
   Diga "ah."

5. Close it, please.
   Ciérrela Vd., por favor.

6. Stick out your tongue.
   Saque Vd. la lengua, por favor.

7. I am going to take a throat culture.
   Voy a tomarle un cultivo de la garganta.

8. Today when you cough, please collect in this jar all the phlegm that comes up, so that we can examine it.
   Hoy, cuando tosa, guarde todo el esputo (flema) en este vaso, para que lo (la) examinemos.

9. Breathe deeply through your mouth.
   Respire hondo por la boca.

Neck *El cuello*

1. I am going to examine your neck.
   Voy a examinarle el cuello.

2. Does it hurt you when I bend your neck?
   ¿Le duele cuando le doblo a Vd. el cuello?

3. Please swallow.
   Trague Vd., por favor.

4. Again, please.
   Otra vez, por favor.

Breasts *Los pechos*

1. I am going to examine your breasts.
   Voy a examinarle los pechos.

2. I am going to show you how to do breast self-examination (BSE).
   Voy a enseñarle cómo hacer el autoexamen de los senos.

3. While standing, raise one arm in the air. Use several fingers of the other hand to explore the opposite breast for any unusual lump under the skin. Then repeat on the other side.
   De pie, levante Vd. un brazo. Use unos dedos de la mano del otro brazo para explorar cuidadosamente el seno opuesto para averiguar si siente algún abultamiento o dureza no común debajo de la piel. Entonces, repita el procedimiento con el lado opuesto.

4. In front of a mirror, check both breasts for a nipple discharge, a puckering, or a dimpling. Lean forward to check for any abnormalities in shape.
   Delante de un espejo, con los brazos en los lados, revísese para ver si encuentra un desecho de los pezones, un arrugamiento, u hoyuelo. Entonces, agáchese hacia adelante para ver si encuentra alguna anormalidad en la forma.

5. Lying down on your back, with a pillow under your back and one arm behind your head, inspect the opposite breast using circular movements. Work inward toward the nipple. Check the area surrounding the breast, beginning with the underarm. Repeat on the other side.
   Acostándose con una almohada debajo de la espalda y con un brazo debajo de la cabeza, inspeccione Vd. el seno opuesto, ejerciendo presión en forma circular. Tiente cada pecho, presionando hacia el pezón. Revise las áreas que rodean los pechos, empezando por las axilas. Repita Vd. con el lado opuesto.

Respiratory—Cardiovascular
Respiratorio—Cardiovascular

VITAL SIGNS *SIGNOS VITALES*

1. I am going to examine your lungs.
   Voy a examinarle los pulmones.

2. I am going to examine your heart.
   Voy a examinarle el corazón.

3. I am going to listen to your chest.
   Voy a escucharle el pecho.

4. Take a deep breath.
   Respire Vd. profundo.

5. Breathe slowly.
   Respire Vd. al paso. (colloq)
   Respire Vd. lento.

6. Breathe rapidly.
   Respire Vd. rápido.

7. Raise both arms over your head.
   Levante Vd. los dos brazos sobre la cabeza.

8. Lower your arms.
   Baje Vd. los brazos.

9. Breathe deeply in and out through your mouth.
   Respire Vd. fuertemente hacia dentro y hacia fuera, por la boca.

10. Cough, please.
    Tosa Vd. por favor.

11. Again.
    Otra vez.

12. Once more.
    Una vez más.

13. Please don't breathe for one minute.
    Favor de no respirar por un minuto.

14. Hold your breath.
    Mantenga Vd. la respiración.

15. Now you can breathe.
    Ya Vd. puede respirar.

16. Inhale.
    Inspire Vd.

17. Exhale.
    Espire Vd.

18. Breathe normally.
    Respire Vd. normalmente.

19. Everything is OK.
    Todo está bien.

20. Everything will be OK.
    Todo va a estar bien.

21. Calm down.
    Cálmese Vd.

22. Relax.
   Descanse Vd.
   No se apure Vd. (Chicano)

23. Don't worry.
   No se preocupe Vd.
   No se apure Vd. (Chicano)
   No se apene Vd. (Chicano)

24. I am going to take your blood pressure.
   Voy a tomarle la presión.
   Voy a tomar su presión de la sangre.

25. Roll up your sleeves.
   Arremánguese las mangas, por favor.

26. Relax (physically).
   Afloje Vd. el cuerpo, por favor.

27. Bend your elbow.
   Doble Vd. el codo, por favor.

28. Make a fist.
   Haga Vd. el puño, por favor.
   Cierre Vd. el puño, por favor.

39. Your blood pressure is normal.
   Su presión arterial es normal.

30. Your pressure is too low.
   Su presión está demasiado baja.

31. Your pressure is quite high.
   Su presión arterial está bastante alta.

32. Your pressure is too high.
   Su presión está demasiado alta.

33. Your pressure is higher than normal.
   Su presión está más alta que lo normal.

34. We have to try to determine why you have high blood pressure; although sometimes this is not possible.
   Debemos tratar de determinar por qué tiene Vd. la presión alta, aunque en muchos casos la causa no es conocida.

35. Here is a prescription to reduce your blood pressure.
   Aquí tiene Vd. una receta para reducir la presión arterial.

36. Take one pill every day after breakfast.
   Tome Vd. una píldora cada día después de desayunarse.

37. Let me feel your pulse.
   Déjeme tomarle el pulso.

38. Your pulse is too rapid.
    El pulso está demasiado rápido.

39. Please step on the scale.
    Súbase Vd. en la báscula, por favor.
    Párese Vd. en la báscula, por favor.

TEMPERATURE *LA TEMPERATURA*

1. I am going to take your temperature.
   Voy a tomarle la temperatura.

2. Let me take your temperature.
   Permítame tomarle la temperatura.

3. Moisten your lips, please.
   Por favor, humedezca Vd. los labios.
   Favor de humedecer los labios.

4. Please keep the thermometer in your mouth, under the tongue.
   Por favor, mantenga el termómetro en la boca, bajo la lengua.
   Favor de mantener el termómetro en la boca, bajo la lengua.

5. Open your mouth.
   Abra Vd. la boca, por favor.

6. Don't be afraid.
   No tenga Vd. miedo.

7. You have a high fever.
   Vd. tiene fiebre alta.

8. You have a slight fever.
   Vd. tiene un poco de fiebre.

9. How long have you had fever?
   ¿Desde cuándo tiene Vd. fiebre?

10. Did you have fever last night? Yesterday?
    ¿Tuvo Vd. fiebre (calentura) anoche? ¿ayer?

11. How much?[28]
    ¿Cuánta?

12. Did you take any medicine before coming to the hospital?
    ¿Tomó Vd. alguna medicina antes de venir al hospital?

13. What type?
    ¿Qué clase?

14. How much?
    ¿Cuánta?

Gastrointestinal *Gastrointestinal*

ABDOMINAL EXAM *RECONOCIMIENTO ABDOMINAL*

1. I am going to examine your abdomen (stomach).
   Voy a examinarle el estómago.

2. Sit up and don't cross your legs.
   Siéntese Vd. y no cruce las piernas.

3. Relax please.
   Cálmese Vd., por favor.

4. Lie down.
   Acuéstese, por favor.
   Lie on your right (left) side.
   Acuéstese, por favor, sobre su lado derecho (izquierdo).

5. Extend one leg and bend the other.
   Estire Vd. la pierna (derecha) (izquierda) y doble la otra.

6. Does it hurt when I press here?
   ¿Le duele cuando le aprieto aquí?

7. Does it hurt when I let go?
   ¿Le duele cuando le suelto?

8. Suck in your stomach.
   Succione Vd. el estómago.

9. Inflate it.
   Inflelo. Vd.

10. Relax.
    Descanse Vd.

RECTAL EXAM[29] *RECONOCIMIENTO RECTAL*

11. I am going to examine you rectally.
    Voy a examinarle el recto.

12. Please kneel.
    Póngase Vd. de rodillas, por favor.

13. Turn on your left side and draw your knees up to your chin.
    Póngase Vd. del lado izquierdo y doble Vd. las rodillas hasta la barbilla.

14. Pull your legs toward you.
    Encoja Vd. las piernas.

15. Stay on your back.
    Esté Vd. boca arriba.
    Esté Vd. postrado (-ada).

16. I am going to do a proctoscopic examination.
    Voy a hacerle un examen proctoscópico.

17. Bear down as if you were going to move your bowels.
    Puje Vd. como si fuera a obrar.

18. I am going to examine your rectum with an instrument that I am now putting in.
    Voy a examinar el recto con un instrumento que le voy a introducir.

19. It will probably be slightly irritating.
    Le molestará un poco solamente.

20. Push. (Bear down.)
    Puje Vd., por favor.

21. Don't move.
    No se mueva.

22. Breathe through your mouth.
    Respire con la boca abierta.

23. Don't be afraid.
    No tenga Vd. miedo.

24. I have finished.
    He terminado ya.

25. You have
    Vd. tiene

    ulcerations
    ulceraciones
    an inflammation
    inflamación
    fissures
    grietas (partiduras)
    polyps
    pólipos
    fistulas
    fístulas
    an abscess
    un absceso (apostema)
    a foreign body
    un cuerpo extraño
    a prolapsed rectum
    un prolapso del recto

26. You will also need a stool culture.
    También Vd. necesita un cultivo de heces.

Genitourinary *Génitourinario*

FEMALE GENITALIA *LOS ORGANOS GENITALES FEMININOS*

1. I have to examine you internally.
   Tengo que examinarle por dentro.

2. I am going to do a pelvic examination.
   Voy a hacerle ahora un examen de la pelvis.

3. Put your feet in these stirrups.
   Ponga Vd. los pies en estos estribos.

4. Spread your knees and legs apart.
   Abra Vd. las rodillas y las piernas.

5. Please lie on your back.
   Acuéstese de espaldas, por favor.

6. Scoot closer to the edge of the table.
   Acérquese al borde de la mesa.

7. Try to relax.
   Aflójese un poco.

8. Relax your muscles.
   Relaje los músculos.

9. Don't tighten up.
   No se atiese Vd.
   No se ponga tiesa.

10. I am going to insert a speculum into your vagina in order to do the Pap smear.
    Voy a introducirle un espéculo (espéculum) en la vagina para hacerle el examen de Pap.

11. I am going to take a sample of cells from the cervix and the area around it, with a cotton swab (with a spatula).
    Voy a extraer unas células del cuello del útero y de alrededor de ello con un hisopillo (con una espátula de madera).

12. It may be a little uncomfortable, but it won't last long.
    Sentirá un poco incómoda, pero no durará mucho tiempo.

13. Place your arms at your side and leave them there.
    Acomode los brazos al lado del cuerpo y déjelos allí.

14. The cells are normal (abnormal).
    Las células son normales (anormales).
    Las células son sanas (contienen cáncer).

15. I want to do another Pap test.
    Quiero hacerle otro (segundo) examen de Pap.

16. I am going to do a colposcopy (a visual examination with a special magnifying instrument—a colposcope).
Voy a hacerle una colposcopia (un examen visual del cuello uterino con un instumento especial de aumento -un colposcopio).

17. You need a uterine biopsy.
Vd. necesita una biopsia del útero.

18. I advise you to have a "cone biopsy"/conization.
Le aconsejo que hagan una biopsia de un cono del cuello uterino/una conización.

19. Return in 6 months (next year) for another Pap.
Vuelva Vd. en seis meses (el año que viene) para otro examen de Pap (otro Papanicolau).

20. Stay quiet.
Esté Vd. tranquila.

21. You should not have sexual intercourse.
No debería Vd. tener relaciones sexuales.

22. Do not use any douche.
No se dé Vd. duchas vaginales.

MALE GENITALIA *LOS ORGANOS GENITALES MASCULINOS*

23. I am going to examine your testicles.
Voy a examinarle los testículos.

24. I am going to examine you for hernias.
Voy a examinarle para ver si tiene hernias inguinales.

URINARY *URINARIO*

25. I am going to examine your kidneys.
Voy a examinarle los riñones.

26. Lean forward, please.
Inclínese hacia adelante, por favor.

27. I am going to do a cystoscopy.
Voy a hacerle una cistoscopia.

28. I am going to do an IVP (a retrograde IVP).
Voy a hacerle un pielograma intravenoso (un pielograma intravenoso retrógrado).

29. This will take about twenty minutes.
Esto durará unos veinte minutos.

30. It will be a little painful, but I won't hurt you more than I can help.
Va a dolerle un poco, pero lo haré lo más gentil y cuidadosamente posible.

31. I am going to put this tube into your bladder so that you can urinate.
Voy a ponerle este tubo en la vejiga de modo que podrá orinar.

Musculoskeletal and Extremities
Muscular-esquelético y las extremidades

1. Please stand up.
   Levántese Vd., por favor.

2. Please sit down.
   Siéntese Vd., por favor.

3. Walk a little
   Camine Vd. un poco.

4. Come back, please.
   Vuelva Vd., por favor.
   Regrese Vd.

5. Walk backwards.
   Camine Vd. hacia atrás.

6. Walk on your toes.
   Camine Vd. sobre los dedos.

7. Walk on your heels.
   Camine Vd. sobre los talones.

8. Bend over.
   Dóblese Vd. hacia adelante.

9. Bend backwards.
   Dóblese Vd. hacia atrás.

10. Bend your trunk forward as far as you can.
    Doble Vd. el tronco hacia adelante tanto como pueda.

11. Close your hand.
    Cierre Vd. la mano.

12. Open it.
    Ábrala Vd., por favor.

13. Close your fist.
    Cierre Vd. el puño.

14. Open it.
    Ábralo Vd., por favor.

15. Grip my hands tightly.
    Apriete Vd. mis manos con fuerza.

16. Can't you do it better than that?
    ¿No puede Vd. hacerlo más fuerte?

17. Push against my hand as hard as you can.
    Empuje mi mano tan fuerte como posible.

18. Don't let me move your _____ .
    No me deje mover su _____ !

19. Relax and let me move your _____ .
    Relájese y déjeme mover su _____ .

20. Raise your arms.
    Suba Vd. los brazos.
    Levante Vd. los brazos.

21. Higher.
    Más alto.

22. Raise your arms all the way up.
    Levante Vd. los brazos completamente.
    Suba Vd. los brazos completamente.

23. Lower.
    Más bajo.

24. Raise your left (right) leg.
    Levante Vd. la pierna izquierda (derecha).
    Suba Vd. la pierna izquierda (derecha).

25. Can you move that arm?
    ¿Puede Vd. mover ese brazo?

26. Can you lift that arm?
    ¿Puede Vd. levantar ese brazo?

27. Can you move that leg?
    ¿Puede Vd. mover esa pierna?

28. Can you lift that leg?
    ¿Puede Vd. levantar esa pierna?

29. When did you sprain _____ ?
    ¿Cuándo se torció _____ ?

Neurological Exam *Reconocimiento neurológico*

1. Cross the left leg over the right one.
   Cruce Vd. la pierna izquierda sobre la derecha.

2. Now cross the right leg over the left.
   Ahora cruce Vd. la pierna derecha sobre la izquierda.

3. Bend your right (left) knee.
   Doble Vd. la rodilla derecha (izquierda).

4. Bend your right (left) elbow.
   Doble Vd. el codo derecho (izquierdo).

5. Move a little over to the right.
   Muévase Vd. un poco hacia la derecha.

6. Does it hurt?
   ¿Le duele?

7. Where?
   ¿Dónde?

8. Turn your angle.
   Gire el tobillo.

9. To the right.
   A la derecha.

10. To the left.
    A la izquierda.

11. This way.
    Hacia acá.

12. Stretch your fingers.
    Estire Vd. los dedos.

13. Grasp this object between your fingers.
    Apriete Vd. este objeto entre los dedos.

14. Stretch your legs.
    Estire Vd. las piernas.

15. Flex your feet.
    Flexione Vd. los pies.

16. Close your eyes and keep them shut.
    Cierre Vd. los ojos por favor y manténgalos cerrados.

17. Tell me when you feel something.
    Dígame cuando sienta algo.

18. Where do you feel it?
    Dónde lo siente?

19. Does this feel hot (cold)?
    ¿Siente esto caliente (frío)?

20. Do you feel a prick?
    ¿Siente Vd. algo como un pinchazo?

21. Is it moving upward?
    ¿Se mueve hacia arriba?
    Is it moving downward?
    ¿Se mueve hacia abajo?

22. Close your eyes and don't let me open them.
    Cierre Vd. los ojos por favor y no me deje abrirlos.

23. What does this smell like?
   ¿A qué huele esto?

24. Shrug your shoulders.
   Encójase de hombros.

EXERCISE   *EJERCICIO*

Statements 1–5 in the above section are polite commands (see Verb section, pages 146–149). Several acceptable substitutes exist for the polite command. These involve using some form of *please* and the infinitive. In Spanish several forms of *please* may be used:

haga Vd. el favor de

favor de

tenga la bondad de

sírvase

Rewrite all polite commands in the musculoskeletal and neurological exam sections using the above ways to say *please*.

Bend your head to the right, please. **Doble Vd. la cabeza a la derecha, por favor.**

(Haga Vd. el favor de) _____

Haga Vd. el favor de doblar la cabeza a la derecha.

(Favor de) _____

Favor de doblar la cabeza a la derecha.

(Tenga la bondad de) _____

Tenga la bondad de doblar la cabeza a la derecha.

(Sírvase) _____

Sírvase doblar la cabeza a la derecha.

Continue in this fashion with all the commands listed.

SURGERY

CIRUGIA

Pre-op   *Antes de la operación*

1. You need an operation.[30]
   Vd. necesita una operación.

2. It is not a serious operation.
   No es una operación grave.

3. It is a very serious operation.
   Es una operación muy grave.

4. We have to operate on your _____ so that you will get well.
   Es necesario hacerle una operación a (la _____) (al _____) para que se mejore.

5. There can be no delay.
   Vd. no puede retrasarse.

6. We are going to sew up your wound.
   Vamos a coserle las heridas.

7. We are going to remove your appendix.
   Vamos a sacarle el apéndice.

8. We think that we may have to remove part of your stomach.
   Pensamos que es preciso sacarle una parte de su estómago.

9. We have to amputate your leg (arm, finger).
   Tenemos que amputarle la pierna (el brazo, el dedo).

10. We cannot do this unless you give us your written permission.
    No podemos operar sin su permiso escrito.
    Hay que firmar el permiso para operar.

11. This should be a rather simple operation.
    Esta operación debe ser bastante sencilla.

12. We expect that everything will be fine, but we cannot be absolutely sure.
    Esperamos que todo esté bien, pero no se puede estar completamente seguro.

13. Do you understand?
    ¿Me comprende Vd.?

14. Are you certain that you understand me? Do you have any questions?
    ¿Está seguro(-a) de que me comprende? ¿Tiene Vd. algunas preguntas para mí?

15. Please sign your name here.
    Firme Vd. su nombre aquí, por favor.

16. I am going to make arrangements with the hospital.
    Voy a hacer los arreglos en el hospital.

17. You will go to the hospital on _____.
    Vd. ingresará en el hospital el _____.

18. Take your hospitalization and insurance papers with you.
    Lleve Vd. sus papeles de hospitalización y seguros consigo.

19. We will notify your family of the approximate time that your operation is scheduled.
    Le avisaremos a su familia de la hora aproximada en que la operación está programada.

20. Your family may come to see you before the operation and accompany you to the surgical floor.
    Su familia puede venir a verle antes de la operación y acompañarle al piso quirúrgico.

21. Would you like me to call your family to tell them about your operation?
    ¿Quiere Vd. que yo avise a su familiar (acerca) de su operación?

22. We intend to operate tomorrow, but we may have to postpone it until the next day.
    Pensamos operar mañana, pero quizás es necesario cambiarla hasta el día siguiente.

23. The surgery will be at 6 a.m. and you will be in the recovery room by 9 A.M.
    La cirugía será a las seis de la mañana y Vd. estará en la sala de recuperación a eso de las nueve de la mañana.

24. We do not know exactly how long the surgery will take; it could be several hours.
    No sabemos exactamente cuánto tiempo durará la cirugía; podría ser un par de horas.

25. The anesthesiologist will be here soon to discuss what anesthesia he is going to give you.
    El anestesiólogo estará aquí dentro de poco para discutir qué anestesia va a ponerle.

26. Perhaps he will use a local anesthetic.
    Tal vez usará anestesia local.

27. Do you prefer sodium pentothal?
    ¿Prefiere Vd. el pentotal de sodio?

28. I am going to prepare you for the operation.
    Voy a prepararle (prepararla) para la operación.

29. I have to shave you.
    Tengo que rasurarle. (rasurarla).

30. We are going to give you a sedative before taking you to the operating room.
    Vamos a darle un calmante antes de llevarle (-la) a la sala de operaciones.

31. The nurse will give you an enema.
    La enfermera le pondrá una enema.

32. You will feel better after an enema.
    Vd. se sentirá mejor después de una enema.

33. The patient is in a lot of pain.
    El (la) paciente tiene mucho dolor.

34. This injection will stop your pain.
    Esta inyección le quitará el dolor.

35. You won't feel the pain.
    Vd. no sentirá el dolor.

36. Just relax.
    No se apure.

37. You can't have these injections too often.
    No se le pueden poner estas inyecciones con demasiado frecuencia.

38. When you awaken after the operation, you may have a tube in your throat to help you breathe.
    Al despertarse después de la cirugía, podrá tener un tubo en la garganta para ayudarle (-la) a respirar.

39. Don't worry if you cannot urinate after the operation; the nurse will empty your bladder.
    No se apure Vd. si no puede orinar después de la cirugía; la enfermera le vaciará la vejiga.

40. We will put a tube in your bladder so that you can urinate.
 Le pondremos un tubo en la vejiga para que pueda orinar.

41. I am going to start these fluids in your vein.
 Voy a ponerle estos fluidos (este suero) en la vena.

42. You will feel a little stick.
 Vd. va a sentir un piquete.

43. It may hurt a little, but we have to do it in order to help you.
 Le duela un poco (Sentirá la aguja un poco), pero tenemos que hacerlo para ayudarle(-la).

44. This IV is in your arm in order to feed you.
 Este suero está en el brazo para alimentarle(-la).

45. This IV in your arm is to give you sugar, water, and salt through your veins.
 Este suero en el brazo es para darle azúcar, agua y sal por las venas.

46. The IV must stay there for a while after the operation.
 El suero tiene que quedarse ahí por algún tiempo después de la operación.

47. Please do not remove it.
 No lo quite, por favor.

48. After the operation the IV must stay in your arm until you begin to eat and drink.
 Después de la cirugía, el suero tiene que quedarse en el brazo hasta que empiece a comer y beber.

49. If you do not eat (drink) we will have to put the IV back into your arm.
 Si Vd. no come (bebe), tendremos que ponerle el suero en el brazo de nuevo.

50. After the operation you may have a tube in your stomach so you will not vomit.
 Después de la operación, podrá tener un tubo en el estómago para que no vomite.

51. Do not eat or drink anything after midnight by mouth.
 No coma ni beba nada por boca después de medianoche.

52. The surgeon has just arrived.
 El cirujano acaba de llegar.

53. I will be at the operation.
 Asistiré a la operación.

54. I will come to see you after the operation.
 Vendré a verle(-la) después de la operación.

55. I am going to give you a drug through this mask.
 Voy a poner una droga por medio de esta máscara.

56. Breathe naturally through the mask.
 Respire Vd. naturalmente por la máscara.

57. Take a deep breath.
 Respire Vd. profundo.

58. You will fall asleep soon and be asleep during the surgery.
 Vd. se dormirá dentro de poco y estará dormido(-a) durante la cirugía.

59. I am going to give you a local anesthetic—a shot so that you will feel no pain during the operation.
    Voy a ponerle un anestético local—una inyección para que no sienta ningún dolor durante la operación.

60. I am going to give you a spinal anesthetic (an epidural, a caudal).
    Voy a ponerle anestesia espinal (anestesia epidural, anestesia caudal).

61. I am going to inject a drug into your back so that you will not feel pain during the operation, but you will not be asleep.
    Voy a inyectarle en la espalda, para que no sienta ningún dolor durante la operación, pero Vd. no estará dormido(-a).

62. Please turn on your side at the edge of your bed.
    Acuéstese Vd. sobre el lado, muy cerca del borde de la cama.

63. Bring your knees up to your chest and bend your head down, so that your chin rests on your chest.
    Doble Vd. las rodillas junto al pecho e incline la cabeza de modo que la barbilla esté junto al pecho.

64. That's right.
    Así. Bien.

65. Hold still.
    No se mueva, por favor.
    Esté inmóvil.

66. That is all.
    Es todo.

67. You may relax now.
    Vd. puede aflojarse ahora.

68. Stretch your legs.
    Extienda las piernas.

69. Is this painful?
    ¿Le duele esto?

70. Is this more painful than this? The same? More? Less?
    ¿Le duele esto más que esto? ¿Lo mismo? ¿Más? ¿Menos?

71. Tell me when you feel pain, not just pressure.
    Dígame cuando sienta dolor, no sólo presión.

Post-op *Después de la operación*

72. The operation turned out all right.
    La operación salió bien.

73. You are waking up.
    Vd. está despertándose.

74. You will feel better soon.
    Vd. se sentirá mejor dentro de poco.

75. You are in the Recovery Room.
    Vd. está en la sala de recuperación.

76. When you are fully awake, you will be taken to your room.
    Cuando Vd. esté completamente despierto(-a), le (la) llevarán a su cuarto.

77. You cannot have anything to eat (drink) yet.
    Vd. no puede comer (beber) nada todavía.

78. The patient is out of danger.
    El (la) paciente está fuera de peligro.

79. The patient is not expected to live.
    No se cree que el (la) paciente va a vivir.

80. The patient is going to live.
    El (la) paciente va a vivir.

81. The patient has been taken to the Recovery Room.
    El paciente ha sido llevado a la sala de recuperación.

82. The patient has been taken to Intensive Care (Cardiac Care).
    La paciente ha sido llevada a Cuidado Intensivo (a Cuidado Cardíaco).

83. He will leave Intensive Care tomorrow.
    Saldrá del Cuidado Intensivo mañana.

84. They are not going to operate on him (her) any more.
    No le van a operar más.

85. Your family is waiting outside.
    Su familia está esperando afuera.

86. The doctor has told them that the operation is over.
    El doctor le ha dicho que la cirugía se acabó.

87. You can see your family (husband, wife) when you are back in your room.
    Vd. puede ver a su familia (esposo, esposa) cuando haya vuelto a su cuarto.

88. They can only visit five minutes.
    Puede visitarle(-la) no más de cinco minutos.

89. I am going to remove this tube as soon as you don't need it any longer.
    Voy a quitarle este tubo (esta sonda) tan pronto como no lo (la) necesite más.

90. Your doctor is going to remove your stitches today.
    Su doctor va a quitarle los puntos hoy.
    Su médico va a quitarle las puntadas hoy.

91. Tomorrow the doctor will probably change your dressing.
    Mañana el doctor probablemente le cambiará el vendaje.

92. You are doing very well.
    Vd. va muy bien.

93. When the stitches are taken out, you may have a scar.
    Cuando le quitamos las puntadas, quizás tenga una cicatriz.

94. Don't remove your dressing.
    No se quite el vendaje.

95. Stick to the diet that we gave you.
    Siga Vd. la dieta que le dimos.

96. Don't drive a car for a month.
    No conduzca Vd. el coche por un mes.

97. Don't do any heavy work for two months (weeks).
    No haga ningún trabajo pesado por dos meses (semanas).

MEDICATION AND TREATMENT

MEDICACION Y TRATAMIENTO

1. Whose medicine is this?[31]
   ¿De quién es esta medicina?

2. Whose vaccine is that?
   ¿De quién es esa vacuna?

3. Give me the medicine, please.
   Favor de darme la medicina.

4. Take the medicine today.
   Tome Vd. la medicina hoy.

5. Don't take the medicine tomorrow.
   No tome Vd. la medicina mañana.

6. I am going for the medicine.
   Voy por la medicina.

7. Are you taking the medicine?
   ¿Toma Vd. la medicina?

8. You have to take your medicine, Ma'am.
   Vd. tiene que tomar su medicina, señora.

9. You must take your medicines, or you will not get better.
   Es preciso que Vd. tome sus medicinas, porque si no, no se recuperará.

10. If you don't take them, it will take a long time for you to get well.
    Si no las toma, no se recuperará por mucho tiempo.

11. Take your medicines regularly at the same hour, if possible.
    Debe tomar sus medicinas regularmente, a la misma hora, si es posible.

12. Take only what the nurse gives you.
    Tome Vd. solamente las (medicinas) que le da la enfermera.

13. Do not take any medicine from home.
    No tome Vd. ninguna medicina traída de su casa.

14. Do not take any medicine before coming to the hospital.
    No tome Vd. ninguna medicina antes de venir al hospital.

15. When was your last tetanus shot?
    ¿Cuándo fue su última inyección (vacuna) contra el tétano?

16. I am going to give you an injection.
    Voy a ponerle una inyección.

17. Here is your prescription.
    Aquí tiene Vd. su receta.

18. This is a prescription for your medicine.
    Esta es una receta para su medicina.

19. The doctor will give you a prescription.
    El doctor (La doctora) le dará una receta.

20. You can have it filled at any drugstore.
    Puede comprarla en cualquier farmacia.

21. You can renew it _____ times.
    Vd. puede usarla _____ veces.

22. Take the prescription to your druggist.
    Lleve Vd. esta receta a su farmacéutico.

23. Take this to the hospital pharmacy.
    Lleve Vd. ésta a la farmacia del hospital.

24. Who is taking your prescriptions to the pharmacy?
    ¿Quién lleva las recetas a la farmacia?

25. Come back if you don't feel better.
    Regrese Vd. si no se siente mejor.

26. Call me if you need more.
    Llámeme Vd. por favor, si necesita más.

27. Call the office if you have any questions.
    Llame Vd. al consultorio si tiene algunas preguntas.

28. Call me if you feel worse.
    Llámeme si Vd. se siente peor.

29. Stop the medicine immediately if you have any reactions.
    Deje de tomar la medicina si Vd. tiene cualquier molestia.

30. Do you have this medicine in the house?
    ¿Tiene esta medicina en casa?

31. Have you ever taken it before?
    ¿Jamás la ha tomado antes?

32. When? How much?
    ¿Cuándo? ¿Cuánto? (¿Qué cantidad?)

33. Did it help?
    ¿Le (La) alivió?

34. Did you have any reactions to it?
    ¿Sufrió Vd. algunas reacciones?
    ¿Tuvo algunas molestias?

35. Take this every time you feel pain.
    Tome Vd. esto cada vez que sienta dolor.

36. Take these pills only if you feel pain.
    Tome Vd. estas píldoras solamente si siente dolor.

37. Take this only when absolutely necessary because it is habit-forming.
    Tome esta medicina solamente cuando sea absolutamente necesario (cuando la necesite muchísimo) porque produce hábito.

38. This medicine is not habit-forming.
    Esta medicina no produce hábitos.

39. Take these pills three times daily for a week.
    Tome Vd. estas píldoras tres veces al (por) día por una semana.

40. Take this medicine four times a day.
    Tome esta medicina cuatro veces al día.

41. Take two pills twice a day.
    Tome Vd. dos píldoras dos veces al día.

42. Instead of taking two pills, you can take only one.
    En vez de tomar dos píldoras, puede tomar solamente una.

43. Three times a day.
    Tres veces al día.

44. Every four hours.
    Cada cuatro horas.

45. Take a tablespoonful of this.
    Tome una cucharada de esto.

46. Take a teaspoonful of this.
    Tome Vd. una cucharadita de esto.

47. Whenever it hurts you.
    Cuando le duela.

48. Take one capsule at breakfast.[32]
    Tome Vd. una cápsula con el desayuno.

49. Take one of these tablets before bedtime.
    Tome Vd. una de estas pastillas antes de acostarse.

50. Take this medicine before meals.
    Tome Vd. esta medicina antes de las comidas.
    before breakfast.
    antes de desayunarse.
    before lunch.
    antes de almorzar.
    before dinner.
    antes de cenar.

51. After meals.
    Después de las comidas.

52. Take them with a glass of water, juice, milk.
    Tómelas con un vaso de agua, jugo, leche.

53. I am going to put some (medicine) in your _____.
    Voy a ponerle medicina en _____.

54. I am going to give you the medicine.
    Voy a darle la medicina.

55. The medicine will burn for a moment; then it will feel better.
    La medicina va a quemarle (arderle)(-la) por un momento; después, va a sentirse mejor.

56. I will give you a cream.
    Voy a darle una crema.

57. Apply this to the affected area.
    Aplíquese esto en la parte afectada.

58. Apply the ointment without rubbing
    Apíquese la pomada sin frotarse.

59. Put this over the rash, burn, wound.
    Póngase esto en el sarpullido, en la quemadura, en la herida.

60. Put two drops in each ear; in each eye; in each nostril.
    Póngase dos gotas en cada oído; en cada ojo; en cada ventana de la nariz.

61. Let this lozenge dissolve in your mouth.
    Deje que esta tableta disuelva en la boca.

62. Let these melt on (under) your tongue.
    Deje Vd. que se le derritan en (debajo de) la lengua.

63. Chew them.
    Mastíquelas Vd.

64. Don't chew them.
    No las mastique Vd.

65. Swallow this without chewing.
    Trague Vd. esto sin masticar.

66. Dissolve one tablet in 8 oz. of distilled water.
    Disuelva Vd. una tableta en ocho onzas de agua destilada.

67. Mix 2 tablespoons of the powder with 2 cups of water.
    Mezcle Vd. dos cucharadas de polvo con dos tazas de agua.

68. Dissolve a teaspooon of Epsom salts in a large glass of water.
    Disuelva Vd. una cucharadita de sal inglesa en un vaso grande de agua.

69. Drink the medicine.
    Tome Vd. la medicina.

70. Drink it.
    Tómela Vd.
    Bébala Vd.

71. Gargle with this medicine for the pain.
    Haga Vd. gárgaras con esta medicina para el dolor.

72. Soak your _____ in the dissolved powder.
    Remoje Vd. _____ en el polvo disvelto.

73. Inhale through your nose.
    Inhale (aspire) Vd. por la nariz.

74. Use the spray in your nasal passages daily.
    Use Vd. el spray (atomizador) en las ventanas de la nariz.

75. I want you to apply heat to your back.
    Quiero que Vd. aplique calor a la espalda.

76. You must keep the area clean at all times.
    Vd. tiene que mantener el área limpia todo el tiempo.

77. Change the bandages every day.
    Cambie Vd. los vendajes cada día.

78. Apply a hot, wet compress every hour.
    Póngase Vd. una compresa caliente y húmeda cada hora.

79. Apply a wet bandage every two hours.
    Póngase una venda húmeda cada dos hora.

80. Apply a hot water bag over the _____.
    Aplique una bolsa de agua caliente sobre _____.

81. Put your _____ in warm water.
    Ponga _____ en agua caliente.

82. Bathe with warm (cold) water.
    Báñese con agua caliente (fría).

83. Rub yourself with alcohol.
    Frótese con alcohol.

84. You must wear an elastic bandage.
    Debe llevar una venda elástica.

85. Put on an elastic stocking during the day.
    Póngase Vd. una media elástica por el día.

86. Paint the swelling with this.
    Es preciso que Vd. pinte la hinchazón con esto.

87. Take hot sitz baths every _____ hours.
    Dése Vd. un caliente baño de asiento (semicupio) cada _____ horas.

88. Is there anyone in your house who knows how to give an injection?
    ¿Hay alguien en su casa que sepa poner inyecciones?

89. Use one of these suppositories every evening.
    Póngase uno de estos supositorios (una de estas calillas) cada noche.

90. Insert one of these suppositories using this applicator.
    Introdúzcase uno de estos supositorios (una de estas calillas) por medio de este aplicador.

91. Don't drive a car after taking this.
    No conduzca Vd. un coche después de tomar esto.

92. Don't drink alcohol with this.
    No tome Vd. alcohol con esto.

93. Keep in the refrigerator.
    Guarde en el refrigerador.

94. Do not keep in the freezer.
    No guarde en el congelador.

95. Keep in a cool, dry place.
    Consérvese en un lugar fresco y seco.

96. Keep out of children's reach.
    No se deje al alcance de los niños.

97. Shake well before using.
    Agite Vd. bien antes de usar.

98. Keep away from heat.
    Guarde Vd. la medicina fuera del calor.

99. Keep out of direct (strong) light.
    Guárdela Vd. donde no haya mucha luz (fuerte).

100. You will need a cast.
Vd. va a necesitar un calote (un yeso).

101. You are going to need a bandage.
Vd. va a necesitar un vendaje (venda).

102. I have to give you a sling.
Tengo que ponerle un cabestrillo (una honda para el brazo).

103. Keep your arm in it.
Deje el brazo en él (ella).

104. You have a sprained ankle which you should keep elevated as much as possible to reduce the swelling.
Vd. tiene una dislocadura (torcedura) del tobillo, el cual debe mantener lo más elevado posible para reducir la inflamación (la hinchazón).

105. Apply ice to the torn ligament (pulled muscle) at intervals of 30 minutes for the first 24 hours after the initial injury.
Aplique Vd. hielo al ligamento roto (músculo jalado/rasgado) en intervalos de treinta minutos por las primeras veinticuatro horas.

106. Stay in bed with your foot elevated.
Guarde Vd. cama con una almohada debajo de la pierna.

107. Leave the strapping on until you see the doctor.
Conserve Vd. el vendaje hasta que le vea al (a la) doctor(a).

108. Don't get the tape wet.
No deje mojarse la cinta (venda).

109. If the Ace bandage over the tape becomes loose, remove it and rewrap it starting at the base of the toes.
Si el vendaje de Ace se suelta, quítelo y póngaselo de nuevo comenzando con la base de los dedos.

110. Loosen the Ace bandage if numbness, tingling, swelling, or discoloration occurs.
Suelte el vendaje de Ace si hay adormecimiento, hormigueos, hinchazón, o ennegrecimiento en la piel.

111. Your finger needs to be put in a splint.
Hay que entablillar el dedo.

112. Elevate the affected hand in order to avoid/reduce the swelling.
Levante Vd. la mano afectada para evitar/reducir la hinchazón.

113. Leave the splint on until the doctor sees it.
Conserve Vd. el entablillado hasta que lo vea el doctor (la doctora).

114. Call me if the pain, swelling, and numbness increase.
Avíseme en seguida si le duele más, o se le recrece, o se le entumece.

115. Notify me immediately if there is a change in the skin color of the fingers.
Avíseme Vd. en seguida si hay un cambio en el color de la piel de los dedos.

116. The doctor will put the broken arm in a cast.
    El doctor le pondrá el brazo roto dentro de un yeso.

117. Notify the doctor immediately if there is pain, numbness, or blue color of the fingers.
    Avise Vd. al doctor (a la doctora) en seguida si hay dolor, adormecimiento o si los dedos se ponen morados.

118. The cast will remain on for six weeks.
    Vd. tiene que dejarse puesto el yeso por seis semanas.

119. If the cast hurts you, come back at once.
    Si le duele el yeso, vuelva Vd. inmediatamente.

120. Don't get the cast wet.
    No permite que se moje el yeso.

121. Keep the injured arm elevated and exercise the fingers to reduce the swelling.
    Mantenga el brazo lastimado levantado y haga ejercicios con los dedos para reducir la hinchazón (la inflamación).

122. Don't stay on your feet much with a broken leg.
    No esté Vd. de pie con la pierna rota.

123. Walking casts need to be completely dry before they can bear weight. This takes 48 hours.
    Las enyesaduras para caminar necesitan secarse por completo antes de poder aguantar el peso. Esto toma cuarenta y ocho horas.

124. You will have to use crutches for a while.
    Vd. tendrá que usar muletas por algún tiempo.

125. The nurse will show you how to use them even after the cast is removed.
    La enfermera le enseñará cómo usarlas aún después de quitarle el yeso.

126. You will have to come to physical therapy for diathermy twice a week.
    Vd. tendrá que volver a la (clínica de) fisioterapia para la diatermia dos veces por (a la) semana.

127. You have to massage this leg daily and do an exercise like this.
    Vd. tiene que darle masajes a esta pierna todos los días y también hacer un ejercicio así.

128. Observe your wound to see if bleeding or drainage develops that was not there before.
    Fíjese en su herida y llame al doctor (a la doctora) si aparece hemorragia o secreción (drenaje) que no existía antes.

129. I am putting you on a respirator.
    Voy a unirle(-la) al respirador.

130. The respirator is to help you breathe.
    El respirador es para ayudarle(-la) a respirar.

131. Relax.
    Relájese Vd., por favor.

132. Breathe slowly, with the machine.
    Respire Vd. despacio, con la ayuda del aparato.

133. Don't breathe so fast.
No respire Vd. tan rápido.

134. The tube that is in your throat is to help you breathe.
El tubo que está en la garganta es para ayudarle(-la) a respirar.

135. It must stay in for a while.
Tiene que quedarse allí (por) un rato.

EXERCISE *EJERCICIO*

Substitution Drill. Using the cue given in parenthesis, give the correct instructions for taking medication:

Tome Vd. la medicina.
(hoy)
Tome Vd. la medicina hoy.
(mañana)
Tome Vd. la medicina mañana.
(No)
No tome Vd. la medicina mañana.
(ninguna medicina)
No tome Vd. ninguna medicina mañana.
(alcohol)
No tome Vd. alcohol mañana.

Tome Vd. esta medicina cuatro veces al día.
(dos píldoras)
Tome Vd. dos píldoras cuatro veces al día.
(tres veces)
Tome Vd. dos píldoras tres veces al día.
(cada cuatro horas)
Tome Vd. dos píldoras cada cuatro horas.
(cápsulas)
Tome Vd. dos cápsulas cada cuatro horas.
(estas pastillas)
Tome Vd. estas pastillas cada cuatro horas.
(antes de las comidas)
Tome Vd. estas pastillas antes de las comidas.
(esta medicina)
Tome Vd. esta medicina antes de las comidas.
(después de las comidas)
Tome Vd. esta medicina después de las comidas.
(cuando le duela)
Tome Vd. esta medicina cuando le duela.
(con un vaso de agua)

Tome Vd. esta medicina con un vaso de agua.
(un vaso de jugo)

Tome Vd. esta medicina con un vaso de jugo.
(un vaso de leche)

Tome Vd. esta medicina con un vaso de leche.

ACCIDENTAL POISONINGS

ENVENENAMIENTOS ACCIDENTALES

1. Did you eat or drink something that disagreed with you?
   ¿Comió o bebió algo que le ha sabido mal?

2. What did you (he, she) eat?
   ¿Qué comió?

3. Something from a can?
   ¿Productos enlatados?
   ¿Comidas de lata?

4. What did you (he, she) drink?
   ¿Qué bebió?

5. What did you (he, she) swallow?
   ¿Qué tomó?
   ¿Qué tragó?

6. Do you know?
   ¿Sabe?

7. Was it lead from paint?
   ¿Fue plomo de pintura?

8. Was it lead from batteries?
   ¿Fue plomo de baterías?

9. Was it hair dye?
   ¿Fue tinte para el pelo?

10. When did you (he, she) swallow it?
    ¿Cuándo lo (la) tragó?

11. How much was swallowed?
    ¿Cuánto tragó?

12. The whole bottle?
    ¿La botella entera?

13. Do you still have the bottle that the liquid (pills) came in?
   ¿Todavía tiene la botella en la que el líquido vino (en la que las píldoras vinieron)?

14. Bring me the bottle that it came in.
   Tráigame la botella en la que vino (vinieron).

15. This is very important.
   Esto es importantísimo.

16. Have you (he, she) breathed anything poisonous?
   ¿Ha respirado algo venenoso?

17. Do you see any burns around the lips or mouth?
   ¿Ve Vd. algunas quemaduras alrededor de los labios o la boca?

18. Are your (the victim's) pupils contracted or dilated as the result of poison or an overdose?
   ¿Se contraen las pupilas de los ojos (de la víctima) como consecuencia del veneno o de dosis excesiva de morfina u otra droga?

19. Is there a chemical odor on the breath?
   ¿Hay un mal olor químico en el aliento?

20. Dilute the poison with a glass of water or milk if the victim is conscious and not having convulsions.
   Diluya Vd. el veneno haciendo la víctima injerir un vaso de agua o leche si está consciente y no tiene convulsiones.

21. Induce vomiting with your finger.
   Provóquese Vd. el vómito con el dedo.

22. with this syrup of ipecac.
   con este jarabe de ipecacuana.

23. Induce vomiting in the victim by causing him (her) to retch or by giving him (her) a liquid to drink which causes nausea such as mustard water, soapy water, or milk of magnesia and water.
   Hágale vomitar[33] a la víctima haciendo cosquillas con su dedo en la garganta de la víctima (arcadas) o dándole a beber un líquido que provoque náuseas, como agua con mostaza, agua jabonosa, o agua y leche de magnesia.

24. Have you (has he/she) vomited?
   ¿Ha vomitado?

25. What did you (he/she) vomit?
   ¿Qué vomitó?

26. Save the vomited material for analysis.
   Conserve Vd. una muestra del vómito y tráigala para examen.

27. If you have taken an overdose of drugs that contain opium or alcohol, drink strong coffee or tea.
   Si Vd. ha tomado una dosis excesiva de drogas con contenido de opio o alcohol, beba café o té fuerte.

28. Do not give him (her) any fluids or induce vomiting if the victim is unconscious or having convulsions.

No le administre (dé) líquidos por vía oral ni provoque vómitos (le haga vomitar) si la víctima está inconsciente o tiene convulsiones.

29. Do not induce vomiting if you (the victim) have (has) swallowed a strong acid, alkali, or petroleum product.

No (se) provoque vómitos si (Vd.) (la víctima) ha injerido un ácido fuerte, un álcali fuerte, o productos derivados del petróleo.

30. Turn the victim on his (her) side or on his (her) stomach, if he (she) is vomiting and is unconscious (and has just had a convulsion).

Coloque Vd. a la víctima hacia un lado o sobre el estómago, si vomita y si está inconsciente (y si acaba de tener convulsión).

31. Turn his (her) head so that the vomit drains from his (her) mouth and does not reenter the airway or throat.

Mueva Vd. la cabeza más baja que las caderas de modo que el veneno vomitado no pueda reentrar las vías respiratorias o los pasajes alimenticios.

32. Call the poison-control center nearest you that is listed in the telephone book.

Llame Vd. al centro de control de envenenamiento (intoxicantes) más cercano cuyo número encontrará en la guía de teléfonos

33. Stay calm.

Quédese tranquilo(-a).

34. Keep the victim quiet and covered.

Mantenga Vd. a la víctima quieta y abrigada.

35. Immobilize the extremity bitten by the snake in such a way that it is at or below heart level.

Inmovilice Vd. la extremidad que la víbora (culebra) mordió de tal manera que está al nivel de o debajo del nivel del corazón de la víctima.

36. Apply a constrictive bandage 2 to 4 inches (5 to 10 cm) above the bite if to an extremity. (The bandage should allow a finger to be slipped underneath if it is in place properly.)

Aplique Vd. una venda constrictiva de dos a cuatro pulgadas (cinco a diez centímetros) más alta que la mordedura si es a una extremidad. (Al estar en su lugar, la venda debe permitir que un dedo pueda deslizarse debajo.)

37. Make a straight incision (not cross-cut) along the length of the limb, cutting only the skin.

Haga Vd. una incisión seguida (no cruzada) en el eje mayor del miembro, cortando solamente la piel.

38. Suck the poison from the affected area, either with a suction cup or with your mouth.

Chupe el veneno de la herida o haciendo succión con la copa para succión o usando la boca para chuparlo y escupirlo.

39. Do this for 30 to 60 minutes.

Siga la succión de treinta a sesenta minutos.

40. Wash the bitten area with soap and water, drying it well.
    Lave Vd. la herida con jabón y agua, secándola bien.

41. Do not give any medicines that contain aspirin.
    No dé ningunas medicinas que contengan aspirina.

42. Come immediately to the nearest (this) hospital.
    Venga Vd. inmediatamente al hospital más cercano (a este hospital).

43. Bring him (her) immediately to the hospital.
    Tráigale (-la) en seguida al hospital.

44. Call the Fire Department.
    Llame Vd. al Departamento de Bomberos.

45. Get medical assistance as soon as possible.
    Procure Vd. asistencia médica tan pronto como sea posible.

46. Take the victim to a place in the fresh air.
    Pasee Vd. a la víctima a un lugar de aire fresco.

47. Try to get an ambulance immediately.
    Procure Vd. obtener una ambulancia inmediatamente.

48. I have to put this tube through your nose, into your stomach.
    Tengo que ponerle este tubo por la nariz dentro del estómago.

49. It will go through your nose to your stomach so that I can clean out your stomach.
    Pasará por la nariz al estómago para que yo pueda lavarle el estómago.

50. I need your help for this.
    Necesito su ayuda a insertar este tubo.

51. Calm down.
    Tranquilícese Vd.

52. Swallow.
    Trague Vd. por favor.

53. Take a sip of water.
    Tome Vd. un traguito de agua.

54. Now, swallow again.
    Ahora, trague Vd. otra vez.

55. Relax!
    Cálmese Vd.

56. Very good. That was fine.
    Muy bien. Excelente.

57. You have to (The child has to) stay in the hospital overnight.
    Vd. (El niño/La niña) tiene que quedarse en el hospital esta noche.

58. When you get home, if you have any more questions, don't hesitate to call.
    Después de haber salido del hospital (consultorio), si se le ocurren a Vd. más preguntas, no titubee en llamarme y preguntarme.

59. Medicines cause more poisonings among children under five than any other product.

Las medicinas causan más envenenamientos entre los niños menores de cinco años, que cualquier otro producto químico.

60. Keep all medicines and other poisonous things away from children.

Guarde Vd. (Almacene Vd.) todas las medicinas y cosas peligrosas (tóxicas) fuera del alcance de los niños.

61. Keep all medicines and other dangerous products in a cabinet that locks with a key.

Guarde Vd. (Almacene Vd) todas las medicinas y otros productos peligrosos en un gabinete cerrado con llave.

62. Never leave any medicine out when you go to answer the phone or the door.

Nunca deje ninguna medicina al alcance de la mano cuando vaya a contestar al teléfono o abrir la puerta.

63. Always give a child the correct prescribed dosage.

Siempre déle al niño (a la niña) la cantidad recetada.

64. Read the labels carefully on over-the-counter (OTC) medicines and ask either your pharmacist or your doctor if they are safe for children, should you have any doubts.

Lea las etiquetas cuidadosamente de las medicinas que se venden sin receta (remedios caseros; medicinas patentadas; medicinas auto-prescritas) y consulte a su farmacéutico(-a) o médico(-a) para saber si deben darse o no a los niños si Vd. tiene alguna duda.

65. Ask for a child-proof bottle if your pharmacist doesn't use one automatically because the law requires that most medicines and other potentially dangerous products should be packaged in child-proof bottles.

Pídale Vd. a su farmacéutico(-a) un envase de seguridad si el (ella) no lo usa de costumbre porque la ley requiere que la mayoría de las medicinas, tanto las recetadas como las que se compran sin receta, así como muchos otros productos químicos que puedan ser peligrosos en potencia, estén envasados en forma tal que sólo un adulto pueda abrirlos.

66. When giving a child medicine, never tell him (her) that it is "candy" or that it is something that he (she) may like. When the child is alone, he (she) may try to take more by himself (herself).

Cuando tenga que darle medicina a un niño (una niña), nunca le diga que es un "dulce" o algo que le guste. Cuando esté solo(-a), podría tratar de tomar más por sí mismo(-a).

DRUG OVERDOSE

LA DOSIS EXCESIVA DE DROGAS

1. It is important for you to recognize the signs and symptoms of drug abuse in emergencies.

Es importante que las señales y los síntomas del abuso de drogas sean identificados por Vd. en casos de emergencia.

2. Did he (you, she) take some pills? capsules?
   ¿Tomó pastillas (píldoras)? cápsulas?
   ¿Pildoreó?

3. What kind of pills did you (he, she) take?[34]
   ¿Qué tipo de píldoras tomó?
   ¿Qué tipo de pastillas injerió?

4. How many did you (he, she) take?
   ¿Cuántas tomó?

5. What color were they?[35]
   ¿De qué color (colores) eran?

6. What shape were they?
   ¿De qué forma eran?
   round?
   ¿redondas?
   oval?
   ¿ovales?
   cylindrical?
   ¿cilíndricas?
   triangular?
   ¿triangulares?
   rectangular?
   ¿rectangulares?
   square?
   ¿cuadradas?
   pentagonal?
   ¿pentagonales?
   hexagonal?
   ¿hexagonales?

7. Were they large or small?
   ¿Eran grandes o chiquitas (pequeñas)?

8. Were they flat?
   ¿Eran llanas?

9. Do you know the name of what you took?
   ¿Sabe Vd. el nombre de lo que ha tomado?

10. What time did you (he, she) take them?
    ¿A qué hora las injirió?

11. Did you (he, she) inject something?
    ¿Se inyectó con algo?
    ¿Se picó? (colloq.)
    ¿Se dio un piquete? (slang)

12. Did you find anything that would indicate what was taken—like a teaspoon, wrapping paper, a medicine dropper, a hypodermic needle, ampules, empty gelatinous capsules, needle marks on the skin?

¿Encontró Vd. algo que le indicaría los tipos de drogas injeridas—como una cucharadita, papel de envolver, una cuentagotas, un jaipo, ampollas, cápsulas gelatinosas vacías, o marcas de una aguja hipodérmica en la piel?

13. Call the nearest Drug Abuse Center whose number is listed in the phone book.

Llame al Centro de Abusos de Drogas más cercano cuyo número de teléfono encontrará en la guía telefónica.

14. Save the bottle (hypo) and bring it for examination when you come.

Guarde el envase (la botella) (el jaipo) y tráigalo(-la) para examen cuando venga.

15. You (he, she has) have taken too much, and we are going to try to empty your stomach to prevent your body from absorbing the drugs.

Ha tomado demasiado y vamos a hacer un esfuerzo para vaciarle el estómago a fin de prevenir la absorbción de las drogas por su cuerpo.

16. Do you (does he, she) have any of the following characteristic symptoms?

¿Tiene algunos de los siguientes síntomas característicos?

convulsions?

¿convulsiones?

nausea and vomiting?

¿náusea y vómitos?

increase in blood pressure?

¿aumento de la presión sanguínea?

dilated pupils?

¿dilatación (agrandamiento) de las pupilas?

contracted pupils?

¿pupilas reducidas?

increased/elevated body temperature

¿aumento de la temperatura del cuerpo?

increased palpitations?

¿aumento de las palpitaciones del corazón?

reddishness in the face?

¿rubicundez de la cara? ¿la cara rojiza?

increased nervousness?

¿aumento de la actividad/nerviosidad?

total loss of emotional control?

¿pérdida completa de control emocional?

deep depression?

¿depresión profunda

tension and anxiety?

¿tensión y ansiedad?

paranoid illusions?

¿ilusiones paranoicas?

hallucinations?
¿alucinaciones?
repiratory difficulty?
¿dificultad respiratoria?
irritation of respiratory passages?
¿irritación de las vías respiratorias?
loss of balance?
¿pérdida de equilibrio?
lethargy and reduction of activity?
¿letargo y aumento de la reducción de la actividad y conocimiento?
sleepiness, even prolonged unconsciousness?
¿sueño, aun inconsciencia prolongada?
muscle pains as well as sharp pains in the legs, back, stomach?
¿dolores musculares y dolores punzantes en las piernas, espalda y abdomen?
loss of appetite, loss of weight?
¿pérdida de apetito y pérdida de peso?
confusion?
¿confusión?
disorganization?
¿desorganización?
fear?
¿temor?
aggressiveness and harmful types of antisocial behavior?
¿agresividad y conducto antisocial que puede hacer peligro a otros?
irritability?
¿irritabilidad?
insomnia?
¿insomnia? (no duerme)
catatonia?
¿catatonía?
drainage (of the nose)?
¿goteo (de la nariz)?
dry mouth?
¿boca seca?
dryness (of the mucous membranes or mucosa)?
¿resequedad (de las mucosas)?
fitful sleep?
¿sueño sobresaltado?
giggling?
¿risa tonta? (¿risa falsa?)
goose pimples?
¿carne de gallina? (¿piel erizada?) (¿se pone chinito?)
in a stupor?
¿atolondrado(-a)?
nodding?
¿cabeceo?
self-control?
¿autodominio?

loss of self-control?
¿pérdida del autodominio?
thirst?
¿sed?
an abnormal walk?
¿una marcha anormal?
yawning?
¿bostezo?

17. Are his (her, your) eyes bloodshot and/or glassy?[36]
    ¿Tiene los ojos ensangrentados (inyectados de sangre) y/o vidriosos?

18. Are the pupils constricted?[37]
    ¿Están las pupilas encojidas?
    Pinpointed?
    ¿Están como un punto? ¿Del tamaño de un punto?

19. Are the eyes clear?
    ¿Están los ojos claros? (limpios?)
    watery?
    acuosos? (llorosos?)

20. Does he (she) lurch when walking?
    ¿Anda con un paso vacilante?
    ¿Se balancea hacia un lado u otro o hacia adelante?

21. Does he (she) stumble?
    ¿Tropieza?

22. Does he (she) sway?
    ¿Se bambolea?
    ¿Se tambalea?

23. Does he (she) weave?
    ¿Serpentea?
    ¿Zigzaguea?

24. Does he (she) veer?
    ¿Cambia de dirección de modo repentino?
    ¿Se desvía?

25. Is his (her) speech slurred?
    ¿Habla arrastrando las palabras?
    ¿Habla con pronunciación indistinta?

26. Is his (her) speech incoherent?
    ¿Está incoherente su modo de hablar?

27. Is his (her) speech hesitant?
    ¿Está titubeante su modo de hablar (su lenguaje)?

BLOOD TESTS, LABORATORY TESTS, AND INJECTIONS

ANALISIS DE SANGRE, PRUEBAS LABORATORIAS E INYECCIONES

1. Good morning (good afternoon), I am the technician.
   Buenos días (buenas tardes), yo soy el técnico (la técnica).

2. You need some blood tests.[38]
   Vd. necesita unos análisis de sangre.

3. I am going to take a sample of your blood.[38]
   Voy a tomar una muestra de su sangre.

4. Do you have the doctor's written orders?
   ¿Tiene Vd. las instrucciones escritas del doctor?

5. What type of test are you here for?
   ¿Para qué clase de análisis vino Vd. aquí?
   Blood count?
   ¿Biometría hemática?
   Blood chemistry (analysis of the blood)?
   ¿Análisis de sangre?
   Prothrombin time?
   ¿Análisis de la coagulación de la sangre? (del tiempo de protrombina)?
   White cell count?
   ¿Un recuento de los glóbulos blancos (leucocitos)?
   Triglycerides?
   ¿Un examen de triglicéridos?
   ¿Una prueba de triglicéridos?
   Hematocrit?
   ¿Un análisis del hematócrito?
   Differential blood count?
   ¿La fórmula que indica la proporción de cada tipo de leucocitos?
   Glucose tolerance test?
   ¿Un examen de tolerancia para la glucosa?
   Lipids?
   ¿Un análisis de la distribución de lípidos en la sangre?

6. Don't be nervous.
   No se ponga nervioso (nerviosa).

7. Roll up your sleeve.
   Suba la manga.

8. Make a fist, please.
   Cierre Vd. el puño, por favor.

9. Keep your hand closed.
   Mantenga Vd. la mano cerrada.

10. It will not hurt.
    No le dolerá.

11. I am sorry, but I have to stick you again.
    Lo siento, pero tengo que picarle otra vez.

12. I wasn't able to get enough blood the first time.
    No pude obtener bastante sangre la primera vez.

13. Don't move, please.
    No se mueva, por favor.

14. Open your hand.
    Abra Vd. la mano, por favor.

15. Fold your arm.
    Doble Vd. el brazo, por favor.

16. Keep this Band-Aid on for a few minutes.
    Déjese Vd. esta curita por unos minutos.

17. Do you feel dizzy?
    ¿Se siente mareado (mareada)?

18. Please, lean forward, and put your head down between your legs for a few minutes.
    Favor de inclinarse hacia adelante y poner la cabeza entre las piernas por unos minutos.
    Por favor, inclínese Vd. hacia adelante y coloque Vd. la cabeza entre las piernas por unos minutos.

19. We have to do some tests.
    Tenemos que hacerle algunos análisis.

20. You need
    Vd. necesita
    a cardiac function test.
    una prueba de función cardíaca.
    a cardiac catheterism.
    un cateterismo cardiovascular.
    angiography.
    una radiografía de los vasos sanguíneous (una angiografía).
    a mammogram.
    una radiografía de la mama (una mamografía; un mamograma).
    a CAP test.
    una prueba de CAP para identificar los cambios biotérmicos de las mamas (un colorgrama).
    bronchoscopy.
    un examen bronquial directo con un aparato óptico (una broncoscopia).
    a pulmonary function test.
    una prueba funcionaria de los pulmones.
    a serology test.
    prueba serológica.

a sputum test.
análisis de esputos.
sigmoidoscopy.
una inspección del colon con un espéculo rectal (una sigmoidoscopia).
gastroscopy.
una gastroscopia (una endoscopia gástrica).
an upper GI series.
pruebas del sistema gastrointestinal superior.
a brain scan.
un gammagrama del cerebro.
a liver scan.
un gammagrama del hígado
a liver function test.
una prueba funcionaria hepática (una prueba de la función hepática).
a proctoscopic examination.
un examen proctoscópico (una inspección del recto)
a biopsy
una biopsia.
a culture of your vaginal secretions.
un cultivo de las secreciones vaginales.
a Pap smear.
los untos de Papanicolaou.
los frotis de Papanicolaou.
el test de Papanicolaou.
a pancreatic function test.
una prueba funcional pancreática
una prueba de tolerancia para la glucosa.
a thyroid function analysis.
una prueba funcional tiroidea.
un análisis de la función del tiroides.

21. I want to explain them to you.
    Quiero explicárselos.

22. You have to go to the clinic (laboratory) for the tests.
    Vd. tiene que ir a la clínica (al laboratorio) para los análisis.

23. Tomorrow they will give you a special test.
    Mañana le harán un análisis especial.

24. You cannot eat or drink anything after midnight.
    Vd. no puede comer ni tomar nada después de medianoche.

25. Don't eat or drink anything before the test.
    No coma ni beba nada antes del análisis.

26. It is important to come to the laboratory without eating.
    Es importante venir al laboratorio sin comer.

27. Don't eat anything.
    Venga en ayunas.

28. Have you eaten or drunk since midnight?
¿Ha comido o bebido desde la medianoche?

29. We will bring you breakfast after the test.
Le traeremos el desayuno después del análisis.

30. You need an electrocardiogram, and I am going to take it.
Vd. necesita un electrocardiograma y voy a hacérselo.

31. This machine will record your heartbeats.
Este aparato (esta máquina) registrará las palpitaciones (los latidos) del corazón.

32. The test will only take 30 minutes.
La prueba durará solamente treinta minutos.

33. Please lie still.
Quédese inmóvil, por favor.

34. I am going to put some cream (jelly) on different parts of your body.
Voy a ponerle alguna crema (jalea) en diferentes partes del cuerpo.

35. This helps these leads (wires) to transmit the electricity that comes from the heart.
Esta ayuda estos conductores (cordones) a conducir la electricidad que viene del corazón.

36. These wires will not hurt you.
Estos cordones no le (la) dañarán.

37. I am going to put them loosely on your skin.
Voy a ponérselos sin cohesión sobre la piel.

38. I am going to give you a shot.[39]
Voy a ponerle una inyección (un chot).

39. Stretch out your arm.
Extienda Vd. el brazo, por favor.

40. Roll over on your side.
Voltéese Vd. del lado, por favor.

41. The needle will prick a little, but it is for your pain.
Vd. sentirá un poco esta aguja pero es para aliviar su dolor.

42. I am going to give you an intravenous feeding.
Le voy a aplicar suero.

43. The IV will go into your veins through this needle.
El alimento intravenoso pasará sus venas a través de esta aguja.

44. It is not painful once it is in place.
No duele cuando está en su sitio (una vez que está en su sitio).

45. The IV in your arm is to give you food—sugar, salt, and water.
El suero en el brazo es para darle de comer—azúcar, sal, y agua.

46. We have to do a cystoscopy.
Tenemos que hacerle una cistoscopia (un examen visual de la vejiga urinaria).

47. You need a renal function test.
    Vd. necesita una prueba funcional renal (un análisis de la función de los riñones).

48. The doctor wants you to have a urine culture.
    El doctor (La doctora) quiere que Vd. tenga un cultivo de orina.

49. I am going to do a urinalysis.
    Voy a hacerle un urinálisis (un análisis de la orina).

50. I need a urine specimen from you.
    Necesito una muestra de orina de Vd.

51. You must drink lots of liquids.
    Vd. debe tomar muchos líquidos.

52. When you urinate, fill up this bottle and give it to the nurse on duty.
    Cuando Vd. orine, llene este frasco y déselo a la enfermera de guardia.

53. Collect and bring your urine of the previous 24 hours.
    Recoja y traiga la orina de todo el día.

54. Call when you have to go to the toilet.
    Llame Vd. cuando tenga que ir al inodoro (a los servicios).

55. Go to the bathroom.
    Vaya Vd. al inodoro (a los servicios, al cuarto de baño).

56. Did you urinate?
    ¿Orinó Vd.?

57. You need a barium enema.
    Vd. necesita una enema de bario.

58. You need a stool culture.
    Vd. necesita un cultivo de heces (un cultivo del excremento).

59. Give yourself an enema before coming.
    Póngase una enema antes de venir.

60. Take a laxative the night before.
    Tome Vd. un laxante la noche anterior.

61. Bring me a (recent) specimen of your stools in this container.
    Tráigame una muestra (reciente) de su excremento (sus evacuaciones) en este frasco.

62. I will give you an enema.
    Le pondré una enema.

63. Turn on your left (right) side.
    Acuéstese Vd. sobre el lado izquierdo (derecho).

64. Turn over.
    Voltéese Vd. del otro lado, por favor.

65. You need an x-ray.
    Vd. necesita (tomarse) unas radiografías.

66. Someone will come to take you to x-ray.
 Alguien le (la) llevará al cuarto de rayos X.

67. The x-rays will be taken tomorrow.
 La radiografía se hará mañana.

68. Lie down on the x-ray table.
 Acuéstese Vd. sobre la mesa radiográfica.

69. It may be a little cold.
 Pudiese estar un poco fría.

70. Let me put you in the right position.
 Déjeme ponerle (colocarle) en la postura correcta.

71. In order to take the x-ray you must swallow this mixture.
 Para sacarle la radiografía, Vd. tiene que tomar (tragar) esta mezcla.

72. You need a barium swallow.
 Vd. necesita un trago de bario.

73. Hold the cup up and every time that I say "Drink," take a sip'
 Mantenga el vaso en alto, y cada vez que le diga «Beba,» tome Vd. un trago.

74. It may not taste good.
 Quizás no tenga un buen sabor.

75. Don't drink all the mixture now. Drink only half.
 No tome Vd. toda la mezcla ahora. Beba solamente la mitad.

76. Stand here and place your chest against this plate.
 Párese Vd. aquí y apoye el pecho contra esta placa.

77. Let me put you in the right position.
 Permítame colocarle en la postura correcta.

78. Move a little over to the right (left).
 Muévese Vd. un poco hacia la derecha (izquierda)

79. Rest your chin here.
 Apoye Vd. la barbilla (el mentón) aquí.

80. Put your hands on your hips with the palms facing out, like so.
 Póngase Vd. las manos en las caderas con las palmas hacia afuera, así.

81. Take a deep breath and hold it.
 Respire Vd. profundamente y sostenga la respiración.

82. Don't move, please.
 No se mueva Vd., por favor.

83. Now you may breathe.
 Ahora Vd. puede respirar.

84. Turn your body slowly to the left; to the right.
 Gire Vd. el cuerpo lentamente hacia la izquierda; hacia la derecha.

85. Breathe in.
  Aspire Vd.[40]

86. Breathe out.
  Exhale Vd.

87. Stand perfectly still.
  Párese Vd. perfectamente quieto.

88. We have to take another film.
  Tenemos que sacarle otra placa.

89. Thank you for your cooperation.
  Gracias por su cooperación (colaboración).

90. Your doctor will tell you the results.
  Su doctor le dirá los resultados.

91. Sit down on the wheelchair and wait for the orderly.
  Siéntese Vd. en la silla de ruedas y espere al ayudante.

92. The orderly will take you back to your room.
  El ayudante le (la) llevará a su cuarto.

93. Come back Thursday at 9 A.M.
  Vuelva Vd. el jueves a las nueve de la mañana, por favor.

94. You have an appointment for Monday.
  Vd. tiene una cita para el lunes.

95. I have to do a lumbar puncture.
  Tengo que hacerle una punción lumbar (punción raquídea).

96. I am going to draw some fluids from your spine.
  Voy a sacarle algún fluido de la columna vertebral.

97. Please lie on your side near the edge of the bed.
  Acuéstese de un lado, por favor, cerca del borde de la cama.

98. Bring your knees up to your chest, and bend your head down so that your chin rests on your chest, if possible.
  Doble Vd. las rodillas junto al pecho y baje la cabeza de manera que la barbilla descanse sobre el pecho, si es posible.

99. That's it. Lie perfectly still.
  Así. Échese perfectamente quieto.

100. Don't move at all.
  No se mueva nada.

101. I am all finished.
  Ya acabo de terminar.

102. You may relax and move.
  Vd. puede aflojarse ahora y mover.

EXERCISE *EJERCICIO*

Rewrite all polite commands in this section using the acceptable substitutes of *please* plus the infinitive:

Please $\begin{cases}\textbf{Haga Vd. el favor de} \\ \textbf{Favor de} \\ \textbf{Tenga la bondad de} \\ \textbf{Sírvase}\end{cases}$

No se ponga nervioso, por favor.
(Haga Vd. el favor de) _____
Haga Vd. el favor de no ponerse nervioso.
(Favor de) _____
Favor de no ponerse nervioso.
(Tenga la bondad de) _____
Tenga la bondad de no ponerse nervioso.
(Sírvase) _____
Sírvase no ponerse nervioso.

DENTAL CONVERSATION

CONVERSACION DENTAL

1. Please sit down in the chair and relax.
   Por favor, siéntese Vd. en la silla y relájese.

2. Put your head back.
   Eche Vd. la cabeza para atrás.

3. Open your mouth wide, please.
   Abra Vd. bien la boca, por favor.

4. Wider.
   Más, por favor.

5. Raise your head a bit.
   Levante Vd. un poco la cabeza, por favor.

6. Lower it.
   Bájela Vd., por favor.

7. You have a nice set of teeth.
   Vd. tiene buena dentadura.

8. Where do you feel the pain?
¿Dónde siente Vd. el dolor?

9. Which tooth hurts you?
¿Cuál diente (muela) le duele?

10. How long have you had the pain?
¿Desde cuándo existe el dolor?

11. Does it hurt you when you eat or drink cold things?
¿Le duele cuando come o bebe cosas frías?

12. Does it hurt you when you eat or drink something hot?
¿Le duele cuando come o bebe algo caliente?

13. Does it hurt when you eat sweets?
¿Le duele cuando come dulces?

14. Does it hurt when you chew?
¿Le duele cuando mastica Vd.?

15. Does it hurt when you bite?
¿Le duele cuando muerde Vd.?

16. Does something sour hurt your teeth?
¿Le molesta algo agrio?

17. Do you feel better when you drink cold water? Hot water?
¿Se siente Vd. mejor cuando bebe agua fría? ¿agua caliente?

18. I don't see any cavities.
No veo (ningunas) caries.

19. You have a cavity in one tooth.
Vd. tiene una cavidad en un diente.

20. You have a cavity in a molar.
Vd. tiene una carie en una muela.

21. You have three cavities.
Vd. tiene tres caries.

22. It is a very small cavity.
Es una cavidad (picadura) muy pequeña.

23. I have to fill the tooth.
Tengo que tapar (empastar, emplomar [Arg.]) el diente.

24. I am going to fill it (them) next week.
Voy a empastarla(s) la semana que viene.

25. I hope that I can fill it.
Espero poder empastarla.

26. The cavity is very deep.
La carie está muy honda.

27. This is not going to hurt you at all.
    Esto no le duele nada.

28. I am going to give you a shot to put your gum to sleep.
    Voy a ponerle una inyección para anestesiar la encía.

29. You will feel only a slight prick.
    No sentirá más que un leve pinchazo.

30. Don't be nervous.
    No se ponga nervioso(-a).

31. I am going to put some medicine in the tooth so that it will not hurt you.
    Voy a ponerle una medicina en el diente para que no le duela.

32. Drink some water and rinse your mouth now.
    Beba algún agua y enjuáguese la boca ahora.

33. Spit here.
    Escupa aquí, por favor.

34. What would you like to have it filled with: a silver amalgam, gold, or porcelain?
    ¿Con qué quiere Vd. que se lo tape (empaste, emplome [Arg.], calce)? ¿Con platino, con oro, o con porcelana?

35. A gold inlay is the best filling because it will last the longest.
    Una incrustación (de oro) es el mejor empaste (relleno, tapadura, emplomadura [Arg.]) porque le durará mucho tiempo.

36. Please close your mouth a little.
    Cierre Vd. la boca un poco, por favor.

37. I have to take impressions for the gold inlay.
    Tengo que hacerle impresiones antes de orificarle el diente.

38. I must change the packing.
    Tengo que cambiarle este empaque.

39. Keep your mouth wide open.
    Mantenga Vd. la boca bien abierta, por favor.

40. I am going to put some fast-hardening dental plaster in your mouth to make a model.
    Voy a usar en la boca yeso dentífrico que endurece dentro de momentos para hacerle un molde exacto de la región.

41. Try not to gag.
    Trate de no sentir náuseas.

42. You will hear a pop.
    Vd. oirá un crujido.

43. Don't be frightened.
    No tenga miedo.

44. I am finished for today.
    Estoy terminado (-a) para hoy.

45. Don't eat hard foods for an hour.
    No coma Vd. nada duro por una hora.

46. When I finish with this tooth, I am going to take x-rays of your mouth and also clean your teeth.
    Cuando termine con este diente, voy a hacerle una radiografía dental y también hacerle una limpieza.

47. Do your gums bleed when you brush your teeth?
    ¿Le sangran las encías cuando se cepilla los dientes?

48. My gums are bleeding a lot.
    Las encías me sangran mucho.

49. Do you often have bad breath?
    ¿Tiene Vd. mal aliento con frecuencia?

50. Your gum is infected.
    Vd. tiene la encía infectada.

51. You should use dental floss to clean between your teeth especially where there are pockets.
    Vd. debe usar hilo dental para limpiarse entre los dientes, sobre todo donde hay surcos gingivales (espacios anormales entre la encía y la raíz del diente).

52. Massage your gums often.
    Masajee (sobe) las encías a menudo.

53. You should brush your teeth three times a day.
    Vd. debe cepillarse los dientes tres veces al día.

54. Brush your teeth in the morning, and at bedtime, and if possible after meals.
    Cepíllese Vd. los dientes al levantarse por la mañana y antes de acostarse por la noche, y si es posible, después de cada comida.

55. You have pyorrhea. You must see a periodontist.
    Vd. padece de piorrea. Debe de consultar con un(a) especialista de las encías.

56. You need gum surgery.
    Vd. necesita tener cirugía en las encías.

57. If you do not have it, your teeth will soon loosen and fall out.
    Si Vd. no la tiene, tendrá un desprendimiento de los dientes que dentro de poco se caigan.

58. The nurse is going to show you how you ought to brush your teeth to clean them well.
    La enfermera (higienista) va a enseñarle (-la) cómo Vd. debe cepillarse los dientes para limpiarlos bien.

59. Clean your bridge after every meal, if possible.
    Límpiese el puente después de cada comida si es posible.

60. Store your dentures in a glass of water when you are not wearing them.
    Guarde Vd. su dentadura postiza en un vaso de agua cuando no la esté usando (no la use).

61. Don't remove your bridge until you see me.
    No se quite Vd. el puente hasta que vuelva a verme.

62. I have to remove your wisdom teeth (upper bicuspids).
    Tengo que sacarle las muelas del juicio (los bicúspides superiores).

63. Don't touch the wound with your fingers, tongue, or toothpicks.
    No toque la cicatrización con los dedos, la lengua, o mondadientes.

64. Bite on this gauze for an hour *without* moving it.
    Muerda Vd. a dentelladas esta gasa *sin* moverla.

65. If bleeding is excessive, call me immediately.
    Si (se) desangra, llámeme en seguida.

66. Eat only liquids today.
    Hoy no coma más que líquidos.

67. Don't use straws.
    No use Vd. pajas.

68. Tomorrow begin eating a soft diet.
    Empezando mañana, siga una dieta blanda.

69. Don't rinse your mouth at all for the first 24 hours.
    No se enjuague nada la boca durante las primeras veinticuatro horas.

70. Rinse your mouth with warm salt water every 4 hours.
    Enjuáguese la boca con agua de sal tibia cada cuatro horas.

71. You will have some pain in the form of soreness around the operated area.
    Vd. tendrá algún dolor en la forma de una parte dolorida por toda la súperficie afectada.

72. Take two aspirins if it hurts you a lot.
    Tome Vd. dos aspirinas si le duele mucho.

73. Do not change the dose or frequency of your medication.
    No cambie la dosis o la frecuencia de su medicina.

74. Expect some swelling for about three days. This is normal.
    Cuente con alguna tumefacción que durará unos tres días. Es normal.

75. Apply an ice pack as soon as possible after the surgery.
    Póngase una bolsa de hielo tan pronto como posible después de la cirugía oral.

76. Don't smoke for a few days.
    No fume por unos días.

77. I want you to rest here in the office for an hour before you leave.
    Quiero que Vd. descanse aquí en la oficina por una hora antes de irse.

78. Return for your next appointment in a week.
    Vuelva Vd. para su próxima cita de hoy en ocho.

79. I will remove the stitches then.
    Voy a quitarle las puntadas entonces.

DIET

DIETA

1. What type of work do you do?[41]
   ¿Cómo gana Vd. la vida?

2. What are your working hours?
   ¿Cuántas horas trabaja Vd. por día?

3. How many days a week do you work?
   ¿Cuántos días por semana trabaja Vd.?

4. At what time do you get up in the morning?
   ¿A qué hora se despierta por la mañana?

5. Where do you eat breakfast, at home or in a restaurant?
   ¿Dónde se desayuna Vd? ¿en casa? ¿o en un restorán?

6. What do you eat for breakfast?[42]
   ¿Qué se desayuna?

7. Do you carry lunch?
   ¿Lleva su almuerzo?

8. What do you eat for lunch? for dinner?
   ¿Qué come Vd. para el almuerzo? ¿para la cena?

9. What do you eat between meals?
   ¿Qué come Vd. entre comidas?

10. Do you eat while you watch television?
    ¿Come Vd. mientras mira la televisión?

11. What do you eat before going to bed?
    ¿Qué come antes de acostarse?

12. Have you ever been on a diet before?
    ¿Ha estado Vd. a dieta antes?

13. You will have to follow a _____ diet.
    Vd. tendrá que seguir una dieta _____.

14. Eat three meals a day.
    Coma Vd. tres comidas al día.

15. Do not skip meals. It is very important.
    No salte Vd. comidas. Es muy importante.

16. Drink milk between meals and before going to bed.
    Tome Vd. leche entre comidas y antes de acostarse.

17. Do not overeat raw vegetables of any kind.
    No coma Vd. en exceso ningunas legumbres crudas.

18. Do not use pepper or spice.
   No use Vd. ni pimienta ni especies.

19. Do not use sugar or sweets.
   No use Vd. ni azúcar ni dulces.

20. Do not use salt or baking soda.
   No use Vd. ni sal ni bicarbonato.

21. Use only sweet butter or margarine.
   No use Vd. más que mantequilla sosa o margarina sin sal.

22. Do not eat gravies or sauces.
   No coma Vd. salsas de ninguna clase.

23. Do not eat fried foods.
   No coma Vd. nada frito.

24. Do you have any questions about your diet?[43]
   ¿Tiene Vd. preguntas acerca de su dieta?

25. Do you want to describe the meals that you are used to eating during the day?[44]
   ¿Quiere Vd. describirme las comidas que Vd. acostumbra a tomar durante el día?

26. I will be able to help you plan your meals better (plan your substitutions) when you return home if I have this information.
   Podré ayudarle(-la) a planificar mejor sus comidas (su lista de intercambios) cuando Vd. vuelva a casa si tengo esta información.

LABOR AND DELIVERY
LA LABOR Y EL PARTO

1. When is your expected delivery date? How many more weeks?
   ¿Cuál es la fecha anticipada (esperada) del parto? ¿Cuántas semanas le quedan?

2. Do you have sharp pains in your hip—in the lumbar region?
   ¿Tiene Vd. dolor agudo de la cadera (de la espalda en la región lumbar)?

3. Are you having uterine contractions (abdominal pains) now?
   ¿Tiene Vd. contracciones uterinas (dolores abdominales) ahora?

4. Do the pains come at regular intervals—for example every 10 minutes?
   ¿Le vienen los dolores (de parto) a intervalos regulares—como, por ejemplo, cada diez minutos?

5. Do the pains decrease when you walk?
   ¿Se disminuyen las contracciones uterinas (los dolores abdominales) al caminar?

6. How close together are they? (How many minutes apart are they?)
   ¿Con qué frecuencia le vienen?
   ¿Cuántos minutos hay entre las contracciones (los dolores)?

7. How long do they last?
   ¿Cuánto tiempo le duran?

8. Since this is your first baby, you should come to the hospital when the contractions are five minutes apart.
   Puesto que va a tener su primer bebé, le aconsejo que venga al hospital cuando las contracciones uterinas vengan cada cinco minutos.

9. Since this is not your first baby, I advise you to come to the hospital when your contractions are 10 minutes apart.
   Puesto que Vd. ha tenido más de un bebé, le aconsejo que venga al hospital cuando las contracciones uterinas vengan cada diez minutos.

10. Have your waters broken?
   ¿Se ha roto la bolsa membranosa (que contiene el bebé y el líquido que le rodea)?
   ¿Se le ha quebrado la bolsa de aguas?
   ¿Se rompió la fuente?
   ¿Se reventaron las aguas?

11. Have you noticed a bloody show?
   ¿Se ha fijado en una secreción mucosa mezclada con sangre procedente de la vagina? [45]
   ¿Había ya una muestra de sangre (un tapón de moco)?

12. You are in the first stage of labor—dilation stage.
   Vd. está en la primera etapa de la labor—el período de dilatación.

13. Come to the emergency room entrance and tell the receptionist that you are in labor.
   Venga al hospital, por la entrada de emergencia donde indicará a la recepcionista que Vd. está en labor.

14. You will be sent to the labor area in a wheelchair.
   A Vd. le enviarán en seguida a la sala de labor (parto) en una silla de ruedas.

15. The nurse will take you to the prep room where you will undress and put on a hospital gown.
   La enfermera la llevará al cuarto de preparación donde Vd. se quitará la ropa (se desvestirá y se pondrá una bata de hospital.

16. The nurse will ask you for a urine specimen and will ask you to lie down on the bed so that she will be able to take your blood pressure, pulse, and temperature and check your breathing.
   La enfermera le pedirá que le dé una muestra de orina a ella, y que se acueste en una cama de modo que pueda tomarle la presión arterial, pulso, temperatura y respiraciones.

17. Do you feel like urinating?
   ¿Tiene Vd. deseos de orinar?

18. I am going to take a blood sample that will be sent to the laboratory for routine admission tests.
Voy a sacarle una muestra de sangre para enviar al laboratorio para exámenes rutinarios de admisión.

19. I am going to shave you.
Voy a rasurarla.

20. I am going to shave the lower part of your vulva, which is where you will have an episiotomy.
Voy a afeitarle la parte inferior de la vulva donde será el sitio para hacer la episiotomía (el corte de las partes).

21. I am going to give you an enema.
Voy a ponerle una enema (un lavado intestinal).

22. Your doctor will do a vaginal examination to determine the progress of your labor.
Su doctor(a) le hará un examen vaginal para determinar el progreso de su labor.

23. You are six centimeters dilated.
Vd. tiene seis centímetros de cuello.
La cérvix está dilatada seis centímetros.

24. The child's head is completely down in the birth canal.
La cabecita del niño está completamente abajo en el canal vaginal (canal de nacimiento).

25. Your husband may stay with you during your labor.
Su esposo puede estar aquí a su lado durante su labor.

26. Your cervix is completely dilated and the baby's head is crowning.
La cérvix se abre (se dilata) completamente y la cabecita del niño está coronando.

27. You are going to feel a tremendous pushing sensation.
Va a tener una sensación tremenda de pujo.

28. Do abdominal breathing when you have contractions.
Respire bien lentamente del abdomen cuando haya contracciones.

29. Don't push.
No puje Vd.[46]

30. At the end of the first stage of labor you may feel nauseated. Don't be frightened; it indicates transition to the second stage.
Al fin de la primera etapa de la labor, puede tener náuseas. No se asuste; indica la transición a la segunda etapa.

31. A positive mental attitude is important—concentrate on something pleasant.
Una mentalidad positiva es importante—concentre, medite en algo agradable.

32. The best person to help you during this period is your husband (the baby's father).
La persona más indicada para ayudarla es su esposo (el padre del niño).

33. During the first stage, concentrate on squeezing his hand, don't push.
Durante la primera etapa, concentre Vd. en apretar fuerte la mano del esposo, no puje.

34. Pant—breathe shallowly and rapidly. This helps to prevent tearing.
    Jadee Vd.—respire corto y rápido (jadeo). Esto ayuda a prevenir que se desgarre la abertura.

35. If you anticipate the contractions, you will not feel them so much.
    Si Vd. anticipa la presión, no se siente tanto.

36. At the beginning of the contraction take a deep breath, let it out, and then breathe deeply, slowly, and evenly for the remainder of the contraction.
    Al principio de la contracción haga una aspiración completa y expúlsela (exhálela) y luego respire profunda, lenta y rítmicamente por el resto de la contracción.

37. Abdominal breathing helps keep the abdominal walls relaxed and helps keep them from touching the uterus.
    La respiración abdominal ayuda a mantener las paredes abdominales relajadas y mantener el útero sin tocar (presionar) contra la cavidad abdominal (contra ellas).

38. We are going to move you to the delivery room now that you are dilated.
    Vamos a trasladarla a la sala de partos ya que el cuello de la matriz está completamente dilatado.

39. You are now in the second phase of labor—the expulsion period.
    Vd. está en la segunda etapa de la labor—el período de expulsión.

40. It is a short phase.
    No dura mucho tiempo.

41. With the second stage of labor the muscles of the perineum are flattened or stretched out, the coccyx is pushed back.
    Cuando viene la segunda etapa de la labor, los músculos del perineo se extienden, el cóccix está bien atrás.

42. When the head is crowning, the doctor does an episiotomy—a simple incision in the area between the vagina and the anus.
    Cuando la cabecita está coronando, el doctor (la doctora) le hace la episiotomía—una incisión sencilla en el área entre la vagina y el ano.

43. The episiotomy prevents the rupture or tearing of the perineum and gives the baby more room.
    El corte de las partes (la episiotomía) prohibe la ruptura o un desgarramiento irregular de los tejidos y proporciona más espacio para el bebé.

44. In the delivery room there is a lamp that has a type of mirror so that you can see the child's birth.
    En la sala de partos hay una lámpara que contiene una especie de espejos para que Vd. pueda ver como aparece el niño.

45. Don't push until you are told.
    No puje hasta que se lo diga.

46. Push hard.
    Puje con fuerza.

47. Rest between contractions.
Descanse cuando no tenga contracciones.

48. Normally the baby's head comes out with the face downward.
Normalmente la cabeza sale con la cara hacia abajo.

49. The baby's body is turning in order to allow the shoulders to come out.
El cuerpecito del bebé se ladea para dejar salir los hombros.

50. It is a boy!
Es un niño.
It is a girl!
Es una niña.

51. Everything is turning out fine.
Todo sale bien.

52. The nurses will clean the baby up and put an ID on him (her).
Las enfermeras limpiarán al (a la) bebé y pondrán identificación en el tobillo.

53. Your uterus is going to contract again now that you are in the third phase of labor—the expulsion of the placenta.
El útero va a contraerse de nuevo ahora que está en la tercera etapa de la labor—la expulsión de la placenta (el período placentario).

54. Push.
Puje.

55. I am going to sew you up.
Voy a reparar la incisión ahora.

56. I am going to use dissolving stitches.
Voy a emplear suturas absorbibles.
Voy a utilizar puntos que se absorben.

57. It will not be necessary to remove them.
No faltará quitarlas.
No será necesario levantarlos.

58. Are you going to nurse the baby?
¿Piensa criarle a los pechos?
¿Va a amamantarle?

59. If you are going to bottle feed her (him), I am going to give you an injection to dry up your milk.
Si Vd. va a darle biberón, voy a ponerle inyección para que los senos se sequen y no tengan leche.

60. Your breasts will swell and fill with milk.
Los senos se le hincharán y se llenarán de leche.

61. Wear a good nursing bra both for support and for convenience.
Póngase unos sostenes para criar tanto para darle un apoyo como por conveniencia para criar.

62. During the first days after birth, you will produce calostrum.
En los primeros días después del parto, saldrá un líquido de los pezones llamado calostro.

63. Ask the nurse for help.
Pídale a la enfermera ayuda.

64. Your breasts will become painful and it will help to wear a breast binder.
Los senos le dolerán y va a ayudarle llevar una faja para los pechos.

65. You will need a caeserean.
Necesitará una operación cesárea.

66. The baby will be born through an incision in the abdomen, instead of through the birth canal.
Su bebé nacerá a través de una incisión en su abdomen en lugar de por el conducto natal.

67. Your pelvis is too small.
Vd. tiene la pelvis demasiada pequeña.

68. It is a case of placenta previa.
Se trata de placenta previa.

69. You will have to stay in the hospital a few extra days.
Vd. tendrá que permanecer en el hospital unos días más.

70. After the baby is born, you will be taken to the recovery room.
Después de nacer su niño, se la lleva a una sala de recuperación.

71. When you are back in your own room, tell the nurse if you want to eat, or if the food is no good.[47]
Cuando vuelva a su propio cuarto, dígale a la enfermera si quiere comer o si la comida no le gusta.

72. The dietician will try to plan foods for you to eat that you will like.[47]
La dietista tratará de planear una dieta para Vd. que le gustará.

CONTRACEPTIVE METHODS FOR FAMILY PLANNING[48]

LOS METODOS ANTICONCEPTIVOS PARA LA PLANIFICACION FAMILIAR

1. Are you interested in talking about birth control?
¿Se interesa en hablar de los métodos anticonceptivos (de la prevención del embarazo).

2. Do you know about birth control?
¿Sabe Vd. (algo) de los métodos para no tener hijos (del control de la natalidad)?

3. Are you interested in using some form of birth control?
   ¿Se interesa en usar alguna forma de anticoncepción (contracepción)?

4. Have you ever used it?
   ¿La ha usado Vd. alguna vez?

5. Do you use contraception now?
   ¿Usa Vd. anticonceptivos ahora?

6. Would you like to use them?[49]
   ¿Quisiera Vd. usarlos?

7. Are you satisfied with your present method?
   ¿Está Vd. satisfecha (-o) con su método actual?

8. Would you like to have (more) children?
   ¿Quiere Vd. tener (más) hijos?

9. Do you want to discuss this with your husband (boyfriend)?
   ¿Quiere Vd. discutir esto con su esposo (novio)?

10. Do you want to talk about this with your husband (boyfriend) present?
    ¿Quiere Vd. hablar de esto en la presencia de su esposo (novio)?

11. I advise you to discuss your sexual goals with your spouse (boyfriend) as well as your thoughts about spacing pregnancies, and the number of children you want.
    Le aconsejo que discuta sus metas del sexo con su esposo (novio) así como las del espaciamiento de sus nacimientos y del número de hijos que quisiera.

12. You and your husband will have time to talk and choose the method that is best for you.
    Su esposo y Vd. tendrán tiempo para hablar y escoger el método que sea más satisfactorio para ustedes dos.

13. It is important to know how the reproductive system works.
    Es importante saber cómo funciona el sistema reproductivo.

14. The man has two external parts: the penis and the scrotum (balls), which is a sac that hangs under the penis and contains two testicles that produce sperm.
    El hombre tiene dos partes externas: el pene y el escroto (las bolas), que es un saco que cuelga por debajo del pene y contiene dos testículos que producen la esperma (las semillas).

15. When a man gets excited or "hot," his penis fills with blood and becomes hard (it produces an erection).
    Cuando un hombre se excita, o se "calienta," el pene se llena de sangre y se pone duro (se produce una erección).

16. During sexual excitement the sperm combines with a milky liquid called semen, which is expelled by the erect penis by means of muscular contractions.
    Durante la excitación sexual la esperma se combina con un líquido lechoso, llamado semen, todo lo que es expulsado por el pene erecto mediante contracciones musculares.

17. This process of expelling semen is called ejaculation ("coming"), and the feeling of pleasure is called an orgasm.
    Este proceso de expulsar el semen se llama la eyaculación (el "venirse"), y la sensación de placer se llama un orgasmo.

18. Ejaculation can also occur during a "wet dream," one which excites sexually, or by means of masturbation.[50]

   La eyaculación también puede producirse durante un "sueño mojado," uno que le excite en forma sexual, o por medio de la masturbación.

19. During sexual intercourse the penis penetrates the vagina and gives off semen.

   Durante el acto sexual, el pene penetra en la vagina de la mujer y suelta el semen en ella.

20. The woman has two ovaries, each of which alternately produces an egg cell about once every 28 days.

   La mujer tiene dos ovarios, uno de los cuales produce un óvulo (o célula femenina) más o menos cada veintiocho días.

21. The egg cell moves through the fallopian tube to the uterus (womb).

   El óvulo se mueve por la trompa de falopio hasta el útero (también llamado la matriz).

22. During intercourse sperm are introduced into the vagina and travel upward into the uterus and then into the tubes.

   Durante el acto sexual la esperma se introduce en la vagina y viaja hacia arriba por el útero y de ahí a las trompas.

23. If a sperm unites with an egg cell that has been released, fertilization occurs and a baby begins to develop.

   Si una esperma se encuentra con un óvulo que ha sido desprendido, ocurre la fertilización y un bebé empieza a desarrollarse.

24. If the egg is not united with a sperm, the egg and the lining of the uterus (which would have fed the fertilized egg) are eliminated in the process of menstruation (the "period"), which lasts from 3 to 7 days.[51]

   Si el óvulo no se une a una esperma, el óvulo y el forro del útero (que hubiera alimentado al óvulo fertilizado) se eliminan en la menstruación (o el período de la mujer), que dura de tres a siete días.

25. The basic idea of birth control is to prevent the sperm from meeting the egg in the woman's body.

   La idea básica de control de la natalidad es evitar que la esperma del hombre alcance el óvulo en el cuerpo de la mujer.

26. There are many methods and they are not all equally effective.

   Hay muchos métodos y no son todos igualmente efectivos.

27. If you are having sexual relations, use protection; otherwise you can become pregnant.

   Si tiene relaciones sexuales, use protección; de otro modo, puede estar embarazada.

28. When you resume sexual relations after having your baby, use protection so that you do not become pregnant again immediately.[52]

   Cuando vuelva a tener relaciones sexuales después de dar luz, use protección de modo que no esté embarazada de nuevo inmediatamente.

29. You can buy some of these in a drug store and others from your doctor.

   Vd. puede comprar algunas de estas (protecciones) de una farmacia y otras a través de su médico.

Foam and Condom *Espuma y condón*

30. You can use contraceptive foam and your husband can use a condom. These can be bought in any place where sanitary items are sold.
Vd. puede usar la espuma anticonceptiva y su esposo puede usar un condón. Estos pueden ser comprados en cualquier lugar donde se venden toallas sanitarias.

31. It is best to use foam or contraceptive cream or jelly with a condom.
Es mejor usar la espuma o una crema o jalea anticonceptivas con un condón (un preservativo).

32. Alone they are not very safe.
Solo(-a) no es muy seguro(-a).

33. The cream (or foam) comes in a container that resembles a tampon.
La crema (La espuma) viene en un frasco que parece a un tampón.

34. Fill the applicator and insert it in the vagina no more than a half-hour before intercourse since the heat of the woman's body changes it to liquid.
Llene el aplicador e insértela en la vagina no más de media hora antes de tener relación sexual puesto que el calor del cuerpo se la cambia en forma líquida.

35. Use it *each* time that you have intercourse.
Usela *cada* vez que tenga coito.

36. Do not douche for 8 hours after.
No se dé ducha vaginal (lavaje) durante ocho horas después del coito.

37. The condom is a thin sheath of rubber (or similar material) that fits over the erect penis.
El condón (preservativo, "la goma") es una cubierta delgada hecha de hule (goma) (o de un material semejante), el cual se coloca sobre el pene erecto.

38. Use a condom whenever you enter the vagina, not just before ejaculation.
Use el preservativo cada vez que entre en la vagina, no antes de eyaculación.

39. If the condom has a reservoir tip, so much the better. If not, make a tip by squeezing it.
Si el condón tiene punta de receptáculo, tanto mejor. Si no, haga punta para el líquido, apretándolo.

40. To put it on, place it on the head of the penis and unroll it, making sure that the tip is in the center and about $\frac{1}{2}$ inch from the end of penis.
Para ponérselo, colóquelo en la cabeza del pene y desenróllelo, asegurándose de que la punta está correctamente en el centro y más o menos a media pulgada del final del pene.

41. Withdraw the penis and condom together from the vagina as soon as possible after orgasm to avoid semen escape.
Extráigase el pene junto con el profiláctico de la vagina lo antes posible después del orgasmo para evitar escape del semen.

42. Use a new condom each time there is intercourse.
Use un nuevo profiláctico cada vez que repita el acto sexual.

IUD *El DIU*

43. The IUD is best for the woman who has several children.
    El dispositivo intrauterino (DIU) es mejor para la mujer con varios hijos.

44. There are several types: those made of plastic, in forms of a loop or coil; those containing progesterone; and those made of plastic and copper.
    Hay varios tipos—los hechos de plástico en formas de lupo, coil (muelle); los que con contienen progesterona; y los hechos de plástico y cubre.

45. You must replace the plastic and plastic and copper IUDs every three years, and the IUDs with progesterone every year.
    Vd. debe cambiar el DIU hecho de plástico o de plástico y cubre cada tres años, y el DIU hecho de progesterona cada año.

46. After the IUD is fitted, it can be left in place indefinitely.
    Después de que se coloca el DIU, puede dejarse en el útero indefinidamente.

47. The IUD is inserted during your period.
    Se inserta el DIU durante el período menstrual.

48. When the IUD is well fitted, a string tied to the IUD will hang down from the cervix inside of the vagina.
    Cuando el DIU está bien colocado, un hilo atado al DIU se proyectará (colgará) de la cervix bien adentro de la vagina.

49. You have to check to see that the IUD is in place by inserting either your index or middle finger into your vagina and touching the string, always at the same point.[53] Check once a week.
    Vd. tiene que comprobar que el DIU está en su sitio apropiado al introducir o el dedo índice o el del corazón bien adentro en la vagina y sentir el hilo (tocar el hilo), siempre a la misma distancia. Examínese una vez por semana.

50. Do not pull the string, which could dislocate it.
    No hale Vd. el hilo lo que podría desalojarlo.

51. If you cannot feel the string, or if you can touch the IUD itself, call the doctor, and meanwhile use other contraceptive methods.
    Si Vd. no puede sentir el hilo o puede tocar el DIU sí mismo, llame al médico, y entretanto, use otro método anticonceptivo.

52. Women with vaginal problems or tendencies toward them should not use the IUD since it increase these tendencies.
    Las mujeres con enfermedades vaginales o propensiones para ellas no deben usar el DIU puesto que aumenta estas tendencias.

Diaphragm *El diafragma*

53. The diaphragm is a little round rubber cup, which is used with cream or jelly.
    El diafragma es una redonda gorrita (taza) de goma que se rellena con una gelatina o crema de control de la natalidad.

54. I have to measure you for the correct size.
Tengo que medirla para que le recete el tamaño adecuado.

55. Put a spoonful of cream or jelly in the middle of the diaphragm, squeeze the sides until it folds; with the other hand separate the labia; insert it toward the back and then push upwards behind the pubic bone.[54]
Unte Vd. una cucharadita de crema o jalea en el centro del diafragma, apriete los lados hasta que se doble; con la otra mano separe los labios; introdúzcalo hacia debajo y detrás y entonces, empújelo hacia arriba detrás del hueso púbico.

56. Try inserting it now.
Trate de introducirlo ahora.

57. You can put it in place two hours before sexual intercourse.
Vd. puede ponerlo en su sitio dos horas antes de tener relaciones sexuales.

58. Leave it in place at least eight hours after intercourse.
Déjelo en su lugar por lo menos ocho horas después de las relaciones.

59. Check with your finger to see that it is in place.[54]
Introduzca un dedo para averiguar que está en su lugar.

60. To remove it, grab the rim and pull gently.
Para quitarlo, agárrese del contorno y dé un tirón suave.

61. After using it, wash it with soap and water, and dry carefully, powdering with cornstarch.
Después de usarlo, lávelo con jabón y agua, séquelo cuidadosamente, empolvorándolo con maicena.

The Pill *La píldora*

62. The birth control pill is the best nonpermanent method of birth control.
La píldora (pastilla) (anticonceptiva) es el método no permanente más efectivo de prevenir el embarazo.

63. It is important to follow all instructions when you take the pill.
Es importante seguir todas las instrucciones al usar la píldora.

64. Take the pill at the same time each day. Your partner can remind you.
Tome Vd. la píldora a la misma hora cada día. Su compañero puede recordársela.

65. If you forget to take one pill, the next day, take two.
Si se le olvida tomar una píldora, el día siguiente, tome dos.

66. If you forget two pills, use foam; if you forget three pills in a row, stop using them that month.
Si se le olvidan dos píldoras, use espuma; si se le olvidan tres píldoras deje de usarlas ese mes.

67. The pill comes in two types that are prescribed frequently: packages of 21 and of 28.
La píldora viene de dos clases que se recetan con frecuencia: paquetes de veintiuna y de veintiocho.

68. The first day of your period is the first day that you bleed.
    El primer día de su regla (período) es el primer día que pierde sangre.

69. Take the first pill on the fifth day of your period.
    Tome la primera píldora el quinto día de su regla.

70. Take the pills daily for 21 days.
    Tome Vd. las píldoras cada día por veintiún días.

71. You will begin to menstruate on the second or third day after you finish taking all the pills.
    Comenzará a menstruar (perder sangre) el segundo o tercer día después de terminar tomando todas las píldoras.

72. Stop taking the pills for an entire week before beginning to take them again.
    Deje de tomar las píldoras por una semana entera antes de comenzar a tomarlas de nuevo.

73. If your period skips a month and you have been taking the pills correctly, begin the next package on the correct day as indicated.
    Si se salta una menstruación un mes y si Vd. ha estado tomando las píldoras correctamente, empiece a tomar el próximo paquete en el día correcto como está señalado.

74. Begin the new series of pills on the same day of the week that you began the last series.
    Empiece la nueva serie de píldoras en el mismo día de la semana en que comenzó la serie anterior.

75. If you have a poor memory, your doctor may prescribe a series of 28 pills for you.
    Si Vd. tiene mala memoria, su médico puede recetarle una series de veintiocho píldoras.

76. For 21 days take the white pills. For the next 7 days take the pink ones.
    Por veintiún días tome las píldoras blancas. Por los próximos siete días tome las rosadas.

77. Your period will begin on the second or third day after you begin the pink pills.
    Su regla comenzará el segundo o tercer día después de comenzar las píldoras rosadas.

78. On the eighth day begin a new pack.
    Al octavo día empiece un nuevo paquete.

79. You must take a pill daily when you use the package of 28.
    Vd. tiene que tomar una píldora cada día cuando usa el paquete de veintiocho.

80. If your period does not start while you are taking the pink pills, begin a new pack anyway the day after having taken the last pink pill.
    Si su menstruación no aparece mientras está tomando las píldoras rosadas, de todas maneras empiece un nuevo paquete de píldoras al día siguiente de haber tomado la última píldora rosada.

Rhythm Method *El método del ritmo*

81. This is not effective for all women who are not very regular.
    No resulta efectiva para todas las mujeres que no tengan su regla puntualmente.

82. It is necessary to determine the "unsafe" days of the month and avoid sexual relations on them.
Hay que averiguar cuáles son los días del mes que no son "seguros" y evitarse las relaciones sexuales en ellos.

83. Speak to your doctor if you intend to use this method since "safe days" vary in every woman.
Hable Vd. con su médico si piensa utilizar este método puesto que los "días seguros" varían en cada mujer.

Coitus Interruptus   *El retirarse*

84. The man must withdraw his penis from the vagina before ejaculating.
El hombre debe de retirar el pene de la vagina antes de la eyaculación.

85. This is not effective.
No es efectivo.

Douching[55]   *El lavaje*

86. The use of a vaginal douche immediately after intercourse does not prevent pregnancy.
El uso de un lavaje para tratar de eliminar la esperma de la vagina inmediatamente después de relaciones sexuales no evita el embarazo.

Sterilization   *La esterilización*

87. Sterilization is a *permanent* means of birth control.
La esterilización es un medio *permanente* de control de la natalidad.

88. In a man the process is called a vasectomy: the tubes through which the sperm travel (the vas deferens) are cut surgically.
En el hombre el procedimiento se llama una vasectomía: los conductos por donde se transportan las espermas (los conductos deferentes) se cortan quirúrgicamente.

89. There is no change in the man's sexual desires, appearance, or ability to have intercourse.
No hay ningún cambio en el instinto sexual, en la apariencia ni en la habilidad de tener relaciones sexuales.

90. Use a temporary method of birth control immediately after a vasectomy to avoid pregnancy.
Hay que utilizar un método temporal de anticoncepción inmediatamente después de una vasectomía para prevenir el embarazo.

91. For a woman the procedure is called a tubal ligation: the tubes through which the egg travels from the ovary to the uterus (the fallopian tubes) are cut, separated, and tied.
Para la mujer el procedimiento se llama la ligadura de los tubos: los conductos por los que se transportan los óvulos (las trompas de falopio) se cortan, se separan y se atan.

Notes *Notas*

1. Students may find it helpful to refer to the **Spanish Verb Section**, pages 84–156.

2. The Hispanic family is usually reluctant to give up its responsibility for sick family members and may be very resistant to hospitalization. There are many underlying causes. Despite rapid urbanization, many Hispanics still live in areas where medical facilities are not readily available; the Spanish-speaking as a group tend to be poor, and Anglo medical care is very expensive. Fear of separation from the family is another important factor (see footnote 4). The formality and impersonality of the Anglo health care personnel, the hospital schedules, and unfamiliar foods may be distasteful to Hispanics. Finally, there is the fear of the hospital itself, for it is viewed as the place where people go to die. (See John H. Burma, ed., *Mexican-Americans in the United States: A Reader*, Cambridge: Schenkman Publishing Co., 1970, p. 329; Pedro Poma, "Hispanos: Impact of Culture on Health Care," *Illinois Medical Journal*, Vol. 156, No. 6 [1979], p. 457.)

3. Language differences between English and Spanish show a cultural chasm between the two groups. Hispanic patients increasingly have adopted terms used by professional health workers, such as **presión alta** (high blood pressure) or **vista cansada** (tired eyesight), but have given such terminology different connotative aspects. The former term might refer to symptoms associated with the **edad crítica** (critical age of menopause), or symptoms such as nervousness and propensity toward **cóleras** (anger). Persons with **vista cansada** usually describe such symptoms as burning sensation of the eyes, or overheated eyesight, both possible indicators of poor eyesight. Hispanos often link this to excessive worry, fatigue, or overwork. Consequently, patients and professionals sometimes believe that they are communicating but do not really understand the different meanings attached to the language used. (See S. King, *Perceptions of Illness and Medical Practices*, New York: Russell Sage Foundation, 1962, pp. 227–231; and A. Ordóñez-Plaja et al., "Communication between Physicians and Patients in Outpatient Clinics," *Milbank Memorial Fund Quarterly*, Vol. 46 [April 1968], pp. 161–213.)

Recent Hispanic immigrants often rely upon "on-the-spot" learning. Their adoption of vocabulary or behavioral forms does not ensure full understanding of their meaning or what they are expected to do. Serious misunderstandings can result from factors associated with differing patient and physician concepts about health beliefs and practices. Hispanos often present their own interpretations about the natures of their troubles, unlike the Anglo patients who learn about their diagnosis from the physician. When Hispanos cannot engage in active discourse regarding their own concepts of illness, many adopt a passive attitude, answering politely, even giving responses to questions about which they have little or no understanding. (See L. Cohen, *Culture, Disease, and Stress Among Latino Immigrants*, Washington, D.C.: RIIES Special Study, 1979, pp. 132–159.)

Misunderstandings concerning different cultures and revered values have been among the causes for labeling the Spanish-speaking as irresponsible, lazy, superstitious, untruthful, or some other stereotyped characteristic. First, attitudes about time vary between Hispanos and Anglos. Second, work and efficiency are another area of difference. Anglos value industriousness and success. The Spanish ideal is **ser** rather than **hacer**. Third, Hispanos differ in their attitudes of acceptance and resignation to situations. Many researchers have characterized Latin Americans as passive endurers of stress who tend to avoid direct interpersonal conflict. [See M. Clark, *Health in the Mexican-American Culture* 2nd ed., Berkeley: University of California Press, 1970; J. Samora, "Conceptions of Health and Disease among Spanish-Americans," *American Catholic Sociological Review*, Vol. 22 (Winter 1961), pp. 314–323; R. Díaz-Guerrero, *Psychology of the Mexican*, Austin: University of Texas Press, 1967.] The passive endurance of illness and stress is considered an Hispanic virtue, much to the exasperation of Anglo health-care workers dealing with the chronically sick Hispanos. The latter often "accept" their unpleasant medical problems by withdrawing from contact with those who could render medical service. Finally, Hispanos develop interdependence with their extended family and friends. Unlike the Anglos, they do not look to develop qualities of achieved leadership. The entire community works, in a sense, as a single primary group. Self-sacrifice is expected of all family members, together with dependence, politeness, submission, and **aguante** (the ability to hold up well even in the face of abuse). (See Díaz-Guerrero, *Psychology of the Mexican*, pp. 112–136.)

4. This standard American policy of hospitalization often presents problems for the Hispanic community. Hospitalization often means a separation from family and the temporary loss of the emotional support of kinship. Consequently, family members and close friends may go to the hospital in large numbers to visit the sick individual, thus creating disruptions to hospital regulations. (See P. Poma, "Hispanos: Impact of Culture on Health Care," *Illinois Medical Journal*, Vol. 156 [Dec. 1979], p. 457.)

5. See **Key Diseases**, pages 427–434.

6. For important cultural differences in orientation to time, see note 3, page 386.

7. Spanish-speaking patients use a complicated system of diseases. In terms of their views about medicine, Hispanics fall into three categories. At one extreme is the conservative group, which retains strong social and cultural ties to its country of origin. Its members generally have the lowest incomes and educational levels; they prefer neighborhoods of dense Hispanic population where Spanish is predominant. They have strong faith in the traditional folk medical beliefs and practices, and magic and religion assume great importance in their world. At the other extreme is the highly assimilated group whose educational and income levels approach the medians of the total United States population. They prefer English to Spanish even in the home. Their faith in traditional cures is replaced by reliance on modern medicine. Magic and religion have little importance in their world. Most Hispanos, however, belong to the transitional group, composed of semiskilled or even skilled laborers who are often first- and second-generation Americans. Their cultural beliefs reflect a very heterogeneous mixture of traditional folk beliefs and Anglo-American traits.

Folk concepts of disease are strongly rooted in Hispanic society, dating back hundreds of years to four widely separated sources: medieval Spain, some American Indian tribes, Anglo folk medicine, and "scientific" medical sources. (See L. Saunders, *Cultural Differences and Medical Care*, New York: Russell Sage Foundation, 1954, p. 148.) An important characteristic of this belief system is its capacity to assimilate practices from various folk and "scientific" medical traditions.

Among the peoples of Latin American heritage, beliefs about health and illness have important sociocultural significance. Hispanos view the problems of health and illness as manifestations of closely linked physiologic *and* behavioral disturbance. This view permits them to make judgments about a disease and choices about the selection of practitioner. Although there are numerous syndromes of illness, health practitioners should be aware of disorders of the blood, disorders classified as obstructions of the genitourinary and gastrointestinal tracts, and strong emotional experiences linked with cardiac functioning. Another syndrome is related to the hot and cold theory of disease, which has been discussed elsewhere (see note 15, page 391; note 44, pages 394f; note 47, page 395.)

Disorders of the blood are often associated with behavioral concerns in Hispanic folk medicine. A major diagnostic tool of emergent illness is **la debilidad de la sangre** (weakness of the blood). The Hispano recognizes pale color, sallow skin, or weight loss as symptoms of weak blood. **Decaimiento** (feelings of malaise and low spirits) among adults is attributed to weak blood. Among children correct conduct and academic progress are considered to depend on qualities of the blood. (See L. Cohen, *Culture, Disease, and Stress among Latino Immigrants*, pp. 162–165.) Hispanos take vitamins, tonics, iron, and laxatives, all of which they purchase as over-the-counter medicine, for weaknesses of the blood.

Many of the illnesses that are associated with obstructions of the gastrointestinal and genitourinary tracts are folk diseases and are usually treated within the household or by a folk practitioner. (Digestive problems were part of the expected occurrences of daily life.) Many Hispanos test and share over-the-counter medicines, leftover prescriptions, and antibiotics brought from "home" by newly arrived friends and relatives. Often Hispanos medicate themselves without any understanding of the limitations or risks involved. Home remedies such as tea or oil with honey are often taken as complementary to drugstore medicines.

Many are concerned about cleansing the stomach and purifying the digestive and biliary juices. They feel that it is necessary to periodically purge the stomach and intestinal tract. **Empacho**, correctly termed **impacción**, is the recognized folk disease that results when the stomach is not "clean." **Empacho** is said to be a form of bowel obstruction. However, it applies to any stomach disorder, especially if gas is present. A large ball or knot in the stomach, which produces swelling or lumps in the legs, are symptoms of **empacho**. The disease is most common among children, but attacks adults as well. An herb tea made of mint, camomile and **epazote**, followed by a strong physic, cures the disease. **Empacho** may be caused by poor diet (too many starches) or by eating foods that are not easily tolerated. (See M. Clark, *Health in the Mexican-American Culture*, pp. 164f; A. Rubel, "Concepts of Disease in Mexican-American Culture," *American Anthropologist*, Vol. 62, No. 5 [1960], pp. 795-815.)

Diseases of the heart that were associated with strong emotional experience reflect a mixture of both folk and scientific medicine. Many Hispanos use the terminology of professional health care workers, such as **palpitaciones** (palpitations) and **presión alta** (high blood pressure), while retaining folk concepts of etiology and prevention (these symptoms are typically associated with nerves or anxiety, not the heart). These disorders are treated by physicians.

With regard to etiologic factors, many ethnomedical researchers follow Saunders, who classifies diseases by origin: empirical, magical, and psychological. Empirical or "natural" diseases are those in which a known external factor operates directly on the organism to produce the illness. Magical diseases are those in which the cause lies beyond empirical knowledge and cannot be verified easily. Psychological diseases are those in which a strong emotional experience causes the appearance of the disease symptoms (Saunders, *Cultural Differences and Medical Care*). Clark has grouped folk illness according to their origins: diseases of dislocation of internal organs (i.e., **caída de la mollera**), diseases of emotional origin (i.e., **susto**), diseases of magical origin (i.e., **mal ojo**), and a residual category containing **empacho** (M. Clark, *Health in the Mexican-American Culture*, pp. 163-183).

Caída de la mollera or **mollera caída**, "fallen fontanelle," occurs in infants. The symptoms are insomnia, loss of appetite, excessive crying, severe diarrhea, and vomiting. The baby may be feverish. A diagnosis is made by feeling the top of the baby's head to detect a depression of the anterior fontanelle. The child is treated by having the adult insert both thumbs into the infant's mouth and gently push upward on the palate. The baby may be held upside down by the ankles, allowing gravity to help push the fontanelle back into place. An alternative treatment utilizes suction. Yet another treatment places a poultice of herbs and raw eggs, or fresh soap shavings, over the fontanelle, in an attempt to "pull" the fontanelle up into place. Clinically this illness resembles dehydration and is usually due to some neglect of the child by the person in charge. (See C. Martínez and H. Martín, "Folk Diseases Among Urban Mexican-Americans," *JAMA*, Vol. 196, No. 2 [April 11, 1966], pp. 148; W. Holland, "Mexican-American Medical Beliefs: Science or Magic?" in Argüiro, ed., *Hispanic Culture and Health Care*, St Louis: C. V. Mosby, 1978, pp. 99-119.)

Common emotional illnesses of natural origin are **bilis** (anger, literally "bile") and **susto** or **espanto** (fright). **Bilis** has nothing to do with the bile produced by the gallbladder. Rather it is an illness to which adults are susceptible; it is caused by strong anger or **coraje**, which then produces an excess of yellow stomach bile. The symptoms are diarrhea, vomiting, sometimes a yellowish complexion, chronic fatigue, and acute nervous tension.

Herbal teas made of rosemary, camomile, and camphor leaf, or a combination of cassia bark, lemon shoots, cinnamon bark, toasted walnut, and whiskey, are among some of the recognized treatments. (See M. Clark, *Health in the Mexican-American Culture*, pp. 175-176; R. Adams and A. Rubel, "Sickness and Social Relations," *Handbook of Middle American Indians*, Vol. 6, Austin: University of Texas Press, 1967, p. 345.)

Susto, or spirit loss due to fright, is one of the most common forms of folk illness in all of Latin America. It is caused by any natural fright, such as almost being hit by a truck or being badly frightened by a snake. **Susto** occurs when an individual is unable to cope with personal experiences. **Espanto** is a more severe form of fright, generally attributed to an encounter with the supernatural, such as seeing a ghost. It should be noted that if a pregnant woman is **asustada** or **espantada** (frightened), her baby will be born with **susto** or **espanto**. (See J. Gillin, "Magical Fright," in *Hispanic Culture and Health Care*, pp. 152-170.)

The child who suffers from **susto** often has horrible nightmares about the fright that caused the illness and often cries, whines, has insomnia, loss of appetite, and is irritable. The adult suffering from this disease also shows similar symptoms: nightmares, general malaise, loss of interest in things, dyspnea, indigestion, palpitations, depression, and anorexia. The patient may develop sores on his body and experience great pain. Some patients have an irregular pulse. Some **curanderos** believe that fright can lead to heart trouble (a heart attack), peptic ulcers, and even mental retardation. (See A. Rubel, "The Epidemiology of Folk Illness: **Susto** in Hispanic America," *Ethnology*, Vol. 3 [1964], pp. 268–283; A. Rubel and C. O'Nell, "The Meaning of **Susto** [Magical Fright]," paper presented at the XLI International Congress of Americanists, Mexico City, 1974, p. 6.)

Advanced fright sickness is known as **susto pasado**. Its symptoms are prolonged exhaustion and coughing, in addition to the above-mentioned symptoms.

Margaret Clark describes a popular cure that uses two branches of sweet pepper trees and incantations by a **curandero** (*Health in the Mexican-American Culture*, p. 177). The **curandero**, as part of the cure, spends a lot of time with the patient, familiarizing himself with the social and familial problems that the patient is experiencing. Then, the **curandero** is able to provide not only a ritual cure, but an emotional support system to help overcome the patient's fear. William Holland describes a different cure, which consists of inserting a piece of garlic into the anus on nine consecutive nights, accompanied by prayers (see Holland, "Mexican-American Medical Beliefs," p. 105.)

Mal ojo, or "evil eye," is another ailment that afflicts children. It has a magical origin and occurs in children to whom affectionate overtures have been made, without physical contact. The possessor of the evil eye projects evil into whomever or whatever he or she admires. Touching the person or thing removes the harmful force of the **mal ojo** according to William Madsen (*Mexican-Americans of South Texas*, New York: Holt, Rinehart, & Winston, 1964, p. 76). Most Hispanos touch a child's head after admiring the child's beauty. Wearing a red ribbon or red clothes usually protects susceptible individuals from the damaging forces of the evil eye. (See P. Poma, "Hispanos," p. 456.) The symptoms of **mal ojo** include vomiting, listlessness, excessive crying, trembling, aches and pains, and even rashes.

Hechicería, or "bewitchment," describes any chronic or unexplained illness. Symptoms include strange, erratic behavior, hallucinations, constant fear, nervousness, and insomnia. (See David Werner, *Donde no hay doctor*, 4th ed., México: Editorial Pax-México, 1980, p. 5.)

Demencia, or "insanity," is considered an illness brought about by witchcraft. A witch casts an evil element into the **aire** (air), directed at a susceptible individual. Persons suffering from **demencia** exhibit amnesia, guilt or persecution complexes, and hallucinations. (See M. Kay, "Health and Illness in a Mexican American Barrio," in Spicers, ed., *Ethnic Medicine in the Southwest*, Arizona: University of Arizona, 1977, p. 140.)

Visiones, or "visions," is a milder mental disturbance caused by witches. The patient sees visions of the witch and his client, who often leave their teeth marks or scratches on the patient's body. (See A. Kiev, *Curanderismo*, New York: Free Press, 1968, p. 98.)

Miedo, or "fear," is a still milder mental disturbance caused by witches. The patient imagines that he sees frightful things that "normal" people cannot see. (See P. Poma, "Hispanos," p. 455.)

Melarchic(h)o, which corresponds to a reactive depression, is an illness that occurs following the death of a loved one. Symptoms include tearfulness, anorexia, insomnia, and listlessness. (See A. Kiev, *Curanderismo*, p. 95.)

Mal aire, or "bad air," is thought to be the result of evil spirits that dwell in the air, particularly the night air, and have the power to cause the victim to fall ill. Night air, **sereno**, is especially dangerous to children. It frequently causes pus to form in a baby's eyes or make them run. Symptoms of **mal aire** include back pain, muscle contractions, muscle paralysis. Pneumonia may ensue, as may tuberculosis. The treatment involves eliminating the bad air by massage or by cupping. (See P. Poma, "Hispanos," p. 456.)

Aire, or "air," applies to earaches, colds, stiff necks, headaches, and even dizziness. **Aire** occurs when air enters the body through one of its openings. Severe cases of **aire** often produce paralysis, twisted mouth, or some form of mental incapacity. (See R. Currier, "The Hot–Cold Syndrome and Symbolic Balance in Mexican and Spanish-American Folk Medicine," *Ethnology*, Vol. 5 (1966), pp. 251–263.)

Congestion is another folk-defined disease. It is a vulgar term that applies equally to a headache, a pain in the chest, a stomachache, or general body aches. It also applies to food poisoning, allergic reactions, and breathing problems—asthma, pneumonia, and obstructions of the throat. It has even been used to refer to heart attacks, convulsions, seizures, tetanus, meningitis, polio, and emboli.

Congestión is caused by eating the "wrong" food, by a cold, or by not following the prescribed post-partum **dieta** (see note 47, p. 395). (See D. Werner, *Donde no hay doctor*, p. 23.)

Latido, or "palpitations of the heart," is caused by abstaining from food for a long time. In its advanced stages this serious, often fatal disease is accompanied by high fever, cough, even blood-tinged sputum. It is characterized by severe emaciation, which makes it possible to feel the normal pulsation of the abdominal aorta upon deep palpitation. (See M. Clark, *Health in the Mexican-American Culture*, p. 178.) Ralph Beals (*Cheran: A Sierra Tarascan Village*, Washington, D.C.: Publications of the Institute of Social Anthropology, 1946) reported that "the disease may be caused if the person arrives somewhere very agitated and drinks cold water or something cold, **fresca**."

Fiebre, or "fever," technically refers to an elevation of body temperature to a point higher than normal. In rural areas, **fiebre** refers to a number of illnesses that cause a rise in body temperature: malaria, typhoid fever, typhus, hepatitis, pneumonia, rheumatic fever, postpartum fever, and brucellosis. (See D. Werner, *Donde no hay doctor*, pp. 26–27.)

Bolitas, or "little balls" (lumps) that occur in the extremities, are considered to be dislocated nerves. They are treated with massage or physical manipulation.

Chipil (literally "cry-baby") occurs when a nursing mother becomes pregnant before weaning her infant. The contaminated milk causes digestive disturbances and anger in the child, who often shows an inability to suck and cries excessively. Herbal teas and affection are the best cure. (See R. Currier, "The Hot–Cold Syndrome," p. 259; W. Madsen, *Mexican-Americans*, p. 75.)

Nervios, or "nerves," is an ailment believed to be caused by sexual perversions such as fellatio and cunnilingus, as well as by premature ejaculation. (See A. Kiev, *Curanderismo*, p. 94.)

Dolor de ijar, or "loin pain," occurs in women in the stomach, abdomen, or waist. Among the causes of this disease are urinary tract infections, ovarian or cervical cysts, appendicitis, or severe bowel cramps. (See D. Werner, *Donde no hay doctor*, p. 22.)

Dolor de costado, or "side pain," refers to any passing pain that comes on suddenly. In rural areas this may refer to appendicitis, gallbladder problems, tuberculosis, or a liver involvement due to amebic dysentery. (See M. Clark, *Health in the Mexican-American Culture*, p. 180; and D. Werner, *Donde no hay doctor*, p. 28.)

The most common techniques of curing consist of "cupping" (**ventosas**), massage (**sobadas**), oral administration of herb teas, topical application of herbs, oils, liniments, the use of purges, recitation of prayer, and floral offerings either to God or the saints. Any or all of these techniques can be used to treat a particular disease.

8. Depending on the degree of acculturation, the typical Hispano uses a variety of curing patterns. Whether rural or urban, many Hispanos work at low-level, low-income jobs, requiring a minimum of specialized skills or education. There are many Hispanic doctors, dentists, and attorneys, but they usually assume the general social class characteristics of the dominant Anglo society.

Hispanos look to kin, friends, and employers for consultative and prescriptive advice. Women treat most minor ailments for their family and are frequently consulted by neighbors as "home medical specialists." For folk diseases a folk practitioner is frequently sought. One such specialist is the **curandero** (see note 6, p. 194). Another is the **sobador(a)**, a folk practitioner who is adept at massage. For all serious illnesses—gynecologic and genitourinary problems, persistent digestive disorders, problems thought to be of the heart and blood—a medical specialist is generally consulted. (See L. Cohen, *Culture, Disease, and Stress among Latino Immigrants*, pp. 136–140.) Curing often draws on a wide range of treatment sources, including patent remedies, herbs, over-the-counter medicines, and prescription medicines.

A widespread Hispanic custom exists of borrowing prescriptions proven effective for relatives and friends, as well as using leftover medicines for symptoms that seem similar. (See V. G. de Pineda, *La medicina popular en Colombia*, Bogotá: Universidad Nacional de Colombia, Monografías Socio-lógicas, Vol. 8 [Oct. 1961], pp. 54–55.) Friends and relatives returning from "back home" replenish supplies of antibiotics and other drugs administered only by physician's prescription in the United States, but sold readily over-the-counter elsewhere. (See L. Cohen, *Culture, Disease, and Stress*, pp. 171–177.)

Weaver summarizes the findings of many ethnomedical investigations about the Hispanic illness referral systems. Folk curers are consulted only after the resources of the family have been exhausted. If folk curers are consulted, it is always before official scientific doctors. The physician is consulted only after the folk curer fails. (See T. Weaver, "Use of Hypothetical Situations in a Study of Spanish-American Illness Referral Systems," *Human Organization*, Vol. 29, No. 2 [1970], pp. 140–154; also J. Kreisman, "The **Curandero's** Apprentice: A Therapeutic Integration of Folk and Medical Healing," *American Journal of Psychiatry*, Vol. 132, No. 1 [Jan. 1975], pp. 81–83.)

This combined use of household curing and physicians may be partly related to financial circumstances. When it becomes economically possible for Hispanos living in the United States to get care from health facilities and medical institutions, they quickly avail themselves of this care. (See M. Kay, "Health and Illness," p. 164; W. Gliebe and L. Malley, "Use of the Health Care Delivery System by Urban Mexican-Americans in Ohio," *Public Health Reports*, Vol. 94, No. 3 [May, June, 1979], pp. 226–230.)

9. See Chapter 9 for a fuller list of Key Diseases. In order to elicit the best responses and build patient trust, before beginning either the medical history or the physical, it is often helpful to request the Hispanic patient's permission to ask personal questions and to examine him/her. This display of courtesy requires professionals to use the phrases **Con su permiso** (*With your permission*) and **Sin querer ser indiscreto(-a)** . . . (*Without wanting to be indiscreet* . . .).

10. In rural areas Hispanics often use the word **cáncer** to refer to any serious skin infection, especially infected wounds or gangrene. The term **lepra** refers to any sore that spreads on the skin. This frequently causes confusion for health care personnel. Among the diseases that are called **lepra** are impetigo, boils, allergic skin reactions, scabies, insect bites, skin ulcers, chronic sores, skin cancer, and even skin TB or leprosy.

11. See Chapter 2, pages 137–138.

12. In some places the literal translations, **está caliente** and **está frío** are vulgar and have sexual connotations.

13. **Constipado(-a)** also can be used. It means either to have a cold or to be constipated.

14. When a person sneezes, Spanish-speaking people often say "**¡Jesús!**" The phrase originated in the Middle Ages as a supplication for divine help in time of trouble.

15. Hispanos regard pregnancy and childbirth as a woman's normal obligation. When pregnant, a woman may be **enferma con niño** (ill with child); when she delivers, **se sana** (she is healed) (M. Kay, "Health and Illness," p. 155). Hispanic women generally do not have early prenatal medical help unless they experience complications such as elevated blood pressure, kidney disease, or prolonged dizziness and nausea. This is because they look to the female members of their family for advice.

Much of a pregnant woman's behavior is culturally prescribed to assure an easy birth. Pregnancy is thought to be a dangerous time for the fetus, and so the pregnant woman avoids distress whenever possible. Hispanic women may be careful to avoid "hot" foods or medication during this period in order to prevent her baby from being born with an "irritation" (a rash or red skin). These women may "refresh" themselves with "cool" medicines such as milk of magnesia or commercial antacids, especially during the first and second trimesters. (See A. Harwood, "Hot Cold Theory of Disease," *JAMA*, Vol. 216, No. 7 [May, 1971] p. 1157.) Iron tablets, calcium pills, and other essential medicines are often shunned by pregnant women as a consequence of the avoidance of "hot" substances during pregnancy. These women should be encouraged to "neutralize" these needed medicines with fruit juice or herb tea, which are considered "cold." (See N. Galli, "The Influence of Cultural Heritage on the Health Status of Puerto Ricans," *Journal of School Health*, Vol. XLV, No. 1 [Jan., 1975], p. 13.) Traditional beliefs suggest that the mother-to-be not gain too much weight, lest the baby be too big, or "stick" to the sides of the womb, and need to be delivered with instruments. It is felt that if the mother sleeps too much, the baby will also "stick" to the uterus. Finally, sexual activity is encouraged until labor is imminent "to keep the birth canal lubricated" (Kay, "Health and Illness," p. 154). Massages and castor oil purges become a regular part of the pregnancy, increasing in frequency toward the last stages. Hispanic women in general tend to be "embarrassed" by the final months of pregnancy and prefer the privacy of their homes, frequently attempting to conceal their condition.

Hispanic women often prefer home deliveries to hospital ones. This is in part attributed to the presence of the **partera**, or midwife, who stays by the side of the new mother from the beginning of labor until after delivery and administers tea, gives oil massages for relaxation, and shows warm concern. Recent licensing requirements in the southwestern United States have resulted in a decline of this type of practitioner who had had an important role in the health of Spanish-speaking women. (See M. Kay, "Health and Illness," p. 152.)

A Mexican tradition involves rubbing the new mother's back with warm olive oil and powdered sulphur in order to assure healthy breasts and a good milk supply. It is believed that the colostrum is not good for the baby, and babies are given olive oil or castor oil, to promote evacuation. Nursing is encouraged, and many feel that bottle feeding causes children to suffer from stomach trouble later in life. Most babies, however, are soon given formula during the day and only nursed at night, often past a year of age. (If the pediatrician puts the baby on a formula that contains "hot" evaporated milk as a base, many mothers will put their baby on "cold" whole milk or, after feeding the baby formula, "refresh" the child's stomach with various cool foods, like weak tea, barley water, or magnesium carbonate. This often is a source of diarrhea in infants because some of these substances act as diuretics.) (See Harwood, "Hot-Cold Theory," p. 1155–1156; Kay, "Health and Illness," p. 156.)

16. Many Hispanics believe that syphilis comes from mere physical contact.

17. Persons of Spanish descent frequently have names that, upon first glance, seem confusing to English-speaking Americans. Often they have several given names or **nombres de pila (nombres de bautismo)**. Moreover, both paternal and maternal surnames are retained. The paternal surname precedes the maternal one. Neither is ever considered to be a middle name. Only in the case of an illegitimate child is the maternal surname alone used. Sometimes these family names are connected by the conjunction **y** (and), or by a hyphen; generally they are not. Occasionally, the maternal family name is abbreviated, in which case the first initial of the mother's last name follows the father's last name. In cases where the paternal family name is extremely common (the Spanish equivalent of "Smith" or "Jones") it is either abbreviated or omitted. Thus, in the case of Jaime José Alfredo Fernández y García, the first three names are given names, Fernández is the surname of the father, and García is the surname of the mother.

In addition, the following variations may be found: Jaime José Alfredo Fernández García; Jaime José Alfredo Fernández G.; Jaime José Alfredo Fernández; Jaime José Alfredo F. García; Jaime José Alfredo García; Jaime José Alfredo Fernández-García.

A Spanish woman upon her marriage drops her mother's maiden name and replaces it with that of her husband, prefixed by **de**. Thus, María Fernández y Montero becomes María Fernández de González upon her marriage to Juan Carlos González y Ortiz. Should her husband die, she is known as María Fernández Vda. de González. (**Vda.** = **viuda** = widow)

A number of Spanish surnames include the preposition **de**, with or without a definite article, **el**, etc. At one time the preposition **de** indicated nobility, but no such distinction is made now and the use of **de** is optional. However, some families still retain it as part of the surname: del Campo, de la Torre, de la Rosa.

Many famous people, for somewhat diverse reasons, use only one family name. The great Spanish writer Benito Pérez Galdós is known to most as Galdós. Federico García Lorca also retained his maternal name, and is best known as Lorca. However, Jacinto Benavente y Martínez, Miguel de Unamuno y Jugo, and Miguel de Cervantes Saavedra are all known by their paternal surname.

Proper alphabetizing of Spanish surnames requires knowledge of the differences between the English and Spanish alphabets, the former having 26 letters, the latter, 30. The digraphs **ch, ll, ñ,** and **rr,** are considered independent letters, listed after **c, l,** and **n,** respectively.

Surnames precede proper names. Compound surnames are arranged according to the first surname. For those names with a lower case **de, del, de la** or **de los,** these are placed after the name: Ríos, Fernando de los. Upper-case prepositions, which generally indicate surnames of French, Italian, or Portuguese origin, precede the surname: Da Rosa, Carlos. Names of married women are arranged according to the maiden name.

There are many compound first names: Juan Carlos, María Rosa, José Antonio. Often both names are used. The name **María** is especially frequent in compound names honoring the Virgin Mary. Girls bearing one of these compound names are usually known by the latter part of the compound: María de la Concepción = Concepción; María de la Luz = Luz. *María* is frequently used as the second part in compound male names (as are *Jesús* and *Jesús María*): José María, Ramón María, Tomás María.

Nicknames are used in Spanish as in English and may be quite different from the original name: Dolores = Lola; Francisco = Paco; José = Pepe.

18. See page 203.

19. Local telephone numbers in many Spanish-speaking countries are composed of between two and seven digits: Costa Rica—6 digits; El Salvador—6 digits; Guatemala—2-6 digits; Philippines—4-7 digits; Spain—6-7 digits; Venezuela—4-6 digits.

Inhabitants tend to express their telephone numbers in groups of twos. Thus, 230695 > 23-06-95. If the telephone number contains an odd number of digits, the first number is given separately whereas the remaining digits are grouped in twos: 7123445 > 7-12-34-45.

Some Spanish-speakers adopt the U.S. custom of expressing all digits as units numbers: 525-4123 > 5-2-5-4-1-2-3.

20. In Spanish-speaking countries, it is customary to celebrate both one's birthday and one's saint's day, the **día de su santo**, the day of the saint after whom one is named.

21. See **Occupations**, pages 455–457.

22. See **Religions**, pages 454–455.

23. See **Nationalities**, page 455.

24. Hispanics view being able "to hold one's liquor" as a highly masculine virtue. Hispanic society places strict restraints and sanctions on excessive alcohol consumption and inebriation. This apparently accounts for the low rate of alcoholism among the unacculturated Hispanics, especially the Mexican-Americans, and the higher rates among those who are actively seeking to reject the ethnic ways of the past and adopt "American" ways. (See Ari Kiev, *Curanderismo: Mexican-American Folk Psychiatry*. New York: The Free Press, 1968, p. 100.)

25. See **Selected Drug Abuse Vocabulary**, pp. 441–444.

26. In Spain **el piso bajo** or **planta baja** is the ground floor, **el piso principal** is the first floor, and **el primer piso** usually corresponds to the second or third floor in the United States. In Spanish America, however, floors are usually counted the way they are in the United States.

27. This expression means to physically relax; in New Mexico **relájese** is not used because it means "get embarrassed."

28. Remember, many Spanish-speaking people use centigrade temperatures. See pages 204f. for a conversion table.

29. Hispanics may be hesitant to have their children examined too often rectally. This combined with an excessive use of enemas, they worry, may incline a child toward homosexuality. Some believe that masturbation leads to a decrease in strength, and often to insanity. Insanity may also be caused by inadequate sexual gratification. (Excessive sexual gratification deteriorates the nerves.) Pent-up sexual energy may lead to epilepsy.

30. This standard American custom of expecting the patient and physician to make important medical decisions often presents problems for some Hispanic communities, where illness as well as other aspects of daily living involves family or group decisions. Customarily the sick individual consults relatives, both in the United States and in their country of origin, **compadres** (the godparents of their children), friends, and employers before medical consultation. Long-distance consultations are done with the hope of obtaining advice from both worlds, and especially to fill gaps that Hispanos perceive to exist in treatment that they experience in the United States. Their network of consultants is so chosen because it is the family and friends who must help provide funds and services when the individual is too ill to perform normal daily obligations.

Hispanos express confidence in the physician who diagnoses their complaints through a physical examination, x-rays, or other lab work. Those who prescribe without a physical examination or other confirming indicators are criticized by Hispanos. (See L. Cohen, *Culture, Disease, and Stress Among Latino Immigrants*, pp. 178–179.) When the health-care personnel make recommendations such as "You need an operation," the Hispanic patient must consult with those who would have to relieve him or her of daily tasks, and who would have to provide the money, in the case of an adult. Decisions concerning children are also group decisions.

When pressed for immediate decisions, the Hispano often agrees in name only in order to be courteous and to avoid dissention. If, upon family consultation, there is disagreement, appointments are broken. Surgical procedures in particular, are frequently regarded as harmful, dangerous, and unnecessary.

31. See footnote 7, pages 387f.

32. In the southwestern part of the United States, breakfast is often **almuerzo**, lunch is **comida de mediodía**.

33. This is directed to a third party, rather than to the patient.

34. See **Drug Related Vocabulary**, page 441.

35. See **Colors**, page 454.

36. Marijuana makes the eyes appear this way.

37. Opiates (heroin and opium) or downers (amytal, numbutal) constrict pupils. Stimulants or uppers (amphetamines, bennies, cocaine, dexies, whites, etc.) dilate the pupils.

38. There is a widespread Mexican belief that a person must have a large quantity of blood in order to preserve his health, that he will become ill even if he loses a small quantity. "Loss of blood for any reason, even in the small quantity necessary for laboratory tests, is thought to have a weakening effect, particularly in males, whose sexual vigor is thereby believed impaired." (Lyle Saunders, *Cultural Differences and Medical Care*, p. 147.)

39. **Poner** is used to express the idea of putting something into a person, on a specific part of him, or under him. **Dar** is used with something for the person to take (see page 52).

40. **Respirar**—to breathe (normal process of respiration).
    Aspirar—to breathe in, inhale, breathe deeply.

41. See page 455 for listing of occupations.

42. See section on foods, page 457.

43. It might be helpful if hospitals made "Hispanic" foods more readily available to those Hispanic patients who are not on a restricted diet. Serving Spanish rice, pinto beans, tortillas, and hot chili sauce, for example, would liven the taste for these patients.

44. Health workers who deal with nutritional problems must understand theories underlying the diets of their patients; they should recommend the use of different proportions of foods already in the diet of the people rather than encourage complete dietary changes. During times of illness, Hispanos rely greatly on diet modification. (Most of the folk illnesses affect the gastrointestinal tract.) Many illnesses are directly attributed to imbalances of "hot" and "cold" foods. The theory of "hot" and "cold" is one of the most prevalent medical beliefs in Latin America, dating back to the sixteenth-century. The Spaniards subscribed to the Hippocratic theory of a healthy balance between "hot" and "cold" body essences; health maintenance required the proper mixture of hot and cold foods, just as good health required the proper mixture of the hot and cold body humours. (See G. Foster, "Relationships Between Spanish and Spanish-American Folk Medicine," *Journal of American Folklore*, Vol. 66, No. 261 [1953], pp. 201–217; G. Foster & J. Rowe, "Suggestions for Field Recording of Information on the Hippocratic Classification of Diseases and Remedies," in *Kroeber Anthropological Society Papers*, Vol. V [1951], pp. 1–3.) This theory arbitrarily assigned "hot" and "cold" qualities to foods; the thermal state in which foods and herbal remedies are taken is not important. Temperature is the consideration in labeling an illness or body condition "hot" (diarrhea, rashes, ulcers, etc.) or "cold" (arthritis, menstrual periods, common colds, etc.). New foods and drugs are incorporated into the system according to the effect they have on the body. Penicillin often seems to cause a rash ("hot")

and is thus considered "hot." Calcium that might cause muscular spasms would be considered "cold" (A. Harwood, "Hot–Cold Theory of Disease," p. 1154). This belief in hot and cold is gradually becoming modified so that it is less at odds with "modern" scientific ideas—that is, alcohol rubs ("cold") or "cool" baths to reduce high fevers.

Today most people know nothing about hot/cold diseases and hot/cold herbs. Although they often talk about the heat and coldness of foods, medicines, or body states, people now think in terms of actual temperature of foods, rather than in terms of qualities of hot and cold. There is currently a decrease in the therapeutic use of foods to treat hot and cold disorders. These disorders are now often treated with herbal remedies or with topical applications, which either cool or warm the affected area. (See M. Kay, "Health and Illness," pp. 162f; C. Martínez and H. Martín, "Folk Diseases among Mexican-Americans," pp. 161–164; N. Galli, "Influence of Cultural Heritage," pp. 12–13.)

45. Many Hispanic women may not know the word **vagina**. They may use **las partes privadas**, **verijas**, or some similar expression. They may not be too aware of what is occurring in **las partes privadas** because it is not considered "nice" to know.

46. **Pujar**—to push (as in labor or in evacuating the bowels or bladder).

   Empujar—to push, bring (external) pressure on (something).

47. In many parts of Latin America, but especially in Mexico, women strongly believe in the observance of the postpartum **cuarentena dieta**, which is thought to restore the mother to "normal health." Today in the United States, only those young women who are directly under their mother's or mother-in-law's supervision follow all customs of **la dieta**. This is the forty-day convalescence period following delivery during which there is a prolonged period in bed, much freedom from household responsibilities, and abstention from sexual intercourse.

   Modern women find it difficult to observe *all* of the prohibitions and precautions, which in some ways include the same taboos observed during menstruation, such as avoiding bathing and eating foods that are "too acid," or "cool." Many women avoid cool foods after delivery on the grounds that they "impede the blood flow and the emptying of the uterus." To help prevent this blockage, which many once believed caused nervousness or even insanity, women take "hot" substances to strengthen the womb. One such tonic is made of chocolate, garlic, cinnamon, rue, rum, and pieces of cheese. (See A. Harwood, "Hot and Cold Theory of Disease," pp. 1153–1158; N. Galli, "The Influence of Cultural Heritage," pp. 10–16.) Postpartum Hispanic patients frequently complain that the foods on their hospital trays are either "too hot" or "too cold." If dieticians could substitute more familiar choices for these patients, or at least serve these food "taboos" less often, these mothers would not be forced either to violate their food prohibitions or to go hungry. With regard to bathing, most women who have had their babies in the hospital have become used to bathing within a few hours after delivery. There are still some who "because my mother so accustomed me" will go into the shower room, turn on the water, but avoid getting wet. Thus they satisfy both the hospital staff and their own socio-cultural pressures (M. Kay, "Health and Illness," p. 155).

48. Attitudes about sex and sexuality are difficult to discuss. There are many prudish ideas prevalent, as well as considerable embarrassment. In addition, Hispanos use many euphemisms and local **modismos** (idiomatic expressions). Therefore, it might be helpful to have a native speaker present for this type of discussion. It is important that the health-care worker and the patient be of the same sex, because of the modesty and embarrassment of most Hispanic women.

49. Some men object to their wives using contraceptives because they think that it robs them of their "male authority." These men believe that birth control, like any other sexual matter, lies within the man's authority to determine time, form, and frequency of sexual relations. (See N. Galli, "The Influence of Cultural Heritage," pp. 10–16.)

50. Many Latin cultures believe that masturbation can lead to a decrease in strength, cause depression, and possibly even some form of insanity.

51. There are still many myths in the Hispanic culture. Some women believe that washing their hair during menstruation may lead to death, for example.

52. According to the Hispanic culture, women who have just given birth should abstain from having sexual relations for a 40-day period, the **cuarentena**. This is not, however, always completely adhered to. (See footnote 47.)

53. Because of the tendency toward excessive modesty and reluctance to touch oneself, many Hispanic women are hesitant to touch themselves internally as is necessary on a weekly basis when using an IUD.

54. Many Hispanic women have trouble using the diaphragm because they are inhibited about touching the genital area. It is difficult for them to check the IUD on a weekly basis, but impossible for them to insert one or two fingers into the vagina to feel that the cervix is covered properly by a diaphragm both before and after intercourse.

55. Many Hispanic women follow the practice of vaginal douching, common in folk medicine everywhere. A douche is indicated after each menstrual cycle and following postpartum bleeding. A homemade solution of herbs (**chicura**, **tlachichinole**, **damiana**, or rue) may be used. If bleeding is heavy, a douche is made from a solution of boiled nut shells or leaves. (See M. Kay, "Health and Illness," p. 153.)

CHAPTER

Conversations for Administrative Personnel

Conversaciones para personal administrativo

INFORMATION FOR ADMISSION

INFORMACION PARA ADMISION

1. What is the patient's complete and correct name?[1]
   Dígame el nombre completo y correcto del (de la) paciente.
   ¿Cómo se llama el (la) paciente?

2. What is the address and zip code of the patient?
   ¿Cuál es la dirección y la zona postal del (de la) paciente?

3. What is your former address?
   ¿Dónde vivía antes?

4. Is there a telephone?
   ¿Hay teléfono?

5. What is the patient's telephone number?
   ¿Cuál es el número de teléfono del (de la) paciente?

6. What is the sex of the patient?
   ¿Cuál es el sexo del (de la) paciente?

7. To what race does the patient belong?[2]
   ¿A qué raza pertenece el (la) paciente?

8. How old is the patient?
   ¿Qué edad tiene el (la) paciente?
   ¿Cuántos años tiene el (la) paciente?

9. On what day, month, and year was the patient born?
   ¿En qué día, mes y año nació el (la) paciente?

10. Where was the patient born?
    ¿(En) dónde nació el (la) paciente?

11. Tell me the name of the town, the state, and the country.
    Dígame el nombre del pueblo, del estado y del país.

12. How long have you been in the United States?
    ¿Desde cuándo está Vd. en los Estados Unidos?

13. What is the patient's religion?[3]
    ¿Cuál es la religión del (de la) paciente?

14. What is the patient's marital status?
    ¿Qué es su estado civil?

15. If married, what is the spouse's name?
    Si es casado (casada), ¿cómo se llama la esposa (el esposo)?

16. What kind of work does the patient do?[4]
 ¿Qué clase de trabajo hace el (la) paciente?
 ¿Cuál es su ocupación?
 ¿En qué se ocupa el (la) paciente?

17. What is the name of the patient's employer or the responsible party?
 ¿Cómo se llama el patrón del (de la) paciente o el responsable?

18. What is the address of that employer?
 ¿Cuál es la dirección de ese patrón?

19. What is the telephone number there?
 ¿Cuál es el número de teléfono allí?

20. Of what country is the patient a citizen?
 ¿De qué país es el (la) paciente ciudadano (ciudadana)?
 ¿Cuál es su ciudadanía?

21. What is the name of the patient's nearest relative?
 ¿Cómo se llama el pariente más cercano al (a la) paciente?

22. What is his/her address?[5]
 ¿Cuál es su dirección?

23. What is his/her telephone number?[6]
 ¿Cuál es su número de teléfono?

24. What is the relationship with the patient?
 ¿Qué parentesco tiene con el (la) paciente?
 ¿Qué es la relación entre ellos?

25. What is the patient's social security number?[7]
 ¿Cuál es el número de la tarjeta de seguro social del (de la) paciente?

26. To whom shall the bill be sent?
 ¿A quién debemos mandar la cuenta?

27. What is the address and zip code of this person?
 ¿Cuál es la dirección y zona postal de esta persona?

28. When was the patient admitted to the hospital?
 ¿Cuándo fue admitido el paciente (admitida la paciente) al hospital?
 ¿Cuándo ingresó el (la) paciente al hospital?

29. What was the time?
 ¿Qué hora era?

30. When was the patient discharged?
 ¿A qué hora se le dieron de alta al (a la) paciente?

31. Is this his/her first time in the hospital?
 ¿Es ésta la primera vez en el hospital?

32. Was the patient admitted to the hospital within the last six months?
 ¿Tuvo el (la) paciente admisión previa al hospital dentro de los últimos seis meses?
 ¿Fue admitido el paciente (admitida la paciente) al hospital dentro de los últimos seis meses?

33. Does the patient have Blue Cross/Blue Shield?
    ¿Tiene el (la) paciente Blue Cross o Blue Shield?

34. What is the certificate and group number of the patient's Blue Cross?
    ¿Cuál es el número del certificado y del grupo de la Blue Cross del (de la) paciente?

35. What is the name of the policyholder?
    ¿Cómo se llama el tenedor de la póliza?

36. What is the sex of the policyholder?
    ¿Cuál es el sexo del poseedor de la póliza?

37. What is the patient's relation to the policyholder?
    ¿Qué es la relación entre el (la) paciente y el asegurado (la asegurada)?

38. What is the social security number of the policyholder?
    ¿Cuál es el número de la tarjeta de seguro social del tenedor de la póliza?

39. Does the patient have other medical, hospitalization, or health insurance?
    ¿Tiene el (la) paciente algún otro seguro médico, de hospital o de enfermedad?

40. What is the name of his/her insurance company (companies)?
    ¿Cuál es el nombre de su(s) aseguranza(s)?
    ¿Cómo se llama(n) la(s) empresa(s) con que está asegurado (asegurada)?

41. What is the insurance policy number?
    ¿Cuál es el número de su póliza de seguros?

42. What is the name of the policyholder?
    ¿Cómo se llama el tenedor de esta póliza?

43. What is the name of the policyholder's employer?
    ¿Cómo se llama el patrón del tenedor de esta póliza?

44. What is the employer's address?
    ¿Cuál es la dirección del patrón?

45. Was the patient admitted because of an accident?
    ¿Se le admitieron al (a la) paciente a causa de un accidente?

46. When did the accident happen?
    ¿Cuándo ocurrió el accidente?

47. Where did the accident happen?
    ¿Dónde ocurrió el accidente?

48. Was the patient admitted from a general hospital?
    ¿Ingresó el (la) paciente de un hospital general?

49. From home?
    ¿De casa?

50. From an extended-care facility?
    ¿De una institución de cuidado prolongado?

51. What was the admission diagnosis?
¿Cuál fue el diagnóstico al ingresar?

52. Is the condition due to injury or sickness arising from the patient's employment?
¿Es la condición debida a una herida o enfermedad que proviene del empleo del (de la) paciente?

53. If "yes," what is the name and address of the employer?
Si lo es, dígame el nombre y la dirección del patrono.

54. Does the patient want a private room?
¿Desea el (la) paciente un cuarto privado (individual)?

55. A semiprivate room?
¿Un cuarto semiprivado (doble)?

56. A ward?
¿Una crujía (una sala de los enfermos)?

57. What is the name and address of the patient's physician?
Dígame el nombre y la dirección del médico del (de la) paciente.

58. Whom shall we notify in case of emergency?
¿A quién se notifica en caso de emergencia?
¿A quién podemos notificar en caso de emergencia?

59. Is this person a relative? a friend? a neighbor?
¿Es un pariente? ¿amigo? ¿vecino?

60. Where does this person live?
¿Dónde vive esta persona?

61. What is his telephone number?
¿Cuál es el número de su teléfono?

62. Does the patient authorize release of information requested on this form by the above-named hospital?
¿Autoriza el (la) paciente un descargo de la información contenida en este informe por el hospital ya nombrado?

63. Does the patient authorize payment directly to the above-named hospital of any benefits payable in this case, realizing that the patient shall be responsible for the charges not covered?
¿Autoriza el (la) paciente el pago de todos los beneficios aplicables en este caso directamente al susodicho hospital, dándose cuenta de que hay que pagar lo que no paga el seguro?

64. Does the patient consent to and authorize all treatments, surgical procedures, and administration of all anesthetics that in the judgment of his/her physician may be considered necessary for the diagnosis or treatment of this case while a patient in _____ hospital?
¿Da el (la) paciente su consentimiento y autorización para todos los tratamientos, procedimientos quirúrgicos y administración de todas anestesias que crea necesarios su médico para el diagnóstico o tratamiento de este caso mientras estar paciente en _____ hospital?

EMERGENCY ROOM REPORT

INFORME DE LA SALA DE EMERGENCIA

1. Are you the patient?[8]
   ¿Es Vd. el paciente?
   ¿Es Vd. la paciente?

2. What is your name?
   Cómo se llama Vd.?
   Dígame su nombre completo y correcto.

3. What is your last (surname) name?[9]
   ¿Cuál es su apellido?

4. How is it spelled?
   ¿Cómo se deletrea?

5. What is your first name?
   ¿Cuál es su primer nombre?
   ¿Cuál es su nombre de bautismo?

6. What is your middle initial?
   ¿Cuál es su segunda inicial?

7. What is your maiden name?
   ¿Cuál es su nombre de soltera?

8. What is your home telephone number?[10]
   ¿Qué es el número de teléfono de su casa?

9. What is your address?[11]
   ¿Cuál es su dirección?
   ¿Dónde vive Vd.?

10. What is your zip code?
    ¿Cuál es su zona postal?

11. What is the name of your nearest relative?
    ¿Cómo se llama su pariente más cercano (cercana)?

12. What is the relationship with you?
    ¿Qué parentesco tiene con Vd.?
    ¿Qué es la relación entre Vds.?

13. How is she/he related to you?
    ¿Qué es de Vd.?

14. Where does she/he live?
    ¿Dónde vive?

15. What is the zip code there?
    ¿Cuál es la zona postal allí?

16. What is her/his telephone number?
    ¿Qué es su número de teléfono?

17. How old are you?
    ¿Qué edad tiene Vd.?
    ¿Cuántos años tiene Vd.?

18. On what day, month, and year were you born?
    ¿En qué día, mes y año nació Vd.?

19. Where were you born?
    ¿(En) dónde nació Vd.?

20. What is your race?[12]
    ¿A qué raza pertenece Vd.?

21. What is your marital status?
    ¿Qué es su estado civil?

22. Are you married?
    ¿Es Vd. casado (casada)?

23. Are you divorced?
    ¿Es Vd. divorciado (divorciada)?

24. Are you single?
    ¿Es Vd. soltero (soltera)?

25. Are you a widow(er)?
    ¿Es Vd. viudo (viuda)?

26. Are you separated?
    ¿Es Vd. separado (separada)?

27. When were you hurt?
    ¿Cuándo se lastimó?

28. What was the time?
    ¿A qué hora?

29. When did the accident happen?
    ¿Cuándo ocurrió el accidente?

30. What kind of work do you do?[13]
    ¿Qué clase de trabajo hace Vd.?
    ¿Cuál es su ocupación?
    ¿En qué se ocupa Vd.?

31. What is the complete name of your employer?
    Dígame el nombre completo del lugar donde trabaja.

32. What is the address of the place where you work?
    ¿Cuál es la dirección del lugar donde trabaja?

33. What is the zip code?
    ¿Cuál es la zona postal?

34. What is the telephone number where you work?
    ¿Cuál es el número de teléfono donde trabaja?

35. Do you have Blue Cross and/or Blue Shield?
    ¿Tiene Vd. Blue Cross y/o Blue Shield?

36. What is the number of your Blue Cross policy? of your Blue Shield policy?
    ¿Cuál es el número de su certificado de Blue Cross? ¿de Blue Shield?

37. What is the name of the group policyholder?
    ¿Cómo se llama el tenedor de la póliza del grupo?
    Dígame el nombre del asegurado (de la asegurada) del grupo.

38. Do you have a Medicare card?
    ¿Tiene Vd. una tarjeta de Medicare?

39. What is the number of your card? (You must include all the letters, also.)
    ¿Cuál es el número de su tarjeta? (Hay que incluir todas las letras también.)

40. Do you receive public assistance?
    ¿Recibe Vd. el bienestar público?

41. What is the number of your green card?[14]
    ¿Cuál es el número de su tarjeta verde?

42. When does the card expire?
    ¿Cuándo expira la tarjeta?

43. Do you have medical insurance?
    ¿Tiene Vd. seguros médicos?

44. Do you have hospitalization?
    ¿Tiene Vd. seguros de hospital?

45. What type of insurance do you have?
    ¿Qué tipo de seguros tiene Vd.?

46. What is the name of your insurance company?
    ¿Cuál es el nombre de su aseguranza?
    ¿Cuál es el nombre de la empresa con que está asegurado (asegurada)?

47. Where did the injury occur?
    ¿En qué lugar ocurrió la herida?

48. Where was the onset of the illness?
    ¿En qué lugar empezó la enfermedad?

49. Were the police notified?
    ¿Fue notificada la policía?

50. What was the police district nùmber?
   ¿De qué barrio fue la policía?

51. Does it hurt a lot?
   ¿Le duele mucho?

52. You will be OK.
   Vd. va a estar bien.

53. You will (won't) need stitches (sutures).
   Vd. (no) va a necesitar puntadas/costuras (suturas/puntos).

54. When was your last tetanus shot?
   ¿Cuándo fue su última inyección (vacuna) contra el tétano?

55. How did you burn yourself?
   ¿Cómo se quemó Vd.?

56. Hot water, grease, fire, acid, the stove?
   ¿Agua caliente, grasa, fuego,[15] ácido, la estufa/el horno?

57. Tell me if this hurts.
   Dígame si le duele esto.

58. You must keep it clean at all times.
   Vd. tiene que mantenerla limpia todo el tiempo.

59. I want to check it again in a week.
   Quiero examinarla otra vez de hoy en ocho (días).

60. The above instruction(s) have been explained to me as continued care following treatment in the emergency room at ———— Hospital.
   Se me han explicado las antedichas instrucciones como cuidado continuo siguiente el tratamiento en la sala de emergencia a ———— Hospital.

INFORMATION FOR THE CERTIFICATE OF LIVE BIRTH

INFORMACION PARA LA PARTIDA DE NACIMIENTO VIVO

Child *Nene*

1. Tell me the complete and correct name of the child.
   Dígame el nombre completo y correcto del recién nacido.

2. On what day, month, and year was he/she born?
   ¿En qué día, mes y año nació?

3. At what time was the child born?
   ¿A qué hora exacta nació?

4. What is the sex?
   ¿Cuál es su sexo?

5. Was this a single birth, twin, triplet, etc.?
   ¿Fue un parto único, doble, triple, etc.?

6. If this was not a single birth, was this child born first, second, third, etc.? (Specify)
   Si éste no fue un parto único, ¿nació este hijo primero, segundo, tercero, etc.? (Especifique.)

7. In what county was the child born?
   ¿En qué partido nació el nene?

8. Tell me the name of the city, town, township.
   Dígame el nombre de la ciudad, del pueblo, del municipio.

9. Was the child born inside the city?
   ¿Nació el nene dentro de la ciudad?

10. What is the name of the hospital? If the birth did not occur in the hospital, tell me the street and number.
    ¿Cómo se llama el hospital? Si el parto no ocurrió en el hospital, dígame el nombre de la calle y el número allí.

Mother   *Madre*

11. What is your complete and correct maiden name?
    Dígame su nombre completo y correcto de soltera.

12. How old are you at the time of this birth?
    ¿Cuántos años tiene al parir?

13. Where were you born? Tell me the state or foreign country.
    ¿Cuál es su lugar de nacimiento? Dígame el nombre del estado o del país extranjero.

14. In what state is your permanent address?
    ¿En qué estado está su dirección permanente?

15. In what county is your permanent address?
    ¿En qué partido está su dirección permanente?

16. In what city, town, or township do you live?
    ¿En qué ciudad, pueblo, o municipio vive Vd.?

17. Do you live inside the city?
    ¿Vive Vd. dentro de la ciudad?

18. What is your exact address?
    ¿Cuál es su dirección exacta?

19. What is your complete mailing address?
    ¿Cuál es su dirección completa del correo?

20. Is this your first pregnancy?
    ¿Es ésta su primera preñez?
    ¿Es su primer embarazo?

21. How many living children have you had?
    ¿Cuántos hijos vivos ha tenido?

22. How many miscarriages or abortions have you had?
    ¿Cuántos malpartos o abortos ha tenido?

23. How many still births have you had?
    ¿Cuántos nati-muertos ha tenido?

24. What is your blood type?
    ¿Qué tipo de sangre tiene?
    ¿Tiene factor RH?

25. Are you going to nurse the baby?
    ¿Piensa darle el pecho al nene?

Father *Padre*

26. Tell me the complete and correct name of the father.
    Dígame el nombre completo y correcto del padre.

27. How old is the father at the time of this birth?
    ¿Qué edad tiene el padre al nacer su nene?

28. Where was the father born? Tell me the state or foreign country.
    ¿Dónde está el lugar de nacimiento del padre? Dígame el nombre del estado o del país extranjero.

29. Signature of the informant.
    Firma de la informante.

30. What is the relation to the child?[16]
    ¿Qué es la relación entre Vd. y el nene?

REPORT FOR BLUE CROSS/BLUE SHIELD

1. Admitting Date ————————————————————————————

2. Patient's Name ————————————————————————————

3. Blue Cross Certificate Number ————————————————————

The following questions must be answered for all claims which may be "work related" in order for Blue Cross to determine eligible benefits. Thank you for cooperating.

4. Was the condition which required hospital care caused by your employment? If yes, answer only questions 5 through 9.

5. Are you entitled to Workmen's Compensation benefits for this disability?

6. Give reason: ————————————————————————————

7. Briefly explain in what way condition was caused by employment.

8. If you are employed, give the following information:

   What is the name of your employer? ————————————————

   What is his address? ————————————————————————

   In what city and state is he? ————————————————————

   What is the zip code? ——————————————————————

   What is the telephone number where you work? ————————————

9. Signature of informant ————————————————————————

   Date ——— Informant's telephone number ——————————————
   If the response to Question 4 is no, answer only what follows. Skip questions 5–9.

10. Signature of informant.

   Date ——— Informant's telephone number ——————————————

Note carefully: If subsequent investigation reveals your condition is "work related," benefits paid for you by Blue Cross must be returned.

INFORME PARA BLUE CROSS/BLUE SHIELD

1. **Fecha de admisión** _____

2. **Nombre del paciente** _____

3. **Número del certificado de Blue Cross** _____

Hay que contestar a las preguntas que siguen para todas reclamaciones que sean "relacionadas al trabajo" para que Blue Cross determine los beneficios admisibles. Gracias para su cooperación.

4. **¿Fue la condición que necesitó hospitalización causada por su empleo?**
   Si la respuesta es afirmativa, conteste a las preguntas 5 a 9 solamente.

5. **¿Tiene derecho a recibir algunos beneficios de la compensación obrera en cuanto a esta incapacidad?**

6. **Explíqueselo.** _____

7. **Con brevedad explique la manera en que su empleo causó esta incapacidad.**

8. **Si tiene trabajo, dé la información siguiente:**

   ¿Cómo se llama su patrón? _____

   ¿Cuál es su dirección? _____

   ¿En qué ciudad y estado está? _____

   ¿Cuál es la zona postal? _____

   ¿Cuál es el número de teléfono del lugar donde trabaja? _____

9. **Firma del informante** _____

   Fecha _____ **Número de teléfono del informante** _____
   Si la respuesta es negativa, solamente conteste a lo que sigue y omita a las preguntas 5 a 9.

10. **Firma del informante.**

   Fecha _____ **Número de teléfono del informante** _____

Fíjese bien: Si investigación subsecuente revela que su condición es «relacionada al trabajo,» será preciso devolver todos los beneficios pagados por Blue Cross.

Notes *Notas*

1. See note 17, page 392f.

2. Racial problems in the Iberian Peninsula theoretically do not exist because all inhabitants are supposedly of Caucasian background. This is not the case in Latin America. Racial problems originated in the sixteenth century when the Conquistadors came to the New World for "Gold," "Glory," and the "Gospel." Women in the beginning did not come, for the men did not intend to stay permanently. Unions were formed with either native women or with Black slaves who were imported from Africa. New Races resulted:

> Mestizo—offspring of a White and an Indian.
> Mulato—offspring of a White and a Black.
> Zambo—offspring of a Black and an Indian.

In Latin America the indigenous and Black elements play important roles. As for racial identification, a person is frequently called White if he is not Black. (In the United States a person is classified as Black if he is not completely White.) A number of terms are used when referring to color or racial characteristics: the term *negro* (especially in Puerto Rico) is very rarely used. In fact *negra*, or the diminutive *negrita*, are frequently used as forms of affection for someone who is completely white. The most common term used to designate a Black is *de color*. Problems arise, however, in identifying those people who do not belong to either race solely. Official documents such as marriage and baptismal records use several terms: *pardo, moreno, mulato*—but *trigueño* is perhaps the most commonly used term for the group in-between. *Indio* is used for those with Indian characteristics. *Grifo* designates someone with kinky hair, characteristic of Blacks, but who is of light color. (*Pelo malo*, "bad hair," has the same meaning.) *Trigueño*, which literally means wheat colored, often is used to describe a person who has dark color but obviously Caucasoid features.

Race membership is often more closely linked to socio-economic status than to physical characteristics. Identification of a person as *white, colored*, or *trigueño* depends in great part on the attitude of the individual making the identification. Two individuals who are both rather dark and similar in physical characteristics, are often judged differently. If socially acceptable, they are considered *trigueños*; if socially unacceptable they are *de color*. Julian Steward [*People of Puerto Rico* (Champaign: University of Illinois Press, 1946), p. 425] notes that "an individual is 'whiter' in proportion to his wealth." The Mestizo inhabits all economic classes, and now occupies many positions which were formerly held by Whites alone. Racial characteristics are not important, nor do they deter the Mestizo. Education and economics provide for advancement. The Indian is generally a country dweller. He is often poorly educated if not illiterate, poor, and limited in opportunity for future advancement. The Mulato and the Black are found along the coastal regions of South America and in the Caribbean. While poor, and often poorly educated, hope exists for future advancement.

3. See pages 454–455.

4. See pages 455–457.

5. See page 203.

6. See note 19, page 393.

7. See page 203.

8. Because several family members usually accompany the Hispanic patient about to be hospitalized, this question eliminates unnecessary confusion and delay for the person in charge of admitting. See note 4, page 387.

9. See note 17, page 392f.

10. See note 19, page 393.

11. See page 203.

12. See note 2, above.

13. See pages 455–457.

14. Mexicans and others often confuse this "green card" with another one, the **mica**, or *mi*gration *c*ard.

15. **Lumbre** (fire) is used in the southwestern part of the United States.

16. In many Latin American countries the term *illegitimate* is never used. A child born to a married couple is called *legitimate* and is a "legal" child. All other children are often termed "natural." A third term, **hijo reconocido** (recognized child) is coming into use. Some countries, such as Puerto Rico, require the father of such a child, whether he is living with the mother or not, to recognize the child, thus giving the offspring the right to use the father's name, the right to support, and some rights of inheritance.

CHAPTER **8**

Authorizations and Signatures

Autorizaciones y firmas

This chapter contains sample hospital authorization and signature forms. At crucial times patients are shown these forms. Students should practice reading them for fluency and comprehension. Key words and idioms are boldface or underscored in the Spanish texts. The following vocabulary should be helpful.

KEY WORDS AND IDIOMS FOR CONSENT FORMS

PALABRAS Y MODISMOS PRINCIPALES PARA LAS AUTORIZACIONES

abortion **aborto** (m)
  induced abortion **inducción del aborto** (f)
  therapeutic abortion **aborto terapéutico**
above (written) **arriba escrita** (adv)
above named **ya citado** (adj)
administer, to **administrar**
administration **administración** (f)
advantage **ventaja** (f)
adverse results **resultados adversos** (m)
advisable **aconsejable** (adj)
anesthetic **anestético** (m)
apply for admission, to **solicitar admisión a**
appropriate **apropiado** (adj)
assistant **ayudante** (m/f)
assume, to **asumir**
assurance **aseguramiento** (m)
attending physician **médico de atendencia** (m)
authorization **permiso** (m), **autorización** (f)
authorize, to **autorizar**
be capable, to **ser capaz**
be gowned, to **vestirse de bata de hospital**
be guaranteed, to **ser garantizado**
be successful, to **tener éxito**
become pregnant, to **salir encinta (embarazada)**
blood **sangre** (f)
  blood components **componentes de sangre** (m); **componentes sanguíneos** (m)
  blood donors **donantes de sangre** (m/f)
  blood stock **depósito de sangre** (m)
  blood transfusion **transfusión de sangre** (f)
  blood, whole **sangre pura** (f)
body **cuerpo** (m)

certify, to **certificar**
commentary **comentario** (m)
complication **complicación** (f)
component **parte constitutiva** (f)
consent **consentimiento** (m)
consent, to **consentir (ie)**
consider, to **considerar**
cross-matching **prueba cruzada** (f)
daily **por día**
deceased **difunto** (m)
destroyed **destruido** (adj)
detect, to **detectar**
disposal **eliminación** (f)
educational **educacional** (adj)
effects, ill **malos efectos** (m)
8:00 P.M. **las ocho de la noche** (f)
element **elemento** (m)
emergency **emergencia** (f)
examination **examinación** (f)
exception **excepción** (f)
exempt, to (to release) **eximir**
feeding hours **horas de alimentación** (f)
fitness (good health) **buena salud** (f)
free will **libre albedrío** (m)
give up (a claim), to **ceder**
guarantee, to **hacer garantías**
gynecological floor **piso ginecológico** (m)
have children, to **tener niños**
hepatitis **hepatitis** (f)
  infectious hepatitis **hepatitis infecciosa**
  viral hepatitis **hepatitis viral**
incompatible **incompatible** (adj)
incompetent **incompetente** (adj)
lack **falta** (f)
law suit **pleito** (m)
maternity floor **piso de maternidad** (m)
medical purposes **fines médicos** (m)
mentally **mentalmente** (adv)
necessary **necesario** (adj)

newborn **recién nacido** (m/f)
no one **nadie**
occasionally **de vez en cuando**
operating room **quirófano** (m)
operation **operación** (f)
patient **paciente** (m/f)
performance **ejecución** (f)
permanent sterility **esterilidad permanente** (f)
permit **permiso** (m)
photography **fotografía** (f)
physically **físicamente**
plasma **plasma** (f)
procedure **procedimiento** (m)
produce, to **producir**
reaction **reacción** (f)
registered nurse **enfermera registrada** (f)
release **descargo** (m)
request **petición** (f); **pedido** (m)
require, to **requerir**
risk **riesgo** (m)
scientific **científico** (adj)
sixteen years old **dieciséis años** (m)
sterilization **esterilización** (f)
sterilized person **persona estéril** (f)
surgical **quirúrgico** (adj)
test **prueba** (f)
there may be **haya**
tissue **tejido** (m)
transfusion **transfusión** (f)
treatment **tratamiento** (m)
2:00 P.M. **las dos de la tarde** (f)
undersigned **abajo firmado** (adj)
understand, to **comprender**
undertaker **funerarios** (m)
unexpected **inesperado** (adj)
virus **virus** (m)
visiting hours **horas de visita** (f)
visitor **visitante** (m/f)
waiver **renuncia voluntaria** (f)
warrant, to **hacer certificación**
wash one's hands, to **lavarse las manos**
witness **testigo** (m)

AUTHORIZATION FOR SURGICAL AND OTHER PROCEDURES

Date _____

Time _____

    I hereby authorize the following operation _____

_____

             (state nature and extent of operations or procedures)

to be performed upon _____
                      (myself, or name of patient)

under the direction of Dr. _____
                         (surgeon)

and whomever may be designated as his assistants.

    I consent to the performance of all operations and procedures in addition to or different from those now contemplated, whether or not arising from presently unforeseen conditions, which the above-named doctor or his assistants may consider necessary or advisable on the basis of findings during the course of the operation.

    I consent to all necessary, usual, or convenient procedures in connection with the operation including blood transfusions, and I consent to the administration of such anesthetics as may be considered necessary or advisable by the physician responsible for this service. I make the following exceptions: None _____ or Other _____.

    I consent to the photography of the operation procedures to be performed including appropriate portions of my body for medical, scientific, or educational purposes provided identification is not revealed by the pictures or by descriptive texts accompanying them.

    I consent to the admittance of proper professional observers to the operating room.

    I consent to the examination of and disposal by hospital authorities of any tissue or part which may be removed during the operation.

    I hereby certify that I have read and fully understand the above authorization for surgical treatment and possible blood transfusion, the reasons why these procedures are considered necessary, and the advantages and possible complications, which have been explained to me by Dr. _____. I also certify that no guarantee or assurance has been made as to the results that may be obtained.

Witness:

                                    _____
                                      (Signature of patient)

Name _____

                                    _____
                               (Signature of person authorized to

Address _____
                                       consent for patient)

                                    _____
                                       (Relationship to patient)

                                    _____
                                           (Address)

PERMISO PARA PROCEDIMIENTOS QUIRURGICOS Y OTROS PROCEDIMIENTOS

Fecha _____

Hora _____

Por este medio **autorizo** la siguiente **operación** _____

_____
(Declare la naturaleza y extensión de operaciones o **procedimientos**)

que será ejecutada sobre _____
(mí mismo, o nombre de paciente)

bajo la dirección del doctor_____
(cirujano)

y quienquiera que denomine como sus **ayudantes**.

    Consiento en la ejecución de todos los procedimientos y operaciones además de o diferente de los pensados, que pueda ocurrir o no, de condiciones ya **inesperadas**, que el médico ya citado, o sus ayudantes consideren **necesarios** o **aconsejables** a base de descubrimientos durante la operación.

    Consiento en todos los procedimientos necesarios, comunes o convenientes con respecto a la operación incluso **transfusiones de sangre**, y consiento en **la administración** de tales **anestéticos** que el médico responsable para este servicio considere necesarios o **aconsejables**. Hago las siguientes **excepciones**: Ninguna _____ u Otra _____.

    Autorizo **la fotografía** de los procedimientos quirúrgicos que serán ejecutados incluso porciones **apropiadas** de mi **cuerpo** para **fines médicos**, **científicos** o **educacionales** con tal que la identificación no sea revelada por las fotos o por **comentarios** descriptivos que las acompañan.

    Autorizo la admisión de decentes observadores profesionales al **quirófano**.

    Autorizo **la examinación** de y **la eliminación** de cualquier **tejido** o parte que pueda ser **destruido** durante la operación por las autoridades del hospital.

    Por este medio certifico que he leído y que comprendo completamente la **arriba escrita** autorización para **tratamiento quirúrgico** y para posible transfusión de sangre, las razones por qué estos procedimientos son considerados necesarios, **las ventajas** y **las complicaciones** posibles, que me han sido explicadas por el doctor _____. También certifico que ninguna garantía ni **aseguramiento** ha sido hecho en cuanto a los resultados que sean obtenidos.

Testigo:

Nombre _____

Dirección _____

_____
(Firma del paciente)

_____
(Firma de la persona autorizada a
consentir en nombre del paciente)

_____
(Parentesco al paciente)

_____
(Dirección)

REQUEST FOR TRANSFUSION OF WHOLE BLOOD OR ANY OF ITS COMPONENTS

(Consent and Waiver Form)

I, _____, do hereby request Dr. _____ (Attending Physician) and any of his assistants or associates (hereinafter called physician) to administer to me such blood transfusions or any blood components including, but not limited to, plasma, as may be deemed advisable in the judgment of any such physician.

It has been explained to me that it is not always possible to detect the existence or non-existence of some elements occasionally present in blood, such as the virus causing infectious hepatitis or other unusual blood components, and that there is a possibility of ill effects, such as infectious hepatitis resulting from the transmission of its virus or a transfusion reaction resulting from the transmission of unusual blood components. I also understand that there is the possibility of the transmission of the causative agent of other diseases.

It has also been explained to me that emergencies may arise when it is not possible to make adequate cross-matching or other tests and that immediate need may make it necessary to use existing stocks of blood, which may include some incompatible blood types or substances.

I fully understand that the blood supplied in accordance with this agreement is incidental to the rendition of services and that no requirements, guarantee or warranty of fitness, quality or absence of undetectable substances such as viruses, shall apply.

After considering all of the items set forth above and the possibility of adverse results from the said blood transfusions, it is still my desire that one or more transfusions of blood or its components be administered to me, if in the opinion of my physician such transfusions are needed.

I hereby assume any and all risks in connection with any said blood transfusions and release physician and _____ Hospital, its personnel and employees, all blood donors and all other persons, firms and corporations which in any way handled or processed said blood, from any responsibility whatsoever for any resulting contraction of viral hepatitis or any reaction from any such transfusion. I further assume any and all risks in connection with said blood transfusions and agree that I will never bring suit in connection with said transfusions.

Date _____

Witness:

_____ R.N.

_____ M.D.

(Signature of Attending Physician)

_____

(Signature of patient or person authorized
to consent for patient)

_____

(Relationship to patient)

PETICION PARA TRANSFUSION DE SANGRE PURA O DE CUALQUIER DE SUS PARTES CONSTITUTIVAS

(Consentimiento y renuncia voluntaria)

Por este medio yo _____, **autorizo** al Dr. _____ (**médico de atendencia**) y a alguno de sus **ayudantes** o asociados (más adelante llamados «médico») que me administre tales **transfusiones de sangre** o **componentes de sangre** incluso, pero no limitado a **plasma**, que según el juicio del médico sean aconsejables.

Se me explicaron que no es posible siempre **detectar** la existencia o la falta de existencia de algunos **elementos** presentes **de vez en cuando** en la sangre, como por ejemplo **el virus** que cause **la hepatitis infecciosa**, u otros **componentes sanguíneos** no muy comunes y que puede haber la posibilidad de **malos efectos**, tal como la hepatitis infecciosa que resulta de la transmisión de su virus o **una reacción** de transfusión que resulta de la transmisión de extraordinarios componentes sanguíneos. También **comprendo** que **haya** la posibilidad de la transmisión de agentes que causan otras enfermedades.

También se me han explicado que **emergencias** aparezcan cuando no sea posible hacer suficientes **pruebas cruzadas** u otras **pruebas** y que la necesidad inmediata pueda **requerir** la necesidad de usar **el depósito de sangre** que incluya algunos tipos o substancias de sangre que sean **incompatibles**.

Comprendo completamente que la sangre provista de acuerdo con este consentimiento es elemento incidental a la rendición de servicios y que nadie me **hace garantías** ni **certificación** de **buena salud**, cualidad ni falta de substancias ocultas como virus.

Después de **considerar** todo lo que se me ha explicado y la posibilidad **de resultados adversos** de las ya citadas **transfusiones de sangre**, todavía quiero que me sean administradas tantas transfusiones de sangre y sus componentes como mi médico juzgue necesarias.

Por este medio **asumo** cualquier y todos **los riesgos** con respecto a cualquier citada transfusión de sangre y les **eximo** al médico, a _____ Hospital, y a su personal y empleados, a todos **los donantes de sangre** y a todas las personas, firmas y corporaciones que, de cualquier manera hayan manejado o preparado dicha sangre, de cualquier responsabilidad si contraigo **la hepatitis viral** o alguna **reacción** de semejante transfusión. Además asumo cualquier y todos los riesgos con respecto a las citadas transfusiones de sangre y cedo que nunca seguiré **un pleito** con respecto a tales transfusiones.

Fecha _____

Testigo: _____

(Firma de paciente o de la persona
autorizada a dar permiso para paciente)

_____
(Firma de la **enfermera registrada**)

(Parentesco a paciente)

_____, Médico
(Firma del **médico de atendencia**)

AUTHORITY TO PERFORM A
THERAPEUTIC ABORTION

Date _____

This is to certify that I, the undersigned, consent to the administration of whatever anesthetic may be necessary and the performing of a therapeutic abortion upon

Name _____

Address _____

Signature of Patient _____

Signature of Patient's Husband _____

Witness: _____
Name

_____
Address

_____

AUTORIZACION PARA
UN ABORTO TERAPEUTICO

Fecha _____

Esto es para certificar que yo, **la abajo firmada**, **consiento** en la **administración** de cualquier **anestético** que sea necesario y en **la ejecución** de un aborto terapéutico sobre

Nombre _____

Dirección _____

Firma de la paciente _____

Firma del esposo de la paciente _____

Testigo: _____
Nombre

_____
Dirección

RELEASE FROM RESPONSIBILITY
FOR ABORTION

Date _____ 19 _____ Time _____A.M./P.M.

This is to certify that I, _____ , a patient applying for admission to _____
Hospital believe that I am in a condition of abortion. I hereby declare that neither the attending physician nor any person employed by or connected with the said hospital has knowingly performed any act that may have contributed to the induction of the abortion, and I do hereby absolve said persons from any responsibility or liability for my condition.

Witness _____   Signed _____
                                                                                     (Patient or nearest relative)

Witness _____   _____
                                                                                     (Relationship)

Authorization must be signed by the patient, or by the nearest relative when the patient is physically or mentally incompetent.

DESCARGO DE LA RESPONSABILIDAD
PARA UN ABORTO

Fecha _____ Hora _____

Esto es para **certificar** que yo, _____ , una paciente **solicitando admisión a** _____
Hospital, creo estar en condiciones de aborto. Por la presente declaro que ni el médico que me atiende ni ninguna persona empleada por o conectada con este hospital ha realizado ningún acto que haya contribuido a **la inducción del aborto,** y por medio de la presente descargo a estas personas de cualquier responsabilidad por mi condición.

Testigo _____   Firma _____
                                                                                     (Paciente o pariente más cercano)

Testigo _____   _____
                                                                                     (Parentesco)

Autorización debe ser firmada por la paciente o por su pariente más cercano cuando la paciente es **incompetente física o mentalmente.**

STERILIZATION PERMIT

We, the undersigned, husband and wife, hereby authorize Dr. _____ to perform _____ (name of operation) the sole purpose of which is to produce permanent sterility, on _____ (name of patient) which in all likelihood will be the result, but in no case can it be guaranteed. The operation may not be a success.

We voluntarily request this operation and understand that it is intended to result in sterility although this result cannot be guaranteed. Sterilization has been explained to us, and we understand that a sterile person is not capable of becoming pregnant and bearing a child.

Signed _____
(Wife)

_____
(Husband)

Date _____

Witness: _____
Name

Address _____

Date _____

PERMISO PARA ESTERILIZACION

Nosotros, los **abajo firmados**, esposo y esposa, por este medio autorizamos al doctor _____ a hacer _____ (nombre de la operación) con el propósito único de **producir esterilidad permanente** sobre _____ (Esposa) o _____ (Esposo). Con toda probabilidad la operación **tendrá éxito**, pero puede haber la posibilidad de que la operación no tenga éxito.

Nosotros solicitamos esta operación por nuestro **libre albedrío** y **comprendemos** que el propósito de la operación es la esterilización, aunque este resultado no puede **ser garantizado**. Se nos explicó lo que es la esterilización, y entendemos que **una persona estéril** no **es capaz** de **salir encinta (embarazada)** y **tener niños**.

Firma _____
(Esposa)

_____
(Esposo)

Fecha _____

Testigo: _____
Nombre

Dirrección _____

Fecha _____

VISITING POLICY FOR ALL MATERNITY
AND GYNECOLOGY PATIENTS

Fathers and/or husbands are permitted to visit from 2 P.M. to 8 P.M. The father of the baby visiting during feeding hours must wash his hands and be gowned.

Other visitors to Maternity and Gynecology are permitted from 2 P.M. to 3 P.M. and 7 P.M. to 8 P.M.

Maternity and Gynecological patients are permitted two visitors per day, exclusive of the father and/or husband.

No persons under 16 years of age are permitted to visit a maternity or gynecological patient other than the father of the baby or husband of the patient.

HORAS DE VISITA PARA PACIENTES
DEL PISO DE MATERNIDAD Y DEL
PISO GINECOLOGICO

Se permiten visitas de los padres y/o los esposos desde **las dos de la tarde** hasta **las ocho de la noche**. Durante **las horas de alimentación**, el padre **del recién nacido** debe **lavarse las manos** y **vestirse de bata de hospital** si está presente.

Se permiten otros **visitantes** al piso de maternidad y al piso ginecológico desde las dos hasta las tres de la tarde y desde las siete hasta las ocho de la noche.

Además del padre y/o esposo, se permiten dos visitantes a cada paciente de maternidad o de ginecología **por día**.

Nadie de menos de **dieciséis años** pueda visitar a ninguna paciente de maternidad o de ginecología a menos que sea el padre del recién nacido o el esposo de la paciente.

REQUEST FOR POSTMORTEM EXAMINATION

Name _____ Room _____

Age _____ Date _____

Physician _____ Intern _____

I, _____, hereby request _____

Hospital to do a postmortem examination on the body of my _____,
(relationship)

_____, with the removal and retention of diseased tissue.
(name of deceased)

_____
(Special instructions, if any.)

Signed, _____

Witness _____

Witness _____

PEDIDO PARA AUTOPSIA

Nombre _____ Cuarto _____

Edad _____ Fecha _____

Médico _____ Médico residente _____

Yo, _____, por este medio pido al Hospital de _____

que se hace una autopsia del cadáver de mi _____,
(Parentesco)

_____, con el traslado y retención de los **tejidos** enfermos.
(Nombre del difunto)

_____
(Instrucciones especiales, si las hay.)

Firma _____

Testigo _____

Testigo _____

UNDERTAKER'S RELEASE

Date _____

I hereby grant permission to _____ Undertakers to remove the

body of _____ from the _____ Hospital.

The deceased has been a resident of _____ for _____ years,
and has (not) served in the military or naval service of the United States. (If so, what war?)

Social Security Number _____

Signed _____

Relationship _____

Witness _____

DESCARGO PARA LOS FUNERARIOS

Fecha _____

Yo, por este medio doy permiso a los **funerarios** de _____ para que

quiten el cadáver de _____ del Hospital de _____. El difunto

ha sido residente de _____ por _____ años,

y (no) ha servido en el servicio militar o naval de los Estados Unidos. (Si es así, ¿en qué guerra?)

Número de seguro social _____

Firma _____

Parentesco _____

Testigo _____

Crucial Vocabulary for Medical Personnel

Vocabulario crucial para personal médico

CONTENTS

INDICES

Major clinics **Clínicas principales** 427

Key diseases, symptoms, and injuries **Enfermedades, síntomas, y heridas principales** 427

Principal medical abbreviations **Abreviaturas médicas principales** 435

Common medications and treatments **Medicinas y tratamientos comunes** 436

Common poisons **Venenos comunes** 440

Selected drug abuse terminology **Terminología escogida para el abuso de (las) drogas** 441

Excretions **Excreciones** 444

Blood **Sangre** 444

Pregnancy, childbirth, contraception, postnatal care of the mother **Embarazo, parto, contracepción, cuidado posnatal de la madre** 445

Medical specialists **Especialistas médicos** 449

Places in the hospital **Lugares en el hospital** 450

The family **La familia** 450

Bathroom, toilet articles, and personal effects **Artículos para el baño y el tocador y objetos personales** 451

Bedding **Ropa de cama** 453

Clothing **Ropa** 453

Colors **Colores** 454

Practitioners of the major religions **Practicadores de las religiones principales** 454

Countries and nationalities **Países y nacionalidades** 455

Occupations **Ocupaciones** 455

Food and meals **Alimentos y comidas** 457

  Special diets **Dietas especiales** 457

  Cooking terms **Terminología de cocina** 458

  Seasonings **Condimentos** 459

  Soups **Sopas** 459

  Salads **Ensaladas** 459

  Eggs and cereals **Huevos y cereales** 459

  Breads and noodles **Panes y pastas** 459

  Butter and cheese **Mantequilla y queso** 460

  Vegetables **Legumbres y verduras** 460

  Meat **Carne** 461

  Poultry and game **Aves y caza** 461

  Fish and seafood **Pescado y mariscos** 461

  Fruits **Frutas** 461

  Desserts **Postres** 462

  Beverages **Bebidas** 462

  Dishes and utensils **Loza y utensilios** 463

MAJOR CLINICS

CLINICAS PRINCIPALES

Acute Care **primeros auxilios** (m, pl)
Admitting **ingresos** (m, pl)
Allergy **alergia** (f)
Audiology **audiología** (f)
Bronchology **broncología** (f)
Cardiology **cardiología** (f)
  Congential Cardiology **cardiología congénita**
  Rheumatic Cardiology **cardiología reumática**
Central Testing Laboratory **laboratorio central** (m)
Chest **pulmonar** (adj)
Dental **dental** (adj)
  Dentistry **dentistería** (f); **odontología; estomatología** (f)
Dermatology **dermatología** (f)
Diabetic **diabética** (adj)
ECG—Electrocardiogram **electrocardiograma** (m)
EEG—Electroencephalogram (Brain Wave Test) **laboratorio para encefalogramas** (m)
Emergency Room **sala de urgencia** (f)

Employees' Health Service **dispensario de empleados** (m)
Endocrinology **endocrinología** (f)
ENT—Ear, Nose, and Throat **GNO-garganta, nariz, oídos**
Eyes **ojos** (m)
Genetics **genética** (f)
Gerontology **gerontología** (f)
Gynecology **ginecología** (f)
Hematology **hematología** (f)
Immunology **inmunología** (f)
Kidneys—nephritic **riñones-nefrítica**
Maternity **maternidad** (f)
Medicine **medicina** (f); **médica** (adj)
Nephrology **nefrología** (f)
Neurology **neurología** (f)
Obstetrics **obstétrica** (f)
Occupational Therapy **terapia ocupacional** (f)
Oncology **oncología** (f)
Operating Room **sala de operaciones** (f); **quirófano** (m)
Ophthalmology **oftalmología** (f)
Optics **óptica** (f)

Orthopedics **ortopedia** (f)
  Special Orthopedics **ortopedia especial**
Outpatient Clinic **clínica para pacientes ambulatorios** (f)
Pediatrics **pediatría** (f)
Pharmacy **farmacia** (f)
Physical Therapy **fisioterapia** (f)
Psychiatry **psiquiatría** (f)
Pulmonary Disease **enfermedad respiratoria** (f)
Rheumatology **reumatología** (f)
Social Service **servicio social** (m)
Special Seizure **convulsiones** (f)
Speech **del habla** (m)
  Voice, Articulation **voz, articulación** (f)
Surgery **cirugía** (f)
  Plastic Surgery **cirugía plástica**
  Special Surgery **cirugía especial**
Urology **urología** (f)
X-rays **rayos x (equis)** (m)

KEY DISEASES, SYMPTOMS, AND INJURIES

ENFERMEDADES, SINTOMAS, Y HERIDAS PRINCIPALES

abrasion **razpón** (m); **rozadura** (f)
abscess **absceso** (m); **hinchazón** (f, colloq)
accident **accidente** (m)
acne **acné** (f); **espinillas** (f); **cácara** (f, Chicano)
"acute abdomen" **abdomen agudo** (m)[1]
addicted **adicto** (adj)
ailment **dolencia** (f)
alcoholism **alcoholismo** (m)
allergic reaction **trastorno alérgico** (m); **reacción alérgica** (f)
allergy **alergia** (f)
amblyopia **ambliopia** (f)
anemia **anemia** (f); **sangre clara** (f, colloq); **sangre débil** (f, colloq); **sangre pobre** (f, colloq)
  aplastic anemia **anemia aplástica** (f)

  iron deficiency anemia **deficiencia de hierro** (f)
  pernicious anemia **anemia perniciosa** (f)
  sickle cell anemia **anemia drepanocítica** (f); **drepanocitemia** (f)
  thalassemia **talasemia** (f)
aneurysm **aneurisma** (f)
angina **angina** (f)
  angina pectoris **angina del pecho** (f)
angiomata (red dots on skin) **cabecita de vena** (f, Chicano)
anxiety **ansiedad** (f)
aortic insufficiency **insuficiencia aórtica** (f)
aphasia **afasia** (f)
aphonia (hoarseness) **afonia** (f); **ronquera** (f)

apoplexy, stroke **apoplejía** (f)
appendicitis **apendicitis** (f); **panza peligrosa** (f, slang)[2]
arrhythmia, cardiac **arritmia cardíaca** (f)
arteriosclerosis **arteriosclerosis** (f)
arthritis **artritis** (f)
  rheumatoid arthritis **artritis reumatoidea** (f)
asthma **asma** (f); **fatiga** (f, slang); **ahoguío** (m, colloq, Mex.)
  asthmatic attack, seizure **ataque asmático** (m)
  asthmatic wheeze **resuello asmático** (m)
  bronchial asthma **asma bronquial** (f)
astigmatism **astigmatismo** (m)
athlete's foot **pie de atleta** (m); **infección de serpigo** (f)

atrial fibrillation **fibrilación auricular** (f)
atrophy **atrofia** (f)
attack **ataque** (m)
bacterium **bacteria** (f)
bald **calvo** (adj)
  baldness **calvicie** (f)
bearing **porte** (m)
bedbug **chinche** (f)
bedsore **úlcera por decúbito** (f); **llaga de cama** (f)
Bell's palsy **parálisis facial** (f)
bite (animal) **mordedura** (f); **mordida** (f)
  cat bite **mordida de gato** (f)
  dog bite **mordida de perro** (f)
  human bite **mordedura humana** (f)
  scorpion bite[3] **mordedura de escorpión** (f)
  snake bite **mordedura de serpiente** (f)
bite (insect), sting[4] **picadura** (f); **piquete** (m)
black and blue **amoratado** (adj)
blackeye **ojo morado** (m)
blackhead, shin **espinilla** (f)
bleed excessively, to **desangrar**
bleeding **pérdida de sangre (de poca intensidad)** (f); **sangría** (f); **hemorragia** (f)
  bleeding tendencies **tendencias a sangrar** (f)
  internal bleeding **hemorragia interna** (f)
blemish **lunar** (m); **mancha** (f)
blepharitis **blefaritis** (f)
blind **ciego** (adj)
  blind in one eye **tuerto** (adj)
  blindness **ceguera** (f); **ceguedad** (f)
    color blindness **daltonismo** (m); **acromatopsia** (f); **ceguera para los colores** (f)
    night blindness (nyctalopia) **nictalopía** (f); **ceguera nocturna** (f)
    river blindness (oncocerciasis)[5] **oncocercosis** (f); **oncocerciasis** (f); **cerguera del río** (f)
blisters **ampolla** (f); **vesícula** (f); **bulla** (f)
  blister on sole of foot **sietecueros** (m, sg)
blocked intestine **tripa ida** (f)
blood clot **coágulo de sangre** (m); **cuajarón** (m)
blood poisoning **envenenamiento de la sangre** (m); **toxemia** (f); **septicemia** (f); **sepsis** (f)
blood pressure **presión arterial** (f); **tensión arterial** (f); **presión de la sangre** (f); **presión sanguínea** (f)
  high blood pressure **presión arterial alta** (f); **hipertensión arterial** (f)

low blood pressure **presión arterial baja** (f); **hipotensión arterial** (f)
boil **furúnculo** (m); **nacido** (m); **sisote** (m); **tacotillo** (m, Chicano)
bowel obstruction **obstrucción de la tripa** (f); **tripa ida** (f, colloq); **panza peligrosa**[6] (f, slang); **abdomen agudo**[6] (m, slang)
bronchitis **bronquitis** (f)
bruise **contusión** (f); **magulladura** (f); **moretón** (m, Mex., Hond.); **lastimadura** (f)
  bruised **moreteado** (adj, Chicano)
bubo **búa** (f); **ganglio** (m); **incordio** (m); **seca** (f, colloq)
bubonic plague **peste bubónica** (f)
bulging eyes **ojos saltones** (m); **ojos capotudos** (m, Chicano)
bullet **bala** (f)
  bullet wound **balazo** (m)
bunion **juanete** (m)
burn **quemadura** (f); **quemazón** (m)
  acid burn **quemadura por ácido** (f)
  alkali burn **quemadura por álcali** (f)
  chemical burn **quemadura química** (f)
  dry heat burn **quemadura por calor seco** (f)
  scald **escaldadura** (f)
  sunburn **quemadura solar** (f); **solanera** (f); **eritema solar** (m)
bursitis **bursitis** (f)
buzzing in the ears **zumbido de oídos** (m)
callus **callo** (m)
cancer **cáncer** (m)[7]
  cancerous **canceroso** (adj)
canker **úlcera** (f); **llaga ulcerosa** (f); **ulceración** (f)
carcinoma **carcinoma** (m)
cardiac arrest **fallo cardíaco** (m); **paro cardíaco** (m)
caries **caries** (f); **cavidad dental** (f); **diente podrido** (m)
case **caso** (m)
cataract **catarata** (f)
catch a disease, to **contraer una enfermedad**; **agarrar**; **pegarle**
celiac disease **celíaca** (f)
cerebral paralysis **parálisis cerebral** (f)
cerebrospinal meningitis **meningitis cerebroespinal** (f)
chafing **piel roja** (f); **rozadura** (f)
Chagas's disease **enfermedad de Chagas** (f)
chancre **chancro** (m)
  soft chancre **chancro blando** (m)
change of life **cambio de vida** (m)
chapped **rosado** (adj); **cuarteado** (adj)

chap skin, to **rozarse**
cheilosis (sore at corner of mouth) **boquilla** (f)
chicken pox **varicela** (f); **viruelas locas** (f, slang); **bobas** (f); **tecunda** (f, Mex.)
chilblain **sabañón** (m)
chills **escalofríos** (m)
choking **asfixia** (f)
cholera **cólera** (m)
chorea **corea** (f); **mal o baile de San Guido o de San Vito** (m)
chronic **crónico** (adj); **duradero** (adj)
cirrhosis of the liver **cirrosis del hígado** (f); **cirrosis hepática** (f)
cleft palate **paladar partido** (m); **paladar hendido** (m); **grietas en el paladar** (f); **boquineta** (m, Chicano)
club foot **pie zambo** (m); **talipes**
coated tongue **lengua sucia** (f); **lengua saburral** (f)
cold **catarro** (m); **resfriado** (m)
  common cold **resfriado común** (m)
  "stopped-up" head; head cold **constipado** (m)
colic **cólico** (m)
colitis **colitis** (f)
collapse **colapso** (m)
colostomy **colostomía** (f)
coma **coma** (f)
complaint, chronic **alifafe** (m, slang)
complication **complicación** (f); **accidente** (m)
concussion **concusión** (f); **golpe** (m)
congenital **congénito** (adj)
  congenital anomaly **anomalía congenita** (f)
congestion of the chest **ahoguijo** (m); **ahoguío** (m, colloq)
conjunctivitis (pinkeye) **conjunctivitis** (f); **mal de ojo** (m, colloq); **tracoma** (m); **oftalmia contagiosa** (f); **conjunctivitis catarral aguda** (f)
constipation **constipación** (f); **estreñimiento** (m); **entablazón** (f, Chicano)
contagious **contagioso** (adj); **pegadizo** (adj)
contusion **contusión** (f)
convalescence **convalecencia** (f)
convulsion **convulsión** (f); **ataque** (m)
corn **callo** (m)
coronary thrombosis **trombosis coronaria** (f)
corpse **cadáver** (m)
cough **tos** (f)
  smoker's cough **tos por fumar** (f)
  cough, to **toser**

cough up phlegm, to **esgarrar;
desgarrar** (Chicano)
cramps **calambres** (m)
abdominal cramps **retortijón**
(m); **torsón** (m)
cane-cutter's cramps **calambres
de los cortadores de caña** (m)
charley horse **rampa** (f)
heat cramps **calambres
térmicos** (m)
menstrual **dolores del
período** (m)
postpartum **entuertos** (m)
stomach **retortijón de tripas** (m);
torcijón cólico (m, Mex.)
cretinism **cretinismo** (m)
cripple **tullido** (adj, m); **inválido**
(adj, m)
crippled **lisiado** (adj); **cojo** (adj);
empedido (adj)
crippled hand **manco** (adj)
cross-eyed **bizco** (adj); **bisojo** (adj);
turnio (adj)
cross-eyes **bizquera** (f)
croup **crup** (f); **ronquera** (f)
cut **cortada** (f, Sp. Am.);
cortadura (f)
cyst **quiste** (m)
cystic fibrosis **fibrosis
quística** (f)
cystitis **cistitis** (f); **infección de la
vejiga** (f)
dacryocystitis **infección de la
bolsa de lágrimas** (f)
dandruff **caspa** (f)
dead **muerto** (adj, m)
deaf **sordo** (adj)
deaf mute **sordomudo** (m)
deafness **sordera** (f);
ensordecimiento (m)
death **muerte** (f); **fallecimiento** (m)
death rattle **estertor agónico** (m)
defect **defecto** (m)
deficiency **carencia** (f); **deficiencia**
(f)
deformed **deforme** (adj);
eclipsado (adj, colloq, Sp. Am.);
inocente (adj, Mex.)
deformity **deformidad** (f)
dehydration **deshidratación** (f);
desecación (f)
delirium **delirio** (m)
delouse, to **espulgar**
dementia **demencia** (f)
dengue **dengue** (m); **fiebre
rompehuesos** (f)
depressed **deprimido** (adj)
depression **depresión** (f);
abatimiento (m)
dermatitis **dermatitis** (f)
detached retina **retina
desprendida** (f)
diabetes **diabetes** (f)
diabetes insipidus **diabetes
insípida** (f)
diabetes mellitus **diabetes

mellitus (f); **diabetes
sacarina** (f)
diabetic **diabético** (m, adj)
diagnosis **diagnóstico** (m);
diagnosis (f)
diarrhea **diarrea** (f); **cursera** (f,
slang); **turista** (f, slang); **chorro**
(m, slang); **asientos** (m, slang);
chorrillo (m, slang); **cámara** (f,
slang); **soltura** (f, Chicano);
corredera (f, Chicano); **cagadera**
(f, vulgar, Chicano)
diphtheria **difteria** (f); **garrotillo**
(m)
disability **inhabilidad** (f);
incapacidad (f); **invalidez** (f)
disc, calcified **disco calcificado**
(m)
disc, slipped **disco desplazado** (m);
disco intervertebral luxado (m)
discharge **secreción** (f); **flujo** (m);
supuración (f); **desecho** (m);
descarga (f)
bloody discharge **derrame** (m)
vaginal discharge **flujo
vaginal** (m)
white discharge **flores blancas**
(f, colloq); **flujo blanco** (m)
discomfort **malestar** (m)
disease **enfermedad** (f); **mal** (m);
dolencia (f)
disease due to an act of
witchcraft **enfermedad
endañada** (f, Chicano, Mex.)
disease that is "going around"
enfermedad de andancia (f,
Chicano)
notifiable disease **enfermedad
de notificación** (f)
reportable disease **enfermedad
obligatoria** (f)
dislocated **dislocado** (adj);
zafado (adj, Sp. Am.)
dislocation **dislocación** (f);
luxación (f)
diverticulitis **diverticulitis** (f);
colitis ulcerosa (f)
dizziness **vértigo** (m); **vahído** (m);
tarantas (f, Mex. Hond.)
Down's syndrome **mal de Down**
(m); **mongolismo** (m)
drainage **supuración** (f); **drenaje**
(m)
draining, dripping
escurrimiento (m)
dropsy **ahogamiento** (m);
hidropesía (f)
drowsiness **modorra** (f)
drug addict[8] **drogadicto** (m, f);
adicto a las drogas (m, f)
drug addiction[8] **narcomanía** (f);
dependencia farmacológica (f)
drug overdose[8] **sobredosis de
drogas** (f)
drunk **borracho** (adj); **pisto** (adj);
tacuache (adj); **tlacuache** (adj);

tronado (adj); **alumbrado** (adj,
slang, Chicano); **rascado** (adj,
Ven.)
to be/get drunk **andar bombo**;
andar eléctrico; **andar en la
línea**; **andar loco**; **estar
mediagua**; **ponerse alto**
(colloq); **rascar** (Sp. Am.)
drunkenness **borrachera** (f)
dwarf **enano** (m, f)
dysentery **disentería** (f)
ameobic dysentery **disentería
amebiana** (f)
bacillary dysentery **disentería
bacilar** (f)
dysmenorrhea **dismenorrea** (f);
menstruación dolorosa (f)
dyspnea **dificultad al respirar** (f)
dysuria **dolor al orinar** (m)
earache **dolor de oído** (m)
earwax, impacted **tapón de cera**
(m)
eczema **eccema** (f); **rezumamiento**
(m)
edema **edema** (m)
emaciation **enflaquecimiento** (m);
demacración (f)
embolism **embolismo** (m);
embolia (f)
emergency **emergencia** (f);
urgencia (f); **caso urgente** (m)
emphysema **enfisema** (f)
encephalitis **encefalitis** (f)
enlargement **ensanchamiento** (m);
ampliación (f), **agrandamiento** (m)
epidemic **epidémico** (adj);
epidemia (f)
epilepsy **epilepsia** (f); **ataque (de
epilepsia)** (m)
epileptic attack **ataque
epiléptico** (m); **convulsión** (f)
eruption **erupción** (f)
erysipelas **erisipela** (f); **dicipela** (f,
Chicano)
exhaustion **agotamiento** (m);
fatiga (f)
fainting spell **desmayo** (m);
mareo (m, colloq); **vértigo** (m);
desvanecimiento (m);
desfallecimiento (m)
fallen fontanel[9] **caída de la
mollera** (f)
farsighted **présbita** (adj)
farsightedness **presbicia** (f);
hipermetropía (f), **presbiopía** (f)
fatigue **fatiga** (f)
fear **miedo** (m)
fever[10] **fiebre** (f); **calentura** (f)
acute infectious adenitis **fiebre
ganglionar** (f)
breakbone fever **fiebre
rompehuesos** (f); **dengue** (m)
Colorado tick fever **fiebre de
Colorado** (f); **fiebre tra(n)smitida
por garrapatas** (f)
enteric fever **fiebre entérica** (f)

fever blister **llaga de fiebre** (f);
herpe febril (m, f)
glandular fever **fiebre
glandular** (f)
hay fever **fiebre de(l) heno** (f);
alergia (f); **jey fíver** (m, f);
catarro constipado (m, Chicano)
intermittent fever **fiebre
intermitente** (f)
malarial fever **fiebre palúdica**
(f); **chucho** (m, Arg., Chile)
Malta fever **fiebre de Malta** (f);
fiebre ondulante (f);
brucelosis (f)
paratyphoid fever **fiebre
paratifoidea** (f); **fiebre
paratífica** (f)
parrot fever **fiebre de las
cotorras** (f)
rabbit fever **fiebre de conejo** (f)
rat-bite fever **fiebre por mordedura
de rata** (f)
rheumatic fever **fiebre
reumática** (f)
Rocky Mountain fever **fiebre
de las Montañas Rocosas** (f);
**maculosa de las Montañas
Rocosas** (f)
scarlet fever **fiebre escarlatina**
(f)
spotted fever **fiebre purpúrea (de
las Montañas Rocosas)** (f);
tifus exantemático (m); **fiebre
manchada** (f)
thermic fever **fiebre térmica** (f)
typhoid fever **fiebre tifoidea** (f);
tifus abdominal (m)
typhus **tifus** (m); **tifo** (m);
tifus exantemático (m);
úrzula (f, Chicano)
undulant fever **fiebre ondulante**
(f)
valley fever (coccidioidomycosis)
fiebre del valle (f)
yellow fever **fiebre amarilla** (f);
tifus icteroides (m); **fiebre
tropical** (f); **tifo de América**
(m); **vómito negro** (m)
fibroma **fibroma** (m)
fissure **fisura** (f); **grieta** (f);
partidura (f)
fistula **fístula** (f)
fit **convulsión** (f); **arrebato** (m);
paroxismo (m)
flat foot **pie plano** (m); **planovegus**
(m)
flatus **flato** (m); **ventosidad** (f);
pedo (m, slang)
flea **pulga** (f)
floater **mosca volante** (m);
mancha volante (f)
flu **influenza** (f); **gripe** (f); **gripa** (f)
Asiatic flu **influenza asiática** (f)
folk illness[11] **enfermedad casera**
(f)
foul-smelling **apestoso** (adj)

fracture **fractura** (f); **quebradura
de huesos** (f)
complicated fracture **fractura
complicada** (f)
compound fracture **fractura
compuesta** (f)
green stick fracture **fractura en
tallo verde** (f)
multiple fracture **fractura
múltiple** (f)
open fracture **fractura abierta**
(f)
pathologic fracture **fractura
patológica** (f)
serious fracture **fractura mayor**
(f)
simple fracture **fractura simple**
(f)
spontaneous fracture **fractura
espontánea** (f)
freckle **peca** (f)
frigidity **frigidez** (f)
frostbite **congelación** (f); **daño
sufrido por causa de la helada** (m)
fungus **hongo** (m)
athlete's foot **pie de atleta** (m);
infección de serpigo (f)
moniliasis **candidiasis** (f);
boquera (f); **muguet** (m, f);
moniliasis (f)
ringworm/tinea **culebrilla** (f);
tiña (f); **empeine** (m); **serpigo**
(m); **sisote** (m, Chicano)
tinea corporis **jiotes** (f, colloq)
furuncle **furúnculo** (m)
gait **marcha** (f)
gallbladder attack **ataque
vesicular** (m); **dolor de la vesícula**
(m)
gallstone **cálculo en la vejiga** (m);
cálculo biliar (m) **piedra en la
vejiga** (f)
gangrene **gangrena** (f); **cangrena**
(f)
gash **cuchillada** (f)
gastritis **gastritis** (f)
germ **germen** (m); **microbio** (m)
German measles **rubéola** (f);
sarampión alemán (m); **fiebre de
tres días** (f); **alfombría** (f,
Chicano); **alfombrilla** (f,
Chicano); **sarampión bastardo**
(m)
glaucoma **glaucoma** (m)
goiter **bocio** (m); **buche** (m, slang);
güegüecho (m)
gonorrhea **gonorrea** (f);
purgación (f, slang); **blenorragia**
(f); **chorro** (m, colloq)
gout **gota** (f)
hallucination **alucinación** (f)
hammertoe **dedo gordo en
martillo** (m)
handicap **impedimento** (m)
hangnail **padastro** (m, colloq);
cutícula desgarrada (f)

hangover **malestar post-
alcohólico** (m)
hard of hearing **duro de oído** (m);
corto de oído (m)
harelip **labio leporino** (m);
cheuto (adj, Chile); **jane** (adj,
Hond.); **labio cucho** (m,
Chicano); **boquineta** (m, Chicano)
harsh, raucous sound **ronquido**
(m)
headache **dolor de cabeza** (m);
jaqueca (f); **cajetuda** (f, Chicano)
heart attack **ataque al corazón**
(m); **ataque cardíaco** (m); **ataque
del corazón** (m); **infarto** (m)
heartbeat **latido (cardíaco)** (m);
palpitación (f)
irregular heartbeat (arrhythmia)
latido irregular (m);
palpitación irregular (f);
arritemia (f)
rhythmical heartbeat
palpitación rítmica (f)
slow heartbeat **palpitación lenta**
(f)
tachycardia (rapid heartbeat)
taquicardia (f); **palpitación
rápida** (f)
heartburn **acedia** (f); **agriera** (f,
Sp. Am.); **agruras** (f); **cardialgia**
(f); **pirosis** (f); **ardor de
estómago** (m)
heart disease **enfermedad del
corazón** (f); **enfermedad
cardíaca** (f); **cardiopatías** (f)
heart failure **insuficiencia
cardíaca** (f); **fallo del corazón**
(m); **paro del corazón** (m)
heart murmur **soplo** (m);
murmullo (m)
heat exhaustion **agotamiento por
calor** (m)
heat stroke **golpe de calor** (m);
insolación (f)
hematuria **hematuria** (f); **sangre
en la orina** (f)
hemophilia **hemofilia** (f)
hemorrhage **hemorragia** (f);
desangramiento (m); **morragia** (f,
Chicano)
hemorrhoids **almorranas** (f);
hemorroides (f, pl)
hepatitis **hepatitis** (f); **inflamación
del hígado** (f); **fiebre** (f, colloq,
Mex.)
hernia **hernia** (f); **quebradura** (f);
desaldillado (m, Mex.);
destripado (m, slang)
femoral hernia **hernia femoral**
(f)
inguinal hernia **hernia inguinal**
(f); **quebradura en la ingle** (f)
umbilical hernia **hernia del
ombligo** (f); **ombligo salido** (m,
slang); **ombligón** (m, slang)
herpes **herpes** (m, f)

hiccough, hiccup **hipo** (m); **hipsus** (m)
high arched foot **pie hueco** (m)
high cholesterol **colesterol elevado** (m)
high triglycerides **triglicéridos elevados** (m)
hives **urticaria** (f); **ronchas** (f)
hoarse **afónico** (adj); **ronco** (adj)
hoarseness **ronquera** (f); **carraspera** (f, colloq)
hot flashes **calores** (m); **llamaradas** (f); **calofrío** (m, Chicano)
hunchback **jorobado** (m, f, adj)
hydrocele **hidrocele** (m, f)
hyperlipidemia **hiperlipidemia** (f)
hypertension (high blood pressure) **presión arterial alta** (f); **hipertensión arterial** (f)
hyperventilation **hiperventilación** (f); **susto con resuello duro** (m, colloq)
hyphema **hifemia** (f); **hemorragia detrás de la córnea** (f)
hypochondria **hipocondría** (f)
hypochondriac **hipocóndrico** (m, adj); **adolorado** (adj, Chicano); **adolorido** (adj, Chicano)
hypopyon **pus detrás de la córnea** (m)
hypotension (low blood pressure) **hipotensión arterial** (f); **presión arterial baja** (f)
hysteria **histeria** (f)
ill **malo** (adj); **enfermo** (adj)
illness **mal** (m); **enfermedad** (f); **padecimiento** (m)
  acute illness **enfermedad aguda** (f)
  chronic illness **enfermedad crónica** (f)
  contagious illness (disease) **enfermedad contagiosa** (f); **enfermedad trasmisible** (f)
  mental illness **enfermedad mental** (f)
  minor illness **enfermedad leve** (f)
  organic illness (disease) **enfermedad orgánica** (f)
  serious illness **enfermedad grave** (f)
  tropical illness (disease) **enfermedad tropical** (f)
immune **inmune** (adj)
immunization **inmunización** (f); **vacuna** (f)
impetigo **impétigo** (m); **erupción cutánea** (f)
impotence **impotencia** (f)
indigestion **indigestión** (f); **mala digestión** (f); **dispepsia** (f); **estómago sucio**[12] (m, Chicano); **insulto** (m, Chicano)

infantile paralysis— polio(myelitis) **parálisis infantil** (f); **polio(mielitis)** (f)
infarct **infarto** (m)
infection **infección** (f); **pasmo** (m)
infectious **infeccioso** (adj)
inflammation **inflamación** (f); **encono** (m)
  inflammation of the throat **garrotillo** (m)
influenza **influenza** (f); **gripe** (f); **gripa** (f)
ingrown nail **uña encarnada** (f); **uña enterrada** (f); **uñero** (m)
injured **herido** (adj); **lisiado** (adj)
injury **herida** (f); **lesión** (f); **lastimadura** (f)
insanity **locura** (f); **demencia** (f)
  manic-depressive **locura de doble forma** (f); **mania-melancolía** (f); **sicosis maníaco-depresiva** (f)
insomnia **insomnio** (m); **pérdida del sueño** (f)
intoxication **embriaguez** (f)
intussusception **intususcepción** (f)
irritability **bilis**[13] (f)
irritation **irritación** (f)
itch **picazón** (f); **comezón** (f); **sarna** (f)
jaundice **derrame biliar** (m); **ictericia** (f); **piel amarilla** (f, colloq)
kidney disease **mal del riñón** (m)
kidney stone **cálculo en el riñón** (m); **ataque vesicular** (m); **dolor de la vesícula** (m); **cálculo renal** (m); **piedra en los riñones** (f)
knot (type of tissue swelling) **bolas** (f. pl, Chicano); **nudo** (m)
laceration **laceración** (f); **desgarradura** (f); **cortada** (f)
lame **lisiado** (adj); **cojo** (adj); **rengo** (adj)
lameness **cojera** (f)
laryngitis **laringitis** (f)
leishmaniasis **roncha mala** (f); **roncha hulera** (f)
leprosy **lepra** (f); **lazarín** (m); **mal de San Lázaro** (m); **mal de Hansen** (m)
lesion **lesión** (f)
  oral lesion **pupa** (f); **afta** (f); **perleche** (f); **boquera** (f)
leukemia **leucemia** (f); **cáncer de la sangre** (m)
limp, to **renguear** (Sp. Am.)
lisp (studder) **tartamudeo** (m); **ceceo** (m)
lockjaw **tétanos** (m); **trismo** (m)
lump **dureza** (f); **protuberancia** (f); **hinchazón** (f, m); **borujo** (m)
  large lump **borujón** (m)
  lump or bump on head **chichón** (m); **pisporr(i)a** (f, Chicano)

mad (insane) **loco** (adj)
madness **locura** (f); **manía** (f)
malaise **malestar** (m)
malaria **malaria** (f); **paludismo** (m); **fríos** (m, Sp. Am.)
malignancy **malignidad** (f)
malignant **maligno** (adj)
malnourished **desnutrido** (adj); **mal nutrido** (adj)
malnutrition **malnutrición** (f); **desnutrición** (f); **mala alimentación** (f)
  kwashiorkor **kwashiorkor** (m); **mala alimentación mojada** (f)
  marasmus **marasmo** (m); **mala alimentación seca** (f)
mania **manía** (f)
maniac **maníaco** (adj)
masturbation **masturbación** (f); **casqueta** (f, Chicano)
measles **sarampión** (m); **morbilli**; **tapetillo de los niños** (m, colloq); **granuja** (f, slang)
melancholia **melancolía** (f)
membrane **membrana** (f); **tela** (f)
Meniere's disease **enfermedad de Meniere** (f)
meningitis **meningitis** (f)
menopause **menopausia** (f); **cambio de vida** (m); **período climatérico** (m)
mental retardation **retraso mental** (m)
metastasis **metástasis** (f)
migraine **migraña** (f); **jaqueca** (f)
mild **leve** (adj)
mirror writing **escritura como en un espejo** (f)
mold **moho** (m)
mononucleosis **mononucleosis infecciosa** (f)
mucus **moco** (m); **frío** (m, slang, Mex.)
multiple sclerosis **esclerosis múltiple** (f); **esclerosis en placa** (f)
mumps **paperas** (f); **farfallota** (f, P.R.); **parótidas** (f, pl); **bolas** (f, Chicano); **coquetas** (f, Mex.); **buche** (m, Mex.); **mompes** (m, pl, Chicano)
muscular dystrophy **distrofia muscular progresiva** (f)
mute **mudo** (adj)
myocardial infarct **infarto miocárdico** (m)
myopia **miopía** (f)
myopic **miope** (adj)
nasal drip **goteo nasal** (m); **moqueadera** (f, Chicano)
nausea **náusea** (f); **basca** (f)
  morning nausea **malestares de la mañana** (m); **asqueo** (m); **enfermedad matutina** (f)
nearsighted **miope** (adj); **corto de vista** (adj)
nearsightedness **miopía** (f)

nephritis **nefritis** (f)
nervous breakdown **desarreglo nervioso** (m); **colapso** (m); **neurastenia** (f)
nervous disorder **desorden nervioso** (m)
nervousness **nerviosidad** (f)
neuralgia **neuralgia** (f)
neurasthenia **neurastenia** (f)
neurasthenic **neurasténico** (adj)
neuritis **neuritis** (f)
neurosis **neurosis** (f)
neurotic **neurótico** (adj)
nightmare **pesadilla** (f)
noninfectious **no infeccioso** (adj)
nosebleed **hemorragia nasal** (f); **salirle sangre de la nariz**
nose bleeding **epistaxis** (f)
numb **adormecimiento** (m)
obese **obeso** (adj); **gordo** (adj)
obeseness **obesidad** (f); **gordura** (f)
obstruction **obstrucción** (f); **impedimento** (m)
  nasal obstruction **mormación** (f, Chicano)
  stomach obstruction **entablazón** (f, Chicano)
old age **senectud** (f); **vejez** (f)
one-eyed **tuerto** (adj); **virulo** (adj, Chicano)
ophthalmia (inflammation of the eye) **oftalmía** (f); **inflamación de los ojos** (f)
osteomyelitis **osteomielitis** (f); **inflamación de la médula del hueso** (f)
otitis **otitis** (f)
overdose **dosis excesiva** (f)
overweight **sobrepeso** (m); **exceso de peso** (m)
overweight (adj) **excesivamente gordo** (adj); **excesivamente grueso** (adj)
pain, ache **dolor** (m)
  boring pain **dolor penetrante** (m)
  burning pain **dolor quemante** (m)
  colicky pain **dolor cólico** (m)
  constant pain **dolor constante** (m)
  dull pain **dolor sordo** (m)
  growing pain **dolor de crecimiento** (m)
  labor pain **dolor de parto** (m)
  mild pain **dolor leve** (m)
  moderate pain **dolor moderado** (m)
  phantom limb pain **dolor de miembro fantasma** (m)
  pressure-like pain **dolor opresivo** (m)
  referred pain **dolor referido** (m)
  root pain **dolor radicular** (m)
  severe pain **dolor severo** (m)
  sharp pain **punzada** (f); **dolor agudo** (m)

sharp intestinal pain **torzón** (m)
shooting pain **dolor fulgurante** (m)
steady pain **dolor continuo** (m)
thoracic pain **dolor torácico** (m)
twinge **latido**[14] (m)
palpitation **palpitación** (f); **latido**[14] (m)
palsy **parálisis** (f); **paralización** (f)
  Bell's palsy **parálisis facial** (f)
  cerebral palsy **parálisis cerebral** (f)
  shaking palsy (Parkinson's disease) **enfermedad de Parkinson** (f); **parálisis agitante** (f)
pancreatitis **pancreatitis** (f)
paralysis **parálisis** (f); **paralización** (f)
paranoia **paranoia** (f)
paraplegia **paraplejía** (f); **parálisis de la mitad inferior del cuerpo** (f)
parasite **parásito** (m)
  amoeba **ameba** (f); **amiba** (f)
  ascaris (roundworm) **ascaris** (f); **lombriz grande redonda** (f); **ascáride** (f)
  chigger flea **nigua** (f); **garrapata** (f); **guina** (f, Mex.)
  common name **nombre común** (m)
  cysticercus (bladderworm) **cisticerco** (m)
  distribution **distribución** (f)
  flea **pulga** (f)
  focus of infection **foco de infección** (m)
  form of parasite in feces **forma de los parásitos en heces** (f)
  giardia **giardia** (f)
  gnat **jején** (m, Sp. Am.); **bobito** (m, Chicano)
  louse **piojo** (m)
    crab louse **ladilla** (f)
    nit **liendra** (f)
  metazoos **metazoos** (m)
  mite **ácaro** (m)
  parasitic cyst **quiste** (m); **ladilla** (f)
  pediculosis **pediculosis** (f); **piojería** (f)
  protozoa **protozoarios** (m)
  flagellates **flagelados** (m)
  route of entry **vía de entrada** (f)
  schistosoma **esquistosoma** (f); **bilharzia** (f)
  sporozoa **esporozoarios** (m)
  tapeworm **solitaria** (f); **lombriz solitaria** (f); **tenia** (f)
  solium **solitaria** (f); **gusano tableado** (m)
  threadworms **tricocéfalos** (f); **tricocefalosis** (f); **oxiuro** (m);

  lombriz chiquita afilada (f)
  trichinosis **triquinosis** (f)
  trichocephalus **tricocéfalo** (m); **lombriz de látigo** (f)
  uncinaria (hookworm) **uncinaria** (f); **lombriz de gancho** (f)
  worm **gusano** (m); **lombriz** (f)
    intestinal worm **verme** (m)
pellagra **pelagra** (f)
perforated eardrum **tímpano perforado** (m)
pericarditis **pericarditis** (f)
peritonitis **peritonitis** (f); **panza peligrosa**[15] (f, slang); **abdomen agudo**[15] (m, slang)
pertussis **tos convulsiva** (f); **tosferina** (f); **coqueluche** (f); **tos ferina** (f); **tos ahogana** (f)
pharyngitis **faringitis** (f)
phlebitis **flebitis** (f); **tromboflebitis** (f)
phlegm **flema** (f)
phthisis **tisis** (f); **consunción** (f)
pigeon-toed **patizambo** (adj)
pile **almorrana** (f); **hemorroides** (f, pl)
pimple **grano de la cara, barrillo** (m); **butón** (m); **pústula** (f); **buba** (f)
  blackhead pimple **espinilla** (f); **barro** (m)
pinched nerve **nervio aplastado** (m)
plague **peste** (f); **plaga** (f)
  bubonic plague **peste bubónica** (f); **tifo de oriente** (m)
pleurisy **pleuresía** (f)
pneumonia **pulmonía** (f); **neumonía** (f)
pock **viruela** (f); **postilla** (f) **cacaraña** (f, Guat., Mex.)
poison **veneno** (m, manmade); **ponzoña** (f, natural)
  poison ivy **hiedra venenosa** (f); **chechén** (m); **zumaque venenoso** (f)
poisoning **envenenamiento** (m); **intoxicación** (f)
  botulism poisoning **intoxicación botulínica** (f)
  carbon monoxide poisoning **intoxicación por monóxido de carbono** (f)
  food poisoning **envenenamiento por comestibles** (m); **intoxicación con alimentos** (f)
  lead poisoning **envenenamiento del plomo** (m); **saturnismo** (m); **envenenamiento plúmbico** (f)
  salmonella poisoning **intoxicación por salmonellas** (f)
  staphylococcal poisoning **intoxicación por estafilococos** (f)

polyp **pólipo** (m)
poor health, in **jodido** (adj)
presbyopia **presbiopía** (f);
  presbicia (f); **hipermetropía** (f)
prickly heat **salpullido** (m);
  picazón (f); **erupción debido al
  calor** (f)
proctitis **proctitis** (f)
prostatitis **prostatitis** (f); **tapado
  de orín** (m)
prostration **postración** (f)
heat prostration **postración del
  calor** (f)
psoriasis **soríasis** (f); **mal de
  pintas** (m)
psychosis **sicosis** (f)
psychosomatic **sicosomático** (adj)
psychotic **sicótico** (adj)
pterygium **pterigión** (m);
  carnosidad (f, colloq)
pus **pus** (m)
pustule **pústula** (f); **grano** (m);
  bubón (m)
pyorrhea **piorrea** (f); **mal de las
  encías** (m)
quinsy (sore throat) **esquinancia**
  (f); **amigdalitis supurativa** (f)
rabies **rabia** (f); **hidrofobia** (f)
rape **violación** (f); **rapto** (m,
  Chicano)
rash **salpullido** (m); **erupción** (f);
  alfombra (f, P.R., Cuba);
  sarpullido (m);
diaper rash **pañalitis** (f);
  chincual (m, Mex.)
wheals (hives) **ronchas** (f)
redness **rubor** (m)
relapse **recidiva** (f); **recaída** (f);
  atrasado (adj)
renal **renal** (adj)
rheum **reuma** (m)
rheumatism **reumatismo** (m);
  reumas (m)
rhinitis **rinitis** (f); **escurrimiento de
  la nariz** (m)
rickets **raquitis** (m); **raquitismo**
  (m)
risk **riesgo** (m)
roseola **roséola** (f); **rubéola** (f)
rubella **sarampión alemán** (m);
  rubéola (f); **roséola epidémica** (f);
  fiebre de tres días (f); **peluza** (f,
  Mex.); **alfombría** (f, Chicano);
  alfombrilla (f, Chicano);
  sarampión bastardo (m)
rupture (hernia) **hernia** (f);
  ruptura (f); **relajación** (f); **rotura**
  (f); **reventón** (m); **quebradura** (f);
  rotadura (f, Chicano)
sarcoma **sarcoma** (f)
scab **postilla** (f); **costra** (f);
  cuerín (m, Chicano); **cuerito** (m,
  Chicano)
scabies **sarna** (f); **guaguana** (f,
  slang); **gusto** (m, slang)
scale **escama** (f)

scar **cicatriz** (f)
schizophrenia **esquizofrenia** (f)
schizophrenic **esquizofrénico** (adj)
sciatica **ciática** (f)
scotoma (spots before the eyes)
  escotoma (m); **manchas frente a
  los ojos** (f)
scratch **rasguño** (m); **rascado** (m);
  raspón (m, Sp. Am.)
to scratch (relieve hurt)
  rascar(se)
to scratch (hurt) **rasguñar**
scurvy **escorbuto** (m)
seasickness **mareo** (m); **mal de
  mar** (m)
seborrhea **seborrea** (f)
seizure **ataque** (m); **convulsión** (f)
senile **senil** (adj)
senility **senilidad** (f); **senectud** (f);
  caduquez (f)
septicemia **septicemia** (f);
  bacteriemia (f); **toxemia** (f);
  piemia (f); **infección en la sangre**
  (f, colloq)
serious **grave** (adj); **serio** (adj)
severe **agudo** (adj); **severo** (adj);
  fuerte (adj)
shingles **zona** (f); **herpes** (m);
  zoster (m)
shock **choque** (m); **sobresalto** (m);
  conmoción nerviosa (f); **susto** (m)
anaphylactic shock **choque
  alérgico** (m, colloq); **choque
  anafiláctico** (m)
sick **enfermo** (adj); **malo** (adj)
short of breath **ahoguío** (m,
  colloq); **ahoguijo** (m, colloq)
shortsighted **miope** (adj); **cegato**
  (adj, colloq)
sickliness **achaque** (m)
sickly **enfermizo** (adj); **pálido**
  (adj); **demacrado** (adj); **cholenco**
  (adj, Chicano)
sickness **enfermedad** (f);
  padecimiento (m); **mal** (m);
  dolencia (f)
simulation **fingimiento** (m)
sinus congestion **congestión** (f);
  sinusitis (f)
sleeping sickness **enfermedad del
  sueño** (f)
smallpox **viruela** (f)
smegma **esmegma** (m); **queso** (m,
  slang)
sore **pena** (f); **dolor** (m);
  aflicción (f)
sore ears **mal o dolor de oídos**
  (m)
sore eyes **dolor de ojos** (m)
sore throat **mal o dolor de
  garganta** (m); **garganta
  inflamada** (f)
sore (wound) **llaga** (f); **úlcera** (f);
  grano (m)
souffle **silbido** (m); **pillido** (m,
  Mex.)

spasm **espasmo** (m); **contracción
  muscular** (f); **latido** (m, Chicano)
spasmodic **espasmódico** (adj);
  intermitente (adj); **irregular** (adj)
spastic **espástico** (adj);
  espasmódico (adj)
splinter (in the eye) **esquirla** (f);
  astilla (en el ojo) (f)
spot **mancha** (f)
spotted sickness **mal de pinto** (m);
  pinta (f)
sprain **torcedura** (f); **dislocación**
  (f); **esguince** (f); **falseo** (m,
  Chicano)
squint-eyed **ojituerto** (adj); **bizco**
  (adj); **bisojo** (adj)
stammering **tartamudeo** (m);
  balbucencia (f)
stiff **tieso** (adj)
stiff ("frozen") joint
  articulación envarada (f);
  articulación trabada (f)
stiff neck **nuca tiesa** (f, colloq);
  torticolis (f); **tortícolis** (m)
sting (of an insect) **picadura** (f);
  piquete (m); **punzada** (f)
ant sting **picadura de hormiga**
  (f)
bee sting **picadura de abeja** (f)
blackwidow spider sting
  picadura de viuda negra (f);
  picadura de ubar (f, colloq)
botfly sting **picadura de
  moscardón** (f)
chigoe/jigger/sandflea sting
  picadura de nigua (f)
flea bite **picadura de pulga** (f)
hornet sting **picadura de
  avispón** (f)
mosquito sting (bite) **picadura
  de mosquito** (f)
scorpion sting (bite) **picadura de
  alacrán** (f)
spider sting **picadura de araña**
  (f)
tick **picadura de garrapata** (f)
wasp sting **picadura de avispa**
  (f)
stomachache **dolor de estómago**
  (m)
strabismus **estrabismo** (m); **bizco**
  (C.A.)
strain **tensión** (f); **torcedura** (f)
straining (tenesmus) **pujos** (m,
  colloq)
strep throat **estreptococia** (f);
  **mal o dolor de garganta por
  estreptococo** (m, colloq)
stress **tensión** (f)
stricture **constricción** (f);
  estrictura (f); **estenosis** (f);
  estrechez (f)
stroke **derrame cerebral** (m);
  embolia cerebral (f); **parálisis** (f);
  hemorragia vascular (f); **ataque
  fulminante** (m); **apoplejía** (f);

estroc (m, Chicano); **embolio**
(m, Chicano)
stuffed-up head **constipado** (m)
stuttering **tartamudez** (f);
balbucencia (f)
sty **orzuelo** (m); **perrilla** (f,
colloq)
suffocation **sofocación** (f);
asfixia (f)
suicide **suicidio** (m)
sunstroke **insolación** (f); **soleada**
(f, Am.)
suntanned **bronceado** (adj);
tostado (adj)
suppuration **supuración** (f)
swelling **hinchazón** (f); **tumor** (m);
tumefacción (f)
on the head **chichón** (m)
swollen **hinchado** (adj)
symptom **síntoma** (m)
syndrome **síndrome** (m)
syphilis **sífilis** (f); **sangre mala** (f,
slang); **mal francés** (m, slang);
mal de bubas (m, slang);
infección de la sangre (f, euph);
lúes (f); **avariosis** (f, Sp. Am.)
tachycardia **taquicardia** (f)
tantrum **berrinche** (m, colloq)
temper tantrum **pataletas** (f)
tartar, dental **sarro** (m); **saburra**
(f); **tártaro** (m)
tattoo(ing) **tatuaje** (m)
tetanus **tétanos** (m); **mal de arco**
(m, slang); **trimo** (m)
infantum tetanus **moto** (m,
slang, Mex.); **siete (7) días** (m);
mozusuelo (m, Mex.)
thrombophlebitis **tromboflebitis**
(f); **flebitis** (f)
thrombosis **trombosis** (f)
coronary thrombosis **trombosis**
coronaria (f)
thrush **afta** (f); **algodoncillo** (m,
colloq)
tic **tic** (m); **tirón** (m); **sacudida** (f)
tic douloureux **tic doloroso de**
la cara (m)
tonsillitis **amigdalitis** (f);
tonsilitis (f)
toothache **dolor de muelas** (m);
dolor de dientes (m); **odontalgia**
(f)
tooth decay **caries** (f); **dientes**
podridos (m)
toxemia **toxemia** (f)
tracheostomy **traqueostomía** (f)
trauma **traumatismo** (m);
trauma (m)
tremor **tremor** (m); **tremblor** (m)
tubercular **tuberculoso** (adj);
afectado (adj, Chicano)
tuberculosis **tuberculosis** (f); **tisis**

(f); **manchado del pulmón** (m,
Mex.); **afectado del pulmón** (m,
Chicano, Mex.); **peste blanca** (f)
scrophula (scrofula) **escrófula**
(f)
skin TB **tuberculosis de la piel**
(f)
tumor **tumor** (m); **neoplasma** (m);
neoformación (f); **tacotillo** (m,
Chicano)
tumor on the head **chiporra**
(f, Guat., Hond.)
twisted **torcido** (adj); **zambo** (adj)
ulcer **úlcera** (f)
gastric ulcer **úlcera gástrica** (f)
peptic ulcer **úlcera péptica** (f)
unconscious **inconsciente** (adj);
naqueado (adj, Chicano)
unconsciousness **insensibilidad** (f);
inconsciencia (f)
underweight **peso escaso** (m);
falta de peso (f)
uremia **uremia** (f); **intoxicación de**
orín (f)
urinary problem **mal de orín** (m);
problema de las vías urinarias
(m)
urticaria **urticaria** (f)
uterus prolapse **prolapso de la**
matriz (m); **caída de la matriz** (f);
prolapso del útero (m)
varicose vein **várice** (f); **vena**
varicosa (f); **variz** (m)
venereal disease (VD)
enfermedad venérea (f); **secreta**
(f, slang); **EV** (f)
canker sore **postemilla** (f);
úlcera gangrenosa (f)
chancre **chancro** (m); **grano** (m)
hard **chancro duro** (m);
chancro sifilítico (m)
noninfecting **chancro simple**
(m); **chancro blando** (m)
chlamidia **clamidia** (f)
cold sore **fuegos en la boca no**
los labios (m); **herpes labial** (m)
condyloma **condiloma** (m)
genital wart **verruga genital** (f);
verruga venérea (f)
gonorrhea **gonorrea** (f);
blenorragia (f); **purgaciones** (f,
pl, slang); **gota** (f, slang); **mal**
de orín (m, slang); **chorro** (m,
euph, Chicano)
herpes **herpe(s)** (m, f)
genitalis **herpes genitalis** (m)
menstrualis **herpes**
menstrual (f)
zoster **herpes zoster** (m)
lymphogranuloma venereum
linfogranuloma venéreo (m);
bubones (m)

moniliasis **moniliasis** (f);
algodoncillo (m); **boquera** (f);
candidiasis (f); **muguet** (m, f)
nongonoccocal urethritis
uretritis no gonocal (f)
nonspecific urethritis
uretritis no específica (f);
uretritis inespecífica (f)
sexually transmitted diseases
enfermedades pasadas
sexualmente (f)
syphilis **sífilis** (f); **sangre mala**
(f, slang); **infección de la**
sangre (f, euph)
trichomonas **tricomonas** (f)
venereal lesion **úlcera** (f);
chancro (m); **grano** (m)
vesicular eruption **erupción**
vesicular (f)
victim **víctima** (f)
virus **virus** (m)
vision, blurred **vista borrosa** (f)
vision, double **vista doble** (f)
vitiligo **vitiligo** (m); **ciricua** (f,
colloq); **jiricua** (f, slang)
vomit **vómito** (m); **arrojadera** (f,
vulgar)
wart **verruga** (f); **mezquino** (m,
Mex.)
plantar wart **ojo de pescado** (m,
colloq)
weak **débil** (adj)
weakness **debilidad** (f)
weal (large welt) **verdugón** (m);
cardenal (m)
wen **lobanillo** (m); **lupia** (f)
wheal **roncha** (f); **pápula** (f)
whiplash **lesión de latigazo** (f);
contusión de la columna vertebral
(f); **latigazo** (m, colloq)
whooping cough **tos convulsiva**
(f); **tos ferina** (f); **coqueluche** (f);
tosferina (f); **tos ahogona** (m,
Mex.)
wound **herida** (f); **llaga** (f);
lastimadura (f); **coco** (m)
abrasion **abrasión** (f);
escoriación (f)
chafe **rozadura** (f)
cut **cortadura** (f); **cortante** (f)
incised wound **herida incisa** (f)
incision **incisión** (f); **cisura** (f)
knife wound **filorazo** (m,
Chicano)
laceration **laceración** (f)
open skin wound **grano** (m)
puncture **herida penetrante** (f);
herida punzante (f)
scrape **raspadura** (f)
tear (torn wound) **desgarro** (m)
xerosis **xerosis** (f); **resequedad de**
los ojos (f)

PRINCIPAL MEDICAL ABBREVIATIONS

ABREVIATURAS MEDICAS PRINCIPALES

The following are selected medical abbreviations of Latin or Greek origin that are frequently used in prescription writing.

a a (ana—Greek)	of each	de cada uno (una)
aa	equal parts	a partes iguales
a.c. (ante cibos)	before meals	antes de comer
alt. dieb. (alternis diebus)	every other day	cada dos días
alt. hor. (alternis horis)	every other hour	cada dos horas
alt. noc. (alternis noctus)	every other night	cada dos noches
aq. (aqua)	water	agua
aq. dest. (aqua destillata)	distilled water	agua destilada
bib (bibe)	drink	beba
b.i.d. (bis in die)	twice a day	dos veces al (por) día
b.i.n. (bis in noctus)	twice a night	dos veces a la (por) noche
c̄ (cum)	with	con
cap. (capsula)	capsule	cápsula
et (et)	and	y
Gtt., gtt. (guttae)	drops	gotas
H. (hora)	hour	hora
h.n. (hac nocte)	tonight	esta noche
h.s. (hora somni)	at bedtime	al acostarse
liq. (liquor)	liquid; fluid	líquido; fluido
no. (numero)	number	número
non rep. (non repetatur)	do not refill; do not repeat	no se repita
noxt. (nocte; noxte)	at night	a la (por la) noche
omn. hor. (omni hora)	every hour	cada hora
omn. noct. (omni nocte)	every night	cada noche
os. (os; ora)	mouth	boca
p.c. (post cibum)	after meals	después de comer
p.r.n. (pro re nata)	as needed	a cada tiempo si es necesario
q.d. (quaque die)	every day	cada día
q.h. (quaque hora)	every hour	cada hora
q.i.d. (quater in die)	four times a day	cuatro veces al (por) día
q. 2h.	every 2 hours	cada dos horas
q. 3h.	every 3 hours	cada tres horas
q. 4h.	every 4 hours	cada cuatro horas
q.l.; q.v.	as necessary	tanto como desee, a voluntad
q.m. (quaque mãne)	every morning	cada mañana
q.n. (quaque nocte)	every night	cada noche
q.s.; q. suff. (quantum sufficiat)	a sufficient quantity	cantidad suficiente
quotid. (quotidie)	every day	cada día
℞ (recipe)	take	tome
rep. (repetatur)	repeat; refill	repítase
S. (signa)	mark	indique
s (sans)	without	sin
Sig. (signetur)	directions	método
s.o.s. (si opus sit)	if necessary	si es necesario
stat. (statim)	immediately	inmediatamente
tab. (tabella)	tablet	tableta
t.i.d. (ter in die)	three times a day	tres veces al (por) día
t.i.n. (ter in nocte)	three times a night	tres veces a la (por la) noche

COMMON MEDICATIONS AND TREATMENTS

MEDICINAS Y TRATAMIENTOS COMUNES

acetaminophen **acetaminofén** (m)
acid **ácido** (m)
  acetylsalicylic acid **ácido acetilsalicílico**
  ascorbic acid **ácido ascórbico**
  boric acid **ácido bórico**
  folic acid **ácido fólico**
  p-aminosalicylic acid (PAS) **ácido paraminosalicílico**
activated charcoal **carbón activado** (m)
adhesive plaster **emplasto adhesivo** (m)
adhesive tape **esparadrapo** (m);
  – **tela adhesiva** (f); **cinta adhesiva** (f)
adrenalin **adrenalina** (f)
alcohol **alcohol** (m)
  rubbing alcohol **alcohol para fricciones** (m)
ammonia **amoníaco** (m)
amphetamine **anfetamina** (f)[16]
ampicillin **ampicilina** (f)
ampule **ampolleta** (f)
analgesic **analgésico** (m, adj)
anesthesia **anestesia** (f)
anesthetic **anestético** (m, adj)
ankle support **tobillera** (f)
antacid **antiácido** (m, adj)
antibiotic **antibiótico** (m, adj)
  broad-spectrum **de alcance amplio; de espectro amplio**
  limited-scope **de alcance reducido; de espectro reducido**
antibody **anticuerpo** (m)
anticholinergic **anticolinérgico** (m, adj)
anticoagulant **anticoagulante** (m, adj)
antidote **antídoto** (m)
antiemetic **antiemético** (m, adj)
antigen **antígeno** (m)
antihemorrhagic **antihemorrágico** (adj)
antihistamine **antihistamínico** (m, adj); **droga antihistamínica** (f)
antimalarial **antipalúdico** (m, adj)
antipyretic **febrífugo** (m); **antipirético** (m)
antiseptic **antiséptico** (m, adj)
antispasmodic **antiespasmódico** (m, adj)
antitetanic; anti-tetanus **antitetánico** (adj)
antitoxin **antitoxina** (f); **contraveneno** (m)
application **aplicación** (f)

arch supports **soportes para el arco del pie** (m)
arsenic **arsénico** (m)
artificial **artificial** (adj); **postizo** (adj)
artificial limb **miembro artificial** (m)
artificial respiration **respiración artificial** (f)
aspirin **aspirina** (f)[17]
  children's aspirin **aspirina para niños** (f)[17]
astringent **astringente** (m, adj)
atropine **atropina** (f)
balsam **bálsamo** (m); **ungüento** (m)
band **cinta** (f); **faja** (f)
Band-Aid **curita** (f); **venda** (f); **parchecito** (m)
bandage **vendaje** (m); **venda** (f)
  elastic bandage **vendaje elástico**
  swathing bandage **faja abdominal** (f)
barbiturate **barbiturato** (m)[18]
bath **baño** (m)
  bran bath **baño de salvado**
  emollient bath **baño emoliente**
  mustard bath **baño de mostaza**
  oatmeal bath **baño de harina de avena**
  potassium permanganate bath **baño de permanganato de potasio**
  saline bath **baño salino**
  shower bath **baño de regadera** (Chicano); **ducha** (f)
  sitz bath **baño de asiento; semicupio** (m)
  sodium bath **baño de sodio**
  sponge bath **baño de esponja; baño de toalla** (Chicano)
  starch bath **baño de almidón**
  sulfur bath **baño de azufre**
  tar bath **baño de brea**
belladonna **belladona** (f)
benzedrine **bencedrina** (f)
benzoin **benjuí** (m); **benzoína** (f)
bicarbonate of soda **bicarbonato de soda** (m)
binder **vendaje abdominal** (m); **cintura** (f); **faja** (f)
bleach **cloro** (m); **blanqueo** (m)
blood **sangre** (f)[19]
  blood plasma **plasma sanguíneo** (m)

blood transfusion **transfusión de sangre** (f)
booster shot **inyección secundaria** (f); **búster** (m); **inyección de refuerzo** (f); **reactivación** (f)
borax **bórax** (m)
bottle **botella** (f); **envase** (m); **frasco** (m)
brace **braguero** (m); **aparato ortopédico** (m)
Brewer's yeast **levadura de cerveza** (f)
bromide **bromuro** (m)
calamine **calamina** (f)
calcium **calcio** (m)
  calcium sulfate **escayola** (f); **sulfato de calcio** (m)
camomile tea **té de manzanilla** (m); **agua de manzanilla** (f)
cane **bastón** (m); **báculo** (m)
  walking cane **bastón de paseo** (m)
capsule **cápsula** (f)
carbon tetrachloride **tetracloruro de carbono** (m)
cast **yeso** (m); **calote** (m); **enyesadura** (f); **vendaje enyesado** (m)
  gypsum cast **vendaje de yeso** (m)
  walking cast **enyesadura para caminar**
cataplasm **cataplasma** (f)
cathartic **purgante** (m)
catheter **catéter** (m); **sonda** (f); **tubo** (m); **drenaje** (m, Chicano)
cauterization **cauterización** (f)
chloramphenicol **cloranfenicol** (m)
chloride **cloruro** (m)
chlorine **cloro** (m)
chloromycetin **cloromicetín** (m); **chloromycetin** (m)
chlorophyll **clorofila** (f)
chloroquinine **cloroquina** (f)
cleanliness **limpieza** (f); **aseo** (m)
coagulant **coagulante** (m, adj)
coal tar **brea de hulla** (f)
cocaine **cocaína** (f); **nieve** (f, slang)[20]
cocoa butter **manteca de cacao** (f)
codeine **codeína** (f)[20]
cold pack **emplasto frío** (m); **compresa fría** (f)
comb, fine-tooth **chino** (m, Mex.)
compress **compresa** (f); **cabezal** (m)

contact lens **lente de contacto** (m);
pupilente (m); **lentilla** (f, Spain)
contamination **contaminación** (f)
contraceptive **contraceptivo** (m);
anticonceptivo (m)[21]
contraceptive pills **pastillas
anticonceptivas** (f)[21]
Coramine **coramina** (f)
corn plaster **emplasto para callos**
(m); **parches para callos** (m)
corticosteroid **corticosteroide** (m)
cortisone **cortisona** (f)
cotton **algodón** (m)
absorbent cotton **algodón
absorbente**
cotton swab **hisopillo** (m);
escobillón (m)
sterile cotton **algodón estéril**
cough drops **gotas para la tos** (f);
pastillas para la tos (f)
cough lozenges **pastillas para la
tos** (f)
cough suppressant **béquico** (m);
calmante para la tos (m)
cough syrup **jarabe para la tos** (m)
crutch **muleta** (f)
cure **cura** (f); **método curativo** (m)
curettage **curetaje** (m); **raspado**
(m)
decongestant **descongestionante**
(m, adj)
dental floss **hilo dental** (m);
cordón dental (m); **seda
encerada** (f)
dentifrice **dentífrico** (m, adj)
deodorant **desodorante** (m, adj)
depilatory **depilatorio** (m, adj)
dextrose **dextrosa** (f); **azúcar de
uva** (f)
dialysis **en diálisis**
diaphragm **diafragma** (m);
diafragma anticonceptivo (m)
digitalin **digitalina** (f)
diphenhydramine **difenhidramina**
(f)
disinfectant **desinfectante** (m, adj)
diuretic **diurético** (m, adj);
píldora diurética (f)
dose **dosis** (f); **medida** (f)
douche **ducha** (f); **ducha interna**
(f); **lavado vaginal** (m); **lavado
interno** (m); **ducha vaginal** (f);
irrigación (f)
DPT **vacuna triple** (f)
drainage **desagüe** (m)
drainage (surgical) **drenaje** (m)
dram **dracma** (f)
dressing **cura** (f); **curación** (f);
apósito (m); **emplaste** (m);
parche (m); **vendaje** (m)
dropper **cuentagotas** (m, sg)
eye dropper **gotero (para los
ojos)** (m, Sp. Am.);
cuentagotas (m)
drops **gotas** (f)
drug **droga** (f); **medicina** (f)

drug store **farmacia** (f, Spain);
droguería (f, Sp. Am.); **botica** (f)
electricity **electricidad** (f)
current **corriente** (adj)
ground(ing) **a tierra**
lead wire **alambre de contacto**
(m)
outlet **salida** (f)
plug **enchufe** (m); **clavija de
contacto** (f)
polarity **polaridad** (f)
socket **enchufe** (m);
tomacorriente (f, Sp. Am.)
electrocardiogram
electrocardiograma (m)
electroencephalogram
electroencefalograma (m)
emetic **emético** (m, adj);
vomitivo (m, adj)
emollient **emoliente** (m, adj)
emulsion **emulsión** (f)
enema **enema** (f); **lavativa** (f);
ayuda (f); **lavado** (m)
enema bag **bolsa para enema** (f)
cleansing enema **(enema) de
limpieza**
retention enema **(enema) de
retención**
soapsuds enema **(enema)
jabonosa**
ephedrine **efedrina** (f)
epidemic **epidemia** (f)
Epsom salt **sal de higuera** (f); **sal
de Epsom** (f)
erythromycin **eritromicina** (f)
estrogen **estrógeno** (m)
eucalyptus leaves **hojas de
eucalipto** (f)
expectorant **expectorante** (m, adj)
expiration date **fecha de caducidad**
(f)
external **externo** (adj)
extract **extracto** (m)
eyecup **copa ocular** (f); **ojera** (f);
lavaojos (m)
eyeglasses **anteojos** (m, pl);
lentes (m, pl); **gafas** (f, pl);
espejuelos (m, pl); **quevedos** (m,
pl)
eye salve **ungüento para los
ojos** (m)
first aid **primeros auxilios** (m, pl);
primera ayuda (f)
flask **frasco** (m)
fluoride **flúor** (m)
foam **espuma** (f)
forceps **pinzas** (f); **fórceps** (m);
gatillo (m, dental); **tenazas** (f)
frozen section **corte por
congelación** (m)
fumigation **fumigación** (f)
fungicide **fungicida** (m, adj)
gargle **gárgara** (f)
gargle, to **hacer gárgaras; hacer
buches** (colloq)
gauze **gasa** (f)

gentian violet **violeta de
genciana** (f)
germicide **germicida** (m, adj)
glass eye **ojo de vidrio** (m)
glucose **glucosa** (f)
glue **goma** (f); **cola** (f)
glycerine **glicerina** (f)
graft **injerto** (m)
guaiacol **guayacol** (m)
hearing aid **aparato para la
sordera** (m); **prótesis auditiva** (f);
prótesis acústica (f); **audífono**
(m); **aparato auditivo** (m);
audiófono (m)
heat **calor** (m)
heat therapy **termoterapia** (f);
tratamiento térmico (m)
hemostat **hemostato** (m)
herbicides **herbicidas** (m);
matayerbas (f)
heroin **heroína** (f)
home cure **curación casera** (f)
home remedy **remedio casero** (m)
hormone **hormón** (m);
hormona (f)
hot water bag **bolsa de agua
caliente** (f)
hydrogen peroxide **agua
oxigenada** (f); **peróxido de
hidrógeno** (m)
hypodermic injection **inyección
hipodérmica** (f)
hypodermic needle **aguja
hipodérmica** (f)
hypodermic syringe **jeringuilla
hipodérmica** (f)
ice **hielo** (m)
ice(bag) pack **bolsa de hielo** (f);
bolsa de caucho para hielo (f)
ichthyol **ictiol** (m)
immunization (vaccine)
inmunización (f); **vacuna** (f)
booster dose **dosis de refuerzo**
(f)
schick test **prueba de schick** (f)
ingredient **ingrediente** (m)
injection **inyección** (f); **indección**
(f, Chicano); **chot** (m, Chicano)
intracutaneous injection
inyección intracutánea (f)
intradermic injection **inyección
intradérmica** (f)
intramuscular injection
inyección intramuscular (f)
intravenous injection
inyección intravenosa (f)
subcutaneous injection
inyección subcutánea (f)
inoculation **inoculación** (f)
insecticide **insecticida** (m, adj)
insect repellent **repelente de
insectos** (m)
instrument, sharp-edged
instrumento afilado (m)
insulin **insulina** (f)
internally **internamente** (adv)

intrauterine device **dispositivo intrauterino** (m); **aparato intrauterino** (m)
intrauterine loop **espiral intrauterino** (m)
iodine **yodo** (m)
iron **hierro** (m)
isolation **aislamiento por cuarentena** (m)
IV (intravenous) solution **solución endovenosa** (f); **suero por la vena** (m)
jelly **jalea** (f)
kilogram **kilogramo** (m)
kit **estuche** (m); **botiquín** (m)
emergency kit **botiquín de emergencia** (m)
first aid kit **botiquín de primeros auxilios** (m); **equipo de urgencia** (m)
knife **cuchillo** (m)
knot **nudo** (m)
label **etiqueta** (f)
laboratory **laboratorio** (m)
laboratory findings **hallazgos de laboratorio** (m)
laboratory test **análisis de laboratorio** (m)
laryngoscope **laringoscopio** (m)
lavage **lavado** (m)
lavatory **lavamanos** (m, sg)
laxative **laxativo** (m); **laxante** (m); **purgante** (m)
lens **lente** (m)
level **al ras**
lindane **lindano** (m)
liniment **linimento** (m)
liquid **líquido** (m)
liter **litro** (m)
liver extract **extracto de hígado** (m)
loop (IUD) **lazo** (m)
lotion **loción** (f); **crema** (f)
lozenge **pastilla** (f); **trocisco** (m); **pastilla de chupar** (f)
LSD **drogas alucinantes** (f); **DAL** (f)
lubricant **lubricante** (m); **lubricativo** (adj)
lukewarm **templado** (adj); **tibio** (adj)
lye **lejía** (f)
magnesia **magnesia** (f)
milk of magnesia **leche de magnesia** (f)
magnifying glass **lupa** (f)
marijuana **mariguana** (f); **yerba** (f); **grifa** (f)
mask **máscara** (f)
massage **masaje** (m)
mattress **colchón** (m)
measure **medida** (f)
measuring cup **taza de medir** (f)
medication **medicación** (f); **medicamento** (m); **medicina** (f)

medicine **medicina** (f); **medicamento** (m); **droga** (f)
medicine cabinet (medicine chest) **botiquín** (m); **despensa** (f, Chicano)
patent medicine **medicina de la farmacia** (f); **medicina de la botica** (f); **medicina patentada** (f); **medicina registrada** (f)
menthol **mentol** (m)
mentholatum **mentolato** (m, Chicano)
Mercurochrome **mercurocromo** (m)
Merthiolate **mertiolato** (m)
methadone **metadona** (f)
milligram **miligramo** (m)
milliliter **mliitro** (m)
mineral **mineral** (m)
mineral water **agua mineral** (f)
mint leaves **hojas de yerbabuena** (f)
mixture **mezcla** (f)
moderate **moderado** (adj)
moist **húmedo** (adj)
morphine **morfina** (f)
mouth wash **lavado bucal** (m); **enjuagatorio** (m); **listerina** (f, colloq)
mouthpiece **bocal** (m); **boquilla** (f)
mustard **mostaza** (f)
mustard bath **baño de mostaza** (m)
mustard plaster **cataplasma de mostaza** (f); **sinapismo** (m)
narcotic **narcótico** (m); **droga somnífera** (f); **droga estupefaciente** (f); **estupefaciente** (m)
needle **aguja** (f)
hypodermic needle **aguja hipodérmica** (f); **jeringa** (f); **jaipo** (m, slang)
nitro(glycerin) **nitro(glicerina)** (f)
novocaine **novocaína** (f)
oil **aceite** (m)
baby oil **aceite para niños** (m)
castor oil **aceite de ricino** (m)
cod liver oil **aceite de hígado de bacalao** (m)
mineral oil **aceite mineral** (m)
ointment **ungüento** (m); **crema** (f); **pomada** (f); **unto** (m)
operation **operación** (f)
ophthalmic **oftálmico** (adj)
ophthalmoscope **oftalmoscopio** (m)
opium **opio** (m); **chinaloa** (f, slang)
oxygen **oxígeno** (m)
pacemaker **aparato cardiocinético** (m); **marcador de paso** (m); **marcapaso** (m); **monitor cardíaco** (m); **marcador de ritmo** (m); **seno auricular** (m)
pain killer **calmante** (m); **analgésico** (m)
palliative **paliativo** (m, adj)

Pap smear **test de Pap** (m); **prueba de Papanicolaou** (m); **untos de Papanicolaou** (m); **frotis de Papanicolaou** (m)
paregoric **paregórico** (m)
patch **parche** (m)
penicillin **penicilina** (f)
pennyroyal leaves **hojas de poleo** (f)
peroxide **peróxido** (m); **agua oxigenada** (f)
hydrogen peroxide **agua oxigenada** (f); **peróxido de hidrógeno** (m)
sodium peroxide **agua oxigenada** (f); **peróxido de sodio** (m)
pesticide **pesticida** (m); **plaguicida** (m)
pharmacy **farmacia** (f); **botica** (f)
phenobarbital **fenobarbital** (m)
pill **píldora** (f); **pastilla** (f)
birth control pill **píldoras para control de embarazo** (f); **pastillas para no tener niños** (f); **píldora anticonceptiva** (f)
sleeping pill **píldora para dormir** (f); **sedativo** (m); **píldora somnífera** (f); **somnífero** (m); **soporífera** (f)
thyroid pill **medicación tiroides** (f)
pillow **almohadilla** (f)
inflatable rubber "doughnut" **almohadilla neumática en forma de anillo** (f)
piperazine **piperazina** (f); **piperawitt** (m, f); **piperidol** (m); **anterobius** (m)
plasma **plasma** (f)
plaster of Paris **yeso mate** (m)
pleural tap **toracentesis** (f); **toracocentesis** (f); **punción quirúrgica de la pared torácica** (f)
poison **veneno** (m); **ponzoña** (f); **intoxicación** (f)
poisonous **venenoso** (adj); **ponzoñoso** (adj)
pomade **pomada** (f)
potassium **potasio** (m)
potassium iodide **yoduro de potasio** (m)
potassium permanganate **permanganato de potasio** (m)
potion **poción** (f); **dosis** (f)
poultice **cataplasma** (f); **emplasto** (m)
powder **polvo** (m)
powdered **en polvo** (adj)
powdery **polvoriento** (adj); **polvoroso** (adj); **empolvado** (adj)
prescribe, to **recetar; prescribir un remedio**
prescription **receta** (f); **prescripción** (f)
prick **pinchazo** (m); **punzada** (f)

prick, to **pinchar**
probe **estilete** (m); **sonda** (f);
tienta (f)
prophylactic **profiláctico** (m, adj)
prosthesis **prótesis** (f); **miembro**
artificial (m)
purgation **purgación** (f)
purgative **purgante** (m); **catártico**
(m, adj)
purge **purga** (f); **purgante** (m);
lavado (m); **lavativo** (m)
quart **cuarto** (m)
quinine **quinina** (f)
radiation shield **blindaje contra la**
radiación (m)
radiation therapy **radioterapia** (f)
radiation treatment **radiaciones** (f)
relief **alivio** (m)
relieve, to **aliviar**
remedy **remedio** (m);
medicamento (m)
restraining device **coercitivo** (m);
medio de restricción (m)
restroom **baño** (m); **cuarto de**
baño (m); **servicios** (m); **WC** (m)
excusado (m)
resuscitation **resucitación** (f)
cardiopulmonary resuscitation
(CPR) **resucitación**
cardiopulmonar (RCP) (f)
mouth-to-mouth resuscitation
resucitación boca a boca (f)
rhythm method **método del ritmo**
(m); **ritmo** (m)
ring (IUD) **anillo** (m)
rub **fricción** (f); **frotación** (f)
rub, to **frotar; restregar**
rubber (condom) **goma** (f);
condón (m); **preservativo** (m)
rubber bulb, syringe **pera de**
goma (f)
rubber gloves **guantes de goma**
(m, pl)
saccharine **sacarina** (f)
saline solution **agua con sal** (f);
agua salina (f)
salt **sal** (f)
salt water **agua salada** (f)
iodized salt **sal yodada** (f)
noniodized salt **sal corriente** (f)
smelling salts **sales aromáticas**
(f, pl); **sales perfumadas** (f, pl)
salve **pomada** (f); **ungüento** (m)
sample **muestra** (f)
sanitary napkin **kotex** (m);
servilleta sanitaria (f); **almohadilla higiénica** (f);
absorbente higiénico (m)
scalpel **escalpelo** (m); **bisturí** (m)
sedative **sedante** (m); **sedativo** (m);
calmante (m)
serum **suero** (m)
antivenin serum **suero**
antiviperino (m)
black widow spider antivenin
serum **suero antialacrán** (m)

shield (IUD) **escudo** (m)
shot **inyección** (f); **chot** (m,
Chicano)
silver nitrate **nitrato de plata** (m)
size **tamaño** (m)
assorted size **tamaño surtido** (m)
large size **tamaño grande** (m)
small size **tamaño pequeño** (m)
sling **cabestrillo** (m); **honda** (f)
soap **jabón** (m)
sodium pentothal **pentotal de**
sodio (m); **pentotal sódico** (m)
solution **solución** (f)
soporific **soporífico** (m);
narcótico (m)
specimen **muestra** (f); **espécimen**
(m)
spectacles **anteojos** (m, pl, general
term); **lentes** (m, pl, Mex.);
espejuelos (m, pl, Cuba); **gafas**
(f, pl); **quevedos** (m, pl, wire-
rimmed)
spermaticide, vaginal
espermaticida vaginal (f)
spinal puncture (spinal tap)
punción lumbar (f)
spiral (IUD) **espiral** (m)
splint **tablilla** (f); **férula** (f)
in a splint **entablillado** (adj)
spoonful **cucharada** (f)
spray **rociador** (m); **pulverizador**
(m); **pulverización** (f)
stain (staining) **coloración** (f);
colorante (m)
acid-fast stain **coloración**
acidorresistente (f)
Giemsa's stain **coloración de**
Giemsa (f)
Gram's stain **coloración de**
Gram (f)
methylene blue stain **coloración**
de azul de metileno (f)
Wright's stain **coloración de**
Wright (f)
Ziehl-Neelsen stain **colorante de**
Ziehl-Neelsen (m)
steam **vapor** (m)
sterile **estéril** (adj); **infecundo** (adj)
sterility **esterilidad** (f);
infecundidad (f)
sterilization **esterilización** (f)
sterilized **esterilizado** (adj)
sterilizer **esterilizador** (m)
stethoscope **estetoscopio** (m);
fonendoscopio (m)
stimulant **estimulante** (m)
stitch **sutura** (f); **punto** (m);
puntada (f)
stocking, elastic **calceta elástica** (f)
stomach pump **bomba estomacal**
(f)
streptomycin **estreptomicina** (f)
stylet **estilete** (m)
substitute **substituto** (m)
sugar **azúcar** (m)
sulfathiazole **sulfatiazol** (m)

sulphur **azufre** (m)
sulphur powder **polvo de**
azufre (m)
sunglasses **gafas de sol** (f, pl);
anteojos oscuros (m, pl)
suntan lotion **crema para el sol** (f);
loción bronceadora (f)
support **apoyo** (m); **soporte** (m);
sostén (f)
supporter, athletic **suspensorio** (m)
suppository **supositorio** (m);
cala (f); **calilla** (f)
vaginal suppository **óvulos** (m,
pl)
suture **sutura** (f); **puntada** (f)
sweetner **dulcificante** (m)
sweets **dulces** (m, pl); **golosinas**
(f, pl)
syringe **jeringa** (f); **jeringuilla** (f)
disposable syringe **jeringa**
descartable (f); **jeringa**
desechable (f)
glass cylinder syringe **jeringa**
con cilindro de cristal (f)
hollow needle syringe **jeringa**
con aguja hueca (f)
hypodermic syringe **jeringuilla**
hipodérmica (f); **jaipo** (m,
slang)
piston, plunger of syringe
émbolo (m)
syrup of ipecac **jarabe de ipeca**
(m); **jarabe de ipecacuana** (m)
tablespoonful **cucharada** (f)
tablet **comprimido** (m); **tableta** (f);
pastilla (f)
tampon **tampón** (m); **tapón** (m)
tea **té** (m)
camomile tea **té de manzanilla**
(m), **agua de manzanilla** (f)
croton tea **té de pionillo** (m)
damiana tea **té de damiana**
desert milkweed tea **té de**
hierba del indio (m)
elderberry and lavender tea **té**
de flor de sauz y hojas de
alhucema (m)
herb rose tea **té de rosa de**
castilla (m)
"Mormon" tea **té de cañutillo**
(del campo) (m)
parsley tea **té de oshá** (m)
sarsaparilla tea **té de cocolmeca**
(m)
spasm herb tea **té de hierba del**
pasmo (m)
spearmint tea **té de yerbabuena**
(m)
spider milkweed tea **té de**
inmortal (m)
swamp root tea **té de hierba del**
manzo
tansy mustard herb tea **té de**
pamita
wild marjoram tea **té de**
orégano

wormseed tea **té de epazote** (m);
té de México (m); **té borde** (m)
teaspoonful **cucharadita** (f)
level teaspoonful **cucharadita
llena al ras** (f)
tepid **tibio** (adj)
Terramycin **terramicina** (f)
test **examen** (m); **prueba** (f);
análisis (m)
serology test **prueba serológica**
(f)
skin test **reacción cutánea** (f)
sputum test **análisis de
esputos** (m)
test tube **tubo de ensayo** (m)
tuberculin test **tuberculina** (f)
urinalysis **urinálisis** (m);
análisis de la orina (m)
tetanus **tétano(s)** (m); **mal de
arco** (m); **pasmo seco** (m)
tetracycline **tetraciclina** (f)
therapeutic **terapéutico** (adj)
therapy **terapia** (f); **tratamiento**
(m)
thermometer **termómetro** (m)
oral **oral** (adj)
rectal **rectal** (adj)
tongue depressor **pisa-lengua** (f);
abate lengua (f); **depresor de la
lengua** (m)
tonic **tónico** (m)
tourniquet **torniquete** (m); **liga** (f)

traction **tracción** (f)
tranquilizer **tranquilizante** (m);
calmante (m); **apaciguador** (m)
transfusion **transfusión** (f)
transmission **transmisión** (f)
droplet transmission **transmisión por gotillas** (f)
transmission by contact **transmisión mediante contacto** (f)
vector transmission **transmisión mediante vector** (f)
vehicle **vehículo** (m)
treatment **tratamiento** (m)
truss **braguero** (m); **faja** (f)
turpentine **trementina** (f)
ultraviolet lamp **lámpara de rayos
ultravioletas** (f)
unguent **pomada** (f); **ungüento** (m)
urinalysis **urinálisis** (m);
análisis de la orina (m)
midstream urinalysis **urina
recogida a mitad de la micción**
(f); **uricultivo** (m)
vaccination **vacunación** (f);
inoculación (f)
booster **refuerzo** (m)
DPT **triple** (f)
vaccine, immunization **vacuna** (f);
inmunización (f)
oral polio vaccine **vacuna oral
contra polio** (f); **gotas para
polio** (f)

Vaseline **vaselina** (f)
vermifuge **vermífugo** (m, adj);
antihelmíntico (m, adj)
vial **vial** (m); **botella** (f); **frasco**
(m); **ampolla** (f)
vinegar **vinagre** (m)
vitamin **vitamina** (f)
calcium **calcio** (m)
iron **hierro** (m); **sulfato
ferroso** (m)
niacin **niacina** (f)
vitamin B_1 **tiamina** (f)
vitamin B_2 **riboflavina** (f)
vitamin B_6 **piridoxina** (f)
vitamin C **ácido ascórbico** (m)
vomitive **vomitivo** (m, adj);
emético (m, adj)
walker **andador** (m)
warm **tibio** (adj)
warmer **más caliente** (adj);
calentador (m)
weight **peso** (m)
wheelchair **silla de ruedas** (f)
wrapping in a cold (wet) sheet
**empacamiento en sábana fría
(mojada)** (m)
x-ray **radiografía** (f); **rayo equis**
(m); **retrato del x-ray** (m,
Chicano)
x-ray therapy **radioterapia** (f)

COMMON POISONS

VENENOS COMUNES

Inhaled Poisons Venenos aspirados

gas **gas** (m)

smoke **humo** (m)

vapor **vapor** (m)

Injected Poisons Venenos inyectados

rat bites **picadas de ratones** (f)
scorpion bites **picadas de
escorpión** (f)

snake bite **mordedura de culebra**
(f)

snake bite, poisonous
mordedura de víbora venenosa
(f)

Oral Poisons Venenos tomados por la boca

acetic acid **ácido acético (puro)** (m)
ammonia **amoníaco** (m)
arsenic acid **ácido arsénico** (m)
ascorbic acid **ácido ascórbico** (m)
bichloride of mercury **cloruro
mercúrico** (m)
camphor **alcanfor** (m)

carbolic acid **ácido carbólico**
(m)
carbon tetrachloride **tetracloruro
de carbono** (m)
cyanic acid **ácido cianótico** (m)
detergents **detergentes** (m)
disinfectant **desinfectante** (m)

furniture polish **pulimento para
muebles** (m)
hydrochloric acid **ácido
clorhídrico** (m)
hydrofluoric acid **ácido
fluorhídrico** (m)
iodine **yodo** (m)

kerosene **keroseno** (m); **querosén** (m); **queroseno** (m)
lye **lejía** (f)
mushrooms **hongos** (m)
nitric acid **ácido nítrico** (m)
oil of wintergreen **aceite de gaulteria** (m)
oxalic acid **ácido oxálico** (m)
phosphoric acid **ácido fosfórico** (m)

pine oil **aceite de pino** (m)
rubbing alcohol **alcohol para fricciones** (m)
silver nitrate **nitrato de plata** (m)
sodium carbonate **carbonato de sodio** (m)
sodium hydroxide **hidróxido de sodio** (m)
sodium hypochlorite (bleach)

hipoclorito de sodio (m) **(blanqueador de ropa**, m)
sodium sulfate (in toilet cleaners) **sulfato de sodio** (m) **(en limpiadores de inodoros)**
strychnine **estricnina** (f)
sulfuric acid **ácido sulfúrico** (m)
turpentine **esencia de trementina** (f)

ANTIDOTES
ANTIDOTOS

cause vomiting, to **provocarse el vómito**
drink plenty of, to **beber mucho (-a)**
egg white **clara de huevo** (f)
flour **harina** (f)
ground chalk in water **creta pulvarizada en agua** (f)
hot coffee **café caliente** (m)
milk **leche** (f); **milque** (f, Chicano)
mustard water **agua con**

mostaza (f)
salt water **agua salada** (f)
soapy water **agua jabonosa** (f)
starch **almidón** (m)
stomach pump **bomba estomacal** (f)
strong tea **té cargado** (m); **té fuerte** (m)
syrup of ipecac **jarabe de ipecacuana** (m)

universal antidote **antídoto universal** (m)
animal carbon—2 parts **carbón animal—dos partes**
calcined magnesia—1 part **magnesia calcinada—una parte**
tannic acid—1 part **ácido tánico—una parte**
vomit, to **vomitar; dompear** (Chicano); **arrojar** (colloq)

SELECTED DRUG ABUSE TERMINOLOGY
TERMINOLOGIA ESCOGIDA PARA EL ABUSO DE (LAS) DROGAS—PARA LOS ESTUPEFACIENTES [22]

Acapulco gold (Marijuana) **colombiana; grifa; grifo; Juana; Juanita; lucas; mariguana** [23] **, monte; mota; yerba; yesca; zacate; sinsemilla**
acid (LSD) **ácido; aceite; azúcar; LSD** [24]
addict (drug) **adicto; adicto a droga(s); adicto a las drogas narcóticas; drogadicto; morfinómano; tecato; toxicómano; yeso**
addict in search of a fix **buscatoques** (sg)
addiction (drug) **adicción; drogadicción; farmacodependencia; hábito; toxicomanía**

administer marijuana to someone, to **amarihuanar; engrifar; enmarihuanar**
amphetamine **anfetamina; ácido; a; bombido; estimulante; naranjas**
amphetamine + heroin + barbiturates IV amphetamines **bombita**
ampule **pomo**
angel dust (PCP) **cucuy; fencycladina; líquido; PCP** [25] **; polvo**
artillery **equipo hipodérmico; estuche; herramienta; herre; R**
bad trip **mal viaje; experiencia mala en el uso de drogas**

bag **bolsita; paquete** (m)
balloon (of heroin) **cimbomba; globo**
bang, to **clavarse; componerse; curarse; filerearse; jincarse; picarse; rayarse; shootear**
barbiturate (pill) **barbitúrico; barbiturato; cacahuate** (m); **colorada; globo**
barrels (green)/(the) beast **aceite** (m); **ácido; azúcar; LSD** [26]
be carrying narcotic drugs, to **andar carga; andar cargado (-da); cargar; traer carga**
be (non-)habit forming, to **(no) crear vicio**

bennies (benz, benzies— amphetamines) **anfetaminas; benzedrinas; blancas**

be on the nod, to (be under the influence of heroin) **cotorear**

big C (cocaine) **carga; coca; cocaína; nieve (f); perico** (Cuba); **talco** (Texas, Cuba)

bindle (quantity of marijuana or narcotics) **bolsita, paquete** (m)

blasted, to be **andar botando; andar hypo; andar loco (-a); andar locote; andar pasado; andar prendido; andar servido; andar hasta las manitas; hasta las manos; elevado a-mil; subido a-mil**

blow snow, to **aspirar cocaína**

blue angels (blue devils, blue dolls, blue heavens, blues— amobarbital sodium) **amital; cápsulas azules**

blue star (morning-glory seeds) **dompedro; semillas de dondiego de día**

boy (heroin) **azúcar** (Arizona, Texas); **caballo; carga; chiva; cohete; heroína**

brick (usually a kilogram of marijuana or narcotics) **ladrillo**

burn out, to **doblar(se)**

busted, to be **ser arrestado; ser torcido**

buzz, to get a **agarrar onda**

buzz, to have a (effect of a drug) **sonarse**

buzzed, to be see "high, to be," "blasted, to be"

caffeine **cafeína**

candy (barbiturates) **barbitúricos**

(cocaine) **carga; coca; cocaína; nieve** (f); **perico** (Cuba); **talco** (Texas, Cuba)

cap (capsule) **cachucha; cápsula; deque** (m); **gorra**

charged up, to be see "high, to be," "blasted, to be"

chip, to (to use narcotics infrequently) **chipiar, chipear**

cigarette butt **bachica** (esp. marijuana); **tecolota; tecla**

clean, to be **andar derecho; andar limpio**

clear up, to **cortarse el vicio; kikear; quitear**

coast, to see "high, to be," "blasted, to be"

cocaine[27] **acelere; aliviane; alucine; arponazo; azúcar; blanca nieves; carga; coca; cocacola; cocada; cocazo; coco; coka; cotorra; cucharazo; chutazo; doña blanca; glacis** (m); **knife** (m); **marizazo; nice; nieve**

(f); **nose; pase** (m); **pepsicola; pericazo; perico** (Cuba); **polvo; polvito; talco** (Texas, Cuba); **tecata**

codeine[28] **codeína**

cold turkey **a la brava; a lo bronco**

croaker, hungry[29] **matasanos avaricioso**

deal in drugs, to **dilear; diliar**

depressant **deprimente; debilitante**

devils (seconal, barbiturates) **coloradas; diablos; rojas**

dexedrine (dexies—dextro-amphetamine) **dexedrina; dextroanfetamina**

dime **diez dólares; diez años de prisión; sinónimo para diez**

dime bag (envelope of heroin, cocaine, or marijuana) **paquete de drogas**

dope **droga; estupefaciente; fármaco; narcótico; nombre inglés para mariguana** (see below)

dope pusher **narcotraficante; burro; madre; pusheador**

doper **mariguano; moto; quemón; yesco**

downer (downs—barbiturate) **calmante; sedativo; tranquilizante**

drag (puff of marijuana cigarette) **toque** (m)

drop (n) **entrega; lugar donde se deja o se esconde una droga**

drug **droga; estupefaciente** (m); **fármaco; narcótico**

drug, to **endrogar**

drug abuse **abuso de las drogas, de los estupefacientes**

drugged **endrogado; prendido**

drug habit **morfinomanía**

drug supply **cachucha**

drug traffic **venta y tráfico de drogas**

dump, to (to get rid of) **dompear**

dust (cocaine, PCP) **cucuy; fencycladina; líquido; PCP[30]; polvo**

falling out (overdose of narcotics or sedatives) **durmiéndose; durmiéndose a medias**

fit (outfit—tools necessary for injection of drugs: needle, syringe [eyedropper and rubber bulb] cooker, cotton and matches, tie off) **equipo hipodérmico; estuche** (m); **herramienta; herre** (f); **R** (f)

fix (an IV injection of drugs) **abuja; abujazo; cura** (f); **filerazo; gallazo**

fix, to (to inject drugs) **clavarse; componerse; curarse; filerearse;**

jincarse; picarse; rayarse; shootear

fix up, to (to heat and mix heroin) **arreglar; cuquear**

flashing, to be[31] **oler cola**

flip, to **volverse loco**

floating, to be see "high, to be," "blasted, to be"

flying saucers (morning-glory seeds) **dompedro; semillas de dondiego de día**

freak out, to see "high, to be," "blasted, to be"

gallery (place to take drugs) **galería**

gas (nitrous oxide) **gas exhilarante; gas hilarante; óxido nitroso**

get down, to (to acquire drugs) **tomar drogas; usar drogas**

get in the groove, to **ponerse al tanto**

glass eyes (drug addict) see "addict (drug)"

glue **cola; goma**

glue sniffer **glufo**

gluey **drogadicto a cola**

goofballs (sedatives, especially barbiturates) **cápsulas de drogas**

gravy (a mixture of blood and heroin) **salsa**

gun **equipo hypodérmico; estuche; herramienta; herre; R**

H (heroin) **azúcar** (Arizona, Texas); **caballo; carga; chiva; cohete; heroína**

habit **adicción; drogadicción; farmacodependencia; hábito; habituación; toxicomanía**

hallucinogen **alucinante; alucinógeno**

hangover, to have **andar crudo**

hash (hashish) **hachís; hachich; haschich** (m)

heroin[32] **adormidera; achivia; amor; ardor; arpon; arponazo; azúcar, azufre; banderilla; blanco; blanca; borra blanca; ca-ca; caballo; cagada** (vulgar); **carga; cáscara; cohete; cristales; cura; chiva; chutazo; dama blanca; golpe; goma; gato; H; helena; heroica; heroína; la cosa; la duna; lenguazo; manteca; nieve; papel; papelito; pericazo; piquete; polvo; polvo amargo; polvo blanco; pasta; stufa; tecata**

heroin capsule **cachucha; capa; gorra; timba**

heroin user (addict) **tecato**

high, to be **andar botando; andar hypo; andar loco; andar locote; andar pasado; andar prendido; andar servido; andar hasta las**

manitas; hasta las manos;
elevado a-mil; subido a-mil
high, to get **agarrar onda; andar
botando; andar hypo; andar loco;
andar locote; andar pasado; andar
prendido; andar servido; sonarse**
high from glue sniffing **glufo** (adj)
high from sniffing paint thinner
tiniado (adj)
high on (marijuana) (turned on)
motiado (adj)
high on (narcotics) **alivianado;
caballón; loco; locote;
sonámbulo; sonado**
high on pills **píldoro**
hit up, to **clavarse; componerse;
curarse; filerearse; jincarse;
picarse; rayarse; shootear**
hooked on drugs **prendido**
hook on narcotics, to **prender**
hot shot ([often fatal]) overdose)
**dosis excesiva; sobredosis;
sobredosis tóxica**
hype (an addict who uses
subcutaneous injections)
**adicto; adicto a drogas;
drogadicto; tecato**
hypo, to having the see "bang, to"
hypodermic needle used to inject
drugs **jaipo**
ingest narcotic pills, to
pildorear(se); pildoriar(se)
inhalant **inhalante**
inhale glue, to **aspirar cola;
inhalar cola; respirar cola**
injection (of a narcotic substance)
abuja; abujazo; inyección; piquete
(m)
inject oneself with drugs, to
**clavarse, componerse; curarse;
filerearse; darse un piquete;
inyectarse; jincarse; picarse;
rayarse; shootear**
in need, to be **andar enfermo**
in transit **tripeando**
jab, to jack off, to "inject
oneself with drugs, to," see
"inject oneself with drugs, to"
jagged up, to be (under the
influence of drugs) "blasted, to
be"
jerk off, to see "inject oneself
with drugs, to"
jive stick (marijuana cigarette)
**charuto; cigarro de mariguana;
frajo; frajo de seda; leño;
leñito; pito**
joint (marijuana cigarette) **abuja;
charuto; cigarro de mariguana;
frajo; frajo de seda; leño; pito**
jolly pop, to (to use drugs
infrequently) **chipiar; chipear**
joy pop, to (to use drugs
infrequently) **chipiar; chipear**
junkie (narcotic addict) **adicto;
adicto a drogas; drogadicto;**

morfinómano; tecato;
toxicómano; yeso
kick **patada**
kick the habit, to **cortarse el
vicio, kikear, quitear**
kit see "fit"
lactose (used to cut heroin)
lactosa
layout see "fit"
letdown **bajón**
loaded, to be see "blasted, to be"
loaded, to get **agarrar onda;
sonarse**
load of narcotics **carga**
LSD[33] **aceite; aceitunas; acelide;
ácido(s); alucinantes; avándaro;
azúcar; blanco de España; bomba;
cápsulas; cohete; colorines;
cristales; chochos; diablos;
divina; droga alucinante; dulces;
elefante blanco; en onda; gis;
grasas; la salud; lluvia de
estrellas; mica; mureler; nave;
orange; papel; paper; piedrita de
la luna; pit; purple haze;
saturnos; sugar; sunshine;
tacatosa; terrones; trip; viaje;
viaje en las nubes; white ácido
lisérgico; droga LSD; ALD;
café**
machinery see "fit"
magic mushrooms (psilocybin)
hongos
mainline, to **inyectar drogas
directamente en la vena principal
del brazo**
mainliner **jaipo; jaipa**
manicure, to (clean and prepare
marijuana for rolling into
cigarettes) **limpiar (mariguana)**
marijuana[34] **achicalada; alfalfa;
bacha; bailarina; café;
campechana verde; canabis;
cáñamo; carrujo; cartucho;
cochornis; coffee; colombiana;
cosa; cris; chara; chester;
chiclona; chichara; chira; chupe;
churus; de la buena; diosa verde;
doña Juanita; epazote; fitoca;
flauta; flor de Juana; frajo;
ganga; ganja; gavos; golden;
griefo; grifa; grifo; grilla; grass;
guato; güera; habanita; hashi;
hierba; hoja verde; huato; índice;
jani; Jefferson; joint; Juana;
Juanita; Kris Kras; la verde;
lucas; macoña; mafufa; mani;
Margarita; mari; María; María
Juanita; Mariana; mariguana;
marihuana; marijuana; marinola;
mariola; marquita;Mary Jane;
Mary Popins; meserole;
monstruo verde; monte; mora;
mostaza; mota; oro verde,
panetela; pasto; pastura;
pepita verde; petate; petate del**

soldado; pitillo; pito; pochola;
pod; polillo; pot; queta; rollo; té;
toque; tromadora; verdosa; yedo;
yerba; yerba verde; yerba de oro;
yerba del diablo; yerba santa;
yerbavuena; yesca; zacate (low-
grade variety)
marijuana smoker **yesco**
marijuana user **grifo; mariguano;
marihuano; marijuano; moto;
quemón; yesco**
marks see "tracks"
member of police narcotics squad
narco
mescaline[35] **mescalina**
morning glory seeds[36] **semillas de
dondiego del día; dompedro**
morphine[37] **morfi; morfina**
nail (needle for drug injection)
**abuja; aguja; filero; hierro;
jeringuilla; punta**
narcotic **narcótico; droga;
estupefaciente; fármaco**
narcotic pills **pinguas**
narcotic substitute **la otra cosa**
nebbis[38] (barbiturates) **amarillas;
gorras amarillas**
need, to be in **andar enfermo**
needle **abuja; aguja; filero; hierro;
jeringuilla; punta**
OD, to (to overdose) **doblar(se);
dar una dosis excesiva**
opiate **opiáceo; opiado**
opium[39] **goma; material negro;
opio**
outfit see "fit"
overdose **dosis excesiva;
sobredosis; sobredosis tóxica**
overdosed **sobredosado**
packet of heroin **gramo**
paraphernalia see "fit"
paregoric **paregórico**
PCP[40] **cucuy; fencycladina;
líquido; PCP[41]; polvo**
peddler (drug dealer)[42] **burro;
madre; pusheador; traficante;
vendedor de drogas;
narcotraficante**
person high on drugs **cócono**
pill freak **píldoro**
pill head **píldoro**
pill popper **píldoro**
pop, to (to inject with a needle)
see "inject oneself with drugs, to"
poppy **amapola**
Product IV **combinación de PCP
y LSD**
provide an addict with a fix, to
curar
psilocybin[43] **las mujercitas; los
niños; hombrecitos; hongos**
psychedelic **droga psicodélica;
sicodélico**
push, to **pushar**
put heroin in capsules, to **capear;
capiar**

roach (butt of a marijuana cigarette) **bacha; bachilla; colilla; cucaracha; tecla; tecolota; tocola**

runner (carrier of drugs)[44] **caballo; mula**

scoff, to **ingerir/injerir narcóticos**

scoop, to **aspirar narcóticos**

score, to see "inject oneself with drugs, to"

seconal[45] **seconal; colorada; diablo; roja**

sedative **calmante; sedativo**

shoot (up), to see "inject oneself with drugs, to"

shoot oneself, to see "inject oneself with drugs, to"

skin, to **inyectar narcóticos**

sleep walker (heroin addict) **tecato; adicto a heroína**

smoke marijuana, to **motear; motiar; tronar(se); quemar**

sniff glue, to **aspirar cola; hacer(se) a la glu(fa); inhalar cola; respirar cola; sesonar**

snort, to (to sniff residue of powdered narcotics) **estufear; estufiar; aspirar narcóticos por la nariz**

snow bird **adicto a cocaína**

soaring, to be see "blasted, to be"

spaced (out), to be see "blasted, to be"

spike (a hypodermic needle) **abuja; aguja; filero; hierro; jeringuilla; punta**

stash, to (to hide supply of drugs) **clavar; plantar**

stimulant **estimulante; exitante**

stoned, to be see "blasted, to be"

strung out, to be see "blasted, to be"

syringe see "spike"

take (drugs), to **ingerir; injerir; administrarse; tomar**

take a hit, to (to take a puff from a joint) **quemar; tronarse; tronársela**

take marijuana, to **amarihuanarse, enmarihuanarse, engrifarse**

take up, to see "take a hit, to"

tolerance **tolerancia**

track marks see "tracks"

tracks (marks and scars caused by use of hypodermic needle) **marcas; trakes; traques**

traffic in drugs, to **dilear; diliar; traficar**

tranquilizer **ansiolítico; tranquilizante**

trip, to **tripear**

trip out, to **agarrar onda; sonarse**

user **adicto; adicto a drogas; drogadicto; tecato; toxicómano; yeso**

of marijuana, cocaine and morphine **maricocaimorfi**

of morphine **morfiniento**

of pills **pildoriento**

weed, to blow (to smoke marijuana) **motear; motiar; tronar**

wired, to be see "inject oneself with drugs, to"

yage[46] **ayahuasca**

zonked, to be see "blasted, to be"

EXCRETIONS
EXCRECIONES

excretion **excreción** (f); **miércoles** (m, sg, euph)

feces **"aguas mayores"** (f); **caca** (f, slang); **cagada** (f, vulgar); **cámara** (f); **deposiciones** (f); **evacuación del vientre** (f); **excrementos** (m); **heces fecales** (f, pl); **materia fecal** (f); **miércoles** (m, sg, euph); **mierda** (f, vulgar); **pase del cuerpo** (m)

stool see "feces"

stool specimen **muestra de excremento** (f); **muestra de heces fecales** (f)

sweat **sudor** (m)

urine **"aguas menores"** (f); **chi** (f, vulgar); **orín** (m); **orina** (f); **orines** (m)

collection of the specimen **acumulación de la muestra** (f); **toma de la muestra** (f); **recolección de la muestra** (f)

color of the urine **color de la orina** (f)

straw **de paja**

yellow **amarillo**

urine constituents **componentes de orina** (m)

acetone **acetona** (f)

albumin **albúmina** (f)

ammonia **amoníaco** (m)

bile **bilis** (f)

bilirubin **bilirrubina** (f)

blood **sangre** (f)

calcium **calcio** (m)

chlorides **cloruro** (m)

creatine **creatina** (f)

crystal(s) **cristal(es)** (m)

glucose **glucosa** (f)

phosphate **fosfato** (m)

solids **sólidos** (m)

total nitrogen **nitrógeno total** (m)

total sulphur **azufre total** (m)

urea **urea** (f)

urobilin **urobilina** (f)

urobilirubin **urobilirrubina** (f)

BLOOD
SANGRE

antibody **anticuerpo** (m)

antigen **antígeno** (m)

bleeding **pérdida de sangre de poca intensidad** (f); **sangría** (f); **flujo de sangre** (m)

bleeding tendencies **tendencias a sangrar** (f)

bleeding time **tiempo de hemorragia** (m); **tiempo de sangría** (m)

blood **sangre** (f); **colorada** (f, slang, Chicano)

blood bank **banco de sangre** (m)

blood chemistry (analysis of blood) **análisis de sangre** (m)

blood clot **coágulo de sangre** (m); **cuajarón de sangre** (m) blood component **componente de sangre** (m); **componente sanguíneo** (m)

dessicated red blood cells **hematíes desecados** (m)

fresh blood **sangre fresca** (f)

oxalated blood **sangre oxalatada** (f)

platelet enriched blood **sangre enriquecida en plaquetas** (f)

stored (frozen) blood **sangre conservada** (f)

whole blood **sangre pura** (f)

blood corpuscles **corpúsculos de la sangre** (m)

blood count **biometría hemática** (f); **recuento hemático** (f); **recuento sanguíneo** (m); **cifra de los elementos formes de la sangre** (f); **hematimetría** (f)

blood culture **hemocultivo** (m)

blood donor **donante de sangre** (m, f); **donador(a) de sangre** (m, f)

plasmapheresis donor **donante para plasmaféresis**

blood exchange **exanguino-transfusión** (f)

blood flow **corriente sanguínea** (f)

blood formula **fórmulo hemática** (f)

blood group **grupo sanguíneo** (m)

universal donor **donante universal** (m, f)

universal recipient **receptor(a) universal** (m, f)

blood-grouping **determinación de los grupos sanguíneos** (f)

blood lavage **lavado de la sangre** (m)

blood oxygen analyzer **analizador del oxígeno de la sangre** (m)

blood path **vía sanguínea** (f)

blood picture **cuadro hemático** (m); **fórmula hematológica** (f)

blood pigment **pigmento sanguíneo** (m)

blood plasma **plasma sanguíneo** (m)

blood platelet (blood plaque) **plaqueta** (f)

blood poisoning **intoxicación de la sangre** (f); **toxemia** (f); **septicemia** (f); **sepsis** (f); **envenenamiento de la sangre** (m)

blood pressure **presión de la sangre** (f); **presión arterial** (f); **tensión arterial** (f)

blood pressure cuff (sphygmomanometer) **esfigmomanómetro** (m); **manguito de presión sanguínea** (m)

blood pressure gauge **hemodinamómetro**

blood serum **suero sanguíneo** (m)

blood smear **frotis sanguíneo** (m); **extensión de sangre** (f)

bloodstained **sanguinolento** (adj)

blood stock **depósito de sangre** (m)

bloodstream **torrente circulatorio** (m)

blood studies **exámenes hematológicos** (m)

blood sugar **azúcar sanguíneo** (m); **glucemia** (f)

blood supply **aporte de sangre** (m); **irrigación** (f)

blood test **examen de la sangre** (m); **análisis de sangre** (m)

SMA **análisis múltiple secuencial** (m)

blood transfusion **transfusión sanguínea** (f)

blood type **grupo sanguíneo** (m)

blood typing **determinación del grupo sanguíneo** (f)

blood urea **urea** (f)

blood vessel **vaso sanguíneo** (m)

clot reaction time **tiempo de retracción del coágulo** (m)

coagulation time **tiempo de coagulación** (m)

cross match **pruebas cruzadas** (f)

determination of circulation time **determinación del tiempo de circulación** (f)

erythrocytes (red blood cells) **eritrocitos** (m); **glóbulos rojos** (m); **hematíes** (m)

fibrin **fibrina** (f)

hemoglobin **hemoglobina** (f)

leukocytes (white blood cells) **leucocitos** (m); **glóbulos blancos** (m)

nucleated leukocytes **leucocitos nucleados** (m)

acidophiles **acidófilos** (m)

basophiles **basófilos** (m)

blood platelets **plaquetas sanguíneas** (f)

eosinophiles **eosinófilos** (m)

lymphocytes **linfocitos** (m)

monocytes **monocitos** (m)

polymorphonuclear neutrophiles **neutrófilos polimorfonucleares** (m)

"polymorphs" **"polimorfos"** (m)

reticulocytes **reticulocitos** (m)

thrombocytes **trombocitos** (m)

plasmapheresis **plasmaféresis** (f)

prothrombin time **tiempo de protrombina** (m)

RBC (red blood count) **numeración de glóbulos rojos** (f); **NGR** (f)

sedimentation **sedimentación** (f)

erythrosedimentation **eritrosedimentación** (f)

unit of blood **unidad de sangre** (f)

WBC (white blood count) **numeración de glóbulos blancos** (f); **NGB** (f)

PREGNANCY, CHILDBIRTH, CONTRACEPTION, POSTNATAL CARE OF THE MOTHER

EMBARAZO, PARTO, CONTRACEPCION, CUIDADO POSNATAL DE LA MADRE

abortion **aborto** (m)

induced abortion **aborto inducido** (m); **aborto provocado** (m)

spontaneous abortion **aborto espontáneo** (m)

therapeutic abortion **aborto terapéutico** (m)

threatened abortion **amenaza de aborto** (f)

abscess **absceso** (m)

abscessed (adj) **apostemado** (adj)

abstain from sexual relations, to **abstenerse de las relaciones sexuales**

add, to **añadir; agregar**

afterbirth **secundinas** (f, pl, Mex.); **placenta** (f); **segundo parto** (m, Chicano)

alcohol **alcohol** (m)
rubbing alcohol **alcohol para fricciones** (m)

amenorrhea **amenorrea** (f)

amniocentesis **amniocentesis** (f); **prueba del saco amniótico** (f)

amniotic sac **saco amniótico** (m)

amniotic fluid **agua del amnios** (f)

anesthesia **anestesia** (f)
block **anestesia de bloque** (f)
caudal **anestesia caudal** (f)
epidural **anestesia epidural** (f)
general **anestesia total** (f)
inhalation **anestesia por inhalación** (f)
local **anestesia local** (f)
regional **anestesia regional** (f)
saddle block **anestesia en silla de montar** (f)
spinal **anestesia espinal** (f); **anestesia raquídea** (f)
twilight sleep **sueño crepuscular** (m)

apron **delantal** (m)

baby, infant **criatura** (f); **bebé** (m); **nene** (m); **nena** (f); **guagua** (m, f, Chile, Ec., Peru, Bol., Arg., Ur.); **tierno** (m, C.A.)

bag of waters **fuente** (f, colloq); **bolsa de las aguas** (f); **bolsa membranosa** (f); **aguas** (f, pl)

bathe, to **bañar**

bear down, to **pujar; hacer bajar por fuerza**

become bloated, to **abotagar**

bed **cama** (f); **lecho** (m)

bilirubin **bilirrubina** (f)

bind, to **atar; amarrar**

binder **cintura** (f); **faja** (f)
"belly" binder **ombliguero** (m)

birth **nacimiento** (m)
at term **a término**
multiple birth **nacimiento múltiple** (m)
post-term **nacimiento tardío** (m)
premature **nacimiento prematuro** (m)

birth, to give **dar a luz; parir; alumbrar; sanar** (euph); **salir de su cuidado** (Chicano); **aliviarse** (Chicano)

birth canal **canal del parto** (m)

birth certificate **certificado de nacimiento** (m); **partida de nacimiento** (f)

birth control **control de la natalidad** (f)
Billing's method **método de Billing** (m)

cervical cap **gorro cervical** (m)

coil **coil** (m, Chicano)

coitus interruptus **interrupción de coito** (f); **retirarse** (m); **salirse** (m, slang)

condom **condón** (m); **hule** (m, slang); **forro** (m, vulgar, Arg.); **preservativo** (m, slang); **goma** (f)

diaphragm **diafragma (anticonceptivo)** (m)

IUD **DIU** (m); **dispositivo intrauterino** (m); **aparato intrauterino** (m); **aparatito** (m, Chicano)
loop **alambrito** (m); **lupo** (m); **asa** (f)
pill **píldora** (f); **pastilla** (f)
rhythm **ritmo** (m); **método de ritmo** (m)
rubber **goma** (f); **forro** (m, vulgar, Arg.); **hule** (m, slang)
sterilization **esterilización** (f)
tubal ligation **ligadura de trompas** (f)
vaginal cream **crema vaginal** (f)
vaginal foam **espuma vaginal** (f)
vaginal jelly **jalea vaginal** (f)
vasectomy **vasectomía** (f)

birthmark **lunar** (m)

birth weight **peso del nacimiento** (m)

bladder **vejiga** (f)

blanket **frazada** (f)

bleed in excess, to **desangrar**

bleeding **flujo de sangre** (m); **périda de sangre de poca intensidad** (f); **hemorragia** (f); (hemorrhage); **sangría** (f)

bleeding (adj) **sangrante** (adj)

bleeding, breakthrough **hemorragia inesperada** (f); **flujo de sangre por la vagina inesperadamente** (m)

bleeding to excess **desangramiento** (m)

bloated **aventado** (adj); **hinchado** (adj); **abotagado** (adj)

blood **sangre** (f)
blood circulation **circulación sanguínea** (f)
blood clot **coágulo sanguíneo** (m); **cuajarón** (m)
blood count **hematimetría** (f); **recuento sanguíneo** (m)
blood donor **donante de sangre** (m, f)
blood group **grupo sanguíneo** (m)
blood plasma **plasma sanguíneo** (m)
bloodstain **mancha de sangre** (f)
bloodstained **manchado de sangre** (adj)
blood transfusion **transfusion de sangre** (f)

blood, whole **sangre entera** (f)

bloody **cruento** (adj); **sangriento** (adj)

bloody show **muestra de sangre** (f); **tapón de moco** (m, Mex.); **secreción mucosa mezclada con sangre** (f); **mucosidad teñida de sangre** (f)

blotches, skin **manchas oscuras en la piel** (f)

boil the bottles, to **hervir las botellas**

bottle, baby **biberón** (m); **bote** (m, slang, Chicano); **botella** (f); **mamadera** (f, Sp. Am.); **pacha** (f, Chicano); **tele** (f, Chicano)

breast **seno** (m); **pecho** (m); **teta** (f); **chichi** (f, Mex.); **chichas** (f, pl, C.R.); **tele** (f, Chicano)
breast of a wet nurse **chiche** (m, Mex. Guat.)
caked breast **mastitis por estasis** (f)
painful breasts **senos dolorosos** (m)

breastfeed, to **dar el pecho; dar de mamar; dar chiche; criar con pecho** (Chicano)

breastfeeding **lactancia maternal** (f)

breast pump **mamadera** (f); **bomba de ordeñar** (f); **tiraleches** (f)

breechbirth (frank breech) **presentación trasera** (f); **presentación de nalgas** (f)

burp **eructo** (m); **regüeldo** (m)

burp, to **eructar; repetir** (i); **sacar aire** (Chicano); **urutar** (Chicano)

buttock[47] **nalga** (f); **culo** (m, colloq. Arg.); **salvohonor** (m, colloq); **bombo** (m, Ur.)

caeserean delivery **parto cesáreo** (m); **parto por operación** (m)

caesarean section **operación cesárea** (f); **sección cesárea** (f)

can opener **abrelatas** (m)

catheter **catéter** (m); **sonda** (f)

catheterize **cateterizar**

cervix **cerviz** (f); **cuello de la matriz** (m); **cuello del útero** (m); **cérvix** (f)

childbirth **parto** (m); **alumbramiento** (m)

chloasma (facial discoloration) (mask of pregnancy) **paño** (m); **mancha del embarazo** (f); **mancha de la preñez** (f); **cloasma** (f)

circumcise, to **circuncidar**

circumcision **circuncisión** (f)

clitoris **clítoris** (m); **bolita** (f, slang); **pelotita** (f, slang)

coitus **coito** (m)

colic **cólico** (adj)

colostrum **calostro** (m)
conceive, to **concebir** (i)
conception **concepción** (f);
fecundación del huevo (f)
confinement **puerperio** (m);
cuarentena[48] (f); **riesgo** (m);
alumbramiento (m)
congential malformations
malformaciones congénitas (f)
constipation **estreñimiento** (m)
continue working, to **seguir**
trabajando (i)
contraceptive **anticonceptivo** (m,
adj); **contraceptivo** (m, adj)
contractions **contracciones de la**
matriz (f); **dolores de parto** (m)
cord **cordón** (m)
  umbilical cord **cordón**
  umbilical (m); **cordón del**
  ombligo (m)
cotton **algodón** (m)
  cotton swab **hisopo de**
  algodón (m)
crack, to **agrietar; rajar**
cramps (menstrual) **calambres**
(m); **dolores del período** (m)
(muscular) **calambres** (m)
(postpartum pains) **entuertos**
(m)
crib **camilla de niño** (f); **cuna** (f)
  warming crib **camilla**
  calentadora de niño (f);
  incubadora (f); **estufa** (f);
  armazón de calentamiento (f)
crown, to **coronar; estar**
coronando
crowning **coronamiento** (m)
curettage **curetaje** (m); **raspado**
(m)
D&C **raspa** (f, colloq); **legrado**
(m, colloq)
dangle one's legs, to **colgar las**
piernas (ue)
deliver, to **dar a luz; parir; tener**
el niño; aliviarse (Chicano)
delivery **parto** (m)
  abdominal **parto abdominal** (m)
  breech **extracción de nalgas** (f)
  delivery room **sala de partos** (f)
  forceps **extracción con fórceps**
  (f)
  premature **parto prematuro** (m)
diaper **pañal** (m); **braga** (f);
zapeta (f, Mex.); **pavico** (m,
Chicano)
diaper, to **cambiar el pañal;**
renovar el pañal de (ue);
proveer con pañal
diaper rash **salpullido** (m);
escaldadura (en los bebés) (f);
chincual (m, Mex., Chicano)
diet **dieta** (f); **régimen** (m)
  be on a diet, to **estar a dieta**
  put on a diet, to **poner a dieta**
dilation (of cervix) **dilatación del**
cuello de la matriz (f)

dirty, to be **estar caquis maquis**
(euph)
discharge **flujo** (m); **secreción** (f);
supuración (f); **desecho** (m);
descarga (f)
discharge (bloody) **derrame** (m)
discharge (from the hospital), to
dar de alta
dissolve, to **disolver (ue)**
douche **lavado vaginal** (m); **ducha**
(f)
drop **gota** (f)
dry, to **secar**
duct **conducto** (m)
eclampsia **eclampsia** (f)
edema **edema** (m); **hinchazón** (f)
ejaculate, to **eyacular; venirse**
(slang)
elbow **codo** (m)
embryo **embrión** (m)
enema **enema** (f)
  barium **enema de bario** (f);
  enema opaca (f)
  soapsuds **enema jabonosa** (f)
engorgement **estancamiento** (m)
episiotomy **corte de las partes** (m);
episiotomía (f; **tajo** (m, slang)
estrogen **estrógeno** (m)
exercise moderately, to **hacer**
ejercicios moderado
expulsion **expulsión** (f)
eyepads **paños en los ojos** (m);
toallas en los ojos (f)
eye shield **escudo ocular** (m)
fainting spell **desvanecimiento** (m)
during pregnancy **achaque** (m,
C.R.)
family **familia** (f)
  family planning **planificación de**
  la familia (f); **planificación**
  familiar (f)
feed, to **alimentar**
fetal heart tone **latido del**
corazón fetal (m)
fetoscope **estetescopio fetal** (m);
fetoscopio (m)
fetus **feto** (m)
fever **fiebre** (f); **calentura** (f, Mex.,
Chicano)
fill, to **llenar**
fissure **fisura** (f); **cisura** (f)
fontanel **fontanela** (f); **mollera** (f)
forceps (obs.) **fórceps** (m)
formula **fórmula** (f)
forty days following parturition
cuarentena (f)[49]
fundus **fondo del útero** (m)
funnel **embudo** (m)
gestation **gestación** (f); **gravidez**
(f)
glass (drinking) **vaso** (m)
glucose water **agua con azúcar** (f)
go down in the birth canal, to
encajarse
gynecologist **ginecólogo** (m)
hair **pelo** (m); **cabello(s)** (m)

pubic hair **vello púbico** (m);
pelo púbico (m); **pendejos** (m,
slang, Arg.)
heartbeat **latido cardíaco** (m)
heartburn **acedía** (f); **agriera** (f,
Sp. Am.); **agruras** (f); **pirosis** (f);
acidez (f)
heating pad, electric **almohadilla**
caliente eléctrica (f)
hemorrhoids **hemorroides** (f);
almorranas (f)
hormone **hormona** (f); **hormón** (m)
hymen **himen** (m)
ice **hielo** (m)
  ice bag **bolsa de hielo** (f)
  ice pack **aplicación de hielo**
  empaquetado (f)
inch **pulgada** (f)
incision **incisión** (f); **cortada** (f)
incubator **incubadora** (f); **estufa** (f)
infant **infante** (m/f); **nene** (m);
nena (f)
infection **infección** (f)
infertile **infértil** (adj); **estéril** (adj);
capón (adj, Chicano)
intercourse **relación sexual** (f)
jar **frasco** (m); **envase** (m)
labor **parto** (m); **trabajo de parto**
(m); **labor** (f)
  artificial **parto artificial** (m)
  be in labor, to **estar de parto;**
  enfermarse (Chicano)
  complicated **parto complicado**
  (m)
  dry **parto seco** (m)
  false **parto falso** (m)
  first stage of **primer período del**
  parto (m)
  immature **parto inmaturo** (m)
  induced **parto inducido** (m)
  instrumental **parto instrumental**
  (m)
  multiple **parto múltiple** (m)
  pains **dolores de parto** (m)
  premature **parto prematuro** (m)
  prolonged **parto prolongado** (m)
  room, labor **sala de partos** (f);
  sala prenatal (f)
  second stage of **segundo**
  período del parto (m)
  spontaneous **parto espontáneo**
  (m)
  third stage of **tercer período del**
  parto (m)
lactation **lactancia** (f)
length of pregnancy (LOP)
duración del embarazo (f)
lump **tumorcito** (m); **bola** (f);
bulto (m); **protuberancia** (f)
lying-in after childbirth
sobreparto (m)
massage **masaje** (m)
massage, to **sobar; dar masaje**
masturbate, to **masturbar(se);**
puñetear (vulgar); **hacerse la**
casqueta (Chicano)

maternity **maternidad** (f); **de maternidad** (adj)
maternity clothes **ropa de maternidad** (f)
maternity floor **piso de maternidad** (m)
maternity hospital **casa de maternidad** (f)
measure, to **medir (i)**
measuring cup **taza de medir** (f)
menarche **primera regla menarquia** (f)
menstruate, to **menstruar; perder sangre (ie); estar mala; estar indispuesta; tener el mes; estar mala de la luna; estar mala de la garra; tener/traer la garra**
menstruation **menstruación** (f, general term); **mes** (m); **período** (m, colloq); **administración** (f, Mex.); **regla** (f, Mex., P.R.); **costumbre** (f); **luna** (f, Chicano); **enferma** (f, euph); **tiempo del mes** (m, colloq)
mentally retarded **retardado** (adj); **simple** (adj, euph); **inocente** (adj, euph)
mental retardation **retardo mental** (m); **retraso mental** (m)
midwife (quack) **rinconera** (f) (trained) **partera** (f) (untrained) **comadrona** (f)
miscarriage **malparto** (m); **parto malogrado** (m)
mix, to **mezclar**
morning sickness **vómitos del embarazo** (m); **enfermedad matutina** (f); **mal de madre** (m); **ansias matutinas** (f)
navel **ombligo** (m)
nipple (breast) **pezón** (m); **chichi** (f, Arg.)
nipple, cracked **grieta del pezón** (f)
nipple, engorged (caked) **pezón enlechado** (m)
(of a baby nursing bottle) **tetilla** (f); **chupón** (m); **mamadera** (f); **tetina** (f); **tetera** (f, Mex. Cuba, P.R.)
nipple shield **escudo para el pezón** (m); **pezonera** (f)
nurse **enfermera** (f)
baby nurse **nodriza** (f); **ama de cría** (f); **niñera** (f)
nursemaid **niñera** (f)
wet nurse **nodriza** (f); **chichi** (f, colloq, Mex., Guat.); **chichigua** (f, vulgar, Sp. Am.)
nurse, to **amamantar; dar el pecho al niño; criar a los pechos; dar de mamar**
nursery **cuarto de los niños** (m)
newborn nursery **sala de los recién nacidos** (f)
nursing **amamantamiento** (m);

crianza (f); **lactante** (adj); **de crianza** (adj)
nursing bottle **biberón** (m); **mamadera** (f); **tetera** (f)
nursing bra **sostén de maternidad** (m)
nursing pad **almohadita** (f)
obstetric **obstétrico** (adj)
obstetrical **obstétrico** (adj)
obstetrician **obstétrico** (m, f); **médico partero** (m, f); **tocólogo** (m, f)
obstetrics **obstetricia** (f, sg); **tocología** (f)
oil **aceite** (m)
ointment **ungüento** (m); **pomada** (f)
orgasm **orgasmo** (m)
ounce **onza** (f)
outpatient **paciente externo** (m, f); **paciente ambulatorio** (m, f)
ovary **ovario** (m)
overdue **atrasado** (adj)
ovulate, to **ovar**
ovulation **ovulación** (f)
ovum **óvulo** (m); **huevo** (m)
oxytocic **oxitócico** (m)
oxytocin **oxitocina** (f)
pacifier **chupete** (m); **mamón** (m, Chicano)
pain **dolor** (m)
bearing-down **sensación de pesantez en el perineo** (f)
expulsive **dolores expulsivos** (m)
false **dolores falsos** (m)
hunger **dolores de hambre** (m)
intermenstrual **dolores intermenstruales** (m)
labor **dolores de parto** (m)
premonitory **dolores premonitorios** (m)
shooting **dolor fulgurante** (m)
wandering **dolor errante** (m)
pant, to **jadear; resollar (ue)**
panting **jadeante** (adj)
pediatric **pediátrico** (adj)
pediatrician **pediatra** (m, f)
pediatrics **pediatría** (f, sg)
pelvic **pelviano** (adj); **pélvico** (adj)
pelvimeter **pelvímetro** (m)
pelvis **pelvis** (f)
perforation **perforación** (f)
perineal **perineal** (adj)
perineum **perineo** (m)
physician **médico** (m); **doctor (doctora)** (m, f)
attending physician **médico de cabecera** (m); **médico a cargo** (m); **médico asistente** (m)
consulting physician **médico consultor** (m); **médico de apelación** (m)
resident physician (house) **médico residente** (m)
pitocin **pitocín** (m); **pitocina** (f)
PKU (phenylketonuria) **prueba del pañal** (f); **fenilcetonuria** (f);

fenilquetonuria (f)
placenta **placenta** (f); **secundinas** (f); **segundo parto** (m, Chicano); **lo demás** (slang)
placenta previa **placenta previa** (f)
placental **placentario** (adj)
planned parenthood **procreación planeada** (f); **natalidad dirigida** (f)
postnatal care **cuidado postnatal** (m)
pounds **libras** (f)
pregnancy **preñez** (f); **embarazo** (m); **gravidez** (f); **estado interesante** (m, euph)
ectopic pregnancy **embarazo ectópico** (m); **embarazo fuera de la matriz** (m)
false **embarazo falso** (m)
hysteria **embarazo histérico** (m)
incomplete **embarazo incompleto** (m)
tubal pregnancy **embarazo tubárico** (m); **embarazo en los tubos** (m)
pregnant **preñada** (adj); **gruesa** (adj, colloq); **embarazada** (adj); **encinta** (adj); **grávida** (adj); **panzona** (f, vulgar)
premature **prematuro** (adj); **sietemesino** (literally "seven months")
prenatal **prenatal** (adj)
prenatal care **cuidado prenatal** (m)
prescribe, to **recetar; prescribir**
prescription **receta médica** (f); **prescripción** (f)
presentation **presentación** (f)
procreate **procrear**
progeny **prole** (f); **progenie** (f)
progesterone **progesterona** (f)
prolapse **prolapso** (m); **caída de la matriz** (f)
prophylactic **profiláctico** (adj)
puerile **pueril** (adj)
puerperal **puerperal** (adj)
puerperal fever **fiebre puerperal** (f)
puerperium **puerperio** (m); **riesgo** (m)
pull back foreskin of penis, to **pelársela** (colloq)
pull up (one's) knees, to **encoger las rodillas**
pump, to **sacar (leche) por medio de una bomba**
push, to **pujar**
quadruplet **cuatrillizo** (m); **cuadrúpleto** (m)
quintuplet **quintillizo** (m); **quíntuplo** (m)
rabbit test **examen de conejo** (m)
recessive **recesivo** (adj)
recessive character **carácter recesivo** (m)
rectal **rectal** (adj)

rectocele **rectocele** (m)
rectum **recto** (m)
reddish **rojizo** (adj); **bermejizo** (adj, hair)
red-haired **pelirrojo** (adj)
reduce, to **reducir(se)**
reducing exercises **ejercicios físicos para adelgazar; ejercicios físicos para reducir peso**
relation **pariente** (f); **parentesco** (m) **relación** (f)
relations, to have sexual **tener relaciones sexuales; dormir con alguien; estar con alguien; chingar** (vulgar); **cojer/coger** (vulgar, P.R., Mex. Arg.); **conocer; hacer cositas** (euph, Chicano); **dar una atascada** (vulgar); **echar un palito** (Chicano); **chopetear** (slang); **dar pa' dentro** (vulgar); **tumbar**
relationship **relación** (f); **parentesco** (m)
relax, to **relajar; aflojarse; relajar el cuerpo**
relaxation **relajación** (f); **descanso** (m)
relaxation of tension **disminución de la tirantez** (f)
Rh factor **factor Rh** (m); **factor Rhesus** (m)
Rh negative **Rh-negativo** (adj)
Rh positive **Rh-positivo** (adj)
rinse, to **enjuagar**
rub, to **frotarse; pasar la mano sobre la superficie de**
rubbing alcohol **alcohol para fricciones** (m)
sanitary pad **kotex** (m); **servilleta**

sanitaria (f)
shave, to **rasurar; afeitar**
sitz bath **baño de asiento** (m); **semicupio** (m)
soap **jabón** (m)
soft **suave** (adj)
specimen, urine **muestra de la orina** (f)
speculum **espejo vaginal** (m); **espéculo** (m)
sperm **semen** (m); **espermatozoide** (m); **semilla** (f, Mex. slang); **mecos** (m, slang); **esperma** (f)
spotting **manchado** (m); **manchas de sangre** (f)
squat, to **acuclillarse; ponerse de cuclillas**
sterility, female **frío de la matriz** (m)
sterilize, to **castrar; esterilizar**
sterilize the bottles, to **esterilizar botellas**
sterilizer **esterilizador** (m)
stillbirth **parto muerto** (m); **nati-muerto** (m)
stillborn **nacido muerto** (adj); **mortinato** (adj)
stir, to **revolver (ue)**
stretch marks (strias) **estrias** (f)
subtract, to **sustraer; deducir**
suck, to **mamar; chupar**
supplementary feedings **alimentación suplementaria** (f)
suture **sutura** (f)
dissolving suture **sutura absorbible** (f)
swallow, to **tragar**
tampax **tampax** (m)
tampon **ta(m)pón** (m)

tear **desgarramiento** (m)
tie the tubes, to **ligar trompas; ligar los tubos de Falopio; ligar los tubos uterinos**
toxemia **toxemia** (f)
of pregnancy **toxemia del embarazo** (f)
triplet **trillizo** (m)
tub **tina de baño** (f); **bañera** (f)
tube **tubo** (m)
Fallopian tube **trompa de Falopio** (f); **tubo de Falopio** (m)
(for feeding) **sonda** (f)
twin **gemelo** (m); **mellizo** (m); **jimagua** (m, f), **cuate** (m, f, Mex.)
umbilical cord **cordón umbilical** (m); **cordón del ombligo** (m)
umbilicus **ombligo** (m)
urine specimen **muestra de la orina** (f)
uterus **útero** (m); **matriz** (f)
vagina **vagina** (f)[50]
vaginal **vaginal** (adj)
vaginitis **vaginitis** (f)
varicose **varicoso** (adj)
varicose vein **várice** (f); **variz** (m); **vena varicosa** (f)
varicosity **varicosidad** (f)
vulva **vulva** (f)
wash, to **lavar**
wean, to **destetar**
weigh, to **pesar**
well-being **bienestar** (m)
wet **mojado** (adj)
womb **matriz** (f); **útero** (m)
x-ray, chest **radiografía del tórax** (f); **rayo X del pecho** (m)

MEDICAL SPECIALISTS

ESPECIALISTAS MEDICOS

anesthesiologist **anestesiólogo**
attending physician **médico de cabecera; médico a cargo; médico de atendencia**
bacteriologist **bacteriólogo**
biologist **biólogo**
cardiologist **cardiólogo**
charge nurse **enfermera de cargo**
chiropodist **quiropodista; pedicuro; callista**
chiropractor **quiropráctico; quiropractor**
consulting physician **médico consulator; médico de apelación**
cytologist **citólogo**
day nurse **enfermera de día**

dentist **dentista**
dermatologist **dermatólogo**
dietician **dietista**
doctor **médico, doctor**
druggist **farmacéutico; boticario**
ear, nose and throat specialist (otorhinolaryngologist) **otorrinolaringólogo**
embryologist **embriólogo**
endocrinologist **endocrinólogo**
endodontist **endodontista**
general duty nurse **enfermera general**
general practitioner **médico general**
gynecologist **ginecólogo**

head nurse **jefa de enfermeras**
hematologist **hematólogo**
histologist **histólogo**
homeopathist **homeópata**
house staff **personal médico**
house surgeon **cirujano asistente; médico interno**
hygienist **higienista**
intern **interno; médico practicante**
internist **internista**
midwife (trained) **partera** (untrained) **comadrona**
neurologist **neurólogo**
neuropsychiatrist **neuropsiquiatra**
neurosurgeon **neurocirujano**
night nurse **enfermera de noche**

nurse **enfermero, enfermera**
nurse on duty **enfermera de guardia**
nurse's aide **ayudante de enfermera**
obstetrician **obstétrico, médico partero, tocólogo**
occulist **oculista**
ophthalmologist **oftalmólogo**
optician **óptico**
optometrist **optometrista**
oral surgeon **cirujano oral**
orderly **ayudante (de hospital)**
orthodontist **ortodontista**
orthopedist **ortopedista**
orthoptist **ortóptico**
osteopath **osteópata**
otolaryngologist **otolaringólogo**
otologist **otólogo**

paramedic **paramédico**
pathologist **patólogo**
pediatrician **pediatra; pedíatra**
pedodontist **pedodontista**
periodontist **periodontista**
pharmacist **farmacéutico; boticario**
pharmacologist **farmacólogo**
physician **médico; doctor**
physiotherapist **fisioterapeuta**
plastic surgeon **cirujano plástico**
podiatrist **podiatra**
practical nurse **enfermera no diplomada; enfermera práctica**
private nurse **enfermera privada**
psychiatrist **psiquiatra**
psychoanalyst **psicoanalista**
psychologist **psicólogo**

public health nurse **enfermera de salud pública**
radiologist **radiólogo**
registered nurse **enfermera registrada; enfermera diplomada**
social worker **trabajador(-a) social**
stretcher bearer **camillero**
surgeon **cirujano, quirurgo**
therapist **terapeuta**
tocologist **tocólogo**
traumatologist **traumatólogo**
urologist **urólogo**
venereologist **especialista en enfermedades venéreas**
veterinarian **veterinario**
visiting nurse **enfermera ambulante**

PLACES IN THE HOSPITAL

LUGARES EN EL HOSPITAL

basement **sótano** (m)
cafeteria **cafetería** (f); **cafetín** (m, colloq); **lonchería** (f, Chicano)
cashier **departamento de caja** (m)
chapel **capilla** (f)
department of welfare **departmento de bienestar**
doctor's office **consultorio**
elevator **elevador** (m); **ascensor** (m)
emergency room **sala de emergencia; sala de urgencia**
floor **piso**
front desk **recepción** (f)

home health agency **agencia de salud doméstica**
hospital care **cuidado en el hospital**
infirmary **enfermería**
laboratory **laboratorio**
lobby **salón principal** (m); **vestíbulo** (m); **zaguán** (m)
lounge **salón de entrada** (m)
medical records **departamento de archivo clínico**
mental health department **departamento de enfermedades mentales**

nursery **guardería**
nursing home care **cuidado en los asilos; cuidado en un hospicio para ancianos**
operating room **sala de operaciones; quirófano**
personnel department **departamento de personal**
pharmacy **farmacia**
snack shop **tienda de refrescos** (f)
stairway **escalera** (f)
waiting room **sala de espera; cuarto de estar**
ward **crujía; pabellón** (m)

THE FAMILY[51]

LA FAMILIA

Many nouns of relationship ending in -*o* change it to -*a* to form the feminine.

the bachelor **el soltero**
the boy **el muchacho**
the brother **el hermano**
the brother-in-law **el cuñado**
the cousin (m) **el primo**
the father-in-law **el suegro**
the fiancé **el novio**
first cousin **el primo hermano**
the grandfather **el abuelo; el abue** (Chicano)
the grandson **el nieto**

the bachelorette **la soltera**
the girl **la muchacha**
the sister **la hermana**
the sister-in-law **la cuñada**
the cousin (f) **la prima**
the mother-in-law **la suegra**
the fiancée **la novio**
the first cousin **la prima hermana**
the grandmother **la abuela; la abue** (Chicano)
the granddaughter **la nieta**

the great grandfather **el bisabuelo**	the great grandmother **la bisabuela**
the great grandson **el biznieto**	the great granddaughter **la biznieta**
the great great grandfather **el tatarabuelo**	the great great grandmother **la tatarabuela**
the great great grandson **el tataranieto**	the great great granddaughter **la tataranieta**
the half brother **el medio hermano**	the half sister **la media hermana**
the husband **el esposo**	the wife **la esposa**
the little boy **el niño**	the little girl **la niña**
the nephew **el sobrino**	the niece **la sobrina**
the son **el hijo**	the daughter **la hija**
the son-in-law **el yerno**	the daughter-in-law **la nuera**
the stepbrother **el hermanastro**	the stepsister **la hermanastra**
the stepson **el hijastro**	the stepdaughter **la hijastra**
the uncle **el tío**	the aunt **la tía**
the widower **el viudo**	the widow **la viuda**

Other nouns of relationship must be memorized.

adult **el adulto**
ancestor **el antepasado**
baby **el bebé; la criatura; el(la) nene (-a); el(la) guagua** (Chile, Ec., Peru, Bol., Arg., Ur.)
dad **el papá; el tata**
daddy **papí**
deceased **difunto**
dependent **dependiente** (m/f)
descendant **descendiente** (m/f)
divorced **divorciado (-a)**
family name **apellido**
father **el padre**
female **hembra**
first name **el primer nombre**
foster child **hijo de leche**
foster mother **ama de leche**
friend **amigo**
godchild **ahijado**

godfather **el padrino**
godmother **la madrina**
guardian **guardián**
lover **el amante**
maiden name **nombre de soltera**
male **el varón**
man **hombre**
marital status **estado civil**
marriage **el casamiento; matrimonio**
middle name **segundo nombre**
mom **mamá**
mommy **mamita; mami**
mother **la madre**
newly wed **recién casado**
nickname **mote; apodo**
older child **hijo mayor**
orphan **huérfano (-a)**
parenthood **paternidad**

puberty **la pubertad**
quadruplets **cuádruples**
quintuplets **quintillizos**
race **la raza**
relationship (family) **parentesco**
relatives **parientes; familiares**[52]
stepfather **padrastro**
stepmother **madrastra**
surname **apellido**
survivor **sobreviviente**
triplets **trillizos**
twins **mellizos; gemelos**
under age **menor de edad**
virgin **virgen**
woman **mujer**
young person **joven**
youth **juventud**

NOTE: Nouns designating relationship are used in the masculine plural to denote individuals of both sexes.

the parents, the fathers **los padres**

the brothers, the brother and sister, the brothers and sisters **los hermanos**

BATHROOM, TOILET ARTICLES, AND PERSONAL EFFECTS

ARTICULOS PARA EL BAÑO Y EL TOCADOR Y OBJETOS PERSONALES

ashtray **cenicero** (m)
bag **bolsa** (f); **cartera** (f); **saco** (m)
bath powder **polvos de baño** (m, pl)
beautify oneself, to **embellecerse**

bedpan **bacín** (m); **bidet** (m); **cuña** (f); **chata** (f); **cómodo** (m, Mex.); **paleta** (f); **pato** (m); **silleta** (f); **taza** (f)
billfold **cartera** (f); **billetera** (f)

bleach, to **blanquear**
bobby pin **horquilla** (f); **clip** (m)
book **libro** (m)
bracelet **brazalete** (m); **pulsera** (f)

brush one's teeth, to **cepillarse los dientes**
checkbook **talonario (de cheques) (m); chequera (f); libreta de cheques (f)**
cigar **cigarro (m); puro (m); tabaco (m); habano (m)**
cigarette **cigarrillo (m); pitillo (m, Spain); cigarro (m, Sp. Am.)**
cigarettes, carton of **cartón de cigarrillos (m)**
cleansing cream **crema limpiadora (f)**
clippers **maquinilla para cortar (f)**
coat hanger **percha (f); gancho (m, Mex.)**
cold cream **crema facial (f)**
cologne **agua de colonia (f); colonia (f)**
comb **peine (m)**
comb, to **peinar(se)**
compact **polvera (f)**
contact lenses **lentes de contacto (m); pupilentes (m); lentillas (f, Spain)**
  hard **duro (adj)**
  soft **suave (adj)**
  contact lens case **estuche (m)**
cosmetic **cosmético (adj)**
cosmetics **cosméticos (m, pl); productos de belleza (m, pl)**
cream **crema (f)**
curlers **rizadores (m); rollos (m); rulos (m); tubos (m)**
cut hair, to **cortar el pelo**
dental floss **hilo dental (m)**
denture cup **recipiente para guardar la dentadura (m)**
deodorant **desodorante (m)**
depilatory **depilatorio (m)**
drug **droga (f)**
drugstore **farmacia (f, Spain); droguería (f, Sp. Am.); botica (f)**
dry, to **secar**
dye **tintura (f); tinte (m)**
dye, to **teñir (i)**
earring **arete (m); zarcillo (m); pantalla (f, P.R.)**
  earring, drop **pendiente (m); arracada (f)**
emery board **lima para las uñas (f)**
emesis bowl **riñonera (f); vasija para vomitar (f)**
envelope **sobre (m)**
face powder **polvo facial (m)**
facial tissues **servilletas faciales (f); pañuelos faciales (m); kleenex (m)**
flowers **flores (f)**
foot powder **polvos para los pies (m)**
glasses **anteojos (m, pl); gafas (f, pl); lentes (m, pl, Mex.); espejuelos (m, pl, Cuba)**
  glass case **estuche (m); funda de gafas (f)**

sunglasses **gafas de sol (f, pl)**
hairbrush **cepillo para el pelo (m); cepillo de cabeza (m)**
haircut **corte de pelo (m)**
hairdresser **peluquero (-a) (m, f)**
hair dye **tinte para el pelo (m)**
hair net **redecilla (f)**
hairpin **horquilla (f); gancho para el pelo (m); sujetador (m)**
hair spray **fijador para el pelo (m)**
hair tonic **tónico para el pelo (m)**
handbag **saquito de mano (m)**
hand cream **crema para las manos (f)**
hankie, handkerchief **pañuelo (m)**
jewelry **joyas (f, pl)**
key **llave (f)**
Kleenex **kleenex (m); pañuelo de papel (m)**
lather **espuma (f)**
lather the face, to **enjabonar la cara; dar jabón en la cara**
letter **carta (f)**
lipstick **lápiz labial (m); pintura de labios (f); lápiz para los labios (m)**
lotion **loción (f); crema (f, Mex.)**
magazine **revista (f)**
makeup **maquillaje (m)**
makeup, to put on **maquillarse**
manicure **manicura (f); arreglo de uñas (m)**
mascara **máscara (f); rímel (m)**
match **fósforo (m); cerilla (f, Spain); cerillo (m, Mex.)**
medicated soap **jabón medicinal (m)**
medicine **medicina (f)**
mirror **espejo (m)**
mouth wash **lavado bucal (m); enjuague (m)**
nail file **lima para las uñas (f)**
nail polish **esmalte de uñas (m); pintura de uñas (f); barniz (m); laca de uñas (f)**
nail polish remover **quitador de esmalte de uñas (m)**
necklace **collar (m); gargantilla (f)**
needle **aguja (f)**
newspaper **periódico (m); diario (m)**
package **paquete (m); cajetilla (f)**
perfume **perfume (m)**
permanent wave **ondulación permanente (f); ondulado permanente (m)**
pin **alfiler (m); prendedero (m)**
pipe **pipa (f); cachimba (f, Sp. Am.)**
pitcher **jarra (f)**
pocketbook **cartera (f); portamonedas (f, sg); bolsa (f); bolso (m)**
postcard **tarjeta postal (f)**
powder **polvo (m)**
powder puff **mota para empolvarse (f); borla (f);**

bellota (f)
purse **monedero (m); bolso (m); bolsa (f)**
put up one's hair, to **ponerse los rulos**
razor **navaja de afeitar (f); cuchilla de afeitar (f)**
razor, safety **máquina de afeitar (f); maquinilla de afeitar (f); maquinilla de seguridad (f)**
razor blade **hoja de afeitar (f); navajita (f); gillette (m, C.A.)**
ring **anillo (m); sortija (f); argolla (f, parts of Sp. Am.)**
  engagement ring **anillo de prometida (m); anillo de compromiso (m, Mex.)**
  wedding ring **alianza (f); anillo (o sortija) de matrimonio, de boda, de casamiento (m)**
rinse **enjuagador (m)**
rinse, to **enjuagar; aclarar**
rouge **colorete (m)**
rubber gloves **guantes de goma (m)**
safety pin **imperdible (m); alfiler de seguridad (m)**
sanitary napkin **servilleta sanitaria (f); kotex (m); almohadilla higiénica (f); absorbente higiénico (m)**
scissors **tijeras (f, pl)**
set (setting) **peinado (m)**
set, to **marcar**
shampoo **champú (m); shampoo (m)**
shave **afeitada (f); rasuración (f)**
shave (oneself), to **afeitar(se); rasurar(se)**
shaving cream **crema de afeitar (f)**
shower **ducha (f); regadera (f, Mex.); baño de China (m, Arg.)**
shower, to **ducharse**
smoke, to **fumar; pitar (Arg., Chile)**
  smoke a pipe, to **fumar en pipa; pipar**
soap **jabón (m)**
stamp (postage) **timbre (m, Mex.); estampilla (f, Sp. Am.); sello (m, Spain)**
stationery **papel de escribir (m)**
suitcase **maleta (f); velis (m, Mex.)**
suntan lotion **loción/crema para el sol (f); loción bronceadora (f)**
talcum powder **polvo de talco (m)**
tampon **tampón (m); tapón (m)**
thread **hilo (m)**
tie clasp **alfiler de corbata (m)**
toilet paper **papel sanitario (m); papel de baño (m); papel de inodoro (m); papel higiénico (m)**
toothbrush **cepillo de dientes (m)**
toothpaste **pasta dental (f); dentífrico (m); pasta dentífrica (f)**

tooth powder **polvo dental** (m)
towel **toalla** (f)
  clean **toalla limpia** (f)
  dirty **toalla sucia** (f)
truss **braguero** (m)
tube **tubo** (m)
tweezer **pinzas** (f)

urinal **orinal** (m)
vaseline **vaselina** (f)
wallet **cartera** (f); **billetera** (f);
  portamonedas (m, pl)
wash, to **lavar(se)**
washbasin **basija** (f); **jofaina** (f);
  ponchera (f, C.A.); **palanga** (f,

Mex.); **lavabo** (m)
washcloth **paño de lavarse** (m);
  toallita (f)
waste basket **papelera** (f)
watch **reloj** (m)
  wristwatch **reloj de pulsera** (m)
wig **peluca** (f)

BEDDING
ROPA DE CAMA

bed **cama** (f)
bedboard **tabla para la cama** (f)
bed pad **colchoncillo para la**
  cama (m)
blanket **frazada** (f); **manta** (f);
  cobija (f, Mex.)
  electric blanket **frazada**
  eléctrica (f)
cot **catre** (m)
cover **cubierta** (f)
covers **cobertores** (m, pl); **cobijas**

(f, pl, Mex. and elsewhere)
crib **cuna** (f); **camita de niño** (f)
hammock **hamaca** (f)
mattress **colchón** (m)
  air mattress **colchón de aire** (m);
  colchón de viento (m)
  (inner)spring mattress **colchón de**
  muelles (m)
mosquito net **mosquitero** (m)
pad **cojincillo** (m); **almohadilla** (f)
pillow **almohada** (f)

feather pillow **edredón** (m)
pillowcase **funda (de almohada)**
  (f); **almohada** (f)
quilt **colcha** (f); **sobrecama**
  acolchada (f); **edredón** (m)
sheepskin **zalea** (f)
sheet **sábana** (f)
  plastic sheet **sábana de plástico** (f)
side rail **riel del costado** (m);
  baranda protectora (f)

CLOTHING
ROPA

apron **delantal** (m)
bathing suit **traje de baño** (m);
  bañador (m, Spain)
bathrobe **bata (de baño)** (f);
  salida (f, Arg.)
  (terrycloth) **albornoz** (m)
bedclothes **ropa de cama** (f);
  tendido (m, Col Ec. Mex.)
belt **cinto** (m); **cinturón** (m)
blouse **blusa** (f); **camiseta** (f)
blue jeans **pantalones vaqueros**
  (m, pl); **mezclillas** (f, Mex.)
boot **bota** (f); **botín** (m, Arg.)
bra (brassiere) **sostén** (m);
  sostenedor (m); **portabustos** (m);
  corpiño (m, Arg.); **ajustador** (m);
  justillo (m)
buckle **hebilla** (f)
button **botón** (m)
button, to **abotonar; abrochar**
cap **gorra** (f); **montera** (f);
  cachucha (f, Mex.)
change clothes, to **mudarse de**
  ropa; cambiarse la ropa
cloth **tela** (f); **paño** (m); **tejido** (m)
  batiste **batista** (f)

calfskin **becerro** (m)
cotton **algodón** (m)
dark **oscuro** (adj)
heavyweight **grueso** (adj)
light **claro** (adj)
lightweight **delgado** (adj)
linen **lienzo** (m); **lino** (m); **hilo**
  (m)
satin **raso** (m)
silk **seda** (f)
wool **lana** (f)
woolen **de lana** (adj)
clothes, apparel **ropa** (f, sg);
  vestimenta (f)
coat **abrigo** (m)
  fur **abrigo de piel** (m)
  jacket **chaqueta** (f)
  lightweight **abrigo de**
  entretiempo (m)
  overcoat **abrigo** (m);
  sobretodo (m)
  rain **impermeable** (m)
collar **cuello** (m)
corset **corsé** (m)
diaper **pañal** (m)
dress **vestido** (m); **traje** (m, Perú,

Pan.)
dress, house **vestido para la casa**
  (m)
  maternity **vestido de maternidad**
  (m)
  wash **vestido que puede**
  lavarse (m)
dress, to **vestir(se) (i)**
dry clean, to **limpiar en seco**
fade, to **desteñir (i)**
fur **piel** (f)
galoshes **galochas** (f); **chanclo** (m,
  Spain)
garter **liga** (f)
garter belt **portaligas** (m)
girdle **ceñidor** (m); **cinturón** (m);
  faja (f)
gloves **guantes** (m)
handkerchief **pañuelo** (m)
hat **sombrero** (m)
heel **tacón** (m); **taco** (m, Arg.)
hook **gancho** (m)
hose **medias** (f, pl)
  pantyhose **medias** (f, pl);
  medias pantalón (f);
  pantimedias (f, pl)

jacket **chaqueta** (f); **saco** (m);
americana (f)
ski **gamberro** (m); **anorak** (m)
jeans **pantalones vaqueros** (m, pl);
mesclillas (f, Mex.); **pantalones de
mesclilla** (m, pl)
leather **cuero** (m)
light (color) **claro** (adj)
(weight) **delgado** (adj)
lingerie **ropa interior de mujer** (f)
necktie (tie) **corbata** (f)
nightgown **camisón de dormir** (m);
camisa de noche (f); **bata** (f)
nylon **nilón** (m)
oxfords **zapatos bajos** (m, pl);
zapatos de estilo Oxford (m)
pair **par** (m)
pajama **pijama** (f/m); **piyama**
(f/m)
panties **bragas** (f); **calzones** (m,
pl); **pantalones interiores de
mujer** (m); **pantaleta** (f)
pants (men's) **pantalones** (m)
rubber heel **tacón de goma** (m)
rubber overshoe **chanclo** (m,

Spain); **zapato de goma** (m, Sp.
Am.), **zapato de hule** (m, Mex.)
rubber pants **pantalones
plásticos** (m, pl)
sandals **sandalia** (f); **guaraches** (m,
Mex.); **caites** (m, C.A.) **ojotas** (f,
Chile, Ec., Perú, Bol.)
scarf **bufanda** (f)
shawl **chal** (m); **rebozo** (m, Mex.)
shirt **camisa** (f)
sweat **camisa enguatada** (f)
under **camiseta** (f)
(T-shirt) **polera** (f, Sp. Am.)
shoe **zapato** (m)
high-heeled shoes **zapatos de
tacones altos** (m, pl)
low-heeled shoes **zapatos de
tacones bajos** (m, pl)
shorts **calzones cortos** (m)
shorts, under **calzoncillos** (m)
skirt **falda** (f); **saya** (f); **sayuela**
(f); **pollera** (f, Arg., Chile)
sleeve **manga** (f)
slip **combinación** (f); **enagua** (f);
refajo (m); **fondo** (m, Spain)

slipper **zapatilla** (f); **chinela** (f);
chancleta (f)
sneaker **zapato de goma** (m);
zapato de gimnasio (m); **tenis**
(m, Mex.)
sock **calcetín** (m); **media** (f, Arg.)
sole (of shoe) **suela** (f)
stockings **medias** (f)
suit **traje** (m); **vestido** (m, Perú,
Pan.)
sweater **sweater** (m); **suéter** (m);
jersey (m)
trousers **pantalones** (m)
trunks **calzones de baño** (m);
shorts (m)
unbutton, to **desabotonar**;
desabrochar
underpants **calzoncillos** (m)
undershirt **camiseta** (f)
underwear **ropa interior** (f)
uniform **uniforme** (m)
wash, to **lavar**
wrinkle **arruga** (f)
zipper **cierre automático** (m);
cierre relámpago (m)

COLORS

COLORES

beige **beige**
black **negro**
blonde **rubio**; **chelo** (Mex.)
blue **azul**
brown **moreno**; **pardo**; **carmelita**
(Cuba, Chile)
brunette **moreno**; **trigueño**
chestnut **castaño**; **pardo**
clear **incoloro**
color **color** (m)

cranberry **arándano**
dark **oscuro**
gold **dorado**
gray **gris**
green **verde**
light (color) **claro**
maroon **rojo obscuro**; **marrón**
opaque **opaco**
orange **anaranjado**
pale **pálido**

pink **rosado**
purple **púrpura**; **purpúreo**
red **rojo**
ruby **rubí**
silver **plateado**
transparent **transparente**
violet **violeta**; **morado**
white **blanco**
yellow **amarillo**

PRACTITIONERS OF THE MAJOR RELIGIONS

PRACTICADORES DE LAS RELIGIONES PRINCIPALES

Agnostic **agnóstico**
Anglican **anglicano**
Atheist **ateo**
Baptist **bautista**
Born-again Christian **cristiano
renacido**

Buddhist **budista**
Catholic **católico**
Greek Catholic (Greek
Orthodox) **católico de rito
griego**
Roman Catholic **católico**

romano
Christian **cristiano**
Christian Scientist **miembro de la
ciencia cristiana**
Congregationalist
congregacionalista

Covenanter **covenantario;
pactante**
Evangelical Covenanter
**covenantario evangélico;
miembro del Pacto**
Episcopalian **episcopalista**
Evangelist **evangelista**
Hindu **hindú**
Jehovah's Witness **testigo de**

Jehová
Jew **judío**
Lutheran **luterano**
Methodist **metodista**
Mormon **mormón**
Moslem **mahometano,
musulmán, islámico**
Presbyterian **presbiteriano**
Protestant **protestante**

Quaker **cuáquero, cuákero**
Seventh-Day Adventist
adventista del séptimo día
Shintoist **sinoísta**
Taoist **taoísta**
Unitarian **unitario**
Zoroastrian **zoroástrico**

COUNTRIES AND NATIONALITIES

PAISES Y NACIONALIDADES

Países	*Habitantes*[53]	*Capitales*[54]	*Habitantes*
México⎫	mexicano⎫	México⎫	mexicano ⎫
Méjico⎭	mejicano⎭	Méjico⎭	mejicano ⎭
Cuba	cubano	La Habana	habanero
Puerto Rico	puertorriqueño	San Juan	sanjuanero
La República Dominicana	dominicano	Santo Domingo	santodominicano
Guatemala	guatemalteco	Guatemala	guatemalteco
El Salvador	salvadoreño	San Salvador	sansalvadoreño
Honduras	hondureño	Tegucigalpa	tegucigalpense
Nicaragua	nicaragüense	Managua	managüense
Costa Rica	costarricense	San José	(san)josefino
Panamá	panameño	Panamá	panameño
Colombia	colombiano	Bogotá	bogotano
Venezuela	venezolano	Caracas	caragueño
El Ecuador	ecuatoriano	Quito	quiteño
El Perú	peruano	Lima	limeño
Bolivia	boliviano	La Paz	paceño
Chile	chileno	Santiago	santiaguino
(La) Argentina	argentino	Buenos Aires	bonaerense
El Uruguay	uruguayo	Montevideo	montevideano
El Paraguay	paraguayo	Asunción	asunceño
El Brasil	brasileño	Brasilia	brasileño
España	español	Madrid	madrileño

OCCUPATIONS[55]

OCUPACIONES

actor **actor**
actress **actriz**
administrator **administrator;
gobernante**
advertiser **anunciador;
anunciante**
adviser, advisor **consejero;
consultor**
agent **agente; represente**
architect **arquitecto**
artist **artista**
assistant **asistente; ayudante**

athlete **atleta**
attorney **abogado; procurador**
author **autor**
babysitter **niñera por horas**
baker **panadero; hornero**
ballplayer **pelotero; beisbolista**
banker **banquero**
barber **barbero; peluquero**
bartender **cantinero; tabernero**
beautician **cosmetólogo (a)**
biologist **biólogo**
bookkeeper **tenedor de libros;**

contable
bookseller **librero; vendedor de
libros**
broker **cambista; intermediario**
builder **constructor; arquitecto**
bullfighter **torero; matador**
bus driver **conductor de
ómnibus**
businessman **hombre de negocios;
comerciante; negociante**
businesswoman **mujer de
negocios; mujer de empresa**

butcher **carnicero**
cab driver **taxista; cochero**
carpenter **carpintero**
cashier **cajero**
chauffeur **chófer; chofer** (Sp. Am.)
chef **cocinero; jefe de cocina**
chemist **químico; farmacéutico**
civil servant **funcionario público;
empleado del estado**
cleaner **tintorero; lavandero**
cleaning woman **criada que
limpia la casa**
clergyman **clérigo; sacerdote;
ministro, pastor; rabí**
clerk **oficinista, empleado de
oficina, secretario** (offices);
**dependiente, empleado de tienda,
vendedor** (stores); **escribano** (law)
coach **maestro particular** (tutor);
entrenador (sports)
coal miner **minero de carbón**
conductor **conductor, guía,
director** (music); **recogedor de
billetes** (train)
construction worker **trabajador
de edificación**
cook **cocinero (-a)**
correspondent **correspondiente;
corresponsal**
counselor **consejero; abogado
consultor**
dancer **bailador(a); danzante**
day laborer **jornalero; bracero**
dental technician **técnico dental**
detective **detective; investigador**
diagnostician **experto en hacer
diagnósticos**
dietician **dietista**
director **director; administrador;
dirigente**
dishwater **lavaplatos; lavador(a)
de platos**
dockhand **estibador; cargador**
doctor **doctor**
domestic **doméstico; criado;
sirviente**
draftsman **dibujante; diseñador;
bosquejador**
dressmaker **modista; costurera**
driver **piloto; conductor; cochero;
maquinista**
druggist **farmacéutico; boticario**
editor **redactor titular**
(newspaper); **editor** (literary)
educator **educador; maestro;
pedagogo; instructor**
electrician **electricista**
engineer **ingeniero**
engraver **grabador**
exporter **exportador**
farmer **agricultor; hacendado**
farmhand **labrador; campesino**
fireman **bombero**
fisherman **pescador**
florist **florista**
garbage collector **basurero**

gardener **jardinero**
guide **guía**
handyman **hacelotodo; factótum**
hard-hat **operario de
construcción**
helper **ayudante; asistente**
hired hand **mozo de campo**
housekeeper **ama de llaves; ama
de gobierno; casera**
housewife **ama de casa; madre de
familia**
houseworker **doméstico; criado;
sirviente**
husband **esposo; marido**
industrialist **industrialista**
inspector **inspector; supervisor**
instructor **instructor; profesor;
maestro**
insurance agent **agente de
seguros**
interior decorator **decorador de
interiores**
interpreter **intérprete**
inventor **inventor; creador**
investigator **investigador;
indagador**
ironworker **herrero**
janitor **portero; conserje**
jeweler **joyero**
journalist **periodista; cronista**
junk dealer **chatarrero**
laboratory technician **técnico de
laboratorio**
laborer **obrero; trabajador;
jornalero; bracero**
lathe operator **tornero**
laundress **lavandera**
lawman **agente de policía;
alguacil**
lawyer **abogado; letrado;
licenciado**
librarian **bibliotecario**
lifeguard **salvavidas**
longshoreman **estibador;
cargador**
machinist **mecánico; maquinista**
maid **criada; sirvienta**
mail carrier **cartero**
manager **gerente; director;
administrador; superintendente**
manicurist **manicuro; manicura**
manual laborer **obrero de mano**
mason **albañil**
masseur **masajista**
mathematician **matemático**
mechanic **mecánico**
merchant **mercader; comerciante;
negociante**
messenger **mensajero; mandadero;
recadero**
metalworker **metalario; metalista**
minister (religion) **ministro;
clérigo; pastor; sacerdote; cura;
rabí**
(diplomat) **ministro; enviado**
motorcyclist **motociclista**

motorman **andinista; alpinista**
mover **empleado de una casa de
mudanzas**
musician **músico**
navigator **navegador; navegante**
newsboy **vendedor de periódicos;
diariero**
newscaster **cronista de
noticiarios; comentarista
radiofónico**
newsman **repórter; periodista**
notary (public) **escribano
(público); notario (público)**
nun **monja; religiosa**
nursemaid **niñera; aya; ama**
occupational therapist **terapeuta
ocupacional; ergoterapeuta**
office boy **mandadero; mensajero**
office clerk **oficinista; escribano**
office manager **jefe de oficina**
officer **funcionario; oficial;
policía; agente**
oil field worker **obrero petrolero**
oilman **petrolero**
operator **operador; telefonista**
painter **pintor**
patrolman **policía; guardia**
peddler **buhonero; mercachifle**
pharmacist **farmacéutico;
boticario; farmaceuta** (Sp. Am.)
photographer **fotógrafo;
fotógrafa**
physical therapist **fisioterapeuta**
physicist **físico**
pilot **piloto; guía**
plasterer **enlucidor; revocador**
plowman **arador; labrador;
yuguero**
plumber **plomero; cañero**
policeman **policía** (m); **vigilante**
(Ven.); **guardia; gendarme** (Mex.)
policewoman **mujer policía**
politician **político; estadista**
porter **portero; conserje**
presser **planchador**
priest **sacerdote; presbítero;
clérigo; cura**
principal **director; rector;
principal**
printer **impresor; tipógrafo**
publisher **editor; publicador**
rabbi **rabí**
ranchman **hacendado; ganadero**
ranger **vigilante**
reader **lector**
realtor **corredor de bienes raíces**
receptionist **recibidor(a);
recepcionista**
registrar **registrador; archivista;
jefe de registros civiles**
repairman **reparador; mecánico de
reparaciones**
reporter **repórter; reportero;
noticiero**
retailer **menorista** (Sp. Am.);
comerciante al por menor

retired **jubilado** (adj)
road worker **peón caminero**
sailor **marinero**
salesclerk **vendedor(a);
dependiente; dependienta**
saloonkeeper **tabernero;
cantinero**
scavenger **basurero**
schoolteacher **maestro (-a) de
escuela**
scientist **científico**
scrubwoman **fregona**
seamstress **costurera; modistilla**
secretary **secretario (-a)**
serviceman **mecánico; reparador;
militar**
sheriff **alguacil de policía**
shipping clerk **dependiente
encargado del envío de
mercaderías**
shoemaker **zapatero**
shopkeeper **tendero; almacenista**
singer **cantante; cantatriz**
social worker **asistente social;
trabajador social**
soldier **soldado**
solicitor **solicitador**
steelworker **obrero en una fábrica
de acero**
stenographer **estenógrafo;
taquígrafo**
stevedore **estibador**
stockbroker **bolsista; corredor de
bolsa**

street cleaner **barredor de calles**
supervisor **superintendente**
surveyor **topógrafo**
switchman **guardagujas**
tailor **sastre**
taxi driver **taxista, chofer de taxi**
(Sp. Am.)
teacher **maestro (-a); profesor;
instructor**
teamster **carretero**
technician **técnico; especialista;
experto técnico**
telephone operator **telefonista**
teller **pagador; cajero**
therapist **terapeuta**
ticket agent **agente de viajes;
taquillero**
timekeeper **cronometrador (-a)**
toreador **torero**
trackman **guardavía**
tradesman **tendero; comerciante
al por menor**
train dispatcher **despachador de
trenes**
translator **intérprete; traductor**
travel agent **agente de viajes**
treasurer **tesorero (-a)**
truck driver **camionero;
conductor de camión**
trunk dealer **baulero; cofrero**
trustee **consignatario; fiduciario**
tutor **preceptor; maestro
particular**
typesetter **compositor; tipógrafo**

typist **mecanógrafo (-a);
dactilógrafo (-a); tipiadora**
undertaker **funerario; agente de
entierros**
unemployed **cesante** (adj)
unskilled laborer **peón de pico y
pala**
unskilled workman **obrero no
especializado**
upholsterer **tapicero**
valet **asistente personal**
varnisher **barnizador; charolista**
vendor **vendedor; buhonero**
vocalist **cantante; vocalista**
waiter **mozo; camarero; mesero**
(Mex.)
waitress **moza de restaurante;
camarera**
warden **carcelero**
warehouse keeper **guardalmacén**
washer **lavandero (-a)**
watchmaker **relojero**
watchman **sereno; guardián**
weatherman **meteorologista**
weaver **tejedor (-a)**
welder **soldador**
wet nurse **nodriza; ama de
crianza**
white-collar worker **oficinista
profesional**
wholesaler **mayorista** (Sp. Am.);
comerciante al por mayor
wigmaker **fabricante de pelucas**

FOODS AND MEALS
ALIMENTOS Y COMIDAS

Special diets *Dietas especiales*

absolute diet **dieta absoluta**
acid-ash diet **dieta de residuo
ácido**
alkali-ash diet **dieta de residuos
alcalinos**
balanced diet **dieta balanceada**
bedtime snack, feeding **colación** (f)
bland diet **dieta blanda**
diabetic diet **dieta para los
diabéticos**
diet to control weight **dieta para
controlar el peso**
diet to gain weight **dieta para
aumentar el peso**
diet to lose weight **dieta para
perder peso**
elimination diet **dieta de
eliminación**
fat-free diet **dieta sin grasa**

gallbladder diet **dieta para la
vesícula**
gluten-free diet **dieta libre de
gluten**
high-carbohydrate diet **dieta rica
en carbohidratos**
high-fat diet **dieta rica en grasas**
high-protein diet **dieta de elevado
contenido proteico; dieta rica en
proteína**
high-residue diet **dieta de elevado
residuo**
iron-enriched diet **dieta rica en
hierro**
light diet **dieta ligera**
liquid diet **dieta de líquidos; dieta
líquida**
    clear liquid diet **dieta de
    líquidos claros**

full (nourishing) liquid diet
**dieta de líquidos nutritivos;
dieta de líquidos espesos**
low-calorie diet **dieta de pocas
calorías**
low-carbohydrate diet **dieta baja
en carbohidratos**
low-fat diet **dieta de escaso
contenido graso**
low-protein diet **dieta de escaso
contenido proteico; dieta baja en
proteína**
low-residue diet **dieta de escaso
residuo; dieta gástrica**
low-salt diet **dieta con escaso
contenido de sal**
mineral enriched diet **dieta rica
en minerales**
nutritional diet **dieta alimenticia**

purine-free diet **dieta sin purinas**	**desclorurada**	ulcer diet **dieta para las úlceras**
restricted diet **dieta rigurosa**	smooth diet **dieta pobre en**	vitamin-enriched diet **dieta rica**
salt-free diet **dieta sin sal; dieta**	**celulosa**	**en vitaminas**

Cooking terms   *Terminología de cocina*

appetite **apetito** (m)
appetizing **apetitoso** (adj)
aversion **aversión** (f);
  repugnancia (f)
bake, to **asar en horno; hornear;**
  cocer en horno
baked **al horno; horneado** (adj)
beaten **batido** (adj)
bitter **amargo** (adj)
boil, to **hervir (ie)**
boiled **cocido** (adj); **hervido** (adj)
boil in water, to **cocer**
breaded **empanado** (adj)
breakfast **desayuno** (m)
breakfast, to have, to eat
  desayunar(se)
broiled **asado; asado a la parrilla**
  (adj)
browned **dorado** (adj)
calorie **caloría** (f)
can **lata** (f)
canned **enlatado** (adj); **en**
  conserva (prep)
chew, to **masticar**
chop, to **picar**
cold **frío** (adj)
cook, to **guisar; cocinar**
cookbook **libro (manual) de**
  cocina (m)
cooked **cocinado** (adj)
crushed **machacado** (adj)
cut, to **cortar**
defrost, to **deshelar (ie)**
delicious **delicioso** (adj)
diced **cortado en cuadritos**
diet **dieta** (f); **régimen** (m)
diet, to **estar a dieta**
dinner **cena; comida** (f)
dinner, to have **cenar**
dish **plato** (m)
dry, dried **seco** (adj)
eat, to **comer**
eat heartily, to **comer por cuatro**
enjoy eating or drinking, to
  saborear
enriched **enriquecido** (adj)
entrée **principio** (m); **entrada** (f)
feed, to **alimentar; dar de comer**
feeding **alimentación** (f)
flavor **sabor** (m)
food **alimento** (m); **comestibles**
  (m, pl); **vianda** (f)
food stamps **cupones de comida**
  (m)
fortify **fortalecer**

freeze, to **congelar; helar (ie)**
fresh **fresco** (adj)
fried **frito** (adj)
frosted **azucarado** (adj)
frozen **helado; congelado** (adj)
fry, to **freír (i)**
grated **rallado** (adj)
gravy (au jus) **salsa** (f)
greasy **grasiento** (adj); **con grasa**
  (prep)
grilled **asado a la parrilla** (adj)
grind, to **moler (ue)**
ground **molido** (adj)
heat, to **calentar (ie)**
hot **caliente** (adj)
juicy **jugoso** (adj)
kosher **cácher** (adj); **kosher** (adj)
larded **mechado** (adj)
lean **magro** (adj)
lunch **almuerzo** (m)
lunch, to eat **almorzar (ue)**
marinate, to **marinar; escabechar**
mashed **amasado** (adj); **majado**
  (adj)
measure **medir (i)**
medium **medio** (adj)
mince, to **desmenuzar**
mix, to **mezclar**
mixed **mezclado** (adj)
not agree, to **caer mal**
nourish, to **alimentar**
nourishment **alimentación** (f);
  alimento (m)
nutriment **alimento** (m)
nutritious **alimenticio; nutritivo**
  (adj)
pat **cuadrado** (m)
peel, to **pelar**
pickled **encurtido; en escabeche**
  (adj)
poach **escalfar**
poached **escalfado** (adj)
pour, to **verter (ie)**
precooked **precocinado** (adj)
protein **proteína** (f)
puree **puré** (m)
put on weight, to **engordar**
rare (meat) **poco asado; poco frito;**
  poco hecho; medio crudo; poco
  cocido (adj)
raw **crudo** (adj)
relish **entremés** (m)
rind **cáscara** (f)
rinse, to **enjuagar**
ripe **maduro** (adj)

roast, to **asar**
roasted **asado** (adj)
rough **áspero** (adj)
round slice **rueda** (f)
salty **salado** (adj)
sauce **salsa** (f)
sauté **salteado** (adj)
scrape, to **raspar**
scrub, to **restregar**
season, to **condimentar; sazonar**
shred, to **desmenuzar**
sip **trago** (m); **sorbo** (m)
sip, to **sorber**
slice **rebanada** (f); **tajado** (f)
slice, to **rebanar; tajar**
smoke, to (food) **ahumar**
smoked **ahumado** (adj)
smooth **blando** (adj)
snack **merienda** (f)
soak, to **remojar**
soft **blando** (adj)
solid **sólido** (adj)
sour **agrio** (adj)
spicy **picante; condimentado** (adj)
starch **almidón** (m)
steamed **cocido** (adj)
stew, to **estofar; guisar**
stewed **guisado** (adj)
strain, to **colar**
strip **lonja** (f)
stuffing **relleno** (m)
supper **cena** (f)
supper, to eat **cenar**
swallow, to **tragar**
sweet **dulce** (m, adj)
sweetness **dulzura** (f)
taste, to **saborear**
tasteless **sin sabor; insípido** (adj)
temperature, at room **al tiempo**
  (adj); **natural** (adj)
tender **tierno** (adj)
thaw, to **deshelar (ie)**
thick (liquid) **espeso** (adj)
toast, to **tostar**
toasted **tostado** (adj)
victuals **viandas** (f)
wash, to **lavar**
wean, to **destetar**
well cooked **bien cocinado** (adj)
well done (steak) **bien frito** (adj);
  bien asado (adj); **bien cocida** (adj)
whipped **batido** (adj)
wrap, to **envolver (ue)**

Seasonings *Condimentos*

anise seed **anís** (m)
basil **albahaca** (f)
bay leaves **hojas de laurel** (f)
black pepper **pimienta** (f)
butter **mantequilla** (f)
catsup **salsa de tomate** (f)
chile **ají** (m); **chile** (m)
chile powder **polvo de chile** (m)
cinnamon **canela** (f)
cloves **clavos** (m)
condiment **condimento** (m)
corn oil **aceite de maíz** (m)
cornstarch **maicena** (f)
cottonseed oil **aceite de semillas de algodón** (f)
cumin seed **comino** (m)
fat **manteca** (f); **grasa** (f)
garlic **ajo** (m)
ginger **jengibre** (m)

grease **grasa** (f); **manteca** (f)
honey **miel** (f)
horseradish **rábano picante** (m)
hot sauce **salsa picante** (f); **picante** (m)
jelly **jalea** (f)
lard **manteca** (f)
lemon **limón** (m)
margarine **margarina** (f)
majoram **orégano** (m)
marmalade **mermelada** (f)
mayonnaise **mayonesa** (f); **salsa mayonesa** (f)
MSG **glutamato monosódico** (m)
mushroom **seta** (f); **hongo** (m)
mustard **mostaza** (f)
nutmeg **nuez moscada** (f)
oil **aceite** (m)
olive oil **aceite de oliva** (m)

paprika **pimentón** (m)
red pepper **pimiento** (m)
red pepper sauce (Mex.) **mole** (m)
saccharine **sacarina** (f)
saffron **azafrán** (m)
salt **sal** (f)
  iodized **sal yodada**
  noniodized **sal corriente**
sauce **salsa** (f)
sesame oil **aceite de sésame** (m); **aceite de ajonjolí** (m)
spice **especia** (f)
sugar **azúcar** (m)
  brown sugar **panocha** (f, Mex.)
tarragon **tarrago** (m)
thyme **tomillo** (m)
vinegar **vinagre** (m)
Worcestershire sauce **salsa inglesa** (f)

Soups *Sopas*

broth **caldo** (m)
chicken soup (with noodles) **sopa de gallina (con fideos)** (f); **caldo de pollo (con fideos)** (m)
consomme **consomé** (m)

cream of tomato soup **crema de jitomate** (f)
onion soup **sopa de cebollas** (f)
oyster soup **caldo de ostras** (m); **sopa de ostiones** (f)

tomato soup **sopa de tomate** (f)
vegetable soup **sopa de vegetales** (f); **caldo de vegetales** (m)

Salads *Ensaladas*

cucumber and tomato **pepinos con tomates** (m)
fruit salad **ensalada de frutas** (f)

lettuce with mayonnaise **lechuga con mayonesa** (f)

mixed green salad **ensalada mixta** (f)

Eggs and cereals *Huevos y cereales*

barley **cebada** (f)
bran **acemite** (m); **salvado** (m)
cooked cereal **cereal cocido** (m)
cornflakes **copos de maíz** (m)
corn flour **maicena** (f)
cream of wheat **crema de trigo** (f)
dry cereal **cereal seco** (m)
egg **huevo** (m); **blanquillo** (m, Mex.)
  egg shell **cáscara de huevo** (f)
  egg white **clara de huevo** (f)

egg yolk **yema de huevo** (f)
fresh egg **huevo fresco** (m)
fried eggs **huevos fritos** (m)
hard-boiled eggs **huevos duros** (m); **huevos hervidos** (m); **huevos cocidos** (m)
omelette with ham **tortilla con jamón** (f)
poached eggs **huevos escalfados** (m); **huevos blandos** (m)
rotten eggs **huevos podridos** (m)

scrambled eggs **huevos revueltos** (m)
soft-boiled eggs **huevos pasados por agua** (m); **huevos tibios** (m)
grits **sémola** (f)
hot cereal **cereal caliente** (m)
millet **mijo** (m)
oatmeal **avena** (f)
rice **arroz** (m)
sorghum **sorgo** (m)
wheat **trigo** (m)

Breads and noodles *Panes y pastas*

biscuit **bizcocho** (m); **galleta** (f); **rosca** (f)
bread **pan** (m)
  bran bread **acemita** (f)
  cassava bread (or cake) **cazabe** (m, Sp. Am.)

corn bread **pan de maíz** (m)
dark bread **pan negro** (m); **pan moreno** (m)
French bread **pan francés** (m)
fresh bread **pan del día** (m); **pan tierno** (m)

home-made bread **pan casero** (m)
rye bread **pan de centeno** (m)
stale bread **pan duro** (m); **pan sentado** (m)
white bread **pan blanco** (m)

whole wheat bread **pan de trigo entero** (m); **pan de grano integral** (m)
cracker **galleta** (f); **galletica** (f)
soda cracker **galleta salada** (f)
crumb **miga(ja)** (f)
crust **corteza** (f)
fiber (natural) **fibra (natural)** (f)
hot cakes **queques** (m, pl, Mex.); **panqueques** (m, pl, Sp. Am.); **tortitas calientes** (f, pl)
macaroni **macarrones** (m, pl)

nixtamal (corn processed for making tortillas) **nixtamal** (m, Mex.)
noodle **fideo** (m); **tallarín** (m)
pancake, cornmeal and cheese **panocha** (f, Col., C.R., Chile)
pasta **pasta** (f)
roll **panecillo** (m); **bollo de pan** (m); **bolillo** (m, Mex.)
sandwich **sandwich** (m); **emparedado** (m); **bocadillo** (m, Spain)

slice **rebanada** (f); **tajada** (f)
spaghetti **espaguetis** (m, pl); **tallarín** (m)
sweet roll **pan dulce** (m, Mex.)
toast **tostada de pan** (f); **pan tostado** (m); **tostadas** (f, pl, Spain)
French toast **tostada al estilo francés** (f)
waffles **queques** (m, pl, Mex.); **wafles** (m)

Butter and cheese   *Mantequilla y queso*

butter **mantequilla** (f); **manteca de vaca** (f, Spain)
cheese **queso** (m)
cottage cheese **requesón** (m); **naterón** (m); **názula** (f)
cream cheese **queso de crema** (m)

goat's cheese **queso de cabra** (m)
headcheese **queso de cerdo** (m)
cooking fat **grasa de cocinar** (f); **aceite de comer** (m)
dairy products **productos lácteos** (m)
fat **manteca** (f); **grasa** (f)

lard **manteca (de puerco)** (f)
margarine **margarina** (f); **mantequilla artificial** (f)
peanut butter **mantequilla de maní** (f); **crema de cacahuete** (f);
vegetable oil **aceite vegetal** (m)

Vegetables   *Legumbres y verduras*

artichoke **alcachofa** (f)
asparagus **espárragos** (m, pl)
avocado **aguacate** (m)
bean **haba** (f); **judía** (f); **habichuela** (f); **frijol** (m)
dried beans **habichuelas secas** (f)
French beans **habichuela** (f)
green beans **habichuelas verdes** (f); **ejotes** (m)
kidney beans **habichuela** (f); **frijol** (m)
lima beans **habas** (f, pl)
navy beans **frijol blanco común** (m)
soy beans **soya** (f); **soja** (f)
string beans **habichuelas verdes** (f); **judías verdes** (f); **ejotes** (m, pl, Mex.); **chauchas** (f, pl, Arg.)
beet **remolacha** (f); **betabel** (m)
broccoli **brécol** (m)
brussels sprouts **col de Bruselas** (m)
cabbage **col** (m); **repollo** (m)
carrot **zanahoria** (f)
cauliflower **coliflor** (f)
celery **apio** (m)
chard **acelga** (f)
chick pea **garbanzo** (m)
collards **berzas** (f)
corn **maíz** (m)

corn on the cob (sweet corn) **elote** (m, Mex.)
green corn **maíz tierno** (m)
sweet corn **choclo** (m, Sp. Am.)
cucumber **pepino** (m)
dandelion **amargón** (m)
eggplant **berenjena** (f)
endive **escarola** (f)
green pepper **pimiento verde** (m)
greens **verduras** (f)
green vegetables **hortalizas de hoja verde** (f)
dark green vegetables **verduras de hojas verde-claras** (f)
kale **berza** (f); **col rizada** (f)
legumes **legumbres** (f)
lentil **lenteja** (f)
lettuce **lechuga** (f)
maize **maíz** (m)
mushroom **hongo** (m); **seta** (f); **champiñón** (m, Chicano)
okra **quimbombó** (m); **quinbombó** (m)
onion **cebolla** (f)
parsley **perejil** (m)
pea **guisante** (m); **alverjas** (f, pl, Sp. Am.); **chícharo** (m); **arveja** (f, Sp. Am.)
green pea **guisante** (m); **chícharo** (m)
split pea **arveja seca** (f)

pickle **pepinillo** (m); **encurtido** (m); **picles** (m)
potato **patata** (f); **papa** (f, Sp. Am.)
baked potatoes **papas asadas** (f)
fried (French fried) **papas fritas** (f)
mashed potatoes **puré de papas** (m); **puré de patata** (m)
sweet potato **camote** (m, Mex.); **batata** (f); **buniato** (m)
radish **rábano** (m); **rabanito** (m)
rutabaga(s) **nabo de Suecia** (m)
sauerkraut **berza** (f); **col agria** (f)
spinach **espinaca** (f)
squash **calabaza** (f)
tomato **tomate** (m); **jitomate** (m, Mex.)
stewed tomatoes **puré de tomates** (m)
turnip **nabo** (m)
turnip greens **hojas de nabo** (f)
vegetables **vegetales** (m); **hortalizas** (f); **legumbres** (f); **verduras** (f)
yellow vegetables **vegetales de pulpa amarilla** (m)
watercress **berro** (m)
yam **batata** (f); **buniato** (m)

Meat *Carne*

bacon **tocino** (m)
barbecue **barbacoa** (f)
beef **carne de vaca** (f); **carne de res** (f)
  beefsteak **bistec** (m); **biftec** (m); **filete** (m); **bife** (m, Arg.)
  broiled (beef)steak **churrasco** (m, Arg., Chile)
  roast beef **rosbif** (m); **carne asada** (f)
brains **sesos** (m, pl)
chop, cutlet **chuleta** (f); **costilla** (f)
cold cuts **fiambres** (m, pl)
frankfurter **salchicha** (f)
giblets **menudillo** (m)
ground meat **carne molida** (f)
ham **jamón** (m)
hamburger **hamburguesa** (f)
hot dog **perro caliente** (m)
kid **cabrito** (m)
kidneys **riñones** (m pl)

lamb **cordero** (m); **borrego** (m, Chicano)
  lamb meat **carne de cordero** (f)
liver **hígado** (m)
meatballs **albóndigas** (f, pl)
meatpie **empanada** (f)
meat stew and ají (Chile) **ajiaco** (m)
mutton **carnero** (m)
  leg of mutton **pierna de carnero** (f)
pork **cerdo** (m); **carne de puerco** (f); **chancho** (m, Sp. Am.)
  pork rind (roast pork) **chicharrón** (m, Peru)
  stew of pork, corn and chile **pozole** (m, Mex.)
  young pig **lechón** (m); **lechoncillo** (m)
ribs **costillas asadas** (f)
  baked ribs **costillas al horno** (f)

barbecued ribs **costillas a la parrilla** (f)
roast **asado** (m, adj)
sausage **salchicha** (f)
  blood sausage **morcilla** (f)
  bologna **salchichón** (m)
  pork sausage **chorizo** (m)
sirloin **solomillo** (m)
stew **cocido** (m); **estofado** (m); **guisado** (m)
sweetbreads **mollejas** (f, pl)
tenderloin **filete** (m)
  tenderloin tips **puntas de filete** (f)
tongue **lengua** (f)
tripe **mondongo** (m); **callos** (m, pl)
veal **carne de ternera** (f)
  breaded veal cutlet **milanesa** (f); **ternera apanada** (f)

Poultry and game *Aves y caza*

capon **capón** (m)
chicken **pollo** (m)
  boiled chicken **pollo cocido** (m)
  breast of chicken **pechuga de pollo** (f)
  broiled chicken **pollo a la parrilla** (m)

fried chicken **pollo frito** (m)
roast chicken **pollo asado** (m)
stuffed chicken **pollo relleno** (m)
duck **pato** (m)
  wild duck **pato silvestre** (m)
fowl **ave** (f)
goose **ganso** (m)

hare **liebre** (f)
hen **gallina** (f)
partridge **perdiz** (f)
pheasant **faisán** (m)
rabbit **conejo** (m)
turkey **pavo** (m); **guajolote** (m, Mex.); **guanajo** (m, Cuba)

Fish and seafood *Pescado y mariscos*

anchovies **anchoas** (f)
bass **mero** (m); **lobina** (f)
bluepoint **ostra pequeña** (f)
caviar **caviar** (m)
clam **almeja** (f)
cod (fish) (baked) **bacalao** **(guisado)** (m)
crab **cangrejo** (m); **jaiba** (f, Sp. Am.)
eel **anguila** (f)
fish (living) **pez** (m)
fish (already caught) **pescado** (m)
  pickled fish **escabeche** (m)
fishbone **espina** (f)

flounder **lenguado** (m)
haddock **róbalo** (m)
hake (a type of bass) **merluza** (f)
herring (smoked) **arenque** **(ahumado)** (m)
lobster **langosta** (f)
mackerel **pejerrey** (m); **caballa** (f)
octopus **pulpo** (m)
oyster **ostra** (f); **ostión** (m, Mex.)
perch **percha** (f)
prawn **langostino** (m)
red snapper **huachinango** (m, Mex.); **pargo** (m, Cuba)
roe **hueva** (f)

salmon **salmón** (m)
sardines **sardinas** (f)
scallop **pechina** (f); **venera** (f)
shellfish **marisco** (m)
shrimps **camarones** (m); **gambas** (f)
snapper **pargo** (m)
sole **lenguado** (m)
squid **calamar** (m)
trout **trucha** (f)
tuna fish **atún** (m)
turtle **tortuga** (f)
white fish **corégono** (m)

Fruits *Frutas*

apple **manzana** (f)
apricot **albaricoque** (m); **chabacano** (m)
avocado **aguacate** (m, Mex., C.A.); **palta** (Sp. Am.)
banana **banana** (f); **plátano** (m); **guineo** (m)

berry, wild **baya silvestre** (f)
blackberry **zarza** (f)
blueberry **vaccinio** (m)
cherry **cereza** (f)
citrus fruit **fruta cítrica** (f)
currant **grosella** (f)
date **dátil** (m)

fig **higo** (m)
gooseberry **grosela blanca** (f)
grape **uva** (f)
grapefruit **toronja** (f); **pomelo** (m, Sp. Am.)
guava **guayaba** (f)
lemon **limón** (m)

lime **lima** (f)
mango **mango** (m)
melon **melón** (m)
nut **nuez** (f)
orange **naranja** (f); **china** (f, P.R.)
papaya **papaya** (f); **fruta bomba** (f,
   Cuba—AVOID use of *papaya* in
   this country!)
peach **melocotón** (m); **durazno**
   (m)

pear **pera** (f)
   prickly pear **tuna** (f)
pineapple **piña** (f); **ananá** (m/f)
pit **hueso** (m)
plantain **plátano** (m); **banana** (m)
plum **ciruela** (f)
pomegranate **granada** (f)
prune **ciruela seca** (f); **ciruela**
   pasa (f); **pruna** (f, Chicano)
pumpkin **calabaza** (f)

quince **membrillo** (m)
raisin **pasa** (f)
raspberry **frambuesa** (f)
seed **pepita** (f)
skin (of fruit) **cáscara** (f)
strawberry **fresa** (f); **frutilla** (f,
   Sp. Am.)
tangerine **mandarina** (f)
watermelon. **sandía** (f)

Desserts *Postres*

bonbon **bombón** (m)
cake **torta** (f); **bizcocho** (m);
   queque (m)
   cheese cake **quesadilla** (f)
   small pastry cake **bollo** (m)
candy **dulces** (m, pl); **confites** (m,
   pl)
chewing gum **chicle** (m)
chocolate bar **barra de chocolate**
   (f)
cookie **galleta** (f); **galletica** (f);
   pasta (f)

custard **flan** (m); **natillas** (f)
dessert **postre** (m)
doughnut **rosquilla** (f); **donut** (m,
   Chicano); **buñuelo** (m)
eclair **pastelillo de crema** (m)
ice cream **helado** (m); **mantecado**
   (m); **nieve** (f)
jello **gelatina** (f)
lollipop **caramelo en un palito** (m);
   paleta (f); **pirulí** (m)
meringue **merengue** (m)
nut **nuez** (f)

pastry **pasta** (f); **pastel** (m)
   sweet pastry **quesadilla** (f)
pie **pastel** (m)
pudding **pudín** (m)
rice pudding **arroz con leche** (m)
sherbet **sorbete** (m); **nieve** (f,
   Mex.)
sweet **dulce** (m)
syrup **jarabe** (m)
tapioca **tapioca** (f)
whipped cream **nata batida** (f)

Beverages *Bebidas*

alcohol **alcohol** (m)
ale **cerveza inglesa** (f)
atole (drink made with cornmeal
   gruel) **atole** (m, Sp. Am.)
beer **cerveza** (f); **helada** (f,
   Chicano)
beverage **bebida** (f)
   cold beverage **refresco** (m)
brandy **coñac** (m); **aguardiente** (m)

champagne **champaña** (f)
chocolate **chocolate** (m)
   chocolate milk **leche con**
      chocolate (f)
   cocoa **cacao** (m)
   hot chocolate **chocolate caliente**
      (m)
cider **sidra** (f)
   can cider **guarapo** (m)
   fruit cider, fermented maize
      chicha (f, Sp. Am.)
cocktail **coctel** (m)
coffee **café** (m)
   black coffee **café solo** (m); **café**
      puro (m); **café tinto** (m, Col.)
   coffee with cream **café con**
      crema (m)
   coffee with cream and sugar
      café con azúcar y crema (m)
   coffee with milk **café con**
      leche (m)
   coffee with sugar **café con**
      azúcar (m)
   decaffeinated coffee **café**
      descafeinado (m)

instant coffee **café instantáneo**
   (m); **nescafé** (m)
strong coffee **café fuerte** (m);
   café cargado (m)
weak coffee **café débil** (m); **café**
   claro (m); **café simple** (m);
   café suave (m); **café ralo** (m)
cream **crema** (f)
drink **bebida** (f); **trago** (m, usually
   alcoholic)
carbonated drink **gaseosa** (f)
cold drink **bebida fría** (f)
hot drink **bebida caliente** (f)
gin **ginebra** (f)
juice **jugo** (m)
   apple juice **jugo de manzana** (m)
   cranberry juice **jugo de**
      arándano (m)
   grape juice **jugo de uvas** (m)
   grapefruit juice **jugo de**
      toronja (m)
   lemon juice **jugo de limón** (m)
   lime juice **jugo de lima** (m)
   orange juice **jugo de naranja** (m)
   pineapple juice **jugo de piña** (m)
   prune juice **jugo de ciruela** (m)
   tomato juice **jugo de tomate** (m)
lemonade **limonada** (f)
liqueur **licor** (m)
milk **leche** (f)
   buttermilk **leche agria** (f);
      suero de leche (m)
   condensed milk **leche**
      condensada (f)
   cow's milk **leche de vaca** (f)

dry milk **leche en polvo** (f)
evaporated milk **leche**
   evaporada (f)
malted milk **leche malteada** (f)
pasteurized milk **leche**
   pasteurizada (f)
skim milk **leche desnatada** (f);
   leche sin crema (f); **leche**
   descremada (f)
orangeade **naranjada** (f)
pop **soda** (f); **gaseosa** (f); **coca**
   cola (f)
punch **ponche** (m)
refreshment **refresco** (m)
rum **ron** (m)
tea **té** (m)
   iced tea **té helado** (m)
   Paraguay tea **yerba mate** (f, Sp.
      Am.)
   strong tea **té fuerte** (m); **té**
      cargado (m)
   weak tea **té débil**; **té claro**; **té**
      simple; **té suave**; **té ralo** (m)
water **agua** (f)
   carbonated water **agua**
      gaseosa (f)
   drinking water **agua potable** (f)
   mineral water **agua mineral** (f)
   seltzer water **agua de Seltz** (f)
   soda water **agua de soda** (f)
whiskey **whiskey** (m)
wine **vino** (m)
   claret, red wine **vino tinto** (m)
   white wine **vino blanco** (m)

Dishes and utensils *Loza y utensilios*

bowl **escudilla** (f)
china **loza** (f); **porcelana** (f)
coffeepot **cafetera** (f)
cup **taza** (f)
dish **plato** (m); **platico** (m)
fork **tenedor** (m)
frying pan **sartén** (f)
glass **vaso** (m)
jar **jarra** (f)
jug **jarra** (f)
knife **cuchillo** (m)

ladle **cucharón** (m)
lid **cobertera** (f)
napkin **servilleta** (f)
pepper shaker **pimentero** (m)
plate **plato** (m)
platter **fuente** (f)
pot **caldera** (f); **olla** (f); **puchero** (m), **pote** (m)
salt shaker **salero** (m)
saucepan **cacerola** (f)
saucer **platico** (m); **platillo** (m)

spoon **cuchara** (f)
straw **pajiza** (f); **popote** (m)
tablespoon **cuchara grande** (f); **cuchara de sopa** (f)
teapot **tetera** (f)
teaspoon **cucharita** (f); **cucharilla** (f); **cuchara de café** (f)
tray **bandeja** (f); **charola** (f); **charol** (m, Sp. Am.)

Notes *Notas*

1. This may refer to appendicitis, peritonitis, or a bowel obstruction.

2. See note 1.

3. In northwestern Mexico a poisonous lizard is called a scorpion.

4. See "sting," page 433.

5. This illness is found in southern Mexico, the high plateaus of Guatemala, and eastern Venezuela.

6. This may also refer to appendicitis or peritonitis.

7. In rural areas, especially of Mexico and Puerto Rico, peasants often call any serious skin disease, especially infected wounds or gangrene, **cancer.**

8. See **Selected Drug Abuse Vocabulary,** pages 441–444.

9. See page 388 for a discussion of this and other folk illnesses.

10. See page 390 for a discussion of "fever."

11. For a fuller discussion of folk illnesses, see note 7, pages 387–390.

12. See pages 387f.

13. This "disease" has nothing to do with bile.

14. See page 390.

15. See note 1.

16. See **Selected Drug Abuse Vocabulary,** pages 441–444.

17. A common brand of aspirin in Latin America is **mejoral** or **mejoralito,** for children.

18. See **Selected Drug Abuse Vocabulary,** page 441.

19. See pages 444–445.

20. See **Selected Drug Abuse Vocabulary,** pages 441–444.

21. See **Pregnancy, Childbirth, Contraception, Postnatal Care of the Mother,** pages 445–449; and Chapter 6, pages 378–385.

22. This is new vocabulary, not necessarily listed nor yet recognized by the Royal Academy of Spanish Grammar. It is understood that this vocabulary is primarily slang. Unless otherwise indicated, the gender of nouns is assumed to be obvious.

23. I have followed the spelling given in the *Diccionario de la lengua española,* RAE, 19th edition, 1970. Spanish does recognize variations using **j** and **h.**

24. Use the Spanish pronunciation of these letters.

25. See note 24.

26. See note 24.

27. As of 1980–1981, the English street terminology for *cocaine* includes: angel dust, Bernice gold dust, bernies, big C, blow, burese, C, candy, c-game, C & H, carrie, Cecil, Charlie, cholly, coca, coke,

Corine, dream, dust, dynamite, flake, gin, girl, gold dust, happy dust, heaven dust, her, jelly, joy powder, King's habit, killer stuff, lady, lady snow, leaf, love affairs, M & C, Merck, nose, nose candy, nose powder, one & one, paradise, rich man's heroin, rock, schmeck, schoolboy code, sleigh ride, snow, snowbird, speedball, star dust, thing, white lady, white stuff, whiz bang.

28. Street terminology generally uses "syrup" (terpinhydrate) and terps for codeine.

29. A croaker is a physician who dispenses prescriptions for drugs.

30. See note 24.

31. A flash is the euphoric initial reaction to IV narcotics.

32. As of 1980–1981 the English street terminology for *heroin* includes: a-bomb, big H, blanks, boss, boy, brother, brown, ca-ca, caballo, carga, C & H, China white, Chinese red, chiva, cobics, crap, dogie, doojee, doojie, dope, duji, dynamite, dyno, eighth, Frisco speedball, girl, goods, gravy, H, hairy, hard stuff, harry, H-caps, Henry, him, hochs, horse, joy powder, junk, ka-ka, killer stuff, lemonade, love affairs, Mexican brown, Mexican horse, Mexican mud, noise, peg, poison, scag, scar, schmeck, shit, skag, smack, smeck, snow, speedball, stuff, sugar, tecata, thing, TNT, white junk, white lady, white stuff, whiz bang.

33. As of 1980–1981 the English street terminology for LSD includes: acid, barrels, (the) beast, big D, blue acid, blue cheer, blue heavens, blue mist, blue sky, blue tab, blue wedge, brown dots, California sunshine, cherry dome, cherry top, (the) chief, chocolate chips, Christmas acid, clear-light, coffee, contact lens, crackers, crystals, cube, cupcakes, deeda, dome, dots, double dimples, electric kool-aid, fifty, flats, gammon, (the) Ghost, grape parfait, grays, green barrels, (the) hawk, haze, heavenly blue, hit, instant Zen, L, LSD 25, Lucy in the sky (with diamonds), lysergide, mellow yellows, micro dots, mikes, mind detergent, oranges, orange mushrooms, orange sunshine, orange wedge, Owsley's acid, Ozzie's stuff, paper acid, peace, peace acid, peace pills, pearly gates, pellets, pink wedge, product IV, psychedelic, purple barrels, purple dome, purple dots, purple haze, purple microdots, purple ozoline, purple wedge, royal blue, smears, squirrels, Stanley's stuff, strawberry field, sunshine, tabs, ticket, trips, turtle, twenty-five, wedge, white lightning, window pane (paine) yellow dimples.

34. As of 1980–1981 the English street terminology for *marijuana* includes: a-bomb, a-stick, Acapulco gold, ace, African black, Alice B. Toklas, baby, bale, bar, bhang, black gunion, boo, brick, broccoli, buddha sticks, bush, butter flower, can, Canadian black, cannabis, cannabis sativa, charge, cocktail, colombo, Colombian, Colombian red, C.S. dagga, dawamesk, doobee, dope, dry high, dube, duby, fatty, finger lid, flower tops, fuma d'Angola, funny stuff, gage, Gainesville green, ganga, gangster, ganja, giggle weed, giggles-smoke, goblet of jam, gold, gold Colombian, golden leaf, gold star, goof but, grass, grasshopper, green, grefa, greta, griefo, griefs, grifa, griffo, gunga, gungeon, gunja, haircut, has, Hawaiian, hay, hemp, herb, hooch, Indian hay, Indian hemp, intsaga, intsagu, J, Jane, jay, jay smoke, jive, jive stick, Juana, Juanita, Juanita weed, juja, kaif, Kansas grass, kauii, kee, key, ki, kick sticks, kif, killer weed, kilter, light stuff, loaf, loco, locoweed, loveweed, mach, macon, maconha, marihuana, mariguana, Mary, Mary Anne, Mary Jane, Mary Warner, Mary Werner, Mary Wearver, Mary Worner, match box, mauii, Mex, Mexican, Mexican brown, Mexican green, Mexican locoweed, M.J., mohasky, moocah, moota, mooters, mootie, mor a grifa, mota, moto, mu, muggles, muta(h), nail, nigra, number, Panama gold, Panama red, panatella, pin, pod, pot, potlikker, P.R. (Panama red), Puff the Dragon, rainy day woman, red dirt marijuana, reefer, righteous bush, roach, root, rope, Rose Maria, rough stuff, sativa, seeds, shit, sinsemilla, skinny, smoke, smoke Canada, snop, stack, stems, stick, super pot, Sweet Lucy, T, tea, Texas tea, thrupence bag, thumb, tustin, twist, weed, wheat, yesca.

35. As of 1980–1981 the English street terminology for *mescaline* includes: anhalonium, beans, big chief, blue caps, blue devils, buttons, cactus, full moon, hikori, huatari, mesc, mescal, mescal buttons, moon, plants, seni.

36. As of 1980–1981 the English street terminology for *morning glory seeds* includes: badoh negro, blue star, flying saucers, glory seeds, heavenly blues, pearly gates, pearly whites, seeds.

37. As of 1980–1981 the English street terminology for *morphine* includes: cobies, dope, emsel, first line, goods, hard stuff, hocus, junk, M, morf, morphie, morpho, morphy, mud, sister, Miss Emma, mojo, cube.

38. Also known as nembutol, nimbies, nemish, nimby.

39. As of 1980–1981 the English street terminology for *opium* includes: black, black stuff, gow, gum, hop, leaf, Mash Allah.

40. As of 1980–1981 the English street terminology for PCP includes: amoeba, angel dust, angel hair, animal tranquilizer, cadillac, C.J., crystal, crystal joints, cyclones, dead on arrival, D.O.A., dust, elephant tranquilizer, goon, hog, horse tranquilizer, killer weed, K.J., mist, peace pill, pig tranquilizer, rocket fuel, scuffle, sheets, snorts, soma.

41. See note 24.

42. Other slang terms include: dealer, mother, pusher.

43. As of 1980–1981 the English street terminology for *psilocybin* includes: hombrecitos, little children, little men, little women, magic mushroom, las mujercitas, mushrooms, los niños, noble princess of the waters.

44. Other slang terms include: mule.

45. As of 1980–1981 the English street terminology for *seconals* include: bullets, devils, M & M, red devils, reds.

46. As of 1980–1981 the English street terminology for *yage* includes: ayahuasca, caapi, drug, jungle drug.

47. For a more complete listing, see **Anatomical Vocabulary**, page 225.

48. This is the forty-day period following delivery during which there is a prolonged period in bed, much freedom from household responsibilities, and abstention from sexual intercourse.

49. See note 48.

50. See **Anatomical Vocabulary** (page 227) for slang terminology.

51. All of the words in this vocabulary belong to "standard" Spanish, understood by all who know Spanish. Yet many variants exist for all of these nouns, depending upon the influence of the many distinct and unrelated Indian dialects that have entered the language. An example of this is seen in the different forms Hispanic America has for *little boy*: Argentina—**pibe**; Chile—**cabro**; Colombia— **pelado**; Cuba—**chico**; El Salvador—**cipote**; Guatemala—**patojo**; Mexico—**chamaco**; Panamá—**chico**.

52. In the Spanish-speaking world, it is common to have relatives living in a household—grandparents, aunts, and uncles—along with the nuclear family. The typical Hispanic attitude is that older people are happiest when with their children. An elderly parent *or* relative who is chronically sick will be cared for at home as long as possible.

   For most Hispanics family gatherings are a very important part of their social life. The extended family members often live within a few blocks of each other. Family members usually stick together, but especially in times of trouble.

53. Some nouns or adjectives of nationality—like **nicaragüense**—have only one form; others—like **boliviano**—change the masculine *-o* to *-a* for the feminine; those ending in a consonant add *-a* for feminine: **español/española**.

54. Today, 14,605,883 Americans (about 6.5% of the total U.S. population) are Hispanic Americans— most with ancestries in Mexico, Puerto Rico, and Cuba. Hispanic Americans are many peoples with their own histories, beliefs, life-styles, and cultures. Millions of Americans have roots in Central and South America and many Caribbean Islands: *Venezuela*—9 million in a resource-rich land: pre- dominantly mestizos, 10% black, 10% white, 5% Indians. *Colombia*—about 20 million: 70% mestizos, 20% white, 5% Indians, 5% black; Colombian Spanish is the purest Castilian in America. *Ecuador*— 5 million: half Indian and 10–15% white; a poor nation with endless political strife. *Peru*—over 12 million: 50% Indians, 35% mestizos, 10% white, few blacks; their largest export is fishmeal. *Bolivia*— 4 million: almost all Indian and mestizo; landlocked and hungry nation. (Revolutionary "Che" Guevara was killed in Bolivia in 1967.) *Brazil*—90 million in half of all South American territory; colonized by Portugal, perhaps half Europeans and 40% black or mulatto. *Paraguay*—about 2½ million almost entirely of Spanish and Guarini Indian blood; it is the least populated South American nation. *Uruguay*—about 3 million: majority Spanish and Italian; half the population lives in the capital city

of Montevideo. *Argentina*—almost 25 million: mostly of Spanish and Italian extraction. (From 1860 to 1940, 3 million Italian and 2 million Spanish immigrants moved to Argentina.) *Chile*—over 9 million: a blend of Spanish and Araucanian Indians. (Chile has been a large melting pot with an exceptionally high rate of literacy.) *Panama*—only 1½ million: 75% mulatto, the rest black and white, with few Indians. (It was created by U.S. action in 1903.) *Costa Rica*—just under 2 million: 80% of European descent; the most highly educated Central American nation. *Nicaragua*—about 2 million: 3–4% Indians, 10% black, and the rest mestizos. (It has large empty spaces.) *El Salvador*—3½ million; it is the smallest, most densely populated, and industrialized Central American nation. *Honduras*—2½ million: largely Indians, blacks, mixed. (It is the poorest Central American nation.) *Guatemala*—5 million: 55% Indians of Mayan stock, 45% mestizos, less than 1% Spanish ancestry. *The Dominican Republic*— 5½ million: 73% mulatto, 16% white, 11% black. *Puerto Rico*—almost 3½ million: 99% Hispanic. (A commonwealth associated with the U.S.) **Puertorriqueños** are U.S. citizens and many travel freely to and from the mainland. *Cuba*—almost 10 million; an island some 90 miles off the coast of the U.S. (Most Cuban immigrants came to the U.S. after the 1959 Communist revolution; as of 1977 some 68,000 were admitted as permanent U.S. residents under the Refugee Act, and in 1980 more than 125,000 Cubans landed in southern Florida aboard the "Freedom Flotilla.") *Mexico*—65¾ million people: 60% mestizos, 30% Indians, 10% whites; originally extended over large areas of presently owned U.S. land. Since the Mexican-American War, many Mexicans have immigrated to the U.S. legally. Large numbers of workers continue to cross the border illegally in search of seasonal employment. Their numbers have been estimated to be as high as 12 million, but a more realistic figure probably would be between 5 and 6 million. (Statistics from the *World Almanac*, 1981, the *Chicago Tribune*, November 2, 1980, Sec. 2, p. 14, col. 1, the 1980 U.S. Census, and John Quiñones, CBS News, a personal interview on January 27, 1981.)

55. There is a tendency to differentiate gender of nouns of occupation. New feminine forms are rapidly being incorporated into the Spanish language (e.g., **abogada, arquitecta, presidenta**). See page 38.

APPENDIX

English–Spanish Vocabulary

Vocabulario inglés–español

ABBREVIATIONS

ABREVIATURAS

adj	adjetive	**adjetivo**
adv	adverb	**adverbio**
colloq	colloquial	**coloquial**
euph	euphemism	**eufemismo**
f	feminine noun	**sustantivo feminino**
m	masculine noun	**sustantivo masculino**
m, f	masculine or femine noun	**sustantivo masculino o feminino**
pl	plural	**plural**
sg	singular	**singular**

Unless specified, words ending with **a** are feminine, words ending with **o** are masculine.

SPECIAL WORDS USED TO INDICATE REGIONAL OCCURRENCES

PALABRAS ESPECIALES USADAS PARA INDICACION REGIONAL

Arg.	Argentina	**la Argentina**
Bol.	Bolivia	**Bolivia**
C.A.	Central America (Guatemala, El Salvador, Honduras, Costa Rica, Nicaragua)	**Centroamérica (Guatemala, el Salvador, Honduras, Costa Rica, Nicaragua)**
Carrib.	(Cuba, Puerto Rico, Dominican Republic)	**(Cuba, Puerto Rico, la República Dominicana)**
Chicano	Chicano (southwestern U.S.)	**Chicano**
Chile		
Col.	Colombia	**Colombia**
C.R.	Costa Rica	**Costa Rica**
Cuba		
Ec.	Ecuador	**el Ecuador**
Guat.	Guatemala	**Guatemala**
Hond.	Honduras	**Honduras**
Mex.	Mexico	**México**
Nic.	Nicaragua	**Nicaragua**
Pan.	Panama	**Panamá**
Para.	Paraguay	**Paraguay**
Perú		
P.R.	Puerto Rico	**Puerto Rico**
Ríopl.	Rio de la Plata region (Eastern Argentina, Uruguay)	**Río de la Plata (la Argentina oriental, el Uruguay)**
Sal.	El Salvador	**el Salvador**
Sp. Am.	Spanish America	**América del Sur**
Spain		
Ur.	Uruguay	**el Uruguay**
Ven.	Venezuela	**Venezuela**

abdomen abdomen (m); panza (colloq); vientre (m)
abortion aborto
  abortion, induced aborto inducido; aborto provocado
  abortion, spontaneous aborto espontáneo
  abortion, therapeutic aborto terapéutico
  abortion, threatened amenaza de aborto
abrasion razpón (m); rozadura
abscess absceso; hinchazón (f)
abscessed apostemado (adj)
abstain from sexual relations, to abstenerse de las relaciones sexuales
accident accidente (m)
acetaminophen acetaminofén (m)
acid ácido
  acid, acetic ácido acético (puro)
  acid, acetylsalicylic ácido acetilsalicílico
  acid, arsenic ácido arsénico
  acid, ascorbic ácido ascórbico
  acid, boric ácido bórico
  acid, cyanic ácido ciánico
  acid, folic ácido fólico
  acid, p-aminosalicylic (PAS) ácido paramino salicílico
acne acné (f); cácara (Chicano); espinillas (f)
acrylic acrílico (adj)
activated charcoal carbón activado (m)
acupuncture acupuntura
acute abdomen abdomen agudo (m)
Adam's apple bocado de Adán; manzana (Mex.); nuez de Adán (f)
add, to agregar; añadir
addict (drug) adicto; adicto a droga(s); adicto a las drogas narcóticas; drogadicto; morfinómano; toxicómano; yeso
addicted adicto (adj)
addict in search of a fix buscatoques (sg)
addiction (drug) toxicomanía
adenoids vegetaciones adenoideas (f)
adhesive plaster emplasto adhesivo
adhesive tape cinta adhesiva; esparadrapo; tela adhesiva
administer marijuana to someone, to engrifar; enmarihuanar; marihuanar
adrenalin adrenalina
advantage ventaja
adverse results resultados adversos (m)
afterbirth placenta; secundinas (f, pl, Mex.); segundo parto (Chicano)

ailment dolencia
albumen albúmina; albumen (m)
alcohol alcohol (m)
  alcohol, rubbing alcohol para fricciones (m)
alcoholism alcoholismo
alertness viveza
allergic reaction reacción alérgica (f); trastorno alérgico
allergy alergia
alveoli alvéolos
amalgam amalgama
amenorrhea amenorrea
amino acids aminoácidos
ammonia amoníaco
amniocentesis prueba del saco amniótico
amniotic sac saco amniótico
amniotic fluid agua del amnios
amoebic dysentery disentería amibiana
amphetamine anfetamina
  amphetamine, heroin, and barbiturate class IV bombita
  amphetamines a; ácido (sg) bombido: naranjas; pepas (slang)
ampicillin ampicilina
ampoule ampolleta
amuse oneself, to have a good time divertirse (ie)
analgesic analgésico
anemia anemia; sangre clara (colloq); sangre débil (f, colloq); sangre pobre (f, colloq)
  anemia, aplastic anemia aplástica
  anemia, iron deficiency deficiencia de hierro
  anemia, pernicious anemia perniciosa
  anemia, sickle cell anemia drepanocítica; drepanocitemia
  anemia, thalassemia talasemia
anesthesia anestesia
  anesthesia, block anestesia de bloque
  anesthesia, caudal anestesia caudal
  anesthesia, epidural anestesia epidural
  anesthesia, general anestesia total
  anesthesia, inhalation anestesia por inhalación
  anesthesia, local anestesia local
  anesthesia, regional anestesia regional
  anesthesia, saddle block anestesia en silla de montar
  anesthesia, spinal anestesia espinal; anestesia raquídea
  anesthesia, twilight sleep sueño crepuscular

anesthetic anestético (m, adj)
aneurysm aneurisma (m)
anger cólera; coraje (m); rabia
angina angina
angina pectoris angina del pecho
angiomate (red dots on skin) cabecita de vena (Chicano)
anguish angustia; congoja
ankle tobillo
ankle support tobillera
antacid antiácido (m, adj)
antibiotic antibiótico (m, adj)
  antibiotic, broad-spectrum antibiótico de alcance amplio; antibiótico de espectro amplio
  antibiotic, limited-spectrum antibiótico de alcance reducido; antibiótico de espectro reducido
antibody anticuerpo
anticholinergic anticolinérgico (m, adj)
anticoagulant anticoagulante (m, adj)
antidote antídoto
  antidote, universal antídoto universal
antiemetic antiemético (m, adj)
antigen antígeno
antihemorrhagic antihemorrágico (adj)
antihistamine antihistamínico (m, adj); droga antihistamínica
antimalarial antipalúdico (m, adj)
antipyretic antipirético; febrífugo
antiseptic antiséptico (m, adj)
antispasmodic antiespasmódico (m, adj)
antitetanic; anti-tetanus antitetánico (adj)
antitoxin antitoxina; contraveneno
anus ano; agujero (vulgar, Chicano); chicloso (vulgar, Chicano); chiquito (vulgar, Chicano); fundillo (Mex.); istantino (colloq)
anxiety ansiedad (f)
aortic insufficiency insuficiencia aórtica
aphasia afasia
aphonia (hoarseness) afonía; ronquera
apoplexy (stroke) apoplejía
apparatus, prosthetic aparato prótesis
appendicitis apendicitis (f); panza peligrosa (slang); abdomen agudo (m, slang)
appendix apéndice (m); apendix (f); tripita (colloq)
appetite apetito (m)
application aplicación (f)
apply for admission, to solicitar admisión a
appointment cita; turno

apron delantal (m)
aqueous humor humor acuoso (m)
arch supports soportes para el arco del pie (m)
arm brazo
arm, bend of the flexura del brazo
armpit arca (Mex.); axila; sobaco
arrhythmia, cardiac arritmia cardíaca
arsenic arsénico
arteriosclerosis arteriosclerosis (f)
arthritis artritis (f)
articulation articulación (f); coyuntura
artificial artificial (adj); postizo (adj)
artificial limb miembro artificial
artificial respiration respiración artificial (f)
Asiatic flu influenza asiática
ask (for) (to request) pedir (i)
aspirin aspirina
aspirin, children's aspirina para niños
assume, to asumir
asthma ahoguío (colloq, Mex.); asma; fatiga (slang)
asthma, bronchial asma bronquial
asthmatic attack (seizure) ataque asmático (m)
asthmatic wheeze resuello asmático
astigmatism astigmatismo
astringent astringente (m, adj)
asymptomatic asintomático (adj)
atrial fibrillation fibrilación auricular (f)
atrophy atrofia
atropine atropina
attack ataque (m)
authorization autorización (f); permiso
authorize, to autorizar
baby (infant) bebé (m); criatura; guagua (m, f, Chile, Ec., Perú, Bol., Arg., Ur.); nene (m, f)
back dorso; espalda
backbone columna vertebral
bacterium bacteria
bag of waters aguas (f); bolsa de las aguas; bolsa membrosasa; fuente (f, colloq)
bald calvo (adj)
baldness calvicie (f)
balloon (of heroin) globo
balsam bálsamo; ungüento
band cinta; faja
bandage venda; vendaje (m)
bandage, to fajar; vendar
bandage, elastic vendaje elástico
bandage, swathing faja abdominal
Bandaid curita; parchecito; venda
barbiturate barbiturato

barbiturate (pill) barbiturato; barbitúrico; cacahuate (m); colorada; globo
base of the cranium base del cráneo (f)
bath baño
bath, bran baño de salvado
bath, emollient baño emoliente
bath, mustard baño de mostaza
bath, oatmeal baño de harina de avena
bath, potassium permanganate baño de permanganato de potasio
bath, saline baño salino
bath, shower baño de regadera (Chicano); ducha
bath, sitz baño de asiento; semicupio
bath, sodium baño de sodio
bath, sponge baño de esponja; baño de toalla (Chicano)
bath, starch baño de almidón
bath, sulfur baño de azufre
bath, tar baño de brea
bathe, to bañar
bathe, to (take a bath, to) bañar(se)
be—years old tener—años
be afraid, to tener miedo
be ashamed, to tener vergüenza
be blue, to tener murria
be called, to (be named, to) llamarse
be careful, to tener cuidado
be carrying narcotic drugs, to andar carga; andar cargado (-a); traer carga
be cold, to tener frío
be gowned, to vestirse de bata de hospital (i)
be guaranteed, to ser garantizado (-a)
be guilty, to (be at fault, to) tener la culpa
be (non)habit forming, to (no) crear vicio
be high, to andar/ponerse + adj (see "high")
be hungry, to tener hambre (f)
be in a hurry, to tener prisa
be in the habit of, to soler (ue)
be late, to tener retraso
be on the road to recovery, to estar recuperándose
be quiet, to callarse
be right, to tener razón
be sleepy, to tener sueño
be successful, to tener éxito
be thirsty, to tener sed (f)
be under the weather, to estar pachucho (-a) (Spain)
be up and about after an illness, to andar andando
be warm, to tener calor (m)
be wrong, to no tener razón

beard barba
bear down, to hacer bajar por fuerza; pujar
bearing porte (m)
become (something), to hacerse + noun of profession
become (turn) + adj to ponerse + adj of emotional/mental state
become bloated, to abotagar
bed cama; lecho
bedbug chinche (f)
bedsore llaga de cama; úlcera por decúbito
beg, to rogar (ue)
begin, to comenzar (ie); empezar (ie)
belch, to eructar; regoldar; regurgitar
belladonna belladona
Bell's palsy parálisis facial (f)
belly barriga; panza (colloq)
"belly" binder fajero; ombliguero
bend over, to agacharse; doblarse
benzedrine bencedrina
benzoin benzoína; benjuí (m)
bewitch, to echar al bote
bicarbonate of soda bicarbonato de soda; salarete (m)
biceps bíceps (m); conejo (slang, Chicano); mollero (colloq)
bichloride of mercury cloruro mercúrico
bile bilis (f); hiel (f)
bile salt sal biliar (f)
bilirubin bilirrubina
bind, to amarrar; atar
binder cintura; faja; vendaje abdominal (m)
birth (childbirth) acostada (Sp. Am.); alumbramiento; nacimiento; parto
birth, at term a término
birth, multiple nacimiento múltiple
birth, post-term nacimiento tardío
birth, premature nacimiento prematuro
birth, to give alumbrar; dar a luz; parir; salir de su cuidado (Chicano); sanar (euph)
birth canal canal del parto (m)
birth certificate certificado de nacimiento; partida de nacimiento
birth control control de la natalidad (m)
Billing's method método de Billing
cervical cap gorro cervical
coil coil (m, Chicano)
coitus interruptus interrupción de coito (f); retirarse (m); salirse (m, slang)
condom condón (m); forro (vulgar, Arg.); goma; hule (m,

slang); preservativo;
profiláctico
diaphragm diafragma
(anticonceptivo) (m)
IUD aparatito (Chicano);
aparato intrauterino; DIU
(m); dispositivo intrauterino
loop alambrito; asa; lupo
pill pastilla; píldora
rhythm método de ritmo; rimto
rubber forro (vulgar, Arg.);
goma; hule (m, slang)
sterilization esterilización (f)
tubal ligation ligadura de
trompas
vaginal cream crema vaginal
vaginal foam espuma vaginal
vaginal jelly jalea vaginal
vasectomy vasectomía
birthmark lunar (m)
birthweight peso del nacimiento
bite (animal) mordedura;
mordida
bite, cat mordida de gato
bite, dog mordida de perro
bite, human mordedura humana
bite, scorpion mordedura de
escorpión
bite, snake mordedura de
serpiente
bite (insect), sting picadura;
piquete (m)
spider picadura de araña
bite, to morder (ue)
black and blue amoratado (adj)
black eye ojo morado
blackhead, shin espinilla
bladder vejiga; vesícula
blanket cobija; frazada; manta
bleach blanqueo; cloro
bleed, to sangrar
bleed excessively, to (bleed in
excess, to) desangrar
bleeding flujo de sangre;
hemorragia
bleeding (adj) sangrante (adj)
bleeding, breakthrough flujo de
sangre por la vagina
inesperadamente; hemorragia
inesperada
bleeding, internal hemorragia
interna
bleeding tendencies tendencias a
sangrar (f)
bleeding time tiempo de
hemorragia
bleeding to excess desangramiento
blemish lunar (m); mancha
blepharitis blefaritis (f)
blind ciego (adj)
blind in one eye tuerto (adj)
blindness ceguedad (f); ceguera
blindness, color acromatopsia;
ceguera para los colores;
daltonismo
blindness, night (nyctalopia)

ceguera nocturna; nictalopia
blindness, river (onchocerciasis)
ceguera del río; oncocercosis
blink, to parpadear
blister ampolla; bulla; vesícula
blister on sole of foot sietecueros
(m, sg)
bloated aventado (adj); hinchado
(adj); abotagado (adj)
block, to bloquear; obstruir
block the nerve, to
obstruir el nervio
blockage obstrucción (f)
blocked intestine tripa ida
blood colorada (slang, Chicano);
sangre (f); sanguíneo (adj)
blood bank banco de sangre
blood chemistry (analysis of
blood) análisis de sangre (m)
blood circulation circulación
sanguínea (f)
blood clot coágulo de sangre;
coágulo sanguíneo; cuajarón
(m); cuajarón de sangre (m)
clot reaction time tiempo de
retracción del coágulo
blood, coagulation time tiempo
de coagulación
blood component componente
de sangre (m); componente
sanguíneo (m)
blood count biometría
hemática; hematimetría;
recuento sanguíneo
blood culture hemocultivo
blood donor donante de sangre
(m, f)
blood group grupo sanguíneo
universal donor donante
universal (m, f)
universal recipient receptor
universal (m, f)
blood, oxalated sangre
oxalatada (f)
blood oxygen analyzer
analizador del oxígeno de la
sangre (m)
blood plasma plasma
sanguíneo (m)
blood poisoning
envenenamiento de la sangre;
intoxicación de la sangre (f);
sepsis (f); septicemia;
toxemia
blood pressure presión arterial (f);
presión sanguínea (f)
high hipertensión arterial (f);
presión arterial alta
low hipotensión arterial (f);
presión arterial baja
blood, screening prueba selecta
de sangre
blood smear frotis sanguíneo (m);
extensión de sangre (f)
bloodstain mancha de sangre
bloodstained manchado de

sangre (adj)
bloodstock depósito de sangre
blood sugar azúcar sanguíneo
(m); glucemia
blood test examen de la sangre
(m)
blood transfusion transfusión de
sangre (f); transfusión
sanguínea (f)
blood type grupo sanguíneo
blood typing determinación del
grupo sanguíneo
blood vessel vaso sanguíneo
blood, whole sangre entera (f);
sangre pura (f)
bloody cruento (adj); sangriento
(adj)
bloody show muestra de sangre;
tapón de moco (m, Mex.);
secreción mucosa mezclada con
sangre (f)
blotches, skin manchas oscuras en
la piel (f)
blow one's nose, to sonarse la
nariz; soplarse la nariz
body cuerpo
body, ciliary cuerpo ciliar
boil furúnculo; nacido; sisote
(m); tacotillo (Chicano)
boil the bottles, to hervir las
botellas (ie)
bone hueso
booster shot búster (m); inyección
de refuerzo (f); inyección
secundaria (f); reactivación (f)
borax bórax (m)
borderline case caso límite
bosom senos (m, pl)
bothersome incómodo (adj)
bottle botella; envase (m); frasco
bottle, baby biberón (m); bote
(m, slang, Chicano); botella;
mamadera (Sp. Am.); pacha
(Chicano); tele (Chicano)
bowel intestino inferior
bowel obstruction abdomen agudo
(m, slang); obstrucción de la
tripa (f); panza peligrosa (slang)
bowels entrañas (f); tripa (colloq)
brace braguero
braces aparato ortodóntico;
frenos (Mex.)
brains sesos
breast agarraderas (f, Chicano);
busto; chichas (f, pl, C.R.);
chiche (f); chichi (f, Mex.);
pecho; seno; tele (f, slang)
breast, caked mastitis por
estasis (f)
breast, of a wet nurse chiche
(m, Mex., Guat.)
breast, painful seno doloroso
breastbone esternón (m)
breastfeed, to criar con pecho
(Chicano); dar chiche; dar de
mamar; dar el pecho

breastfeeding lactancia maternal
breast pump bomba de ordeñar; mamadera; tiraleches (f)
breast self-examination (BSE) auto exploración de las mamas (f); autoexamen mensual de los senos (m)
breath aliento
breathe, to resollar (ue); respirar
breathing respiración (f); resuello
breechbirth (frank breech) presentación de nalgas (f); presentación trasera (f)
brewer's yeast levadura de cerveza
bridge (dental) puente (m)
  bridge (dental), fixed puente fijo
  bridge (dental), removable puente movible
bromide bromuro
bronchia bronquios (m)
bronchitis bronquitis (f)
bruise contusión (f); lastimadura; magulladura; morete (m, Mex., Hond.); moretón (m)
bruised moreteado (adj, Chicano)
brush one's teeth, to cepillarse los dientes
bubo búa; ganglio; incordio; seca (colloq)
bubonic plague peste bubónica (f)
bulging eyes ojos capotudos (Chicano); ojos saltones
bullet bala
bullet wound balazo
bunion juanete (m)
burn (oneself), to quemar(se)
burn quemadura; quemazón (m)
  burn, acid quemadura por ácido
  burn, alkali quemadura por álcali
  burn, chemical quemadura química
  burn, dry heat quemadura por calor seco
  burn, scald escaldadura
  burn, sun eritema solar (m); quemazón (f); solanera
  burn, sunburn quemadura solar
burp eructo; regüeldo
burp, to eructar; repetir (i); sacar aire (Chicano); urutar (Chicano)
burr fresa
bursitis bursitis (f)
buttock anca; aparato (Chicano); bombo (Ur.); buche (m, vulgar, Chicano); común (m, Mex.); culo (colloq, Arg.); fondillo (Cuba); fondongo (slang); fundillo (Mex.); nalga; olla (slang, Chicano); pellín (m, Chicano); salvohonor (m, colloq) sentadera
buzzing in the ears zumbido de oídos

caesarean delivery parto cesáreo; parto por operación
caesarean section operación cesárea (f); sección cesárea (f)
caffeine cafeína
calamine calamina
calcium calcio
calcium sulfate escayola; sulfato de calcio
calloused calloso (adj)
callus callo
calm down, to calmar(se)
camphor alcanfor (m)
cancer cáncer (m)
cancerous canceroso (adj)
cane báculo; bastón (m)
canker llaga ulcerosa; úlcera; ulceración (f)
canker sore postemilla; ulceración (f)
can opener abrelatas (m)
capillary capilar (m); vaso capilar
capsule cápsula
carbohydrate carbohidrato
carbolic acid ácido carbólico
carbon tetrachloride tetracloruro de carbono
carcinoma carcinoma (m)
cardiac arrest fallo cardíaco; paro cardíaco
cardiac care cuidado cardíaco
cardiopulmonary resuscitation resucitación cardiopulmonar (f)
cardiopulmonary resuscitator resucitador cardiopulmonar (m)
cardioscope cardioscopio
careless (neglected) descuidado (adj)
caries caries (f); cavidad dental (f); diente podrido (m)
carrier portador (-a) de enfermedad (m, f)
cartilage cartílago
case caso
cast calote (m); yeso; enyesadura
  cast, gypsum vendaje de yeso (m)
cataplasm cataplasma
cataract catarata; granizo
catch, to (come down with a disease) caer con algo
catch a disease, to contraer una enfermedad; agarrar; pegarle
cathartic purgante (m)
catheter catéter (m); drenaje (m, Chicano); sonda; tubo
catheterize, to cateterizar
caucasian caucasiano (adj)
cause vomiting, to provocarse el vómito
cauterization cauterización (f)
cavity carie (f); cavidad (f); diente cariado (m); diente picado (m); picadura
celiac disease celíaca
cell célula

cell, ciliated célula ciliada
cell, sickle célula falciforme
cementum cemento
cerebral cortex corteza cerebral; materia gris (colloq)
cerebral hemisphere hemisferio cerebral
cerebral paralysis parálisis cerebral (f)
cerebrospinal meningitis meningitis cerebroespinal (f)
cerebrum cerebro
  cerebrum, anterior chamber of cámara anterior del cerebro
  cerebrum, posterior chamber of cámara posterior del cerebro
certify, to certificar
cervix cérvix (f); cerviz (f); cuello de la matriz; cuello del útero
chafing piel roja (f); rozadura
Chagas's disease enfermedad de Chagas (f)
chancre chancro
chancre, soft chancro blando
change (oneself), to cambiar(se)
change of life cambio de vida; menopausia
chapped cuarteado (adj); rosado (adj)
chap skin, to rozarse
chart diagrama (m)
checkup chequeo (Chicano)
cheek cacha; cachete (m); carrillo; mejilla
cheekbone pómulo
cheilosis (sore at corner of mouth) boquilla
chest pecho; tórax (m)
chew, to mascar; masticar
chicken pox bobas; tecunda (Mex.); varicela; viruelas locas (slang)
chigger flea garrapata; güina (Mex.); nigua
chilblain sabañón (m)
childbirth alumbramiento; parto
chill escalofrío
chin barba; barbilla; mentón (m); piocha; talache (m)
chloasma (facial discoloration, mask of pregnancy) cloasma (m); mancha de la preñez; mancha del embarazo; paño
chloramphenicol cloranfenicol (m)
chloride cloruro
chlorine cloro
chloromycetin chloromycetín (m); cloromicetín (m)
chlorophyll clorofila
chloroquinine cloroquina
choke, to ahogarse; atorarse; atragantarse
choking asfixia
cholecystogram colecistograma (m)
cholera cólera (m)

cholesterol colesterol (m); grasa en las venas
choose, to elegir (i)
chorea corea; mal/baile de San Guido/de San Vito (m)
chorioid corioides (f, sg)
chronic crónico (adj); duradero (adj)
cigarette butt bachica (esp. marijuana); tecla; tecolota
circulation circulación (f)
circumcise, to circuncidar
circumcision circuncisión (f)
cirrhosis of the liver cirrosis del hígado (f); cirrosis hepática (f)
clasp gancho
cleaning limpieza
cleanliness aseo
clean oneself, to limpiarse
cleft palate boquineta (m, Chicano); grietas en el paladar paladar hendido (m); paladar partido (m)
climb up, to subirse
clitoris bolita (slang); clítoris (m); pelotita (slang); pepa (slang)
close, to cerrar (ie)
clot, to cuajar
coagulant coagulante (m, adj)
coal tar brea de hulla
coarse grueso (adj)
coated tongue lengua saburral; lengua sucia
cocaine acelere; aliviane; alucine; arponazo; azúcar; blanca nieves; carga; coca; cocacola; cocada; cocaína; cocazo; coco; coka; cotorra; cucharazo; chutazo; doñ a blanca; glacis; knife; marizazo; nice; nieve; nose; pase; pericazo; pepsicola; perico (slang, Cuba); polvito; polvo; talco (Texas, Cuba); tecata
coccyx cóccix (m, Chicano); colita; coxis (m); rabadilla
cocoa butter manteca de cacao
codeine codeína
coitus coito
cold catarro; resfriado
  cold, common resfriado común
  cold, "stopped-up" head constipado
cold pack compresa fría; emplasto frío
colic cólico (adj)
colitis colitis (f)
collapse colapso
  collapse, physical colapso físico
collar bone (clavicle) clavícula; cuenca
colon colon (m)
colostomy colostomía
colostrum calostro
coma coma (m)
comb, fine-tooth chino (Mex.)

comb one's hair, to peinarse
come, to venir
comfortable cómodo (adj)
communicate a disease, to contagiar
compete, to competir (i)
complain, to quejarse
complication accidente (m); complicación (f)
compress cabezal (m); compresa
conceive, to concebir (i)
conception concepción (f); fecundación del huevo (f)
concussion concusión (f); golpe (m)
confess, to confesar (ie)
confinement alumbramiento; cuarentena; puerperio; riesgo
congenital congénito (adj)
  congenital anomaly anomalía congenita
  congenital malformations malformaciones congénitas (f)
congested (stuffed up) constipado (adj)
congestion congestión (f)
congestion of the chest ahoguijo; ahoguío (colloq)
conjunctiva conjuntiva
conjunctivitis conjuntivitis (f); mal de ojo (m, colloq); tracoma (m)
connect, to conexionar
consent, to consentir (ie)
constipated estreñ ido (adj)
constipation constipación (f); entablazón (f, Chicano); estreñimiento
contact contacto
contact lens lente de contacto (m); microlentilla; pupilente (m)
contagious contagioso (adj); pegadizo (adj); pegajoso (adj, colloq)
contamination contaminación (f)
continue working, to seguir trabajando (i)
contraceptive anticonceptivo (adj); contraceptivo (adj)
contraceptive pills pastillas anticonceptivas
contractions contracciones de la matriz (f); contracciones uterinas (f); dolores de parto (m)
control, to controlar; regular
contusion contusión (f)
convalescence convalecencia
convalescent convaleciente (m, f)
convert, to convertir (ie)
convulsion ataque (m); convulsión (f)
coramine coramina
cord cordón (m)
  cord, umbilical cordón del ombligo; cordón umbilical
corn callo

cornea córnea
corn plaster emplasto para callos; parches para callos (m)
coronary coronario (adj)
coronary thrombosis trombosis coronaria (f)
corpse cadáver (m)
corticosteroid corticoesteroide (m)
cortisone cortisona
cost, to costar (ue)
cotton algodón (m)
  cotton, absorbent algodón absorbente
  cotton, sterile algodón estéril
cotton swab escobillón (m); hisopillo; hisopo de algodón
cough tos (f)
cough drops gotas para la tos; pastillas para la tos
cough lozenges pastillas para la tos
cough suppressant béquico; calmante para la tos (m)
cough syrup jarabe para la tos (m)
cough, smoker's tos por fumar (f)
cough, to toser
cough up phlegm, to desgarrar (Chicano); esgarrar
count, to contar (ue)
crack, to agrietar; rajar
cramps calambres (m)
  charleyhorse rampa
  cramps, abdominal retortijón (m); torsón (m)
  cramps, cane-cutter's calambres de los cortadores de caña
  cramps, heat calambres térmicos
  cramps, menstrual dolores del período (m); calambres
  cramps, muscular calambres
  cramps (postpartum pains) entuertos
  cramps, stomach retortijón de tripas (m); torcijón cólico (m, Mex.)
cretinism cretinismo
crib camilla de niño; cuna
  crib, warming armazón de calentamiento (f); camilla calentadora de niño; estufa; incubadora
cripple inválido (m, adj); tullido (m, adj)
crippled cojo (adj); empedido (adj); lisiado (adj)
crippled hand manco (adj)
cross-eyed bisojo (adj); bizco (adj); turnio (adj)
cross-eyes bizquera
cross match pruebas cruzadas
crotch entrepiernas (f, pl)
croup crup (f); ronquera
crown corona

crown of the head mollera
crown of tooth corona; filete (m)
crown, acrylic jacket corona acrílica
crown, porcelain jacket corona de porcelana
crown, to coronar; estar coronando
crowning coronamiento
crow's feet patas de gallo
crush, to machucar
crutch muleta; sobaquera (colloq)
cry, to llorar
crystalline cristalino
cure cura; método curativo
cure-all sanalotodo (Chicano)
cure from the evil eye, to desaojar
cure, to aliviar
curettage curetaje (m); raspado
cut cortada (Sp. Am.); cortadura
cut (oneself), to cortar(se)
cut teeth, to dentar (ie); echar dientes; endentecer
cuticle cutícula
cyst quiste (m)
cystic fibrosis fibrosis quística (f)
cystitis cistitis (f); infección de la vejiga (f)
cystoscope cistoscopio
dacryocystitis infección de la bolsa de lágrimas (f)
daily cotidiano (adj); diario (adj); por día
damage daño
D&C legrado (colloq); raspa (colloq)
dandruff caspa
dangerous peligroso (adj)
dangle one's legs, to colgar las piernas (ue)
dead muerto (m, adj)
deaden the nerve, to adormecer el nervio
deaf sordo (adj)
deaf-mute sordomudo
deafness ensordecimiento; sordera
deal in drugs, to dilear; diliar
death fallecimiento; muerte (f)
death rattle estertor agónico
decongestant descongestionante (m, adj)
deep profundo (adj)
defecate, to andar el cuerpo; correr el cuerpo; evacuar; hacer caca; hacer caquis maquis; hacer el cuerpo; ir al inodoro (colloq); obrar (Mex.); tirar (la) basura (slang)
defect defecto
defibrillator defibrilador (m)
deficiency carencia; deficiencia
deformed deforme (adj); eclipsado (adj); inocente (adj, Mex.)
deformity deformidad (f)
dehydrate, to deshidratar; perder

fluidos del cuerpo (ie)
dehydration desecación (f); deshidratación (f)
delirium delirio
deliver, to aliviarse (Chicano); dar a luz; parir; tener el niño
delivery parto
delivery, abdominal parto abdominal
delivery, breech extracción de nalgas (f)
delivery, forceps extracción con fórceps (f)
delivery, premature parto prematuro
delivery room sala de partos
delivery table mesa del parto
delouse, to espulgar
dementia demencia
demonstrate, to (show, to) demostrar (ue)
dengue dengue (m); fiebre rompehuesos (f)
dental artery arteria dental
dental drill taladro; torno; trépano
dental floss cordón dental (m); hilo dental; seda encerada
dental forceps gatillo; pinzas; tenazas de extracción
dental hygienist higienista dental (m, f)
dental impression mordisco
dental nerve nervio dental
dental office clínica dental
dental vein vena dental
dentifrice dentífrico (m, adj)
dentine dentina
dentition dentadura
denture dentadura (postiza)
denture, full dentadura completa
denture, partial dentadura parcial
deny, to negar (ie)
deodorant desodorante (m, adj)
depilatory depilatorio (m, adj)
depressed deprimido (adj)
depression abatimiento; depresión (f)
deprive, to privar
dermatitis dermatitis (f)
desire (to), to tener deseos (de)
destroyed destruido (adj)
detached retina retina desprendida
detect, to descubrir; detectar
detergents detergentes (m)
determination of circulation time determinación del tiempo de circulación (f)
dextrose azúcar de uva (m); dextrosa
diabetes diabetes (f)
diabetes insipidus diabetes insípida

diabetes mellitus diabetes mellitus; diabetes sacarina
diabetic diabético (m, adj)
diagnose, to diagnosticar
diagnosis diagnosis (f); diagnóstico
dialysis en diálisis
diaper braga; pañal (m); pavico (Chicano); zapeta (Mex.)
diaper rash chincual (m); escaldadura (en los bebés); pañalitis (f); salpullido
diaper, to cambiar el pañal; proveer con pañal; renovar el pañal de (ue)
diaphragm diafragma anticonceptivo (m)
diarrhea asientos (m, slang); cagadera (vulgar, Chicano); cámara; corredera (Chicano); cursera (slang); chorrillo (slang); chorro (slang); diarrea; soltura (Chicano); turista (slang)
diastole diástole (f)
die, to morir (ue)
diet dieta; régimen (m)
diet, liquid dieta de líquidos
diet, be on a—, to estar a dieta
diet, put on a—, to poner a dieta
digest, to digerir (ie)
digestion digestión (f)
digestive system aparato digestivo
digitalin digitalina
digitalis digital (f)
dilation (of cervix) dilatación del cuello de la matriz (f)
diphenhydramine difenhidramina
diphtheria difteria; garrotillo
dirty, to be estar caquis maquis (euph)
disability incapacidad (f); inhabilidad (f); invalidez (f)
disc disco
disc, calcified disco calcificado
discern, to discernir (ie)
discharge flujo; secreción (f); supuración (f); desecho; descarga
discharge, bloody derrame (m)
discharge, vaginal flujo vaginal
discharge, white flores blancas (f); flujo blanco
discharge (from the hospital), to dar de alta
discomfort incomodidad (f); malestar (m)
discovery descubrimiento
disease dolencia; enfermedad (f); mal (m)
disease due to act of witchcraft enfermedad endañada (f, Chicano)
disease, notifiable enfermedad de notificación (f)

disease, reportable enfermedad obligatoria (f)
disease that is "going around" enfermedad de andancia (f, Chicano)
disinfectant desinfectante (m, adj)
disorder desorden (m)
dissolve, to disolver (ue)
diuretic diurético (m, adj); píldora diurética
diverticulitis colitis ulcerosa (f); diverticulitis (f)
dizziness tarantas (f, Mex., Hond.); vahido; vértigo
dizzy atarantado (adj); vertiginoso (adj)
doctor's bag maletín (m)
dope pusher narcotraficante (m, f)
dosage dosificación (f); dosis (f)
dose dosis (f); medida
douche ducha; ducha interna; ducha vaginal; irrigación (f); lavado interno; lavado vaginal
Down's syndrome mal de Down (m); mongolismo
DPT vacuna triple
drag (puff of [marijuana] cigarette) toque (m)
drainage desagüe (m); drenaje (m); supuración (f)
drainage (surgical) drenaje (m)
draining (dripping) escurrimiento
dram dracma (m)
dream (of), to soñar (con) (ue)
dress (oneself), to vestir(se) (i)
dressing apósito; cura; curación (f); emplaste (m); parche (m); vendaje (m)
drill, to perforar; taladrar
drink plenty of ... beber mucho ...
drop gota
drop back into, to retroceder
dropper cuentagotas (m)
dropsy ahogamiento; hidropesía
drowsiness mordorra; somnolencia
drug droga; medicina
  drug abuse abuso de (las) drogas
  drug addict adicto a las drogas (m, f); drogadicto (m, f)
  drug addiction dependencia farmacológica; narcomanía
  drug habit morfinomanía
  drug, hallucinogenic alucinógeno; droga alucinadora
  drug overdose sobredosis de drogas (f)
  drugstore botica; droguería (Sp. Am.); farmacia (Spain)
  drug supply cachucha
drunk alumbrado (adj, slang, Chicano); bolo (adj, C.A.); borracho (adj); caneco (adj, Arg., Bol.); intoxicado (adj);

pisto (adj); rascado (adj, Ven.); tacuache (adj); tlacuache (adj); tronado (adj)
drunk, to be (to get) andar bombo; andar eléctrico (-a); andar en la línea; andar loco (-a); estar mediagua; ponerse alto (colloq); rascar (Sp. Am.)
drunkenness borrachera
dry, to secar
duct conducto
duodenum duodeno
dwarf enano (m, f)
dye tinte (m)
dying moribundo (adj)
dysentery disentería
  dysentery, amoebic disentería amibiana
  dysentery, bacillary disentería bacilar
dysmenorrhea dismenorrea; menstruación dolorosa (f)
dyspnea dificultad al respirar (f)
dysuria dolor al orinar (m)
ear oreja
ear (organ of hearing) oído
  auditory auditivo (adj)
  earlobe lóbulo; pulpejo
  external ear aurícula; oído externo; pabellón externo de la oreja (m)
    eardrum (tympanic membrane) tímpano
    external ear canal canal de la oreja (m, colloq); conducto auditivo externo
  inner ear oído interno
    cochlea caracol (m); cóclea
    earwax cera de los oídos; cerilla; cerumen (m)
    earwax, impacted tapón de cera (m)
    Eustachian tube trompa de Eustaquio
    saccule sáculo
    semicircular canal conducto semicircular
  middle ear oído medio
    anvil (incus) yunque (m)
    hammer (malleus) martillo
    stirrup (stapes) estribo
earache dolor de oído (m)
eat breakfast, to desayunarse
eclampsia eclampsia
eczema eccema; rezumamiento; lepra (colloq)
edema edema (m); hinchazón (f)
egg white clara de huevo
ejaculate, to eyacular; venirse (slang)
elbow codo
electricity electricidad (f)
  electrical current corriente (adj)
  electrical ground(ing) polaridad (f)

electrical lead wire alambre de contacto (m)
electrical outlet salida
electrical plug clavija de contacto; enchufe (m)
electric polarity polaridad (f)
electric socket enchufe (m); tomacorriente (f, Sp. Am.)
electric valve válvula
electrocardiogram electrocardiograma (m)
electroencephalogram electroencefalograma (m)
emaciation demacración (f); enflaquecimiento
embolism embolia; embolismo
embryo embrión (m)
emergency caso urgente; emergencia; urgencia
emesis basis riñonera
emetic emético (m, adj); vomitivo (m, adj)
emollient emoliente (m, adj)
emphysema enfisema (m)
empty, to vaciar
emulsion emulsión (f)
enamel esmalte (m)
encephalitis encefalitis (f)
endoscope endoscopio
enema ayuda; enema; lavado; lavativa
  enema bag bolsa para enema
  enema, barium enema de bario; enema opaca
  enema, cleansing enema de limpieza
  enema, retention enema de retención
  enema, soapsuds enema jabonosa
energy energía
engorgement estancamiento
enlargement agrandamiento; ampliación (f); ensanchamiento
enzyme enzima; jugo digestivo
ephedrine efedrina
epidemic epidemia; epidémico (adj)
epidermis epidermis (f)
epilepsy ataque (de epilepsia) (m); epilepsia
epileptic attack ataque epilético (m); convulsión (f)
episiotomy corte de las partes (m); episiotomía; tajo (slang)
epsom salt sal de epsom (f); sal de higuera (f)
erysipelas dicipela (Chicano); erisipela
erythrocytes (red blood cells) eritrocitos; glóbulos rojos; hematíes (m)
erythromycin eritromicina
esophagus esófago; tragante (m, Chicano)
estrogen estrógeno

estrogen replacement therapy terapia sustitutoria con estrógeno
eucalyptus leaves hojas de eucalipto
every cada (adj)
exam, medical examen médico (m)
examination examinación (f); reconocimiento; chequeo (Chicano)
examine, to examinar
excessive excesivo (adj)
exchange list lista de intercambios
excretion excreción (f); excremento; miércoles (m, slang)
exempt, to (release, to) eximir
exercise moderately, to hacer ejercicios moderado
exhaustion agotamiento; fatiga
expectorant expectorante (m, adj)
expel anal gas, to tirarse flato; tirarse un pedo
expiration date fecha de caducidad
expulsion expulsión (f)
external externo (adj)
extract extracto
extraction extracción (f)
eye ojo
  chorioid corioides (f, sg)
  cone cono
  conjunctiva conjuntiva
  cornea córnea
  dropper (medicine dropper) cuentagotas (m); goteador (m); gotero (para los ojos) (Sp. Am.)
  eyeball globo del ojo; globo ocular; tomate (m, slang, Chicano)
  eyebrow ceja
  eye cup copa ocular; lavaojos (m); ojera
  eyelash pestaña
  eyelid párpado
  eyepads paños en los ojos; toallas en los ojos
  glasses anteojos (pl); espejuelos (pl); gafas (pl); lentes (pl); quevedos (pl)
  iris iris (m)
  lachrymal lacrimal (adj); lagrimal (adj)
  lens cristalino
  pupil niña del ojo; pupila
  retina retina
  rod bastoncillo
  salve ungüento para los ojos
  sclera esclerótica
  shield escudo ocular
  tear duct conducto lagrimal
  tear sac bolsa de lágrimas
face cara; carátula (slang, Chicano); rostro
faint, to desmayarse

fainting spell desfallecimiento; desmayo; desvanecimiento; mareo (colloq); vértigo
fainting spell during pregnancy achaque (m, C.R.)
fall, to caer
  fall asleep, to (doze off, to) dormirse (ue)
  fall down, to caerse
  fallen fontanel caída de la mollera
fallopian tubes trompas de Falopio; tubos
family / familia
  family planning planificación de la familia (f); planificación familiar (f)
farsighted présbita (adj)
farsightedness hipermetropía; presbicia; presbiopía
fasting ayuno
fasting blood sugar glucemia en ayunas
fat gordo (adj); grasa
fatigue fatiga
fauces fauces (f, pl)
fear miedo
features facciones (f)
feces (stool) "aguas mayores" (f); caca (slang); cagada (vulgar); cámara; deposiciones (f); evacuación del vientre (f); excrementos (m); heces fecales (f, pl); materia fecal; pase del cuerpo (m)
feeble enfermizo (adj)
feed, to alimentar
feeding alimentación (f)
feel, to (regret, to) sentir (ie)
feel (emotion/pain), to sentirse (ie)
feel (touch), to tocar
feel like, to tener ganas (de)
feel nothing, to no sentir nada (ie)
femur fémur (m)
fester, to enconarse
fetal heart tone latido del corazón fetal
fetoscope estetoscopio fetal; fetoscopio
fetus feto
fever calentura; fiebre (f)
  fever, acute infectious adentitis fiebre ganglionar
  fever blister herpe febril (m, f); llaga de fiebre
  fever, breakbone fiebre rompehuesos
  fever, Colorado tick fiebre de Colorado; fiebre tra(n)smitida por garrapatas
  fever, enteric fiebre entérica
  fever, glandular fiebre glandular
  fever, hay alergia; catarro constipado (Chicano); fiebre de(l) heno; jey fíver (m, f)

  fever, intermittent fiebre intermitente
  fever, malarial chucho (Chile, Arg.); fiebre palúdica
  fever, Malta brucelosis (f); fiebre de Malta; fiebre ondulante
  fever, paratyphoid fiebre paratífica; fiebre paratifoidea
  fever, parrot fiebre de las cotorras
  fever, rabbit fiebre de conejo
  fever, rat bite fiebre por mordedura de rata
  fever, rheumatic fiebre reumática
  fever, Rocky Mountain spotted fiebre de las Montañas Rocosas; maculosa de las Montañas Rocosas
  fever, scarlet fiebre escarlatina
  fever, spotted fiebre manchada; tifus exantemático (m)
  fever, thermic fiebre térmica
  fever, typhoid fiebre tifoidea; tifo abdominal
  fever, typhus tifo; tifus (m); tifus exantemático (m); úrzula (Chicano)
  fever, undulant fiebre ondulante
  fever, valley (coccidioidomycosis) fiebre del valle
  fever, yellow fiebre amarilla; fiebre tropical; tifo de América; tifus icterodes (m); vómito negro
fibrin fibrina
fibroid fibroideo (adj)
fibroma fibroma (m)
fibula peroné (m)
file down, to limar
fill, to calzar; empastar; emplomar (Arg.); llenar; rellenar; tapar
fill with gold, to orificar
filling empastadura; empaste (m); emplomadura (Arg.); relleno; tapadura
  filling, temporary empaque (m, Chicano); empaste provisional
filter, to filtrar
find, to encontrar (ue)
finger dedo
  finger, fleshy tip of the yema
  finger, index índice (m)
  finger, knuckle nudillo
  finger, little meñique (m)
  finger, middle dedo del corazón; dedo del medio
  finger, ring dedo anular
  finger, thumb dedo gordo; pulgar (m)
  ball of pulpejo
first aid primera ayuda; primeros auxilios (m, pl)

fissure cisura; fisura; grieta; partidura
fist puño
fistula fístula
fit arrebato; convulsión (f); paroxismo
fitness (good health) buena salud (f)
fix (slang) abuja; abujazo; cura; gallazo
flank costado
flask frasco
flat foot pie plano (m); planovegus (m)
flatus aire (m); flato; pedo slang); ventosidad (f); viento
flea pulga
flesh carne (f)
floater mancha volante; mosco volante
flour harina
flow, to fluir
flu gripa; gripe (f); influenza
fluoride fluor (m)
flushed enrojecido (adj)
foam espuma
folk illness enfermedad casera (f)
follicle folículo
follow, to seguir (i)
fontanel fontanela; mollera
foot pie (m)
foot, sole of the planta del pie
forceps (obstetric) fórceps (m); (dental) gatillo; tenazas
forearm antebrazo
forehead frente (f)
foreskin prepucio
formula fórmula
forty days following parturition cuarentena
fossa fosa
foul-smelling apestoso (adj)
fovea centralis fóvea central
fracture fractura; quebradura de huesos
  fracture, complicated fractura complicada
  fracture, compound fractura compuesta
  fracture, green stick fractura en tallo verde
  fracture, multiple fractura múltiple
  fracture, open fractura abierta
  fracture, serious fractura mayor
  fracture, simple fractura simple
  fracture, spontaneous fractura espontánea
fracture, to fracturar; quebrarse
freckle peca
free gratis (adj)
free will libre albedrío
frenum of the tongue frenillo
frigidity frigidez (f)
frontal frontal (adj)

frostbite congelación (f); daño sufrido por causa de la helada
frozen section corte por congelación (m)
fumigation fumigación (f)
fundus fondo del útero
funeral entierro
funeral home funeraria
fungicide fungicida (m, adj)
fungus hongo
  athlete's foot infección de serpigo (f); pie de atleta (m)
  moniliasis boquera; candidiasis (f); moniliasis (f); muguet (m)
  ringworm (tinea) culebrilla; empeine (m); serpigo; sisote (m, Chicano); tiña
  tinea corporis jiotes (f, colloq)
funnel embudo
furniture polish pulimento para muebles
gain weight, to engordar
gait marcha
gallbladder vejiga de la bilis; vesícula biliar
gallbladder attack ataque vesicular (m); dolor de la vesícula (m)
gallstone cálculo biliar; cálculo en la vejiga; piedra en la vejiga
ganglion ganglio
gangrene cangrena; gangrena
gargle gárgara
gargle (liquid) gargarismo
gargle, to hacer buches (de sal) (colloq); hacer gárgaras
gas gas (m)
gash cuchillada
gastric juice jugo gástrico
gastritis gastritis
gauze gasa
genitals órganos genitales; partes (f, slang); partes ocultas (f, slang); verijas
genitourinary system aparato genito-urinario
gentian violet violeta de genciana
germ germen (m); microbio
German measles alfombría (Chicano); alfombrilla (Chicano); fiebre de tres días (f); peluza (Mex.); rubéola; sarampión alemán (m); sarampión bastardo (m)
germicide germicida (m)
gestation gestación (f); gravidez (f)
get angry, to enfadarse; enojarse
get close, to acercarse
get drunk, to jalarse (Sp. Am.)
get frightened, to asustarse
get goose bumps, to—enchinarse la piel; ponerse chinito
get married, to (marry) casarse con
get sick, to enfermarse

get tired, to cansarse; fatigarse
get undressed, to desvestirse (i)
get up, to (stand up, to) levantarse
get up, to (wake up, to) despertarse (ie)
get well, to aliviarse, sanarse
give up (a claim), to ceder
gland glándula
  gland, adrenal glándula suprarrenal
  gland, carotid glándula carótidea
  gland, endocrine glándula endocrina
  gland, lymph glándula linfática
  gland, mammary glándula mamaria
  gland, parathyroid glándula paratiroides
  gland, prostrate glándula de la próstata; glándula prostática; próstata
  gland, sebaceous glándula sebácea
  gland, sweat glándula sudorípara
  gland, thyroid glándula tiroides
glans (penis) bálano; cabeza (slang); glande (m)
glass (drinking) vaso
glass eye ojo de vidrio
glaucoma glaucoma (m)
glucagon glucagón (m)
glucose glucosa
glucose water agua con azúcar
glue cola; goma
glue sniffer glufo
gluteal region gluteo; región glutea (f)
glycerine glicerina
glycogen glicógeno
gnat bobito (Chicano); jején (m, Sp. Am.)
goal meta; objectivo
go away, to irse; marcharse
go down in birth canal, to encajarse
goiter bocio; buche (m, slang); gueguecho
gold oro
gonorrhea blenorragia; chorro (colloq); gonorrea; purgación (f, slang)
go to bed, to acostar(se) (ue)
gout gota
gown bata; camisón (m)
graft injerto
green card (migration card) mica
groin empeine (m); ingle (f); aldilla
ground chalk in water creta pulvarizada en agua
guaiacol guayacol (m)
guarantee, to hacer garantías
gums encías

gynecological floor piso ginecológico
gynecologist ginecólogo
hair cabello(s); chimpa (Chicano); pelo
  hair, curly pelo chino
  hair, kinky pelo grifo
  hair, prematurely gray canas verdes
  hair, pubic pelo púbico; pendejos (slang, Arg.); vello púbico
  hair, straight pelo liso
  hair, wavy pelo quebrado
hairy peludo (adj); tarántula (Chicano)
hallucination alucinación (f)
hallucinogen alucinógeno; droga alucinadora
hammertoe dedo gordo en martillo
hand mano
  hand, back of the dorso de la mano
  hand, palm of the palma de la mano
handicap impedimento
hang, to colgar (ue)
hangnail cutícula desgarrada; padastro (colloq)
hangover malestar post-alcohólico (m)
hangover, to have andar crudo (-a)
hard of hearing corto de oído; duro de oído
harelip boquineta (m, Chicano); cheuto (adj, Chile); jane (adj, Hond.); labio cucho (Chicano); labio leporino
harsh, raucous sound ronquido
hash (hashish) hachich (m); hachís (m); haschich (m)
have to, to (must) tener que + infinitive
headache cajetuda (Chicano); dolor de cabeza (m); jaqueca
headrest apoyo para la cabeza
heal, to curar; sanar
healing curación (f)
hearing aid aparato auditivo; aparato para la sordera; audífono; prótesis acústica (f); prótesis auditiva (f)
heart corazón (m)
  heart, apex of punta del corazón
heart attack ataque al corazón (m); ataque cardíaco (m); ataque del corazón (m); infarto
heartbeat latido cardíaco; palpitación (f)
  heartbeat, irregular (arrhythmia) arritmia; latido irregular; palpitación irregular
  heartbeat, rapid (tachycardia) palpitación rápida taquicardia

heartbeat rhythmical palpitación rítmica
heartbeat, slow palpitación lenta
heartburn acedía; agriera (Sp. Am.); agruras (f); ardor de estómago (m); cardialgia; pirosis (f)
heart disease cardiopatías (f); enfermedad cardíaca (f); enfermedad del corazón (f)
heart failure fallo del corazón; insuficiencia cardíaca; paro del corazón
heart murmur murmullo; soplo
heart valve válvula del corazón
heat calor (m)
heat exhaustion agotamiento por calor
heating pad, electric almohadilla caliente eléctrica
heat stroke insolación (f); golpe de calor (m)
heat therapy termoterapia; tratamiento térmico
heel calcañar (m); talón (m)
hematuria hematuria; sangre en la orina (f)
hemoglobin hemoglobina
hemophilia hemofilia
hemorrhage desangramiento; hemorragia; morragia (Chicano)
hemorrhoids almorranas; hemorroides (f, pl)
hemostat hemostato
hepatitis fiebre (f, colloq, Mex.); hepatitis (f); inflamación del hígado (f)
  hepatitis, infectious hepatitis infecciosa
  hepatitis, viral hepatitis viral
herbicides herbicidas (m) matayerbas
hernia desaldillado (Mex.); hernia; quebradura
  hernia, femoral hernia femoral
  hernia, inguinal hernia inguinal; quebradura en la ingle
  hernia, umbilical hernia del ombligo; ombligón (m, slang); ombligo salido (slang); desombligado (adj, colloq)
heroin adormidera; achivia; amor; ardor; arpon; arponazo; azúcar; azufre; banderilla; blanco(a); borra blanca; caballo; ca-ca; cagada (vulgar); carga; cáscara; cohete; cura; cristales; chiva; chutazo; dama blanca; golpe; goma; gato; H; helena; heróica; heroína; la cosa; la duna; lenguazo; manteca; nieve; papel; papelito; pericazo; piquete; polvo; polvo amargo; polvo blanco; pasta; stufa; tecata

heroin capsule cachucha; capa; gorra
heroin user tecato
herpes herpes (m, f)
hiccough (hiccup) hipo; hipsus (m)
hide, to esconderse
high arched foot pie hueco (m)
high cholesterol colesterol elevado (m)
high from glue sniffing glucó (adj)
high from sniffing paint thinner tiniado (adj)
high (turned on) **on marijuana** motiado (adj)
high on narcotics (turned on) alivianado (adj); caballón (adj); loco (adj); locote (adj); sonado (adj); sonámbulo (adj)
high on pills píldoro (adj)
high triglycerides triglicéridos elevados (m)
hip cadera; cuadril (m, Mex., Chicano)
hit oneself, to golpearse
hives ronchas, urticaria
hoarse afónico (adj); ronco (adj)
  hoarse, chronically carrasposo (adj)
  hoarse, to be carraspear
hoarseness carraspera (colloq); ronquera
home remedy remedio casero
hooked on drugs prendido (adj)
hook on narcotics, to prender
hormone hormón (m); hormona
hospital hospital (m); nosocomio (Chicano)
hot coffee café caliente (m)
hot flashes bochornos; calofrío (Chicano); calores (m); fogajes (m, P.R.); llamaradas; sofocones (m)
hot water bag bolsa de agua caliente
humerus húmero
hunchback jorobado (m, f, adj)
hurt, to (ache, to) doler (ue)
hydrocele hidrocele (f)
hydrochloric acid ácido clorhídrico
hydrofluoric acid ácido fluorhídrico
hymen himen (m)
hyperlipidemia hiperlipidemia
hypertension hipertensión (f)
hyperventilation hiperventilación (f); susto con resuello duro (colloq)
hyphemia hemorragia detrás de la córnea; hifemia
hypochondria hipocondría (f)
hypochondriac adolorado (m, adj, Chicano); adolorido (m, adj, Chicano); hipocóndrico (m, adj)
hypodermic needle jaipo
hypoglycemia hipoglicemia

hypopyon pus detrás de la córnea (m)
hypotension hipotensión (f)
hysteria histeria
ice hielo
  ice bag (ice pack) aplicación de hielo empaquetado (f); bolsa de caucho para hielo; bolsa de hielo
ichthyol ictiol (m)
ileum íleon (m)
ill enfermo (adj); malo (adj)
illness enfermedad (f); mal (m); padecimiento
  illness, acute enfermedad aguda
  illness, chronic enfermedad crónica
  illness (disease), **contagious** enfermedad contagiosa; enfermedad trasmisible
  illness, mental enfermedad mental
  illness, minor enfermedad leve
  illness (disease), **organic** enfermedad orgánica
  illness, serious enfermedad grave
  illness (disease), **tropical** enfermedad tropical
imbalance desequilibrio
immobilization inmovilización (f)
immune inmune (adj)
immunization inmunización (f); vacuna
  immunization—booster dose dósis de refuerzo (f)
  immunization—Schick test prueba de Schick
impaction impacción (f)
impetigo erupción cutánea (f); impétigo
impotence impotenc'~
impression impresión (f)
improve, to (get better, to) mejorarse
inch pulgada
incision cortada; incisión (f)
incompatible incompatible (adj)
increase (persist), **to** (fever) cargar la calentura (Chicano)
incubator estufa; incubadora
indigestion dispepsia; estómago sucio (Chicano); indigestión (f); insulto (Chicano); mala digestión (f)
infant infante (m, f); nena; nene (m)
infantile paralysis parálisis infantil (f)
infarct infarto
infect, to contagiar; infectar
infection infección (f); pasmo
infectious infeccioso (adj)
infertile capón (adj, Chicano); estéril (adj); infértil (adj)
inflame, to inflamar

inflammation encono; inflamación (f)
  inflammation of the throat garrotillo
influenza gripa; gripe (f); influenza
ingest narcotic pills, to pildorear(se); pildoriar(se)
ingredient ingrediente (m)
ingrown toenail uña encarnada; uña enterrada; uñero
inject (oneself), to inyectar(se)
inject oneself with drugs, to darse un piquete; inyectarse; picarse
injection indección (f, Chicano); inyección (f); chot (m, Chicano)
  injection (of a narcotic substance) abuja; abujado; piquete (m)
  injection, hypodermic inyección hipodérmica
  injection, intracutaneous inyección intracutánea
  injection intradermic inyección intradérmica
  injection, intramuscular inyección intramuscular
  injection, intravenous inyección endovenosa; inyección intravenosa
  injection, subcutaneous inyección subcutánea
injure, to hacer daño; lastimar; herir (ie); lesionar
injured herido (adj); lisiado (adj)
injury herida; lastimadura; lesión (f)
inlay incrustación (f); orificación (f)
inoculation inoculación (f)
insanity demencia; locura
  insanity, manic-depressive locura de doble forma; maniamelancolía; sicosis maníacodepresiva (f)
insecticide insecticida (m)
insect repellent repelente de insectos (m)
insidious insidioso (adj)
insomnia insomnio; pérdida del sueño
instep empeine (m)
instrument, sharp-edged instrumento afilado
insulin insulina; insulínico (adj)
intensive care cuidado intensivo
intercourse relación sexual (f)
internally internamente (adv)
interval intervalo
intestine intestino
  intestine, large intestino grueso
  intestine, small intestino delgado
intolerance intolerancia
intoxication embriaguez (f)
intrauterine device (IUD) aparato intrauterino; DIU (m);

dispositivo intrauterino
intrauterine loop espiral intrauterino (m)
intussusception intususcepción (f)
iodine yodo
iron hierro
irritability (not related to bile) bilis (f)
irritate, to irritar
irritation irritación (f)
isolate, to aislar; apartar
isolation aislamiento por cuarentena
itch comezón (f); picazón (f); sarna
itching escozor (m); picor (m); prurito
IV (intravenous solution) solución endovenosa (f); suero por la vena
IVP (intravenous pyelogram) P.I.V./pielograma intravenoso (m)
jar frasco
jaundice derrame biliar (m); ictericia; piel amarilla (f, colloq)
jaw mandíbula; quijada
  jaw bone mandíbula
  jaw, broken quijada/mandíbula rota
jejunum yeyuno
jelly jalea
jog, to trotar
jogger trotador (-a)
joint articulación (f); coyuntura
joint (of a narcotic cigarette) abuja
junkie tecato
kerosene keroseno; querosén (m)
ketosis quetosis (f)
kick patada
kidney ri ón (m)
kidney disease mal de riñón (m)
kidney stone cálculo en el riñón; cálculo renal; cálculo urinario piedra en los riñones
kilogram kilogramo
kit botiquín (m); estuche (m)
  kit, emergency botiquín de emergencia
  kit, first aid botiquín de primeros auxilios; equipo de urgencia
knee rodilla
  knee, back of the corva; flexura de la pierna
kneecap choquezuela; rótula
knife cuchillo
knot nudo
knot (type of tissue swelling) bolas (f, pl, Chicano)
label etiqueta
labor labor (f); parto; trabajo de parto
  labor, artificial parto artificial
  labor, complicated parto complicado

labor, dry parto seco
labor, false parto falso
labor, first stage of primer período del parto
labor, immature parto inmaturo
labor, induced parto inducido
labor, instrumental parto instrumental
labor, multiple parto múltiple
labor pains dolores de parto (m)
labor, premature parto prematuro
labor, prolonged parto prolongado
labor room sala de partos; sala prenatal
labor, second stage of segundo período del parto
labor, spontaneous parto espontáneo
labor, third stage of tercer período del parto
labor, to be in enfermarse (Chicano); estar de parto
laboratory laboratorio
laboratory findings hallazgos de laboratorio
laboratory test análisis de laboratorio (m)
labored dificultoso (adj)
laceration cortada; desgarradura; laceración (f)
lactation lactancia
lame cojo (adj); lisiado (adj); rengo (adj)
lameness cojera
lap regazo
laryngitis laringitis (f)
laryngoscope laringoscopio
larynx laringe (f)
laugh, to reír (i)
lavage lavado
lavatory lavamanos (m, sg)
lawsuit pleito
laxative laxante (m); laxativo; purgante (m)
lazy (indolent) indolente (adj)
leave, to (go away, to) jalarse (P.R.); salir
leg pierna
leg, calf of the canilla; chamorro (Chicano); pantorrilla
leishmaniasis roncha hulera; roncha mala
length of pregnancy (LOP) duración del embarazo (f)
lens lente (m)
leprosy lepra; lazarín (m); mal de Hansen (m); mal de San Lázaro (m)
lesion lesión (f)
lesion, oral afta; pupa; perleche (f)
let go of, to soltar (ue)

leukemia cáncer de la sangre (m); leucemia
leukocytes (white blood cells) glóbulos blancos; leucocitos
level al ras
lie, to mentir (ie)
lie down, to acostarse (ue)
lift, to levantar
ligament ligamento
light, to (turn on, to) encender (ie)
limb extremidad (f); miembro
limp, to (hobble, to) cojear; renguear (Sp. Am.)
lindane lindano
lingual lingual (adj)
liniment linimento
lip labio
liquid líquido
lisp (stutter) ceceo; tartamudeo
listen (to), to escuchar
liter litro
liver hígado
liver extract extracto de hígado
load of narcotics carga
lockjaw tétanos (m); trismo
loin lomo
look (appear) **well, to** tener buena cara
loop (IUD) lazo
lose, to perder (ie)
lose weight, to adelgazar; perder peso (ie)
lotion loción (f)
lower the cholesterol count, to bajar el nivel del colesterol
lozenge pastilla; pastilla de chupar; trocisco
LSD aceite; aceitunas; acelide; ácido; ácido lisérgico; ácidos; alucinantes; avándaro; azúcar; blanco de España; bomba; café; cápsulas; cohete; colorines; cristales; chochos; dal; diablos; divina; droga alucinante; droga LSD; dulces; elefante blanco; en onda; gis; grasas; la salud; lluvia de estrella; mica; mureler; nave; orange; papel; paper; piedrita de la luna; pit; purple haze; saturnos; sugar; sunshine; tacatosa; terrones; trip; viaje; viaje en las nubes; white
lubricant lubricante (m); lubricativo (adj)
lukewarm templado (adj); tibio (adj)
lump bola; borujo; bulto; dureza; hinchazón (f); protuberancia; tumorcito
lump, large borujón (m)
lump (bump) **on the head** chichón (m); pisporr(i)a (Chicano)
lunch, to have almorzar (ue)
lung bofe (m, Chicano, Sp. Am.); pulmón (m)
lye lejía

lying-in after childbirth sobreparto
lymph glands glándulas linfáticas
lymph node nódulo linfático; nudo linfático (colloq)
mad (insane) loco (adj)
madness locura; manía
magnesia magnesia
magnesia, milk of leche de magnesia (f)
magnifying glass lupa
"mainliner" jaipa; jaipo
make better, to aliviar
make-up, to put on maquillarse
make worse, to empeorar
malaise malestar (m)
malaria fríos (Sp. Am.); malaria; paludismo
malignancy malignidad (f)
malignant maligno (adj)
malnourished desnutrido (adj); mal nutrido (adj)
malnutrition desnutrición (f); mala alimentación (f); malnutrición (f)
malnutrition—kwashiorkor kwashiorkor (m); mala alimentación mojada
malnutrition—marasmus mala alimentación seca; marasmo
malpractice impericia; malpraxis (f); práctica impropia (inhábil)
mammogram mamografía; mamograma (m)
mania manía
maniac maníaco (adj)
marijuana achicalada; alfalfa; bacha; bailarina; carrujo; cáñamo; cartucho; cochornis; coffee; colombiana; cosa; cris; chara; chester; chícara; chiclona; chira; chupe; churus; doñajuanita; epazote; fitoca; flauta; flor de juana; frajo; ganga; ganja; gavos; griefo; grifa; grife; grilla; guato; guera; habnaita; hashi; hierba; huato; índico; jani; Jefferson; joint; juana; juanita; Kris Kras; leña; lucas; macoxa; mafufa; mani; Margarita; María; María Juanita; Mariana; mariguana; marijuana; marinola; mariola; Mary Popins; meserole; monte; mota; orégano; panatela; petate; petate del soldado; pitillo; pito; pochola; podo; polillo; pot; queta; rollo; té; tronadora; yedo; yerba; yesca; zacate
marijuana cigarette frajo de seda; leñito
marijuana smoker yesco
marijuana user grifo; mariguano; marihuano; moto
marrow médula; tuétano

mask máscara
massage masaje (m)
massage, to dar masaje; masajar;
  masajear; masar; sobar
masturbate, to hacerse la
  casqueta (Chicano); masturbarse;
  puñetear (vulgar)
masturbation casqueta (Chicano);
  masturbación (f)
maternity de maternidad (adj);
  maternidad (f)
  maternity clothes ropa de
   maternidad
  maternity floor piso de
   maternidad
  maternity hospital casa de
   maternidad
mattress colchón (m)
maturity madurez (f)
maxillar maxilar (adj)
measles granuja (slang); morbilli
  (f); sarampión (m); tapetillo de
  los niños (colloq)
measure medida
measure, to medir (i)
measuring cup taza de medir
medical purposes fines médicos (m)
medical records archivo clínico
medication medicación (f)
medicine droga; medicamento;
  medicina; medicación
  medicine, patent medicina de la
   botica; medicina de la
   farmacia; medicina patentada;
   medicina registrada
  medicine cabinet (medicine chest)
   botiquín (m); despensa
   (Chicano)
melancholia melancolía
member of police narcotics squad
  narco
membrane membrana; tela
menarche primera regla
  menarquia
Ménière's disease enfermedad de
  Ménière (f)
meningitis meningitis (f)
menopause cambio de vida;
  menopausia; período climatérico
menstruate, to estar indispuesta;
  estar mala; estar mala de la
  garra; estar mala de la luna;
  menstruar; perder sangre (ie);
  tener el mes; tener/traer la garra
menstruation administración (f,
  Mex.); costumbre (f); enferma
  euph); luna (Chicano);
  menstruación (f, general); mes
  (m); período (colloq); regla
  (Mex., P.R.); tiempo del mes
  (colloq)
mentally retarded inocente (adj,
  euph); retardado (adj); simple
  (adj, euph)
mental retardation retardo
  mental; retraso mental

menthol mentol (m)
mentholatum mentolato
  (Chicano)
Mercurochrome mercurocromo;
  sangre de chango (f, Chicano)
Merthiolate mertiolato
mescaline mescalina ·
metabolize, to metabolizar
metastasis metástasis (f)
methadone metadona
midwife (quack) rinconera
  midwife (trained) partera
  midwife (untrained) comadrona
migraine jaqueca; migraña
mild leve (adj)
milk leche (f); milque (f, Chicano)
  milk of magnesia leche de
   magnesia (f)
milligram miligramo
milliliter mililitro
mineral mineral (m)
mineral water agua mineral
mint leaves hojas de yerbabuena
mirror writing escritura en espejo
miscarriage malparto; parto
  malogrado
mix, to mezclar
mixture mezcla
moderate moderado (adj)
moist húmedo (adj)
mold moho
mole (birthmark) lunar (m)
mononucleosis mononucleosis
  infecciosa (f)
morning sickness ansias matutinas
  (f); enfermedad matutina (f); mal
  de madre (m); vómitos del
  embarazo (m)
morphine morfi (f); morfina
moustache bigote (m); mostacho
mouth boca
mouth breathing respiración
  bucal (f)
mouth mirror odontascopio
mouthpiece bocal (m); boquilla
mouth-to-mouth resuscitation
  resucitación boca a boca (f)
mouthwash enjuagatorio; lavado
  bucal; listerina (colloq)
move, to mover (ue)
mucus frió (slang, Mex.); moco
multiple sclerosis esclerosis en
  placa (f); esclerosis múltiple (f)
mumps bolas (Chicano); buche
  (m, Mex.); coquetas (Mex.);
  farfallota (P.R.); mompes (m, pl,
  Chicano); paperas; parótidas
  (f, pl)
muscle músculo
  muscle, involuntary músculo
   involuntario
  muscle, smooth músculo liso
  muscle, striated músculo
   estriado
  muscle, voluntary músculo
   voluntario

muscular dystrophy distrofia
  muscular progresiva
mushrooms hongos (m)
mustard mostaza
  mustard bath baño de mostaza
  mustard plaster cataplasma de
   mostaza; sinapismo
  mustard water agua con
   mostaza
mute mudo (adj)
myocardial infarct infarto
  miocardiaco; infarto
  miocardíaco
myocardium miocardio
myopia miopía
myopic miope (adj)
nail uña
nape of neck cogote (m); nuca
narcotic droga estupefaciente;
  droga somnífera; narcótico (m,
  adj)
  narcotic pills pinguas (f, pl)
  narcotic substitute, any la otra
   cosa
nasal drip goteo nasal;
  moqueadera (Chicano)
nausea basca; náusea
  nausea, morning asqueo;
   enfermedad matutina (f);
   malestares de la mañana (m)
navel ombligo
nearsighted corto de vista (adj);
  miope (adj)
nearsightedness miopía
neck cuello
needle aguja
  needle, hypodermic aguja
   hipodérmica; jeringa
neglect, to descuidar
negroid negro (adj)
nephritis nefritis (f)
nerve nervio
  nerve, cranial nervio craneal
  nerve, motor nervio motor
  nerve, parasympathetic nervio
   parasimpático
  nerve, sensory nervio sensorial
  nerve, sympathetic nervio
   simpático
nervous breakdown colapso;
  desarreglo nervioso; neurastenia
nervous disorder desorden
  nervioso (m)
nervous system, autonomic
  sistema nervioso autónomo (m)
nervous system, central sistema
  nervioso central (m)
neuralgia neuralgia
neurasthenia neurastenia
neurasthenic neurasténico (adj)
neuritis neuritis (f)
neurosis neurosis (f)
neurotic neurótica (adj)
nightmare pesadilla
nipple (breast) chichi (f, Arg.);
  pezón (m)

nipple, cracked grieta del pezón
nipple, engorged (caked) pezón enlechado (m)
nipple (female) chichi (f, slang); pezón (m)
nipple (male) tetilla
nipple (of a baby nursing bottle) chupón (m); mamadera; tetera (Mex., Cuba, P.R.); tetilla; tetina
nipple shield escudo para el pezón; pezonera
nitric acid ácido nítrico
nitro(glycerin) nitro(glicerina)
noninfectious no infeccioso (adj)
no one nadie
nose nariz (f); nayotas (f, pl, slang)
nosebleed hemorragia nasal; salirle sangre de la nariz
nose bleeding epistaxis (f)
nostril fosa nasal; ventana de la nariz; ventanilla de la nariz
Novocaine novocaína
nucleated leukocytes leucocitos nucleados
acidophiles acidófilos
basophiles basófilos
blood platelets plaquetas sanguíneas
eosinophiles eosinófilos
lymphocytes linfocitos
monocytes monocitos
polymorphonuclear neutrophiles neutrófilos polimorfonucleares
"polymorphs" "polimorfos"
reticulocytes reticulocitos
thrombocytes trombocitos
numb adormecido (adj); adormecimiento; entumecido (adj); entumido (adj)
numbness adormecimiento
nurse (for the sick) enfermera
nurse (nursemaid) niñera
nurse, baby ama de cría; niñera; nodriza
nurse, wet chichi (f, colloq, Guat., Mex.); chichigua (vulgar, Sp. Am.); nodriza
nurse, to amamantar; criar a los pechos; dar de mamar; dar el pecho al niño
nursery cuarto de los niños
nursery, newborn sala de los recién nacidos
nursing amamantamiento; crianza; de crianza (adj); lactancia; lactante (adj)
nursing (for the sick) asistencia a los enfermos
nursing bottle biberón (m); mamadera; tetera
nursing bra sostén de maternidad (m)
nursing care cuidados auxiliares

nursing home clínica de reposo; hospicio para ancianos
nursing pad almohadita
obese gordo (adj); obeso (adj)
obesity gordura; obesidad (f)
obstetric(al) obstétrico (adj)
obstetrician obstétrico (m, f); médico partero (m, f); tocólogo (m, f)
obstetrics obstetricia (sg); tocología
obstruction impedimento; obstrucción (f)
obstruction, nasal mormación (f, Chicano)
obstruction, stomach entablazón (f, Chicano)
obtain, to (get, to) conseguir (i)
occipital occipital (adj)
occlusion oclusión (f)
oil aceite (m)
oil, baby aceite para niños
oil, castor aceite de ricino
oil, cod liver aceite de hígado de bacalao
oil, mineral aceite mineral
oil of wintergreen aceite de gaulteria
ointment crema; pomada; ungüento; unto
old age senectud (f); vejez (f)
olfactory olfatorio (adj)
one-eyed tuerto (adj); virulo (adj, Chicano)
onset ataque (m); comienzo; principio
operating room quirófano; sala de operaciones
operation operación (f)
ophthalmia (inflammation of the eye) inflamación de los ojos (f); oftalmía
ophthalmic oftálmico (adj)
ophthalmoscope oftalmoscopio
opium chinaloa (slang); opio
optic nerve nervio óptico
organ órgano
orgasm orgasmo
oriental oriental (adj)
osteomyelitis inflamación de la médula del hueso (f); osteomielitis (f)
otitis otitis (f)
ounce onza
outpatient paciente ambulatorio (m, f); paciente externo (m, f)
outside of fuera de (prep)
ovary ovario
overdose dar una dosis excesiva; dosis excesiva (f)
overdue atrasado (adj)
overweight exceso de peso; sobrepeso
overweight (adj) excesivamente gordo (adj); excesivamente grueso (adj)

ovulate, to ovar
ovulation ovulación (f)
ovum huevo; óvulo
oxalic acid ácido oxálico
oxygen oxígeno
oxytocic oxitócico
oxytocin oxitocina
pacemaker aparato cardiocinético; marcador de paso (m); marcador de ritmo (m); marcapaso; monitor cardiaco (m); seno auricular
pacifier chupete (m); mamón (m, Chicano)
packet of heroin gramo
pad cojín (m); cojincillo
pain dolor (m)
pain, ache dolor
pain, bearing-down sensación de pesantez en el perineo (f)
pain, boring dolor penetrante
pain, burning dolor quemante
pain, colicky dolor cólico
pain, constant dolor constante
pain, dull dolor sordo
pain, expulsive dolores expulsivos
pain, false dolores falsos
pain, growing dolor de crecimiento
pain, hunger dolores de hambre
pain, intermenstrual dolores intermenstruales
pain killer calmante (m)
pain, labor dolor de parto; dolores de parto
pain, mild dolor leve
pain, moderate dolor moderado
pain, phantom limb dolor de miembro fantasma
pain, premonitory dolores premonitorios
pain, pressure-like dolor opresivo
pain, prickling hormigueo
pain, referred dolor referido
pain, root dolor radicular
pain, severe dolor severo
pain, sharp dolor agudo; dolor clavado; punzada
pain, sharp internal torzón (m)
pain, shooting dolor fulgurante
pain, smarting escozor (m)
pain, steady dolor continuo
pain, thoracic dolor torácico
pain, twinge latido (m)
pain, wandering dolor errante
painful doloroso (adj)
palate paladar (m); cielo de la boca
palate, hard bóveda ósea del paladar
palate, soft velo del paladar
pale pálido (adj)
palliative paliativo (m, adj)
palpitation latido (Chicano); palpitación (f)

palsy parálisis (f); paralización (f)
(f)
palsy, Bell's parálisis facial
palsy, cerebral parálisis
cerebral
palsy, shaking (Parkinson's
disease) enfermedad de
Parkinson (f); parálisis
agitante
pancreas páncreas (m)
pancreatitis pancreatitis (f)
pant, to jadear; resollar (ue)
panting jadeante (adj)
paralyzed, to be estar paralizado
(-a)
Pap smear frotis de Papanicolaou
(m); untos de Papanicolaou (m)
paralysis parálisis (f);
paralización (f)
paranoia paranoia
paraplegia parálisis de la mitad
inferior de cuerpo (f); paraplejía
parasite parásito
amoeba ameba; amiba
ascaris (roundworm) ascáride
(f); ascaris (f); lombriz grande
redonda (f)
chigger flea garrapata; güina
(Mex.); nigua
common name nombre común
(m)
cysticercus (bladderworm)
cisticerco
distribution distribución (f)
feces, form of—in forma de los
parásitos en heces
flea pulga
focus of infection foco de
infección
giardia giardia
gnat bobito (Chicano); jején
(m, C.A.)
louse piojo
louse, crab ladilla
louse, nit liendra
metazoos metazoos
mite ácaro
parasitic cyst ladilla; quiste (m)
pediculosis (infestation)
pediculosis (f); piojería
protozoa protozoarios
protozoa, flagellates
flagelados
route of entry vía de entrada
schistosoma bilharzia;
esquistosoma
solium (tapeworm) gusano
tableado; solitaria
sporozoa esporozoarios
tapeworm lombriz solitaria (f);
solitaria; tenia
threadworms lombriz chiquita
afilada (f); oxiuro
trichinosis triquinosis (f)
trichocephalus lombriz de
látigo (f); tricocéfalo

uncinaria (hookworm) lombriz
de gancho (f); uncinaria
worm gusano; lombriz (f)
worm, intestinal verme (m)
paregoric paregórico
parotid gland glándula parótida
pass on (a disease), to pegar
pass over, to atravesar (ie); pasar
por
patch parche (m)
PCP amiba; polvo
pear-shaped piriforme (adj)
pediatric pediátrico (adj)
pediatrician pediatra (m, f)
pediatrics pediatría (sg)
pellagra pelagra
pelvic pelviano (adj); pélvico (adj)
pelvimeter pelvímetro
pelvis pelvis (f)
penicillin penicilina
penis balone (m, Chicano); chale
(m, vulgar, Chicano); chalito
(vulgar, Chicano); chicote (m,
slang); chile (m, slang); chorizo
(vulgar); güine (m, vulgar);
miembro; palo (slang); pene (m);
picha (vulgar); pichón (m,
vulgar); pija (slang, Arg.);
pilinga (vulgar); pito (slang);
reata/riata (vulgar); verga (slang)
pennyroyal leaves hojas de poleo
perforated eardrum tímpano
perforado
perforation perforación (f)
pericarditis pericarditis (f)
perineal perineal (adj)
perineum perineo
periosteum periostio
peritonitis abdomen agudo (m,
slang); panza peligrosa (slang);
peritonitis (f)
permit permiso
peroxide agua oxigenada;
peróxido
peroxide, hydrogen agua
oxigenada; peróxido de
hidrógeno
persist, to persistir (en)
person high on drugs cócono
perspiration sudor (m)
perspire, to sudar
pertussis coqueluche (f); tos
convulsiva (f); tos ferina (f);
tosferina
pesticide pesticida (m); plaguicida
(m)
phalanx falange (f)
phallus falo
pharmacy botica; farmacia
pharyngitis faringitis (f)
pharynx faringe (f)
phenobarbital fenobarbital (m)
phlebitis flebitis (f);
tromboflebitis (f)
phlegm flema; mocosidad (f);
moquera (colloq)

phosphoric acid ácido fosfórico
phosphorus fósforo
photography fotografía
phthisis consunción (f); tisis (f)
physically físicamente (adv)
physician doctor (m); doctora;
médica; médico
physician, attending médico (-a)
a cardo (m, f); médico
asistente (m); médico (-a) de
cabecera (m, f)
physician, consulting médico
(-a) consultor (-a) (m, f);
médico (-a) de apelación (m, f)
physician, resident (house)
médico (-a) residente (m, f)
pigeon-toed patizambo (adj)
pile almorrana; hemorroides (f,
pl)
pill pastilla; píldora
pill, birth control pastillas para
no tener niños; píldora
anticonceptiva; píldoras para
control de embarazo
pill, sleeping píldora para
dormir; píldora somnífera;
sedativo; somnífero;
soporífera
pill, thyroid medicación
tiroides (f)
pillow almohadilla
pillow (inflatable rubber
"doughnut") almohadilla
neumática en forma de anillo
pimple barrillo; buba; butón (m);
grano de la cara; pústula
pimple, blackhead barro;
espinilla
pinched nerve nervio aplastado
pine oil aceite de pino (m)
pinkeye conjuntivitis catarral
aguda (f); mal de ojo (m);
oftalmía contagiosa
piperazine anterobius (m);
piperawïtt (m, f); piperazina;
piperidol (m)
pitocin pitocín (m); pitocina
pituitary gland glándula pituitaria
PKU (phenylketonuria)
fenilcetonuria; fenilquetonuria;
prueba del pañal
place, to colocar; poner
placenta lo demás; placenta;
secundinas
placenta previa placenta previa
placental placentario (adj)
plague peste (f); plaga
plague, bubonic peste bubónica;
tifo de oriente
planned parenthood natalidad
dirigida (f); procreación
planeada (f)
plaque placa
plasma plasma (m)
plaster of Paris yeso mate
plate placa

platelet plaqueta
pleural tap toracentesis (f)
pleurisy pleuresía; inflamación de los bofes (f, Chicano)
pneumonia neumonía; pulmonía
pock cacaraña (Mex., Guat.); postilla; viruela
point to, to indicar; señalar
poison intoxicante (m); ponzoña; veneno
poisoning envenenamiento; intoxicación (f)
  poisoning, botulism intoxicación botulínica
  poisoning, carbon monoxide intoxicación por monóxido de carbono
  poisoning, food envenenamiento por comestibles; intoxicación con alimentos
  poisoning, lead envenenamiento plúmbico; envenenamiento del plomo; saturnismo
  poisoning, salmonella intoxicación por salmonellas
  poisoning, staphylococcal intoxicación por estafilococos
poison ivy chechén (m); hiedra venenosa; yedra venenosa; zumaque venenoso (m)
poison (oneself), to envenenar(se); emponzoñar; intoxicar
poisonous ponzoñoso (adj); venenoso (adj)
polio(myelitis) parálisis infantil (f); poliomielitis (f)
polish, to limar
polyp pólipo
pomade pomada
poor health, in jodido (adj)
porcelain porcelana
pore poro
postnatal care cuidado postnatal
potassium potasio
  potassium iodide yoduro de potasio
  potassium permanganate permanganato de potasio
potbellied panzón (adj)
potion dosis (f); poción (f)
poultice cataplasma; emplasto
pound libra
powder polvo
powdered en polvo (adj)
powdery empolvado (adj); polvoriento (adj); polvoroso (adj)
precipitate, to precipitar
predisposition predisposición (f)
pregnancy embarazo; estado interesante (euph); gravidez (f); preñez (f)
  pregnancy, ectopic embarazo ectópico; embarazo fuera de la matriz
  pregnancy, false embarazo falso

pregnancy, hysteria embarazo histérico
pregnancy, incomplete embarazo incompleto
pregnancy, tubal embarazo en los tubos; embarazo tubárico
pregnant embarazada (adj); encinta (adj); grávida (adj); gruesa (adj, colloq); panzona (vulgar); preñada (adj)
premature prematuro (adj); sietemesino (literally "seven months") (adj)
prenatal prenatal (adj)
  prenatal care cuidado prenatal
presbyopia hipermetropía; presbicia; presbiopía
prescribe, to prescribir; prescribir un remedio; recetar
  prescribe for oneself autorecetarse
prescription prescripción (f); receta; receta médica
presentation presentación (f)
pressure presión (f)
  pressure, exert—on, to ejecer presión sobre
pressure sensations sensaciones de ser apretado (-a)
prevent, to impedir (i)
prick pinchazo; punzada
prick, to pinchar
prickly heat erupción debida al calor (f); picazón (f); sarpullido
probe estilete (m); sonda; tienta
problem problema (m); trastorno
procedure procedimiento
procreate, to procrear
proctitis proctitis (f)
produce, to producir
progeny progenie (f); prole (f)
progesterone progesterona
prolapse caída de la matriz; prolapso
prophylactic profiláctico (m, adj)
prostatitis prostatitis (f); tapado de orín
prosthesis miembro artificial; prótesis (f)
prostration postración (f)
  prostration, heat postración del calor
prothrombin time tiempo de protrombina
prove, to (test, to; try out, to) probar (ue)
provide an addict with a fix, to curar
psilocybin hongos; mujercitas; niños
psoriasis mal de pintas (m); soríasis (f)
psychedelic droga psicodélica; sicodélico (adj)
psychosis sicosis (f)

psychosomatic sicosomático (adj)
psychotic sicótico (adj)
pterygium carnosidad (f, colloq); pterigión (m)
pubic hair pelitos (m, pl, Chicano)
pubic region partes ocultas (f); verijas (pl)
puerile pueril (adj)
puerperal puerperal (adj)
puerperium puerperio; riesgo
pull, to jalar
pull back foreskin of penis, to pelársela
pull out, to extraer
pull up (one's) knees, to encoger las rodillas
pulp pulpa
pulpotomy pulpotomía
pulse pulso
pump, to sacar (leche) por medio de una bomba
purgation purgación (f)
purgative catártico (adj); purgante (m)
purge lavado; lavativo; purga; purgante (m)
pursue, to perseguir (i)
pus pus (m)
push, to empujar
pustule bubón (m); grano; pústula
put heroin in capsules, to capear; capiar
put in a plaster cast, to enyesar
put on (clothing), to ponerse + noun
put to sleep, to adormecer por anestesia
pyorrhea mal de las encías (m); piorrea
quadruplet cuadrúpleto; cuatrillizo
quarrel, to reñir (i)
quart cuarto
quinine quinina
quinsy (sore throat) amigdalitis supurativa (f); esquinancia
quintuplet quintillizo; quíntuplo
rabbit test examen de conejo (m)
rabies hidrofobia; rabia
radiation shield blindaje contra la radiación (m)
radiation therapy radioterapia
radiation treatment radiaciones (f)
radius radio
rale estertor (m)
rape rapto (Chicano); violación (f)
rash alfombra (P.R., Cuba); erupción (f); salpullido; sarpullido
  rash, diaper pañalitis (f)
  wheals (hives) ronchas
rat bite mordedura de ratones
RBC (red blood count) NGR (f); numeración de glóbulos rojos (f)
recessive recesivo (adj)

recessive character carácter recesivo (m)
recover, to curarse; sanar
rectal rectal (adj)
rectocele rectocele (m)
rectum recto
recur, to repetirse (i); volver a ocurrir (ue)
red blood cells hematíes (m)
reddish bermejizo (adj, hair); rojizo (adj)
red-haired pelirrojo (adj)
redness rubor (m)
reduce, to reducir(se)
reduce a fracture, to enderezar
reducing exercises ejercicios físicos para adelgazar; ejercicios físicos para reducir peso
refer, to referir (ie)
refined refinado (adj)
reflex reflejo
regenerate, to regenerar
regulate, to regular
regurgitation regurgitación (f)
reimplantation reimplantación (f); reinjertación (f)
relapse atrasado (adj); recaída; recidiva
relapse, cause to suffer atrasar
relapse, to have atrasarse
relation parentesco; pariente (f); relación (f)
relations, to have sexual coger or cojer (vulgar, Arg., P.R., Mex.); conocer; chingar (vulgar); chopetear (slang); dar una atascada (vulgar); dar pá dentro (vulgar); dormir con alguien (ue); echar un palito (Chicano); estar con alguien; hacer cositas (euph, Chicano); tener relaciones sexuales; tumbar
relationship parentesco; relación (f)
relax, to, aflojarse; calmarse; relajar el cuerpo; relajarse
relaxation descanso; relajación (f)
relaxation of tension disminución de la tirantez (f)
release descargo
release, to deprender
relief alivio
relieve, to aliviar
remedy medicamento; remedio
remember, to acordarse (ue); acordarse de (ue); recordar (ue)
remove, to quitar
remove the nerve, to matarle el nervio a alguien; sacarle el nervio a alguien
renal renal (adj)
repeat, to repetir (i)
repent, to arrepentir(se) (ie)
request petición (f)
require, to requerir (ie)

respiratory system aparato respiratorio
rest reposo
rest, to descansar
restraining device coercitivo; medio de restricción
restroom baño; comodidades (f, pl); cuarto de baño; excusado; servicios (m); WC (m)
resuscitation, cardiopulmonary (CRP) resucitación cardio-pulmonar (f); RCP (f)
return, to (come back, to) volver (ue)
return, to (give back, to) devolver (ue)
RH factor factor RH (m); factor Rhesus (m)
RH negative RH-negativo (adj)
RH positive RH-positivo (adj)
rheum reuma (m)
rheumatism reumas (m); reumatismo
rheumatoid arthritis artritis reumatoidea (f)
rhinitis escurrimiento de la nariz; rinitis (f)
rhogam rogam (m)
rhythm method método del ritmo; ritmo
rib costilla
rib, false (floating) costilla falsa (flotante)
rib, true costilla verdadera
rickets raquitis (m); raquitismo
ridge elevación (f); reborde (m)
ring (IUD) anillo
rinse (out), to enjuagar(se)
rise, to subir
risk riesgo
roll up one's sleeve, to arremangarse subirse las manga
roof of the mouth cielo de la boca; paladar (m)
root raíz (f)
root canal canal radicular (m)
root canal work curación del nervio (f); extracción del nervio (f)
roseola roséola; rubéola
rough áspero (adj); raposo (adj)
rub fricción (f); frotación (f)
rub, to frotar; frotarse; pasar la mano sobre la superficie de; restregar
rubella alfombría (Chicano); fiebre de tres días (f); peluza (Mex.); roséola epidémica; rubéola; sarampión alemán (m)
rubber (condom) condón (m); goma; hule (m); preservativo
rubber bulb, syringe pera de goma
rubber gloves guantes de goma (m, pl)
rubbing alcohol alcohol para fricciones (m)

rupture (hernia) hernia; quebradura; relajación (f); reventón (m); rotadura (Chicano); rotura; ruptura
rupture, to (burst, to) romper
ruptured roto (adj)
sac saco
saccharine sacarina
sacroiliac sacroilíaco (adj)
sacrum sacro
saline solution agua con sal; agua salina
saliva esputo; expectoración (f); saliva
salivary gland glándula salival
salt sal (f)
salt, iodized sal yodada
salt, noniodized sal corriente
salts, smelling sales aromáticas sales perfumadas
salt water agua salada
salve pomada; ungüento
sample muestra
sanitary napkin absorbente higiénico (m); almohadilla higiénica; kotex (m); servilleta sanitaria
sanitary pad kotex (m); servilleta sanitaria
sarcoma sarcoma (m)
say goodbye, to despedirse (de) (i)
scab costra; cuerín (m, Chicano); cuerito (Chicano); postilla
scabies guaguana (slang); gusto (slang); sarna
scale escama
scalp casco; cuero cabelludo; piel de la cabeza (f)
scalpel bisturí (m); escalpelo
scar cicatriz (f)
scarred cicatrizado (adj)
schizophrenia esquizofrenia
schizophrenic esquizofrénico (adj)
sciatic ciático (adj)
sciatica ciática
scorpion bite mordedura de escorpión
scotoma (spots before the eyes) escotoma (m); manchas frente a los ojos
scratch rascado; rasguño; raspón (m, Sp. Am.)
scratch to (relieve itch) rascar(se)
scratch, to (hurt) rasguñar
scrotum bolsa de los testículos; escroto
scrub (surgically), to fregar; lavar; refregar
scurvy escorbuto
seasickness mal de mar (m); mareo
seborrhea seborrea
seconal capsule colorada
secrete, to secretar
sedative calmante (m); sedante (m); sedativo

sedimentation sedimentación (f)
erythrosedimentation
eritrosedimentación (f)
seizure ataque (m); convulsión (f)
semen esperma; leche (f, vulgar);
mecos (m, pl, vulgar); semen (m)
seminal vesicle vesículo seminal
senile senil (adj)
senility caduquez (f); senectud (f);
senilidad (f)
sense sentido
  sense, of feel (tactile) sentido
del tacto
  sense, of hearing (auditory)
sentido del oído
  sense, of sight (visual) sentido
de la vista
  sense, of smell (olfactory)
sentido del olfato
  sense, of taste (gustatory)
sentido del gusto
sensorial sensorial (adj)
septicemia bacteriemia; infección
en la sangre (f, colloq); piemia;
septicemia; toxemia
septum tabique (m)
serious grave (adj); serio (adj)
serum suero
  serum, antivenin suero
antiviperino
  **serum, black widow spider
antivenin** suero antialacrán
serve, to servir (i)
set a fracture, to componer una
fractura; reducir una fractura
severe agudo (adj); fuerte (adj);
severo (adj)
shave, to afeitar(se); rasurar(se)
shield (IUD) escudo
shin canilla; espinilla
shinbone tibia
shingles herpes (m, f); zona;
zoster (f)
shiver, to temblar; tiritar
shock choque (m); conmoción
nerviosa (f); sobresalto; susto
  shock, anaphylactic choque
alérgico (colloq); choque
anafiláctico
shortness of breath ahoguijo;
ahoguío (colloq)
shortsighted cegato (adj, colloq);
miope (adj)
shot chot (m, Chicano); inyección
(f)
shoulder hombro
shoulder blade (scapula) escápula;
espaldilla; omóplato; paletilla
show, to mostrar (ue)
shower, to (take a shower, to)
ducharse
show one's teeth, to enseñar los
dientes (colloq); mostrar los
dientes (ue)
sick enfermo (adj); malo (adj)
sickliness achaque (m)

sickly cholenco (adj, Chicano);
demacrado (adj); enfermizo
(adj); farruto (adj, Arg., Bol.,
Chile); pálido (adj)
sickness dolencia; enfermedad
(f); mal (m); padecimiento
side costado; lado
  side, left lower lado izquierdo
inferior
  side, left upper lado izquierdo
superior
  side, right lower lado derecho
inferior
  side, right upper lado derecho
superior
silver nitrate nitrato de plata
simulation fingimiento
single out, to separar
sinus seno
sinus congestion congestión nasal
(f); sinusitis (f)
sit down, to sentarse (ie)
sitz bath baño de asiento;
semicupio
size tamaño
  size, assorted tamaño surtido
  size, large tamaño grande
  size, small tamaño pequeño
skeleton armazón (m); esqueleto
skin cuero (colloq); piel (f)
  skin, flap of the pellejo
  skin of the face cutis (m)
skinned (complexioned), **light**
despercudido (adj)
skinned (complexioned), **olive**
trigueño (adj)
**skinned, very dark, lacking negroid
features** pinto (adj); retinto
(adj)
skull calavera (Chicano);
cráneo
  skull, top of tapa de los sesos
(colloq)
sleep, to dormir (ue)
sleeping sickness enfermedad del
sueño (f)
sling cabestrillo; hondo
slipped disc disco desplazado;
disco intervertebral luxado
smallpox viruela
smear cultivo
smegma esmegma (m); queso
(slang)
smell, to oler (ue)
smile, to sonreir (i)
smoke humo
smoke, marijuana, to motear;
motiar; tronar
smooth, to limar
snake bite mordedura de culebra
sneeze, to estornudar
sniff glue, to hacer(se) a la glu(fa);
sesonar
**sniff residue of powdered narcotics,
to** estufear; estufiar
soak, to remojar

soap jabón (m)
soapy water agua jabonosa
sodium carbonate carbonato de
sodio
sodium hydroxide hidróxido de
sodio
sodium hypochlorite (bleach)
blanqueador de ropa (m);
hipoclorito de sodio
sodium pentothal pentotal sódico
(m); pentotal de sodio (m)
sodium peroxide agua oxigenada;
peróxido de sodio
sodium sulfate (in toilet cleaners)
sulfato de sodio (en limpiadores
de inodoros)
soft blando (adj); suave (adj)
soft (pliant) blando (adj)
solution solución (f)
soporific narcótico; soporífico
sore aflicción (f); dolor (m); pena
sore (wound) grano; llaga; úlcera
sore ears mal (dolor) de oídos (m)
sore eyes dolor de ojos (m)
sore throat garganta inflamada;
mal (dolor) de garganta (m)
souffle pillido (Mex.); silbido
sound (harsh, raucous) ronquido
spasm contracción muscular (f);
espasmo; latido (Chicano)
spasmodic espasmódico (adj);
intermitente (adj); irregular (adj)
spastic espasmódico (adj);
espástico (adj)
specimen espécimen (m); muestra
  specimen, urine muestra de la
orina
spectacles anteojos (general
term); espejuelos (Cuba); gafas;
lentes (m, pl, Mex.); quevedos
(m, wire-rimmed)
speculum espéculo; espejo vaginal
spell, to deletrear
sperm espermatozoide (m);
mecos; semen (m); semilla
(slang, Mex.)
spermaticide, vaginal
espermaticida vaginal (m)
sphincter esfínter (m)
spinal column columna vertebral;
espinal dorsal
spinal cord médula espinal
spiral (IUD) espiral (m)
spit in the bowl, to escupir en la
taza
spleen bazo; esplín (m, Chicano)
splint férula; tablilla
splint, in a entablillado (adj)
splinter (in the eye) astilla (en el
ojo); esquirla
spoonful cucharada
spot mancha
spotted sickness mal de pinto (m);
pinta
spotting manchado; manchas de
sangre

sprain dislocación (f); esguince (f); falseo (Chicano); torcedura
sprain, to desconcertar; falsear; torcer (ue)
spray pulverización (f); pulverizador (m); rociador (m)
spread (out), to tender (con) (ie)
spread limbs, to extender (ie)
sputum esputo; desgarro (Sp. Am.); gargao; pollo (Chicano); saliva
squat, to acuclillarse; ponerse de cuclillas
squeeze, to apretar (ie)
squint-eyed bisojo (adj); bizco (adj); ojituerto (adj)
stain (staining) coloración (f); colorante (m); tinción (f)
  stain, acid-fast coloración acidorresistente
stand up, to levantarse; parar(se); ponerse de pie
starch almidón (m)
starchy almidonado (adj); amiláceo (adj)
stay, to quedarse
stay awake, to desvelarse
steam vapor (m)
sterile estéril (adj); infecundo (adj)
sterility esterilidad (f); infecundidad (f)
  sterility, female frío de la matriz
  sterility, permanent esterilidad permanente
sterilization esterilización (f)
sterilize, to castrar; esterilizar
sterilize the bottles, to esterilizar las botellas
sterilized esterilizado (adj)
sterilizer esterilizador (m)
stethoscope estetoscopio; fonendoscopio
stick to clavar; picar
stick out, to sacar
stiff tieso (adj)
stiff neck nuca tiesa (colloq); torticolis (m); tortícolis (m)
stiff ("frozen") joint articulación envarada (f); articulación trabada (f)
stillbirth nati-muerto; parto muerto
stillborn mortinato (adj); nacido muerto (adj)
stimulant estimulante (m)
sting (of an insect) picadura; piquete (m); punzada
  sting, ant picadura de hormiga
  sting, bee picadura de abeja
  sting, black widow spider picadura de ubar (colloq); picadura de viuda negra
  sting, botfly picadura de moscardón

  sting, chigoe, jigger, sandflea picadura de nigua
  sting, flea picadura de pulga
  sting, hornet picadura de avispón
  sting, mosquito picadura de mosquito
  sting, scorpion picadura de alacrán
  sting, spider picadura de araña
  sting, tick picadura de garrapata
  sting, wasp picadura de avispa
sting, to picar
stir, to revolver (ue)
stitch puntada; punto; sutura
stocking, elastic calceta elástica
stomach estómago; panza (Chicano); vientre (m)
stomach, on an empty en ayunas
stomach, pit of boca del estómago; epigstrio
stomach ache dolor de estómago (m)
stomach pump bomba estomacal
stomach ulcer úlcera del estómago
stool softener cápsula para ablandar evacuaciones
stool specimen muestra de excremento; muestra de heces fecales
stop, to pararse
strabismus bizco (C. A.), estrabismo
straighten the teeth, to enderezar los dientes
strain tensión (f); torcedura
straining, tenesmus pujos
strength fuerza
strep throat estreptococia; mal (dolor) de garganta por estreptococo
streptomycin estreptomicina
stretch, to (unfold, to) tender (ie)
stretch marks (strias) estrias
stricture constricción (f); estenosis (f); estrechez (f); estrictura
stroke accidente cerebral (m); apoplejía; ataque fulminante (m); derrame cerebral (m); embolia cerebral; embolio (Chicano); estroc (m, Chicano); hemorragia vascular; parálisis (f)
strong tea té cargado (m); té fuerte (m)
strychnine estricnina
stuttering balbucencia; tartamudez (f)
sty orzuelo; perrilla (colloq)
stylet estilete (m)
sublingual gland glándula sublingual
submaxillary gland glándula submaxilar

subside, to calmarse
substitute substituto
subtract, to deducir; sustraer
suck, to chupar; mamar
sudden súbito (adj)
suffer, to padecer (de); sufrir (de)
suffocation asfixia; sofocación (f)
sugar azúcar (m)
sugary azucarado (adj)
suggest, to sugerir (ie)
suicide suicidio
sulfathiazole sulfatiazol (m)
sulfonyluria sulfoniluria
sulfuric acid ácido sulfúrico
sulfur powder polvo de azufre
sulphur (sulfur) azufre (m)
sunglasses anteojos oscuros; gafas de sol
sunstroke insolación (f); soleada (Sp. Am.)
suntan lotion loción bronceadora (f); loción para el sol (f)
suntanned bronceado (adj); tostado (adj)
supplementary feedings alimentación suplementaria (f)
support apoyo; soporte (m); sostén (m)
supporter faja medical
supporter, athletic suspensorio
suppository cala; calilla; supositorio
suppository, vaginal óvulos
suppuration supuración (f)
surface superficie (f)
surgical quirúrgico (adj)
suture comisura; puntada; sutura
  suture, dental sutura
  suture, dissolving sutura absorbible
swallow trago
swallow, to tragar
sweat sudor (m)
sweetener dulcificante (m)
sweets dulces (m, pl); golosinas (f, pl)
swell, to hinchar
swelling hinchazón (f); tumefacción (f); tumor (m)
  swelling on the head chichón (m)
swollen hinchado (adj)
symptom síntoma (m)
syndrome síndrome (m)
syphilis avariosis (f, Sp. Am.); infección de la sangre (f, euph); lúes (f); mal de bubas (m, slang); mal francés (m, slang); sangre mala (f, slang); sífilis (f)
syringe jeringa; jeringuilla
  syringe, disposable jeringa desechable; jeringuilla descartable
  syringe, glass cylinder jeringa con cilindro de cristal

syringe, hollow needle jeringa con aguja hueca
syringe, hypodermic jeringuilla hipodérmica
syringe-piston, plunger émbolo
syrup of ipecac jarabe de ipeca (m)
systole sístole (f)
tablespoonful cucharada
tablet comprimido; pastilla; tableta
tachycardia taquicardia
tactile tácil (adj)
take, to tomar
  take advantage of, to aprovecharse de
  take (drugs), to administrarse; ingerir (ie); tomar
  take care of, to cuidar
  take hold, to agarrar
  take marijuana, to amarihuanarse; engrifarse; enmarihuanarse
  take off, to (undress, to) quitarse
  take place, to tener lugar
Tampax tampax (m)
tampon ta(m)pón (m)
tantrum berrinche (m, colloq)
  tantrum, temper pataletas
tartar sarro
  tartar, dental saburra; sarro; tártaro
taste saber; saborear
taste, to (try, to) probar (ue)
taste good (bad), to tener buen (mal) sabor
tasteless desabrido (adj)
tattoo(ing) tatuaje (m)
tea té (m)
  tea, camomile agua de manzanilla; té de manzanilla
tear desgarramiento
tear, to romper
tear gland glándula lagrimal
tears lágrimas
teaspoonful cucharadita
  teaspoonful, level cucharadita llena al ras
teeth dientes (m); mazorca (sg, slang)
  teeth, artificial (false) dientes postizos
  teeth, bicuspids bicúspides (m); premolares
  teeth, canine (eyeteeth) canino; colmillo
  teeth, deciduous dientes de leche
  teeth, even dientes parejos
  teeth, front (incisors) incisivos
  teeth, lacking chimuelo (adj, Chicano)
  teeth, molars molares (m)
  teeth, stained dientes manchados

teeth, third molar tercer molar
teeth, white dientes blancos
teeth, wisdom muelas cordales (f); muelas del juicio (f)
teethe, to dentar (ie); echar dientes; endentecer
teething dentición (f); salida de los dientes
tell, to (say, to) decir
temperature calentura; temperatura
temple sien (f)
tendon tendón (m)
tepid tibio (adj)
Terramycin terramicina
test examen (m); prueba
  test of análisis de (m)
  test, angiography angiografía; radiografía de los vasos sanguíneos
  test, cardiac function prueba de función cardíaca
  test, serology prueba serológica
  test, sputum análisis de esputos
  test, tuberculin tuberculina
  test, urinalysis análisis de la orina; urinálisis (m)
test, to examinar; poner a prueba
testicle blanquillo (slang, Chicano); bolas (f, pl, slang, Chicano); compañones (m, pl, slang); cuates (m, pl, slang, Chicano); huevos (m, pl, slang); testículo
tetanus mal de arco (m, slang); pasmo seco; tétano(s); trimo
  tetanus, infantum moto (slang, Mex.); mozusuelo (Mex.); siete días (7 días) (m)
tetracycline teraciclina
therapeutic tetrapéutico (adj)
therapy terapia; tratamiento
  therapy, x-ray radioterapia
thermometer termómetro
  thermometer, oral termómetro oral
  thermometer, rectal termómetro rectal
thicken, to espesar
thigh muslo
think, to pensar (ie)
thoracic cavity caja torácica
thorax tórax (m)
throat garganta
thrombophlebitis flebitis (f); tromboflebitis (f)
thrombosis trombosis (f)
  thrombosis, coronary trombosis coronaria
thrombus coágulo; cuajo; cuajarón (m)
thrush afta; algodoncillo (colloq)
thymus timo
thyroid tiroides (m); tiroideo (adj)
tic tic (m); tirón (m); sacudida

tic douloureux tic doloroso de la cara
tie the tubes, to ligar los tubos de Falopio; ligar los tubos uterinos; ligar trompas
tingling hormigueo
tinnitus zumbido del oído
tire, to cansar(se)
tissue tejido
toe dedo (del pie)
  toe, big dedo grueso
toilet baño; común (m); excusado; inodoro; privado; retrete (m, Spain); servicios
tolerance tolerancia
tongue lengua
tongue depressor abate lengua (f); depresor de la lengua (m); pisa-lengua
tonic tónico
tonsilitis amigdalitis (f); tonsilitis (f)
tonsils amígdalas; anginas (Mex., Ven.); tonsils (m, Chicano)
tooth diente (m)
  tooth, baby diente de leche; diente mamón
  tooth, back muela
  tooth decay caries (f); dientes podridos
  tooth, impacted diente impactado
  tooth, large, misshapened diente de ajo (colloq)
  tooth, lower diente inferior
  tooth, neck of cuello
  tooth, socket alvéolo
  tooth, upper diente superior
toothache dolor de dientes (m); dolor de muelas (m); odontalgia
toothbrush cepillo de dientes
toothpaste pasta de dientes; pasta dentífrice
toothpick mondadientes (m); palillo de dientes
touch, to tocar
tourniquet liga; torniquete (m)
toxemia toxemia
  toxemia of pregnancy intoxicación del embarazo (f); toxemia del embarazo
trachea gaznate (m); tráquea
tracheostomy traqueostomía
traction tracción (f)
trade, to cambiar
traffic in drugs, to dilear; diliar; traficar
tranquilizer apaciguador (m); calmante (m); tranquilizante (m)
transfer, to transferir (ie)
transfusion transfusión (f)
transmission transmisión (f)
  transmission by contact transmisión mediante contacto
  transmission, droplet transmisión por gotillas

transmission, vector transmisión mediante vector
transmission vehicle vehículo
trauma trauma (m); traumatismo
treatment tratamiento
tremor temblor (m); tremor (m)
triplet trillizo
truss braguero; faja
tub bañera; tina de baño
tube tubo
  tube, fallopian trompa de Falopio; tubo de Falopio
tube (for feeding) sonda
tubercular afectado (adj, Chicano); tuberculoso (adj)
tuberculosis afectado del pulmón (Chicano, Mex.); manchado del pulmón (Mex.); peste blanca (f); tisis (f); tuberculosis (f)
tumefaction edema (m); hinchazón (f); tumefacción (f)
tumor neoformación (f); neoplasma (m); tacotillo (Chicano); tumor (m)
  tumor on the head chiporra Guat., Hond.)
tuning fork diapasón (m)
turn (over), to darse vuelta; volverse (ue)
turn around (over), to voltearse
turn into, to convertir(se) (ie)
turpentine esencia de trementina; trementina
twin cuate (m, f, Mex.); gemelo; mellizo
twist, to (bend, to) bornear
twist, to (turn, to) torcer (ue)
twisted torcido (adj); zambo (adj)
ulcer úlcera
  ulcer, gastric úlcera gástrica
  ulcer, peptic úlcera péptica
ulna cúbito
ultrasound ultrasonda
ultraviolet lamp lámpara de rayos ultravioletas
umbilical cord cordón umbilical (m)
umbilical hernia, (to have) (estar) des ombligado (-a)
umbilicus ombligo
unconscious inconsciente (adj)
unconsciousness inconsciencia; insensibilidad (f)
undernourished desnutrido (adj, colloq)
underside superficie inferior (f)
undersigned abajo firmado (adj)
understand, to comprender; entender (ie)
underweight falta de peso; peso escaso
undress, to desnudarse; desvestirse (i); encuerarse (Chicano)
unguent pomada; ungüento
untreated no tratado (adj)

uremia intoxicación de orín (f); uremia
ureter uréter (m)
urethra canal urinario (m); caño urinario; uretra
urinalysis análisis de la orina (m); urinálisis (m)
urinary bladder vejiga de la orina
urinary problem mal de orín (m)
urinary tract vías urinarias
urinate, to hacer agua (Chicano); hacer (la) chi(s) (vulgar, Chicano); hacer (la) pipi (pipí); mear; tirar (el) agua (slang)
urine "aguas menores" (f); chi (f, vulgar); orín (m); orina; orines (m, pl)
urine, collection of the specimen acumulación de la muestra (f)
urine, color—straw de paja (adj)
urine, color—yellow amarilla (adj)
urine, frequent urinating meadera (Chicano); orinar muy de seguido
urine constituents componentes (m)
  acetone acetona
  albumin albúmina
  ammonia amoníaco
  bile bilis (f)
  bilirubin bilirrubina
  blood sangre (f)
  calcium calcio
  chlorides cloruro
  creatine creatina
  crystal(s) cristal(es) (m)
  glucose glucosa
  phosphate fosfato
  solids sólidos (m)
  total nitrogen nitrógeno total
  total sulfur azufre total (m)
  urea urea
  urobilin urobilina
  urobilirubin urobilirrubina
urticaria urticaria
user of pills pildoriento
user of marijuana, cocaine, morphine maricocaimorfi
user of morphine morfiniento
uterus matriz (f); útero
uterus prolapse caída de la matriz; prolapso de la matriz; prolapso del útero
uvula campanilla (colloq); galillo (colloq); úvula
vaccinate, to vacunar
vaccination inoculación (f); vacunación (f)
  vaccination, booster refuerzo
  vaccination, DPT triple (f)
vaccine, immunization inmunización (f); vacuna
vaccine, oral polio gotas para polio; vacuna oral contra polio

vagina agujero (vulgar, Chicano); concha (vulgar, Arg., Chile, Urug.); cueva (slang, vulgar, Chicano); linda (slang); pan (m, slang, vulgar); panocho (slang); partida (vulgar); vagina
vaginal vaginal (adj)
vaginitis vaginitis (f)
valve válvula
vapor vapor (m)
varicose varicoso (adj)
varicose vein várice (f); variz (m); vena varicosa
varicosity varicosidad (f)
vas deferens conducto deferente
vaseline vaselina
vein vena
venereal disease enfermedad venérea (f); secreta (slang)
  canker sore postemilla; úlcera gangrenosa
  chancre chancro; grano
  chancre, hard chancro duro; chancro sifilítico
  chancre, noninfecting chancro blando; chancro simple
  chlamidia clamidia
  cold sore fuegos en la boca (en los labios); herpes labial (m)
  conduloma condiloma (m)
  genital wart verruga genital; verruga venérea
  gonorrhea blenorragia; chorro (euph, Chicano); gonorrea; gota (slang); mal de orín (m, slang); purgaciones (f, pl, slang)
  herpes herpe(s) (m, f)
  herpes genitalis herpes genital
  herpes menstrualis herpes mestrual
  herpes zoster herpes zoster
  lymphogranuloma venereum bubones (m); linfogranuloma venéreo (m)
  moniliasis algodoncillo; boquera; candidiasis (f); moniliasis (f); muguet (m)
  nongonococcal urethritis uretritis no gonococal (f)
  nonspecific urethritis uretritis inespecífica (f); uretritis no específica (f)
  sexually transmitted diseases enfermedades pasadas sexualmente (f)
  syphilis infección de la sangre (f, euph); sangre mala (f, slang); sífilis (f)
  trichomonas tricomonas
  venereal lesion chancro; grano; úlcera
  vesicular eruption erupción vesicular (f)

vermifuge antihelmíntico (m, adj);
vermifugo (m, adj)
vertebra vértebra
vial ampolla; botella; frasco; vial
(m)
victim víctima
vinegar vinagre (m)
virus virus (m)
vision, blurred vista borrosa
vision, double vista doble
vitamin vitamina
vitamin B₁ tiamina
vitamin B₂ riboflavina
vitamin B₆ piridoxina
vitamin C ácido ascórbico
vitamin, calcium calcio
vitamin, iron hierro; sulfato
ferroso
vitamin, niacin ácido nicotínico;
niacina
vitiligo ciricua (colloq); jiricua
(slang); vitíligo
vitreous humor humor vitreo (m)
vocal cord cuerda vocal
vomit (vomiting) arrojadera
(vulgar); basca; vómito
vomit, to arrojar (colloq);
dompear (Chicano); vomitar;
tirar las tripas
vomitive emético (m, adj);
vomitivo (m, adj)
vulva panocha (slang); rajada
(vulgar); vulva
waist cintura
wait (for), to esperar
waiver renuncia voluntaria
wake up, to despertar(se) (ie)
walk, to andar; caminar
walker andador (m)

walking cane bastón de paseo (m)
want, to (love, to) querer (ie)
warm templado (adj); tibio (adj)
warmer calentador (m); más
caliente (adj)
warn, to advertir (ie)
warning aviso
warning sign signo de
advertencia
warrant, to hacer certificación
wart mezquino (Mex.); verruga
wart, plantar ojo de pescado
(colloq)
wash, to lavar
wash oneself, to lavarse
waste desecho
watch, to (care for, to) cuidar
water pick limpiador de agua a
presión (m)
watery aguoso (adj); blandito (adj)
WBC (white blood count) NGB
(f); numeración de glóbulos
blancos (f)
weak débil (adj)
weakness debilidad (f)
weal (large welt) cardenal (m);
verdugón (m)
wean, to destetar
weigh, to pesar
weight peso
well-being bienestar (m)
wen lobanillo; lupia
wet mojado (adj)
wet the bed, to mojar
wheal pápula; roncha
wheelchair silla de ruedas
wheeze, to respirar
asmáticamente; respirar con
dificultad

whooping cough (pertussis)
coqueluche (f); tos ahogona (f,
Mex.); tos convulsiva (f); tos
ferina (f); tosferina
wire, to atar con alambre
witness testigo
womb matriz (f); útero
worry pena; preocupación (f)
worry, to apenarse (Chicano);
preocuparse
wound herida; llaga; coco
wound, abrasion abrasión (f)
wound, chafe rozadura
wound, cut cortadura
wound, incised herida incisa
wound, incision cisura;
incisión (f)
wound, knife filorazo (Chicano)
wound, laceration laceración (f)
wound, open skin grano
wound, puncture herida
penetrante; herida punzante
wound, scrape raspadura
wound, tear (torn wound)
desgarro
wound, to (hurt, to) herir (ie)
wrapping in a cold (wet) sheet
empacamiento en sábana fría
(mojada)
wrinkle arruga
wrist muñeca
xerosis resequedad de los ojos (f);
xerosis (f)
x-ray radiografía; rayo equis;
retrato del x-ray (Chicano)
x-ray, chest radiografía del
tórax; — del pecho
x-ray, to radiografiar
zinc oxide radióxido de zinc

APPENDIX

Spanish–English Vocabulary

Vocabulario español–inglés

ABBREVIATIONS

ABREVIATURAS

adj	adjective	**adjetivo**
adv	adverb	**adverbio**
colloq	colloquial	**coloquial**
euph	euphemism	**eufemismo**
f	feminine noun	**sustantivo feminino**
m	masculine noun	**sustantivo masculino**
m, f	masculine or femine noun	**sustantivo masculino o feminino**
pl	plural	**plural**
sg	singular	**singular**

Unless specified, words ending with **a** are feminine, words ending with **o** are masculine.

SPECIAL WORDS USED TO INDICATE REGIONAL OCCURRENCES

PALABRAS ESPECIALES USADAS PARA INDICACION REGIONAL

Arg.	Argentina	**la Argentina**
Bol.	Bolivia	**Bolivia**
C.A.	Central America (Guatemala, El Salvador, Honduras, Costa Rica, Nicaragua)	**Centroamérica (Guatemala, el Salvador, Honduras, Costa Rica, Nicaragua)**
Carrib.	(Cuba, Puerto Rico, Dominican Republic)	**(Cuba, Puerto Rico, la República Dominicana)**
Chicano	Chicano (southwestern U.S.)	**Chicano**
Chile		
Col.	Colombia	**Colombia**
C.R.	Costa Rica	**Costa Rica**
Cuba		
Ec.	Ecuador	**el Ecuador**
Guat.	Guatemala	**Guatemala**
Hond.	Honduras	**Honduras**
Mex.	Mexico	**México**
Nic.	Nicaragua	**Nicaragua**
Pan.	Panama	**Panamá**
Para.	Paraguay	**Paraguay**
Peru		
P.R.	Puerto Rico	**Puerto Rico**
Ríopl.	Rio de la Plata region (Eastern Argentina, Uruguay)	**Río de la Plata (la Argentina oriental, el Uruguay)**
Sal.	El Salvador	**el Salvador**
Sp. Am.	Spanish America	**América del Sur**
Spain		
Ur.	Uruguay	**el Uruguay**
Ven.	Venezuela	**Venezuela**

a (f) amphetamines
a término at term (birth)
a tierra electrical grounding
abajo firmado (adj) undersigned
abate lengua tongue depressor
abatimiento depression
abdomen (m) abdomen
   abdomen agudo (slang) acute abdomen; bowel obstruction; peritonitis; appendicitis
aborto abortion
   aborto espontáneo spontaneous abortion
   aborto inducido induced abortion
   aborto provocado induced abortion
   aborto terapéutico therapeutic abortion
abotagar to become bloated
   abotagarse to bloat; to swell
abrasión (f) abrasion
abrelatas (m) can opener
absceso abscess
absorbente higiénico sanitary napkin
abstenerse de las relaciones sexuales to abstain from sexual relations
abuja fix; injection (of a narcotic substance); joint (of a narcotic substance)
abujazo fix; injection (of a narcotic substance)
abuso de (las) drogas drug abuse
acabarse (C.A., Mex., Ríopl.) to decline in health
ácaro parasite; mite
accidente (m) accident; complication
   accidente cerebral stroke
acedía heartburn
aceite (m) oil
   aceite de gaulteria oil of wintergreen
   aceite de hígado de bacalao cod liver oil
   aceite de pino pine oil
   aceite de ricino castor oil
   aceite mineral mineral oil
   aceite para niños baby oil
acercarse to get close
acetaminofén (m) acetaminophen
acetona acetone
acidez (f) heartburn
ácido acid
   ácido (slang) amphetamines
   ácido acético (puro) acetic acid
   ácido acetilisalicílico acetylsalicylic acid
   ácido arsénico arsenic acid
   ácido ascórbico ascorbic acid; vitamin C
   ácido bórico boric acid
   ácido carbólico carbolic acid

   ácido clorhídrico hydrochloric acid
   ácido fluorhídrico hydrofluoric acid
   ácid fólico folic acid
   ácido fosfórico phosphoric acid
   ácido lisérgico LSD
   ácido nicotínico niacin
   ácido nítrico nitric acid
   ácido oxálico oxalic acid
   ácido paramino salicílico p-aminosalicylic acid (PAS)
   ácido sulfúrico sulphuric acid
   ácido tánico tannic acid
   ácido úrico uric acid
acidófilos acidophiles
acné (f) acne
acordarse de (ue) to remember
acostarse (ue) to go to bed; to lie down
acrílico (adj) acrylic
acromatopsia color blindness
acuclillarse to squat
acumulación de la muestra (f) collection of the (urine) specimen
acupunctura acupunture
achaque (m) (C.R.) sickliness; fainting spell during pregnancy
adelgazar to lose weight
adicto addict (drug)
   adicto (adj) addicted
   adicto a droga(s) drug addict
   adicto a las drogas narcóticas adddict (drug)
administración (f, Mex.) menstruation
administrarse to take (drugs)
adolorado (adj, Chicano) hypochondriac
adormecer el nervio to deaden the nerve
adormecer por anestesia to put to sleep
adormecido (adj) numb
adormecimiento numb; numbness
adrenalina adrenalin
advertir (ie) to warn
afasia aphasia
afectado (adj, Chicano) tubercular
afectado del pulmón (Chicano, Mex.) tuberculosis
afecto de (adj) suffering from
afeitar(se) to shave
aflicción (f) sore
aflojarse to relax
afonia aphonia; hoarseness
afónico (adj) hoarse
afta oral lesion; thrush
agacharse to bend over
agarraderas (Chicano) breast
agotamiento exhaustion
   agotamiento por calor heat exhaustion
agrandamiento enlargement

agregar to add
agriera (Sp. Am.) heartburn
agrietar to crack
   agrietarse to chap
agruras heartburn
agua water
   agua con azúcar glucose water
   agua con mostaza mustard water
   agua con sal saline solution
   agua de amnios amniotic fluid
   agua de manzanilla camomile tea
   agua jabonosa soapy water
   agua mineral mineral water
   agua oxigenada peroxide; hydrogen peroxide; sodium peroxide
   agua salada salt water
   agua salina saline solution
   "aguas mayores" feces; stool
   "aguas menores" urine
agudo (adj) severe
aguja needle
   aguja hipodérmica needle, hypodermic
agujero (vulgar, Chicano) anus; vagina
aguoso (adj) watery
ahogamiento dropsy
ahogarse to choke
ahoguijo congestion of the chest; shortness of breath
ahoguío (colloq) congestion of the chest; shortness of breath; asthma (colloq, Mex.)
aislamiento por cuarentena isolation
aislar to isolate
al ras level
alambre de contacto (m) (electrical) lead wire
alambrito loop
albúmina albumin
alcanfor (m) camphor
alcohol (m) alcohol
   alcoholismo alcoholism
   alcohol para fricciones rubbing alcohol
alergia allergy; hay fever
alfombra (P.R., Cuba) rash
alfombría (Chicano) German measles; rubella
alfombrilla (Chicano) German measles
algodón (m) cotton
   algodón absorbente absorbent cotton
   algodón estéril sterile cotton
algodoncillo (colloq) thrush; moniliasis
aliento breath
alimentación (f) feeding
   alimentación suplementaria supplementary feeding
alimentar to feed

alivianado (adj) "high" on narcotics; "turned on"
aliviar to cure; to make better; to relieve
  aliviarse to get well; (Chicano) to deliver a child
alivio relief
almidón (m) starch
almidonado (adj) starchy
almohadilla pillow
  almohadilla caliente eléctrica electric heating pad
  almohadilla higiénica sanitary napkin
  almohadilla neumática en forma de anillo inflatable rubber "doughnut"
  almohadita nursing pad
almorrana pile; hemorrhoid
almorzar(ue) to have lunch
alucinación (f) hallucination
alucinógeno hallucinogenic drug; hallucinogen
alumbrado (adj, slang, Chicano) drunk
alumbramiento childbirth; confinement
alumbrar to give birth
alvéolo tooth socket; alveolus
ama de cría baby nurse
amalgama amalgam
amamantamiento nursing
amamantar to nurse (breastfeed)
amarihuanarse to take marijuana
amarilla (adj) yellow
amarrar to bind
ambliopia amblyopia
ameba amoeba
amenaza de aborto threatened abortion
amenorrea amenorrhea
amiba (slang) amoeba; PCP
amígdalas tonsils
amigdalitis (f) tonsilitis
  amigdalitis supurativa quinsy (sore throat)
amiláceo (adj) starchy
aminoácidos amino acids
amoníaco ammonia
amoratado (adj) black and blue
ampicilina ampicillin
ampliación (f) enlargement
ampolla blister; vial
ampolleta ampoule
analgésico (m, adj) analgesic
análisis (m) test
  análisis de esputos sputum test
  análisis de laboratorio laboratory test
  análisis de orina urinalysis
  análisis de sangre blood chemistry (analysis of blood)
analizador del oxígeno de la sangre (m) blood oxygen analyzer
anca buttock
andador (m) walker

andar to walk
  andar + adj to be high (see **high** Appendix A)
  andar andando to be up and about after an illness
  andar bombo to be drunk; to get drunk
  andar carga to be carrying narcotic drugs
  andar cargado(-a) to be carrying narcotic drugs
  andar crudo(-a) to have a hangover·
  andar el cuerpo to defecate
  andar eléctrico(-a) to be drunk; to get drunk
  andar en la línea to be drunk; to get drunk
  andar loco(-a) to be drunk; to get drunk
anemia anemia
  anemia aplástica aplastic anemia
  anemia drepanocítica sickle cell anemia
  anemia perniciosa pernicious anemia
anestesia anesthesia
  anestesia caudal caudal anesthesia
  anestesia de bloque block anesthesia
  anestesia en silla de montar saddle block anesthesia
  anestesia epidural epidural anesthesia
  anestesia espinal spinal anesthesia
  anestesia local local anesthesia
  anestesia por inhalación inhalation anesthesia
  anestesia raquídea spinal anesthesia
  anestesia regional regional anesthesia
  anestesia total general anesthesia
anestético (m, adj) anesthetic
aneurisma (m) aneurysm
anfetamina amphetamine
angina angina; (Mex., Ven.) tonsil
  angina de pecho angina pectoris
angustia anguish
anillo IUD ring
ano anus
anomalía congénita congenital anomaly
ansias matutinas morning sickness
ansiedad (f) anxiety
antebrazo forearm
anteojos (m, pl, general term) eyeglasses; spectacles
  anteojos oscuros sunglasses
anterobious (m) piperazine

antiácido (m, adj) antacid
antibiótico (m, adj) antibiotic
  antibiótico de alcance amplio broad-spectrum antibiotic
  antibiótico de espectro amplio broad-spectrum antibiotic
anticoagulante (m, adj) anticoagulant
anticolinérgico (m, adj) anticholinergic
anticonceptivo (m, adj) contraceptive
anticuerpo antibody
antídoto antidote
  antídoto universal universal antidote
antiemético (m, adj) antiemetic
antiespasmódico (m, adj) antispasmodic
antígeno antigen
antihelmíntico (m, adj) vermifuge
antihemorrágico (adj) antihemorrhagic
antihistamínico (m, adj) antihistamine
antipalúdico (m, adj) antimalarial
antipirético (m, adj) antipyretic
antiséptico (m, adj) antiseptic
antitetánico (adj) antitetanic; anti-tetanus
antitoxina antitoxin
añadir to add
apaciguador (m) tranquilizer
aparatito (Chicano) IUD
aparato apparatus; system; (Chicano) buttock
  aparato auditivo hearing aid
  aparato cardiovascular cardiovascular system
  aparato circulatorio circulatory system
  aparato digestivo digestive system
  aparato endócrino endocrine system
  aparato gastrointestinal gastrointestinal system
  aparato genitourinario genitourinary system
  aparato intrauterino intrauterine device
  aparato para la sordera hearing aid
  aparato reproductivo reproductive system
  aparato respiratorio respiratory system
apartar to isolate
apenarse (Chicano) to worry
apéndice (m) appendix
apendicitis (f) appendicitis
apendix (f) appendix
apestoso (adj) foul-smelling
apetito appetite
aplicación (f) application

aplicación de hielo empaquetado
ice pack
apoplejía apoplexy; stroke
apósito dressing
apostemado (adj) abscessed
apoyo support
apoyo para la cabeza headrest
apretar (ie) to squeeze
arca (Mex.) armpit
ardor de estómago (m) heartburn
armazón (m) skeleton
armazón de calentamiento (f)
warming crib
arrebato fit
arrepentirse (ie) to repent
aritmia irregular heartbeat;
arrhythmia
arritmia cardíaca cardiac
arrhythmia
arrojadera (vulgar) vomit;
vomiting
arrojar (colloq) to vomit
arruga wrinkle
arsénico arsenic
arteria dental dental artery
arteriosclerosis (f) arteriosclerosis
articulación (f) articulation; joint
articulación envarada stiff or
"frozen" joint
articulación trabada stiff or
"frozen" joint
artificial (adj) artificial
artritis (f) arthritis
artritis reumatoidea rheumatic
arthritis
asa loop
ascáride (f) ascaris; roundworm
ascaris (f) ascaris; roundworm
aseo cleanliness
asfixia suffocation, choking
asientos (slang) diarrhea
asintomático (adj) asymptomatic
asma asthma
asma bronquial bronchial
asthma
áspero (adj) rough
aspirina aspirin
aspirina para niños children's
aspirin
asqueo morning nausea
astigmatismo astigmatism
astilla (en el ojo) splinter (in the
eye)
astringente (m, adj) astringent
asumir to assume
asustarse to get frightened
ataque (m) attack; convulsion;
onset; seizure
ataque (de epilepsia) epilepsy
ataque al corazón heart attack
ataque asmático asthmatic
attack; seizure
ataque cardíaco heart attack
ataque del corazón heart attack
ataque epiléptico epileptic
attack

ataque fulminante stroke
ataque vesicular gallbladder
attack
atar to bind
atar con alambre to wire
atarantado (adj) dizzy
atorarse to choke
atragantarse to choke
atrasado (adj) overdue; relapse
atrasar to cause to suffer a relapse
atrasarse to have a relapse
atravesar (ie) to pass over
atrofia atrophy
atropina atropine
audífono hearing aid
auditivo (adj) auditory
aurícola external ear
autorización (f) authorization
autorizar to authorize
avariosis (f, Sp. Am.) syphilis
aventado (adj) bloated
axila armpit
ayuda enema
ayunas, en fasting
ayuno fasting
azúcar (m) sugar
azúcar de uva dextrose
azúcar sanguíneo blood sugar
azucarado (adj) sugary
azufre (m) sulphur; (slang) heroin
azufre total total sulphur
bacteria bacterium
bacteriemia septicemia
báculo cane
bachica cigarette butt (esp.
marijuana)
bajar el nivel del colesterol to
lower the cholesterol count
bala bullet
bálano glans (penis)
balazo bullet wound
balbucencia stuttering
balone (m, Chicano) penis
bálsamo balsam
banco de sangre blood bank
bañar to bathe
bañar(se) to bathe; to take a bath
bañera tub
baño bath; restroom; toilet
baño de almidón starch bath
baño de asiento sitz bath
baño de azufre sulphur bath
baño de brea tar bath
baño de esponja sponge bath
baño de harina de avena oatmeal
bath
baño de mostaza mustard bath
baño de permanganato de
potasio potassium
permanganate bath
baño de regadera (Chicano)
shower bath
baño de salvado bran bath
baño de sodio sodium bath
baño de toalla (Chicano) sponge
bath

baño emoliente emollient bath
baño salino saline bath
barba beard; chin
barbilla chin
barbiturato barbiturate;
barbiturate pill
barbitúrico barbiturate pill
barriga belly
barrillo pimple
barro pimple, blackhead
basca nausea
base del cráneo (f) base of the
cranium
basófilos basophiles
bastón (m) cane
bastón de paseo walking cane
bastoncillo rod (of the retina)
bata gown, robe
bazo spleen
bebé baby; infant
beber mucho ... to drink plenty
of ...
bellandona belladonna
bencedrina benzedrine
benjuí (m) benzoin
benzoína benzoin
béquico cough suppressant
bermejizo (adj) reddish (hair)
berrinche (m, colloq) tantrum
biberón (m) baby bottle; nursing
bottle
bicarbonato de soda bicarbonate
of soda
bíceps (m) biceps
bicúspide (m, adj) bicuspid
bienestar (m) well-being
bigote (m) moustache
bilharzia schistosoma
bilirrubina bilirubin
bilis (f) bile; irritability (not
related to bile)
biometría hemática blood count
bisojo (adj) cross-eyed;
squint-eyed
bisturí (m) scalpel
bizco (m, adj, C.A.) cross-eyed;
squint-eyed; strabismus
bizquera cross-eyes; strabismus
blandito (adj) watery
blando (adj) soft (pliant)
blanqueador de ropa (m) sodium
hypochlorite (bleach)
blanqueo bleach
blanquillo (slang, Chicano)
testicle
blefaritis (f) blepharitis
blenorragia gonorrhea
blindaje contra la radiación (m)
radiation shield
bloquear to block
bobas chicken pox
bobita (Chicano) gnat
boca mouth
boca del estómago pit of
stomach
bocado de Adán Adam's apple

bocal (m) mouthpiece
bocio goiter
bofe (m, Chicano, Sp. Am.) lung
bola lump
bolas (Chicano) mumps; knot (type of tissue swelling); (slang Chicano) testicle
bolita (slang) clitoris
bolo (adj, C.A.) drunk
bolsa bag
  bolsa de agua caliente hot water bag
  bolsa de caucho para hielo ice bag; ice pack
  bolsa de hielo ice bag; ice pack
  bolsa de lágrimas tear sac
  bolsa de las aguas bag of waters
  bolsa de los testículos scrotum
  bolsa membranosa bag of waters
  bolsa para enema enema bag
bomba pump
  bomba de ordeñar breast pump
  bomba estomacal stomach pump
bombido (slang) amphetamines
bombita (slang) amphetamine + heroin + barbiturate IV amphetamine
bombo (Ur.) buttock
boquera fungus; moniliasis
boquilla cheilosis (sore at corner of mouth); mouthpiece
boquineta (m, Chicano) cleft palate; harelip
bornear to twist; to bend
borujo lump
borujón (m) large lump
borrachera drunkenness
borracho (adj) drunk
bote (m, slang, Chicano) baby bottle
botella bottle; baby bottle; vial
botica drug store; pharmacy
botiquín (m) kit; medicine cabinet; medicine chest
  botiquín de emergencia emergency kit
  botiquín de primeros auxilios first-aid kit
bóveda ósea del paladar hard palate
braga diaper
braguero brace; truss
brazo arm
brea de hulla coal tar
bromuro bromide
bronceado (adj) suntanned
bronquios bronchia
bronquitis (f) bronchitis
brucelosis (f) Malta fever
búa bubo
buba pimple
bubón (m) pustule
bubones lymphogranuloma venereum
buche (m, Mex.) mumps; (slang)

goiter; (vulgar, Chicano) buttock
buena salud (f) fitness (good health)
bulto lump
bulla blister
bursitis (f) bursitis
buscatoques (m, f, sg, slang) addict in search of a fix
búster (m) booster shot
busto breast
butón (m) pimple
caballete (m) bridge (of the nose)
caballo heroin
caballón (adj) "high" on narcotics; "turned on"
cabecita de vena (Chicano) angiomata (red dots on skin)
cabello hair
cabestrillo sling
cabeza (slang) glans (penis); head
cabezal (m) compress
caca (slang) feces; stool
ca-ca (slang) heroin
cacahuate (m) barbiturate pill
cácara (Chicano) acne
cacaraña (Mex., Guat.) pock
cachete (m) cheek
cachucha drug supply; heroin capsule
cada every
cadáver (m) corpse
cadera hip
caduquez (f) senility
caer to fall
  caer con algo to catch; to come down with a disease
caerse to fall down
café (m, slang) LSD
  café caliente hot coffee
cafeína caffeine
cagada (vulgar) feces; stool; heroin
cagadera (vulgar, Chicano) diarrhea
caída de la matriz prolapse; uterus prolapse
caída de la mollera fallen fontanel
caja torácica thoracic cavity
cajetuda (Chicano) headache
cala suppository
calambres (m) cramps; menstrual cramps; muscular cramps
  calambres de los cortadores de caña cane-cutter's cramps
  calambres térmicos heat cramps
calamina calamine
calavera (Chicano) skull
calcañar (m) heel
calceta elástica elastic stocking
calcio calcium
cálculo stone
  cálculo biliar gallstone
  cálculo en el riñón kidney stone

  cálculo en la vejiga gallstone
  cálculo renal kidney stone
calentador (m) warmer
calentura fever; temperature
calmante (m) pain killer; sedative; tranquilizer
  calmante para la tos cough suppressant
calmar(se) to calm down
calmarse to relax
calofrío (Chicano) hot flashes
calor (m) heat
  calores hot flashes
calostro colostrum
calote (m) cast
calvicie (f) baldness
calvo (adj) bald
calzar to fill
callarse to be quiet
callo callus; corn
calloso (adj) calloused
cama bed
cámara chamber; (slang) diarrhea; feces; stool
  cámara anterior del cerebro anterior chamber of cerebrum
  cámara posterior del cerebro posterior chamber of cerebrum
cambiar to trade
  canbiar el pañal to diaper
  cambiar(se) to change (oneself)
  cambio de vida change of life; menopause
camilla calentadora de niño warming crib
camilla de niño crib
caminar to walk
camisón (m) gown
campanilla (colloq) uvula
canal (m) canal; duct
  canal de la oreja (colloq) external ear canal
  canal del parto birth canal
  canal radicular root canal
  canal urinario urethra
canas (verdes) (premature) gray hair
cáncer (m) cancer
  cáncer en la sangre leukemia
canceroso (adj) cancerous
candidiasis (f) fungus, moniliasis
cangrena gangrene
canilla calf of the leg; shin
canino canine tooth; eyetooth
cansado (adj) tired
cansar to tire
  cansarse to get tired
cano urinario urethra
capa (slang) heroin capsule
capear to put heroin in capsules
capiar to put heroin in capsules
capilar (m) capillary
capón (adj, Chicano) infertile

cápsula capsule
  cápsula para ablandar evacuaciones stool softener
cara face
caracol (m, colloq) cochlea
carácter recesivo (m) recessive character
carátula (slang, Chicano) face
carbohidrato carbohydrate
carbón activado (m) activated charcoal
carbonato de sodio sodium carbonate
carcinoma (m) carcinoma
cardenal (m) weal (large welt)
cardialgia heartburn
cardiopatías heart disease
cardioscopio cardioscope
carencia deficiency
carga (slang) load of narcotics
cargar la calentura (Chicano) to increase; persist (fever)
carie (f) cavity; caries; tooth decay
carne (f) flesh
carnosidad (f, colloq) pterygium
carraspera (colloq) hoarseness
carrillo cheek
cartílago cartilage
casa de maternidad maternity hospital
casarse (con) to get married; to marry
casco scalp
caso case
  caso límite borderline case
  caso urgente emergency
caspa dandruff
casqueta (Chicano) masturbation
castrar to sterilize
cataplasma cataplasm; poultice
  cataplasma de mostaza mustard plaster
catarata cataract
catarro cold
  catarro constipado (Chicano) hay fever
catártico (m, adj) purgative
catéter (m) catheter
cateterizar to catheterize
caucásico (adj) caucasian
cauterización (f) cauterization
cavidad (f) cavity
  cavidad dental caries
ceceo lisp; stutter
ceder to give up (a claim)
cegato (adj, colloq) shortsighted
ceguedad (f) blindness
ceguera blindness
  ceguera del río river blindness
  ceguera nocturna night blindness
  ceguera para los colores color blindness
ceja eye, eyebrow
celíaca celiac disease

célula cell
  célula ciliada ciliated cell
  células falciformes sickle cell
cemento cementum
cepillarse los dientes to brush one's teeth
cepillo de dientes toothbrush
cera de los oídos earwax
cerebro cerebrum
cerilla earwax
cerrar (ie) to close
certificado de nacimiento birth certificate
certificar to certify
cerumen (m) earwax
cerviz (f) cervix
ciática sciatica
ciático (adj) sciatic
cicatriz (f) scar
cicatrizado (adj) scarred
ciego (adj) blind
cielo de la boca roof of the mouth
cinta band
  cinta adhesiva adhesive tape
cintura binder; waist
circulación (f) circulation
  circulación sanguínea blood circulation
circuncidar to circumcise
circuncisión (f) circumcision
ciricua (colloq) vitiligo
cirrosis del hígado (f) cirrhosis of the liver
  cirrosis hepática cirrhosis of the liver
cirugía surgery
cisticerco cysticercus; bladderworm
cistitis (f) cystitis
cistoscopio cystoscope
cisura fissure; incision
cita appointment
clamidia chlamidia
clara de huevo egg white
clavar to stick
clavícula collar bone; clavicle
clavija de contacto electrical plug
clínica clinic; private hospital; doctor's office
  clínica dental (f) dental office
  clínica de reposo (f) nursing home
clítoris (m) clitoris
cloasma (m) chloasma (facial discoloration); mask of pregnancy
cloranfenicol (m) chloramphenicol
cloro bleach; chlorine
clorofila chlorophyll
cloromicetín (m) chloromycetin
cloromicetina chloromycetin
cloroquina chloroquinine
cloruro chlorine
  cloruro mercúrico bichloride of

mercury
coagulante (m, adj) coagulant
coágulo sanguíneo blood clot
cocaína cocaine
cóccix (m, Chicano) coccyx
cóclea cochlea
cócono person high on drugs
codeína codeine
codo elbow
coercitivo restraining device
coger (cojer) (vulgar, Arg., P.R., Mex.) to have sexual relations
coil (m, Chicano) coil
coito coitus
cojear to limp; to hobble
cojera lameness
cojincillo pad
cojo (adj) crippled; lame
cola (slang) glue
colapso collapse; nervous breakdown
  colapso físico physical collapse
colchón (m) mattress
colecistograma (m) cholecystogram
cólera (f) anger; (m) cholera
colesterol (m) cholesterol
  colesterol elevado high cholesterol
colgar (ue) to hang
  colgar las piernas to dangle one's legs
cólico (adj) colic
colita (slang) coccyx
colitis (f) colitis
  colitis ulcerosa diverticulitis
colmillo canine tooth; eyetooth
colocar to place
colon (m) colon
color (m) color
coloración (f) stain, staining
colorada barbiturate pill; seconal capsule; (slang, Chicano) blood
colorante (m) stain, staining
colostomía colostomy
columna vertebral backbone; spinal column
coma (m) coma
comadrona midwife (untrained)
comenzar (ie) to begin
comezón (f) itch
comienzo onset
comisura suture
cómodo (adj) comfortable
compañones (m, slang) testicle
competir (i) to compete
complicación (f) complication
componente (m) constituent; component
  componente de sangre blood component
  componente sanguíneo blood component
componer una fractura to set a fracture

comprender to understand
compresa compress
  compresa fría cold pack
comprimido tablet
común (m) toilet; (Mex.) buttock
concebir (i) to conceive
concepción (f) conception
concha (vulgar, Arg., Chile, Urug.) vagina; (colloq) external ear
concusión (f) concussion
condiloma (m) condyloma
condón (m) rubber; condom
conducto duct; canal
  conducto auditivo external ear canal
  conducto deferente vas deferens
  conducto lacrimal tear duct
  conducto lagrimal tear duct
  conducto semicircular semicircular canal
conejo (slang, Chicano) biceps
conexionar to connect
confesar (ie) to confess
congelación (f) frostbite
congénito (adj) congenital
congestión (f) congestion
  congestión nasal sinus congestion
congoja anguish
conjuntiva conjunctiva
conjuntivitis (f) conjunctivitis
  conjuntivitis catarral aguda pinkeye
conmoción nerviosa (f) shock
cono cone
conocer to have sexual relations
conseguir (i) to obtain; to get
consentir (ie) to consent
constipación (f) constipation
constipado (m, adj) "stopped-up"; head cold
constricción (f) stricture
consunción (f) phthisis
contacto contact
contagiar to communicate a disease; to infect
contagioso (adj) contagious
contaminación (f) contamination
contar (ue) to count
continuar to continue
contracción muscular (f) spasm
contracciones de la matriz (f) contractions
contraceptivo (m, adj) contraceptive
contraer una enfermedad to catch a disease
contraveneno antitoxin
control de la natalidad (m) birth control
controlar to control
contusión (f) bruise; contusion
convalecencia convalescence
convaleciente convalescent
convertir (ie) to convert

convertir(se) (ie) to turn into
convulsión (f) convulsion; epileptic attack; fit; seizure
copa ocular eyecup
coqueluche (f) whooping cough; pertussis
coquetas (Mex.) mumps
coraje (m) anger
coramina coramine
corazón (m) heart
cordón (m) cord
  cordón del ombligo umbilical cord
  cordón dental dental floss
  cordón umbilical umbilical cord
corea chorea
corioides (f) chorioid
corona crown; crown of tooth
  corona acrílica acrylic jacket crown
  corona de porcelana porcelain jacket crown
coronamiento crowning
coronar to crown
coronario (adj) coronary
corredera (Chicano) diarrhea
correr el cuerpo to defecate
corriente (f, adj) electrical current
cortada incision; laceration; (Sp. Am.) cut
cortadura cut
cortarse to cut (oneself)
corte de las partes (m) episiotomy
corte por congelación frozen section
corteza cerebral cerebral cortex
corticoesteroide (m) corticosteroid
cortisona cortisone
corto de oído hard of hearing
corto de vista nearsighted
corva back of the knee
costado flank; side
costar (ue) to cost
costilla rib
  costilla flotante false (floating) rib
  costilla verdadera true rib
costra scab
costumbre (f) menstruation
cotidiano (adj) daily
coxis (m) coccyx
coyuntura articulation; joint
cráneo skull; cranium
creatina creatine
crema ointment
  crema vaginal vaginal cream
creta pulverizada en agua ground chalk in water
cretinismo cretinism
crianza nursing; lactation period
criar a los pechos to nurse (a baby)
criar con pecho (Chicano) to breastfeed
criatura baby; infant
cristal(es) (m) crystal(s)

cristalino crystalline; lens of eye
crónico (adj) chronic
cruento (adj) bloody
crup (f) croup
cuadril (m, Mex., Chicano) hip
cuadrúpleto quadruplet
cuajar to clot
cuajarón (m) blood clot
  cuajarón de sangre blood clot
cuarentena forty days following parturition; confinement
cuarteado (adj) chapped
cuarto quart; room
  cuarto de baño restroom
  cuarto de los niños nursery
cuate (Mex.) twin
cuates (m, pl, slang, Chicano) testicle
cuatrillizo quadruplet
cúbito ulna
cucharada spoonful; tablespoon
cucharadita teaspoon
  cucharadita llena al ras level teaspoonful
cuchillada gash
cuchillo knife
cuello neck; neck of tooth
  cuello de la matriz cervix
  cuello del útero cervix
cuenca (Chicano) collar bone; clavicle
  cuenca de los ojos eye socket
cuentagotas (m) eye dropper; medicine dropper
cuerda vocal vocal cord
cuerín (m, Chicano) scab
cuero skin
  cuero cabelludo scalp
cuerpo body
cuertito (Chicano) scab
cueva (slang, vulgar, Chicano) vagina
cuidado care
  cuidado cardíaco cardiac care
  cuidado intensivo intensive care
  cuidado postnatal postnatal care
  cuidado prenatal prenatal care
cuidar to take care of; to watch; to care for
culebrilla fungus; ringworm; tinea
culo (colloq, Arg.) buttock
cuna crib
cura cure; dressing; fix; (m) priest
curación (f) dressing; healing
  curación del nervio root canal work
curar to heal; (slang) to provide an addict with a fix
curarse to recover
curetaje (m) curettage
curita Band-Aid
cursera (slang) diarrhea
cutícula cuticle
  cutícula desgarrada hangnail

cutis (m)   skin (of the face)
chale (m, vulgar, Chicano)   penis
chalito (m, vulgar, Chicano)
   penis
chamorro (Chicano)   calf of the
   leg
chancro   chancre; veneral lesion
   chancro blando   soft chancre
   chancro duro   hard chancre
   chancro silfilítico   hard chancre
   chancro simple   non-infecting
   chancre
chechén (m)   poison ivy
cheuto (adj, Chile)   harelip
chi (f, vulgar)   urine
chichas (f, pl, C.R.)   breast
chiche (m, Mex., Guat.)   breast of
   a wet nurse
chichi (f, colloq, Arg.)   nipple (of
   female breast); (Guat., Mex.)
   wet nurse; (Mex.) breast
chichigua (vulgar, Sp. Am.)   wet
   nurse
chichón (m)   lump; bump on
   head; swelling on the head
chicloso (vulgar, Chicano)   anus
chicote (m, slang)   penis
chile (m, slang)   penis
chimpa (Chicano)   hair
chimuelo (adj, Chicano)   lacking
   teeth
chinaloa (slang)   opium
chinche (f)   bedbug
chingar (vulgar)   to have sexual
   relations
chino (Mex.)   fine-tooth comb
chiporra (Guat., Hond.)   tumor on
   the head
chiquito (vulgar, Chicano)   anus
chiva (slang)   heroin
cholenco (adj)   sickly
chopetear (slang)   to have sexual
   relations
choque (m)   shock
   choque alérgico (colloq)
   anaphylactic shock
   choque anafiláctico
   anaphylactic shock
choquezuela   kneecap
chorizo (vulgar)   penis
chorrillo (slang)   diarrhea
chorro (euph.)
   gonorrhea; (slang) diarrhea
chot (m, Chicano)   shot, injection
chucho (Chile, Arg.)   malarial
   fever
chupar   to suck
chupete (m)   pacifier
chupón (m)   nipple (of a baby
   nursing bottle)
DAL (f)   LSD
daltonismo   color blindness
daño   damage
   **daño sufrido por causa de la
   helada**   frostbite
dar   to give

dar a luz   to give birth; to
   deliver
dar chiche   to breastfeed
dar de alta   to discharge (from
   the hospital)
dar de mamar   to breastfeed; to
   nurse
dar el pecho   to breastfeed
dar el pecho al niño   to nurse
dar pá dentro (vulgar)   to have
   sexual relations
dar una atascada (vulgar)   to
   have sexual relations
dar una dosis excesiva   to
   overdose
darse un piquete   to inject
   oneself with drugs
darse vuelta   to turn (over)
de crianza (adj)   nursing
de maternidad (adj)   maternity
de paja (adj)   straw
débil (adj)   weak
debilidad (f)   weakness
decir   to tell; to say
dedo   finger
   dedo anular   ring finger
   dedo del corazón   middle finger
   dedo del medio   middle finger
   dedo (del pie)   toe
   dedo gordo   thumb
   dedo gordo en martillo
   hammertoe
   dedo grueso   big toe
deducir   to substract
defecto   defect
defibrilador (m)   defibrillator
deficiencia   deficiency
   deficiencia de hierro   anemia;
   iron deficiency
deforme (adj)   deformed
deformidad (f)   deformity
delantal (m)   apron
deletrear   to spell
delirio   delirium
demacración (f)   emaciation
demacrado (adj)   sickly
demencia   dementia; insanity
demostrar (ue)   to demonstrate;
   to show
dengue (m)   dengue
dentadura   dentition
   dentadura (postiza)   denture
   dentadura completa   full denture
   dentadura parcial   partial
   denture
dentición (f)   teething
dentífrico (m, adj)   dentifrice
dentina   dentine
dependencia farmacológica   drug
   addiction
depilatorio (m, adj)   depilatory
deposiciones (f)   feces; stool
depósito de sangre   blood stock
depresión (f)   depression
depresor de la lengua (m)   tongue
   depressor

deprimido (adj)   depressed
dermatitis (f)   dermatitis
derrame (m)   discharge (bloody)
   derrame biliar   jaundice
   derrame cerebral   stroke
desabrido (adj)   tasteless
desagüe (m)   drainage
desaldillado (Mex.)   hernia
desangramiento   bleeding to
   excess; hemorrage
desangrar   to bleed excessively; to
   bleed in excess
desaojar   to cure from the evil eye
desarreglo nervioso   nervous
   breakdown
desayunarse   to eat breakfast
descansar   to rest
descanso   relaxation; (Chile)
   toilet
descargo   release
desconcertar (ie)   to sprain
descongestionante (m, adj)
   decongestant
descubrimiento   discovery
descubrir   to detect
descuidado (adj)   careless;
   neglected
descuidar   to neglect
desecación (f)   dehydration
desecho   waste; secretion
desequilibrio   imbalance
desfallecimiento   fainting spell
desgarradura   laceration
desgarramiento   tear
desgarrar (Chicano)   to cough up
   phlegm
desgarro   tear, laceration; (Sp.
   Am.) sputum
deshidratación (f)   dehydration
deshidratar   to dehydrate
desinfectante (m, adj)   disinfectant
desmayarse   to faint
desmayo   fainting spell
desnudarse   to undress
desnutrición (f)   malnutrition
desnutrido (adj)   malnourished;
   (colloq) undernourished;
   emaciated
desodorante (m, adj)   deodorant
desorden (m)   disorder
   desorden nervioso   nervous
   disorder
despedirse (de) (i)   to say goodbye
despensa (Chicano)   medicine
   cabinet; medicine chest
despercudido (adj)   light-skinned
   (complexioned)
despertar(se) (ie)   to wake up
desprender   to release
destetar   to wean
destruido (adj)   destroyed
desvanecimiento   fainting spell
desvelarse   stay awake, to
desvestirse (i)   to get undressed
detectar   to detect
detergentes (m)   detergents

determinación del grupo sanguíneo (f) blood type
determinación del tiempo de circulación determination of circulating time
dextrosa dextrose
diabetes (f) diabetes
  diabetes insípida diabetes insipidus
  diabetes mellitus diabetes mellitus
  diabetes sacarina diabetes mellitus
diabético (m, adj) diabetic
diafragma (m) diaphragm
  diafragma anticonceptivo diaphragm (birth control device)
diagnosis (f) diagnosis
diagnosticar to diagnose
diagnóstico (m, adj) diagnosis
diagrama (m) chart
diapasón (m) turning fork
diario (adj) daily
diarrea diarrhea
diástole (f) diastole
dicipela (Chicano) erysipelas
diente (m) tooth
  diente cariado cavity
  diente de ajo (colloq) large, misshapened tooth
  diente de leche baby tooth
  diente impactado impacted tooth
  diente inferior lower tooth
  diente mamón baby tooth
  diente picado cavity
  diente podrido caries
  diente superior upper tooth
  dientes blancos white teeth
  dientes de leche (pl) deciduous teeth
  dientes manchados stained teeth
  dientes parejos even teeth
  dientes podridos tooth decay
  dientes postizos artificial (false) teeth
dieta diet
  dieta de líquidos liquid diet
difenhidramina diphenhydramine
dificultad al respirar (f) dyspnea
dificultoso (adj) labored
difteria diphtheria
digerir (ie) to digest
digestión (f) digestion
digitalina digitalin
dilatación del cuello de la matriz (f) dilation (of cervix)
dilear to deal in drugs; to traffic in drugs
diliar to deal in drugs; to traffic in drugs
discernir (ie) to discern
disco disc
  disco calcificado calcified disc
  disco desplazado slipped disc

disco intervertebral luxado slipped disc
disentería dysentery
  disentería amebiana amoebic dysentery
  disentería amibiana amoebic dysentery
  disentería bacilar bacillary dysentery
dislocación (f) sprain
dismenorrea dysmennorrhea
disminución de la tirantez (f) relaxation of tension
disolver (ue) to dissolve
dispepsia indigestion
dispositivo intrauterino intrauterine device; IUD
distribución (f) distribution
distrofia muscular progresiva muscular distrophy
DIU (m) IUD
diurético (m, adj) diuretic
diverticulitis (f) diverticulitis
divertirse (ie) to amuse oneself; have a good time
doblarse to bend over
doctor physician
doctora physician
dolencia ailment; disease; sickness
doler (ue) to hurt; to ache
dolor (m) pain; ache; sore
  dolor agudo sharp pain
  dolor al orinar dysuria
  dolor cólico colicky pain
  dolor constante constant pain
  dolor continuo steady pain
  dolor de cabeza headache
  dolor de crecimiento growing pain
  dolor de dientes toothache
  dolor de estómago stomachache
  dolor de la vesícula gallbladder attack
  dolor de miembro fantasma phantom limb pain
  dolor de muelas toothache
  dolor de oído earache
  dolor de ojos sore eyes
  dolor de parto labor pain
  dolor errante wandering pain
  dolor fulgurante shooting pain
  dolor leve mild pain
  dolor moderado moderate pain
  dolor opresivo pressure-like pain
  dolor penetrante boring pain
  dolor quemante burning pain
  dolor radicular root pain
  dolor referido referred pain
  dolor severo severe pain
  dolor sordo dull pain
  dolor torácico thoracic pain
  dolores de hambre hunger pain
  dolores de parto contractions; labor pains

  dolores del período menstrual cramps
  dolores expulsivos expulsive pain
  dolores falsos false pain
  dolores intermenstruales intermenstrual pain
  dolores premonitorios premonitory pain
doloroso (adj) painful
dompear (Chicano) to vomit
donador de sangre blood donor
donante de sangre blood donor
  donante universal universal donor
doña juanita (slang) marijuana
dormir (ue) to sleep
  dormir con alguien (ue) to have sexual relations
dormirse (ue) to fall asleep; to doze off
dorso back
  dorso de la mano back of the hand
dosificación (f) dosage
dosis (f) dosage; dose; potion
  dosis de refuerzo booster dose
  dosis excesiva overdose
dracma (m) dram
drenaje (m, surgical) drainage; (Chicano) catheter
droga drug; medicine
  droga alucinadora hallucinogenic drug; hallucinogen
  droga antihistamínica antihistamine
  droga estupefaciente narcotic
  droga LSD LSD
  droga psicodélica psychedelic
  drogma somnífera narcotic
drogadicto addict; drug addict
droguería (Sp. Am.) drugstore
ducha shower; bath; douche
  ducha interna douche
  ducha vaginal douche
ducharse to shower; to take a shower
dulces (m, pl) sweets
dulcificante (m) sweetener
duodeno duodenum
duración del embarazo (f) length of pregnancy (LOP)
duradero (adj) chronic
dureza lump
duro de oído hard of hearing
eccema eczema
eclampsia eclampsia
eclipsado (adj) deformed
echar al bote to bewitch
echar un palito (Chicano) to have sexual relations
edema (m) edema; tumefaction
efedrina ephedrine
ejercer presión sobre to exert pressure on

ejercicios físicos para adelgazar reducing exercises
ejercicios físicos para reducir peso reducing exercises
electricidad (f) electricity
electrocardiograma (m) electrocardiogram
electroencefalograma (m) electroencephalogram
elegir (i) to choose
elevación (f) ridge
embarazada (adj) pregnant
embarazo pregnancy
  embarazo ectópico ectopic pregnancy
  embarazo en los tubos tubal pregnancy
  embarazo falso false pregnancy
  embarazo fuera de la matriz ectopic pregnancy
  embarazo histérico hysteria pregnancy
  embarazo incompleto incomplete pregnancy
  embarazo tubárico tubal pregnancy
embolia embolism
embolia cerebral stroke
embolio (Chicano) stroke
embolismo embolism
émbolo piston; plunger of syringe
embriaguez (f) intoxication
embrión (m) embryo
embudo funnel
emergencia emergency
emético (m, adj) emetic; vomitive
emoliente (m, adj) emollient
empacamiento en sábana fría (mojada) wrapping in a cold (wet) sheet
empaque (m, Chicano) filling, temporary
empastadura filling
empastar to fill
empaste (m) filling
  empaste provisional temporary filling
empedido (adj) crippled
empeine (m) instep; groin; ringworm; tinea
empeorar to make worse
empezar (ie) to begin
emplaste (m) dressing
emplasto poultice
  emplasto adhesivo adhesive plaster
  emplasto frío cold pack
  emplasto para callos corn plaster
emplomadura (Arg.) to fill (teeth)
empolvado (adj) powdery
empujar to push
emulsión (f) emulsion
en diálisis dialysis

en polvo (adj) powdered
enano dwarf
encajarse to go down in birth canal
encefalitis (f) encephalitis
encender (ie) to light; to turn on
enchufe (m) electrical plug; electrical socket
encías gums
encinta (adj) pregnant
encoger las rodillas to pull up (one's) knees
enconarse to fester
encono (Chile) inflammation
encontrar (ue) to find
encuerarse (Chicano) to undress
enderezar los dientes to straighten the teeth
endoscopio endoscope
enema enema
  enema de bario barium enema
  enema de limpieza cleansing enema
  enema de retención retention enema
  enema jabonosa soapsuds, enema
  enema opaca barium enema
energía energy
enfadarse to get angry
enferma (euph.) menstruation
enfermarse to get sick; (Chicano) to be in labor
enfermedad (f) disease; illness; sickness
  enfermedad aguda acute illness
  enfermedad cardíaca heart disease
  enfermedad contagiosa contagious illness (disease)
  enfermedad crónica chronic illness
  enfermedad de andancia (Chicano) disease that is "going around"
  enfermedad de Chagas Chagas's disease
  enfermedad de Ménière Ménière's disease
  enfermedad de notificación notifiable disease
  enfermedad de Parkinson shaking palsy; Parkinson's disease
  enfermedad del corazón heart disease
  enfermedad del sueño sleeping sickness
  enfermedad endañada (Chicano) disease due to act of witchcraft
  enfermedad grave serious illness
  enfermedad leve minor illness
  enfermedad matutina morning sickness; morning nausea
  enfermedad mental mental illness

  enfermedad obligatoria reportable disease
  enfermedad orgánica organic illness (disease)
  enfermedad tra(n)smible contagious illness (disease)
  enfermedad tropical tropical illness (disease)
  enfermedad venérea venereal disease (VD)
  enfermedades pasadas sexualmente sexually transmitted diseases
enfermera nurse
enfermería infirmary; patients of a hospital
enfermizo (adj) feeble; sickly
enfermo (adj) ill; sick
enfisema (m) emphysema
enflaquecimiento emaciation
engordar to gain weight
engrifar to administer marijuana to someone
engrifarse to take marijuana
enjuagar to rinse
enjuagar(se) to rinse (out)
enjuagatorio mouthwash
enmarihuanar to administer marijuana to someone
enmarihuanarse to take marijuana
enojarse to get angry
enrojecido (adj) flushed
ensanchamiento enlargement
enseñar los dientes (colloq) to show one's teeth
ensordecimiento deafness
entablazón (f, Chicano) constipation; stomach obstruction
entablillado (adj) in a splint
entender (ie) to understand
entierro funeral
entrañas bowels
entrepiernas (pl) crotch
entuertos postpartum pains; cramps
entumecido (adj) numb
envenenamiento poisoning
  envenenamiento de la sangre blood poisoning
  envenenamiento del plomo lead poisoning
  envenenamiento plúmbico lead poisoning
  envenenamiento por comestibles food poisoning
envenenar(se) to poison (oneself)
enyesar to put in a plaster cast
enzima enzyme
eosinófilos eosinophiles
epidemia epidemic
epidémico (adj) epidemic
epidermis (f) epidermis
epidídimo epididymis
epilepsia epilepsy

episiotomía episiotomy
epistaxis (f) nosebleeding
equipo de urgencia first-aid kit
erisipela erysipelas
eritema solar (m) sunburn
eritrocitos erythrocytes (red blood cells)
eritromicina erythromycin
eritrosedimentación (f) sedimentation; erythrosedimentation
eructar to belch; to burp
eructo burp
erupción (f) rash
   erupción cutánea impetigo
   erupción debida al calor prickly heat
   erupción vesicular vesicular eruption
escaldadura scald
   escaldadura (en los bebés) diaper rash
escalofrío chill
escalpelo scalpel
escama scale
escápula shoulder blade; scapula
escarrar to cough up phlegm
escayola calcium sulfate
esclerosis en placa (f) multiple sclerosis
   esclerosis múltiple multiple sclerosis
esclerótica sclera
escobillón (m) cotton swab
esconderse to hide
escorbuto scurvy
escotoma scotoma; spots before the eyes
escozor (m) itching
escritura en espejo mirror writing
escroto scrotum
escuchar to listen (to)
escudo shield (IUD)
   escudo ocular eye shield
   escudo para el pezón nipple shield
escupir en la taza to spit in the bowl
escurrimiento draining; dripping
   escurrimiento de la nariz rhinitis; runny nose
esencia de trementina turpentine
esfínter (m) sphincter
esguince (f) sprain
esmalte (m) enamel
esmegma (m) smegma
esófago esophagus
espalda back
espaldilla shoulder blade; scapula
esparadrapo adhesive tape
espasmo spasm
espasmódico (adj) spasmodic; spastic

espástico (adj) spastic
espécimen (m) specimen
espéculo speculum
espejo vaginal speculum
espejuelos (pl) eyeglasses; (Cuba) spectacles
esperar to wait (for)
esperma semen
espermaticida vaginal (m) vaginal spermaticide
espermatozoide (m) sperm
espesar to thicken
espina dorsal spinal column
espinilla blackhead; shin
   espinillas acne
espiral (m) spiral (IUD)
   espiral intrauterino intrauterine loop
esporozoarios sporozoa
espulgar to delouse
espuma foam
   espuma vaginal vaginal foam
esputo saliva; sputum
esqueleto skeleton
esquinancia quinsy (sore throat)
esquirla splinter (in the eye)
esquistosoma schistosoma
esquizofrenia schizophrenia
esquizofrénico (adj) schizophrenic
estado interesante (euph.) pregnancy
estancamiento engorgement
estar to be
   estar a dieta to be on a diet
   estar con alguien to have sexual relations
   estar coronando to crown
   estar de parto to be in labor
   estar indispuesta to menstruate
   estar mala to menstruate
      estar mala de la garra to menstruate
      estar mala de la luna to menstruate
   estar mediagua to be (to get) drunk
estenosis (f) stricture
estéril (adj) infertile; sterile
esterilidad (f) sterility
   esterilidad permanente permanent sterility
esterilización (f) sterilization
esterilizado (adj) sterilized
esterilizador (m) sterilizer
esterilizar to sterilize
   esterilizar las botellas to sterilize the bottles
esternón (m) breastbone
estertor (m) rale
   estertor agónico death rattle
estetoscopio stethoscope
   estetoscopio fetal fetoscope
estilete (m) probe; stylet
estimulante (m) stimulant
estómago stomach
   estómago sucio (Chicano)

indigestion
estornudar to sneeze
estrabismo strabismus
estrechez (f) stricture
estreñido (adj) constipated
estreñimiento constipation
estreptococia strep throat
estreptomicina streptomycin
estrías stretch marks (strias)
estribo stirrup; stapes
estricnina strychnine
estrictura stricture
estroc (m, Chicano) stroke
estrógeno estrogen
estuche (m) kit
estufa warming crib; incubator
estufear sniff residue of powdered narcotics
estufiar sniff residue of powdered narcotics
etiqueta label
evacuación del vientre (f) feces; stool
evacuar to defecate
examen (m) test
   examen de conejo rabbit test
   examen de la sangre blood test
examinación (f) examination
examinar to examine; to test
excesivamente gordo (adj) overweight
excesivamente grueso (adj) overweight
excesivo (adj) excessive
exceso de peso overweight
excreción (f) excretion
excremento excretion; feces; stool
excusado toilet
eximir to exempt; to release
expectoración (f) saliva
expectorante (m, adj) expectorant
expulsión (f) expulsion
extender (ie) to spread limbs
externo (adj) external
extracción (f) extraction; removal
   extracción con fórceps forceps delivery
   extracción de nalgas breech delivery
   extracción del nervio root canal work
extracto extract
   extracto de hígado liver extract
extraer to pull out
extremidad (f) limb
eyacular to ejaculate
facciones (f) features
factor RH (m) RH factor
   factor rhesus RH factor
faja band; binder; truss
   faja abdominal swathing bandage
   faja medical supporter
fajero "belly" binder

falange (f) phalanx
falo penis; phallus
falseo (Chicano) sprain
falta de peso underweight
fallecimiento death
fallo cardíaco cardiac arrest
fallo del corazón (m) heart failure
familia family
farfallota (P.R.) mumps
faringe (f) pharynx
faringitis (f) pharingitis
farmacia pharmacy; (Spain) drugstore
fatiga exhaustion; fatigue; (slang) asthma
fatigarse to get tired
fauces (f, pl) fauces
febrífugo (m, adj) antipyretic
fecundación del huevo (f) conception
fecha de caducidad expiration date
fémur (m) femur
fenilcetonuria phenylketonuria (PKU)
fenilquetonuria phenylketonuria (PKU)
fenobarbital (m) phenobarbital
férula splint
feto fetus
fetoscopio fetoscope
fibrilación auricular (f) atrial fibrillation
fibrina fibrin
fibroideo (adj) fibroid
fibroma (m) fibroma
fibrosis quística (f) cystic fibrosis
fiebre (f) fever; (colloq, Mex.) hepatitis
   fiebre amarilla yellow fever
   fiebre de Colorado Colorado tick fever
   fiebre de conejo rabbit fever
   fiebre de las cotorras parrot fever
   fiebre de las Montañas Rocosas Rocky Mountain spotted fever
   fiebre de Malta Malta fever
   fiebre de tres días German Measles; rubella
   fiebre de(l) heno hay fever
   fiebre del valle valley fever; coccidioidomycosis
   fiebre entérica enteric fever
   fiebre escarlatina scarlet fever
   fiebre ganglionar acute infectious adenitis fever
   fiebre glandular glandular fever
   fiebre intermitente intermittent fever
   fiebre manchada spotted fever
   fiebre ondulante Malta fever; undulant fever
   fiebre palúdica malarial fever
   fiebre paratífica paratyphoid fever

   fiebre paratifoidea paratyphoid fever
   fiebre por mordedura de rata rat-bite fever
   fiebre purpúrea (de las montañas) spotted fever
   fiebre reumática rheumatic fever
   fiebre rompehuesos dengue; breakbone fever
   fiebre térmica thermic fever
   fiebre tifoidea typhoid fever
   fiebre tra(n)smitida por garrapatas Colorado tick fever
   fiebre tropical yellow fever
filete (m) crown of tooth
filorazo (Chicano) knife wound
filtrar to filter
fines médicos (m) medical purposes
fingimiento simulation
físicamente (adv) physically
fístula fistula
fisura fissure
flagelados flagellates
flato flatus
flebitis (f) phlebitis
flema phlegm
flexura de la pierna back of the knee
flexura del brazo bend of the arm
flores blancas (f) white discharge
fluir to flow
flujo discharge
   flujo blanco white discharge
   flujo de sangre bleeding
   flujo de sangre por la vagina inesperada breakthrough bleeding
   flujo vaginal vaginal discharge
flúor (m) fluoride
foco de infección focus of infection
folículo follicule
fondillo (Cuba) buttock
fondo del útero fundus
fondongo (slang) buttock
fonendoscopio stethoscope
fontanela fontanel
fórceps (m) forceps (obs.)
fórmula formula
forro (vulgar, Arg.) condom; (vulgar, Arg.) rubber
fosa fossa
   fosa nasal nostril
fosfato phosphate
fósforo phosphorus
fotografía photography
fóvea central fovea centralis
fractura fracture
   fractura abierta open fracture
   fractura complicada complicated fracture
   fractura compuesta compound fracture

   fractura en tallo verde green-stick fracture
   fractura espontánea spontaneous fracture
   fractura mayor serious fracture
   fractura múltiple multiple fracture
   fractura simple simple fracture
fracturar to fracture
frajo de seda marijuana cigarette
frasco flask; jar; vial
frazada blanket
fregar to scrub (surgically)
frenillo frenum of the tongue
frente (f) forehead
fresa burr
fricción (f) rub
frigidez (f) frigidity
frío cold; (slang, Mex.) mucus
   frío de la matriz female sterility
frios (Sp. Am.) malaria
frontal (adj) frontal
frotación (f) rub
frotar to rub
   frotarse to rub
frotis de Papanicolaou (m) Pap smear
frotis sanguíneo (m) blood smear, film
fuegos en la boca (en los labios) cold sore
fuente (f, colloq) bag of waters
fuera de (prep) outside of
fuerte (adj) severe
fuerza strength
fumigación (f) fumigation
fundillo (Mex.) buttock
funeraria funeral home
fungicida (m, adj) fungicide
furúnculo boil
gafas (pl) eyeglasses; spectacles
   gafas de sol sunglasses
galillo (colloq) uvula
gallazo fix
gancho clasp
ganglio bubo; ganglion
gangrena gangrene
garganta throat
   garganta inflamada sore throat
gárgara gargle
gargarismo gargle (liquid)
garrapata chigger flea
garrotillo diphtheria; inflammation of the throat
gas (m) gas
gasa gauze
gastritis (f) gastritis
gaznate (m) trachea
gemelo twin
germen (m) germ; sperm (slang)
germicida (m, adj) germicide
gestación (f) gestation
giardia parasite—giardia
ginecólogo gynecologist
glande (m) glans (penis)

glándula gland
  glándula de la próstata
    prostate gland
  glándula lagrimal tear gland
  glándula linfática lymph gland
  glándula mamaria mammary
    gland
  glándula paratiroides para-
    thyroid gland
  glándula parótida parotid gland
  glándula pituitaria pituitary
    gland
  glándula prostática prostrate
    gland
  glándula salival salivary gland
  glándula sebácea sebaceous
    gland
  glándula sublingual sublingual
    gland
  glándula submaxilar sub-
    maxillary gland
  glándula sudorípara sweat gland
  glándula suprarrenal adrenal
    gland
  glándula tiroides thyroid gland
glaucoma (m) glaucoma
glicerina glycerine
glicógeno glycogen
globo balloon (of heroin);
  barbiturate pill
  globo del ojo eyeball
  globo ocular eyeball
glóbulos blancos leukocytes
  (white blood cells)
glóbulos rojos erythrocytes
  (red blood cells)
glucagón (m) glucagon
glucemia blood sugar
  glucemia en ayunas fasting
    blood sugar
glucosa glucose
glufo (adj) glue sniffer; "high"
  from glue sniffing
gluteo gluteal region
golosinas (pl) sweets
golpe (m) concussion
  golpe de calor heat stroke
golpearse to hit oneself
goma condom; rubber; glue
gonorrea gonorrhea
gordo fat; obese
gordura obesity
gorra (slang) heroin capsule
gorro cervical cervical cap
gota drop; gout; (slang)
  gonorrhea
  gotas para la tos cough drops
  gotas para polio oral polio
    vaccine
goteador (m) eye dropper;
  medicine dropper
goteo nasal nasal drip
gotera (para los ojos) (Sp. Am.)
  eye dropper; medicine dropper
gramo (slang) packet of heroin
granizo cataract

grano pustule; open skin wound;
  sore (wound); chancre;
  venereal lesion
  grano de la cara pimple
grasa fat
  grasa en las venas cholesterol
gratis (adj) free
grave (adj) serious
grávida (adj) pregnant
gravidez (f) gestation; pregnancy
griefo marijuana
grieta fissure
  grieta del pezón cracked
    nipple
  grietas en el paladar cleft palate
grifa marijuana
grifo marijuana user
gripa influenza; flu
gripe (f) flu; influenza
gruesa (adj, colloq) pregnant
grueso (adj) coarse; stout
grupo sanguíneo blood group
guagua (Chile, Ec., Perú, Bol., Arg.,
  Ur.) infant baby
guaguana (slang) scabies
guantes de goma (m, pl) rubber
  gloves
guayacol (m) guaiacol
güegüecho goiter
güina (Mex.) chigger flea
güine (m, vulgar) penis
gusano worm
  gusano tableado solium;
    tapeworm
gusto (slang) scabies
hacer to do; to make
  hacer agua (Chicano) to
    urinate
  hacer bajar por fuerza to bear
    down
  hacer buches (colloq) to gargle
    hacer buches de sal to gargle
  hacer caca (Chicano) to
    defecate
  hacer caquis maquis to defecate
  hacer certificación to warrant
  hacer cositas (euph., Chicano)
    to have sexual relations
  hacer daño to injure
  hacer ejercicios moderadamente
    to exercise moderately
  hacer el cuerpo to defecate
  hacer garantías to guarantee
  hacer gárgaras to gargle
  hacer (la) chi(s) (vulgar, Chicano)
    to urinate
  hacer (la) pipi (pipí) to urinate
  hacer(se) a la glu(fa) to sniff
    glue
  hacerse la casqueta (Chicano)
    to masturbate
  hacerse + noun of profession
    to become (something)
hachís (m) hash; hashish
hallazgos de laboratorio
  laboratory findings

harina flour
haschich (m) hash; hashish
heces fecales (f, pl) feces; stool
hematíes (m) erithrocytes (red
  blood cells)
hematimetría blood count
hematuria hematuria
hemisferio cerebral cerebral
  hemisphere
hemocultivo blood culture
hemofilia hemophilia
hemoglobina hemoglobin
hemorragia bleeding; hemorrhage
  hemorragia detrás de la córnea
    hyphemia
  hemorragia inesperada break-
    through bleeding
  hemorragia interna internal
    bleeding
  hemorragia nasal nosebleed
  hemorragia vascular stroke
hemorroides (f, pl) hemorrhoids;
  pile
hemostato hemostat
hepatitis (f) hepatitis
  hepatitis infecciosa infectious
    hepatitis
  hepatitis viral viral hepatitis
herbicidas (m) herbicides
herida injury; wound
  herida incisa incised wound
  herida penetrante puncture
    wound
  herida punzante punture wound
herido (adj) injured
herir (ie) to wound; to hurt
hernia hernia; rupture
  hernia del ombligo umbilical
    hernia
  hernia femoral femoral hernia
  hernia inguinal inguinal hernia
heroína heroin
herpe(s) (m, f) herpes; shingles
  herpe febril fever blister
  herpes genital herpes genitalis
  herpes labial cold sore
  herpes menstrual herpes
    menstrualis
  herpes zoster herpes zoster
hervir las botellas (ie) to boil the
  bottles
hidrocele (f) hydrocele
hidrofobia rabies
hidropesía dropsy
hidróxido de sodio sodium
  hydroxide
hiedra venenosa poison ivy
hiel (f) bile
hielo ice
hierba (slang) marijuana
hierro iron
hifemia hyphemia
hígado liver
higienista dental dental hygienist
hilo dental dental floss
himen (m) hymen

hinchado (adj) bloated; swollen
hinchar to swell
hinchazón (m, f) abscess, swelling; edema; lump
hiperlipidemia hyperlipidemia
hipermetropía farsightedness; presbyopia
hipertensión (f) hypertension
 hipertensión arterial high blood pressure
hiperventilación (f) hyperventilation
hipo hiccough; hiccup
hipoclorito de sodio sodium hypochlorite (bleach)
hipocondría hypochondria
hipocóndrico (adj) hypochondriac
hipoglicemia hypoglycemia
hipotensión (f) hypotension
 hipotensión arterial low blood pressure
hipsus (m) hiccough; hiccup
hisopillo cotton swab
hisopo de algodón cotton swab
histeria hysteria
hojas de eucalipto eucalyptus leaves
hojas de poleo pennyroyal leaves
hojas de yerbabuena mint leaves
hombro shoulder
hongo fungus
 hongos (slang) mushrooms; magic mushrooms; psilocybin
hormigueo tingling
hormón (m) hormone
hormona hormone
hueso bone
huevo ovum
 huevos (pl, slang) testicle
hule (m, slang) condom; "rubber" (birth control)
húmedo (adj) moist
húmero humerus
humo smoke
humor acuoso aqueous humor
humor vítreo vitreous humor
ictericia jaundice
ictiol (m) ichthyol
íleum (m) ileum
impacción (f) impaction
impedimento handicap; obstruction
impedir (i) to prevent
impericia malpractice
impétigo impetigo
impotencia impotence
impresión (f) impression
incapacidad (f) disability
incisión (f) incision
incisivos front teeth; incisors
incomodidad (f) discomfort
incómodo (adj) bothersome
incompatible (adj) incompatible
inconsciencia unconsciousness
inconsciente (adj) unconscious
incordio bubo

incrustación (f) inlay
incubadora warming crib
indección (f, Chicano) injection
índice (m) index finger
indigestión (f) indigestion
indolente (adj) lazy (indolent)
infante (m, f) infant
infarto heart attack; infarct
 infarto miocardíaco (miocardiaco) myocardial infarct
infección (f) infection
 infección de la bolsa de lágrimas dacryocystitis
 infección de la sangre (euph.) syphilis
 infección de la vejiga cystitis
 infección de serpigo athlete's foot
 infección en la sangre (colloq) septicemia
infeccioso (adj) infectious
infectar to infect
infecundidad (f) sterility
infecundo (adj) sterile
infértil (adj) infertile
inflamación (f) inflammation
 inflamación de la médula del hueso osteomyelitis
 inflamación de los ojos ophthalmia (inflammation of the eye)
 inflamación del hígado (f) hepatitis
inflamar to inflame
influenza flu; influenza
 influenza asiática Asiatic flu
ingerir (ie) (slang) to take (drugs)
ingle (f) groin
ingrediente (m) ingredient
inhabilidad (f) disability
injerir (ie) (slang) to take (drugs)
injerto graft
inmovilización (f) immobilization
inmune (adj) immune
inmunización (f) vaccine; immunization
inocente (adj, euph.) mentally retarded; (Mex.) deformed
inoculación (f) inoculation; vaccination
inodoro restroom; toilet
insecticida (m) insecticide
insensibilidad (f) unconsciousness
insidioso (adj) insidious
insolación (f) heat stroke; sunstroke
insomnio insomnia
instrumento afilado sharp-edged instrument
insuficiencia aórtica aortic insufficiency
insuficiencia cardíaca heart failure
insulina insulin
insulínico (adj) insulin

insulto (Chicano) indigestion
intermitente (adj) spasmodic
internamente (adv) internally
interrupción de coito (f) coitus interruptus
intervalo interval
intestino intestine
 intestino ciego caecum
 intestino delgado small intestine
 intestino grueso large intestine
 intestino inferior bowel
intolerancia intolerance
intoxicación (f) poisoning
 intoxicación botulínica botulism poisoning
 intoxicación con alimentos food poisoning
 intoxicación de la sangre blood poisoning
 intoxicación de orín uremia
 intoxicación del embarazo toxemia of pregnancy
 intoxicación por estafilococos staphylococcal poisoning
 intoxicación por monóxido de carbono carbon monoxide poisoning
 intoxicación por salmonellas salmonella poisoning
intoxicado (adj) drunk
intususcepción (f) intussusception
invalidez (f) disability
inválido (adj) cripple
inyección (f) shot; injection
 inyección de refuerzo booster shot
 inyección endovenosa intravenous injection
 inyección hipodérmica hypodermic injection
 inyección intracutánea intracutaneous injection
 inyección intramuscular intramuscular injection
 inyección intravenosa intravenous injection
 inyección secundaria booster shot
 inyección subcutánea subcutaneous injection
inyectar(se) to inject (oneself)
 inyectarse (slang) to inject oneself with drugs
ir al inodoro (colloq) to defecate
iris (m) iris
irregular (adj) spasmodic
irrigación (f) douche
irritación (f) irritation
irritar to irritate
irse to go away
istantino (colloq) anus
jabón (m) soap
jadeante (adj) panting
jadear to pant

jaipo (slang) "mainliner"; hypodermic needle used to inject drug
jalar to pull
jalarse (Sp. Am.) to get drunk; (P.R.) to leave; to go away
jalea jelly
  jalea vaginal vaginal jelly
jane (adj, Hond.) harelip
jaqueca headache; migraine
jarabe de ipeca (m) syrup of ipecac
jarabe para la tos (m) cough syrup
jején (m, Sp. Am.) gnat
jeringa hypodermic needle; syringe
  jeringa con aguja hueca hollow needle syringe
  jeringa con cilindro de cristal glass cylinder syringe
  jeringa desechable disposable syringe
jeringuilla syringe
  jeringuilla descartable disposable syringe
  jeringuilla hipodérmica hypodermic syringe
jey fíver (m, Chicano) hay fever
jimagua twin
jiotes (f. colloq) tinea corporis
jiricua (slang) vitiligo
jodido (adj) in poor health
jorobado (adj) hunchback
juanete (m) bunion
juanita marijuana
jugo digestivo enzyme
jugo gástrico gastric juice
keroseno kerosene
kilogramo kilogram
kotex (m) sanitary napkin; sanitary pad
kwashiorkor (m) kwashiokor (malnutrition)
la otra cosa any narcotic substitute
labio lip
  labio cucho (Chicano) harelip
  labio leporino harelip
labor (f) labor
laboratorio laboratory
laceración (f) laceration
lacrimal (adj) lachrymal
lactancia lactation
  lactancia maternal breastfeeding
lactante (adj) nursing
ladilla crab louse; parasitic cyst
lado side
  lado derecho inferior lower right side
  lado derecho superior upper right side
  lado izquierdo inferior lower left side
  lado izquierdo superior upper left side

lagrimal (adj) lachrymal
lágrimas tears
lámpara de rayos ultravioletas ultraviolet lamp
laringe (f) larynx
laringitis (f) laryngitis
laringoscopio laryngoscope
lastimadura bruise; injury; wound
lastimar to injure
latido twinge of pain; (Chicano) palpitation; spasm
  latido cardíaco heartbeat
  latido del corazón fetal fetal heart tone
  latido irregular irregular heartbeat; arrhytmia
lavado enema; lavage; purge
  lavado bucal mouth wash
  lavado interno douche
  lavado vaginal douche
lavamanos (slang) lavatory
lavaojos eye cup
lavar to scrub (surgically); to wash
  lavarse to wash oneself
lavativa enema
lavativo purge
laxante (m) laxative
laxativo laxative
lazarín (m) leprosy
lazo loop (IUD)
leche (f) milk; (vulgar) semen
  leche de magnesia milk of magnesia
lecho bed
legrado (colloq) D & C
lejía lye
lengua tongue
  lengua saburral coated tongue
  lengua sucia coated tongue
lente (m) lens
  lente de contacto contact lens
  lentes (pl) eye glasses; (Mex.) spectacles
lentilla contact lens
leña marijuana
leñito marijuana cigarette
lepra leprosy
lesión (f) injury; lesion
leucemia leukemia
leucocitos leukocytes (white blood cells)
levadura de cerveza Brewer's yeast
levantar to lift
  levantarse to get up; to stand up
leve (adj) mild
líquido liquid
libra pound
libre albedrío free will
liendra louse; nit
liga tourniquet
ligadura de trompas tubal ligation
ligamento ligament

ligar los tubos de falopio to tie the tubes
ligar los tubos uterinos to tie the tubes
ligar trompas to tie the tubes
limar to file down; to polish; to smooth
limpiador de agua a presión (m) waterpick
limpiarse to clean oneself
limpieza cleanliness; cleaning
linda (slang) vagina
lindano lindane
linfocitos lymphocytes
linfogranuloma venéreo (m) lymphogranuloma venereum
lingual (adj) lingual
linimento liniment
lisiado (adj) crippled; injured; lame
lista de intercambios exchange list
listerina (colloq) mouth wash
litro liter
lo demás placenta
lobanillo wen
lóbulo earlobe
loción (f) lotion
  loción bronceadora suntan lotion
  loción para el sol suntan lotion
loco (adj, slang) "high" on narcotics; "turned on"; mad; insane
locote (adj, slang) "high" on narcotics; "turned on"
locura insanity; madness
  locura de doble forma manic-depressive insanity
lombriz (f) worm
  lombriz chiquita afilada threadworms
  lombriz de gancho uncinaria; hookworm
  lombriz de látigo trichocephalus
  lombriz grande redonda ascaris; roundworm
  lombriz solitaria tapeworm
lomo loin
lubricante (m) lubricant
lubricativo (adj) lubricant
lúes (f) syphilis
luna (Chicano) menstruation
lunar (m) birthmark; blemish; mole
lupa magnifying glass
lupia wen
lupo loop
llaga sore; wound
  llaga de cama bedsore
  llaga de fiebre fever blister
  llaga ulcerosa canker sore
llamaradas hot flashes
llamarse to be called; to be named

llenar to fill
llorar to cry
maculosa de las Montañas Rocosas
  Rocky Mountain spotted fever
machucar to crush
madurez (f) maturity
magnesia magnesia
magulladura bruise
mal (m) disease; illness;
  sickness
  mal de arco (slang) tetanus
  mal de bubas (slang) syphilis
  mal de Down Down's syndrome
  mal (dolor) de garganta sore
    throat
    mal (dolor) de garganta por
      estreptocco strep throat
  mal de Hansen leprosy
  mal de las encías pyorrhea
  mal de madre morning sickness
  mal de mar seasickness
  mal (dolor) de oídos (m) sore
    ears
  mal de ojo (colloq)
    conjunctivitis
  mal de orín urinary problem;
    (slang) gonorrhea
  mal de pintas psoriasis
  mal de pinto spotted sickness
  mal de riñón kidney disease
  mal (baile) de San Guido (de San
    Vito) chorea
  mal de San Lázaro leprosy
  mal francés (slang) syphilis
  mal nutrido (adj)
    malnourished
mala alimentación (f)
  malnutrition
  mala alimentación mojada
    kwashiorkor (malnutrition)
  mala alimentación seca
    marasmus (malnutrition)
mala digestión (f) indigestion
malaria malaria
malestar (m) discomfort; malaise
  malestar de la mañana morning
    nausea
  malestar post-alcohólico
    hangover
malformaciones congénitas (f)
  congenital malformations
malignidad (f) malignancy
maligno (adj) malignant
malnutrición (f) malnutrition
malo (adj) ill; sick
malparto miscarriage
malpraxis (f) malpractice
mamadera breast pump; nipple (of
  of a baby nursing bottle);
  nursing bottle; (Sp. Am.) baby
  bottle
mamar to suck
mamón (m, Chicano) pacifier
mancha blemish; spot
  mancha de la preñez chloasma
    (facial discoloration)

mancha de la sangre blood stain
  stain
mancha del embarazo chloasma
  (facial discoloration)
mancha volante floater
manchas de sangre spotting
manchas frente a los ojos
  scotoma; spots before the eyes
manchas oscuras en la piel
  skin blotches
manchado spotting; stained
  manchado de sangre (adj)
    bloodstained
  manchado del pulmón (Mex.)
    tuberculosis
manco (adj) crippled hand
mandíbula jawbone; jaw
manía madness; mania
maníaco (adj) maniac
maniamelancolía manic-depressive
  insanity
mano (f) hand
manteca de cacao cocoa butter
manzana (Mex.) Adam's apple
maquillarse to put on makeup
marasmo marasmus
marcador de paso pacemaker
marcador de ritmo pacemaker
marcapaso pacemaker
marcha gait
marcharse to go away
mareo seasickness; fainting spell
María Juanita marijuana
maricocaimorfi user of marijuana,
  cocaine, morphine
mariguana marijuana
mariguano marijuana user
marihuanar to administer
  marijuana to someone
marihuano marijuana user
marijuana marijuana
mariola marijuana
martillo hammer (malleus)
más caliente (adj) warmer
masajar to massage
masaje (m) massage
masajear to massage
masar to massage
mascar to chew
máscara mask
mastitis por estasis (f) caked
  breast
masturbación (f) masturbation
masturbar(se) to masturbate
matarle el nervio a alguien to
  remove the nerve
matayerbas herbicides
materia matter
  materia fecal feces; stool
  materia gris (colloq)
    cerebral cortex
maternidad (f) maternity
matriz (f) uterus; womb
maxilar (adj) maxillary
mazorca (slang) teeth
meadera (Chicano) frequent

urination
mecos (pl, vulgar) semen
médica; médico physician
  médico(-a) a cargo attending
    physician
  médico(-a) asistente attending
    physician
  médico(-a) consultor(a)
    consulting physician
  médico(-a) de apelación
    consulting physician
  médico(-a) de cabecera
    attending physician
  médico(-a) forense coroner
  médico(-a) partero(-a)
    obstetrician
  médico(-a) residente resident
    (house) physician
medicación (f) medication
  medicación tiroides thyroid pill
medicamento medicine; remedy
medicina drug; medicine
  medicina de la botica patent
    medicine
  medicina de la farmacia patent
    medicine
  medicina deportiva sports
    medicine
  medicina interna internal
    medicine
  medicina patentada patent
    medicine
  medicina profiláctica preventive
    medicine
  medicina registrada patent
    medicine
  medicina socializada socialized
    medicine
medida dose
medio de restricción restraining
  device
medir (i) to measure
médula marrow
  médula espinal spinal cord
mejilla cheek
mejorarse to improve; to get
  better
melancolía melancholia
mellizo twin
membrana membrane
meningitis cerebroespinal (f)
  cerebrospinal meningitis
menopausia menopause
menstruación (f) menstruation
  menstruación dolorosa
    dysmenorrhea
menstruar to menstruate
mentir (ie) to lie
mentol (m) menthol
mentolato (Chicano)
  mentholatum
mentón (m) chin
meñique (m) little finger
mercurocromo mercurochrome
mertiolato merthiolate
mes (m) menstruation

mesa del parto delivery table
mescalina mescaline
meta goal
metabolizar to metabolize
metadona methadone
metástasis (f) metastasis
metazoos metazoos
método method
  método curativo cure
  método de Billing Billing's
  method of birth control
  método del ritmo rhythm
  method
mezcla mixture
mezclar to mix
mezquino (Mex.) wart
microbio germ
miedo fear
miembro penis; limb
  miembro artificial artificial
  limb; prosthesis
miércoles (m, euph.) excretion;
  feces; stool
mierda (vulgar) feces; stool
migraña migraine
miligramo milligram
mililitro milliliter
milque (f, Chicano) milk
mineral (m) mineral
miocardio (adj) myocardium
miope (adj) myopic; nearsighted;
  shortsighted
miopía myopia; nearsightedness
moco mucus
moderado (adj) moderate
modorra drowsiness
moho mold
mojado (adj) wet
mojar to wet the bed
molares (m) molars
mollera fontanel; crown of the
  head
mompes (m, pl, Chicano) mumps
mondadientes (m) toothpick
mongolismo Down's syndrome
moniliasis (f) moniliasis
monitor cardíaco pacemaker
monocitos monocytes
mononucleosis infecciosa (f)
  mononucleosis
moqueadera (Chicano) nasal drip
morbilli (f) measles
mordedura bite (animal)
  mordedura de culebra snake bite
  mordedura de escorpión
  scorpion bite
  mordedura de ratones rat bite
  mordedura de serpiente
  snakebite
  mordedura humana human bite
morder (ue) to bite
mordida (animal) bite
  mordida de gato cat bite
  mordida de perro dog bite
mordisco dental impression
morete (m, Mex., Hond,) bruise
moreteado (adj, Chicano) bruised

moretón (m) bruise
morfi (f, slang) morphine
morfina morphine
morfiniento user of morphine
morfinomanía drug habit
morfinómano addict (drug)
moribundo (adj) dying
morir (ue) to die
mormación (f, Chicano) nasal
  obstruction
morragia (Chicano) hemorrhage
mortinato (adj) stillborn
mosco volante floater
mostacho moustache
mostaza mustard
mostrar (ue) to show
  mostrar los dientes (ue) to show
  one's teeth
mota (slang) marijuana
motear to smoke marijuana
motiado (adj) "high"; turned on
  marijuana
motiar to smoke marijuana
moto marijuana user; (slang,
  Mex.) infantum tetanus
mover (ue) to move
mozusuelo (Mex.) infantum
  tetanus
mudo (adj) mute
muela back tooth
  muelas cordales wisdom teeth
  muelas de juicio wisdom teeth
muerte (f) death
muerto (adj) dead
muestra sample; specimen
  muestra de excremento stool
  specimen
  muestra de heces fecales
  stool specimen
  muestra de la orina urine
  specimen
  muestra de la sangre bloody
  show
muguet (m) moniliasis
mujercitas psilocybin
muleta crutch
muñeca wrist
murmullo heart murmur
músculo muscle
  músculo estriado striated
  muscle
  músculo involuntario
  involuntary muscle
  músculo liso smooth muscle
  músculo voluntario voluntary
  muscle
muslo thigh
nacido (inflamed) boil; (adj)
  born
  nacido muerto (adj) stillborn
nacimiento birth
  nacimiento múltiple multiple
  birth
  nacimento prematuro
  premature birth
  nacimiento tardío post-term
  birth

nadie no one
nalga buttock
naqueado (adj, Chicano)
  unconscious
naranjas (slang)
  amphetamines
narco member of police narcotics
  squad
narcomanía drug addiction
narcótico (m, adj) narcotic;
  soporific
narcotraficante dope pusher
nariz (f) nose
natalidad dirigida (f) planned
  parenthood
nati-muerto stillbirth
náusea nausea
nayotas (pl, slang, Chicano) nose
nefritis (f) nephritis
negar (ie) to deny
negro (adj) negroid
nena infant
nene (m) infant
neoformación (f) tumor
neoplasma (m) tumor
nervio nerve
  nervio aplastado pinched nerve
  nervio craneal cranial nerve
  nervio dental dental nerve
  nervio motor motor nerve
  nervio óptico optic nerve
  nervio parasimpático
  parasympathetic nerve
  nervio sensorial sensory nerve
  nervio simpático sympathetic
  nerve
neumonía pneumonia
neuralgia neuralgia
neurastenia nervous breakdown;
  neurasthenia
neurasténico (adj) neurasthenic
neuritis (f) neuritis
neurosis (f) neurosis
neurótico (m, adj) neurotic
neutrófilos polimorfonucleares
  polymorphonuclear neutrophiles
NGB (f) WBC (white blood
  count)
NGR (f) RBC (red blood count)
niacina niacin
nictalopia night blindness;
  nyctalopia
nieve (f, slang) heroin; cocaine
nigua chigger flea
niña del ojo pupil of eye
niñera nursemaid; baby nurse
niños (slang) psilocybin
nitrato de plata silver nitrate
nitro(glicerina) nitro(glycerin)
nitrógeno total total nitrogen
no infeccioso (adj) noninfectious
no sentir nada (ie) to feel nothing
no tener razón to be wrong
no tratado (adj) untreated
nodriza baby nurse; wet nurse
nódulo linfático lymph node
  nombre común (m) common name

novocaína Novocaine
nuca nape of neck
  nuca tiesa (colloq) stiff neck
nudillo knuckle
nudo knot; node; protuberance
  nudo linfático (colloq) lymph
  node
nuez de Adán (f) Adam's apple
numeración de glóbulos blancos (f)
  WBC (white blood count)
numeración de glóbulos rojos (f)
  RBC (red blood count)
órgano organ
  órganos genitales genitals
óvulo ovum
  óvulos (pl, Sp. Am.) vaginal
  suppository
obesidad (f) obesity
obeso (adj) obese
objetivo goal
obrar (Mex.) to defecate
obstetricia (sg) obstetrics
obstétrico (adj) obstetric;
  obstetrical
obstétrico (m, f) obstetrician
obstrucción (f) blockage;
  obstruction
  obstrucción de la tripa bowel
  obstruction
obstruir to block
  obstruir el nervio to block the
  nerve
occipital (adj) occipital
oclusión (f) occlusion
odontalgia toothache
oftalmía ophthalmia;
  inflamation of the eye
  oftalmía contagiosa pinkeye
oftálmico (adj) ophthalmic
oftalmoscopio ophthalmoscope
oído ear (organ of hearing)
  oído externo external ear
  oído interno inner ear
  oído medio middle ear
ojera eye cup
ojituerto (adj) squint-eyed
ojo eye
  ojo de pescado (colloq) plantar
  wart
  ojo de vidrio glass eye
  ojo morado blackeye
  ojos capotudos (Chicano)
  bulging eyes
  ojos saltones bulging eyes
oler (ue) to smell
olfatorio (adj) olfatory
olla (slang, Chicano) buttock
ombligo navel; umbilicus
  ombligo salido (slang) umbilical
  hernia
  ombligón (m, slang) umbilical
  hernia
  ombliguero "belly" binder
omóplato shoulder blade;
  scapula
oncocercosis (f) river blindness;
  onchocerciasis

onza ounce
operación (f) operation
  operación cesárea caesarean
  section
opio opium
oreja ear
orgasmo orgasm
orificación (f) inlay
orificar to fill with gold
orín (m) urine
orina urine
orines (m, pl) urine
oro gold
orzuelo sty
osteomielitis (f) osteomyelitis
otitis (f) otitis
ovar to ovulate
ovario ovary
ovulación (f) ovulation
oxígeno oxygen
oxitócico oxytocic
oxitocina oxytocin
oxiuro threadworms
pabellón externo de la oreja
  external ear
paciente ambulatorio outpatient
paciente externo outpatient
pacha (Chicano) baby bottle
padastro (colloq) hangnail
padecimiento illness; sickness
paladar (m) palate; roof of the
  mouth
  paladar hendido cleft palate
  paladar partido cleft palate
paletilla shoulder blade; scapula
paliativo (m, adj) palliative
pálido (adj) pale; sickly
palillo de dientes toothpick
palma de la mano palm of the
  hand
palo (slang) penis
palpitación (f) heartbeat;
  palpitation
  palpitación irregular irregular
  heartbeat; arrhythmia
  palpitación lenta slow heartbeat
  palpitación rápida rapid
  heartbeat; tachycardia
  palpitación rítmica rhythmical
  heartbeat
paludismo malaria
pan (m, slang, vulgar) vagina
páncreas (m) pancreas
panocha (slang) vulva
panocho (slang) vagina
pantorrilla calf of the leg
panza (Chicano) stomach;
  (colloq) abdomen; belly
  panza peligrosa (slang) bowel
  obstruction; peritonitis;
  appendicitis
panzón (adj) potbellied
panzona (vulgar) pregnant
paño chloasma (facial
  discoloration); (mask of
  pregnancy)
  paños en los ojos eyepads

pañal (m) diaper
pañalitis (f) diaper rash
paperas mumps
pápula wheal
parálisis (f) palsy; paralysis;
  stroke
  parálisis agitante palsy;
  shaking; Parkinson's disease
  parálisis cerebral cerebral
  paralysis
  parálisis de la mitad inferior del
  cuerpo paraplegia
  parálisis facial Bell's palsy
  parálisis infantil infantile
  paralysis; polio(myelitis)
paralización (f) palsy; paralysis
paranoia paranoia
paraplejía paraplegia
parar(se) to stand up; to stop
parásito parasite
parche (m) dressing; patch
  parchecito Band-Aid
  parches para callos corn plaster
paregórico paregoric
parentesco relation; relationship
pariente (m, f) relation
parir to give birth; to deliver
paro cardíaco cardiac arrest
paro del corazón heart failure
parótidas (f, pl) mumps
paroxismo fit
parpadear to blink
párpado eyelid
partes (f, slang) genitals
  partes ocultas (slang) genitals
partida (vulgar) vagina
partida de nacimiento birth
  certificate
partidura fissure
parto childbirth; delivery; labor
  parto abdominal abdominal
  delivery
  parto artificial artificial labor
  parto cesáreo caesarean
  delivery
  parto complicado complicated
  labor
  parto espontáneo spontaneous
  labor
  parto inducido induced labor
  parto inmaturo immature labor
  parto instrumental instrumental
  labor
  parto malogrado miscarriage
  parto muerto stillbirth
  parto múltiple multiple labor
  parto por operación caesarean
  delivery
  parto prematuro premature
  labor; premature delivery
  parto prolongado prolonged
  labor
  parto seco dry labor
pasar la mano sobre la
  superficie de to rub
pasar por to pass over
pase del cuerpo (m) feces; stool

pasta de dientes toothpaste
pasta dentífrice toothpaste
pastilla (birth control) pill; lozenge; tablet
pastilla de chupar lozenge
pastillas anticonceptivas contraceptive pills
pastillas para la tos cough drops; cough lozenges
pastillas para no tener niños birth control pill
patada kick
pataletas temper tantrum
patas de gallo crow's feet
patizambo (adj) pigeontoed
pavico (Chicano) diaper
peca freckle
pecho breast; chest
pediatra pediatrician
pediatría (sg) pediatrics
pediátrico (adj) pediatric
pediculosis (f) pediculosis; infestation
pedir (i) to ask (for); to request
pedo (slang) flatus
pegadizo (adj) contagious
pegar to pass on (a disease)
peinarse to comb one's hair
pelagra pellagra
pelársela (Chicano) to pull back foreskin of penis
peligroso (adj) dangerous
pelirrojo (adj) red-haired
pelitos (pl, Chicano) pubic hair
pelo hair
pelo crespo curly hair
pelo chino curly; (Col.) straight hair
pelo grifo (Chicano) kinky hair
pelo liso straight hair
pelo púbico pubic hair
pelo quebrado wavy hair
pelotita (slang) clitoris
peludo (adj) hairy
peluza (Mex.) German measles; rubella
pelviano (adj) pelvic
pélvico (adj) pelvic
pelvímetro pelvimeter
pelvis (f) pelvis
pellejo flap of skin
pellín (m, Chicano) buttock
pena sore; worry
pendejos (slang, Arg.) pubic hair
pene (m) penis
penicilina penicillin
pensar (ie) to think
pentotal de sodio (m) sodium pentothal
pentotal sódico (m) sodium pentothal
pepa (slang) clitoris
pera de goma rubber bulb; syringe
perder (ie) to lose
perder fluidos del cuerpo (ie) to dehydrate

perder peso (ie) to lose weight
perder sangre (ie) to menstruate
pérdida del sueño insomnia
perforación (f) perforation
perforar to drill
pericarditis (f) pericarditis
perineal (adj) perineal
perineo perineum
período (colloq) menstruation
período climatérico menopause
periostio periosteum
peritonitis (f) peritonitis
perleche (m) oral lesion
permanganato de potasio potassium permanganate
permiso authorize; permit
peroné (m) fibula
peróxido peroxide
peróxido de hidrógeno hydrogen peroxide
peróxido de sodio sodium peroxide
perrilla (colloq) sty
perseguir (i) to pursue
persistir (en) to persist
pesadilla nightmare
pesar to weigh
peso weight
peso del nacimiento birthweight
peso escaso underweight
pestaña eyelash
peste (f) plague
peste blanca tuberculosis
peste bubónica bubonic plague
pesticida (m) pesticide
petición (f) request
pezón (m) nipple of female (breast)
pezón enlechado engorged nipple (caked)
pezonera nipple shield
picadura cavity; bite (of insect); sting (of insect)
picadura de abeja bee sting
picadura de alacrán scorpion sting
picadura de araña spider bite; spider sting
picadura de avispa wasp sting
picadura de avispón hornet sting
picadura de garrapata tick sting
picadura de hormiga ant sting
picadura de moscardón botfly sting
picadura de mosquito mosquito sting
picadura de nigua chigoe, jigger, sandflea sting
picadura de pulga flea sting
picadura de ubar (colloq) black-widow spider sting
picadura de viuda negra black-widow spider sting

picadura de zancudo (Mex.) mosquito sting
picar to stick
picarse (slang) to inject oneself with drugs
picazón (f) itch
picor (m) itching
picha (vulgar) penis
pichón (m, vulgar) penis
pie (m) foot
pie de atleta athlete's foot
pie hueco high arched foot
pie plano flat foot
piedra en la vejiga gallstone
piedra en los riñones kidney stone
piel (f) skin
piel amarilla (colloq) jaundice
piel de la cabeza scalp
piel roja chafing
piemia septicemia
pierna leg
pija (slang, Arg.) penis
píldora (birth control) pill
píldora anticonceptiva birth control pill
píldora diurética diuretic
píldora para control de embarazo (f) birth control pill
píldora para dormir sleeping pill
píldora somnífera sleeping pill
pildorear(se) to ingest narcotic pills
pildoriar(se) to ingest narcotic pills
pildoriento user of pills
píldoro (adj, slang) "high" on pills
pilinga (vulgar) penis
pillido (Mex.) souffle
pinchar to prick
pinchazo prick
pinguas (pl) narcotic pills
pinta spotted sickness
pinto (adj) very dark-skinned; lacking negroid features
pinzas (pl) dental forceps
piocha chin
piojería pediculosis; infestation
piojo louse
piorrea pyorrhea
piperawitt (m, f) piperazine
piperazina piperazine
piperidol (m) piperazine
piquete (m) (insect) bite; sting (from an insect); (slang) injection (of a narcotic substance)
piridoxina vitamin B-6
piriforme (adj) pear-shaped
pirosis (f) heartburn
pisa-lengua (m) tongue depressor
piso floor
piso de maternidad maternity floor

piso ginecológico gynecological floor
pisporr(i)a (Chicano) lump; bump on head
pisto (adj) drunk
pito (slang) penis
pitocín (m) pitocin
pitocina pitocin
PIV (pielograma intravenoso (m) IVP (intravenous pyelogram)
placa plaque; plate
placenta afterbirth; placenta
placenta previa placenta previa
placentario (adj) placental
plaga plague
plaguicida (m) pesticide
planificación de la familia (f) family planning
planificación familiar (f) family planning
planovegus (m) flat foot
planta del pie sole of the foot
plaqueta platelet
plaquetas sanguíneas blood platelets
plasma (m) plasma
plasma sanguíneo blood plasma
pleito lawsuit
pleuresía pleurisy
poción (f) potion
podo marijuana
polaridad (f) polarity
poliomielitis (f) polio(myelitis)
pólipo polyp
polvo powder; (slang) PCP; cocaine
polvo de azufre sulphur powder
polvoriento (adj) powdery
polvoroso (adj) powdery
pollo (Chicano, Arg.) sputum
pomada ointment; pomade; salve; unguent
pómulo cheekbone
poner to place
poner a dieta to put on a diet
poner a prueba to test
ponerse + adj of emotion (mental state) to become; turn + adj
ponerse + noun to put on (clothing)
ponerse alto (colloq) to be drunk; to get drunk
ponerse de pie to stand up
ponzoña poison
ponzoñoso (adj) poisonous
por día daily
porcelana porcelain
poro pore
portador (-a) de enfermedad carrier
porte (m) bearing
postemilla canker sore
postilla pock; scab
postizo (adj) artificial
postración (f) prostration

postración del calor heat prostration
potasio potassium
práctica impropia (inhábil) malpractice
precipitar to precipitate
predisposición (f) predisposition
prematuro (adj) premature
premolares (f) bicuspids
prenatal (adj) prenatal
prender (slang) to hook on narcotics
prendido (adj, slang) hooked on drugs
preñada (adj) pregnant
preñez (f) pregnancy
preocupación (f) worry
preocuparse to worry
prepucio foreskin
presbicia farsightedness; presbyopia
presbiopía farsightedness; presbyopia
présbita (adj) farsighted
prescribir to prescribe
prescribir un remedio to prescribe
prescripción (f) prescription
presentación (f) presentation
presentación de nalgas breechbirth (frank breech)
presentación trasera breechbirth (frank breech)
preservativo condom
presión (f) pressure
presión arterial alta high blood pressure
presión arterial baja low blood pressure
primer período del parto first stage of labor
primera ayuda first aid
primera regla menarquia menarche
primeros auxilios (pl) first aid
principio onset
privado toilet
privar to deprive
probar (ue) to prove; to test; to try out
procedimiento procedure
procreación planeada (f) planned parenthood
procrear to procreate
proctitis (f) proctitis
producir to produce
profiláctico (m, adj) prophylactic; condom
profundo (adj) deep
progenie (f) progeny
progesterona progesterone
prolapso prolapse
prolapso de la matriz uterus prolapse
prolapso del útero uterus prolapse
prole (f) progeny

próstata prostate gland
prótesis (f) prosthesis
prótesis acústica hearing aid
prótesis auditiva hearing aid
protozoarios protozoa
protuberancia lump
proveer con pañal to diaper
provocarse el vómito to cause vomiting
prueba test
prueba del pañal PKU (phenylketonuria)
prueba selecta de la sangre blood screening
prueba serológica serology test
pruebas cruzadas cross match
prurito itching
pterigión (m) pterygium
puente (m) bridge (dental)
puente fijo fixed dental bridge
puente movible removable dental bridge
pueril (adj) puerile
puerperal (adj) puerperal
puerperio confinement; puerperium
pujar to bear down; to push
pujos straining; tenesmus
pulga flea
pulgada inch
pulgar (m) thumb
pulimento para muebles furniture polish
pulmón (m) lung
pulmonía pneumonia
pulpa pulp
pulpejo ball of thumb; earlobe
pulpotomía pulpotomy
pulso pulse
pulverización (f) spray
pulverizador (m) spray
puntada stitch; suture
punta del corazón apex of heart
punto stitch
punzada sharp pain; prick; sting (of an insect)
puñetear (vulgar) to masturbate
puño fist
pupa oral lesion
pupila pupil (eye)
purga purge
purgación (f) purgation; (slang) gonorrhea
purgante (m) cathartic; laxative; purgative; purge
pus (m) pus
pus detrás de la córnea hypopyon
pústula pimple; pustule
quebradura hernia; rupture
quebradura de huesos fracture
quebradura en la ingle inguinal hernia
quebrarse to fracture
quedarse to stay
quejarse to complain

quemadura burn
  quemadura por ácido acid burn
  quemadura por álcali alkali
  burn
  quemadura por calor seco dry
  heat burn
  quemadura química chemical
  burn
  quemadura solar sunburn
quemarse to burn oneself
quemazón (f) sunburn; burn
querer (ie) to want; to love
queso (slang) smegma
quetosis (f) ketosis
quevedos (pl) (wire-rimmed)
  eyeglasses; spectacles
quijada jaw
  quijada (mandíbula) rota broken
  jaw
quinina quinine
quintillizo quintuplet
quíntuplo quintuplet
quirófano operating room
quirúrgico (adj) surgical
quiste cyst; parasitic cyst
quitar to remove
  quitarse to take off; to undress
rabadilla coccyx
rabia anger; rabies
radiaciones (f) radiation
  treatment
radio radius
radiografía x-ray
  radiografía del tórax chest
  x-ray
  radiografiar to x-ray
radioterapia radiation therapy;
  x-ray therapy
radióxido de zinc zinc oxide
raíz (f) root
rajada (vulgar) vulva
rajar to crack
rampa charleyhorse
raposo (adj) rough
rapto (Chicano) rape
raquitis (m) rickets
raquitismo rickets
rascado (adj, Ven.) drunk; (m)
  scratch
rascar (Sp. Am.) to be drunk; to
  get drunk
  rascar(se) to scratch (relieve
  itch)
rasguñar to scratch (hurt)
rasguño scratch
raspa (colloq) D & C
raspado curettage
raspadura scrape
raspón (m, Sp. Am.) scratch
rasurar(se) to shave
rayo equis x-ray
razpón (m) abrasion
reación alérgica (f) allergic
  reaction
reactivación (f) booster shot
reata (riata) (vulgar) penis

reborde (m) ridge
recaída relapse
receptor universal (m, f) universal
  recipient
recesivo (adj) recessive
receta prescription
  receta médica prescription
recetar to prescribe
recidiva relapse
reconocimiento examination
recordar (ue) to remember
rectal (adj) rectal
recto rectum
rectocele (m) rectocele
recuento sanguíneo blood count
reducir(se) to reduce
  reducir una fractura to set a
  fracture
referir (ie) to refer
refinado (adj) refined
reflejo reflex
  reflejo de convergencia
  convergence reflex
refregar to scrub (surgically)
refuerzo booster shot
regazo lap
regenerar to regenerate
régimen (m) diet
región glútea (f) gluteal region
regla (Mex., P.R.) menstruation
regoldar to belch
regüeldo burp
regular to control; to regulate
regurgitación (f) regurgitation
regurgitar to belch
reimplantación (f) reimplantation
reinjertación (f) reimplantation
reír (i) to laugh
relación (f) relation; relationship
  relación sexual intercourse
relajación (f) relaxation; rupture
  (hernia)
relajar el cuerpo to relax
  relajarse to relax
rellenar to fill
relleno filling
remedio remedy
  remedio casero home remedy
remojar to soak
renal (adj) renal
rengo (adj) lame
renguear (Sp. Am.) to limp
renovar el pañal de (ue) to diaper
renuncia voluntaria waiver
reñir (i) to quarrel
repelente de insectos (m) insect
  repellent
repetir (i) to repeat; (colloq) to
  burp
  repetirse (i) to recur
reposo rest
requerir (ie) to require
resequedad de los ojos (f) xerosis
resfriado cold
  resfriado común common cold
resollar (ue) to breathe; to pant

respiración (f) breathing;
  respiration
  respiración artificial artificial
  respiration
respirar to breath
  respirar asmáticamente to
  wheeze
  respirar con dificultad to wheeze
restregar to rub
resucitación boca a boca (f)
  mouth-to-mouth resuscitation
resucitación cardiopulmonar (RCP)
  cardiopulmonary resuscitation
  (CPR)
resucitador cardiopulmonar (m)
  cardiopulmonary resuscitator
resuello breathing
  resuello asmático asthmatic
  wheeze
resultados adversos adverse
  results
retardado (adj) mentally retarded
retardo mental mental retardation
reticulocitos reticulocytes
retina retina
  retina desprendida detached
  retina
retinto (adj) very dark-skinned,
  lacking negroid features
retirarse (m) coitus interruptus
retortijón (m) abdominal cramps
  retortijón de tripas stomach
  cramps
retraso mental mental retardation
retrato del x-ray (Chicano) x-ray
retrete (m, Spain) restroom;
  toilet
retroceder to drop back into
reuma (m) rheum
reumas (m) rheumatism
reumatismo rheumatism
reventón (m) rupture; hernia
revolver (ue) to stir
rezumamiento eczema
rh-negativo (adj) rh negative
rh-positivo (adj) rh positive
riboflavina vitamin B-2
riesgo confinement; puerperium
rinconera midwife (quack)
rinitis (f) rhinitis
riñón (m) kidney
riñonera emesis basis
ritmo rhythm method
rociador (m) spray
rodilla knee
rogar (ue) to beg
rojizo (adj) reddish
romper to rupture; to burst; to
  tear
roncha wheal; hive
  roncha hulera leishmaniasis
  roncha mala leishmaniasis
ronco (adj) hoarse
ronquera aphonia; hoarseness;
  croup
ronquido harsh, raucous sound

ropa de maternidad maternity clothes
rosado (adj) chapped
roséola roseola
  roséola epidémica rubella
rostro face
rotadura (Chicano) rupture; hernia
roto (adj) ruptured
rótula kneecap
rotura rupture; hernia
rozadura abrasion; chafing; chafe
rozarse to chap skin
rubéola German measles; roseola; rubella
rubor (m) redness
ruptura rupture (hernia)
sabañón (m) chilblain
saborear to taste
saburra dental tartar
sacar to take; to stick out
  sacar aire (Chicano) to burp
  sacarle el nervio a to remove the nerve
  sacar (leche) por medio de una bomba to pump
sacarina saccharine
saco sac
  saco amniótico amniontic sac
sacro sacrum
sacroilíaco (adj) sacroiliac
sacudida tic
sáculo saccule
sal (f) salt
  sal biliar bile salt
  sal corriente noniodized salt
  sal de epsom epsom salt
  sal de higuera epsom salt
  salyodada iodized salt
  sales aromáticas smelling salts
  sales perfumadas smelling salts
sala room
  sala de los recién nacidos newborn nursery
  sala de operaciones operating room
  sala de partos delivery room; labor room
  sala prenatal labor room
salida exit; electrical outlet
  salida de los dientes teething
salir to leave (exit)
  salir de su cuidado (Chicano) to give birth
  salirle sangre de la nariz nosebleed
  salirse (m, slang) coitus interruptus
saliva saliva; sputum
salpullido diaper rash; prickly heat; rash
salvohonor (m, colloq) buttock
sanar to heal; to recover; (euph.) to give birth
  sanarse to get well
sangrante (adj) bleeding

sangrar to bleed
sangre (f) blood
  sangre clara anemia
  sangre débil (colloq) anemia
  sangre de chango (Chicano) mercurochrome
  sangre en la orina hematuria
  sangre entera whole blood
  sangre mala (slang) syphilis
  sangre oxalatada oxalated blood
  sangre pobre (colloq) anemia
  sangre pura whole blood
sarampión (m) measles
  sarampión alemán German measles; rubella
  sarampión bastardo German measles
sarcoma (m) sarcoma
sarna itch; scabies
sarpullido rash
sarro tartar; dental tartar
saturnismo lead poisoning
seborrea seborrhea
seca (colloq) bubo
secar to dry
sección cesárea (f) caesarean section
secreción (f) discharge
secreta (slang) venereal disease (VD)
secretar to secrete
secundinas placenta; (Mex.) afterbirth
seda encerada dental floss
sedante (m) sedative
sedativo sleeping pill; sedative
sedimentación (f) sedimentation
seguir (i) to follow
  seguir trabajando (i) to continue working
segundo parto (Chicano) afterbirth
segundo período del parto second stage of labor
semen (m) semen
semicupio sitz bath
semilla (slang, Mex.) sperm
senectud (f) old age; senility
senil (adj) senile
senilidad (f) senility
seno breast; sinus
  seno auricular pacemaker
  seno doloroso painful breast
  senos (pl) bosom
sensación de pesantez en el perineo (f) bearing-down pain
sensaciones de ser aprestado (-a) pressure sensations
sensorial (adj) sensorial
sentadera buttock
sentarse (ie) to sit down
sentido sense
  sentido de la vista sense of sight (visual)
  sentido del gusto sense of taste (gustatory)

sentido del oído sense of hearing (auditory)
sentido del olfato sense of smell (olfactory)
sentido del tacto sense of feel (tactile)
sentir (ie) to feel; to regret
sentirse (ie) to feel (emotion, pain)
separar to single out
sepsis (f) blood poisoning
septicemia blood poisoning; septicemia
ser garantizado to be guaranteed
serio (adj) serious
serpigo ringworm; tinea
servicios restroom; toilet
servilleta sanitaria sanitary napkin; sanitary pad
servir (i) to serve
sesonar (slang) to sniff glue
sesos brains
severo (adj) severe
sicodélico (adj) psychedelic
sicosis (f) psychosis
  sicosis maníacodepresiva manic-depressive insanity
sicosomático (adj) psychosomatic
sicótico (adj) psychotic
sien (f) temple
siete (7) días (m) infantum tetanus
sietecueros (slang) blister on sole of foot
sietemesino (adj) premature (literally "seven month")
sífilis (f) syphilis
signo de advertencia warning sign
silbido souffle
silla de ruedas wheelchair
simple (adj, euph.) mentally retarded
sinapismo mustard plaster
síndrome (m) syndrome
síntoma (m) symptom
sinusitis (f) sinus congestion
sisote (m) boil; (Chicano) ringworm; tinea
sistema nervioso autónomo (m) autonomic nervous system
sistema nervioso central (m) central nervous system
sístole (f) systole
sobaco armpit
sobar to massage
sobredosis de drogas (f) drug overdose
sobreparto lying-in after childbirth
sobrepeso overweight
sobresalto shock
sofocación (f) suffocation
solanera sunburn
soleada (Sp. Am.) sunstroke
soler (ue) to be in the habit of

solicitar admisión a to apply for admission
sólidos solids
solitaria solium; tapeworm
soltar (ue) to let go of
soltura (Chicano) diarrhea
solución (f) solution
  solución endovenosa IV (intravenous solution)
somnífero sleeping pill
somnolencia drowsiness
sonado (adj) "high" on narcotics; "turned on"
sonámbulo (adj, slang) "high" on narcotics; "turned on"
sonarse la nariz to blow one's nose
sonda catheter; probe; tube (for feeding)
sonreír (i) to smile
soñar (con) (ue) to dream (of)
soplarse la nariz to blow one's nose
soplo heart murmur
soporífera sleeping pill
soporífico soporific
soporte (m) support
  soportes para el arco del pie arch supports
sordera deafness
sordo (adj) deaf
sordomudo deaf mute
soríasis (f) psoriasis
sostén (m) support
  sostén de maternidad nursing bra
suave (adj) soft
subir to rise
  subirse to climb up
  subirse la manga to roll up one's sleeve
súbito (adj) sudden
substituto substitute
sudar to perspire
sudor (m) sweat; perspiration
sueño crepuscular twilight sleep anesthesia
suero serum
  suero antialacrán black widow spider antivenom serum
  suero antiviperino antivenom serum
  suero por la vena IV (intravenous solution)
  suero sanguíneo blood serum
sugerir (ie) to suggest
suicidio suicide
sulfatiazol (m) sulfathiazole
sulfato de calcio calcium sulfate
sulfato de sodio sodium sulfate (in toilet cleaners)
sulfato ferroso iron
sulfoniluria sulfonyluria
superficie (f) surface
  superficie inferior underside
supositorio suppository

supuración (f) discharge; drainage; suppuration
suspensorio atheltic supporter
susto shock
  susto con resuello duro (colloq) hyperventilation
sustraer to subtract
sutura stitch; suture; suture (dental)
  sutura absorbible dissolving suture
tableta tablet
tablilla splint
tácil (adj) tactile
tacotillo (Chicano) boil; tumor
tacuache (adj) drunk
tajo (slang) episiotomy
talache (m) chin
taladrar to drill
taladro dental drill
talasemia anemia, thalassemia
talón (m) heel
tamaño size
  tamaño grande large size
  tamaño pequeño small size
  tamaño surtido assorted size
tampax (m) Tampax
tampón (m) tampon
tapa de los sesos (colloq) top of skull
tapado de orín prostatitis
tapadura filling
tapar to fill
tapón (m) tampon
  tapón de cera impacted earwax
  tapón de moco (Mex.) bloody show
taquicardia rapid heartbeat; tachycardia
tarantas (Mex., Hond.) dizziness
tarántula (Chicano) hairy
tartamudeo lisp; stutter
tartamudez (f) stuttering
tártaro dental tartar
tatuaje (m) tattoo(ing)
taza de medir measuring cup
té (m) tea; (slang) marijuana
  té cargado strong tea
  té de manzanilla camomile tea
  té fuerte strong tea
tecato heroin user; junkie
tecla cigarette butt
tecolota cigarette butt
tecunda (Mex.) chicken pox
tejido tissue
tela membrane
  tela adhesiva adhesive tape
tele (f, Chicano) baby bottle; breast
temblar to shiver
templado (adj) lukewarm
tenazas de extracción (pl) dental forceps
tendencias a sangrar bleeding tendencies

tender (con) (ie) to spread (out); to stretch; to unfold
tendón (m) tendon
tener to have
  tener ... años to be ... years old
  tener buen (mal) sabor to taste good (bad)
  tener buena cara to look (appear) well
  tener calor (m) to be warm
  tener cuidado to be careful
  tener deseos (de) to desire (to)
  tener el mes to menstruate
  tener el niño to deliver
  tener éxito to be successful
  tener frío to be cold
  tener ganas (de) to feel like
  tener hambre (f) to be hungry
  tener la culpa to be guilty; to be at fault
  tener (traer) la garra to menstruate
  tener lugar to take place
  tener miedo to be afraid
  tener murria to be blue
  tener prisa to be in a hurry
  tener que + infinitive to have to (must)
  tener razón to be right
  tener relaciones sexuales to have sexual relations
  tener retraso to be late
  tener sed (f) to be thirsty
  tener sueño to be sleepy
  tener vergüenza to be ashamed
tenia tapeworm
tensión (f) strain
terapéutico (adj) therapeutic
terapia therapy
tercer molar (m) third molar
tercer período del parto third stage of labor
termómetro thermometer
  termómetro oral oral thermometer
  termómetro rectal rectal thermometer
termoterapia heat therapy
terramicina Terramycin
testículo testicle
testigo witness
teta (slang) breast
tétanos tetanus; lockjaw
tetera nursing bottle; (Mex., Cuba, P.R.) nipple (of baby nursing bottle)
tetilla male nipple; nipple (of a baby nursing bottle)
tetina nipple (of a baby nursing bottle)
tetraciclina tetracycline
tetracloruro de carbono carbon tetrachloride
thromboflebitis (f) phlebitis
tiamina vitamin B1

tibia shinbone
tibio (adj) lukewarm; tepid; warm
tic (m) tic
  tic doloroso de la cara tic
  douloureux
tiempo de coagulación coagulation
time
tiempo de hemorragia bleeding
time
tiempo de protrombina
prothrombin time
tiempo de retracción del coágulo
clot reaction time
tiempo del mes (colloq)
menstruation
tienta probe
tieso (adj) stiff
tifo typhus fever
  tifo abdominal typhoid fever
  tifo de América yellow fever
  tifo de oriente bubonic plague
tifus (m) typhus fever
  tifus exantemático spotted
  fever; typhus fever
  tifus icterodes yellow fever
timba (slang) heroin capsule
timo thymus
tímpano eardrum; tympanic
membrain
  tímpano perforado perforated
  eardrum
tina de baño tub
tinción (f) stain; staining
tiniado (adj, slang) "high" from
sniffing paint thinner
tinte (m) dye
tiña ringworm; tinea
tiraleches (f) breast pump
tirar (el) agua (slang) to urinate
tirar (la) basura (slang) to
defecate
tirarse flato to expel anal gas
tirarse un pedo to expel anal gas
tiritar to shiver
tiroides (m) thyroid
tirón (m) tic
tisis (f) phthisis; tuberculosis
tlacuache (adj) drunk
toallas en los ojos eyepads
tobillera ankle support
tobillo ankle
tocar to feel; to touch
tocología obstetrics
tocólogo obstetrician
tolerancia tolerance
tomacorriente (f, Sp. Am)
electrical socket
tomar to take; (slang) to take
(drugs)
tomate (m, slang, Chicano)
eyeball
tónico tonic
tonsilitis (f) tonsilitis
tonsils (m, Chicano) tonsils
toque (m) drag; puff of
(marijuana) cigarette

toracentesis (f) pleural tap
tórax (m) chest; thorax
torcedura sprain; strain
torcer (ue) to sprain; to twist; to
turn
torcido (adj) twisted
torcijón cólico (m, Mex.) stomach
cramps
torniquete (m) tourniquet
torsón (m) abdominal cramps
torticolis (m) stiff neck
torzón (m) sharp internal pain
tos (f) cough
  tos ahogona (Mex.) whooping
  cough; pertussis
  tos convulsiva whooping
  cough; pertussis
  tos ferina whooping cough;
  pertussis
  tos por fumar smoker's cough
toser to cough
tosferina whooping cough;
pertussis
tostado (adj) suntanned
toxemia blood poisoning;
septicemia; toxemia
  toxemia del embarazo
  toxemia of pregnancy
toxicomanía (drug) addition
toxicómano (drug) addict
trabajo de parto labor
tracción (f) traction
tracoma (m) conjunctivitis
traer carga (slang) to be carrying
narcotic drugs
traficar (slang) to traffic in drugs
tragante (m, Chicano) esophagus
tragar to swallow
trago swallow
tranquilizante (m) tranquilizer
transferir (ie) to transfer
transfusión (f) transfusion
  transfusión de sangre blood
  transfusion
  transfusión sanguínea blood
  transfusion
transmisión transmission
  transmisión mediante contacto
  transmission by contact
  transmisión mediante vector
  vector transmission
  transmisión por gotillas droplet
  transmission
tráquea trachea
traqueostomía tracheostomy
trastorno alérgico allergic
reaction
tratamiento therapy; treatment
  tratamiento térmico heat
  therapy
trauma (m) trauma
traumatismo trauma
tremblor (m) tremor
trementina turpentine
tremor (m) tremor
tricocéfalo trichocephalus

tricomonas trichomonas
triglicéridos elevados high
triglycerides
trigueño (adj) olive-skinned
(complexioned)
trillizo triplet
trimo tetanus
tripa (colloq) bowels
  tripa ida blocked intestine
tripita (colloq) appendix
triple (f) DPT vaccination
triquinosis (f) trichinosis
trismo lockjaw
trocisco lozenge
trombocitos thrombocytes
tromboflebitis (f)
thrombophlebitis
trombosis (f) thrombosis
  trombosis coronaria coronary
  thrombosis
trompa de eustaquio eustachian
tube
trompa de Falopio fallopian tube
tronado (adj) drunk
tronar to smoke marijuana
trotador (-a) jogger
trotar to jog
tuberculina tuberculin test
tuberculosis (f) tuberculosis
tuberculoso (adj) tubercular
tubo catheter; tube
  tubo de ensayo test tube
  tubo de Falopio fallopian tube
  tubos fallopian tubes
tuerto (adj) blind in one eye;
one-eyed
tullido (adj) cripple
tumbar to have sexual relations
tumefacción (f) swelling;
tumefaction
tumor (m) swelling; tumor
tumorcito lump
turista (slang) diarrhea
turnio (adj) cross-eyed
turno appointment
úlcera canker; sore (wound);
ulcer
  úlcera del estómago stomach
  ulcer
  úlcera gangrenosa canker sore
  úlcera gástrica gastric ulcer
  úlcera péptica peptic ulcer
  úlcera por decúbito bedsore
ulceración (f) canker sore
ultrasonda ultrasound
uncinaria uncinaria; hookworm
ungüento balsam; ointment;
salve; unguent
  ungüento para los ojos eye salve
unto ointment
untos de Papanicolaou Pap smear
uña nail
  uña encarnada ingrown toenail
  uña enterrada ingrown toenail
uñero ingrown toenail
urea urea

uremia uremia
uréter (m) ureter
uretra urethra
uretritis inespecífica (f)
  nonspecific urethritis
  uretritis no específica
    nonspecific urethritis
  uretritis no gonococal
    nongonoccocal urethritis
urgencia emergency
urinálisis (m) urinalysis
urobilina urobilin
urobilirrubina urobilirubin
urticaria hives; urticaria
urutar (Chicano) to burp
úrzula (Chicano) typhus fever
útero uterus; womb
úvula uvula
vaciar to empty
vacuna immunization vaccine
  vacuna oral contra el polio oral
    polio vaccine
  vacuna triple DPT vaccination
vacunación to vaccinate
vagina vagina
vaginal (adj) vaginal
vaginitis (f) vaginitis
vahído dizziness
válvula valve
  válvula del corazón heart valve
vapor (m) steam; vapor
várice (f) varicose vein
varicela chicken pox
varicosidad (f) varicosity
varicoso (adj) varicose
variz (m) varicose vein
vasectomía vasectomy
vaselina vaseline
vaso drinking glass
  vaso capilar capillaries
  vaso sanguíneo blood vessel
vehículo vehicle
vejez (f) old age
vejiga bladder
  vejiga de la bilis gallbladder
  vejiga de la orina urinary
    bladder
velo del paladar soft palate

vello púbico pubic hair
vena vein
  vena dental dental vein
  vena varicosa varicose vein
venda Band-Aid; bandage
vendaje (m) bandage; dressing
  vendaje abdominal binder
  vendaje de yeso gypsum cast
  vendaje elástico elastic
    bandage
veneno poison
  venenos aspirados inhaled
    poisons
  venenos comunes common
    poisons
  venenos inyectados injected
    poisons
  venenos tomados por la boca
    oral poisons
venenoso (adj) poisonous
venir (ie) to come
venirse (ie) (slang) to ejaculate
ventaja advanatage
ventana de la nariz nostril
ventanilla de la nariz nostril
ventosidad (f) flatus
verdugón (m) weal (large welt)
verga (slang) penis
verme (m) intestinal worm
vermífugo (adj) vermifuge
verruga wart
  verruga genital genital wart
  verruga venérea genital wart
vértebra vertebra
vertiginoso (adj) dizzy
vértigo dizziness; fainting spell
vesícula bladder; blister
  vesícula biliar gallbladder
  vesículo seminal seminal
    vesicle
vestir(se) (i) to dress (oneself)
  vestirse de bata de hospital (i) to
    be gowned
vía de entrada route of entry
vial (m) vial
vías urinarias (f) urinary tract
víctima victim
vientre (m) abdomen; stomach

vinagre (m) vinegar
violación (f) rape
violeta de genciana gentian violet
viruela pock; smallpox
  viruelas locas (slang) chicken
    pox
virulo (adj, Chicano) one-eyed
virus (m) virus
vista vision
  vista borrosa blurred vision
  vista doble double vision
vitamina vitamin
vitíligo vitiligo
viveza alertness
voltearse to turn around (over)
volver (ue) to return; to come
  back
vomitar to vomit
vomitivo (m, adj) emetic; vomitive
vómito vomit; vomiting
  vómito negro yellow fever
  vómitos del embarazo morning
    sickness
vulva vulva
xerosis (f) xerosis
yedo marijuana
yedra venenosa poison ivy
yema fleshy tip of the finger
yerba marijuana
yesca marijuana
yesco marijuana smoker
yeso (drug) addict; cast
  yeso mate plaster of Paris
yeyuno jejunum
yodo iodine
yoduro de potasio potassium
  iodide
yunque (m) anvil (incus)
zacate (m) marijuana (low-grade
  variety)
zambo (adj) twisted
zapeta (Mex.) diaper
zona shingles
zoster (f) shingles
zumaque venenoso (m) poison ivy
zumbido de oídos buzzing in the
  ears

Selected Bibliography

Bibliografía selecta

Adams, R. *Cultural Surveys of Panama, Nicaragua, El Salvador, Honduras.* Washington, D.C.: Pan American Sanitary Bureau, 1957.

————, and Rubel, A. J. "Sickness and Social Relations." *In* M. Nash, ed., *Handbook of Middle American Indians.* Vol. 6: *Social Anthropology.* Austin: University of Texas Press, 1967.

Argüiro Martínez, R., ed. *Hispanic Culture and Health Care: Fact, Fiction, Folkore.* St. Louis: C. V. Mosby, 1978.

Aguilar, I., and Wood, V. N. "Aspects of Death, Grief and Mourning in the Treatment of Spanish-Speaking Mental Patients." *Journal of the National Association of Social Workers*, Vol. 21 (1976), 49–54.

Atencio, T. "Mental Health and the Spanish Speaking." *Mental Health Planning Conference for the Spanish Speaking.* Rockville, Md.: National Institute of Mental Health, 1972.

Baca, J. E. "Some Health Beliefs of the Spanish Speaking." *American Journal of Nursing*, Vol. 69, No. 10, 2172–2176.

Barker, G. C. *Pachuco: An American-Spanish Argot and Its Social Functions in Tucson, Arizona.* Tucson: University of Arizona, 1950, reissued 1970.

Beals, R. L. *Cheran: A Sierra Tarascan Village.* Publications of the Institute of Social Anthropology, No. 2. Washington, D.C.: Smithsonian Institution, 1946.

Bender, P. C., and Ruiz, R. A. "Race and Class as Differential Determinants of Underachievement and Underaspiration Among Mexican Americans." *Journal of Educational Research*, Vol. 68 (1974), 51–56.

Bowen, J. D., and Ornstein, J., eds. *Studies in Southwest Spanish.* Mass.: Newbury House Publishers, Inc., 1976.

Brand, E. S., Ruiz, R. A., and Padilla, A. M. "Ethnic Identification and Preference: A Review." *Psychological Bulletin*, Vol. 81 (1974), 360–390.

Burma, J. H., ed. *Mexican-Americans in the United States: A Reader.* Cambridge, Mass.: Schenkman Publishing Co., 1970.

Carlos, M. L., and Sellers, L. "Family, Kinship Structure, and Modernization in Latin America." *Latin American Research Review*, Vol. 7 (1972), 95–124.

Carrier, J. M. "Cultural Factors Affecting Urban Mexican Male Homosexual Behavior." *Archives of Sexual Behavior*, Vol. 5 (1976), 103–124.

————, "Family Attitudes and Mexican Male Homosexuality." *Urban Life*, Vol. 5 (1976), 359–375.

Casavantes, E. J. *El Tecato: Social and Cultural Factors Affecting Drug Use Among Chicanos.* Washington, D.C.: National Coalition of Spanish-Speaking Mental Health Organizations, 1976.

Castillo de Lucas, A. *Folkmedicina.* Madrid: Editorial Dossat, 1958.

Chandler, C. R. "Value Orientations Among Mexican Americans in a Southwestern City." *Sociology and Social Research*, Vol. 58 (1974), 262–271.

Clark, M. *Health in the Mexican American Culture.* 2nd ed. Berkeley: University of California Press, 1970.

————, and Mendelson, M. "Mexican-American Aged in San Francisco: A Case Description." *Gerontologist*, Vol. 9 (1969), 90–95.

Cohen, A. D. *A Sociolinguistic Approach to Bilingual Education: Experiments in the American Southwest.* Mass.: Newbury House Publication, 1975.

Cohen, L. M. *Culture, Disease and Stress Among Latino Immigrants.* Research Institute on Immigration and Ethnic Studies Special Study. Washington, D.C.: The Catholic University of America, 1979.

Cohen, R. "Principles of Preventive Mental Health Programs for Ethnic Minority Populations: The Acculturation of Puerto Ricans to the U.S." *American Journal of Psychiatry*, Vol. 128, No. 12 (June, 1972), 79–83.

Currier, R. L. "The Hot–Cold Syndrome and Symbolic Balance in Mexican and Spanish-American Folk Medicine." *Ethnology*, Vol. 5 (1966), 251–263.

Díaz-Guerrero, R. "A Mexican Psychology." *American Psychologist*, Vol. 32 (1977), 934–944.

———. "Neurosis and the Mexican Family Structure." *American Journal of Psychiatry*, Vol. 112 (1955), 411–417.

———. *Psychology of the Mexican.* Austin: University of Texas Press, 1967.

Edgerton, R. B., and Karno, M. "Mexican-American Bilingualism and Perception of Mental Illness." *Archives of General Psychiatry*, Vol. 24 (March, 1971), 286–290.

———, and Fernández, I. "Curanderismo in the Metropolis: The Diminishing Role of Folk-Psychiatry Among Los Angeles Mexican Americans." *American Journal of Psychotherapy*, Vol. 24 (1970), 124–134.

Fabrega, H., Jr. "Mexican Americans of Texas: Some Social Psychiatric Features." In E. B. Brody, ed., *Behavior in New Environments: Adaptation of Migrant Populations.* Beverly Hills: Sage Publications, 1970.

Fernández-Marina, R. "The Puerto Rican Syndrome: Its Dynamic and Cultural Determinants." *Psychiatry*, Vol. 24 (1961), 79–82.

Firth, R. "Acculturation in Relation to Concepts of Health and Disease." *In* I. Goldston, ed., *Medicine and Anthropology.* No. XXI of the New York Academy of Medicine Lectures to the Laity. New York: Books for Libraries Press, 1971.

Fitzpatrick, J. P. *Puerto Rican Americans: The Meaning of Migration to the Mainland.* Ethnic Groups in American Life Series. New Jersey: Prentice-Hall, Inc., 1971.

Foster, G. M. "Relationships between Spanish and Spanish-American Folk-medicine." *Journal of American Folklore*, Vol. 66, No. 261 (1953), 201–217.

———, and Rowe, J. H. "Suggestions for Field Recording of Information on the Hippocratic Classification of Diseases and Remedies." *Kroeber Anthropological Society Papers*, Vol. V (1951), 1–3.

Fried, J. "Acculturation and Mental Health Among Indian Migrants in Peru." *In* M. K. Opler, ed., *Culture and Mental Health.* New York: Macmillan Co., 1959.

Fuentes, D., and López, J. A. *Barrio Language Dictionary: First Dictionary of Caló.* La Puente, Calif., El Barrio Publications, 1974.

Galli, N. "The Influence of Cultural Heritage on the Health Status of Puerto Ricans." *Journal of School Health*, Vol. 45 (1975), 10–16.

Garrison, V. "The 'Puerto Rican Syndrome' in Psychiatry and Espiritismo." *In* V. Crapanzano and V. Garrison, eds., *Case Studies in Spirit Possession.* New York: Wiley, 1977.

Gillin, J. "Magical Fright." *Psychiatry*, Vol. 11 (1948), 387–400.

Gliebe, W., Malley, A., and Lynn, R. "The Use of Health Care Delivery System by Urban Americans in Ohio." *Public Health Reports*, Vol. 94, No. 3 (May–June, 1979), 226–230.

Hanson, R., and Beech, M. "Communicating Health Arguments Across Cultures." *Nursing Research*, Vol. 12, No. 4, 237–241.

Harwood, A. "Hot and Cold Theory of Disease." *JAMA*, Vol. 216, No. 7 (May 17, 1971), 1153–1158.

Hernández-Chávez, E., Cohen, A. D., and Beltramo, A. F. *El Lenguaje de los Chicanos: Regional and Social Characteristics Used by Mexican Americans*. Virginia: Center for Applied Linguistics, 1975.

Hidalgo, H. and Hidalgo Christensen, E. "The Puerto Rican Lesbian and the Puerto Rican Community." *Journal of Homosexuality*, Vol. 2, No. 2 (Winter 1976–77), 109–121.

Holland, W. R. "Mexican-American Medical Beliefs: Science or Magic?" *Arizona Medicine*, Vol. 20 (1963), 89–101.

Hughes, C. C. "Health and Well-Being Values in the Perspective of Sociocultural Change." *In* H. W. Peter, ed., *Comparative Theories of Social Change*. Ann Arbor: Foundation for Research on Human Behavior, 1966.

Humphrey, N. D. "Some Dietary and Health Practices of Detroit Mexicans." *Journal of American Folklore*, Vol. 58, No. 220, 255–258.

Jaco, E. G. "Mental Health of the Spanish American in Texas." *In* M. K. Opler, ed., *Culture and Mental Health*. New York: Macmillan Co., 1950.

Jarvis, D. C. *Folk Medicine*. New York: Holt, Rinehart & Winston, 1958.

Johnson, C. "Mexican American Women in the Labor Force and Lowered Fertility." *American Journal of Public Health*, Vol. 66, No. 12 (Dec. 1976), 1186–1188.

——. "Nursing and Mexican American Folk Medicine." *Nursing Forum*, Vol. 3, No. 2 (1964), 104–113.

Karno, M., and Edgerton, R. B. "Perception of Mental Illness in a Mexican American Community." *Archieves of General Psychiatry*, Vol. 20 (1969), 233–238.

———, and Morales, A. A. "A Community Mental Health Service for Mexican Americans in a Metropolis." *Comprehensive Psychiatry*, Vol. 12 (1971), 116–121.

———, Ross, R. N., and Caper, R. A. "Mental Health Roles of Physicians in a Mexican American Community." *Community Mental Health Journal*, Vol. 5 (1969), 62–69.

Kelly, C., and Kraly, E. "Recent Net Alien Immigration to the United States: Its Impact on Population Growth and Native Fertility." *Demography*, Vol. 15, No. 3 (Aug., 1978), 267–283.

Kelly, I. *Folk Practices in North Mexico*. Institute of Latin American Studies. Austin: University of Texas Press, 1965.

Kiev, A. *Curanderismo: Mexican-American Folk Psychiatry*. New York: The Free Press, 1968.

——. *Transcultural Psychiatry*. New York: The Free Press, 1972.

King, S. *Perceptions of Illness in Medical Practice*. New York: Russell Sage Foundation, 1962.

Kline, L. Y. "Some Factors in the Psychiatric Treatment of Spanish Americans." *American Journal of Psychiatry*, Vol. 125 (1969), 1674–1681.

Kreisman, J. J. "The *Curandero's* Apprentice: A Therapeutic Integration of Folk and Medical Healing." *American Journal of Psychiatry*, Vol. 132 (1975), 81–83.

Leighton, A. H. *My Name is Legion*. New York: Basic Books, 1959.

Levi, L., ed. *Society, Stress and Disease*. New York: Oxford University Press, 1971.

LeVine, E. S., and Padilla, A. M. *Crossing Cultures in Therapy: Pluralistic Counseling for the Hispanic*. California: Brooks/Cole Publishing Co., 1980.

Lewis, O. *La vida: A Puerto Rican Family in the Culture of Poverty—San Juan and New York*. New York: Random House, 1966.

———. *Life in a Mexican Village: Tepoztlán Restudied*. Urbana: University of Illinois Press, 1963.

———. *The Children of Sánchez: An Autobiography of a Mexican Family*. New York: Random House, 1961.

Logan, M. H. "Humoral Medicine in Guatemala and Peasant Acceptance of Modern Medicine." *Human Organization*, Vol. 32 (Winter, 1973), 385–395.

Lubchansky, I., Egri, G., and Stokes, J. "Puerto Rican Spiritualists View Illness: The Faith Healer as a Paraprofessional." *American Journal of Psychiatry*, Vol. 127 (1970), 312–321.

Mack, C. N., James, L. E., Ramírez, J., and Bailey, J. *The Attitudes of Mexican American "Non-Help Seekers" Regarding Help for Personal Problems: A Pilot Study*. Paper presented at the Southwestern Psychological Association. El Paso, Texas, May 4, 1974.

Madsen, M. C. "Development and Cross-Cultural Differences in the Cooperative and Competitive Behavior of Young Children." *Psychology*, Vol. 2 (1971), 365–371.

Madsen, W. "Health and Illness." *Society and Health in the Lower Río Grande Valley*. Texas: Hogg Foundation for Mental Health, 1961.

———. "Hot and Cold in the Universe of San Francisco Tecospa, Valley of Mexico." *Journal of American Folklore*, Vol. 68 (1955), 123–129.

———. "Mexican-Americans and Anglo-Americans: A Comparative Study of Mental Health in Texas." *In* S. C. Ploy and R. E. Edgerton, eds., *Changing Perspectives in Mental Illness*. New York: Holt, Rinehart & Winston, 1969.

———. "The Alcoholic Agringado." *American Anthropologist*, Vol. 66 (1964), 355–361.

———. *The Mexican-Americans of South Texas*. 2nd ed. New York: Holt, Rinehart & Winston, 1973.

———. "Value Conflicts and Folk Psychiatry in South Texas." *In* A. Kiev, ed., *Magic, Faith, and Healing*. New York: The Free Press, 1964.

Maloney, C., ed. *The Evil Eye*. New York: Columbia University Press, 1976.

Marcos, L. R., Urcuyo, L., Kesselman, M., and Alpert, M. "The Language Barrier in Evaluating Spanish-American Patients." *Archives of General Psychiatry*, Vol. 29 (1973), 655–659.

Martínez, C., and Martín, H. W. "Folk Diseases Among Urban Mexican-Americans: Etiology, Symptoms, and Treatment." *JAMA*, Vol. 196, No. 2 (April 11, 1966), 161–164.

Martínez, J. L. "Cross-Cultural Comparison of Chicanos and Anglos on the Semantic Differential: Some Implications for Psychology." *In* J. L. Martínez, ed., *Chicano Psychology*. New York: Academic Press, 1977.

Martínez, M. *Las plantas medicinales de México*. 5th ed. México, D. F.: Ediciones Botas, 1969.

McFeely, F. "Some Aspects of Folk Curing in the American Southwest." *Anthropological Quarterly*, Vol. 30 (Oct., 1957), 95–110.

McLemore, S. D. "Ethnic Attitudes toward Hospitalization: An Illustrative Comparison of Anglos and Mexican Americans." *Southwestern Social Science Quarterly*, Vol. 43 (1963), 341–346.

McWilliams, C. *North from Mexico: The Spanish-Speaking People of the United States.* New York: Greenwood Press, 1968.

Meadow, A., and Stoker, D. "Symptomatic Behavior of Hospitalized Patients." *Archives of General Psychiatry*, Vol. 12 (March, 1965), 267–277.

Moustafa, A. T. and Weiss, G. "Health Status and Practices of Mexican Americans." *Advance Report 11*. Los Angeles: University of California, Mexican American Study Project, 1968.

Murillo, N. "The Mexican American Family." *In* C. A. Hernández, M. J. Haug, and N. N. Wagner, eds., *Chicanos: Social and Psychological Perspectives.* 2nd ed. St. Louis: C. V. Mosby, 1976.

Nall, F., and Speilberg, J. "Social and Cultural Factors in the Responses of Mexican Americans to Medical Treatment." *Journal of Health and Social Behavior*, Vol. 8 (1967), 299–308.

Nelson, C. "Reconceptualizing Health Care." *In* V. Olesen, ed., *Women and Their Health: Research Implications for a New Era.* Washington, D.C.: U.S. Department of Health, Education, and Welfare. National Center for Health Services Research Publications No. (HRA) 77–3138, 1975.

O'Nell, C. W. "An Investigation of Reported 'Fright' as a Factor in the Etiology of SUSTO, 'Magical Fright.'" *Ethos* Vol. 3 (Spring, 1975), 41–63.

Padilla, A. M., Carlos, M. L., and Keefe, S. E. "Mental Health Service Utilization by Mexican Americans." *In* M. R. Miranda, ed., *Psychotherapy with the Spanish-Speaking: Issues in Research and Service Delivery.* Los Angeles: University of California, Spanish Speaking Mental Health Center, Monograph No. 3, 1976.

Padilla, E. R. "The Relationship Between Psychology and Chicanos: Failures and Possibilities." *In* C. A. Hernández, M. J. Haug, and N. N. Wagner, eds., *Chicanos: Social and Psychological Perspectives.* 2nd ed. St. Louis: C. V. Mosby, 1976.

Padrón, F. *El médico y el folklore.* San Luis Potosí, México: Talleres Gráficos de la Editorial Universitaria, 1956.

Pan American Health Organization. *Health Conditions in the Americas: 1969–1972.* Washington, D.C.: Pan American Health Organization, 1974.

Peñalosa, F. "Mexican Family Roles." *Journal of Marriage and the Family*, Vol. 30 (1968), 680–689.

Pineda, V. G. de. *La medicina popular en Colombia.* Colombia: Facultad de Sociología, Universidad Nacional de Colombia. Monografías Sociológicas, No. 8, 1961.

Poma, P. "Hispanos: Impact of Culture on Health Care." *Illinois Medical Journal*, Vol. 156, No. 6 (Dec., 1979), 451–458.

Press, I. "Physicians, Curers and Dual Use in Bogotá." *Journal of Health and Social Behavior*, Vol. 10 (Sept., 1969), 209–218.

Ramos, R. "A Case in Point: An Ethnomethodological Study of a Poor Mexican American Family." *Social Science Quarterly*, Vol. 53 (1973), 905–919.

Reichel-Dolmatoff, G. and A. *The People of Aritama.* Chicago: University of Chicago Press, 1961.

Richardson, M., and Bode, B. *Popular Medicine in Puntarenas, Costa Rica: Urban and Societal Features.* New Orleans: Middle American Research Institute, Tulane University Publication 24, 1971.

Roemer, M. I. "Medical Care and Social Class in Latin America." *The Milbank Memorial Fund Quarterly*, Vol. 42 (July, 1964), 54–64.

Romano, V., O. I. "Charismatic Medicine, Folk Healing, and Folk-Sainthood." *American Anthropologist*, Vol. 67 (1965), 1151–1173.

Rubel, A. J. *Across the Tracks: Mexican Americans in a Texas City.* Austin: University of Texas Press, 1966.

———. "Análisis functional y efectos negativos de algunas creencias acerca de la causación de enfermedades." *Anuario indigenista*, México, D. F., XXIX (1969), 269–275.

———. "Concepts of Disease in Mexican American Culture." *American Anthropologist*, Vol. 62, No. 5 (1960), 795–815.

———. "The Epidemiology of a Folk Illness: *Susto* in Hispanic America." *Ethnology*, Vol. 3 (1964), 268–283.

———, and O'Nell, C. W. "The Meaning of SUSTO (Magical Fright)." Paper presented at the XLI International Congress of Americanists, Mexico City, 1974.

Sabagh, G. "Fertility Planning Status of Chicano Couples in Los Angeles." *American Journal of Public Health*, Vol. 70, No. 1 (Jan., 1980), 56–61.

Samora, J. "Conceptions of Health and Disease Among Spanish Americans." *American Catholic Sociological Review*, Vol. XXII, No. 4 (1961), 314–323.

———. *Los Mojados: The Wetback Story.* Notre Dame, Indiana: University of Notre Dame Press, 1971.

———, ed. *La Raza: Forgotten Americans.* Notre Dame, Indiana: University of Notre Dame Press, 1966.

Saunders, L. *Cultural Difference and Medical Care.* New York: Russell Sage Foundations, 1954.

———. "Culture and Nursing Care." *In* E. G. Jacob, ed., *Patients, Physicians, and Illness.* Glencoe: The Free Press, 1958.

———. "Healing Ways in the Spanish Southwest." *In* E. G. Jaco, ed., *Patients, Physicians, and Illness.* Glencoe: The Free Press, 1958.

———, and Hewes, G. W. "Folk Medicine and Medical Practice." *Journal of Medical Education*, Vol. 28, No. 9 (1953), 43–46.

———, and Samora, J. "A Medical Care Program in a Colorado County." *In* B. D. Paul, ed., *Health, Culture and Community.* New York: Russell Sage Foundation, 1955.

Serrano, A. C., and Gibson, G. "Mental Health Services to the Mexican-American Community in San Antonio, Texas." *American Journal of Public Health*, Vol. 63 (1973), 1055–1057.

Simmons, O. G. "Popular and Modern Medicine in Mestizo Communities of Coastal Peru and Chile." *Journal of American Folklore*, Vol. 68 (1955), 57–71.

Snow, L. "Folk Medical Beliefs and Their Implications for Care of Patients." *Annals of Internal Medicine*, Vol. 81 (1974), 82–96.

Spicers, E. H., ed. *Ethnic Medicine in the Southwest.* Arizona: University of Arizona Press, 1977.

Stekert, E. "Focus for Conflict: Southern Mountain Medical Beliefs in Detroit." *In* A. Paredes and E. Stekert, eds., *The Urban Experience and Folk Tradition.* Austin: University of Texas Press, 1971.

Stenger-Castro, E. "The Mexican American: How His Culture Affects His Mental Health." *In* R. Argüijo Martínez, ed., *Hispanic Culture and Health Care: Fact, Fiction, Folklore.* St. Louis: Mosby, 1978.

Teller, C. H. "Access to Medical Care of Migrants in a Honduran City." *Journal of Health and Social Behavior*, Vol. 14 (Sept., 1973), 214–226.

Torrey, E. F. *The Mind Game: Witchdoctors and Psychiatrists.* New York: Emerson Hall, 1972.

Turner, P. R., ed. *Bilingualism in the Southwest.* Tucson: University of Arizona Press, 1973.

———— and Turner, S. *Dictionary: Chontal to Spanish-English, Spanish to Chontal.* Tucson: University of Arizona Press, 1971.

Walker, G. M. "Contraceptive Utilization in the United States: 1973–1976." *Advance Data*, Vol. 36 (Aug. 18, 1978).

————. "Utilization of Health Care: The Laredo Migrant Experience." *American Journal of Public Health*, Vol. 69, No. 7 (July, 1979), 667–671.

Weaver, T. "Use of Hypothetical Situations in a Study of Spanish American Illness Referral Systems." *Human Organization*, Vol. 29, No. 2 (1970), 140–154.

Werner, D. *Donde no hay doctor.* 4th ed. México: Editorial Pax-México, 1980.

Uzzell, D. "*Susto* Revisited: Illness as a Strategic Role." *American Ethnologist*, Vol. 1 (May, 1974), 369–378.

Zalamea, L. "The Modern Spirit of *Santería*." *Nuestro Magazine*, Vol. 2, No. 3 (1978), 61–63.

Essential Grammar Index

Indice de Gramatica Basica

ENGLISH

(Numbers refer to pages.)

a
  with certain verbs, 172
  contraction with *el*, 81
  personal **A**, 164
  uses of, 163
absolute superlative, 79, 166
accents, 19, 43
adjectives, 28-29, 71-84
  absolute superlative of, 79
  agreement, 71
  apocopation, 77
  clauses, subjunctive or
    indicative, 154
  comparison, 78
  definite article, 80
  demonstrative, 76
  gender of, 71
  interrogative, 73
  indefinite article, 83
  idiomatic use of, 73
  plural of, 72
  position of, 72
  possessive, 74
adjective clauses, 154
adverbs, 29, 154-156, 156-161
  absolute superlative, 161
  comparison, 160
  of intensity, 159
  of manner, 157
  of place, 158
  sentence modifiers, 159
  of time, 157
adverb clauses, 154
affirmative words, 33
age, 96
al + infinitive, 164
AR verbs, 85, 99, 102, 106, 111, 115,
    123, 124, 139, 142, 144, 150
article, definite
  contractions with, 81
  in dates, 216
  with days of week, 82, 216
  forms, 80
  omission of, 81
  with parts of body and clothing,
    81
  in time expressions, 209
  with titles, 81
article, indefinite
  forms, 83
  uses, 83

become, *to*, 134

by: translated by **para**, 170
  translated by **por**, 168

capitalization, 24
ciento, apocopation of, 77
cognates, 17
commands
  familiar, 148
  first person plural, 147
  indirect, 148
  irregularities, 147
  position of object pronouns
    with, 147
  of stem-changing verbs, 146
  with Vd., Vds., 146
comparison
  adjectives, 78
  adverbs, 161
  of equality, 79, 161
compound tenses, 123, 124, 145
con, 166, 173
conjugations, 84
conjunctions
  coordinate, 177
  correlative, 180
  subordinate, 179
contractions, 81
¿**cuál?**, 62

dar, 147
dates, 216
dative of interest, 59, 83
days of the week, 215
de
  + *el*, 81
  + noun, 166
  + number, 78
  meaning *in* , 167
  to show possession, 64, 166
  in time expressions, 213
  verbs requiring, 174
definite article, *see* article, definite
demonstrative adjectives, 76
demonstrative pronouns, 64
diminutives and augmentatives, 44
diphthongs, 16
direct object, 48
direct object pronouns
  position, 49
  use, 48
double object pronouns, 57

e for **y**, 177

equality, comparison of, 79, 160
ER verbs, 87, 99, 102, 106, 111, 115,
    123, 124, 132, 139, 142, 144,
    150
estar, 94, 95
este, ese, aquel, 76
éste, ése, aquél, 64
exclamatory words, 30

familiar commands, 148
familiar forms of address, 47
feminine gender
  adjectives, 71
  nouns, 38, 39
for: translated by **para**, 170
  translated by **por**, 168
future
  formation, 115
  irregularities, 116
  special use of, 116

gender
  of adjectives, 71
  of nouns, 38
gerund, *see* present participle
gran(de), 77
gustar, 54

haber (auxiliary verb)
  pluperfect indicative, 124
  pluperfect subjunctive, 145
  present perfect indicative, 123
  present perfect subjunctive, 145
hacer, 89, 103, 122
  in expressions of time, 137
hurt, *to*, 136

imperative, 148
imperfect indicative tense,
    106
  formation of, 107
  irregularities, 107
in (after superlative), 79
indefinite article, *see* article,
    indefinite
indirect object, 51
indirect object pronoun, 51
infinitive, 117
interrogation, 31
interrogative
  adjective, 73
  pronouns, 62
  word order, 30

-IR verbs, 87, 100, 102, 106, 111, 115, 123, 124, 132, 139, 142, 144, 150
irregular verbs, 88-92
ísimo, 79

masculine noun endings, 39
más, 78, 169
mejor, 78, 160
months, 215

negation
  imperatives, 147
  sentences, 32
  words, 33
neuter, 64
No, 32
nouns, 28, 37-45
  accents, 43
  adjectives used as, 73
  diminutives and augmentatives, 44
  gender of
    by ending, 39
    by meaning, 38
  past participle used as, 127
  plural, 41
  prepositions used before, 166
noun clause, subjunctive in, 149

object pronouns, 48-59
  direct, 48
  indirect, 51
  order, 57
  position, 49, 52
order, word, 30

para, 170
participle
  past participle, 122
    formation of, 122
    irregularities, 122
    uses, 123
  present participle, 118
    position of object pronouns
      with, 118
    progressive tenses, 120
    uses of, 119
passive voice, 127, 128
  alternates for, 130
  true passive, 128
past subjunctive, 144
pero, 177
personal **a**, 164
personal pronouns
  direct object, 48
  indirect object, 51
  prepositional pronouns, 61
  reflexive, 59, 110
    prepositional forms of, 61

subject, 46
pluperfect indicative, 124
pluperfect subjunctive, 145
plural
  adjectives, 72
  nouns, 41
por, 168
position
  adjectives, 72
  numbers, 200
  object pronouns, 49, 57
possession, 166
possessive adjectives, 74
  stressed forms, 74
possessive pronouns, 69
prepositional pronouns, 61
  forms of reflexive pronouns, 61
prepositions, 29, 161-177
  a, 162, 163, 172
  compound, 162
  con, 166, 173
  de, 163, 166, 174
  en, 175
  before infinitives, 171
  por and **para**, 168, 170
  simple, 162
present indicative, 84
present participle, 118
present perfect indicative, 123
present perfect subjunctive, 145
preterite
  formation of, 102
  irregularities, 103
  orthographic changes, 103
  stem changes, 104
  uses of, 104
progressive tenses, 120
pronouns, 28, 46-71
  chart, 63
  demonstrative, 64
  direct object, 48
  double object, 57
  indirect object, 51
  interrogative, 62
  object of prepositions, 61
  order, 49
  possessive, 69
  reflexive, 59
    prepositional forms of, 61
    reciprocal use of, 60
  relative, 66
  se for **le** or **les**, 57
  subject, 46
pronunciation, 5
punctuation, 23

¿qué?, 63
que
  relative, 67

than, 78
questions, 31
quien, 67
¿quien?, 64
quotation marks, 24

reflexive pronouns, 59, 110
reflexive verbs, 110
  to express passive voice, 130
  uses of, 113
relative pronouns, 66
  compound, 68

Se
  for **le** and **les**, 57
  reflexive, 59, 110
ser, 92, 95
stem changing verbs
  command forms, 146
  past subjunctive, 144
  pluperfect subjunctive, 145
  present indicative, 98
    class I, 99
    class II, 100
    class III, 100
  present participle, 118
  present subjunctive, 140
  preterite, 104
stress, 19
su, sus, clarification of, 74
subjunctive mood
  after **acaso, tal vez, quizá(s)**, 149
  in adjective clauses, 154
  in adverb clauses, 154
  in commands, 146
  in noun clauses, 149
  after **ojalá**, 149
  past, 144
  pluperfect, 145
  in polite statements, 149
  present, 139
    of irregular verbs, 143
    orthographic changes, 142
    of stem changing, 140
  present perfect, 145
  sequence of tenses, 145
superlative, 79, 161
syllabication, 21

tan...como, 79
tanto...como, 79
tantos...como, 79
tener, 91, 96, 97

usted, 47
ustedes, 47

verbs
  auxiliary, 123, 124, 145

conjugation, 84
formation and use of compound
tense, 123, 124, 129, 145
formation and use of simple
tense, 84, 102, 106, 115
future, 115
imperfect, 106
infinitive, 117
irregular, 88-92
orthographic irregularities,
103, 132, 142
passive, 123

past participle, 122
past subjunctive, 144
pluperfect indicative, 124
pluperfect subjunctive, 145
present participle, 118
present perfect indicative, 123
present perfect subjunctive, 145
preterite, 102
progressive tenses, 120
reflexive, 110
special uses of selected verbs, 134
stem changing, 98, 104, 118, 140,

144, 146
subjunctive mood, 138

word order
of adjectives, 72
in commands, 147
of numbers, 200
in questions, 30
in statements, 30

you, 47

ESPAÑOL

(Los números refieren a las páginas.)

a
con ciertos verbos, 172
contracción con el, 81
A personal, 164
usos de, 163
el superlativo absoluto de, 79, 166
los acentos, 19, 43
adjetivos, 28-29, 71-84
el superlativo absoluto de, 79
concordancia de, 71
apócope de, 77
cláusulas, subjuntivo o indicativo,
154
comparativo, 78
artículo definido, 80
demostrativo, 76
género de, 71
interrogativo, 73
artículo indefinido, 83
uso idiomático de, 73
plural de, 72
posición de, 72
posesivo, 74
cláusulas que sirven de adjetivos, 154
adverbios, 29, 154-161
el superlativo absoluto de, 161
comparativo, 160
que expresan cantidad, 159
que expresan modo, 157
que determinan lugar, 158
modificativos de oraciones, 159
que concretan tiempo, 157
cláusulas adverbiales, 154
palabras afirmativas, 33
edad, 96
al + el infinitivo, 164

verbos en *-AR*, 85, 99, 102, 106, 111,
115, 123, 124, 139, 142, 144,
150
artículo definido
contracciones con, 81
con fechas, 216
con los días de la semana, 82, 216
formas de, 80
omisión de, 81
con las partes del cuerpo y la ropa,
81
en expresiones de la hora, 209
con títulos, 81
artículo indefinido
formas de, 83
usos de, 83

equivalentes de *to become*, 134
traducción de *para*, 170
traducción de *por*, 168
uso de letras mayúsculas, 24
ciento, apócope de, 77
cognatos, 17
mandatos
el imperativo, 148
el mandato con "nosotros", 147
el mandato indirecto, 148
irregularidades, 147
posición de los pronombres
objetivos con, 147
de los verbos que cambian de
radical, 146
con *Vd., Vds.*, 146
comparativo
adjetivo, 78
adverbio, 161

de igualdad, 79, 161
tiempo compuesto, 123, 124, 145
con, 166, 173
conjugaciones, 84
conjunciones,
coordinantes, 177
correlativas, 180
subordinantes, 179
contracciones, 81
¿cuál?, 62

dar, 147
fechas, 216
dativo de interés, 59, 83
días de la semana, 215
de
+ *el*, 81
+ sustantivo, 166
+ número, 78
en superlativo, 167
en expresión de posesión, 64, 166
en expresiones horarias, 213
verbos que requieren, 174
artículo definido, *ver artículo
definido*
adjetivos demostrativos, 76
pronombres demostrtivos, 64
diminutivos y aumentativos, 44
diptongos, 16
objeto directo, 48
pronombres objetivos directos
posición de, 49
uso de, 48
dos pronombres objetivos, 57

e en vez de y, 177

comparativo de igualdad, 79, 160
verbos en **-ER**, 87, 99, 102, 106, 111,
  115, 123, 124, 132, 139, 142,
  144, 150
estar, 94, 95
este, ese, aquel, 76
éste, ése, aquél, 64
interjecciones, 30

el imperativo, 148
uso de **tú**, 47
género femenino
  adjetivos, 71
  sustantivos, 38, 39
traducción de *para*, 170
  traducción de *por*, 168
tiempo futuro
  formación de, 115
  irregularidades, 116
  uso especial de, 116

género
  de adjetivos, 71
  de sustantivos, 38
el gerundio, *ver* participio
gran(de), 77
gustar, 54

haber
  pluscuamperfecto de indicativo
    124
  pluscuamperfecto de subjuntivo,
    145
  perfecto de indicativo, 123
  perfecto de subjuntivo, 145
hacer, 89, 103, 122
  en expresiones temporales, 137
equivalentes de *to hurt*, 136

el imperativo, 148
tiempo imperfecto de indicativo, 106
  formación de, 107
  irregularidades, 107
de en superlativo, 79
artículo indefinido, *ver* artículo
  indefinido
objeto indirecto, 51
pronombre objetivo indirecto, 51
infinitivo, 117
interrogación, 31
interrogativo
  adjetivo, 73
  pronombre como, 62
orden de palabras, 30
verbos en **-IR**, 87, 100, 102, 106, 111,
  115, 123, 124, 132, 139, 142,
  144, 150
verbos irregulares, 88-92
-ísimo, 79

terminaciones de sustantivos
  masculinos, 39
más, 78, 160
mejor, 78, 160
los meses, 215

negación
  del imperativo, 147
  en oraciones, 32
  palabras negativas, 33
neutro, 64
No, 32
sustantivos, 28, 37-45
  acentos, 43
  adjetivos usados como, 73
  diminutivos y aumentativos, 44
  género de
    según la terminación, 39
    según la significación, 38
  el participio pasivo usado como,
    127
  plural, 41
  con *de*, 166
subjuntivo en la cláusula sustantiva,
  149

pronombres objetivos, 48-59
  directos, 48
  indirectos, 51
  orden de, 57
  posición de, 49, 52
  orden de palabras, 30

para, 170
participio
  el participio pasivo, 122
    formación de, 122
    irregularidades, 122
    usos, 123
  el gerundio, 118
    posición de los pronombres
      objetivos con, 118
    los tiempos progresivos, 120
    usos de, 119
  la voz pasiva, 127, 128
    alternativos para la voz pasiva, 130
    la verdadera voz pasiva, 128
el imperfecto de subjuntivo, 144
pero, 177
a personal, 164
pronombres personales
  objeto directo, 48
  objeto indirecto, 51
pronombres preposicionales, 61
reflexivo, 59, 110
  formas preposicionales de, 61
  nominativo, 46
el pluscuamperfecto de indicativo,
  124

el pluscuamperfecto de subjuntivo,
  145
plural
  de adjetivos, 72
  de sustantivos, 41
por, 168
posición
  de adjetivos, 72
  de pronombres objetivos, 49, 57
  de números, 200
posesión, 166
adjetivos posesivos, 74
  las formas largas, 74
pronombres posesivos, 69
pronombres preposicionales, 61
  formas de los pronombres
    reflexivos, 61
preposiciones, 29, 161-177
  a, 162, 163, 172
  compuestas, 162
  con, 166, 173
  de, 163, 166, 174
  en, 175
  antes de infinitivos, 171
  por y para, 168, 170
  sencillas, 162
tiempo presente de indicativo, 84
el gerundio, 118
el perfecto de indicativo, 123
el perfecto de subjuntivo, 145
tiempo pretérito
  formación de, 102
  irregularidades, 103
  cambios ortográficos, 103
  cambios de radical, 104
  usos de, 104
los tiempos progresivos, 120
pronombres, 28, 46-71
  gráfica, 63
  demostrativos, 64
  objetivos directos, 48
  dos pronombres objetivos, 57
  objetivos indirectos, 51
  como interrogativos, 62
  preposicionales, 61
  orden de, 49
  posesivos, 69
  reflexivos, 59
    formas preposicionales de, 61
    uso recíproco de, 60
  relativos, 66
  conversión de *le* o *les* en *se*, 57
  nominativos, 46
pronunciación, 5
puntuación, 23

¿qué?, 63
que
  relativo, 67

en formación del comparativo, 78, 288
preguntas, 31
quien, 67
¿*quién?*, 64
comillas, 24

pronombres reflexivos, 59, 110
verbos reflexivos, 110
    alternativo para la voz pasiva, 130
    usos de, 113
pronombres relativos, 66
    compuestos, 68

Se
    conversión de *le* o *les* en *se*, 57
    reflexivo, 59, 110
ser, 92, 95
verbos que cambian de radical
    formas del mandato, 146
    imperfecto de subjuntivo, 144
    pluscuamperfecto de subjuntivo, 145
    presente de indicativo, 98
        1ª clase, 99
        2ª clase, 100
        3ª clase, 100
    el gerundio, 118
    presente de subjuntivo, 140
    pretérito, 104
énfasis, 19
su, sus, clarificación de, 74
pronombre personal nominativo
    el modo subjuntivo
        después de *acaso, tal vez*,

quizá(s), 149
    en cláusulas adjetivas, 154
    en cláusulas adverbiales, 154
    en el mandato, 146
    en cláusulas substantivas, 149
    después de *ojalá*, 149
    el imperfecto de subjuntivo, 144
    el pluscuamperfecto de subjuntivo, **145**
    en ruegos corteses, 149
    el presente de subjuntivo, 139
        de verbos irregulares, 143
        cambios ortográficos, 142
        de verbos que cambian de radical, 140
    el perfecto de subjuntivo, 145
    secuencia de tiempos, 145
superlativo, 79, 161
silabeo, 21

tan...como, 79
tanto...como, 79
tantos...como, 79
tener, 91, 96, 97

usted, 47
ustedes, 47

verbos
    auxiliares, 123, 124, 145
    conjugación, 84
    formación y uso del tiempo compuesto, 123, 124, 129, 145
    formación y uso del tiempo simple, 84, 102, 106, 115

el tiempo futuro, 115
el tiempo imperfecto, 106
el infinitivo, 117
irregulares, 88-92
irregularidades ortográficas, 103, 132, 142
la voz pasiva, 123
el participio pasivo, 122
el imperfecto de subjuntivo, 144
el pluscuamperfecto de indicativo, 124
el pluscuamperfecto de subjuntivo, 145
el gerundio, 118
el perfecto de indicativo, 123
el perfecto de subjuntivo, 145
el pretérito, 102
los tiempos progresivos, 120
reflexivos, 110
usos especiales de verbos escogidos, 134
verbos que cambian de radical, 98, 104, 118, 140, 144, 146
el modo subjuntivo, 138

orden de las palabras
    de adjetivos, 72
    en el mandato, 147
    con números, 200
    en preguntas, 30
    en oraciones declarativas, 30

usted, ustedes, tú, vosotros, 47

Index

Indice

ENGLISH

Abortions, 301, 419, 420
Accentuation, 19, 43
Adjectives, 28, 71
Adverbs, 29, 156
Admission
    information for, 398
    of patient to room, 242
Ailments, 260, 427
    alphabetical order, 427
Allergy, 246, 263, 312, 344
Alphabet, 2
Ambulance, 242
Ambulation, 249
Anatomy and physiology, 221
    anatomical pictures, 5, 223, 225,
        226, 227, 229, 230, 232-239
Anesthesia, 338
    caudal, 340
    effectiveness of, 338
    epidural, 340
    general, 339
    local, 340
    spinal, 340
Authorizations and signatures, 413
    abortion release, 420
    blood transfusion, 417
    postmortem, 423
    sterilization permit, 421
    surgical consent, 415
    therapeutic abortion, 419
    undertaker's release, 424
    visiting policy, 422

Bathing, 250
Bibliography, 517
Birth control, 381, 445
Blood
    pressure, 327, 374
    tests, 360, 375
    transfusion, request for, 417
Blue Cross/Blue Shield, 400, 404,
    408
Body, parts of, 221
Breast, 278, 325
    breast self-examination, 278, 325

Calendar, 215
Capitalization, 24
Cardiovascular system, 283, 325
Clinics, 427
Clothing, 453
Cognates, 17
Colors, 280, 300, 454
Common expressions, 180
Complaints

alphabetical order of, 427
by history, 254
by physical examination, 321
Conjunctions, 30, 177
Consent forms, 413
Contraceptive devices
    coitus interruptus, 385
    diaphragm, 382
    discussion of reproductive system,
        379
    female, 380
    male, 379
    douching, 385
    foam and condom, 381
    IUD, 382
    pill, 383
    rhythm method, 384
    sterilization, 385
Conversion
    Fahrenheit/centigrade, 204
    metric/decimal, 205
Countries of origin, 455
Cultural information and notes, 184,
    194-195, 386-396, 410-411,
    463-466

Date, 215
Dentistry
    amalgams and inlays, 369
    cavities and cavity preparation,
        368
    dental history, 277
    dental needs, 244
    general dental conversation, 367
    impression taking, 369
    oral surgery, 381
    prophylactic, 370
    vocabulary, 228
Diagnosis, 251
Diagnostic studies, 360
    see also special procedures
Diarrhea, 293
Diet, 245, 286, 457
Diphthongs, 16
Discharge instructions
    appointments, 252
    cast care, 349
    diagnosis/prognosis, 251
    instructions on smoking,
        drinking, 252
    prescriptions, 343
    prohibitions, 252
    sprain care, 348
    wound care, 349
Diseases

alphabetical order of, 427
folk diseases, 186, 387, 394
by history, 260
by physical examination, 321
Drug abuse and overdose
    drug indentification, 356
    signs and symptoms of, 355, 357
    use, 314
    vocabulary, 441

Ears, 275, 323
Elimination, 290, 444
Emergency room report, 402
Endocrine system, 309
Enemas, 338, 364, 375
Evaluating the patient
    by history, 267
    by physical examination, 321
Extremities, 305, 333
Eyes, 272, 322

Family, 318
    address, telephone number, 398,
        402
    consent for operation, 337
    duration of surgery, 338
    medical history of, 318
    names of specific relatives, 450
    visiting, 247, 341
Family planning, 378
    discussion of contraceptive
        devices, 381
    discussion of reproductive
        systems, 379
Female problems, 298, 300, 301, 303,
    304
Food, 457

Gastrointestinal system, 286, 329
Genitourinary system, 294, 332
Grammar, 27
Greetings, 187
    communication, 188
    farewells, 192
    introducing oneself, 187, 242
    morning rounds, 190
    polite expressions, 192
Gynecological system, 298, 331

Head, 270, 321
History
    family, 318
    past medical, 260
    personal, 309
    present medical, 254

social, 316
see also Review of systems
Hospitalization, 263, 274
Hygiene, 250

Identifying the patient
age, 310, 398, 403
doctor, 401
education, 312
home, 203, 309, 398, 402
marital status, 310
name, 309, 398, 402
Illness
folk, 186, 387, 394
past medical, 260
present, 254
Immunizations and vaccinations,
262
Information
admission, 398
birth certificate, 405
Blue Cross/Blue Shield, 400, 404,
408
emergency room, 402
Instructing the patient
about appointments, 252
about bathroom, 244
about bed, 243
about call light, 243
about clergy, 245
about collection of urine
specimen, 243
about dentures, 244
about meals, 245
about operation, 258, 336
about patient discharge, 253
about post-operative care, *see*
Post-operative care and
instructions
about room, 245
about supplies, 245, 253
about telephone calls, 244
Insurance, 399, 408
Interjections, 30
Interviewing the patient, *see* Review
of systems
Introducing oneself, 187, 242

Laboratory tests, 360

Medication and treatment, 342
casts and slings, 348
crutches, 349
dosage, 344
dressing changes, 346
history of, 344
instructions for
fractures, 348
sprains, 348
wounds, 349

lozenges, 345
ointments, 345
pills, 344
prohibitions, 347, 355
sprays, 346
suppositories, 347
syrups and liquids, 346
warnings, 347
Menopause, 303
Menstruation, 298, 299
Morning rounds, 180
Mouth and throat, 277, 324
Musculoskeletal system, 308, 333

Nationality, 455
Neck, 278, 324
Negation, 32
Neurological system, 306, 334
Nose and sinuses, 276
Nouns, 28, 37
Numbers and numerical
expressions, 197
cardinals, 198
dates, 215
decimals, 203, 205
dimensions, 204
fractions, 201
metric, 205
ordinals, 199
social security, 203
street addresses, 203
symbols, 202
telephone, 204, 393
temperature, 204
time, 209
Nursing care, 248

Occupations, 309, 455
Operations, 336
anesthesiologist, 338
caesarean, 378
cancellation of, 338
consent, 337
consent forms, 413
duration of, 338
explanation of, 336
informing the family, 337
preparing for post-operative tubes,
339
"prepping" the patient, 338
previous, 265
surgeon, 339
see also Post-operative instructions
Orthopedic exam, 333

Pain, 254, 281, 283, 289, 295, 297,
303, 305, 308
Parents, *see* Family
Parts of the body, 221
Parts of speech, 28
Past medical history, 260

Personal history, 309
Physical examination, 321
abdomen, 329
breasts, 325
chest, 325
ears, 323
extremities, 333
eyes, 322
gastrointestinal, 329
genitourinary, 332
head, 321
limbs, 333
lungs, 325
mental status, 258, 306
mouth, 324
musculoskeletal, 333
neck, 324
neurological, 334
pain, 335
pelvic, 331, 332
rectal, 329
sensation, 335
temperature, 328
testicles, 332
throat, 324
vital signs, 325
Pills, 202, 253, 255, 263, 274, 312,
314, 315, 342, 351, 356, 364,
383
Poisoning, accidental, 351, 440
determining the poison, 351
determining the symptoms, 352
giving the antidote, 352
instructions for snake bites, 353
Polite expressions, 187
Post-operative care and instructions
ambulation, 249
bedrest, 249
dressing change, 342
extubation, 341
family visits, 247, 341
foley cathether, 332, 338
intravenous, 339, 363
NPO instructions, 339, 341, 362
nasogastric tube, 339, 350
PO intake, 339
prohibitions, 341, 342
respirators, 349
restraints, 244
Pregnancy
abortion, release from
responsibility for, 420
delivery
caeserean, 378
vaginal, 376
labor, 373
preparation, 374
stages of, 375
nursing of child, 377
prenatal history, 301

sterilization permit, 421
therapeutic abortion,
    authorization for, 419
visiting policy, 422
vocabulary, 445
Preparation for physical
    examination, 320
Prepositions, 29, 161
Pronouns, 28, 46
Pronunciation, 1
    accentuation, 19, 43
    alphabet, 2
    cognates, 17
    dialectal variations, 12
    diphthongs, 16
    rules, 5
    Spanish phonetics, 3
    syllabication, 21
Public aid, 404
Punctuation, 23

Rectal examination, 329
Relatives, *see* Family
Religion, 398, 454
Respiratory system, 279, 325
Review of systems, 269
    abortions, 301
    accidents, 265
    age, 310
    age of children, 301, 310
    allergies, 263, 312
    angina, 279
    aphasia, 307
    bleeding, 270, 280, 292, 296, 302
    bladder habits, 294
    bowel habits, 290
    breasts, 278
    cancer, history of, 262, 319
    cardiac history, 283
    cardiovascular, 283
    chronic diseases, 307
    constipation, 293
    cough, 280
    diabetes, 295, 302, 309, 315, 319
    discharges from the body, 273,
        275, 278, 300, 304
    doctor, 264
    drinking habits, 286, 313
    drug allergy, 263
    drug identification, 314, 315, 356
    drug ingestion, 292, 314, 351
    dysphagia, 278, 290
    dyspnea, 279, 285
    ears, 275
    eating, 286, 312
    edema, 285, 308
    endocrine system, 309
    extremities, 305
    eyes, 272

family, 310
fever, 328
gastroenteritis, 287
gastrointestinal system, 286
genitourinary system, 294
gynecological system, 298
habits
    drinking, 286, 312
    drug, 314
    eating, 286, 312
    sleeping, 285
    smoking, 281, 313
    travel, 265
hair, 269
head, 270
heart attack, 284
home, 310, 317
hospitalization, 263
hypertension, 286, 302
hypotension, 303
infection, 273, 296, 297
insurance, 316
itching, 269, 291
labor, 302
medicines, 264, 284, 302, 342
menopause, 303
menstruation, 298, 299
mental status, 258, 306
mouth, 277
musculoskeletal, 308
name, 309, 392
nausea, 289
neck, 278
neurological system, 306
nose, 276
obstetrical history, 301
occupation, 254, 311, 455
occupational exposure, 263, 311
operations, 264
orthopnea, 279, 285
pain, 254, 281, 283, 289, 295,
    297, 303, 305, 308
paroxysmal nocturnal dyspnea,
    279, 285
poisoning
    drug, 351
    food, 351
pregnancy, 301
reproductive systems, 297, 298, 301
respiratory system, 279
sinuses, 276
skin, 269
sleeping habits, 285
sputum, 280
surgical history, 264
syncope, 254, 271, 306, 307
throat, 277
transfusions, 265
trauma, 265

tuberculosis, 260, 319
urological history, 294
venereal problems, 297, 300, 304
vertigo, 270, 306
vomiting, 289, 290
weight change, 267, 309, 312
worm infection, 292
X-rays, 281, 293

Skin, hair, 269
Smoking, 281, 313
Social history, 316
Spanish surnames, 392
Special procedures
    barium swallow, 365
    bladder catheterization, 332, 338
    blood tests, 360
    blood pressure, 327
    caudal anesthesia, 340
    colposcopy, 332
    cone biopsy, 332
    cystoscopy, 332, 363
    electrocardiogram, 363
    endoscopy, 329, 330
    epidural anesthesia, 340
    esophagoscopy, 329
    general instructions, 362
    intravenous, 339, 363
    IPPB, 349
    IVP, 332
    list of various tests, 361
    lumbar puncture, 340, 366
    nasogastric intubation, 354
    Pap smear, 331
    pelvic, 331
    proctoscopy, 330
    pulse, 327
    sigmoidoscopy, 329
    spinal, 340
    stomach pump, 354
    stool culture, 364
    temperature, 328
    urinalysis, 364
    venepuncture, 361
    X-ray studies, 364
Speech, dialectal variations of,
    12
Surgery, 336, 413
Syllabication, 21
Systems
    cardiovascular, 283, 325
    endocrine, 309
    gastrointestinal, 286, 329
    genitourinary, 294, 332
    musculoskeletal, 308, 333
    neurological, 306, 334
    reproductive, 379
    respiratory, 279, 325
    see also Review of systems

Temperature, 204, 328
Tests, 360
Time
  day, 213, 215
  month, 215
  season, 215
  telling time, 209
Transportation for tests, 246, 366
Treatment, 342

Useful expressions for morning
  rounds, 190

Venereal disease, 261, 304, 445
Verbs, 28, 84
Visiting hours, 247, 341, 422

Vocabulary
  anatomic and physiological, 221
  bathroom, toilet articles and
    personal effects, 451
  bedding, 453
  blood, 444
  clinics, 427
  clothing, 453
  colors, 454
  countries and nationalities, 455
  dental, 228
  diseases, symptoms and injuries,
    427
  drug abuse, 441
  English-Spanish, 467
  excretions, 444

  family, 450
  food and meals, 457
  medical abbreviations, 435
  medical specialists, 449
  medications and treatments, 436
  occupations, 455
  places in the hospital, 450
  poisons, 440
  pregnancy, childbirth,
    contraception, 445
  religions, 454
  Spanish-English, 491

Word order, 30

X-ray, 281, 293, 364

ESPAÑOL

Abortos, 301, 419, 420
Acentuación, 19, 43
Adjetivos, 28, 71
Admisión
  al cuarto del paciente, 242
  información para, 398
Adverbios, 29, 156
Alergia, 246, 263, 312, 344
Alfabeto, 2
Ambulancia, 242
Anatomía y fisiología, 221
  cartas anatómicas, 5, 223, 225,
    226, 227, 229, 230, 232-239
Anestesia, 338
  caudal, 340
  eficacia de, 338
  epidural, 340
  espinal, 340
  general, 339
  local, 340
Apellidos españoles, 392, n.17
Autorizaciones y firmas, 413
  aborto terapéutico, 419
  descargo para un aborto, 420
  descargo para los funerarios, 424
  horas de visita, 422
  pedido para autopsia, 423
  permiso para esterilización, 421
  permiso para procedimientos
    quirúrgicos, 415
  transfuión de sangre, 417

Baños, 250
Bibliografía, 517

Bienestar público, 404
Blue Cross/Blue Shield, 400,
  404, 408
Boca y garganta, 277, 324

Cabeza, 270, 321
Capitalización, 24
Cirugía, 336, 413
Clínicas, 427
Cognatos, 17
Colores, 280, 300, 454
Comidas, 457
Conjunciones, 30, 177
Contenido, viii
Control de la natalidad, 381, 445
Conversión
  Fahrenheit/centígrado, 204
  métrico/decimal, 205
Cuello, 278, 324
Cuerpo, partes de, 221
Cuidado e instrucciones
  postoperatorios
  anclajes, 244
  cambio de los vendajes, 342
  catéter, 332, 338
  descanso encamado, 249
  extubación, 341
  ingestion por vía oral, 339
  intravenoso, 339, 363
  nada por boca, 339, 341, 362
  prohibiciones, 341, 342
  respiradores, 349
  tubo nasogástrico, 339, 350
  tratamiento ambulatorio, 249

Cuidados auxiliares, 248

Dentistería
  amalgamas y rellenos, 369
  caries y preparación de la cavidad,
    368
  cirugía oral, 381
  conversación dental general, 367
  historia dental, 277
  limpieza profiláctica, 370
  mordisco, 369
  necesidades dentales, 244
  vocabulario dental, 228
Diagnosis, 251
Diarrea, 293
Dieta, 245, 286, 457
Diptongos, 16
Dolor, 254, 281, 283, 289, 295, 297,
  303, 305, 308
Drogas, ver Medicación
Drogas, abuso de y dosis excesiva de
  identificaión de, 356
  señales y síntomas de, 355, 357
  uso, 314
  vocabulario, 441

Eliminación, 290, 444
Embarazo
  aborto, descargo para, 420
  aborto terapéutico, autorización
    para, 419
  historia prenatal, 301
  horas de visita, 422
  labor, 373

etapas de, 375
  preparación para, 374
lactancia, 377
partida de nacimiento vivo, 405
parto
  cesáreo, 378
  vaginal, 376
  permiso para esterilización, 421
  vocabulario, 445
Enemas, 338, 364, 375
Enfermedad
  actual, 254
  casera, 186, 387, 394
  historia de, 260
  orden alfabético de, 427
  previa, 260
  reconocimiento físico, 321
  venérea, 261, 304, 445
Envenenamiento accidental, 351,
    440
  dando el antídoto, 352
  determinación de los sintomas,
    352
  determinación del veneno, 351
  instrucciones para mordidas de
    víboras, 353
Estudios diagnósticos, 360
  ver también Procedimientos
    especiales
Evaluación del paciente
  por la historia médica, 267
  por el reconocimiento físico, 321
Expresiones
  comunes, 180
  horarias
    día, 215
    divisiones horarias, 213
    estación, 215
    hora, 209
    mes, 215
Extremidades, 305, 333

Familia
  consentimiento quirúrgico, 337
  dirección y número de teléfono
    de, 398, 402
  duración de la cirugía, 338
  historia médica, 318
  nombres de parientes específicos,
    450
  visitas, 247, 341
Fecha, 215
Fiebre, 204, 328, 429
Fumar, 281, 313

Garganta, 277, 324
Gramática, 27

Higiene, 250
Historia

enfermedad actual, 254
  familiar, 318
  personal, 309
  previa médica, 260
  social, 316
  ver también Repaso de sistemas
Horas de visitas, 247, 341, 422
Hospitalización, 263, 274

Identificación del paciente
  doctor, 401
  domicilio, 203, 309, 398, 402
  edad, 310, 398, 403
  educación, 312
  estado civil, 310
  nombre, 309 398, 402
Información para
  admisión, 398
  Blue Cross/Blue Shield, 400, 404,
    408
  partida de nacimiento vivo, 405
  sala de emergencia, 402
Inmunizaciones y vacunas, 262
Instrucciones al darse de alta
  citas, 252
  cuidado de dislocaduras, 348
  cuidado de heridas, 349
  cuidado de yesos, 349
  diagnosis, 251
  instrucciones acerca de fumar
    y beber alcohol, 252
  prohibiciones, 252
  recetas, 343
Instrucciones para el paciente acerca
    de
  la cama, 243
  citas, 252
  clerecía, 245
  las comidas, 245
  cuarto, 245
  cuarto de baño, 244
  cuidado postoperatorio, *ver*
    Cuidado e instrucciones
    postoperatorios
  darle de alta al paciente, 253
  dentaduras, 244
  la luz para llamadas, 243
  llamadas telefónicas, 244
  materiales, 245, 253
Interjecciones, 30

Medicación y tratamiento, 342
  atomizadores, 346
  avisos, 347
  cambios de los vendajes, 346
  dosis, 344
  historia de, 344
  instrucciones para
    dislocaduras, 348
    fracturas, 348

heridas, 349
jarabes y líquidos, 346
muletas, 349
píldoras, 344
prohibiciones, 347, 355
supositorios, 347
tabletas, 345
ungüentos, 345
yesos y cabestrillos, 348
Menopausia, 303
Menstruación, 298, 299
Métodos anticonceptivos
  el diafragma, 382
  el DIU, 382
  discusión del sistema
    reproductivo, 379
  de la mujer, 380
  del varón, 379
  espuma y condón, 381
  la esterilización, 385
  el lavaje, 385
  el método del ritmo
  la píldora
  el retirarse

Nariz y senos, 276
Nacionalidad, 455
Negación, 32
Notas e información culturales, 184,
    194-195, 386-396, 410-411,
    463-466
Números y expresiones numéricas
  cardinales, 198
  decimales, 203, 205
  dimensiones, 204
  fechas, 215
  fracciones, 201
  la hora, 209
  métrico, 205
  ordinales, 199
  de seguro social, 203
  señas del domicilio, 203
  símbolos, 202
  teléfono, 204, 393, n.19
  temperatura, 204

Ocupaciones, 309, 455
Odontología, *ver* Dentistería
Oidos, 275, 323
Ojos, 272, 322
Operaciones, 336
  el anestesiólogo, 338
  cancelación de, 338
  cesáreas, 378
  el cirujano, 339
  consentimiento, 337
  dando información a la familia,
    337
  duración de, 338
  explicación de, 336

formas para consentimiento, 413
preparación del paciente, 338
preparación para los tubos
postoperatorios, 339
previas, 265
ver también Instrucciones
postoperatorias
Oración, partes de la, 28
Orden de las palabras, 30

Países de origen, 455
Pechos, 278, 325
autoexamen de los senos, 278, 325
Peticiones y descargos para
consentimiento, 413
Piel y pelo, 269
Píldoras, 202, 253, 255, 263, 274,
312, 314, 315, 342, 351, 356,
364, 383
Planificación familiar, 378
discusión de los métodos
anticonceptivos, 381
discusión del sistema
reproductivo, 379
Preparación para reconocimiento
físico, 320
Preposiciones, 29, 161
Procedimientos especiales
anestesia caudal, 340
anestesia epidural, 340
anestesia espinal, 340
bomba estomacal, 354
catetrización de la vejiga, 332, 338
cistoscopia, 332, 363
colposcopia, 332
conización, 332
endoscopia, 320, 330
esofagoscopia, 329
estudios radiográficos, 364
examen radiológico con contraste
de bario, 365
instrucciones generales, 362
intravenoso, 339, 363
intubación nasogástrica, 354
lista de varias pruebas, 361
pielograma intravenoso, 332
presión arterial, 327
proctoscopia, 330
pruebas hematológicas, 360
pulso, 327
punción lumbar, 340, 366
reconocimiento de la pelvis, 331
respiración con presión positiva
intermitente, 349
sigmoidoscopia, 329
temperatura, 328
test de Papanicolaou, 331
urinálisis, 364
venepuntura, 361
Pronombres, 28, 46

Pronunciación, 1
acentuación, 19, 43
alfabeto, 2
cognatos, 17
diptongos, 16
fonética española, 3
reglas, 5
silabeo, 21
variantes dialectales, 12
Pruebas, 360
Punctuación, 23
Quejas y síntomas
de la historia médica, 254
orden alfabético de, 427
del reconocimiento físico, 321

Rayos X, 281, 293, 364
Reconocimiento físico, 321
abdomen, 329
boca, 324
cabeza, 321
cuello, 324
dolor, 335
estado mental, 258, 306
extremidades, 333
garganta, 324
gastrointestinal, 329
genitourinario, 332
muscular-esquelético, 333
neurológico, 334
oídos, 323
ojos, 322
ortopédico, 333
pechos, 325
pélvico, 331, 332
pulmones, 325
rectal, 329
sensación, 335
signos vitales, 325
temperatura, 328
testículos, 332
tórax, 325
Religión, 398, 454
Repaso de sistemas, 269
abortos, 301
accidentes, 265
afasia, 307
alergias, 263, 312
a drogas, 263
angina, 279
ataque cardíaco, 284
boca, 277
cabeza, 270
cambios de peso, 267, 309, 312
el comer, 286, 312
cuello, 278
diabetes, 295, 302, 309, 315, 319
disfasia, 278, 290
disnea, 279, 285
nocturnal paroxismal, 279, 285

doctor, 264
dolor, 254, 281, 283, 289, 295, 297,
303, 305, 308
domicilio, 310, 317
edad, 310
de los hijos, 301, 310
edema, 285, 308
embarazo, 301
enfermedades crónicas, 307
envenenamiento
por comidas, 351
por drogas, 351
esputo, 280
estado mental, 258, 306
estreñimiento, 293
exposición de trabajo, 263, 311
familia, 310
fiebre, 328
flujo de sangre, 270, 280, 292, 296,
302
flujos del cuerpo, 273, 275, 278,
300, 304
garganta, 277
gastroenteritis, 287
hipertensión, 286, 302
hipotensión, 303
historia de cáncer, 262, 319
historia cardíaca, 283
historia obstétrica, 301
historia quirúrgica, 264
historia urológica, 294
hospitalización, 263
identificación de drogas, 314, 315,
356
infección, 273, 296, 297
de lombrices, 292
ingestión de drogas, 292, 314, 351
labor, 302
medicación, 264, 284, 302, 342
menopausia, 303
menstruación, 298, 299
nariz, 276
náuseas, 289
nombre, 309, 392, n.17
ocupación, 254, 311, 455
oídos, 275
ojos, 272
operaciones, 264
ortopnea, 279, 285
pechos, 278
pelo, 269
piel, 269
picazón, 269, 291
prácticas de
beber, 286, 312
comer, 386, 312
dormir, 285
fumar, 281, 313
injerir drogas, 314
viajar, 265

rayos X, 281, 293
seguros, 316
senos, 276
síncope, 254, 271, 306, 307
sistema
    cardiovascular, 283
    endocrino, 309
    gastrointestinal, 286
    genitourinario, 294
    ginecólogo, 298
    muscular-esquelético, 308
    neurológico, 306
    reproductivo, 297, 298, 301
    respiratorio, 279
tos, 280
transfusiones, 265
trastornos femininos, 298, 300,
    301, 303, 304
trastornos venéreos, 297, 300, 304
trauma, 265
tuberculosis, 260, 319
vértigo, 270, 306
vómitos, 289, 290
Ropa, 453

Saludos, 187
comunicación, 188
despedidas, 192
expresiones de cortesía, 192

presentación, 187, 242
visitas de rutina, 190
Sangre
    análisis de, 360, 375
    petición para transfusión, 417
    presión arterial, 327, 374
Seguros, 399, 408
Silabeo, 21
Sistemas
    cardiovascular, 283, 325
    endocrino, 309
    gastrointestinal, 286, 329
    ginecológico, 298
    muscular-esquelético, 308, 333
    neurológico, 306, 334
    reproductivo, 379
    respirtorio, 279, 325
    ver también Repaso de sistemas
Sustantivos, 28, 37

Temperatura, 204, 328
Transportación a los análisis y
    pruebas, 246, 366
Trastornos femeninos, 298, 300, 301,
    303, 304
Tratamiento, 342

Verbos, 28, 84
Visitas de rutinas, 180

Vocabulario
    abreviaturas médicas, 435
    abuso de las drogas, 441
    alimentos y comidas, 457
    anatómico y fisiológico, 221
    artículos para el baño y el tocador
        y objetos personales, 451
    clínicas, 427
    colores, 454
    dental, 228
    embarazo, parto, contracepción y
        cuidado prenatal, 445
    enfermedades, síntomas y heridas,
        427
    español-inglés, 491
    especialistas médicos, 449
    excreciones, 444
    familia, 450
    inglés-español, 467
    lugares en el hospital, 450
    medicinas y tratamientos, 436
    ocupaciones, 455
    países y nacionalidades, 455
    religiones, 454
    ropa, 453
    ropa de cama, 453
    sangre, 444
    venenos, 440